They Say in Harlan County

They Say in Harlan County

An Oral History

ALESSANDRO PORTELLI

OXFORD
UNIVERSITY PRESS
2011

OXFORD
UNIVERSITY PRESS

Oxford University Press, Inc., publishes works that further
Oxford University's objective of excellence
in research, scholarship, and education.

Oxford   New York
Auckland   Cape Town   Dar es Salaam   Hong Kong   Karachi
Kuala Lumpur   Madrid   Melbourne   Mexico City   Nairobi
New Delhi   Shanghai   Taipei   Toronto

With offices in
Argentina   Austria   Brazil   Chile   Czech Republic   France   Greece
Guatemala   Hungary   Italy   Japan   Poland   Portugal   Singapore
South Korea   Switzerland   Thailand   Turkey   Ukraine   Vietnam

Copyright © 2011 by Oxford University Press, Inc.

Published by Oxford University Press, Inc.
198 Madison Avenue, New York, NY 10016

www.oup.com

Oxford is a registered trademark of Oxford University Press

Library of Congress Cataloging-in-Publication Data
They say in Harlan County : an oral history / Alessandro Portelli.
p. cm.
Includes bibliographical references and index.
ISBN 978-0-19-973568-6
1. Harlan County (Ky.)—History.   2. Harlan County (Ky.)—Social conditions.
3. Harlan County (Ky.)—Economic conditions.   4. Harlan County (Ky.)—Social life and customs.
5. Harlan County (Ky.)—Biography.   6. United Mine Workers of America—History.
7. Labor unions—Organizing—Kentucky—Harlan County—History.   8. Working class—
Kentucky—Harlan County.   9. Oral history—Kentucky—Harlan County.
10. Interviews—Kentucky—Harlan County.   I. Portelli, Alessandro.
F457.H3T447 2010   976.9'154—dc22   2010010364

9 8 7 6 5 4 3 2 1
Printed in the United States of America
on acid-free paper

Frontispiece: Employees' homes in the west end of Benham, Harlan County.
The Kentucky Historical Society, KNU-1987PH2-1607

This book is dedicated to Annie Napier and her family, and to Hazel King

Contents

They Say in Harlan County

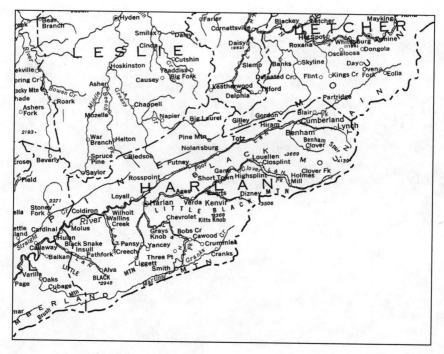

Detail of State of Kentucky: Base Map, U.S. Geological Survey, 1958.

HARLAN COUNTY, 1964–2009

A Love Story

THE MAKING OF A PERSONAL MYTH: THE CLASS STRUGGLE

It was 1988, my fifth visit to Harlan County. I was on the winding road from Harlan to Evarts, driving a borrowed pickup truck, when I began to notice the roadkill. It was a dangerous road, with more than its share of adventurous drivers, and it was getting dark. I began to think of the many ways in which death was a presence in this land: the dead animals, the road accidents, and of course the coal mines. Guns. And black lung.

Let me try to explain what I was doing there that night so far from home. I first heard about Harlan County in, I guess, 1963, from an Almanac Singers recording of "Which Side Are You On?" written by Florence Reece during the dramatic miners' strike of 1931–32. I heard Florence Reece and Pete Seeger sing it again at the great union rally, Solidarity Day, in 1982 in Washington: "They say in Harlan County / There are no neutrals there / You'll either be a union man / Or a thug for J. H. Blair."[1]

In 1964, I bought the New Lost City Ramblers album *Songs from the Depression*, and I heard Aunt Molly Jackson's "Join the CIO": "The bosses ride their big fine white horse while we walk in the mud / Their flag's the old red, white and blue and ours is dipped in blood."[2] I was being educated through music to the history of the American working class. Next was an album of topical songs from the Newport Folk Festival, including Jim Garland singing about Harry Simms, the Communist organizer killed in Kentucky in 1932: "Let's sink this rotten system / In the deepest pits of Hell."[3]

I hadn't realized that such words had ever been uttered in the United States. But in 1970 in Brooklyn I taped Barbara Dane singing another Harlan County song, Sarah Ogan Gunning's "I Hate the Capitalist System."[4] This was the sixties, and many of us dreamed of another world, a different society. I had a passion for America going back to teenage rock and roll, to what I knew of the civil rights movement, and to a year as an exchange student in Los Angeles (where I heard my first hillbilly jokes). So I was also passionately worried about America—about Vietnam, Santo Domingo, the murders of the Kennedys, Malcolm X, Martin Luther King Jr. The image of the United States that prevailed in Italy was that of a society with no history of class conflict, and so these voices from Harlan were a revelation. Harlan was bound to become a point of reference in my imagination: partly mythologized, but full of meaning.

Then I met David Walls, who was working at the University of Kentucky's Appalachian Studies Center, and he took me on a whirlwind drive through towns such as Hazard, Harlan, Hindman, and Whitesburg. It was 1973, and the Brookside strike was on. I remember the coal camps, the strike signs along the road I would take fifteen years later, the one-armed lady in a trailer who talked with David about the strike, and my frustration at being unable to understand what she said. The trip ended at the Highlander Center in New Market, Tennessee, a cradle of progressive unionism in the 1930s, civil rights education in the 1950s and '60s, and the new Appalachian awareness and organizing. I met such inspiring figures as Myles Horton, Helen Lewis, and Guy and Candie Carawan, and I was in Myles's office when Rosa Parks called him on the phone.

I had gone to Harlan on the track of the class struggle. I soon realized that my early inspirations—Sarah Ogan Gunning, Molly Jackson, Jim Garland, Florence Reece—were no longer part of the living memory of Harlan, from which they had been exiled since the thirties. Harlan was more complex and contradictory—which only increased my fascination and my desire to learn. Anyway, the struggle was still on at Brookside and in the Miners for Democracy movement. In Hazard we visited Frances "Granny" Hager in a small house along the railroad tracks, and I recorded the first of the two hundred tapes that went into the making of this book. She spoke of the "roving pickets" of 1962–63, and showed us how the history of the mountains was etched onto the geography of her body:

> HAGER: And I've got scars all over my body, that I can show you, I've got in Harlan. And on my legs and on my arms, where the scabs would try to back us off the picket line, and that here place, I don't guess you can see it too good, that white place, that they pricked the skin up—like that?—and one man held it and held my hand and had them cut that whole chunk out of my hand. And this right here, the doctors once they were afraid it's cancer, but that is where that they held a cigar to my hand till it burned out most through here.
>
> WALLS: In Harlan?
>
> HAGER: Yeah, in the early thirties. And I've got scars all over my legs, you can't see 'em too good, right there's a sunken place, and there's a scar. And I've got scars on my body, where they'd take knife points, you know, sharp knife points, and just barely stick it through the skin where it'd

hurt, and twist it, that way it makes a small hole. Now that's what we went through with our trying to organize, trying to get something out of—for the people.

In 1977, I saw Barbara Kopple's *Harlan County, U.S.A.* in a commercial theater in Rome. When I watched the pickets sing "We Shall Not Be Moved" and Florence Reece sing "We Shall Overcome" at the Evarts Multi-Purpose Center, I sensed that using music to educate myself about American struggles was not entirely a fantasy. So I decided to go back. Through the help of John Stephenson, I obtained a fellowship at the Appalachian Studies Center, where I met my personal spiritual guide into the meaning of the mountains, Gurney Norman, as well as George Ella Lyon, Herb Reid, Alan DeYoung, Dwight Billings, Bill Turner, and many others who improved my education immensely; I also got to know the media and arts center Appalshop, which became my model of practical cultural politics. Back home, I started an Appalachian studies collective in the English Department of the University of Rome. We taught classes, wrote articles and a book of essays, and advised students' dissertations; in three Appalachian festivals we brought over writers, artists, and scholars from the University of Kentucky, the Highlander Center, Appalshop, and Harlan.[5] A faculty exchange program between the University of Kentucky and the University of Rome is still functioning (another participant, Berea College, had to drop out). Since 1986, I've gone back to Harlan every year: an unusual form of longitudinal study and, most important, a living personal relationship.

BEING THERE: PRIDE AND SURVIVAL

In 1986, Bill Turner, a brilliant African American scholar, invited me to stay with his family in Lynch. I fell in love with the wisdom of his father, Earl, and the generosity of his mother, Naomi. It took me half an hour in Lynch to shed some of my more naive expectations. I had expected poverty, and here I was in a former "model" company town. Not that my notions of class struggle were all wrong. A neighbor sported a cap with the slogan "God, Guns, and Guts Made the UMWA," referring to the United Mine Workers of America; another dangled visions of guerrilla warfare in a looming confrontation with the company, a situation that seemed custom-made for a naive radical like me.

But the dominant tone was pride: pride in the living they had achieved through hard work and hard struggles, in the well-kept homes and cars, in the elegant brick church on the corner, in the education received in the old black schools, in the success of friends and relatives who had migrated north. And I was introduced to Willetta Lee and the aptly named black community she had helped create: Pride Terrace.[6]

Guy Carawan, from the Highlander Center, had told me to look up Rebecca Simpson at the Cranks Creek Survival Center, at the opposite end of Harlan

County. I called Becky, and she invited me to come over. (Years later, I learned that she had checked with her sister, Annie Napier; the verdict was, "If he ain't too stuck-up, we'll talk to him." How they decided I wasn't is another story.) Becky's husband, Bob, greeted me at the door of their house, around which the Survival Center had grown. He was at work wiring a new room he had built as an addition to the house, and the room was filled to the ceiling with cans of baby food. I had somehow assumed that the Survival Center would be some kind of cultural organization, and I was jolted into the awareness that in Cranks Creek survival was "not just a word," as Annie Napier put it once, long afterward.

I did see, in and around Cranks Creek, poverty even more distressing than I had imagined. Yet the Survival Center, created after the disastrous 1976 flood, had sprung from an act of pride: the refusal to take lying down the consequences of the strip mining that caused the flood, and the decision to make the coal companies pay for the damage. As Becky and Bob showed me around, I was moved by the affectionate way in which she hovered over him, took his arm, put food on his plate. But it was an hour into the interview when he casually mentioned his "illness," and I asked what it was. "Haven't you realized he's blind?" Becky asked. No, I hadn't, and one wouldn't know from seeing him work and from her interaction with him. Endurance, work, and love: these were the tools of survival in the face of hard times and misfortune.

And then I met Becky's sister, Annie Napier, her husband, Chester, and their daughters and grandchildren. Annie's house became my home in Harlan, her family my Kentucky kinfolks, and she a true sister. For years, she would drop everything and come along with me to interview men and women to whom I would not have had access without her. I managed to invite Annie to our Rome Appalachian festival, and she left a lasting impression on my students; later, at Columbia University, she showed the fellows at the Oral History Research Office's Summer Institute the power of living oral history, always her own proud self, not changing a syllable of her language or her story. She passed away in the summer of 2007, before she could see this book, which is as much hers as mine.

Others gave me advice and guidance and opened doors. I loved Hazel King, in her seventies still fighting for her land and people, climbing mountains to expose strip mining and to organize a democratic opposition. I was helped and enlightened by Joan Robinett, who led the struggle against the chemical pollution of the Cumberland River and of the soil in Dayhoit; by Robert Gipe, Roy Silver, and Theresa Osborne of Southeast Kentucky Community and Technical College, whose cultural organizing is the most effective weapon against the sense of helplessness and defeat that lurks in an area hard hit by unemployment and drugs; by Connie Owens, who took me back to Lynch; and by at least two hundred people who let me into their homes, took time to talk to me, and shared their knowledge and their stories.

TRYING TO GATHER A LITTLE KNOWLEDGE

Harlan greets you with a bullet-ridden "Welcome to Kentucky" sign on top of Black Mountain, and the county has good reasons to be suspicious of academics, missionaries, and other do-gooders. Yet all the time I felt secure and protected (later Hazel King let it slip that when I was on the road, phone calls would be made to see that I arrived safely at my destination). So I got to wondering what I was doing right. I asked Mildred Shackleford, a poet and a working miner.

> PORTELLI: When I first started doing this work I was afraid that people would resent me because I am an outsider. I didn't find much negative reaction. I think basically it's been because I didn't know much and wasn't in a position to teach anybody anything.
> SHACKLEFORD: I'll tell you something else that makes a lot of difference, too. You are not from the United States. You are not from New York or you are not from Chicago or you are not from Louisville and you are not from Lexington or Knoxville.
> PORTELLI: I thought about that, too. I am not from where power comes from.
> SHACKLEFORD: Another thing that would probably—if you were from Wales and you were a coal miner and you come to Harlan County and you was talking to those people about coal mining, they wouldn't resent you. But you're not trying to influence people or anything. All you're doing is trying to gather a little knowledge or get people to tell you stories, and they don't resent that.[7]

It was a lesson in the methodology of fieldwork: the most important things I had to offer were my ignorance and my desire to learn. In Los Angeles I had heard a racist hillbilly joke about an Appalachian "freak" at Harvard, where "he ain't studyin' nothin', they're studyin' him." Well, I was there not to study them but to learn from and about them. It was what I didn't know that encouraged people to talk to me, knowing that they were helping instead of being "helped."

The other lesson had come before I even got to Harlan, from an interview with Julia Cowans in Lexington in 1983. On a tip from Guy Carawan, I had been talking to her husband, Hugh Cowans, a Baptist preacher and union activist from Harlan County. But Julia also had something to teach.

> My grandma, they, they—she was a daughter of s-s-slaves. Her parents were slaves. And they used to sit around and tell things, you know, that happened when they were children and what they parents said. And I'll tell you what that will do for you: although you might not have done a thing in this world to me, but because you're white, of what my parents said...it's put something in my heart, you know: I don't trust you, you know. And so for being misused by a white person, I've never been. But

I've seen conditions of others, you know—blacks as a whole. So I was raised; my grandmother always told us, "I don't care what nobody say, I don't care how good they look, how good they talk, you gon' always be black. There's gonna always be a line."[8]

She probably meant that "I don't trust you" in general, impersonal terms. But I chose to take it personally. Why indeed ought she, a black proletarian Baptist woman from Kentucky, trust me, a white middle-class Catholic-raised but non-believing man from Europe? Fieldwork handbooks always tell you to gain the trust of the interviewee; but it was the distance and difference that made the interview meaningful, while Mrs. Cowans's boldness in speaking across the line and explaining its meaning made it possible. There were lines of age, class, gender, education, religion, language, color, and nationality between myself and most of the women and men who spoke to me in Harlan County. The mutual effort to speak across those lines taught me to think of the interview as an experiment in equality, where trust is achieved not by pretending that we are all the same but by laying the difference and the inequality on the table and making it, as Mrs. Cowans taught me, the implicit subject of the conversation.

So, back to that night on the Evarts road. When I finally got home—that is, to Annie and Chester Napier's—and was sitting on the couch with the stove and the TV going full blast, I took out my notebook and scribbled these notes.

What is in question here is the essentials: life, death; the water, the air, the earth. Nature. All is down to the bare bones. The hills slope steeply down to the narrow valleys where there's hardly enough space for anything but the road, the creek, and the railroad tracks, the hillsides either wildly luxuriating with untamed foliage or stripped bare to the coaly bones of the earth. Life is often tangibly violent and extreme, from the frankness of sex to the pervasiveness of death, teenage pregnancies to car wrecks. I am as disturbed by the animals smashed on the slippery, winding roads as by the hillsides torn open by bulldozers. I've hardly met a family without an experience of violent death, disability, blindness, illness. And the supernatural is as dramatic as the natural. Religion is emotional, even dangerous. The preoccupation with snakes and panthers, ghosts and haints, the presence of an obsessive God are the living reminders of a dramatic relationship with the natural and the supernatural worlds that meet in the omnipresence of death.

This stripping bare of life's essentials generates a strident dissonance with the culture of the contrived, the artificial, the "enhanced," the "vitamin-added" that dominates the crust of fast-food places and shopping malls around Harlan, regurgitates from the television sets through the myriad satellite dishes, from the over-sweetened drinks and snacks that are staples in a welfare family's budget. Poor people drink pop because they can no longer drink the water, and because they dimly sense that the superfluous is now a form of the indispensable. Then teeth decay and bellies swell.

Consumer culture covers both the natural and the supernatural with a veneer of the artificial—safer at one level and more poisonous at another. Yet the folk culture seeps subtly through the veins of mass culture. Fast-food places become lounges where people sit and talk and loaf, partly displacing the ideology of fast, impersonal consumption with an older sense of time, of the country store and the courthouse steps. When small children ask for ghost stories or talk endlessly of vampires and werewolves, they reflect the popularity of monster movies as well the echoes of their grandparents' stories of ghosts and haints.

The interface between the natural and the supernatural is death. In Harlan, the culture is imbued with the awareness that "death could come anytime," as Jeff Salman told me in Cincinnati. Because death is always at hand, the culture centers on the struggle to stay alive; survival, indeed, is not just a word. I have always admired the way in which people fight back under great odds and survive, especially in the United States, where one is not supposed to be up against impossible odds. Harlan County does not display much pursuit of happiness. But you see there the persistence of life in the face of danger and death.

My Kentucky friends and "kinfolks" wouldn't call this daily battle class struggle. But that's what it is: their condition is caused and defined by class, and the struggle at this stage is not about means of production but about survival and reproduction, life and death. No longer, alas, in terms of the union, but against deadly drug merchants of many stripes, or the destruction of their homes, water, and air from strip mining, logging, pollution.

JOAN ROBINETT: The laws, they're designed and created by attorneys and companies and people that really don't give a shit about, about their regular American working-class person and we are...

PORTELLI: I was telling Annie this morning, Harlan is the only place in this country where I hear the word *class* on the lips of someone who is not an academic.

ROBINETT (chuckling): Yeah, I know. But... 'cause we've been able to see in pollution issues, and a lot of people say that there is a racial issue, but actually it's class, you know. I mean, we are a prime example of how poor white folk get dumped on, and it's a class [matter].

SPEAKING, WRITING, REMEMBERING—AND EDITING

This book attempts to paint a huge canvas, covering the whole swath of U.S. history, with the pointillistic detail of microhistory—and to do so by relying on the inherently redundant medium of orality. Keeping all of this within the space of a reasonable book's covers required many sacrifices and a lot of editing. Much of great worth has been left out, enough to put together at least two other books of equal length. To combine accuracy with thoroughness and readability required taking many (responsible and thoughtful) liberties with the material.

Let me explain. *Oral history* means the telling of historical narratives in oral form. Yet the scholarly practice of oral history consists of transferring this spoken performance to a written text. Elsewhere, I attempted to convey some of the aural quality of oral history narrative in an "essay in sound" coauthored with Charles Hardy III.[9] Here, however, the question of writing the oral returns in all its complications.

In oral history much of the meaning is couched in how things are told as much as in what is told. Yet a passive mechanical transcript systematically betrays the form by turning eloquent oral performances into unreadable texts. There is no such thing as a neutral transcript: each comma is an act of interpretation, and I have used punctuation both to accompany the sentence structure and to suggest, when possible, the rhythm of speech. Thus, one must seek a compromise for which there are no set rules beyond the good faith and the ear of the transcriber/writer. In this book, I have followed only two rules: never putting into people's mouths words they did not actually say (insertions are in brackets), and striving to retain on the written page some of the impact of the spoken performance. I have retained the speakers' choices of vocabulary, grammar, syntax, and construction, including those cases in which speakers use interchangeably the standard and Appalachian forms of certain words (*born/borned, cliff/clift, scrip/script*). I have, however, avoided efforts to reproduce orthographically the sound of Appalachian speech—an endeavor always marred by negative connotations and excessive "othering."[10] Thus, I never use an apostrophe to signal a "missing" final *g*; on the other hand, because this is not a specifically linguistic study, I do not use any of the orthographic conventions used by linguists to signal the pauses and inflections of speech. A lot of this has to be imagined or remembered by the reader.[11]

Ultimately, I am aiming not to reproduce orality in writing but to translate (or transmediate) it—a process that needs to respect the rules of the medium I am using, just as a translation must respect the rules of the translator's language. Thus, I have taken a number of "cutting-room" liberties just as if I were making a film: cutting, splicing, shifting, always doing my honest best to be true to what I took to be the speakers' meaning—and leaving in enough redundancies, false starts, and colloquialisms to remind the reader that these words originated in a dialogic oral performance, not a monologic text. For verification purposes, the original recordings and archival transcripts are available at the University of Kentucky Margaret E. King Library, Louie B. Nunn Center for Oral History, and at the Archivio Sonoro "Franco Coggiola" of the Circolo Gianni Bosio in Rome.

Another effect of turning orality into writing is that all these words now appear as contemporary in the book, but they were actually exchanged at different times over a span of twenty-five years. Thus, when necessary, I have occasionally added to the speakers' names the date of the interviews, their ages, and other information. Otherwise, this information is included in the list of narrators at the end of the book.

This is basically a book of history (and therefore follows a broad chronological drift, with occasional flashes back and forward). Yet this history is told through a multitude of stories spoken by a plurality of voices. Like a film director or the director of an orchestra, I saw my task primarily as constructing a coherent discourse and making my point out of the voices of many others. Thus the primary principle is that of montage (as in cinema), sampling (as in music), or, perhaps more to the point, quilting—a form of bricolage in which a new, significant whole is created out of an array of fragments, bits and pieces (each, in turn, extracted from another, significant whole). I had some literary examples in mind—from Joseph Conrad to John Dos Passos—but my models have been primarily musical: the call and response of individual instruments in a jazz performance, or the complex form of the baroque oratorio, as in Handel or Bach: a sequence of arias (in this case, longish quotes from one voice) and chorales (a quick montage of brief quotes in which they seem to be all sounding at the same time) woven together by the half-sung, half-spoken recitative (in this case, my own narrative voice). Of course, the narrative voice does not explain everything: much is implicit in the inexhaustible articulation of the stories and in their interplay. Much of the meaning is in the gaps and in the silences, to be extracted or filled in by the readers' cooperation and imagination.

Finally, I have as much respect for the accuracy of memory as for occasional departures from the factual toward another type of subjective, cultural accuracy. What people believe and what they forget is as significant as what people recall accurately.[12] Thus, the silences on the National Miners Union or the mythic amplification of the life of Old John Shell are signs of the culture's effort to mold the past to suit a less complicated and more mythic image of itself.[13] I have used archives and secondary literature, therefore, both as fact checks and as clues to the meaning of imagination.

A CONVERSATION

I would like to conclude this introduction with the final exchanges in my conversation with Mossie Johnson, mother of sixteen, widow of a miner killed by a roof fall. The conversation took place in a trailer on Straight Creek, Bell County, the scene of much of the struggle in 1931–32. It is both typical and special, which is why I like it as a conclusion of *this* conversation, too.

> PORTELLI: Okay. You sure gave me a lot of information.
> MOSSIE JOHNSON: Well I, I shouldn't, I shouldn't have talked so much.
> PORTELLI: What do you mean? That's what I came here for.
> JOHNSON: It's a lot of time since I talk that way.
> PORTELLI: Well, I'm glad you did. I mean, I think people should talk more.

JOHNSON: Well I always said I'd like to be a psychiatric and if I had went to school—well I couldn't go to school all the time, because I had to help take care of [my mother]. Daddy, he, he cooked but he didn't make no biscuits or nothing so when I got married I learned how to make biscuits, and, so I just went back and cooked for them and helped take care of her while he worked.

PORTELLI: Okay. Well, I sure thank you. And…would it be okay to use this interview to…if I ever write…

JOHNSON: I don't reckon I've ever, I don't reckon I said nothing that would hurt nobody.

PORTELLI: You certainly didn't. It's more of something that will help…

JOHNSON: I just hope and pray our union don't go down, thrown down. They might get that strike settled, but, I don't know, it's getting awful scary. If it wasn't for God, I don't know what we'd do, we would have nobody to guide us nowhere.

PORTELLI: Thank you.

JOHNSON: You're welcome.[14]

1

THE BEAR AND THE SYCAMORE TREE

CREATION STORIES

ANNIE NAPIER: Well, back then we didn't have no TV, or no radio or anything and at nighttime when it got dark you had to go in on account of snakes. We got rattlesnake and copperheads around here, but at nighttime we'd go in and build a fire in the fireplace and Mommy and my daddy would sit around and tell us stories about when they were growing up. And stories their parents had told *them* about growing up. That's where the storytelling started from.

"I'll start this way. Aley was the first, the one who brought the Ledford name into Kentucky." Like many Harlan Countians, 102-year-old Curtis Burnam begins the telling of his life story by tracing his ancestors: "He was still a boy when they came across the mountains in 1808, traveling in covered wagons from North Carolina, following the trail of Boone to the Bluegrass."[1]

MILDRED SHACKLEFORD: There have always been some of us Shacklefords living in Harlan. When was it? About 1787, when the family first settled in that part of eastern Kentucky. My grandfather's grandfather was a Revolutionary War soldier, who settled in Kentucky at the end of the war. His name was Henry.

JUDITH HENSLEY: The other side of my family, the Hamlins—we don't have any evidence, but it has been stated that one of them was in the boat with George Washington when he crossed the Potomac. That may just be fantasy rather than any actual basis.[2] But we have a lot of relatives named George Washington Hensley.

"It makes you wonder, you know. They tell me that the world's been here nineteen hundred years, but if you went back a hundred years ago you probably found nobody living on Cranks Creek" (*Becky Simpson*). In Harlan County, you feel the nearness of the beginnings. The stories go back to a pristine wilderness, the first migrations and settlements, the Revolution, yet this is a living memory, entrusted to generations of storytellers. The mythic founders merge with the familiar grandfathers; folk memory twines with biblical chronology. Harlan County history, like American history, is short and intense. For one who comes from a land where origins seem to fade into immemorial time, it's exciting to be in a place where the beginning is still within reach of memory.

George Burkhart, a Revolutionary War veteran, claimed that he was born in 1741, came to what is now Harlan County in 1791, and settled at the head of Cranks Creek in 1806. Like Abraham, these founders spawned generations. Burkhart is supposed to have married for the third time in 1841 and to have died in 1847. "The Burkhart families of this area appear to all descend from [him]."[3]

BOBBIE DAVIDSON: I was born and raised across Pine Mountain. I'd like to tell you about my grandmother's great-grandfather. His name was John Shell, and he is supposed to have been the oldest man in the world. He died back in 1922, at the age of 134 years old. He hunted with Daniel Boone. He came to Harlan when Harlan wasn't even settled. It wasn't even Harlan then, it belonged to Virginia.[4] And he had four children, I believe. [READING FROM A PAPER]: "John was too old for service in the Mexican War and Civil War. When he died, his oldest child was ninety-nine years, and his youngest one was only seven. Amid this full life and colorful one, John helped defend the settlement of Harlan against a Flaming Arrow Indian attack." That's all I've got on that.[5]

According to a local historian, "The first permanent settlement in Harlan County was begun by Carr Bailey and his two sons-in-law and their families on a hillside overlooking Evarts back in 1790. Mr. Bailey wrote in his diary that he was coming to a secluded spot like Evarts to seek peace. Having gone through the War of the American Revolution forever more he wanted to avoid war and all forms of strife."[6] Eventually named after Silas Harlan (who was killed by Indians in the Battle of Blue Licks in 1782), Harlan County was mainly settled by veterans. Samuel Howard, who had fought with George Washington at Yorktown, was the first settler in what is now the town of Harlan, in 1796 or 1794.[7] "Supposedly Samuel Howard was the first; I guess they would say, the first white child that was born in Harlan, under a cliff at Cawood, and apparently they came through Cumberland Gap, up Stone Mountain, and settled into this area" (Daniel Howard).

CHESTER CLEM: My mom and her ancestors come from North Carolina, and, my dad's people come from Tennessee. [We] trace back to the seventeens—close to the eighteen hundreds. They come down through North Carolina, Tennessee, Virginia, West Virginia...through Cawood, Cranks and that way...My mom's people finally settled in Wallins Creek. First hung in Harlan was a Clem. They hung him for horse thieving. Hadn't done it. Second one hung was the man that did it.

"When [the Howards] first set foot on Harlan soil in 1796, they found an almost impenetrable forest, interspersed so thickly with cane brakes that in many places they had to cut their way through." "Not having any help to build a house, [Samuel Howard] erected a pole house in what is now Harlan town. Some of the best families in the county trace back to him and feel proud to be descended from so worthy an ancestor."[8] Building a home in the wilderness meant either clearing the forest or becoming part of it. The story of George Burkhart's first home is Harlan's literal roots narrative.

> BECKY SIMPSON: He was the first one that was known to live on Cranks Creek, down here at the mouth of the holler. The sycamore tree was there, that he lived in the trunk of. And he had his stove, he had his table, he had his bed in that tree. That's a good-sized tree, ain't it.

"They had two beds and a fire place with a flue. One of the beds was in one of the roots of the tree where a man could roll up in blankets and sleep comfortably for the night. Burkhart was from Virginia. Isaac Burkhart was born in the sycamore tree house. Isaac told that they had a brush fence around the sycamore tree to keep the bears out. They kept some sheep within the enclosure and bears would come around the fence at night and try to grab the sheep. One night they became very frightened as a bear got inside the enclosure, and put his feet on top of the fence. At this point Isaac's mother grabbed a gun as the bear jumped back. She fired the gun, shot the bear, and killed it."[9]

Stories of pioneers living in hollow trees have been told before in southern frontier tradition. In 1714, the North Carolina historian John Lawson wrote, "I have been informed of a tulip tree that was ten feet in diameter, and another wherein a lusty man had got his bed and household furniture, and lived in it till his labor got him a more fashionable mansion." And according to Kentucky historian Otis K. Rice, hunters and trappers John and Samuel Pringle lived for several years in a large sycamore tree in the Tygart Valley in West Virginia after 1761.[10]

In tall-tale form, these stories reflect the sheer size of the frontier environment, its huge trees, dense forests, and "lusty" pioneers. The Harlan County version, however, also symbolizes the settlers' absorption into the land, a sense of place and literal rootedness, and a dramatic confrontation with nature in the very process of living inside it and becoming a part of it. The pioneer becomes a part of the land but wrests it from its original inhabitants, be they the bears or the Indians.

Thus settlement was not without danger and violence. Samuel Howard's child may have been the first *white* child born in Harlan, but other human beings had used that land before, even if they had settled it sparsely or only used it as a hunting ground. To these early occupants, the very act of surveying the land must have appeared like an encroachment; thus a member of the first party of surveyors, led by Thomas Walker in 1750 (the first to notice the presence of coal in the region), was killed by Indians near a creek that still bears his name, Wallins Creek.[11]

A party of settlers at the head of the Clover Fork was attacked by Indians, and only one survived.[12] Around 1800, Stephen Jones, a Revolutionary War soldier from Virginia, and his family stumbled upon an Indian hunting party near what is now Verda. The cliff under which they took refuge is still known as Jones's Creek. They survived on the scraps left by the Indians, who were aware of their presence but did not molest them. Near Bailey's Creek, the Jonathan Kelly party found the remains of some scouts around a recently abandoned campfire and could not discover whether they had been killed by the Indians or by wild animals.[13]

In 1769, the legendary Daniel Boone led a party through Cumberland Gap, thus opening Kentucky and the trans-Appalachian West to the expansion of the newborn nation.[14] He later came through what is now Harlan County, and one of his sons was killed by Indians on Stone Mountain near Pennington Gap. According to one Harlan family's tradition, Daniel Boone made hunting trips into the area, where he and another man named Yoakum were captured by Indians and taken to what is now the town of Evarts. The tribe's council decided to burn them at the stake, but they started scratching like hens and crowing like roosters, which made the Indians laugh so much that instead of killing them they allowed them to run the gauntlet and to escape. From this incident Yoakum Creek got its name.[15]

PORTELLI: What do they make you read in school? Do they make you learn poems, things—recite things?
DEE DEE NAPIER (AGE 9): They just make us read in our reading book and Kentucky history book.
PORTELLI: So what's Kentucky history about?
NAPIER: It's about Kentucky and the first settlers.
PORTELLI: Do you remember something about Daniel Boone from school?
NAPIER: He freed some slaves in some foreign country, and then he walked back there wherever it is, that wild place, and they call it Boonesboro.
PORTELLI: There's a marker up the road, just a little bit above your house, that's got a story about Daniel Boone and his son?
NAPIER: Uh-huh. I read the part about it, and the teacher told me that his son got killed right up through there.

The memory of these events is inscribed onto the land as names: Wallins Creek, Yoakum Creek, Jones Creek. In Harlan, as throughout the United States, the beginning was a matter of language and names. Like Adam, like Lewis and Clark, the settlers of Harlan clinched discovery and possession of the land with the act of naming.[16] According to the manuscript kept by John Shell's descendants, "Greasy Creek when Kentucky was still part of Virginia was called Licking

Creek, by early hunters, because of the deerlicks that was there. The name was later called Laurel Creek, justified by the laurel that abounded then. Then one day John Shell shot and wounded a Bear on the mountain at the mouth of Shell's Branch, a fork of Laurel Creek. The Bear ran off the mountain and fell into the Blue Hole. The water was so deep that John could not get him out. The Bear, in time, created a greasy scum that rose to the surface of the water for some time. People down stream then re-named the tributary to suit its aspects. This is called Greasy Creek to this day."[17] Place names reiterate the process of discovery, revolution, settlement, development: they commemorate early surveyors (Wallins, Martin's Fork), Revolutionary War veterans (Harlan, Evarts), settlers (Cawood, Cranks), mine owners and their families (ArJay, Verda, Louellen).[18]

> CHESTER CLEM: The man that owned all this was one of the Cawoods, and he had two girls—one was named Mary Helen, and the other one was named Lenna Rue, so that's how [Mary Helen and Lenarue] got named. But everyone called it Turtle Creek because turtles crossed the road all the time down here. They're not as bad now as they was, but you still see 'em a lot.

DARK AND BLOODY GROUND

> ED CAWOOD: [My ancestor] Berry Cawood fought in the Revolutionary War. He was a soldier in George Rogers Clark's expedition and served a year or two, got a pension, and came back and settled in Harlan County.[19] Farming and hunting and a lot of lumber; there was no coal mining then, except for the homes and so forth. They were afraid of the Indians, but the Indians just passed through this country, they didn't settle here. One of my ancestors, they claim, bought an Indian girl for a wife with five bushels of corn. That's just hearsay. Well, there's some Indian blood in the Cawoods I believe.

"My great-grandmother was a full-blooded Cherokee" (*Chester Clem*). One of the few redeeming traits attributed to Appalachian mountaineers by local-color writers, missionaries, and educators was their supposed "pure Anglo-Saxon blood."[20] Harlan, however, adds a twist of irony—if anything, people brag about having "full-blooded" Indian ancestors and "mixed" blood.

> MARTHA NAPIER: My grandmaw on my mother's side was a full-blooded Cherokee Indian. I never did see her, but I know she was a Cherokee Indian. My mom would tell us about how she had worked and slaved and raised her family, raised eight or nine kids. I don't know my grandpa. He must have been Cherokee Indian, my mother being Cherokee Indian. Her mother, full-blooded. Mom wasn't full-blooded.

In the eighteenth century, the Cherokee nation controlled most of the Appalachian region.[21] Its most important settlements were in Georgia and North

Carolina; Kentucky was used mainly as a hunting ground but was an integral part of the Cherokees' territory. When they began to trade deerskins and other commodities with the white settlers and pioneers, they became involved, albeit marginally, in a world commodity chain that made them dependent on exports and no longer self-sufficient. Increasingly, land was contracted away and ceded to (or encroached upon by) white settlers. When the cession of his nation's Kentucky lands to the white settlers was formalized in 1775, Cherokee dissenter Dragging Canoe warned: "You have bought a fair land, but there is a cloud hanging over it. You will find its settlement dark and bloody."[22] So often has there been reason to dub Kentucky a "dark and bloody ground" that this is often assumed to be the meaning of the state's name in Cherokee.[23]

> DEBBIE SPICER: Well, I heard that my granpaw come from the Smoky Mountains when he was seventeen years old. My grandpa. Cherokee. It was my great-great-grandpa, my mother's grandpa. I think when the Indians was run off, my ancestors maybe ran off with them and got over in here some way. You know the Indians is treated bad; the Indians really was treated worse than the colored; the whites run them off their territories and [took] their properties and their lands, all that stuff, you know.

"The Cherokees, if you do know from American history, were living in the Carolinas, and Virginia, and a state called Franklin which is now part of East Tennessee. And they decided they would just be people. They were living in cabins and in houses, very much like whites. And the government ran them out...Trail of Tears, round to Oklahoma" (*Arthur Johnson*). In 1838, the federal government began the removal of the Cherokee nation across the Mississippi, twelve hundred miles away to Oklahoma. While fourteen thousand women and men went through the deadly march that they remembered as the "Trail of Tears," some managed to stay behind. Supposedly, the last to stay in Harlan County was an old man named Sam Whitson, who lived near Black Mountain in the 1930s and came occasionally to Harlan to trade.[24]

> FRED NAPIER (B. 1899): My dad bought a place in this mountain here, and a bunch of Indians lived back there at that time. They had them a big log schoolhouse and a church house.[25] I went to the church, been to the schoolhouse. Then all along the top of this mountain was settled in colored people and Indians. There's an old Indian man come through back when I was just a kid, he put up for the winter with us and got wood and stuff through the winter to keep us a fire and he went off one day [looking for] a mine. The old fellow didn't live, he left his stuff there at my home, his moccasins and stuff. And my dad took the map of this mine and found it.

According to family stories, a band of "friendly" Indians called Quadrules is supposed to have remained around Wallins Creek until the Civil War. In his unpublished history of Harlan, Elmon Middleton also speaks of these "friendly"

Indians who "mingled freely with the whites"—until they were deported to a reservation in the West.[26] "But the Indians is all gone now, they died out and left here, I don't know where they went to, they must've went back to their homes or something" (*Martha Napier*). Of course, this *was* their home; but the image of a "fatal" disappearance of the "vanishing American" allows Indian ancestry—as opposed to African American "blood"—to function as nostalgia and pride rather than shame. Somehow, by claiming the Indians as ancestors, whites can legitimate as lawful inheritance the taking of their land.

> ARTHUR JOHNSON: In one sense, the Indians are still here. Before they ran them out, many of them had married into white families. They were handsome men and beautiful women, and they intermarried. So, if you get to running family trees, you look back and you come to a great-grandmother that you didn't have, because they didn't list them in the census. So a lot of them were assimilated.[27]

VARMINTS

The Indians were not the only living beings on the land—indeed, to some of the settlers they were only part of the "wildlife" they had to chase, expel, or tame in order to take possession of the land. Thus, hunting and animal stories and tall tales are a staple in Harlan County folk memory.

> ANNIE NAPIER: That was our second grandpa Dan. From what they've told me he had this dog, small dog, and he come to a cave and he'd send the dog in and he'd lay down in front of the mouth of the cave and when the dog run the bear out, he'd gut it as it came out. Stab it.
> PORTELLI: He didn't shoot it?
> NAPIER: No, he used a knife. I don't guess he even had a gun.

Chester Napier tells the story of a man who was running from a bear and was so scared that instead of climbing a tree to escape, he kept running around its base: "When they found him and they finally got him calmed down enough, he says, 'Wait till I come down outta the tree.' And one of 'em says, 'Hell, you're not up in the tree. You're sitting on the ground.' He had got so scared that he couldn't climb the tree. But he was thinking he was up in the tree." The relationship is reversed, but the protagonists are the same as in George Burkhart's tale: the bear and the tree as symbols of a confrontation with nature's dangers. Burkhart's hollow tree combines life and death: its size gives shelter, but its hollowness suggests that it is itself dead. Death and hollow trees are connected in other stories, too. A hollow tree shelters Curtis Burnam's ancestors as they come over Pennington Gap into Cranks Creek, but crushes them to death when it is blown down by the wind.[28] Fred Napier tells of an outlaw killed on Cranks Creek after the Civil War: "They just cut a piece off of him at a time. Ears, nose, tongue, punched his eyes out," and hid his body in a hollow log, where his bones were accidentally found by Fred's grandfather years later.

And then the bear. From Thomas Bangs Thorpe's "The Big Bear of Arkansas" to William Faulkner's *The Bear*, the bear has stood as a metaphor for the land and its possession.[29] Perhaps less articulately and consciously, but no less poignantly, it plays the same role in Harlan's origin tales—the bear melted in the waters in John Shell's tale, the animal stabbed to death in an almost erotic embrace in Chester Napier's story (and in Faulkner's).

Some Harlan bear stories, like Thorpe's classic, combine humor with the flavor of the tall tale. For instance, Ben Campagnari has a story about a poker game: he had lost all his money, no one would lend him any, so he left announcing, "Well, I'll go kill me a bear." And sure enough, under a cliff he saw a big bear coming at him: "I see that big black bear coming, I wheeled and here I went [running] back to the shack and, when I opened the door, I fell, and that old big bear just scooted in over the top of me. They was playing poker. I said, 'Skin him boys, while I go get another!'"[30]

Not all the stories were funny, however. Bob Simpson recalled a story his father used to tell: "This man got up one morning, told his son, 'Come out here son, I wanna show you some.' Snow was on the ground. He got out, walked all around the house, when he found a rabbit track said, 'Son, see this here?' He said, 'Your breakfast is on the other end.' They didn't have a bite to eat in the house."

CHESTER NAPIER: My dad and me, we used to coon hunt, which we didn't kill anything we didn't eat. And that's still the way I see it today. Don't go kill for the sport of it. Don't go kill a deer just to have it mount on the wall. If you're not gonna eat it, don't kill it. If you're not gonna eat it and somebody else wants it, it's all right to kill it and clean it and give it to them. I mean, that's the way the Indians lived. And that's the way I was raised.

In a hunting culture, guns are a part of the way of life: "Usually most boys and girls have learned how to shoot by the time they are twelve" (*Donna Warren*). "My dad would take me on his back, carry me on, and toted me through the mountains. And I've hunted ever since I can remember" (*Chester Napier*). Chester's daughter Marjorie was given her first gun "before I was walking. It's hanging over the door, that's the one I cut my teeth on, literally. I chewed on the butt of the gun to cut my teeth." She grew up to be a sharpshooter in the army.

TILLMAN CADLE (B. 1902): Yeah, the way I got my first gun...I was about ten, maybe eleven years old. I asked my father if I could have a BB gun for Christmas. He said "No, you can't have a BB gun. You might shoot someone [accidentally]." He said, "I'll take you out and I'll learn you how to shoot a gun, the rules of safety when you handle a gun. Then you can have a real gun." Well, he did take a .22 rifle and he'd show me how to [handle] a gun, shoot at a spot, to never point a gun at anybody, and he told me as I was unloading a gun or loading it to always be sure that it was not pointed toward anybody, all the rules of safety on handling guns. After he had learned me all these things, he saw I was capable of handling a gun. He said, "Now when you get the money, you can have you a gun."

PRESTON McLAIN: In the state of Kentucky you can carry a weapon as long as you have that "concealed deadly weapons" card to carry it. It seems that in the mountains of eastern Kentucky everyone carries a gun; it's just a way of life. They've been hunting all their life, they use it for protection, they might carry a pistol, but it just might have a bird shot, to kill a snake. Or a shotgun to scare off a bear. They're not necessarily carrying it for ulterior motives.

SID TIBBS: Well, I'd say it's human nature. Which, the United States has more guns probably than any other country. But what it is, you're gonna have predators; you're always gonna have criminals. And, around here since 1837, since the open law was passed, there's been an Appalachian culture to take your shotgun, to take your rifle to town. Second Amendment says you have the right to bear arms. I don't mean that everybody does. But I'm an advocate for the Second Amendment. I believe we should have the right to protect our family, not just at the front door. So we got that carry-concealed law passed, it's working well, we've had thirteen accidents, killings, you know what I mean, but they've all been justified.[31]

"I used to go to cockfights with Dad when I was a kid. They'd fight a few roosters, not like they do now, you know. They didn't put the knives and the steel spurs on 'em or anything. They just fit 'em natural. It's against the law, to bet money and gamble on 'em, but it's not against the law to fight 'em. [But] some of the roosters, you pay a hundred fifty, a hundred, two hundred dollars, and you're not gonna go fight 'em for the fun of it, watch 'em get killed without trying to make a dollar back on 'em, are you?" (*Chester Napier*). "Oh gosh, it's unreal. It's like this big old room and they got a fence and you go inside this fence and you can't get out once you get in there, where the people fights the chickens. They hold these two roosters, they put like little knives on their legs and them roosters just fly up in the air and whatever rooster hits [the ground] first usually dies 'cause them knives will go into their neck and it will kill them and you can hear people screaming and hollering and going on and they start bidding on them and betting on them and they can win fifty to a hundred dollars" (*Crystal Vanover, int. 2005*).

The hunting culture lived on, from frontier times into modernity. "We might have seen maybe three bears, but we see a lot of bears' track, and if a bear doesn't want you to see him, you won't see him. But, yes, we have bears up on the mountains" (*Preston McLain, int. 2006*).[32] "Buddy, there was every kind of animal in the world at one time on this mountain. Wild hogs and boars and bears. And wildcats and panthers. Yeah, these mountains were full of 'em, but they didn't bother us much. Plenty of snakes and plenty of snake shit. There's this snaky place, I found a bunch of copperheads in there this year. Stone Mountain side is so rocky, ain't nothing over there but rocks and clifts, and that's where an old snake likes to stay at" (*Henry Farmer*). "And I tell you I have ate every kind of wild game there is in these mountains, I've ate rattlesnake, opossum, ground-hog, coon, rabbit, squirrel, deer, bear, turtle, frog legs, I love frog legs, I love rabbit. I love squirrel gravy" (*Crystal Vanover*). "A lot of people in the cities will look down on ya eating squirrel, but I don't see anything the matter with it. I've eat it all my life. I've eat snapping turtles, frog legs. And, I wouldn't eat possum anymore, but I've eat it when I's growing up. Lot of people eat rattlesnakes. They catch 'em, cut their heads off, skin 'em, and eat 'em. I ate it one time. Not exactly like a fish. I ate a small amount, didn't like it" (*Chester Napier*).

Eating snake meat is more a symbolic act than a nutritional one: another test of identification with the earth and of the ability to handle the danger that lurks in it. Snake stories were part of my own induction to Harlan. The first time I saw Annie Napier, she was standing on the house steps calling, "Come in, children, it's getting dark, and they're crawwwlin'." Later, Chester lectured me on the variety of snakes in their yard.

> We have two poison snakes, called rattlesnakes and copperheads. And we had a lot of the nonpoisonous snakes, we call them a garter snake, black-snakes, ring snakes, milk snakes. I usually kill two or three a year, copper-heads, here in the yard. They stay around close where people lives. So, if I'm out here working and I see one, I take the shotgun and shoot it. Now last spring, I was out in this old house below me, used to throw garbage there, there's some cans there, so I hear the cans make a noise. I think, "That's a rat in there." I go over, and I kicked the cans—this copperhead. So I take the pistol and I try to shoot. Three times, and it wouldn't fire. I just reached out and cut me a stick off the apple tree, a branch of the apple tree, and whacked the snake with it. Killed it.[33]

After worrying me with the snakes in the yard, Chester went on to teach about their relationship with humans. At first he reassured me: "A copperhead will run from you, they are afraid of us more than we are of them." But then:

> Now, see, this month is dog days. They won't run from you this month. I've been told they're blind this month [because they are shedding skin]. They don't hear us, a snake doesn't hear. It goes by the vibrations. But the rattlesnake is the gentleman snake, because a rattlesnake he will warn you, to stay away. That's the gentleman of all snakes, is the rattlesnakes. We have what we call the timber rattler here, and the diamondback. The

timber rattler, he will get in small shrubbery, off the ground. So I guess the timber rattler is more dangerous than the diamondback. The diamondback will grow bigger than a timber rattler. My dad and me we used to catch 'em and we give 'em to preachers, they'd take them to church and have what they call the snake handlers. We don't do that anymore.

The handling of poisonous snakes in church is a test of faith and grace, just as catching them in one's yard is a test of prowess and courage.[34] The deathly presence of the snake parallels the daily danger in the mines, and the culture takes a sort of ironic pride in its ability to handle it. Thus, in the Appalachian storytelling, snake stories are a privileged genre.

CHESTER CLEM (INT. 2006): We've killed thirty-eight copperheads from down in the middle of the camp to Mary Helen. When they tore the tipples about a half mile up the road they killed a little over thirty then, and then we've killed two rattlesnakes, so...[35]
MEGAN CLEM (AGE 15): And then they found, like, how many, thirty maybe? Down at one of the schools in the vending machines.
CHESTER: This year we've killed three rattlesnakes, we killed one big 'un by Mom's and two just across the creek there, big as my arm. The biggest one I know of they killed in Mary Helen, I think it was, fifty-two inches long or fifty-four inches long. This last one we killed this year, had seven rattlers on a button, and it was black as all get-out. But people eat it. Yeah, people eat it.

CHESTER NAPIER: Yeah, there's a lot of snake stories. I was born in a log house, only one big room. One night, about six months after I was born, a rattlesnake got into the house, through a hole in the logs. Between the logs we just had the clay mud to keep the weather out. Sometimes the mud would fall out. So the snake he gets in bed with Dad and me. Ever time we would move the snake would start rattling. [In the morning] Dad gets out and he goes on to work at the coal mines. Mother, she gets up and sets all of us kids out the window. We had one window in the house. So she sits us all out. She starts looking for the snake again. So she hears something outside, and she goes; we had what we called a fireplace. It was where we kept the flour. It was just a chimbley with about a six-foot logs in it to keep the old house warm, and so she goes out there and the snake had bit a rat. And the rat was making a noise. And the snake was half in the house and half out of the house where it crawled through the logs. So, she gets what we call a hoe that we work in the garden with. She chops the snake's head off. And my two oldest brothers, they bury the snake. And it still comes back later in the day to the top of the ground out from under where they buried it. So, maybe six months later on, Mother was out barefooted, and where she had knocked the fang out of the head when she cut it off, she stepped on the fang. And she was in bed for a couple of months with that. Almost died, I guess it was same as a rattlesnake bite. So that was one of our experiences when I was just a kid. I slept with him.

CHESTER CLEM: The snakes don't bother me, once you get used to them. Before I could even walk...I handled snakes then. Mom said that there's one that got in the camp house at Mary Helen where we lived, and she said I was standing beside the bed—this was before I learnt to walk—and she said I'd reach and get ahold of his tail and pull it back down towards where I was at, and by the time he'd turn around to bite me, I'd let go of him. And she was washing dishes, and all she'd hear me say was, "Ooh!" And when he started crawling off again I'd reach and get ahold of it again and pull it back down towards where I was standing. I let go and it and it'd crawl back up through there and I'd go, "Ooh!" So she got curious and stepped out of the kitchen, to the bedroom...screamed, awful scream!...and my dad was in the other room watching TV or talking, so he grabbed a poker and killed the snake—on the bed, even though Mom had just put the new sheets and new [quilts] on the bed.[36]

Sleeping with the snake, even more than eating it, is an eloquent representation of the very intimate presence of danger. The snake is both something radically other and a household presence. According to local historian Mabel Condon, old-time mountaineers kept snakes around the house for protection from rats.[37] "We used to have a black snake come in the kitchen all the time behind the stove where it was warm. Robert, Becky's boy, killed one at the back of his house had fourteen rattles on it. Great big thing, I mean, it was bigger that your fist" (*Annie Napier*). "I killed one clear across the porch there one day. Then I killed one out here in the garden one time. My wife was out there picking beans. And I seen that big snake. I said, 'Now don't get scared honey but, there's a snake right there.' I said, 'Run in there and get my pistol.' And she brought it out there, and that snake's looking at me right in the eye. Boom! Buddy I just shot that thing in the head, head off. It was a big whole long snake. But she never picked another bean after that" (*Lloyd Stokes*).

GHOSTIES AND HAINTS

A counting rhyme, told by Dee Dee Napier at age nine:

One o'clock, two o'clock, three o'clock, rock
Seven o'clock, eight o'clock, nine o'clock, rock
Ten o'clock, eleven o'clock, midnight
Peaches, pumpkin, apple pie
If the ghosts in the graveyard ain't ready
Holler "aye"!

"Used to, people'd get to somebody's house, and they'd tell ghost stories. They call it haints, and they'd tell haint tales. Had the kids scared to death" (*Frank Majority*). "I like ghosts, there are still a bunch of us we used to go out to the graveyards to see if we could see them, and we called it ghost hunting" (*Donna Warren, int. 2005*). If the snake represents the domestic presence of earthly danger, ghosts stand for the domestic supernatural.

MILDRED SHACKLEFORD: My mother was awful bad about telling ghost stories. There was the story about the deaf and dumb people that got runned over on the railroad tracks, 'cause they couldn't hear and they couldn't talk to each other, they had their backs to the train and they couldn't hear the train coming. And they'd tell us if we wasn't good children and stayed off the railroad tracks, then the deaf and dumb couple would get us. Their ghost would come back and get us. Of course, it never worked. We would take those stories and we would go up to the graveyard with 'em when it was dark and we would imagine the bodies coming out of the graves, the tombstones would fall over. Of course all of the people that was in the graveyard were my father's relatives, grandparents, great-grandparents.

"Ghosties" are family, then. One dark and stormy winter night in Annie Napier's isolated house on top of Stone Mountain, she asked me, "Do you believe in ghosties?" Of course I said no. "I don't either," she said. "However..."

ANNIE NAPIER: I have no idea what it is, but we definitely have a ghost. The kids has seen it. They've heard it.
DEE DEE NAPIER: I've seen two of them. Two boys go past the window.
PORTELLI: How did you know they were ghosts?
DEE DEE: 'Cause they was real pale.[38]
ANNIE: There's one that goes across the porch that wears a red shirt. And sometimes Shorty [the dog], he'd sit in front of the swing out there and look at the swing like somebody was sitting there petting him, but there ain't a soul out there. But now, this thing, whatever's here, it walks in the house, and from time to time, believe it or not, it'll hide things. I mean, they'll just be absolutely gone, and then all of a sudden they'll come back. You know, I was raised you don't believe in ghosts, ghosts don't exist. But whatever it's worth, there's definitely something here.

As in Toni Morrison's *Beloved*, a ghost in the house is a metaphor for a memory that—like Chester's snake tooth—will not let itself be buried. Many of the ghosts that walk around in Harlan are indelible "damned spots" from its troubled history, attached to objects and things that carry memories.

HAZEL KING: It was like a freshet from a storm, a movement; you just felt the wind, like something was passing in front of you, the pressure from the movement. Someone had been killed [in this house], and they didn't have ambulances and transportation back in those days, so they'd taken this door off another building, and they'd put the man on the board, and there was a lot of blood on that board where he had bled. Anyway, when they carried him across the mountain and down far enough until they could get a wagon to pick him up, they just threw the board over the hill-side. And this board was supposed to been used then for a door for this [other] building, and the blood wouldn't come off the door.

ANNIE NAPIER: The first time I ever heared it, it was when we bought that first place up in Big Branch. That was back in '72. And when we sold that place in Big Branch, and bought a brand-new trailer and set it on the back lot out here, it moved with us. And when we built this house and sold the trailer, he moved in the house with us.

I got three items, and I wouldn't take nothing for none of them. We've got an old .41 Colt pistol that was used in the union organizing. It belonged to Chester's third grandfather down, and it was patented in 1888, '92, and '93. They ain't no way I'd get rid of that gun. It was used in the union orga-nizing. There was five men killed in one night with it over here at Crummies. This one man killed five men with it in one night, 'cause it's got the handles notched. And then later, he dropped the gun and it went off and killed him.[39] When we got it, I just wanted it 'cause it was old. And we traced it back, and it belonged to Chester's third grandfather down. But I got that, an old rocking chair, and an old magazine table.

It's just an old antique rocking chair that—actually, it ain't worth nothing to nobody else but me. I just liked it. And from time to time, it'll start rocking by itself. Nobody close to it and it'll rock by itself. They say sometimes something favorite of somebody's, their spirit will attach to it, but, now, I don't know if that's true or not.[40]

PORTELLI: So the ghosts are connected to these things and have fol-lowed them.

ANNIE: Everywhere we move, it goes with us. But, you know, to me it's not scary. It's been with us so long. That was '72 and this is '96. But now, the weird part about it, when something bad's going to happen, it'll start walking, it'll walk more often. Like maybe two or three weeks before something bad happens in the family, it'll walk constantly. It's like a warning that something's going to happen, and it normally does. But, you know, it's just one of them things that you can't explain it to people. A lot of people that's come here has really got terrified of it when it walks.

These are not mere relics from archaic folklore. As Dee Dee Napier's transfor-mation of "Rock Around the Clock" into a ghostly counting rhyme indicates, folk imagination incorporates popular culture. A twenty-four-year-old hitchhiker near Wallins Creek: "I like scary movies. Like *Nightmare on Elm Street, Friday the Thirteenth*" (*Lowell Hanson*). A nineteen-year-old girl at the Harlan literacy center: "Scary movies. Ghost stories. Suspense stories. I think that young kids now like Freddy Krueger and Jason and *Howl*. Me, I like to hear an old-fashioned ghost story" (*Nancy Mayer [name changed]*). At a musical evening at her sister Becky's house, Annie Napier and her kinfolks picked and sang John Duffey's "Bringing Mary Home," a country music version of the legend of the ghostly hitchhiker: "Down a lonely road on a dark and stormy night" a motorist picks up a little "pale" girl and takes her home. But when he gets there she has disappeared, and her mother explains that she died in a car wreck thirteen years ago and that he is the "thirteenth one that's been here bringing Mary home."[41] In a Pine Mountain variant, the ghost of a murdered girl appeared on a bus on October 13, 1956, and disappeared in midtrip.[42]

> WILL GENT: [There]'s supposed to be a young girl was killed round the turn of the century, round 1900, was killed and never did find out who killed her. They caught her coming home from the road. She lived up on the bank, had to go 'bout half a mile from where she lived from the road. Musta been a couple of men caught her and they probably wanted to take liberties. And so they just wound up killing her and I don't reckon they [were] ever found out. [Then a] ghost appeared. Girl got on [a bus]. It rolled up, got down a ways and when [the driver] looked back wadn't a soul on it. He jumped off the bus, left it to run and took off and quit his job. That's one of the stories I heared.

LIVING THE FRONTIER

> CHESTER NAPIER: My ancestors, they come to this country, it was all wilderness, wild, you know. And it's still, back into where I was raised, it is still; nobody lives back there, still wilderness. You can drive a four-[wheel-]drive vehicle back there. It's approximately five miles off of the highway.

Historical time is not homogeneous; history and modernity do not proceed at the same linear pace everywhere. Not all that takes place at the same time is "contemporary."[43] When William Goodell Frost in 1899 labeled Appalachians "contemporary ancestors" frozen in the eighteenth century, the twentieth century was staring him in the face from the sawmills, the railroads, the early stirring of the mining industry. Indeed, not only does time flow at different paces in different places, but it may do so in the *same* place. Rather than locating a people and a culture outside history, the persistence of the past may itself be a form of history and an aspect of a stratified modernity.

> PRESTON MCLAIN: As you talk to older people or you look to our county, some people think they step back in time. In a way, that is true, and that's

the way we want to keep it. But, in a way, we're just as modern and up to date as anyone else—as far as Internet, education, better working conditions in the coal mines. [We want] everyone [to] have that, and [also] keep our heritage like we have it.

The wilderness, the animals, the ghosts live on in the machine age, side by side with the railroad, the automobile, film, television, the longwall mining machine. "Like I said, when I was a kid we was raised just about like the pioneers," said Chester Napier. "So much like the beginnings and yet so modern, too." Chester's father, like many others, lived in a log cabin with a dirt floor, but when he left it in the morning, it was not to go bear hunting but to go to work in the coal mine.

MILDRED SHACKLEFORD: I was born at home [in 1950], 'cause my family was still so poor at that time that we did not, you know, go to the hospital or stuff, and I was what my mother always referred to as a blue baby.[44] So when I was born they put me in the oven; they wrapped me up, shoved me in the oven, to warm me up. My mother always thought it was because she ate so much ice when she was carrying me.

My sister and myself both were born at home. And I guess we was the last generation in our family that were. Most of the ones borned after that were born in the hospital. We growed up pretty wild and woolly. Considering [what] most of the United States was economically and socially at that time, I'd say that me and my sisters were probably fifty to sixty years behind what the rest of the country was. Kid going to school those days would take Mickey Mouse lunch boxes, with bologna sandwiches made on white bread. We didn't have any of that; we made our own bread, we made our own soap, sewed our own clothes, made our own bedcovers—a lot of the stuff that pioneer people did, we were still doing, in the fifties. Sort of like growing up on two worlds, one world you'd go to school and there was this modern-day stuff like television and telephones, people's talking 'bout rocket ships, and we'd come home from school and here my grandfather'd been born in a one-room log cabin with a dirt floor, and my grandmother had been a little better off than he was, but not much. And it was just like living a hundred years in the past and then in the future, too.

2

OF HARDSHIP AND LOVE

WHAT YOU RAISED IS ALL YOU HAD

JUDITH HENSLEY: The Hensley Settlement, that's where my relatives formed a settlement, on top of Brush Mountain in the Cumberland Gap area. They still have the log cabins and they've still tried to maintain the authenticity of their lifestyle. It's a thousand-acres plateau on the very top of the mountain. So they were very much isolated from other people and quite self-sufficient. It's a beautiful, beautiful place.[1]

The land between the Cumberland and Kentucky rivers south of Ohio, roughly corresponding to present-day Kentucky, was established as a county of Virginia in 1776, then as a separate state in 1792. Harlan County was established in 1819, on an area carved from parts of Knox and Floyd counties. At the time, it included parts of what later became Letcher and Bell counties, including historic Cumberland Gap. The county seat was originally named Mount Pleasant; it was changed to Harlan Court House in the 1870s and Harlan in 1910.

"Sometimes it'd be a mile from a house to a other. There weren't too many people" (*Debbie Spicer*). Harlan County's population was 1,961 in 1820 and 5,278 in 1880. Throughout the nineteenth century, its density was never more than ten people per square mile.[2] Even after the increase brought by logging, mining, and the railroads (up to 10,566 in 1910), it remained a sparsely populated area of small, relatively isolated farms: "When my grandparents Hall lived, if they let their fire go out, they'd walk for over a mile and get some fire at a neighbor's house and walk back and build their own fire" (*Annie Napier*). "Now, the only way they had to get across [Pine] Mountain then were by horse and buggy. And, I remember my grandmother telling me that they would go shopping to Pineville, which is thirty-four miles from here. It would take them two days. They would go down, and whoever's house they were at when it got dark, they would spend the night. Then they would shop and they'd come home the next day" (*Bobbie Davidson*).

ED CAWOOD (B. 1906): My grandfather's told me he had a store up in Cumberland, and he had to drive all the way to Mount Vernon to get his goods for his store. About 150 miles. They hauled all their freight by wagons. They were rough built, had wooden wheels with big iron or steel rim on 'em and so forth. And then, people from Harlan County, they had to go to Hagan, Virginia. They had a road across the Stone Mountain, the mountain between Kentucky and Virginia. It's a great trip to go to Hagan. One time [my grandfather] said, "[I've] never been anyplace, I've never been out the United States but one time I went to Hagan, Virginia, with Pap."

"It was rough roads, these steep mountains. They used some mules but since back as I can remember, they had them big ol' horses, some of them would weigh two thousand pounds apiece, that they learned to keep getting a move on these steep mountains" (*Ben Lewis*). "[My wife's father] was running a store— just goods like sugar and coffee and stuff like that, and salt. When the railroad got to Pineville in '88 he drove [a wagon] to the top of Tanyard Hill, twenty-two miles from Harlan, and spent the night under the wagon, and drove to Pineville the next day and load it up. It took three days to get a thousand pounds into Harlan" (*Bryan Whitfield*).

ANNIE NAPIER (B. 1942): We were teetotaled isolated from the rest of the world. Now that's what I call growing up illiterate. We didn't have no TV, no newspapers. In fact we didn't have no electricity at all. Growing up in Cranks Creek, it was a world of its own. We didn't know anything about what was in Harlan, even. We didn't go there but once or twice a year anyway.

The image of isolated Appalachia dominated local-color and travel literature for more than a century. Isolation, however, was relative: since the colonial period, Appalachia had been incorporated into the expanding world markets as a peripheral supplier of raw materials. Before industrialization, however, Harlan was even more isolated than most Appalachian counties. Set at the non-navigable headwaters of the Cumberland River, it could not be reached by water and was linked to Hagan and Pineville only by wagon trails.[3] As the *New York Times* reported in 1889, Harlan is located "near the centre of the most mountainous of Kentucky mountains," where "the whistle of the locomotive has never been heard by many of its inhabitants" (the railroad reached Harlan in 1910).[4] Thus Harlan had few of the small industrial activities (sawmills, tanneries) or marketable staples (such as salt) that diversified the economy elsewhere in Appalachia.

Harlan-born writer G. C. Jones notes in his autobiography: "The valleys were very narrow, most of them not being wide enough for a road and the creek. You had to use the creek bed for a road."[5] "In Harlan County the hills are really high and the ridges are steeper, and the spaces between ridges are narrower. It is more dark, in terms of four o'clock in the afternoon; the sun is gone 'cause it's past beyond the mountaintops" (*Faith Holsdorf*). As a country song puts it, in Harlan "the sun comes up about ten in the morning / And the sun goes down about three in the day."[6]

"I had heard about Harlan County, and when I got there I had never seen any hillsides that were as steep as in Kentucky. It made an incredible impression on me. And I remember the corn growing there, and I remember that gardens were growing on these hillsides that seemed to be straight up" (*Faith Holsdorf*). Small family farms engaged in subsistence agriculture, using even the most marginal available land, prevailed in Harlan well into the twentieth century. Farms measured usually less than one hundred acres, divided between clear bottom land planted in corn, oats, and wheat, open pastureland and hayfields, and forest.[7]

> PLENNIE HALL (B. 1900): It wasn't nothing but what you raised is all you had, what you raised that's what you eat. I was living on Cranks Creek. I remember that before I went to the mines, my daddy he'd go to town once a year and get a hundred dollars out of the bank and when he sheared the sheep and get the wool, he'd sell them and he'd come home and pay the bank off. And if there was any left, that's what he'd get his blankets and things like that, you know, extra. But you raised everything. You raised your meat and your corn and everything, chickens. All we had to buy was our coffee and a little dab of sugar and stuff like that. I had everything that I had to have. There wasn't nobody but me and my mother. And me and her raised what we had, what we lived on we raised it.

"You just about eat what you raised, raised what you eat" (*Debbie Spicer*) is a recurring statement of pride and hardship in memories of farming and growing up. "We always grew about everything we ate. We didn't have money, you know. But we always had plenty to eat" (*Annie Napier*). "We had food. Not good food, but food" (*Chester Napier*). Sheep and hog raising, for sale or family consumption, flourished in Harlan as long as there was a viable farming economy.

> FRED NAPIER: Back when I was just a kid [in the early 1900s], big enough to remember anything, most everyone had a gang of sheep, and they'd take these shears, and get the wool off it; "Kentucky jeans," they called it. They'd make clothes out of it. I seen boys ten or eleven years old going around in their shirttails, buddy, nothing but their shirts on. If she didn't make it at home, you didn't eat, there was no money in circulation enough for them to buy [anything]. About all they had to buy was flour, sugar, and coffee. You didn't have to fatten no hog: you planted a chestnut tree and them hogs would get so fat they couldn't hardly walk, and they'd kill their hogs off. Awful good sweet meat it was.

"All they had to have money...they'd pay their taxes, when the taxes was low 'cause the land, timber and everything, there was nothing to sell, and I don't guess their taxes was over to three dollars a year on a whole big farm" (*Ben Lewis*). Insisting on self-sufficiency is a way of rejecting an image of poverty that implies a stigma of failure and shiftlessness. Though they hardly had money, they had food and a roof over their heads, and they worked hard for it; therefore they were not poor in that sense. Yet the rural population was not entirely isolated from the monetary economy, the market, and the state. John and Lottie Caldwell ran a self-sufficient farm on Pine Mountain but also had a store where they would sell "sugar 'n' coffee and just about everything anybody would need in a country: medicines and a few dry goods" (*Lottie Caldwell*). Plennie Hall's father dealt with banks and credit and bought staples with money earned working as a hired hand or selling wool.

To make ends meet, the work of all family members was necessary. "We [children] had our chores to do, too. We had to carry coal, a sack of coal every day, through the summer, so we'd have enough to last through the winter. And there was wood to be cut, then I went to working around the mines when I was twelve or thirteen" (*James Wright*).

ARTHUR JOHNSON: We children used to work in the fields and have to carry off rocks. We thought we were growing those rocks, because every year you had to carry rocks off the hillside to the potato patch. The littlest and the biggest ones, they would all join in and do that, and they would also carry water. Sometimes we had to carry water to livestock; little, little children would carry like a four-pound bucket, we'd save all our large buckets for things like that. We didn't throw away much, things didn't come in plastic containers. There was very little throwaway, very little littering in those days.

So...churning, I learned to churn. We had a churn about knee high, but it was almost shoulder high to me when I learned to churn. It was a square churn that sat in a frame, had a big wheel and a little wheel, the big wheel had a crank handle on it. And I was so fast [with] that piece of machinery atop that churn, that my mother thought I wanted to make a toy out of it.

"Back then if a farmer was farming and he got sick and he couldn't work his ground his neighbor'd come in and he just cleared up everything real good for him, and—and, they helped each other. Now people's selfish with each other" (*Debbie Spicer*). The practice of mutual help engendered a tradition of neighborly solidarity that would be sustained in later industrial conflicts.[8]

ANNIE NAPIER: Growing up on Noe's Branch, those three families seemed to live harder than anybody. And each family had a cow. And about two or three months every year they'd go dry for a while, till they could calve. But they would schedule them; Mommy would schedule hers so she'd have her cow before the Garrick neighbors. And then when our cow was dry, Miss Jones and Ruth Garrick would give us milk. And when one of their cows went dry, we'd give them milk, till their cow come in. And if it hadn't been for that, we'd all have starved to death.

In a sparsely populated area, cooperation and reciprocity were also occasions of socialization and entertainment: "They call it barn raising: somebody want to build a barn, the neighbors from all over the country, from all around, they'd gather in and put his barn up in one day. They'd make it a favorite spot to be there; they'd have it planned away ahead of time, and just about everybody would be there, that lived in the country" (*Ben Lewis*).

FRANK MAJORITY: The fall of the year they'd have a corn shucking. Everybody'd get together and shuck off corn and they'd have them play music with moonshine to drink. Sometimes they'd have a house raising or log rolling and they'd go and clear a whole new field—cut all the timber, dig out the roots so the farmer could plant corn or something for next year. And that's when they had a good time.

BOBBIE DAVIDSON: We would have stir-offs in the fall. That's where they make molasses, out of sugar cane. Cane is grown like corn, and when they harvest it, they take a horse, and tie him to a big wheel, and he goes around continuously; they feed the cane stalks into the wheel, it squeezes out all the sap and makes molasses, which is something like syrup. And that was a big to-do, especially when I was growing up. Everybody in the community would be there, you'd have music, and it was just a big party. It was a social occasion, they don't necessarily need help. It was just an excuse to get together.

Activities such as hunting, fishing, and gathering preserved the closeness to the land and supplemented diet and income. "You'd kill wild meat, took a lot of wild meat in the mountains and plenty fish in the river, and [picked] some currants" (*Debbie Spicer*). "[My mother] she picked salad greens—'sallit,' they call it; she would pick poke [and] they'd sell it down at Harlan, that's the biggest thing everybody eats.[9] My grandfather used to say: 'When you see those women going around the hill with their buckets and knives'—they'd carry a butcher knife to cut the greens—'you know spring is here'" (*Arthur Johnson*). Ginseng was one crop that could be sold outside the region and even abroad: "You use the mountains for ginsenging; we have another herb that's in the spring of the year, we call bear's lettuce, it's a very nice greens for cooking, because you pour some hot grease over it and you can use the bacon mixed in with this, but it's delicious. It's a small green plant and it grows in the hollers where it's damp. But all these things were just natural in the mountains, and people that used the mountains, took all this for granted" (*Hazel King*).[10]

Folk knowledge regulated the cycles and times by planting "by the signs," matching the zodiac signs to the phases of the moon: "My dad, the first three days of May, he called the barren days. He didn't plant nothing; but after that, we went to planting corn. I had a sister watched them signs. Signs in the moon and sun, new moon and old moon, light nights and dark nights: don't set out no shrubs on light nights, wait for dark nights" (*Debbie Spicer*). Harlan-born poet Vivian Shipley writes of the times when hogs were slaughtered or taken to market when the moon was high, so that their meat would weigh more.[11]

Folk knowledge does not necessarily mean best agricultural practices. "The family farm in Appalachia was destroyed because of lack of knowledge in cultivation. Didn't know much about fertilization, didn't know anything about crop rotation. It wasn't all that good a land either, but it didn't take long for them to wear the land out: one of the major crops was corn, and corn is terrible, terribly hard on the soil. If you don't put soybeans on it, or you don't rotate it, that land would be completely worn out. Then they would move, they'd clear another area, clear-cut it, cut everything down and then plant again" (*James B. Goode*). On one hand, the frontier assumption that space was inexhaustible did not encourage the preservation of the land; on the other, farmers did not own enough land to allow fields to remain fallow and to rotate crops, especially as farm families were usually large and farms became increasingly fragmented with each generation.[12]

> BEN LEWIS: My dad lived on the Poor Fork River across the mountain on the highway side. And his daddy moved in the head of what they call Little Harlan. And they had twelve children, nine boys and three girls. And then my dad, which was one of the boys, he married my mother. There was ten of us altogether but they are dead, most of them died young. Before the logging started, everything was farming, and when they had good pieces of land, they just cut the timber down, rolled up and burnt it, they'd clear up that land, raised their crops. All the time [the family was] getting bigger and he had to divide the farm.

Rural Appalachia had been no egalitarian heaven to begin with. The first families that settled in the region secured the largest land grants. At the beginning of the Civil War, 43 percent of rural families had no title to land; by 1892, more than 60 percent of the land in Harlan and nearby Letcher and Rowan counties was owned by nonresidents—a pattern that would be reinforced by the appropriation of land by logging and mining companies. This originated a landless proletariat or forced small farmers to seek extra income by working outside the farm. "I worked many a day, a many a day for a dime, and fifteen cents. Worked all day long; sometimes they give me a quarter. On a farm" (*Bobby Simpson*). "[Before] the Depression hit, we could make a dollar a day if we went out and hoed corn all day, ten hours for somebody that had a big field of corn, or had a big garden that would need work in it" (*Granny Hager*). Debbie Spicer's family raised all they ate, but did not get to eat all they raised: "We didn't own no land, we just rented. We paid money for our house rent, rented us a house, rented the fields, and we'd give a third of our corn to the renter, for the rent." Yet the inequalities of hiring out and tenancy did not generate a sense of class difference: Debbie Spicer remembers her landlords as "just people, just more or less our neighbors."[13] By the time industry came to Appalachia, subsistence farming was in decline. As the population grew, farm sizes shrank, and the standard of living declined, former subsistence farmers were ready to become available as a low-wage workforce for the logging and mining industries.[14] Jim Garland, union activist and folk singer, wrote: "Though my earliest Kentucky ancestors were landowners like most of the first white settlers, we had to turn to sharecropping as land became more and more concentrated in the hands of fewer and fewer Kentuckians. Later, as the family grew and farming on a small scale became an impossible way to make a living, we worked in the coal mines."[15]

"So much of our property here is owned by absentee ownership. Probably about 75 percent. You will find very few areas that are owned by private individuals on Black Mountain. There rest are owned by companies out of here" (*Daniel Howard*). By 1980, only 2 percent of the land in Harlan was used for farming. The 1974 agricultural census listed only forty-six farmers, many near retirement age, most holding several jobs, earning inadequate incomes. Meanwhile, new threats had come upon the land in the guise of strip mining and clear-cutting. The creeks filled with silt, floods became frequent, and acid drainage ruined the water: "Folks can't farm anymore, because the clay mud has washed over the soil; the land no longer absorbs water" (*Becky Simpson*).[16]

FAMILY VALUES: I DONE HAD A NATION

DANIEL HOWARD: Everybody raised chickens. Everybody and, I guess, some of the memorable occasions was after Thanksgiving, the first time the frost would come on, and the whole family would come together and slaughter probably from eight to ten hogs, now. Of course every family has a black sheep. But then the black sheep always stayed a part of that family whether they liked him, or whether they didn't. It's been the closeness—you're poor, but you don't realize you're poor, and you make it up in family ties and family values.

"I ain't got much but I've got family and I'm one of the well-blessed people on earth" (*Robert Simpson*). "We had nothing but hard times and each other" (*Annie Napier*). "We may not a-had much, but we had love" (*Chester Napier*). Among Appalachian children, Harvard child psychiatrist Robert Coles found need and deprivation, but also a "a greater sense of family," a stronger allegiance to parents and grandparents, a closer and noncompetitive relationship to siblings as well as cousins and neighbors, and a clearer sense of their own identity than in city children. "Even before adolescence," researchers concluded, "mountain children learn that a family is no laughing matter."[17]

"Kinfolks," "ancestors," "generations," and the icons of the family farm or the "home place" are key words and images in a family-centered culture. Many families have been on the land for generations—"My mother's side of the family, they had homesteaded the place. This makes about the fifth generation. I guess it's why I worked so hard to [save it]" (*Becky Simpson*)—and each nuclear family is part of a broad, intricate kinship network. As late as the 1980s, sociologist Shaunna Scott found that in one of the Harlan communities in which she conducted her fieldwork, "many of the 180 residents were related...and over half were descended from four original settling families."[18]

CHARLOTTE NOLAN: We are related in many instances, and you will find in these mountains here double first cousins. Brothers married sisters and their children are double first cousins. The way you find out we are related real fast, when election time comes around, they'll shake your hand and remind you we're third cousins, which means that you're a little bit obliged to vote for me. I mean, after all, right? Kinfolks hafta stick together—and you may not know this man from Adam. But still, you're related, and you always brag on your kinfolk.

ED CAWOOD: I've heard of a family up here at Cawood that were Swanson and Osborne. I heard that six Swansons married six Osbornes. There are a lot of double cousins here, double first cousins. I can name you several of them. They're proud of it, but you know back when the pioneer load first came in, people couldn't get out very well. If you [wanted] a girlfriend, you had to go with some of your relatives maybe, that was the only choice you had. There's not much of it anymore. A lot of new people have come in. Foreigners and...people who go away to college, they marry these girls.[19]

Decades of industrialization and migration have spread kinship over broader spaces. Sons and daughters have moved far away and left children to be raised by grandparents, who sometimes ended up adopting them. Yet it remains a powerful factor of identity, preserved by the ritual of family reunions: "Just everybody gets together on the homecoming, everybody takes some kind of food with 'em, and we all get together and eat and talk, well, do more talking than we do eating. As the saying goes, there'll be enough food to feed Jackson's army" (*Chester Napier*).

ARTHUR JOHNSON: And sometimes people were married for years before they found out that they were related. See, if you lived at Smith, you can come down from Smith toward Cawood and Harlan and get a job; you can come in by Wallins, at Black Star, and you can get a job. Or you can go and get a job down in Bell County. Okay now, if one brother went down one creek [and a second brother went down another], then the grandchildren think they are different sets, and they get going around and later on we had drive-in restaurants and the movies and then you meet a real nice girl from down in Bell County named Lewis, and you just go wild about her, that's a different set, that's Bell County Lewises, and nobody bothers to investigate, this young couple gets married, he is twenty-one, she is eighteen, he's got a good job at the mine or somewhere, and...they have been married several years and then one of the great-grandparents dies and they both go to the same funeral, and they find out—"Well, wait a minute!"—maybe they are third cousins.

DEBBIE SPICER: How did we meet? He lived here in Louellen camp, a young man and he worked in the mines. And I lived at Clover Splint. We bought a piece of property here at Highsplint, and we'd go and farm that ground, and we walked the road. I guess I had a hole on my back when he seed me the first time. He told his mother, said, "Who is that little old girl?" She said, "That's little old baby Bean." He said, "That little old baby Bean's mine." I was the only girl that he ever went with. I was sixteen years old when I married him. He was nineteen.

MOSSIE JOHNSON: So we just started walking down the street together and the first thing I knowed we was married, and the next thing I knowed we had sixteen children. Well, we didn't have them all at one time. I was sixteen. I was married nine months and fifteen days when I had my baby. And...everything seemed to be all right in the world at that time, of course I didn't realize what trouble was. It was in the Depression. In twenty-one years we had sixteen children. But one of them was a miscarriage. And then my baby was four and a half when [my husband] got killed with that rock, slate rock. And we have had a real happy life if it hadn't been for that. We had a daughter that died from childbirth, and...she had had eleven children, but when she had her twelfth child, it come too early and killed her. Then I had another girl that shot herself with a pistol, and...I don't know if she done it intentionally or accidentally because it went through her liver and the doctors worked with her but they couldn't [help] her. So...

"Back then people got married really young, and [my grandmother] she was just a baby, twelve years old, and had two kids, she was a baby; well, twelve years old with one, and then she had another one" (*Charlene Dalton*). "A lot of them get married at fourteen, fifteen, some thirteen. There was [one] in the paper here a while back that was eleven. She married a thirty-one-year-old man. Now if I'd been that parent, I would have put my foot down, I would have said, 'No, you ain't either.' That's too young, you're knocking them out of their childhood. Up until well when I was growing up, girls didn't need no education. Anybody can rock, all girls were any good for was housework, cooking, and raise the babies and rock them. Wait on their husband hand and foot. Now that's all changing a whole lot" (*Annie Napier*).[20]

> JULIA COWANS: When I married the first time, it wasn't to a man that I loved, it was a man I was forced for security reasons, a coal miner. He was twenty-eight years older than myself, and I'd always taken care of my momma's children and I didn't ever want any children. And I married and they came two years apart like clockwork. Just baby, baby, baby. I had my first baby in April and I was eighteen in May. We was in the mountains down in Harlan County and, back in the mountains we didn't know nothing about no birth control—never even heard of it. God almighty, I done had a nation. Sometimes I'd have one in my stomach, one in my lap and one by the hand.[21]

Early marriages are not just a holdover from an archaic rural past: in fact, between 1880 and 1910, industrialization lowered the age at which men married and started families.[22] "Some of those miners who had money and were single when they were teenage, and they would work at one mine for a while and stay up at the boarding house, and move to another one and...there were always girls, they had girlfriends...they were working kids, fifteen and sixteen making coal miners' wages and coal miners' wages compared to other wages were pretty good. So sometimes they would marry a girl younger than they were, they'd be seventeen, marry a girl fifteen, and...a year later they'd start fighting and maybe there would be a child on the way...or sometimes they'd run through a couple of bad marriages by the time of their middle twenties. They didn't practice any kind of birth control so they had as many children as...as they had, however it went" (*Arthur Johnson*).

> NANCY MAYER (NAME CHANGED; B. 1966): My sister was fifteen when she got married. And my brother was sixteen when he got married. My mother was married at the age of fourteen. I know mostly young kids—I watch people, I see how they act. And, this one girl got married because she didn't want to stay home. She didn't like her mom or her dad. Or, her parents wouldn't listen to her; or, her dad would—beat on her, something like that. My mother, she had a hard life growing up. Like, her mother had fourteen kids. She lost three in birth. And then she lost one fourteen years ago. He was shot. He was playing with these kids when he got shot, and my mother never got over it.
>
> PORTELLI: Are many of these marriages caused by pregnancies?
>
> MAYER: That's the reason [my sister] she got married. But she gave us a beautiful niece. She's beautiful. And so when you grow up my age—you need cousins and kin. But people here love their kids. They protect them. I know my sister does. She's gonna have another one. She's got two now. She's eighteen.

PORTELLI: How old was your daughter when she got married, the one you said had eleven children?

MOSSIE JOHNSON: Seventeen.

PORTELLI: So how many grandchildren, great-grandchildren, do you have?

JOHNSON: I'll have to get a pencil and a paper and figure out all night. I know I've got fourteen grandsons, and I don't know how many grand-daughters. And I've got some great-grandchildren, and I think I've got three or four great-great-grandchildren. Lots of them I've not even seen, they live some ways away from here. Well, that's what the Bible said, it says fill the world up, so we filled the world up, we helped fill it up. But we had a good life.

WOMAN'S WORK

JOHNNY JONES: [I have] thirteen children. Eight boys and five girls. Baby is thirty-five years old.

PORTELLI: You raised them all here in Lynch?

JOHNNY JONES: I don't believe I could have made it nowhere else. This is a woman's town, here. You take a town where a woman don't work, this is a woman's town.

MRS. JONES: Can you imagine a woman having thirteen children and not working?

"I had six children, and back about '83 I was always nervous, and my sister asked me, 'What's the matter, Becky?' I said, 'I've cooked more rice than a Chinese person, and I've broke so many eggs I'm shell-shocked'" (*Becky Simpson*). "There were thirteen of us in my family. [My mother] she had a real hard time, but she never complained. My mother never complains" (*Bobbie Davidson*). "Growing up in the mountains," said Harlan-born poet and writer George Ella Lyon, "it's a very antifemale culture. It's very patriarchal, the culture as a whole. I think in the mountains there's a strong notion of silence, particularly for women. Because it's a family-centered culture, women have to keep the role they have had, simply because it's harder to make changes."

"Usually, if you think about farming couples, the woman's job is as important as the man's" (*Mildred Shackleford*). "When I was growing up, women did *all* the work. Men just walked in and out of a regular job; they didn't have any responsibility around the house" (*Annie Napier*). "Well my mother was [a] Holiness woman, she went to church and, as far as I remember back, she'd love us, and take care of us, and my dad he'd grunt, laid around drinking" (*J. C. Hall*).

ANNIE NAPIER: Mommy, she liked to sew, quilt, work in the garden. Mommy used to plow out a horse, have a garden, load coal, do whatever come handy. I guess I took that part after her. Mommy worked like a horse. She worked from daylight till dark. She was what you call a slave. 'Cause she worked all day in the cornfield, plowing, come home, milk the cows, cook supper, referee us kids—which was a job. But, she always seemed like she was pretty happy with it. And she went to church every night. She handled snakes—yeah. And she was bit seven times on her hand in one church service, and I don't know how many times she was bitten at. But it didn't hurt her a bit.

MOSSIE JOHNSON: I was used to a lot of kids and, I had always plenty of food in my house, I had my children at home, but I had a lot of neighbors' kids, a lot of kids live around here then, and I'd make big kettles of soup beans, and sometimes I'd make as much as five cakes a day, and I always told all the different people that come in, "I cook it, I leave it in the kettle, you help yourself," and ever[y] child come in seem to fall in line and we didn't see no strangers then. I always figured, if I had beans and potatoes in my house, my house wasn't empty. And I made a lot of homemade candy and stuff like that. And cakes, and we'd have a lot of meat. We killed chickens then, I could kill a chicken a day. I didn't kill one anyway, but my neighbor would chop their heads off if Charlie wasn't home. So we, we just had a normal life, and if God hadn't been with us and worked to death for us, I guess I would have give up at times.

MEEDIA JONES: Didn't have no 'lectric, didn't have no facilities, no automatic washing machines, you scrubbed the clothes on the board; got the water out of the branch, we didn't have a well at one time, we had a little spring, so we later got us a well dug. We never got electric in our home until 1950. I had an old gasoline washing machine, and you'd crank on it half a day to try to get it started and once you got it started you didn't want to turn it off because if you did you'd have to crank it again. The cranking was harder than if you'd actually done the work yourself.

"My mother raised us over an old washboard" (*Henry Farmer*). The evolution from the washboard to the gasoline-operated washing machine to the electric washer is one of the great developments in Harlan County history. "We didn't have no water in the house. We had a well out in the yard by the kitchen door, and we done our washing in a big old washtub and board. Had to wash our clothes on a board, washboard they call it. We didn't have no washer and dryer then, we had to dry our clothes out on the line, in the yard" (*Melinda Slusher*). "My husband got a washing machine when we had our third child, it had wringers on it, it was a button automatic, it was a really nice washing machine. But I'd go through one about every year, I washed so much. Yeah, we had to have a new table set and a new washing machine every year" (*Mossie Johnson*).

CHARLENE DALTON: My grandmother always told me tales because she was always the storyteller of the family. She bathed me and told me stories and all kinds of stuff. She could make beans, corn bread, chicken and dumplings, and she'd tell you how not to stir them, that was the secret. She was married at twelve years old to Jim Daniels, and it was an abusive situation, because he was a pretty fast man, you know.[23] She had two kids that was my mother and her sister, and she left them with his mother, and she left the mountains to come to Cincinnati.

ANNIE NAPIER: What I got from Mommy and a lot of other people, back when they was growing up their grandmothers would hand it down to 'em, their husband treated 'em extremely cruel. All their sexual life was just pain. There was no pleasure in it. It was all for the man and nothing for the woman except pain.[24] And—they've been more or less treated like cattle. Breeding cattle. Which it seems extremely cruel, to me, the way they was treated. And then if they didn't wanna have sex, the husband, they would beat 'em. And it was considered proper for 'em to beat 'em. And some of them actually left their husbands and when they'd go home the husband would tell their daddy, and their daddy would beat 'em. Which I always thought that was cruel—you know. A woman's human too, they can just stand so much pain. And some of 'em would just absolutely, leave—left in the nighttime, when everybody went to sleep, they would get out and maybe walk for fifty miles. In any direction, just to get away from their husband and their parents.

PORTELLI: Were the girls told anything about sex?

ANNIE NAPIER: Oh no, there's nothing, no; no. Nothing was told about sex. We was told absolutely nothing about the normal body functions of a girl at a certain age. [My sisters] knew about it. They knew you was gonna get your period; but they wasn't allowed to tell me. Mommy didn't tell me. And I liked to died, it liked to scared me to death. I thought, "Oh God, I'm dying; I'm bleeding to death," I didn't know what caused it. I can't believe I ever been much more terrified, except when they done snake handling in church. I'd been riding my bicycle, you know, so all of a sudden I was bleeding to death. I went home and lay down. I was scared to death, I didn't know what it was. I was laying on the bed—terrified; just plain terrified. But there's no way in the world I'd have let my girls grow up like that. No, you didn't talk about sex, you didn't talk about your period; the menopause was strictly—nobody knew anything about that. When they started getting hot flashes, nervous from it—they were going nuts; just going crazy. And one man that I know of did have his wife committed to Eastern State. She got real nervous, you know, extremely nervous. He had her committed to Eastern State.

"Used to the babies was borned at home, you didn't go to the hospital. Mine, they was born at home. Oh yeah, and I nursed them on the breast" (*Debbie Spicer*). "They was all borned at home. We had an attendant physician from the coal mines, Peabody Coal Company furnished us doctors, and we also had a hospital at one time. And they delivered—they made house calls, when you were sick, and they delivered babies at home. I could have went to a hospital, but I preferred to be at home, with Mom" (*Meedia Jones*).

PORTELLI: Did you have most of your children at home?
MOSSIE JOHNSON: Let's see, I had Gerald, Downy, and Charlotte, and Junior and Bob and Cork, and Mick and Penney, that's eight, and...Fred is nine, then I...had a miscarriage and then I had ten, eleven, twelve, I had the rest of them in the hospital. But at the hospital that's worse than it is at home. At home you can get up and walk all you want to, if you're ready, but at the hospital they confine you right where you sit, if you went to labor. God sure done a lot of things for me.

ANNIE NAPIER: If it hadn't been for the C-section me and Sherry both would have died. Now, that was a fight with religion. The way I was raised, surgery is completely out, any kind of drugs is out. I went to the doctor all the time, I wanted to make sure that the baby was all right. But he told me, since I was so small most likely I would have had to have a C-section. And I tried desperately to prepare my family for it, because this was a thing we'd never been...But they kept saying, "No, you won't have to do that. No." So the day my water broke I went on to the hospital and this nurse kept telling me, "What're you gonna do, have this baby and no pain?" I said, "No, I don't think so, I'm still planning on some." And then they gave me shots and put me into labor. So, I told this nurse, "They's absolutely something wrong, because the pain's misplaced where it's s'posed to be." And she checked Sherry's heartbeat and she turned as white as her uniform. You know, they can tell by their heartbeat which way the baby is. Then they got trying to round up the surgeon. And all this time my mother was saying: "No; no; absolutely no." And I told Chester, I said, "It's my decision, it's my baby, and if you don't go along with me I'll kill you when I get out if I live through it." I said, "I'm gonna have surgery because I've been carrying this baby for nine months, I've always wanted babies, and if you don't go along with me I'll kill you." And he knowed I was serious, which I was, I was serious as a heart attack. I told that nurse, I said, "Bring me the papers, do the surgery, 'cause I want this baby alive." So finally I told Mommy, "I'm gonna have the surgery, and that's it, that's final; the papers is signed, I'm gonna have it, if I die I'm dead 'cause I'm gon' die anyway. And I want this baby alive." They agreed for Dr. —— to do the surgery. And Dr. —— was drunk. So they kept giving him black coffee to try to sober him up from about two o'clock to seven. They pulled him from the club up at the golf course and him drunk, to do the surgery. And he liked to let me bleed to death. I never will forget what he said. They just give me a spinal. It just paralyzes you from the waistline down; you don't feel anything, so I knew everything that was going on. I never will forget when he cut into the main artery. He said to this [other] doctor, with the mask on and everything, all that you could see was just so much of their eyes, and he—he was very concerned, this other doctor was; but Dr. ——— said, "Well, I'll be goddamn, I think I'm still gonna let her die." It was so comical—after it was over. And this other doctor he said, "Hell no you ain't either." He said, "If you do," he said, "your license is pulled, because I'll make sure of it." So they had this argument going over me, you know. And the blood just standing there like a spigot. So finally they got it clamped off. Now this was before they got the baby out.

"My grandmother was born in 1888. My grandmother used to ride a mule and deliver mail for fifty cents a day. She worked. Now a woman during that time delivering mail was unusual. But she done it. And she would carry it in a Bull Durham tobacco sack tied around her waist with a string" (*Mildred Shackleford*). "Oh I can tell you about Mother. She was a very hardworking lady. She was raised at across Pine Mountain, a two-room house, had a dirt floor. She went to Pine Mountain Settlement School, got an education. She went from there to Berea, and worked her way through there. And she went to Eastern State to get a teacher's certificate. She started teaching. They were very poor. Mother was an ambitious woman. She was very determined. She was interested in the community, her children, just worked like the dickens all of her life" (*Clyde Bennett*).

I asked Hazel King what she thought of the women's liberation movement. "I didn't realize that we weren't liberated already," she said, "'cause I was always rebellious from a child. I wanted to lift as much as my brothers and I wanted to climb as fast and high, do all the active things, hunting and fishing, instead of being in the house listening about babies and cooking." Hazel King never married, joined the air force, and in her old age climbed the hillsides to document and denounce strip mining. Other women drew a sense of power and independence from being able to raise a family in spite of hardships, or from getting an education and earning their own income as teachers, mail carriers, nurses, midwives, office workers, salesclerks, waitresses, truck drivers, or coal miners.[25]

CHARLENE DALTON: Mamie had six husbands, and she outlived them all. [She] was born in eighteen something; when she was twelve years old she had my mom and her sister and they moved to Cincinnati. Mamie, she was a mail lady for a long time in Evarts. Carried the mail and stuff in a car, and then she moved to Cincinnati, and eventually we all kind of followed. She had five husbands, five or six, but she outlived all of them. She was meaner that a snake, bless her heart; I loved her dearly, but she was meaner than a snake.

MILDRED SHACKLEFORD: My grandmother, my dad's mother, never claimed to have any sort of independence whatsoever. She was always one of those people to say, "Let your grandfather decide this" or "Let your grandfather do that." But my grandfather never decided to do anything without asking her permission. Nobody else in the family did either. When she died, she had money on her. None of the rest [of] 'em had. And I can remember lots of times when I was a kid that my grandfather would go to her and ask her for money, and she would carry it in a little tobacco sack tied around a string under her dress. She would turn her back to him and pull her tobacco sack out and count it off and tell him to bring her money back. And he would.

"I was never married. So I was independent, you know, from the beginning. I never wanted to be saddled with a family. I wanted to be free to go on a moment's notice. You know, have tux will travel kind of thing" (*Charlotte Nolan*). Yet a woman interviewed by Shaunna Scott told her: "My status as a single woman, with no children, contributed to my subordinate, dependent position. It seemed that [some people here] did not regard an individual, particularly a woman, as a full adult until they married."[26] "When I was in school, there were very few options for girls to find themselves in ways of developing and exploring their own interests and identities. Your identity came from whose child you were. The social pressures for girls not to be interested in anything, in anything but boys, were strong; it was not okay to be interested in school. You were really ostracized if you showed that kind of interest" (*George Ella Lyon, b. 1949*). Yet things were changing.

MARY NOLAN: Our women teachers were single. And when they got married they would have to resign because the powers that be knew that a woman's first priority was her family and she couldn't do best at both. But the war changed that. People got accustomed to a higher standard of living which required incomes from both the man and the woman. At the time we were married my husband would have been insulted if I had wanted to go out and work. He'd say, "How dare you? I can afford to take care of my family. Your role is to stay at home and when we have children to take care of them." But that changed. The man ceased to have that kind of false pride or whatever you call it, and they enjoy the double income.

LINDA HAIRSTON: Seriously. I talk to you from my heart, because it's serious, it's true. Money makes me happy. I like money. I work because I want money. [Since] I got thirteen years old, I said I'd never marry a man that was gonna beat me or hit for any reason. I can understand why women stayed back there, in those days, with them men. But, today, understand, I have no pity for anyone that will sit back whining, on a monthly check, and say, "I'm on welfare..." What will you do when your kids get older? What kind of life you gonna have? What kind of experience—you're forty-some years old, your kids are all grown, what you gonna do? I wanna know that when I get sixty years old I can get Social Security not from some husband that I've married before, but from myself. That's the reason I'm teaching my kids to be independent. I'm a woman of my own. I can deal with it.

ANNIE NAPIER: Right. I don't like housework. I hate housework. It could be one of the reasons it's such a disaster. I don't like cooking, I don't like housework. But, I love big vehicles. I learned to drive an International K7 log truck when I was about ten years old. It wouldn't've been as big as the school bus I got now, but it was a big vehicle. I made my lessons when I was sixteen. And I've always been, you know, just gung ho for the highway.

WE DIDN'T DREAM OF A WHITE CHRISTMAS

"We grew up hard," says Annie Napier, yet "you grow up with a sense of pride." The harder it was growing up, the greater the pride. *Growing Up Hard in Harlan County*, the title of the autobiography of G. C. Jones, former businessman, logger, and coal miner, means growing up in hardship, but also *becoming* hard, gaining strength, and learning tenderness from that hardship. Annie Napier said: "We growed up hard. But I guess we learned the value of growing up that most people never know. And that's love. We all worked together, we played together, we cried together, and we still do."

NOAH SURGENER: We'd have to get up before daylight to go to work. We were just so rich we didn't have no clock. We had to get up when the chickens crow. When the old rooster crowed the second time, we'd get out of there. We was po' folks, you know.
PORTELLI: There is a lot of pride in that, isn't it?
SURGENER: Well, there's a lot of heartache in it. I mean, a lot of people [talk about] them good old days, but we had a lot of time and no money. Now we've got a little money and no time.

"People now, they got a silver spoon in their mouth. They don't even know how hard times was back then. You walked backwards and forwards to your work, you didn't have nothing but horseback or a wagon, that's all you had to ride. Now kids, they want the school bus to go out under the bed and get them," said Plennie Hall. But he added: "I'm awful proud that I had it to do."

MILDRED SHACKLEFORD: But it wasn't all that bad, really. I think it gave us something that a lot of kids nowdays don't have because we learned to entertain ourselfs; we learned to do things for ourselfs. Didn't have money to buy anything with. We didn't have baseball bats, gloves, or any of that kind of stuff. So if we wanted to play ball, me and my sister would go into the woods and cut a tree down. We would make a baseball [bat] out of that. We would get old green apples or rocks or anything that was hard, and we would put rags around it and wrap black tape on it, and we would make balls out of that. We spent a lot of time swimming, playing in rivers, climbing the mountains, chasing after snakes or any other animals.

"If you think about the way we growed up—actually, it was a miracle that we survived" (*Annie Napier*). The hardship was, in the first place, material. Annie Napier again: "You know that song that a lot of the country singers sing—'I'm dreaming of a white Christmas'? We didn't dream of a white Christmas. It was more like a nightmare."

BOBBY SIMPSON: Many a time, it'd be so cold you couldn't walk, you'd have to run, and I had three-quarters of a mile to go to from the house to the schoolhouse. [One] day, there was three inches of snow on the ground, and I had to foot it back barefooted to the house. Then the next morning when I went back I had to go back to it again, and my teacher bought me a pair of shoes. I don't know where she's at today, but I still won't forget her, her name was Gladys Harper.

SUDIE CRUSENBERRY: I had two to die with quick pneumonia. One of them wasn't but a day old, and the other, she was a little over ten months old. You be sitting like you are here, and that old homemade [curtain] they had, it would blow, you know. It was just like somebody a-beating on the house, and the air would shoot in. And it was real cold, you know. You had an open fireplace, and if you didn't have the money to buy the coal with, you'd have to get out where some had been dumped, the slate, and get your coal out, you know, and pack it in.

"Seemed like that people was more adapted to the weather, they didn't freeze" (*Ben Lewis*). This is more metaphor than fact, another way of saying that hardship hardens. Yet most narratives, including Lewis's, begin with the tale of growing up cold: "I can remember the outhouses and how cold they were. My first home that I can remember, we didn't have any wallpaper or anything, the side[s] of the house were papered with just cardboard boxes" (*Bobbie Davidson*). "Wake up of the morning and brush the snow out of your hair. Buddy it was cold. When I was raised up, we just had two rooms. Four of us all in that one little house. We made it" (*Henry Farmer*).

ANNIE NAPIER: But see, when a baby's born, the first thing is, when a baby's born, all odds in the world is against it, back when I was growing up. The first thing, the house is so cold, they're lucky to survive. Most of them is born underweight because of nutrition. But then after you get the little critters here, they start doctoring them with these homemade remedies. First thing you do is make you a sugar tit. You know what a sugar tit is?[27]

JERRY JOHNSON: Those old remedies were invented to clear the conscience of the parents once the child died. For example, German measles—there was one guy in Harlan County that had sheep. And they assured [him] sheep shit would cure the measles if you made tea of it. And fed the kid. They'd get some sheep shit, they'd boil it; they'd feed it to the kid; the kid died; and they said, "We tried; we really tried to save our child."[28]

MEEDIA JONES: You didn't go to the doctors, you had home remedies—poultices made out of mustard seeds—now that was a hot, hot poultice, you didn't watch you'd burn yourself with it. They took tallow out of groundhogs, betwixt the flesh and the hide, they skinned it off, render it out and put it in a container, they used it as a rub for croups and colds, and what have you. Then spicewood, they took the bark off'n it, to break you with the measles. My mother always made us a tonic in the spring of the year. Cherry bark, and a lot of things, and she brewed it together, strained it. She called it spring tonic; she said her blood was tired from the long winter, and she gave us that tea in the spring of the year, to perk you up. My mother'd always take mullein, have you got mullein in your [country]? It looks like a tobacco plant. She'd take the leaves off it and boil them, it made a good cough syrup. You put sugar in it and drink it; for cough.

"All our clothes was, they was feed sacks. Where they got feed for the stock, and then you make clothes out of that" (*Bobby Simpson*). "I didn't know hardly what a new pair of shoes was. Of course I didn't wear out no pants much" (*James L. Turner*). "Clothes, well we had to buy clothes. Now, when I was a kid we got one pair of shoes a year. Two bib of overalls and two shirts. And the younger ones they'd get jackets from the older ones, handed down for the next winter. And no socks. No one around here wore socks" (*Chester Napier*).

"Little kids didn't have stuff, like today, because their clothes were, for the little boys, long-sleeved, and their shirts came down to their ankles, and what they call brogans, 'cause I've got my daddy's little sister's brogans that died, you know. And so Daddy gave them to me, you know, and I put them away, with my stuff" (*Sudie Crusenberry*). Going barefoot becomes the experience that sums up—materially and symbolically—the experience of growing up hard. "And most kids went barefooted all summer and they wouldn't get but one pair of shoes and they'd get it in the wintertime" (*Ben Lewis*).

BECKY SIMPSON: Bobby told me of a hurtful thing happen to him. His whole family did work for this man, and he came and got Bobby's family one day to help him unload his coal, and Bobby was barefooted, and his feet stuck to the bed of the truck, it had a steel bed in it, and it was so cold that his feet stuck to the steel.

"One of the biggest things that I remember, that stand out the most. Mother would tell us, 'Now children, I know you're going to have to wear patches but if those patches are clean, they're honorable but if they're dirty, they're not. Always try to keep your patches clean'" (*Granny Hager*). In a classic country song, Dolly

Parton sings of a "coat of many colors" that her mother sewed out of a sack of rags received in charity. While the handmade coat is to her a symbol of mother's love, to her schoolmates it is a sign of poverty, to be made fun of.[29]

> SUDIE CRUSENBERRY: And then they was a woman that let Mom have a lot of these colored flowered feed sacks, and Mommy would make them. You know, my little coat, when I started down the primer over here, my grandma made me on that pedal machine in there. She took [some] wine-colored corduroy, and she put me a little white lining in it, and worked the buttonholes on it, and the buttons, and that's the first little coat I remember. That was the year I started in kindergarten.

"I got spanked so many times when I was growing up—I've been tied with a rope and whipped—that now I can hardly ever do it. Every time I start to do it the thought of what I went through flashes right through me and it hurts me more than it does the kids. I just don't believe in it" (*Chester Napier*). In an analysis typical of the "culture of poverty" approach that ends up blaming social ills on the victims' own culture, psychologist David H. Loof explains the high incidence of school phobia in contemporary Appalachia's children with "overly dependent personality disorders" and "symbiotic psychosis" created by overly affectionate and overly indulgent families.[30] Most narratives do insist on family love and closeness, and many families visibly dote on their children; yet there is little overindulgence in memories of growing up.[31]

> PARRIS BURKE: My mother—she was a good Christian woman. She was saved in the Baptist church when she was sixteen years old, and then she got in the Pentecostal way. But she raised her children, she taught them to go to school, and...she believed in the stick, the switch. She really believed in that, and it works, it works, now you can't whip a child in school and anything but I really believe in the rod of correction, for their own good.

A "strict" raising was part of growing up hard, and growing up hard was part of "a good childhood," to be remembered with pride: "We would work, my dad he would [work] us, they were very strict on us. Wouldn't take anything for the way I was raised, I just love it because it was hard, but seemed like you appreciated the world, you appreciate things more when you are raised like that" (*Parris Burke*).

As a favorite phrase in Harlan goes, there are "two sides to everything."[32] Thus love and repression could coexist in the same relationship, in the same context. Children were at risk, and therefore precious; children's work was necessary, and therefore they were bound to strict discipline and early toil. "I started working when I wasn't big enough to even pack the bucket. I was about four years old. That's somewhere about '40. I was born in 1936" (*Bobby Simpson*).

And then gender roles took their toll:

ANNIE NAPIER: My mother's first husband walked out on her three days before her second son was born. He laid out drunk with this other woman for two weeks and he came home and his daughter, she was crazy about her dad and she ran up to him, to snuggle up and pet him, and he had a vicious hangover and he slapped her back so hard she had to learn to walk all over again, he did something to it. So Mom picked up the baby and left. Went back to her parents walking. He followed her up the mountain and caught up with her and tried to slap her. She turned around and pulled a .38 on him, she almost blew his face off. The powder stayed on his face a long time.

"I mean, people grow up here, their parents have beaten them, and they beat their kids, and they just think that's the way it's supposed to be. There is a lot of domestic violence here in Harlan. It's mostly drug- and alcohol-related" (*Marjorie Napier*). Memories of domestic violence are certainly not specific to Harlan (or Appalachia, or the United States), and they are hard and painful to remember and to tell. One young man who I knew had been abused as a child flatly denied that any such thing had happened. But these stories become visible from the point of view of the institutions. Annie Napier sat in a number of such cases as a jury member ("This woman had scalded her little boy. He was three years old and she scalded it, in the bathtub. She scalded his bottom, his behind, his feet"); her daughter Marjorie ran into child abuse while working on the Harlan police force; Bobbie Davidson witnessed it as a hospital nurse ("We got child molesting cases, we got one little boy in...that hurt me the most. He was five years old. His father had shot the top of his head off. He was dead when they brought him in"). Yet Marjorie Napier concludes, "The laws are starting to gradually change. And then eventually some of these kids are going to grow up and realize, 'I'm not supposed to get hit,' and that's where it's going to stop."

ANNIE NAPIER: I think a lot of people is ashamed of the way they was raised. We didn't have good clothes to wear. We wore patches on our breeches 'cause we had to. Now you buy patches, they're designer jeans. They make fun of you, the other children do, for what you wear; what you eat for lunch; and most of 'em can't do any better. But, I think, if you're raised right, you come out from under poverty. We was raised with poverty; and we worked with poverty. Under the circumstances, the older people, my parents, did the best they could.

3

WARS AND PEACE

A PECULIAR INSTITUTION

"If historical trivia interests you, it may be interesting to know how that in this month 130 years ago (July 26, 1853), a 'black female was born into slavery in Harlan County—she was given the name AMERICA.' The family that owned her as well as some of her descendants still live in the region."[1]

> FRED NAPIER: My great-grandfather, he was a slave puncher. He worked slaves, you know, and bought slaves. That's what they called them back in them days: slave puncher. They'd buy these colored fellows and sell them and work them on the farms. If one got till he couldn't do nothing they'd get rid of him, put him out and get rid of him.

In 1901, geographer Ellen Church Semple wrote that Appalachia "is as free from [the negro] as northern Vermont. There is no place for the negro in the mountain economy, and never has been." Actually, blacks had already come to Appalachia along with the early French and Spanish exploration parties in the 1500s; even Daniel Boone's party included some blacks when he crossed Cumberland Gap.[2] Though the mountains did not lend themselves to the plantation economy, slavery did exist in the mountain South, mainly in nonagricultural occupations, including coal mining.[3]

Eastern Kentucky, however, had the lowest percentage of slaves in Appalachia. "They didn't have much work for slaves to do, and people didn't have enough money to afford a slave. Some of 'em sold for a thousand dollars. And that's a fortune to a mountaineer. I know some [descendants] of those slaves that used to be there. Their names were Renfros and Turners. Of course, they got their name from the families that owned 'em. The Turners were a very prominent family in Harlan County and their slaves settled over on Cranks Creek" (*Ed Cawood*). Between them, the Turners, the Renfros, Aley Ledford, John Lewis Sr., and Samuel Howard Sr. owned half the slaves in the county.[4]

> JAMES L. TURNER: I believe my grandmother and my grandfather came here as slaves. I don't know when. I can't remember much beyond my grandmother because I never did see my grandfather 'cause he had already died,

when I was born. But my grandmother owned a whole head of Cranks Creek, and that's where I was born and raised.

EARL TURNER: See, back in the old days, from slavery times on after people was freed, you come out of four hundred years of slavery. They had taken our heritage completely away from us when they brought us here from Africa. You lost your traditions. You lost everything. Those people's names—they come here named Smith and Jones and everything else. I wasn't no Turner. My people wasn't no Turner.[5]

In 1808, Aley Ledford crossed Pennington Gap with his family and "the few slaves they had and their livestock." His descendant Curtis Burnam recalled that Aley "treated them nicely—made his children respect the old ones, called them uncle and aunt. He never would break up a family, wouldn't sell a slave unless he caused a lot of trouble, and not many of them did." Settler George Burkhart "had an awful lot of slaves that he hired out to people to work in the fields. And he worked them in fields and that's where I believe the colored cemetery at Cranks Creek come in at. Mommy said that he was an awful cruel old man to the slaves that he had" (*Annie Napier*).[6] The story of Aley Burnam's "nice" treatment to the slaves may be accurate, or a reflection of the self-absolutory image of slavery as a "paternal" institution. Other voices tell a different, if probably mythic or symbolic, story.

ANNIE NAPIER: Some of Chester's daddy's relatives had slaves and he brung them in after he worked them all day in the field, he'd make them put their tongue out on the back of the chair and he'd take a nail to drive through their tongue, and make them stand there with a nail through their tongue while he eat. Or take a nail and hammer and nail their feet to the floor [so] they could stand in to the back of him and watch him eat. I guess back then they weren't considered human beings like the rest of us.

CHESTER NAPIER: [My father], he wasn't one to talk very much about it. And he said they would be working in the fields, and if one happened to break a leg or get hurt, they would put them in a hollow log, and put them in brush piles and set fire to it and burn them, rather than to have to doctor them. They couldn't work, they just burned them, get it over with. But they tell me when the old man took to his deathbed, that it took him approximately two weeks to die. They tell me they had to chain him to the bed. And they said he was a-howling, "Get these hot chains off of me, they're burning me up." And he would say he could see the devil. And that's about all that I've ever been told about.

Harlan memoirist Harvey Fuson writes of a slaveholder who "directed a woman slave to take a dry beef hide down to the river, place it in the water, and weight it down, to limber up the hide. She did this, but did not weight it sufficiently and the river rose and washed it away. For this deed he beat the colored woman to death. After this, the house became 'hanted.'"[7]

ANNIE NAPIER: Now, the major stories when I was growing up was the slaves. There was one [who] had broke away from somebody, I heared Mommy talk about. And he had some toes [missing]. He was barefooted, and that's how they was tracking him. And he come through the yard where Mommy lived there when she was little. They had been told that colored people eats babies. And they were scared to death anytime they hear, you know, about a black person being loose from its people, who...whoever owned it. And it was either Grandpa Hall or his daddy, he joined in the search for this slave, and I reckon they caught him somewhere over in Virginia. But it went right through the yard where my grandparents lived, and they was terrified for days after that. They sat up with the baby afraid he'd come back and get him.

"My daddy's ancestors were Cherokee Indians, and my mother's ancestors were Caucasians. My mother was a Negro; her ancestors on my granddaddy's side, my mother's daddy, they were Caucasian" (*Nancy Johnson*). Blacks and whites share sometimes a claim to an Indian ancestry—an implicit denial of the pure-race theories of slavery and racism.

WILLETTA LEE: The way we were taught in my home was that we all came from one person, which was God; our original mother and father was Adam and Eve. If it hadn't been for Adam and Eve it wouldn't be no race, so why holler about black and white, green, yellow, whatever. 'Cause if anybody do their family tree, you're gonna find out that there is not a pure race. My grandmother went by Cherokee, her mother and father were Cherokee Indians. My grandfather's mother was Irish. She was not black, she was just as white as snow. She married a black man. So what are we? The races are already mixed.

Cherokees, Willetta Lee goes on, "were sort of slaves to the white man. They went through just as much as some of us blacks did. They take the blacks from their country and bring them to their country and treat them like dogs. They take the Indians' land from them and treat them like dogs. So my family sort of consists of slavery." Some 12 percent of black Appalachians had Cherokee ancestry; nearly one-fourth of those had been owned by Cherokee slave owners.[8]

CHESTER NAPIER: [My mother's grandmother], she would help runaway slaves, whatever. Because her being an Indian, she kind of knew what it was about. Yeah, she was a full Indian, and runaway slaves, they would come in there and she would carry food to 'em, and she would help hide them and take care of them, until they could get farther away, or either, you know, get captured or something. My grandpa, he'd tell me stories about her carrying the food to 'em. And I guess some of the stories was true and prob'ly some of 'em wasn't true, I don't know.

"As soon as Lincoln signed the Emancipation Proclamation, Aley [Ledford] gave all of his slaves their freedom. He also gave a large boundary of land—several thousand acres—in the hollow at the head of Cranks Creek."[9] Most of the former slaves gradually left, however, and only a few of their descendants remain in Harlan. According to local historian Mabel Condon, black people in Harlan were known for telling stories of ghosts and haints.[10] The haunted house in Fuson's story and the tale of the devil on Chester Napier's uncle's deathbed suggest how the unpacified ghost of slavery haunted the memory of the land.

ANNIE NAPIER: There's a cemetery out here on Cranks Creek that must be all slaves. It [has] rock graves, not marble like we do now. There's no tombstone. There's rocks with names scratched in them. And they sound like colored people. Some of them named Jasmine and Jamison and a couple of [others]. Anyway, some of it dates back to the early eighteen hundreds—on the rocks.

"My grandma, they, they—she was a daughter of s-s-slaves. Her parents were slaves" (*Julia Cowans*). If white memory is haunted, black memory is reluctant and angry: it is difficult for Julia Cowans to utter that word, "s-s-slaves." "Old people back down a bit, they kind of turn you off, seem like they...": preacher James L. Turner can't even finish the sentence. The black memory of slavery is etched in sad and angry silences, painful omissions, and periphrases.

BILL LEE: I never met my grandfather, they were all from Alabama, they were slaves.
PORTELLI: Did they used to talk about it?
BILL LEE: Yes they did.
PORTELLI: Can you tell me something about it?
BILL LEE: Yeah, I remember a lot, but I don't like to talk about that, 'cause I get sad all over again. I won't even watch a movie on TV if it has slavery in it.
WILLETTA LEE: It's something you don't like to talk about. I talk it and teach it to my kids, because even though they are still trying to hold us down, we come a long way. And because of our ancestors and what they went through, it keeps the determination in your body to be somebody. Don't ever let that happen again.

EARL TURNER: You ask my mother where she was born, she say, "I was born right where Lee surrendered to Grant after the Civil War: Rockingham County, Virginia." And she'll tell her mother was six years old when slavery time ended. Papa's mother was twenty-one. And she musta been one hundred and five years old when she died. But now, she was—my grandmother was a mulatto. She was fairer-skinned than you are. She was a great big woman, had big blondest-looking hair. Her master was her daddy—she told us about it. Papa's daddy was part a Blackfoot Indian, off of Roanoke Isle. Part Indian-black. My dad was a big man, real curly hair. And he had a big long mustache. And that was out in native country. We come right out of Virginia, you know. At one time, Virginia was the largest slave-owning state in the Union. That's where the first slaves were brought. Right at the James River, right in Virginia. That's where it started. Virginia was what you call a slave market.

PORTELLI: The most famous Virginia Turner was Nat....[11]

EARL TURNER: Yeah, he raised a lot of hell. But they killed 'im and skinned 'im alive. They skinned 'im just like you skin an onion, or a rabbit, or something, and stuffed his body and put it on exhibition, sure did.

BORDER WARFARE

SUDIE CRUSENBERRY: Back then, they had the Rebel and the Yankee, what they called it, War. You've heard of that, I'm pretty sure. Yeah, Grandpa and Daddy both went through that, and Mommy did too. And Granddad Hall, and, you know, they had pretty fair...bad trouble, because one of them was Rebel, and the other was Yankee. I reckon was a war, like, they were into, and I thought several times about going to the library and seeing if I could find a book of it, and all.

"This was on the border, the North and South. They had people here on both sides" (*Sill Leach*). Kentucky did not join the secession, and Harlan's border with Virginia "became a border with another country."[12] Harlan's sympathies lay mostly with the Union (except Clover Fork, closer to the Virginia border); in some memories, the Union that the North fought to save becomes the *labor* union.

MILDRED SHACKLEFORD: I was in high school and I can remember being surprised to find out that Lincoln was a Republican. And I thought, well, that's [why] my family is Republican. I had always been ashamed of it because it was the Democrats that was liberals, that was doing the right thing and the Republicans was the scums, right? So I went home one evening and I said something to my grandfather, about our family being Republicans and that the Republicans were the ones that were fighting to free the slaves and everything. And I can remember my grandfather turning around and looking at me and said, "I'll tell you something right now, girl." He said, "It didn't have anything to do with freeing the niggers." He said, "What it had to do with was preserving the unions. We were Republicans to preserve the unions. It didn't have anything else to do with anything else."

Harlan's border location and mountainous terrain lent itself to guerrilla actions rather than major battles: a raid on a Confederate unit at Poor Fork, an encounter at Wallins Creek in which "the rebels were routed with the loss of four men killed and a good number of them wounded," raids by scouting parties and "bushwhackers." A letter to the Kentucky state government in 1865 complained that "Gurillas" had "nearly laid waste to the county by pillaging Plundering & Robbing…they take arms, clothing, bacon & where they find a man that bitterly opposes them they burn their house furniture and leaves the women and children without clothing or beds to sleep upon."[13] "I've heard my aunt tell about it, when she was a girl, back before I was born. Them rebels come and the old man had a lot of geese, and [they] cut their heads off, and gut them and put mud on them and bake them, and eat them" (*Plennie Hall*).

DANIEL HOWARD: There was a Mr. Nolan here, he was about ninety-seven, he died about two years ago, he was a very good storyteller, and knew a lot of the oral history, and was talking, and what really intrigued me was that there was a large number of people from across the mountain who joined the Union Army, and one reason was that there were a group of renegades that was riding with the Confederacy who—there was a merchant over across the mountain and they decided they'd rob him and after they robbed him they tied him up and whipped him and then finally killed him. And a lot of his folks joined the Union Army to fight against these Rebels. There were parts of this family working with the Confederacy, and parts of this family working with the Union Army, and there were two cousins, one was with the Union and they ambushed in Virginia and he looked in at the guy that [he was about to shoot], it was his cousin from across Pine Mountain. Both those boys wound up just quitting and coming back to Pine Mountain….

CHESTER NAPIER: The raiders, they would come through from either side and take what you had. And you had no telephone, no newspaper or anything, but they'd get word they was coming. Then they would [take] their cows, horses, food, whatever they had, away and hide to keep them from taking it, 'cause they would take everything that you had. Families would hide their belongings, then would not be able to find them and they would be lost. And still today some people, occasionally will find a little jar of silver money that had been hid to keep the raiders from getting it before they maybe killed their family or something.

"My grandmother, she run in front of the [raiders] and warned the people, so they could hide their stuff and what they had. They said they could hear her hollering a mile away. And they had somebody out listening, and when they'd hear her, then they'd get their stuff and hide it" (*Melinda Slusher*). In most stories, it is women who give the warning, as though memory entrusted to them the role of protecting the community from the male scourge of war. Some took up arms ("Nancy, daughter of Moses Cawood, is said to have put on men's clothes and ridden with the Confederate Cavalry"),[14] but most were active primarily in feeding the hungry and tending to the wounded.

> MARTHA NAPIER: My grandmaw Wilson, she was old, she'd set and talk to us kids, but we didn't pay much attention to her back then. She could sit and tell us everything in the world, how she'd done when she was a young girl. How she packed food [for people in hiding]. They had a big [cave], she'd slip food back in there, then she'd come home, to keep the soldiers from finding where they were at. Keep them from being killed. I guess she had, she said maybe a hundred and fifty of them hid out in the mountains way back in towards the butt of the rocks. [They were] the ones, I reckon, she thought was for us, that was fighting for the United States. She said this soldier come through one time with his tongue half cut off, she doctored him and cured him and got him well till he could eat and drink again. I did know his name but I forgot. I was young when she told us about it.

"The courthouse was burned [by the Confederates] during the Civil War in Harlan; so, I guess there's a lot of history here that I don't know about" (*Chester Napier*). As in most of these war narratives, memories are uncertain and plural: some say it was burned by Confederate troops in retaliation for the burning of the Lee County, Virginia, courthouse, others that it was an irregular guerrilla band.[15] Others still blamed "Devil Jim" Turner.

> MILDRED SHACKLEFORD: My dad's mother's grandfather's name was Devil Jim Turner. Did you hear of him? He was a mean old man. According to what my grandfather told me, he was supposed to have killed twenty-two people in his lifetime. He died at the age of ninety-one and he was buried in the state of Washington because he moved out there when life got too tough for him. One of the stories that my grandfather told me—he used to rob people. You know, midwives used to go around delivering babies at that time, I think they got paid a quarter a baby. And one night this old midwife had been out and she happened to get lucky, she delivered twins. So she got fifty cents for that. She was coming home through the woods and Devil Jim stopped her and told her to give him her money. So she gave him a quarter. He said, "No, the other quarter too." He said, "I know you delivered twins tonight and you give me that other quarter." So she lost. But [my grandfather] said one night people got tired of him robbing 'em, beating 'em or whatever he done to 'em, and six of the people in the community got together and decided the world would be a better place without him. So, they attacked him, and they thought they beat him to death. They took him up on the hillside and throwed him in

a brush pile and left him for dead. And he stayed there for two or three days. He recovered enough that he crawled home. It took him six months to get over the beating. And it took him another six months to kill all of 'em. Although Devil Jim Turner was a real person and famous in Harlan, this story is about 95 percent fiction.... My grandfather was very good with a tale.

Devil Jim gathered a guerrilla company on the Union side "and kept up a regular system of murder, robbery and horse stealing throughout the war, southern men being the principal sufferers." Family narratives and oral histories feed into electronic memory. According to a genealogy site, Devil Jim and his gang killed William Middleton in 1869. His widow testified that Jim Turner, his brother William, and Francis Pace had killed William Middleton's brother David. However, they could not be tried because the key witness for the prosecution was killed on Harlan's Main Street.[16] Another Web page reports that on his return from the war Middleton was captured by a gang, tortured, and killed, and his dismembered body was hidden in a hollow log in Devil's Den on Stone Mountain.[17]

"During the Civil War," Fred Napier recalled, "there was a robber, and he'd come through here and he'd take people's money and stuff. He shot one of my dad's [relatives], shot him square through the [head] with an old rifle gun." Some of the victim's relatives traced the robber in Virginia: "They brought him right down here on this creek, they killed him, they cut a piece off of him at a time. Ears, nose, tongue, punched his eyes out. So they killed him and hid him." These may have been the bones that Fred Napier's ancestors found later, on the Martin's Fork side of Stone Mountain.[18]

In 1874, Devil Jim and his accomplices were sentenced to life in prison for the murder of William Middleton. Freed on parole in 1890, he moved to Washington state, where he died in 1909.[19]

MILDRED SHACKLEFORD: There was a lot of hard feelings left over from the Civil War. A lot of people don't realize that when the Civil War was going on, it did separate a lot of families. According to my grandfather, Harlan County was a lot like a frontier town out West; there wasn't much in the way of laws. There were a lot of people that were footloose, that had no family to tie 'em down, so if they were strong enough and mean enough, they would kill people and get what they wanted. But there was also a lot of people that had lost a lot during the Civil War and they didn't have anything and they would take stuff from people. And evidently, old Devil Jim was one of those that was like that. Now his daughter, my great-grandmother, married a doctor, raised a big family, and all of them turned out to be fairly decent people. But the old man, none of the family claimed him, and old Devil Jim wound up going out West somewhere.

EITHER THE TURNERS WILL RULE OR THE HOWARDS

Toward the end of Theodore Dreiser's *Sister Carrie* (1900), George Hurstwood, the heroine's defeated and depressed lover, sits in his room in New York, idly reading a paper. An item draws his attention: "An interesting shooting affray was on in the mountains of Kentucky."[20] About thirty years later, Dreiser himself would witness actual "shooting affrays" in the mountains of Harlan County— but that is another story, and will be told later.

The story Hurstwood read might have been this one, in the October 28, 1899, *New York Times*:

> Harlan Court House, the scene of the present troubles, is near the centre of the most mountainous of Kentucky mountains. The country is wild, and the whistle of the locomotive has never been heard by many of its inhabitants. The town has probably 500 inhabitants. Six years ago one of these residents was Bob Turner, a burly young mountaineer, who wore his trousers stuck in his boots and carried a chronic bad temper. One day, while drunk and boisterous, he threatened to cut the heart out of Wicks Howard, a cousin of Wils Howard, the present leader. Trouble was avoided at the time; but a week later Wicks came to town armed with a musket. He loaded up on home-made whisky, then started out for a fight. The first man he met was Bob Turner. Without a word he raised his gun and sent a charge of bankshot into Turner's heart.[21]

The dead "directly traceable to the feud" between the Turners and the Howards were said to be between twenty-five and fifty. Ten years before, the *New York Times* had informed its readers that Kentuckians, "like the aborigines..., sustain themselves principally by hunting and fishing. They are remarkably good shots and effective assassins." As late as 1941, the *New York Times* explained, "If there is a synonym for vindictiveness it is mountaineer. The highlander never forgets an insult, real or imagined.... The power to forgive and forget is not in him."[22]

Most Appalachian feuds were episodic outbreaks that involved only a fraction of the people, and they were far from the only form of violence and lawlessness in late nineteenth-century America. Yet all of Kentucky's major feuds were long, bloody, and picturesque enough to strike the national imagination.[23] The most famous and romanticized, the Hatfield-McCoy feud on the Tug Fork of Big Sandy River, on the Kentucky-Virginia line (1878–91), is still remembered in Harlan. "The Hatfields and the McCoys started over a hog. The Hatfields lived on the West Virginia side and the McCoys lived on the Kentucky side [of Tug River]. And a hog had went across that river, and got in the McCoys' corn and they killed that hog and they started killing people then" (*Ben Lewis*). This, of course, is folklore: as Cosby Ann Totten, a coal miner from Tazewell, Virginia, recalls, her mother, who was related to the Hatfields, "would get mad when people said the Hatfields and McCoys got in a fuss over a pig. She said it was more a fight over coal rights when the coal companies came into West Virginia."[24]

Feud narratives like to dwell on the discrepancy between trivial causes and tragic consequences: a drunken quarrel, a hog, a dog. The Harlan County feud "officially" began in 1882 with the killing of Little Bob Turner by Wicks Howard on March 7, 1882, "after a dispute over a card game," or, as another version has it, when a Howard charged that a Turner "spoke badly to Mama."[25]

ED CAWOOD: And the Howards and Turners had a great feud back about 1895. And George Briton Turner, he lost all his sons in that feud, five or six of 'em were killed. No one knows for sure, but I've heard it was over a dog. I don't know if that's true. My great-grandfather was killed in that feud. He was riding up the road on his horse and he was shot from the mountains, people up in the woods. Howard and Turner feud, was the name of that, and one of the main Turners is buried right behind the garage over there behind Harlan Motor Company. Not many people know it's there because buildings have been built all around it. You know, you always have two sides and one crowd wants to run the county and to get control, they just fight each other.

As early as 1855, the Howards "had insisted Devil Jim [Turner] be arrested for theft, assault, and rape (wherefore Devil Jim's brother Will killed [Howard ally] Bill Gilbert in retaliation; he was never brought to trial)." There may be more substantial grounds for the rivalry between the landowning Turners and the mercantile Howards: the Turners had bought most of the land on which the town of Harlan was built, and the Howards, an old settler family, saw them as "nouveau riche" and claimed that they were harassing their customers.[26]

DANIEL HOWARD: We, our family had a feud with the Turners, I don't know [about] what, a lot of times families chose not to talk about it. My grandfather always said, "You can't trust the Turners." And that went back to [the] Howard-Turner feud. Now, from what I pieced together, two Howards in Harlan shot a Turner man one night, I don't remember what the disagreement was, but they killed him.

After Little Bob Turner's death, his brother Will attacked the Howards' home, was wounded, and left the state. He returned in 1887 and challenged the Howards to "an open battle in Harlan Courthouse and decide by the arbitraiment of blade and bullet who has the better right to rule the county."[27] In the shootout that followed, Will Turner was mortally wounded. "He was helped to the front porch of the mansion screaming in pain (gut shot). 'Stop that,' his mother snapped. 'Die like a man, like your brother (Little Bob) did.' Will stopped screaming and died." Later, a Howard ally "called on Mrs. Turner to end the violence; walking to the front porch Mrs. Turner pointed at the blood where Will had died. 'You can't wipe out that blood. Either the Turners will rule or the Howards but not both.'"[28]

Howard versus Turner was not the only game in town. In June 1886, two men were killed in "one of the bloodiest battles of modern years...the result of a feud of long standing" on Clover Fork. A family quarrel resulting in multiple killings made the pages of the *Los Angeles Times*.[29] Meanwhile, the feud and the killings went on until the 1890s, mixing with other feuds (like the Cawood-Day feud on Martin's Fork), with brief interludes when the National Guard came to Harlan.[30]

In 1888 county judge Wilson Lewis started a third, "law and order" party to fight the Howards' "whisky ring." When Lewis's posse raided a store owned by Howard allies, "barrels, kegs, and bottles in profusion [were] hustled into the road, where the judge, with all possible coolness, proceeded to knock bungs and heads out with an axe, throwing the contents into the street, while his comrades, about 20 in number, stood guard with their Winchesters." The "whisky party," led by Wils Howards, Wills's brother and successor, "rallied and armed themselves, returned to town yesterday with blood in their eyes. Judge Lewis and his party met them, and a hot encounter took place in the street."[31] In October 1889, Lewis's men attacked the Howard camp.

> *Bullets flew thick and fast. The Howard party suffered from the first volley, one man being killed and six of the party badly wounded. Wills Howard had a close call for his worthless life, a ball from a Winchester plowing a furrow around his neck. His brother, John Howard, received the contents of a gun, and will probably die. James Dean of Howard's band was killed outright. Two of Judge Lewis's posse were wounded, but not seriously. After this fight Judge Lewis took his band to the Court House and is now barricaded therein. Wills Howard threatens to burn the town. The few inhabitants who are not on one side or the other are panic-stricken and want to get away but are afraid to venture across the thirty miles of wild country to the nearest railroad station, which is Pineville. Both sides are armed with Winchesters.*[32]

After the battle, feud leader Wils Howard and his maternal uncle Will Jennings escaped to the West. Wils returned to Harlan in 1890 with a small fortune, possibly the fruit of murders and robberies; he raised a posse, fought Judge Lewis, and fled west again. Arrested for a robbery in California, he was extradited to Missouri and hanged for an 1888 murder.[33]

"And it went on for years and I think they sort of called a truce, but they were hog killing and I think they were together and drinking, and another shooting broke out" (*Daniel Howard*). The feud resumed in 1894, when a Nolan (a former Howard ally) killed two Turners.[34] "The fella sitting up in front of the courthouse told me one time that the Nolan clan was bloodthirsty. And he said that my father was the only one of the bunch that hadn't killed somebody. Another fella told me that my grandfather must be the smartest man in Harlan County because none of his boys who ever got in trouble ever served a day" (*Charlotte Nolan*). By then, however, the spirits of war were waning: "The Turner and Howard feud was over I think in the eighties. I understand [that] shortly after the feud Turners married the Howards, Howards married the Turners. That was the end of that" (*Brian H. Whitfield*).

In 2003, a query about Devil Jim Turner on a Harlan genealogy discussion list spawned dozens of responses. It seems that the house where Devil Jim lived still stands, and it is haunted. According to a correspondent who claimed to be Devil Jim's direct descendant, his ghost was supposed to have appeared in a mirror to a man who lived in the house. A woman bought the house and planned to restore it, but "so many things happened that she abandoned it.... It is sitting empty, doors off and windows broken out. It broke my heart to see it."[35]

Feuds have been explained and interpreted in a variety of ways: carryovers from Civil War enmities, the survival of Old World customs embedded in the mountaineers' "pure Anglo-Saxon blood" (in 1913, a magazine wrote that "mountain homicides...are performed invariably upon some 'point of honor,' and the ethical standards of the feudists always protect women and children"), the inbred vindictiveness of a "race" to whom "bloodshed is a pastime," or the moral depravity caused by poverty, isolation, drunkenness, or ignorance.[36] Actually, all these major feuds, including the Howard-Turner war, were carried out by the most well-to-do and most educated citizens fighting over issues of power and property in a region where law enforcement was weak (no killer was ever sentenced in the Harlan County feud), local politics was nepotistic and often corrupt, and economic prominence was shifting from older to new elites (such as the established settler Howards versus the "nouveau riche" Turners).[37] Yet less illustrious families and more peripheral areas also had their share. Ben Lewis remembers the enmity between two Pine Mountain families that caused thirty-five deaths as late as the 1950s ("I don't know what stopped it: education had a lot to do with it").

> CHESTER NAPIER: When I was a teenager [in the 1950s], Smith and Jones's Creek was the two roughest places around here. I started carrying a pistol when I's about twelve year old, and I've carried one ever since and I still carry one. I guess they was just carryovers, from years gone by. Ever'body'd fight. Didn't believe in no law. There was so many killed [around] Smith. We had a rival with the Middletons. And when we got in their part we'd fight; they'd come to our part, we'd fight. Sometimes it was dangerous to drive a car past their houses where one'd be on one side of the road shooting at the other'n. And sometimes you'd have to stop and wait till they quit shooting. I don't really know what the rivalry was about. It was there when I was [born]. I guess I helped carry it on.

Feuds were family affairs. Kinship networks were wide and interrelated, so neutrals were few and "everybody took sides"; the families' long tenure on the land allowed enmities to be passed on for generations, in the endless retellings of a storytelling culture: "[Feuds were] over the family. Over a piece of land or something or another. Something happen in the family, they held prejudice against one another. They tried to get revenge" (*Fred Napier*).

ANNIE NAPIER: Up in the head of Smith, it's our worst area right now for feuds. The ——— and the ———, they're still feuding. And I'll say they'll be feuding until they die. 'Cause it's come down from generation to generation, the hate part has. And, neither one will give in. I don't really know if they really know now what it come up over, in the beginning. But it's never gonna die. [It's been going on] about two hundred years. It's like the Hatfields and the McCoys. It's just handed down from generation to generation. They tell the story over the years, about what this aunt done to their aunt and what this uncle done to their uncle; and, they do things to agitate each other, keep 'em mad.

"In the head of Smith" in the 1910s, Martha Napier, still a child, was on the way to church when she witnessed the murder of Charles Napier, the father of her future husband, Fred, by his son-in-law. "Fred's daddy, he threw his coat down upon the bank on some rocks, and his knife; he said, 'Fight me fair,' he said; 'I ain't got a thing to fight with, but,' he said, 'fight me fair.' They didn't do it, and they was shooting so much me and my sister laid down in the road so the bullets would go over us to keep from hitting us. When they got done shooting, Daddy said, 'Come on children, he's killed.'" When Fred heard about it, he swore he would not eat or drink until he got revenge. He caught his father's killer in Virginia, as he was getting away on a train.

FRED NAPIER: The train was pulling out, and I run and got on it. I got between the coaches, I had my gun down under my overalls, under my pants belt. I was waiting for him; he come up the steps, and I shot him four times, he fell on the ground, I went down and kicked him and turned over to see if he was dead. I went back upon the train, and the flag man opened the blind to the other side and let me off.

Fred Napier hid in Clay County, dodging the posse that was after him. But after a while he came home to see his mother, and he was arrested and sentenced to twenty years in the penitentiary. He served ten years and eighteen days.

FRED NAPIER: They sent me to work in the lime plant. You don't last very long in them lime plants. That lime eats your lungs up. They sent me to the state farm first, got in some trouble there, and they put me in what they call a sweat box. Kept me in there five days. Had my feet locked on the floor, and that steam burned all my hair. When I come out of there and went back to work I could run my fingers up through my hair [and it would come off] just like same as a scalded hog.

Fred Napier was released in the mid-twenties. Half a century later, one of his sons, who had moved to Michigan, came home to introduce his wife to the family.

ANNIE NAPIER: When Fred got to asking her who her family was, and she got to telling him, he kept getting madder and madder. So I said, "Fred, what's the matter with you? What's wrong?" And he said, "That damn man that killed my daddy, that's his brother's daughter." I told him, "Fred, for God's sake, can't you just let bygones be bygones, forget it? That young'un didn't have nothing to do with that!" So he kept getting louder and louder and yelling—"Martha, you get [her] out of the house; 'cause I don't want her here, because her uncle's the one that killed my daddy." And it started a very bad dispute between [Fred Napier's son and his wife]. And she really loved [him] and she hoped that they could work it out. But they never could. He couldn't let bygones be bygones.

CONTEMPORARY ANCESTORS

In September 1892, the Reverend L. E. Tupper crossed Pennington Gap into Harlan County toward Yoakum Creek. He rode a path dotted with landmarks of feuding and strife: a lumber camp on Martin's Fork run by the brothers of a man killed by the Howards; the place in Catron's Creek where George Turner was shot by Wilts Howard; the creek where James T. Middleton was ambushed and shot; "the house of the father of the Turner boys who were parties to the feud." In Yoakum Creek, he wrote, "Many of the men we have met are homicides." His purpose was to establish an American Missionary Association school and church. He secured fund-raising pledges from local families, selected the place, obtained bonds for the land, and left: "We say good-bye and set out on our return, feeling that a great work has been begun, and the first steps taken towards the redemption of Harlan County from ignorance and sin."[38]

MILDRED SHACKLEFORD: When I was a kid, we had missionaries. Did you know that Harlan County at one time was one of the big missionary posts. We had missionaries from the Baptist. We had missionaries from the Methodist. We had missionaries from churches in Connecticut, New York, Chicago, anyplace in this country. They were sending missionaries to the deepest, darkest Africa to save the savages. They also sent them to Appalachia to save the little hillbilly kids. Did you know that? They would pat you on the head and say, "You may be poor and you may be ignorant, but we are here doing God's duty." They come in to save the soul of the savage. We were the savages and they were going to save us. And, you know, anyplace that God's light hadn't shined, they were there. And, of course, God's light hadn't shined in Appalachia.[39]

"I went to school at Black Mountain Academy in Evarts," Burnam Ledford recalled. "We had the best of teachers—they were Congregationals from New England." The Evarts academy was established in 1892; in 1888, the United Presbyterian Church (Northern) opened an academy in Harlan County. One visitor noted, "The citizens of Harlan, Harlan County, give more to home missions than any church in the Presbytery."[40]

Well-meaning visitors to turn-of-the century Appalachia—missionaries, writers, scholars, educators, philanthropists—saw the mountaineers as "at once noble and ignoble savages...100% Americans of the best stock [or] inbred degenerates, feudists, and moonshiners"—"no better than barbarians," in the words of Arnold Toynbee. Noble or ignoble, they were savages, an absolute other onto whom an America in rapid and problematic modernization projected both nostalgia and anxiety. The fact that the Appalachian population was not racially different made its perceived otherness more intriguing. "Mountaineers," writes cultural historian Henry D. Shapiro, "became at once like us and not like us." Real or imagined cultural survivals were discovered or invented just as the land and its culture were being transformed by land speculation, logging, railroads, and mining. However, the cultural invention of Appalachia as a "discrete land inhabited by a homogeneous population possessing a distinct culture" and the "opposite" of modern America was so necessary that the ongoing changes and the internal differences were blithely ignored.[41]

> In one of the most progressive and productive countries of the world...we find a large area...where the civilization is that of the eighteenth century, where the people speak the English of Shakespeare's time.... The conserving power of the mountains, has caused these conditions to survive, carrying a bit of the eighteenth century intact over into this strongly contrasted twentieth century, and presenting an anachronism all the more marked because found in the heart of the bustling, money-making, novelty-loving United States.[42]

In 1873, Will Wallace Harney labeled Appalachia as "A Strange Land and Peculiar People." Appalachia, Henry Shapiro writes, appeared to writers and travelers as a "terra incognita," whose otherness in space and time generated a sense of displacement and estrangement, not unlike coeval science fiction. According to travel writer John Esten Cooke, Appalachia was indeed another planet—"another world and another race of human beings," defined by its distance and by the imagined strangeness of its inhabitants. Travel to Appalachia was seen as a form of time travel. A short ride into Appalachia, wrote educator William Goodell Frost, was like traveling to the eighteenth century: to him, mountain people were "living anachronisms" and, famously, "our contemporary ancestors." Descriptions of the land mixed the horrific and the sublime, its people either wild feudists and moonshiners or natural aristocrats of unadulterated Anglo-Saxon stock.[43]

Out of time, nature-bound, Appalachians were described as "a people without history," consigned to anthropology and folklore. In 1931, a linguist claimed that the folk speech of the Cumberlands takes us back to Queen Elizabeth's time—though actually the settlement of the region began at least a century after her death. Around the same time, a sympathetic observer described the people of Harlan as primitives surviving in the twentieth century, speaking Elizabethan English and dancing square dances.[44]

The most important trait that Appalachian mountaineers were supposed to have preserved in their frozen history and isolated geography was Anglo-Saxon racial purity. They were supposed to be direct descendants of early colonial settlers, bearing the cultural marks of their ancestry "as plainly as if they had disembarked from their eighteenth-century vessel yesterday."[45] Actually, many Appalachians claim a mixed Cherokee ancestry, and by the time Semple penned these words, Mediterranean and central European immigrants were being recruited to the coal mines. However, the combination of apparent cultural and economic poverty and backwardness, on one hand, and a rich and supposedly uncontaminated Elizabethan culture, on the other, attracted educators and folklorists on a mission to educate and preserve "all that is native and fine" in their heritage. As a Pine Mountain Settlement School publication put it, loggers, miners, missionaries, writers, and folklorists all mined the particular lode in mountain life that best fit with their concerns.[46]

The Pine Mountain Settlement School was established in Harlan County in 1913. "My grandfather's mother's family donated the land for the school. There was no way the children could get an education, so they gave the land to the school for it" (*Bobbie Davidson*). In 1902, Katherine Pettit and other teachers and social workers had established a school in Hindman, Knott County, that combined teaching with other programs and activities on the model of the urban settlement school inaugurated by Jane Addams in Chicago (but minus its involvement in social change). William Creech, a Pine Mountain farmer, offered Pettit land for a similar school on Pine Mountain:[47] "In the earliest years of the school everyone came to it by walking across the mountain to the train or mule back and the visitors were met by a man and a mule to bring them over. The school itself had raised the money to build the only first road across the mountain" (*Burton Rogers, educator*). Pine Mountain Settlement School offered its live-in students both "book larnin'" and "an education for life," teaching trades, crafts, and agricultural practices. "We had the regular classes, but they also taught us woodwork, weaving, home economics; we learned to sew and we made quite a few of our clothes in school" (*Bobbie Davidson*).

Burton and Mary Rogers came to Pine Mountain in 1942, after experiences teaching in China and India: "We wanted badly to have a school that views the interests and abilities of rural children as a medium for their education, so that they could identify with it." They found the local people "lovely. Simple, friendly, a little cautious of accepting you immediately. I think that of all the people we've met here they were the least stamped by 'keeping up with the Joneses' and were much more themselves. And weren't awfully perturbed that when you went to see them, they didn't have a chair for you to sit on or that they'd been found barefoot hoeing the garden. They were gracious, welcoming, and had the right values" (*Mary Rogers*).

BURTON ROGERS: All of them worked up to nineteen and a half hours per week in lieu of any charge for room and board. They all were required to work, jobs keeping the whole school program going, which included the farm, maintenance of buildings, and the dairy herd—milking, handling milk. And for girls, working in the kitchen and in other buildings, cleaning, laundry. Some girls helping in the school's infirmary with the doctor and nurse serving the whole community, and so on. And these jobs had a tremendous significance in the students' opportunity to begin selecting possible vocations and decisions on the future and further education.

Pine Mountain valued the local culture and learned from it. As "Aunt" Sal Creech, who taught spinning, dyeing, and weaving, once said, "I reckon things is about evened up in this world. You've been everywhere and seen everything, and I can spin." While this attitude contributed to the students' sense of identity and pride, the school fostered a selective and often romanticized version of mountain culture, based on a preconceived idea of "genuine" folklore—the handmade crafts for which a market was developing in urban America, the English and Scottish popular ballads recently canonized by Francis James Child, folktales, the dulcimer—and introduced practices that they believed *ought* to have been part of the children's heritage, such as sword dances and other elements of English folklore.[48] The British folklorist Cecil Sharp found Pine Mountain "a prime case for songs" and collected dozens of versions of ballads: in Appalachia, he wrote, "I found myself for the first time in my life in a community in which singing was as common and almost as universal a practice as speaking."[49]

By the time Sharp visited Pine Mountain, the loud banjo was replacing the soft dulcimer as the preferred musical instrument of the mountains, especially in the urban settlements or around the mines and the railroads, but it was considered morally dangerous by respectable people. "The dulcimer [was used] at the settlement schools mainly. But when you get out of those cultural pockets, or cultural influences, you don't see many dulcimers. I never saw one till they started bringing them over to the college" (*Arthur Johnson, musician*). African American music was ignored.[50]

BEN LEWIS: Up here at that school, there is a guy made dulcimers, up till [a] few years back. I think the school ordered the wood they was made of. Jess Cornett, another guy lived up there, made dulcimers. But both of them guys is dead now. There's a guy down on Beach Fork that still makes dulcimers. There is not as many plays them than it used to. And then they used to make their own banjos. Way back when I was a kid there was an old guy he picked the banjo, he had a dozen different songs, "Sourwood Mountain," "Ground Hog," that he picked on the banjo. But some of them old fellows that used to pick the banjo could pick the same thing on the dulcimer.

Ben Lewis has a vague recollection of "Barbarry Allen"—and this is the only trace of ballads from Francis James Child's academically approved canon I ran into in today's Harlan County. Which doesn't mean that the traditional ballads prized by scholars and folklorists hadn't been there. Jim Garland, for instance, writes that "Lord Bateman" and "House Carpenter" were sung in his family; his half sister Molly Jackson remembered hearing "Lord Thomas" and "The Gypsy Davy" from her great-grandmother around 1885; on Pine Mountain in the 1950s Leonard Roberts collected a handful of the ballads included in Child's collection.[51]

The first song I heard in Harlan County was the gospel classic "Life Is Like a Mountain Railroad," performed by Hiram Day at the Cranks Creek Survival Center.[52] On the living room wall, I noted a family tree made of carved wooden hearts, made by Becky Simpson's son Robert. Crafts were the other staple of "genuine" Appalachian culture; they survive today as an economic resource geared to the tourist trade, as well as a form of expression. On top of Pine Mountain, Sid Tibbs gave me a beautiful knife made out of a mine roof bolt. Charlotte Nolan tells of a knife maker who refused to accept more money than he thought his work was worth: "That's the first time I ever bargained with a guy backwards. But that's the way he did it. He just doesn't want to take advantage of ya. He takes pride in his work—and he was paid enough by your just telling him they were beautifully done and wonderfully sharp."

> MELINDA SLUSHER: I've made a lot of quilts in my lifetime and quilted all kinds of quilts. I couldn't hardly tell you how many kinds there are. I pieced and quilted up until my eyes got so I couldn't see how to cut and sew. I guess I was eighty, when I quit quilting. I gave most of mine to the children. That Flower Garden quilt was an awful beautiful quilt. Took a long time to piece it, you know, the pieces were small. Some of my quilts, I'd save the pieces of [my daughter's] dresses and mine, that I had made, and put them in the quilt and keep them that way.

Quilting is the most symbolic of crafts, a useful object, a work of art, a site of memory, and a family heirloom; as Ellen Church Semple conceded, "It does not merely answer a physical need, but is a mode of expression for their artistic sense." It is still a living art, though changed by the availability of synthetic materials and the waning of the social get-togethers that used to go with quilting.[53]

> ANNIE NAPIER: Mommy had a quilt which every one of us had something: some parts of the boys' shirts, parts of their Levi's, part of our dresses. And it was like the whole family, you know, right there together. I use scraps, like

old britches, that some part wore out, you can take the other parts of it, make quilts. We used to get cotton put in between 'em; but you can hardly buy cotton anymore. You can find synthetic, like cotton; but you can't buy the regular cotton no more. Now you get this quilting material, and it works up a lot easier. But now, it's high; it'll run you almost three dollars a yard.

The mountaineers never spoke "Shakespearean English," yet their language had, and still retains, a distinctive local flavor. In Harlan, I heard old words and forms (*poke, fetch, unbeknownst*), high-rolling fancy polysyllables (*humongous, hellacious*), the strong past tense (*holp, clumb, brung*), the eloquent pleonasm (*killed him dead, the biggest majority*), the nonstandard concordance (*used to did, used to could*), the syllabicated plural (*ghosties*), the absent *g* and the *a-* prefix (*a-bornin', a-growin', a-singin', a-courtin', a-weddin', a-churchin', a-plowin', a-ailin', a-dyin', a-buryin'*), reinterpretations of newfangled terms (*physical court* for *fiscal court*, *old-timer's disease* for *Alzheimer's disease*), phonetic changes (*ast* for *ask*, *taters* for *potatoes*, *pillow* for *pillar*, as in "Jesus is my pillow" on the door of Cranks Creek Holiness Church).[54]

Many traits are shared with southern speech in general (e.g., the double negative). Speakers often oscillate between local and standard forms of English within the space of a sentence: "Used to be the babies were *borned* at home... Mine, they was *born* at home" (*Debbie Spicer*). Indeed, the language is still a cultural treasure, rhythmic and expressive, and a marker of identity.[55]

CHARLOTTE NOLAN (ACTRESS, WRITER): The mountain idiom is an expressive and a colorful one. We use many similes in our everyday speech. We say things like, "Honey, you're just as pretty as a picture"; "Why, honey, you're just as welcome as the flowers in May"; "as scarce as hen's teeth"; "hotter'n the hinges of hell"; "cold as a witch's tit." It just rolls off the tongue, and just about everybody speaks in those terms. Folks are anecdotal by nature. They can't buy two dollars' worth of gas without telling the fella that you're very apologetic about not buying more gas, but this is your last two dollar or maybe you've just got ten dollars and need to spend the other eight on something else, and you tell 'im what that is. We swap lies—we spin yarns—we tell stories, you know. We hafta tell a story. It's almost imperative that you tell a story.[56]

The local press brims with colorful episodes and characters from the past; Web pages hark back to traditional stories. Local historians quote handed-down tales: "Dr. M. S. Howard, deceased, of Harlan, Kentucky is authority for the statement that..."; "A story has been handed down in the Kelly family with regard to..."[57] History and memory tend to coincide. The task of the anecdotal society is not to understand the past but to keep talking about it.

GEORGE ELLA LYON (WRITER): I certainly feel that I come out of an oral tradition. Of storytelling and singing that I thought everybody had until I went out into the world. I was really shocked when I went home with a college friend who lived in New Jersey and I was there for a whole weekend and her parents never told a single story. And I asked her when we left, "Are they shy?" She said, "No, why?" And I said, "Because they never told me anything." And she said, "You didn't ask for anything." "Well, I don't mean like information. I mean stories," and she said, "Oh, you mean like your family." And this was a revelation to me. And I was really frightened to think that they didn't have stories.

"And this goes back to the old days when people sat around, potbellied stove, or sat around the cracker barrel in the general store and disseminated information, in this one public place" (*Charlotte Nolan*). "During the summers between semesters of college, I worked for my father in the wholesale grocery business. I drove a truck, and delivered groceries to little country stores. Country stores were, and still are to a limited extent, the hub of small communities in Harlan County. In many instances, these little country stores had a post office where people went, got their mail, and bought groceries. There would be a potbellied stove there, where, in the wintertime, the men would sit around, chew tobacco, spit on the stove, and tell stories" (*Sid Douglass*).

CHARLOTTE NOLAN: If you sit down with ——— at Creech's drugstore, where folks gather to have their coffee and lunch and this kind of thing, he can always say, "I remember your grandmother—I remember her well." Well, 'course you say, "Tell me about it." And he'll tell you some droll little story about your grandmother who smoked a pipe and who made her own Sen-Sen out of dried orange peel and clove so that you couldn't smell the tobacco on her breath. He knows history. He knows about the hanging, he knows anecdote after anecdote. He knows stories about everybody's family. I have numbers of times enjoyed hearing him tell stories.

4

THESE SIGNS SHALL FOLLOW THEM

THEY CAME ON HORSEBACK

ANNIE NAPIER: Well, we've got Catholic, Methodist, Baptist, Presbyterian, Holiness, Mountain Assembly, Church of God, Jesus Only, all different faiths. Everybody's church is the best. But I think that, if everybody's planning on going to heaven, which is my understanding of the whole thing, there's not going to be one little corner for the Holiness and one for the Baptist and one for the Catholic. I don't think it's going to be roped off. So if they're going [to] get along up there, they better start getting along down here.

DONALD HENSLEY: The first religion that came in this country was the Methodists. They came in on horseback, and they were the first ones that came in across the mountains, [preaching] hellfire and brimstone, that you're going to split hell wide open if you are not saved, they scare you half to death, and . . . my mom, when I was real young, she would take me to church, you know, and—you go home, look for the devil under the bed, be afraid to go to sleep.

Appalachian religion is steeped in the emotional and participatory style of religious experience generated in frontier times, in the revivals of the late 1700s that culminated in the great camp meeting at Cane Ridge, Kentucky, in 1800. As the mainline Protestant churches became more centralized and hierarchical and evolved from strict Calvinism toward free will and human agency in salvation, mountain communities became more attracted to the evangelical gospel of sects such as the Old Regular and Primitive Baptists, and later the Campbellites, Church of God, and the Holiness and Pentecostal Churches, which reached Harlan in the early 1900s.[1]

Appalachian religion has been described as a blend of puritanical behavior, religious individualism, fundamentalist doctrines, informality in worship, opposition to the central authority of state and church, and values of grace and humility (as opposed to the mainline churches' focus on individual merit and achievement). Mediating between Calvinist predestination and Arminian free will, Appalachian folk churches mostly shared the persuasion that election

comes from God through grace, but salvation is achieved by human cooperation with grace through faith, conversion, repentance, and belief. Worship practices are typically intense, expressive, and ecstatic, including preaching, singing,
testifying, visions, and dreams. Churches are independent and democratic;
preachers, often unschooled and unpaid, are designated by communal recognition. Even the fatalism often ascribed to Appalachian religious culture can be
seen as a courageous attitude toward life's adversities, as shown, for instance, by
the history of the union movement in the region.[2]

In Harlan, "you're always a stone throw away from a church" (*Joe Scopa Jr.*).
In 1991, a Kentuckians for the Commonwealth almanac listed ninety churches
for a population of fewer than forty thousand. Though all the major national
churches and denominations are present, "mountain religion" sets the tone of
local religious life. Harlan is the only place where I ever go to church myself: for
the intensity of feeling, for the music and the eloquence, for the fellowship with
friends and community, and because I believe that one cannot begin to understand this place without appreciating its religious life and experience.

> NELLIE LEACH: I went to church until February to August and the spirit of
> God was dealing with me, but I wouldn't go pray, and the minister would
> preach about the judgment and about the end of time, and when you
> come up before God you have to have been born again, and he would say,
> "Depart from me, I never knew you, and you'll be cast in hell." And I
> would be afraid to go to sleep at night, I'd be afraid I would die and I'd go
> to hell, so I got back to church again. And they was having a revival meet-
> ing the first night of August. And when they made the altar call I jumped
> up and ran to that altar, and I kneeled down and began to pray and asked
> Jesus to forgive me my sins and to save me and to come into my life. And
> He did, and I have never been the same person since.

THERE'S A BETTER PLACE: MILL CREEK HOLINESS
CHURCH, SEPTEMBER 27, 1997

Whenever I've been to one of Lydia Surgener's churches (Riverside House of
Prayer in Pennington, Lee County, and Mill Creek Holiness Church in Cranks
Creek) there have never been more than eight or ten people in attendance. No
one stands at the altar or the pulpit; the musicians, Hiram and Junior Day, sit on
side benches or behind the altar. The congregation sits mostly on the sides. The
center is empty. I am always reminded of Emily Dickinson's phrase, "an eclipse
they call God"—an exclusively inner presence, evoked by the call-and-response
dialogue of the testimony.

Today a visiting preacher from Tennessee and his wife hold the service. They
stand on the altar. He wears a white shirt, she a flowing white dress with a red
sash; everybody else is in work clothes. He preaches; they sing in harmony, "I've

got a newborn feeling." Then they call for testimony. All the locals are neighbors and kin, and address one another by name: "God is real, ain't he, Brother Hiram?" They ask me to testify but do not call me "brother." They are all elderly except Bryan, a young man in his twenties who has left home and travels with the preachers.

Brother Miller rises, shakes as he speaks, runs back and forth stamping on the wooden floor. Bryan rises, shaking all over, head bent, and walks in a circle, eyes shut, stiff-bodied, feet stamping rhythmically as in a dance. I can almost touch his tension. He wears new, stiff overalls; through his very short hair, I can see a scar-like mark on the back of his head. After the service, some urge him to go home, and tell him everyone needs a mother. But his mother is a hairdresser, and cuts hair; his religion, Lydia explains, "don't believe in cutting women's hair."

A sign behind the altar reads, "There's a better place than this." These words were placed in Lydia's mother's coffin. They express the fundamentalist judg-ment on the world and the hope for an otherworldly alternative. Yet I also read it literally: there are better places than this. Indeed, while they wait for eternity, many migrate in search of better places. Brother Miller (whose testimony con-sistently uses travel and automobile metaphors) says that he and his wife "don't like it here." He has worked all over the country as a tree surgeon but moved back because here is where their children live and where the Lord calls them. They'd like to buy a van and travel in service to the Lord, but can't afford it yet.

Others try to make this a better place. Lydia and her kinfolks are active against strip mining and destructive logging. We are caretakers, not masters of the land, they say. There is a connection between evangelism and ecology. When asked to testify, I talk of the awful white scars of strip mining on the green landscape, and all nod in agreement when I say it's a "sin."

Others still wait for heaven or for the descent of the heavenly city to earth. Brother Miller says, "I'd rather be beat and downtrodden than do something that to me is a sin." Hiram Day testifies on life's dangers—mining accidents, car wrecks—and the sweet hope for the heavenly city. One of his theme songs is "I Can Almost See the Lights of Home," another travel metaphor.

Actually, the members of this congregation tend to do all three—wait, migrate, and organize—each according to individual character and to material conditions. They all must deal with shared poverty: their religion is at odds with the gospel of wealth, which damns them for being poor. The absent center seems to me an allegory for the absence of any institution, religious or political, that represents them. They must represent themselves, in action, in imagination, in faith.

This, of course, is my metaphor. It is easier for me to translate their symbols into my own terms than for them to have a clear sense of mine. They accept me almost like family but find it difficult to articulate my solidarity with my difference. I seek a common ground when asked to testify—environment, peace, fellowship, solidarity, equality—but they must notice that I never mention God. Lydia tries discreetly to save me. Brother Miller has a hard time separating me, a Roman, from the New Testament Romans who killed Jesus Christ, and from the Antichrist, the "mark of the beast"—the Roman Catholic Church.

BORN AGAIN

LYDIA SURGENER: Do you know what being born again means? Well, this baby was borned into my sister's family a year ago, so we know he's real and he's there. And that's the way of being born again a Christian, and I feel like if you're not borned again you cannot be a Christian. The Lord had dealt with me ever since I was a child but you see, whenever I became a Christian I laid aside the world and started walking a new life, so you become a new person in Christ Jesus, borned again Christian, you quit sinning, you quit doing the things that you used to do, and if you loved the world you don't love it anymore.

WILLETTA LEE: I went to a revival, and we all went up to the altar to be prayed for. I just stayed there, because I still felt I had so many burdens to leave there, and the minister did a special prayer for the Holy Spirit to enter my soul and revive me, make me new again. As they would say, be "reborn." You have to die in order to receive Jesus Christ and have a new-born soul. I felt like something just drifted out of me. I felt kind of light-headed like I wanted to drift off. I felt at peace. You don't have any thoughts, you just want to lay there and let the Holy Spirit dwell with you. The Holy Spirit controls your body and you're laying there waiting for Jesus Christ to tell you what to do.

LYDIA SURGENER: I prayed on my knees in a old tent revival. You've seen tents, don't you? They stretch a big old tent and then they put seats in it and put sawdust before the rail and then they put an altar rail, and they make a platform for the preacher to preach from, so that's a tent revival. And I was the second one in that tent to give my heart to God, and I was glad to go to the altar because I was under conviction. I don't know whether a lot of people know what conviction is, but it's being convicted of your sin, it's like you was to do a crime, you was running from the law, you're already convicted in yourself. When the spirit of God is dealing with you, it convicts you of your sins and so, there's something on your trail until you give up to the Lord, surrender to the Lord.

THEA CARTER: Back then we took them out into the river, about waist deep and we baptized them. Put them under water. Immerse them in the water, just like burying someone, lifting them up. Representing death, burial, and resurrection. The way Christ died, was buried, and resurrected. That's what baptism was about. The Bible said we must be born again, he told Nicodemus in the third chapter of St. John, "Nicodemus, you must be born again." And he didn't understand what he meant. "You must be born by the water and of the spirit. Except [you're] born by the water and the spirit you could in no ways enter the kingdom of God."[3]

"When I was little my grandparents took me to a baptize and I had never seen them baptize nobody, you know. They took them to the river and dipped them down in that water and I was wondering whether they were drowning or what they were doing to them" (*Melinda Slusher*). "You're supposed to be baptized and rise to welcome the newness of life. And they believe in total immersion. If one hair on the top of your head is sticking out of the water, then you're not baptized. I was baptized when I was about nine. I was ready because the world was coming to an end tomorrow. And I was going to be sucked up by this thing called hell where people were going to be tortured forever. So, I, to be honest with you, I was scared into [it]" (*James B. Goode*).

LYDIA SURGENER: I experienced something that day, that I never had before. I'll never forget that I was standing there in that water, all at once I began to pray, I said, "Lord, if I'm fit to be baptized, You're able to let me know." And it was a beautiful sunshiny day and there was a bright light shining right through the glory world, and I looked at my hands and I've got awful ugly hands, 'cause they're made like a man's. And when I looked at them they was beautiful and white and glistening. Well, everybody on the creek was just glittering and shiny, they was beautiful, it was kind of like the people on the Mount of Transfiguration. I looked at the water, it was glittering, the trees was most beautiful. That was the most beautiful experience, everybody should have that kind of experience, and it gives you hope to keep traveling on. It's kind of like, you've heard about these mountains; you try to figure out what they'd look like but you just can't explain it; you can make pictures and tapes, but still you can't express in mind and heart what a glory it is.

The record store in the Harlan Mall, early 1990s, has one wall that's blue, one that's black. The blue side holds cassettes of gospel sing-along for churches; the black side has the fiercest type of heavy metal music. I see it as a metaphor. No neutrals in Harlan: Howard or Turner, union or scab, God or the devil. "Only two places to go," says Lydia Surgener. "There's only two that rules in the heart and that's the Lord or the devil. And as long as you're not a born-again Christian you are a servant of the devil, right?"

LYDIA SURGENER: I prayed in my pitiful way and asked the Lord to forgive me, but when He forgive me I felt that old devil leave out of my heart. And he's been gone ever since. He's been gone forty-two years out of my house. But he'll come back and try to get in. He'll come around in every form or fashion.

You probably hear people make remarks that the devil has seven heads and ten horns, but I've never experienced it like that, not really like that.

The devil is real to Harlan's young people. "I don't believe he's taken an actual human form but as far as spiritual and believing, he is there, yes" (*Larry Williamson, b. 1991*); "I don't think he's human, I believe he's somewhat [like] God is, but in the evil presence. [He works through] maybe drugs, there's a lot of ways that he's affected people" (*Mary Beth Lee, b. 1991*). Larry contradicts my dualistic music metaphor—"I listen to a mixture of everything, anywhere from Christian to rap"—only to confirm it a minute later: he likes *Star Wars* because "there's like a dark side of the force and then there's the light side." "In this county people go to the extreme: it's either drugs or religion, it's like they don't want that in-between" (*Bonnie Thomas, b. 1977*). Stories of devil worship overlap with other demons: "I heard of cross burnings and stuff, you know, up in Cumberland. They say they used to burn crosses and they said they used to have devil-worshiping meetings up Lynch Mountain" (*Rick Moore*).[4]

> LYDIA SURGENER: [When you get saved], if you curse you don't curse anymore. If you drink, you don't drink anymore. And if you gamble, you quit your gambling, and if you was a sorry man after women, you quit all of that. Am I talking so you could understand it? Well, you don't go to dances—I don't. And ladies if they get saved they don't wear no short shorts, and they don't wear T straps because they wear their covering. And a lot of things that is modern in these days—most of the ladies cut their hair, and the Bible is really against you cutting your hair. If you get a King James version, you can start in Genesis and go to Revelations and find what they done in the early Bible days, and what they done in the early Bible days we can do today.

"I teach [girl] children in school who have never cut their hair. And I see women in town who have hair piled high on their heads and they're done up in very interesting arrangements. Now, somewhere in the Bible it says that a woman's hair is her crowning glory and they take this literally. This is going to be her crown when she gets to heaven, so she mustn't cut her hair" (*Charlotte Nolan*).[5] "I quit drinking for religion reasons; two years before that, I quit smoking. I was planning in the back of my mind of being saved and I didn't feel like a Christian should smoke. You understand that? Thirty-four years. I gave it up, it was very hard, but I did, I quit cold turkey, I just quit" (*Donald Hensley*).

LEARNING TO LEAN: MACEDONIA BAPTIST CHURCH, CUMBERLAND, OCTOBER 5, 1986

At this revival service in a black Baptist church on Pride Terrace, Cumberland, all the local ministers are in attendance, but the star is "Mother" Melissa Brown, a white lady from Louisville, a classic fire-and-brimstone preacher. "I see you turned the fans on," she begins. "Perhaps you're hot. You'll be much hotter when this is through." No holds are barred in her effort to create an emotional paroxysm, and mainly she succeeds. A few find it undignified: "You don't usually see this kind of things in a Baptist church," they tell me later. But many are caught. A young woman I'd met at a social club dance the night before throws her arms high, shakes all over, falls on all fours. A young preacher sitting next to me on the side of the altar trembles and repeats "amen" at every rhythmic pause in the sermon. The pastor sits by a young girl, puts his arm around her shoulder, whispers. After a few minutes, she rises and goes to the altar while the pastor whispers "salvation" in Mrs. Brown's ear. The choir sings "Learning to Lean," a sweet song of trust and surrender. The preachers gather around the girl, lay hands, anoint her (with Bertolli olive oil: the brand we use at home in Italy to make a salad). The girl collapses, lies on the floor motionless and rigid, eyes closed, an arm raised and bent over her face.

Mother Brown raises the stakes. The preachers, too, she says, need to repent: that you're a preacher doesn't necessarily mean you're filled with the spirit. She sidles up to the young piano player, puts her hand on his head, takes his hands, pulls him toward the altar. I catch myself rooting for him: *Resist, don't give in* . . . He trembles, closes his eyes, but stays put. But Mrs. Brown has set her eyes on bigger game: me. She lays her hand on my head, pulls me up to the altar. Only now does my respect falter. *You don't imagine how far I am from you, sister. Not because I don't believe in your God, but because I can see that this is not about God but about your pride. Imagine if it were known that you converted the white professor from Rome. . . .* She understands and lets me go. One after the other, she gets the preachers to rise, anoints them, lays hands, while the choir repeats "Learning to Lean." Only one closes his eyes and sags on the floor; later, he tells me he did it to impress his congregation.

At last the girl rises from her trance and is pushed to the altar. Someone gives her a microphone. "I am grateful to God because He helped me when I was pregnant: I was afraid I would lose the child, but thanks to Him everything was all right." Two days later, I talk to her. She is fourteen, has a child, lives with her grandmother.

JANICE WILSON (NAME CHANGED): I was scared to go [to the altar]. I couldn't make my mind to do it. My mother has been wanting me to do this for a long time. The other day I said, go ahead and let this be over. Like something told me to go ahead and get it over with. I couldn't stop crying and I had to scream to let it out, and when I screamed it all came out. And my body went light, I couldn't see nothing, so I just laid there. Like I was stuck to the floor, like I didn't want to get up. I could hear people laughing; it's like he's testing you, see what you're gonna do. Felt nice, just to feel good for once.

At night, after the service, I watch television in Earl and Naomi Turner's parlor in Lynch. No face on the screen looks like the faces I saw in church. But there are undercurrents of contamination between those worlds. I look up one of my favorite hymns in the Baptist hymnal on the family piano, number 170: "Are you washed in the blood, in the soul-cleansing blood of the lamb? Are your garments spotless? Are they as white as snow?" It sounds like an ad for some brand of soap—the "whiter than white" detergent of my childhood TV—till I realize that it's the ads that adopt the language of the hymn. Both the revelations of the Bible and the axioms of advertising announce truth beyond proof, to be believed by faith, and both are equally pervasive in this environment. *religious I → commercials*

PENTECOST

THEA CARTER: Well Sandro, I tell you. When I was a young boy, I made a start to serve the Lord. I repented, got saved, and received the baptism of the Holy Ghost. That was in nineteen hundred and thirty. I was fourteen years old. And for sixty years I've been preaching. I started preaching very young; they called me the "Boy Preacher." I had revivals and I lived mostly on free-will offerings that was donated, like love offerings. I preached Cincinnati, Indianapolis, Detroit, and a lot of different places through the state of Kentucky and Tennessee, Virginia, Alabama, Ohio, Michigan, Indiana, Virginia and West Virginia, and in Florida, Brother Sandro. And I've been abroad, I've preached in Rome. And through Europe, Asia, and Africa.

TOMMY SWEATT: I lived here during the time when there were several young boys who were family-pressured to join the church between the ages of eleven, twelve, and thirteen. And as soon as they got them in, they asked them, "Are you called to preach?" And they would have them up in church preaching trial sermons. Many of them [agreed], from pressure or what, that they were called to preach. And by the time they were fifteen years old, they was washed out. I had to stop and think a long time, whether what I was doing was from a higher calling or because people enjoyed seeing me up front. I did my trial sermon back in 1969, going on twenty-one. But I didn't feel an intense calling to preach or to be a minister at that time.

DONALD HENSLEY: I was called to preach September the seventh three years ago. I went to another church one night. There, this man of God, he prophesied for me to step forward, which I refused, I rejected, I was disobedient to it, but I knew it was on me, I could feel it in my heart, I knew that God spoke but I did not want to be a preacher, and I ran from it but I've been in a turmoil and I finally come to the realization I'm not going to be satisfied in this life until I am obedient to God. But I've had God to speak to me. God will speak to you in three ways. He will speak to you in an audible voice, just like you and I are talking now, or He will speak to you with a definite impression upon your heart. And then He will speak to you in that still small voice. It is just a very small audible voice, and He just speaks right in your heart. And you're flooded, you're flooded with peace and joy.

Lydia Surgener: About a year after I was saved, I was sanctified and baptized with the Holy Ghost and fire. A lot of people call it the Holy Spirit, but the Bible calls it the Holy Ghost and fire.[6] You know the calling in your soul, then you begin to read and study your Bible, you don't have to go to no school. I don't have education, and I have to depend fully on the spirit of God. You know, there's a difference between religion and salvation. You can have religion and not even know Christ, but you can't have salvation and not know Him. There's a record kept in heaven of every good and every bad that goes on. And every hair on our heads is numbered and there's not a leaf that falls to the earth but what God knows it.[7] He keeps a record of the whole universe.

Tommy Sweatt: Well, the thing was getting older, getting more settled. And the gradual changes that come with the seasons. As a young person, in our society, the greatest priority that you have is getting out on your own. So you can live like you want to, have some of the things that you want. And the older you get, a lot of the things that you wanted just don't mean too much to you anymore. You read something like Ecclesiastes, there's nothing new under the sun,[8] and you can look at yourself and see where you've worked for years and years to buy a new car and that new car depreciated a thousand dollars when you drove it up the lot. And you worked so hard, trying to keep things, you really don't have anything.

Lydia Surgener: There's a difference in a God-called preacher and a man-called preacher, you understand? There's a lot of preachers, that preaches for a living—say, "Well, I'm gonna go to school, and get me a preacher's degree and I'm going out." You learn how to fit your clothes, you learn how to stand, but you're just a-pleasing man. Now, I've preached with coal dust in my eyes. I used to ride the back of the coal truck, didn't never think to look at my hair, never thought to take a washrag to wipe the coal dust off of me. Preach in Church of God, Pentecostal churches, any church that would let me preach in. Sometimes you might get your gas and sometimes you might not get no gas, but you have to keep traveling on if you're pleasing God.

Tommy Sweatt: I'm a full-time coal miner. The church that [I minister], the church rolls consist of six people. It's a Baptist church on one week, and it's a Methodist church the next week. For that church I put in the general collection ten dollars, each Sunday. They pay me thirty dollars. Then my wife puts in four or five dollars, and we always give the children something to put in. So, from that church I'm taking home maybe fifteen dollars every other Sunday. That's not even enough to take care of my expenses up and down the road. When I go up to Norton, we've got twenty-three people in the church roll. Not all of them are good contributing, or attending. We agreed that I would get fifty dollars each Sunday that I was there. And that I would be sure to have at least twenty dollars to put in that collection plate myself. So I'm netting about seven hundred dollars a year. And I'm not considering the amount that it takes me for transportation back and forth, which is not much more than gas money, a cheap set of tires.

CHARLOTTE NOLAN: I've always thought that churches are very much like theaters. For instance, they've got their marquees. It doesn't say the same things that they say on Broadway, but you do have a marquee out front and it does show the name of the preacher, it does give you the time of the services, and it does give you the title of his next sermon. And he's the star of the show. He's the headliner. That's very theatrical. And several preachers are in love with the sound of their own voice.

TOMMY SWEATT: If you think of it like that, you end up losing sight of what you're up there for. I've seen a lot of people with their props: three-piece suit, handkerchief, diamond stick pin, gold ring, diamond cluster, watches, and they'd get up and stand more or less on display. But the moment that I stand up before a group of people to present a message, and I am so much of a spectacle that the way I look causes their attention to be focused on me rather than what I was saying. The apostle Paul himself was kind of scruffy, rough; he'd been stoned a few times and knocked down; and talked, as they say in westerns, straight from the hip. The part about being theatrical, rocking back and forth, moaning, jumping up and down and some of the stuff, I've seen some of that and I didn't like it. The method of preaching that come from the AME Zion discipline will tell you to state your text, talk of social problems or whatever, and offer Jesus Christ as a solution to those problems. Or as an alternative to the condition of man. And that's what I do.

PORTELLI: Do you believe in the literal truth of the Bible?
THEA CARTER: Yeah. Sure. I don't go for…evolution. I believe that God made Adam and Eve. And that they didn't spring from a monkey or ape. I believe they went [to the moon], yeah. I'm not that dumb.
PORTELLI: Do you think that the Bible ought to be the law of the state?
CARTER: Absolutely. Our Constitution was made from the Bible. In 1776, Benjamin Franklin and all them men they got together, the First Amendment was to give the people their freedom of religion, freedom of speech, the right to worship according to the dictates of their conscience.[9]

MARJORIE NAPIER: "In God we trust" is what this country is built on. [It's] in the Constitution.

PORTELLI: It's on the dollar. The Constitution says, "We the people..."

NAPIER: But the Ten Commandments are in the Constitution.[10]

FIRE IN MY BONES: FIRST PENTECOSTAL CHURCH, WALLINS CREEK, AUGUST 25, 1991

A big church, a congregation of about fifty. Pastor Ed Hanson, a former musician and nightclub singer, stands in full view at the center of the altar. Next to the microphone, on the altar, is a tambourine. Bottles of a brand of cooking oil called Puritan Oil are on sale for fund-raising.

An elder leads in "concert prayer": all kneel and pray individually, in a murmur that sends moving waves of discordant and yet strangely harmonious sound through the air. A man walks to the altar and speaks in unknown tongues. A young man rises abruptly, shouts, "Thank you, Jesus," shaken by sudden tremors. The pastor preaches about "fire shut up in my bones."

A young woman sits at the piano, accompanied by a guitar and bass.

After prayer comes anointing and laying of hands on a member who has suffered a heart attack. In the back, children pay no attention.

Two ladies whisper words about salvation of the soul in my ear.

Then there is testifying. A woman stepped on a rattlesnake and was not bitten. The preacher speaks about people dying in car wrecks. Some go into a trance. The others take turns sustaining them and making sure they don't get hurt. Rather than reaching to the transcendent, trance seems to me a sinking deep into oneself, cutting off the world. Yet while they are "away," the community makes sure they are safe.

A woman keeps interrupting the sermon with a lengthy and incomprehensible prayer and testimony. The preacher accompanies the rise of her enthusiasm, then seizes the moment to call for the musicians to take over. But it takes half an hour before he can resume his sermon.

An elderly, well-dressed lady, coiffed white hair, white shirt, and flowered skirt, dances lightly before the altar, eyes and hands raised high. She weeps; the other ladies touch her. Later she testifies and introduces her daughter, visiting from Chicago.

A lank, gaunt, long-haired lady dances in discotheque style. Once in a while she bends and shakes, stamps her feet in rhythm, vibrates her tongue, making an eerie shrill sound.

A young woman lies on the floor awhile. In testimony, she thanks God because her husband comes to church with her. The preacher raises the hymn "Fire in My Bones."

The pretty young piano player rises, trembles, falls to the floor. The other women surround her, hold her; the music goes on. I had seen her earlier that morning—she was writing a sign, and the only word I could discern was *Satan*.

As I leave, the bass player in the parking lot asks me what I think of the service, then adds: "Don't be deceived. We also have antagonisms and divisions of our own."

MIRACLES

HIRAM DAY: God works miracles, don't He. He works miracles for all of His folks. If you climb in a plane, you don't know whether you're going to make it or not. God sees fit to spare you, you'll land all right. If He don't, you may go down in the sea or something. You go in a coal mine as many years as me and Brother Noe has, you're extra lucky to be here. I'll tell you, God can bring you out of things. He's our only source, Liddy, in this life.[11] If God don't take and keep me, I can't keep myself.

In 1741, Jonathan Edwards preached: "You have nothing to stand upon, nor anything to take hold of; there is nothing between you and hell but the air; it is only the power and mere pleasure of God that holds you up."[12] In the Catholic culture in which I was raised, God is everywhere, but the world goes on in its appointed way sustained by God-made natural law. A miracle is a sudden suspension of that law, an eruption of the supernatural in the ordinary flow of life: if the earth splits under our feet, that's a miracle.[13] But in Harlan, over and over I found traces instead of Jonathan Edwards's vision: the natural world needs to be constantly sustained by the intervention of supernatural power and pleasure of God, and the miracle is that the earth *doesn't* open. "Death could come anytime" (*Jeff Salman*), whether from a car wreck, a slate fall, or a rattlesnake bite; only God's work keeps us alive from moment to moment. The word *miracle* must be taken literally in Harlan: "If a man lasts fifteen, twenty years in the mines, it's a miracle, and then he's dead with black lung and don't even know it" (*Annie Napier*).

SILL LEACH: And the washing machine quit, and an almost new washing machine. She said, "Lord," she said, "we can't afford another washing machine. The washing machine, see, You're going to have to help us and fix it Yourself." So the Lord—she turned [it] back on and it started. She turned [it] back on and it went right off after she prayed over it.
PORTELLI: The Lord fixed your washing machine?
NELLIE LEACH: The Lord fixed it, didn't He.

A domestic God that fixes home appliances is a far cry from Jonathan Edwards's angry God but acts on the same principle. In the Catholic tradition, the sacred is distinct from the workaday world: miracles happen in sacred spaces, and spaces where miracles happen are consecrated. But for Harlan's mountain religion, miracles can be a household occurrence. Brother Coy Miser, a Holiness preacher, confirms: "I didn't get saved in the church, I got saved in my own kitchen. At 10:31 at night." Catholic miracles are about life and death; Harlan miracles can be about refrigerators and cars.[14]

> DELBERT JONES: My son, he was ten years old, he was our baby boy and he was killed in a hunting accident. And we had a refrigerator—we lost it during that fire, but they took some pictures [of it]. One day we got to looking at them pictures and I said, "What is on that refrigerator?" We got to looking and it was Johnny. There's a star, just a bright picture, on that refrigerator. He loved pictures, and when they snapped to take pictures in there, he appeared on that refrigerator. It was a miracle. He appeared on that refrigerator.

> NELLIE LEACH: One time I went to a meeting, we lived five miles from the church and, my gas tank had a hole in it. My gas would leak out, slowly. I got about a third of the way, heading home, and the car began to slow, and I began to pray, I didn't have no money, no way to get any gas, things were closed up anyway, and I began to pray and I said, "Oh dear Lord, the car just died on me out here in this dark, and me out here by myself, just get me inside the town, where the lights are, that's all I ask You to take me." And I kept my foot steady on that gas. It was four mile I went, and soon as I got inside the town, that car died. I called my son, I said, "I'm setting down here at the bridge, I'm out of gas." I said, "I prayed my way this far." He said, "If God brought you that far," he said, "He can bring you the rest of the way home."

This story is a wonderful exercise in literalism. The son's apparently skeptical reply is a literal quotation from "Amazing Grace" ("'twas grace that brought us here so far / And grace shall lead us home"). She, in turn, expects the Lord to take her prayer literally: "I said, 'Well, I didn't ask Him to bring me home, I just asked Him to take me where the light was. That's where He took me.'"

As signs of God's presence in daily life, small providences are more important than big miracles. The Reverend Gary Page mentions briefly that God cured two members of his congregation of cancer, but he goes on at length about how He healed his daughter's broken toe and a rash on his own arm. Appeals to God through prayer become the alternative to worldly medicine. "I was having trouble on my stomach, and I've been going to the veterans' hospital. They had me on an awful lot of medicine. And I went up [to the altar], I looked up and there was a kind of light fog that went across the altar. They were praying for me and I felt a warm feeling come through my stomach, about milk warm. And from then on my stomach was all right. And I quit taking that medicine" (*Sill Leach*).

LYDIA SURGENER: When I was about a year old, I got real sick, and they give me everything that they could find to help me, and Mother said nothing would help and I'd get worse all the time. Now Mother [got] a bunch of Holiness people, to come and pray for her baby. Said, "She sure gonna die, if ain't something done, and medicine ain't helping her." So they came out and prayed and she said they had a bowl full of medicine and the lady preacher she said to my mother, "Does all this medicine belong to your baby?" She said, "Yes, it does." And she said, "Well, now this baby is gonna sleep under the mighty power of God, when she wakes she's gonna eat under the mighty power of God, and you can throw all of her medicine away." Well, when they got supper ready, she wakes me, and I eat, and went right back to sleep. That caused Mother to believe more in God.

LET THE LORD HAVE HIS WAY: MOLUS PENTECOSTAL CHURCH, AUGUST 26, 1991

In Molus, where Florence Reece wrote "Which Side Are You On," the church is all brick and red velvet and stained glass, with a white grand piano and three red plush armchairs on a platform above the altar. The offices and the pastor's study are upstairs. The pastor, who lives in a trailer nearby, explains that the three armchairs represent the Holy Trinity. The church has a fully equipped recording studio, operated by its younger members. They tape the service for me.

On one side, a "wailing wall" is covered with photographs and names of people who do not know Christ yet and are to be prayed for. Across the aisle, the victory wall is empty.

A young man conducts prayer requests and praise. Brother Don Hensley thanks God because his daughter who lives in Georgia has found a Christian babysitter. A young man thanks God because he's found a job. Then, communal prayer: the voices rise in loud heterophony, chanting and wailing. The big church seems empty; the sound cannot fill it as it does in Cranks Creek or Wallins.

The preacher steps to the altar. A young man reads announcements, the musicians and elders take their places on the altar. As the minister begins to speak, the music starts behind him, with hand clapping and tambourines. In the benches, nobody moves; there are no signs of emotion. An old man testifies; some hands are raised in sympathy. A young woman in pink near the altar kneels, barefooted, her back to the church, repeating over and over the same electric hand motions. Then she rises and walks to the back of the church, on the edge of a trance. The church is warming up—"Crying Holy to the Lord," "Let the Lord Have His Way." Someone asks me, "What do you think about Russia?"

Now there are isolated signs of trance: frozen bodies, tears. The sound system drowns out the singing of the congregation. Brother Hensley has noticed the young woman's trance, and he takes her to the altar, calling on others to lay hands and pray over her. Prayer cloths are anointed. The musicians play a few hymns, then the preacher calls for prayers at the altar. After more announcements, the collection plate is passed around.

The text for the sermon is Luke 19, on putting money to work, an allegory of Christ's blood given to us and of the task of making the church grow. "How many believe that we live in the last days?" That is 2 Timothy: the world is full of trouble. The young lady in pink approaches me, saying, "I saw you writing about me." She thinks her father has sent me to spy on her.

The sermon is a complaint about the half-empty church. No call-and-response, hardly an amen. Then the story of Jonah and the whale. Outside the church and on the steps to the recording studio, the young people chat, suck lollipops, do their homework.

The music returns; all are bent in prayer. I talk to a young man, Audie Carroll: "I'm twenty-nine years old, I worked nine years in a coal mine, and I'm beginning to worry—am I going to spend another twenty years underground?" He just found another job, "real good company, benefits and all, it was a blessing. There's nothing pleasant about mining, and it's bad for your health." He has an open, friendly face. The young lady in pink sits at the piano; she can't play or sing, but no one interrupts.

At the Monday morning prayer service, in a corner by the altar, five or six men stand in a circle, head bent, holding hands.

SIGNS

Mark 16:17–20 reads: "And these signs shall follow them that believe: In my name they shall cast out devils; they shall speak with new tongues; they shall take up serpents; and if they drink any deadly thing, it shall not hurt them; they shall lay hands on the sick, and they shall recover."

In 1910, George Went Hensley, a preacher in eastern Tennessee, was moved to take these words literally, and in 1919 he started a Church of God in Pine Mountain, in Harlan County.[15] Since then, the practice of handling serpents in church has taken root in the mountains, not as a "primitive" survival but as an ironic counterpoint to modernization. "A lot of people think it's an old-time mountain religion, but it hasn't always been here. Snake handling came in with some of those groups, the Pentecostal church, about that time" (*Arthur Johnson*).[16]

> J. C. HALL: I believe in handling snakes and believe in the word of God. The Bible say you shall pick up serpents, drink deadly poison, they will not hurt you, so, all my people done it, three generations. My aunts and uncles and my mother, they used to handle snakes and my mother used to go to church handling snakes and hold me in one hand and snakes another. Some of my uncles, they've been bit. They just pray on it, and go sit down and eat a big meal and pray and, Lord, He'll heal.

"To me serpent handling represents God's power over the devil" (*Gary Page*). "It ain't the snake you love, it's the spirit of the Lord. The Bible say that He'd give you power over serpents and scorpions and all the power over the enemy. And so I just leave it in the hands of God" (*Lydia Surgener*). "Snake handling, it's in the Bible and I will not say anything against it, but the only way I can handle them is with a good pole about ten foot long" (*Donald Hensley*). "It's against the law now. They put them in jail, and then they let them out, and they had them over to the courthouse yard and one of these men had a snake on him, and it got [loose] and got away. But I don't think I'd want to get tangled up with that. I'm too scared myself" (*Mossie Johnson*).

In 1938, Hensley was arrested on Greasy Creek for breach of peace by snake handling; in 1940, the practice was outlawed by the state. The police made arrests but failed to stop it, and Preacher Hensley reacted by adding another "sign"—drinking strychnine.[17]

LYDIA SURGENER: [The police] come in and got one of the brothers, down at Pineville. He had his [snake] box with him, but they told him, "If you won't handle anymore we will let you go." He said, "Just step back boys: I feel like handling them right now!" And he threw the lid back, got to holding them right in front of them. The church was all on their knees and praying. My mother was a spirit-filled woman, she went back and laid her hands on [the policeman] and said, "You're doing wrong, this is a child of God." And that man said he'd never arrest another man for handling serpents. He said something hit him when that woman touched him. You know, God's real, son. You take Daniel, he was put in the lion's den because he wouldn't obey man, did you ever read that? Wonder what locked the lion's jaws? It's someone besides man. I have to break down and cry a little when I talk about it; it's more felt that it is told. But it's joy unspeakable and full of glory.

Cawood Holiness Church, June 15, 2009. Before the service, the elders sit near the altar. I can't hear them, but I can see their gestures—"this long," "this big," "open this wide," "this close." They are reminiscing about last night's meeting as calmly as fishermen back from the creek. A man carries a wooden box with a glass lid, a snake inside. Tonight, however, it will stay in the box.

ANNIE NAPIER: They had snakes at Mommy's funeral. I didn't know they had snakes at church that day. Me and Chester went in and sat down, and here come Tony, Becky's little boy, across the room, and all of a sudden he dropped down on his knees and went under this seat, and that's when I seen that snake box. It had a lock in it, but it wasn't locked. It was just hanging in the hasp. And I don't know, from that day I don't know what happened. I remember getting to my feet. The only thing I thought about was Tony, get Tony away from that snake box, 'cause I knew it either had copperheads or rattlers in it, which is, both of them, poison. I remember getting to my feet. Beyond that, I don't remember nothing.

"To me, it's tempting God" (*Mossie Johnson*). "Some people say, if you get bitten [and] it hurts you, you've been doing something wrong" (*Annie Napier*); yet, "I've got not much to say about people getting bit and dying, because I've got a lot of friends that's got bit and died" (*Lydia Surgener*).

ANNIE NAPIER: I was raised with snake handling, all my life, ever since I was about three years old. But I never got used to it. If you've ever seen any films of them, you'll see kids laying on benches like they're asleep. They're not. They're just laying there petrified, afraid somebody's going to get bit and die. Which is very hard, growing up, you know. That makes the children extremely nervous, because they know they're gonna get bit. Almost every Sunday, they had meeting all day, they handled snakes, and fire. They used blowtorches; turn 'em up to real blue, where it'd melt steel, and then they'd run it over their hands, and through their hair, over their clothes, and a lot of times it won't even scorch you. And then sometimes you just about melt the meat right off the bone. The kids is sitting out in the audience, terrified. You just freeze up. It's like your insides die. You sit there on the chair and you're breathing, but you're dead. And you grow up with this fear, and you go to bed at night and you have nightmares about the service you just attended. And you wake up in the morning and you're afraid: "God, we gotta go back tonight to the same thing." And the child just grows up petrified.

Serpent handling can be both a trance-inducing experience and the culmination of a trance generated by the music, the preaching, the excitement. Ethnocentric descriptions teem with terms such as "voodoo," "mad," "savage," "bedlam," and "orgies," or describe a "possession state," a kind of "sensory anesthesia" that enables worshipers to handle snakes and fire.[18]

DONALD HENSLEY: This sister up at Ages, she got down praying in her home and she had an open fire grate. And she said that the spirit of the Lord got on her and she reached in the fire and holding her hand [inside]. And she went to church after that, and they had a potbellied stove and she got over against the stove and it burned her arms. And there was a woman watching her and she thought, she will not have faith now that it burnt her arms. And the Lord spoke to her, and she reached in the stove and got the fire out and walked over and laid it in that lady's lap, and it never even burnt her dress.

"In my name," says Mark, "they shall cast out devils; they shall speak with new tongues." Glossolalia—speaking in unknown tongues—is another sign that follows the faithful. "Now, you're from Rome. You speak Latin. But you're over here talking English. [On Pentecost] there was people from seventeen different nationalities. There was people from Crete, Arabia, and Mesopotamia, Asia, and these people heard these apostles speaking in their own tongues and languages, wherein they were born. Now, fourteenth chapter First Corinthians said, 'He that speaketh an unknown tongue speaketh not unto men, but unto God, and howbeit in the spirit you speak of mysteries yet no man understandeth them.' And that's the unknown tongue" (*Thea Carter*). "Me and my sister, we both got the Holy Ghost, one or two minutes apart. And we were up on that floor shouting and speaking in tongues for about one hour. It was a glorious feeling when I got saved; but when I got the baptism of the Holy Ghost and began to speak with other tongues, that was the most glorious feeling I ever experienced in my life" (*Nellie Leach*).

> GARY PAGE: About six months before the Lord called me to preach, there was a prophet came and I don't know how familiar you are with prophecy. We've got several good prophets in the church and there was a prophet that came and said, "The Lord spoke to me and said that there's a gap coming that I will require you to fill. But now you're poorly prepared." I told the Lord, I said, "Lord, I would do whatever You wanted me to do if You would fill me with the Holy Ghost." And a still, small voice spoke and said, "Would you?" And I said, "Yes, Lord I would. I'd eat bread and water until You give me the Holy Ghost." And I went into a ten-day fast: I'd come home from work and I'd eat one piece of bread. I'd drink a glass of water and then I'd go and pray and go to bed. Seven days into that the Lord spoke to me through another prophet and said, "Your sacrifice has come up before me. And I have found it acceptable." Three days later the Lord filled me with the Holy Ghost. I was praying and I began to feel a cry come out of the pit of my stomach. A tongue—an unknown tongue that spoke, that couldn't be stopped. In a language that I couldn't have described. Words that I didn't know. I was hearing it as it was speaking, as if someone had of been in the room with me. But the most of the time when I've had it to cry out of me was when I was troubled. Maybe the mind would know what was wrong, the heart would feel the grief, but the mouth couldn't form the words to tell God.

Mark connects speaking in tongues with casting out devils. Sill Leach confirms: "I just felt like the old devil was trying to choke me to death, you know. Then I went to beating on to the altar—with my fist; I figured, I ought to beat the old devil's head in, you know, and I went to beating on the altar and, directly I felt like my tongue come back just a little bit. And then I went to talking in a foreign language." The devil chokes Donald Hensley, Janice Wilson had to "scream to let it out": glossolalia and conversion are like the coming free of something pent up inside. "And the only way I could describe it is if maybe if you had your fingers stuck in a hole stopping up water and when you pulled your finger out of that hole the water started and it cut its way through and then it was unstoppable" (*Gary Page*).

> DEBBIE SPICER: I go to Holiness church. They sing and shout and pray; if they get the spirit of God, they dance. I speak in tongues, when the Holy Ghost falls on me. The spirit of the Lord just covers you up, you feel so good, you couldn't explain it, how you feel, when the spirit of the Lord is on you. Some are speaking to the Lord; and sometimes the Holy Ghost tells you what they're saying. That's the spirit of the Lord a-moving it, it's the Lord speaking through you. Yeah. It's real. It's ree-al, it's real.

"My mother, she was handling a copper, he bit her. I believe he bit her about fourteen times, and it never really swelled, not as much as a little boy's scratch would" (*Lydia Surgener*). "Here in a church at Ages, there's an old man, been a-preaching down there for years and years, and he had a boy, and he got him to hold [the] snakes, and one of them bit him and killed him, just a month or two ago" (*Otis King*).[19] "Out here on the hill as you go up towards Harlan, there used to be a church...both of the ministers were snake-bitten and died as a result of it" (*Arthur Johnson*). "We used to have snakes out here in the yard and throw basketballs and them snakes would strike at the basketballs, we used to catch them and sell them to the churches. Yeah, we had rattlesnakes and copperheads out here and we kept 'em in big old cages. We sold them for fifty dollars" (*Crystal Vanover*).

> ANNIE NAPIER: The last one that I know that got bit and died, was [a preacher's] niece, from Baxter. They handled snakes at his funeral wake and she got bitten, died before daylight.[20] They was one kid in Cawood got bit and died, she wasn't hardly fourteen year old. This preacher took this snake out and [put] it in the young'un's hands and it bit her and she died that night. This one preacher I know of, when I was small, he lived at Evarts, he got bit here in Virginia and died. And that was the most horriblest death that I ever heared of. We was up there that evening when he died. His arm was swelled and plumb black and it split. And it's like the ground vibrating, where he was trying to breathe. He was struggling so hard to breathe, it was like the ground was shaking. He never did go to the doctor. His family kept him right there at the house. Till he died.

> GARY PAGE: Been two people bit here in the last six years. Neither one of them serious, but—and I say this with love for them, but they shouldn't have been in the box. They should have left it alone until the Lord moved them. I've handled serpents with them many times and the Lord moved great but—it's important not just to know the law, but to know when to apply it. Most of the time I'll ask—and not always does the Lord say it's all right to take one. If it was up to me, I would have one every night because

there's such a blessing that goes with it, but the Lord doesn't heal people every night. The Bible says in Ecclesiastes there's a time and a season for everything.

"Whatever you're doing in the mountains, it's dangerous. There ain't nothing safe in the mountains. Nothing else, a rattlesnake will bite you and kill you" (*Otis King*). In the snake-handling ritual of Cocullo, in the Abruzzi, St. Paul's statue is carried in procession with snakes crawling all over it—with their poison teeth removed. They are symbolic, and harmless.[21] In more literal-minded Appalachian religion, snakes retain their deadly power: the danger is the thing. Perhaps, by taking up serpents and juggling them around, worshipers express and exorcise the awareness of daily danger by literally taking death and life in their own hands: "the poverty, the unemployment, the yawning strip mines, death in the deep mines have all been harsh, uncontrollable forces for simple people. The handling of serpents is their way of confronting and coping with their very real fears about life and the hardness of reality."[22]

One day on my first visit, snake handling came up in conversation with Jerry Johnson, a Brookside coal miner. "All nonsense," he said. "I grew up with it, I was scared to death every Sunday." His neighbor, a young red-headed lady, snapped back: "Dangerous? What about him [i.e., me] climbing into that plane and flying over across the waters? Isn't that dangerous?" I objected that that there is a rationality to the airplane, I know how it works. Yet the news was full of airplane accidents and crashes, and I wondered whether I really knew about planes any more than snake handlers know about snakes. As she turned to leave, the lady fired her parting shot: "Did you hear, they made twelve nuclear tests in Nevada, this year? What's more dangerous, that or a snake?"

SO MANY MOONS HERE ON EARTH: CUMBERLAND, FIRST BAPTIST CHURCH, OCTOBER 1986

It was my first church service, on my first research visit to Harlan, and I was still too shy to ask permission to record. So as I listened to the sermon by Reverend Baxter (name changed), I just took notes.

When you move your hand, when you walk, you don't do it by your own power. God gave you the power. Some of us have too much faith in automobiles, education, worldly goods, and forget God. God only loaned these things for a short while. I never saw God with my natural eyes, because God is too holy. We will see him if we are faithful in Lord Jesus. But if Christ came back today, the church will be empty.

In America we have people that are starving and the stores are full, but it's so high they can't buy it. There are people that have no jobs. But the Lord provides. It rains on the just and on the unjust, it doesn't mean that because you are born again Christians you won't have to suffer.

Some of us are so high minded they don't know how to humble, our clothes are so good that we can't get on our knees. I'll get on my knees because God can take back those clothes and destroy them, and when I leave this world I won't take more than I brought into it.

I'm glad my children weren't brought up today—drugs, no prayer in the schools, teachers know nothing about God.

Some people are uneasy about the next world war. You better get uneasy. Because if your soul ain't right you may get in trouble. Don't serve Reagan, serve yourself. Because Reagan himself must answer to God. Atomic age, going to the moon—some of it I don't believe, some of it I don't like, there are so many moons here on earth that need to be taken care of. God is the answer to your problem. Don't try to straighten it out, you're the one told the lie—you promised to God I'll be faithful to my wife and vice versa—now maybe she lied—let God straighten you out.

The congregation sings "The Blood Done Sign My Name."

CLASS

"We never had no books in the house—all we had is the Bible. King James Version, you know? That's anti-union, as far as I'm concerned" (*Jerry Johnson*). "Moses, he was a good man, a great union organizer. All them people living in slavery, he went down there and he helped them get organized. There's a passage in the Scripture. It said if you don't work, you don't eat, you know.[23] And I kinda halfway go along with that" (*Rev. Hugh Cowans*).

> SUDIE CRUSENBERRY: I hope to God they put them Bibles back in school. We need them, right along with the union. They's three things I will stand for. That's the Bible and church, and my union, and God. I'm still union, still believe in my Bible.

> DELBERT JONES: I think they got the principle of the union from Christianity. And, to be honest with you, I think just as much of my union as I do religion. Because if it wasn't the union, we wouldn't get treated, get medication—[my wife] wanted to get a wheelchair, we wouldn't have got that. 'Course, we got the Lord, too, on our side. And it's a blessing to have both.

Snake-handling preacher Harvey Valentine joined the Communist-oriented National Miners Union during the strike of 1931–32. So did Jim Garland, a preacher's son and a church deacon, and Tillman Cadle, the son and grandson of preachers. Preachers were on the front line in the UMW campaigns after 1933: "They had mountain religion, the conservative, more literalist sort of religion with a predominantly Pentecostalist people, Old Regular Baptists. My grandfather was a member of that church. And they believe literally in the Bible; their teachers, their preachers were nonpaid, volunteer preachers; some of them couldn't read, but they were fervid in their religion; and they were working class. And some of the preachers from the Old Regular Baptist Church were the leaders in the struggle. And they'd preach on Sunday, this fundamentalist religion, then go out on the picket line all week" (*Myles Horton*).[24]

Theologian Reinhold Niebuhr reported from Harlan and Bell in 1932: "The miners are more religious than any similar body of proletarians.... The religious character of these proletarians would offer a splendid opportunity for the emergence of a real proletarian religion."[25] Things didn't work out as Niebuhr hoped; but class remains a factor in religion in Harlan. Shaunna Scott points out that the anti-materialistic preaching can veer toward either class consciousness or otherworldly passivity: the "interpenetration between Pentecostalism, working-class identity, and patriarchy" implies a "potential to reinforce cultures of resistance" as well as "ideological connection to patriarchy."[26]

"But alas," Niebuhr wrote, "the miners' preachers (who usually dig coal for a living) must preach in company churches." As a West Virginia miner wrote in 1916, company preachers, "instead of preaching the Gospel of the Son of God, they preach the doctrine of union hatred and prejudice."[27] Mostly, however, preachers avoid controversial themes. The only reference to labor I heard in Harlan was an African American minister in Lynch, in 1986, warning his congregation that "we can't afford a strike." Thea Carter recognized that the Pentecostal Church appeals "more to the poor" because "Christ said he came to preach the Gospel to the poor" and the Pentecostal people, like early Christians, are looked down on "as the trash and scoundrel of the earth." Yet when he preached at the funeral of thirty-two men killed in a mine explosion at Fourmile, he taught acceptance of events beyond human control:

THEA CARTER: Jesus told the people, "Consider the tower of Siloam, it fell on eighteen men, and killed them. Suppose ye they were sinners above all men? I tell you nay, except you repent you shall all likewise perish."[28] It's just something that took place, but still yet we are people, except we repent we will perish too.
PORTELLI: Isn't everything that happens God's will?
CARTER: Well...I don't know about that. There's good people that's been killed, and good people destroyed, and good people died in wrecks, and...I believe sometimes the devil has something to do with it.
PORTELLI: And did the company have anything to do with it?
CARTER: Well now, you know, in this section of the country, something like that happens, and they blame it every bit on the owner of the mine. Because he didn't have the safety rules.
PORTELLI: And did people feel that these disasters are caused by the devil?
CARTER: Well, no, they don't blame the devil but, I tell you, I believe the devil has a whole lot to do with it.

The class status and composition of the congregations range from the mainline denominations (Presbyterian, Methodist) on top to the Pentecostal and Holiness at the bottom. Gladys Hoskins, secretary of the Harlan County Chamber of Commerce, admits: "I hate to say that, but I do think that there's still some sort of [social distinction] between churches and that's probably really wrong."

> GEORGE ELLA LYON: I remember at one time at my church some very poor kids came to our Sunday school and they were clearly not welcome; the Sunday school teacher didn't like having them there. That bothered me a lot and the next week, when the kids didn't come back, I asked the teacher about it. She said, "Well, it's really for the best. They wouldn't have been happy here. They're more the Church of God type."

Ironically, "some of the preachers in the cities were talking liberal theology, all the modern interpretations of religion, yet they would side with the [operators]. It was a class division" (*Myles Horton*). In 1935, Methodist minister Carl E. Vogel was forced to leave Harlan after denouncing acts of violence against the striking miners.[29] "I know a Presbyterian [minister] left Cawood because he got involved with a strike. There was a strike about 1957, and he made a public statement that led to his moving out. Usually the big churches took the stand with the coal operators and the lawyers because that was their churches" (*Arthur Johnson*).

"And unto this day, for example during the strip mine struggles in the mountains, the mainline churches in Whitesburg, Harlan—the Baptist, Methodist, Presbyterian—all side with management, against the effort to stop strip mining" (*Myles Horton*). On the other hand, Pentecostal snake handler Lydia Surgener was "bitter against" strip mining and clear cutting, and actively organizing against it: "If they hadn't come union in back when I was a girl, we wouldn't have nothing. And we still got fights to go through. 'Cause God wouldn't want poor people destroyed."

"In the late sixties, when all my friends were quoting Mao," Larry Holcomb recalls, someone asked him how he got from Harlan County to the Washington office of the Appalachian Volunteers. He replied: "I sat on the front pew of the Closplint Missionary Baptist Church and the Pentecostal Church in Black Bottom, and when the preacher talked about when Jesus talked about justice, I made that connection; and I was able to make that connection partly because of Dad's talk about the union."

> JOHNNY WOODWARD: I don't go to church. But I believe in God, and I believe that as long as I am out here helping people, and trying to better people's life, I'm doing His commandments. Jesus was a poor man. And He was kind of an organizer. Martin Luther King, he was a kind of organizer. And His disciples were organizers, and He got crucified for it.

5

FLUSH TIMES AND ROUGH TIMES

THE LITTLE SHEPHERD OF MILLER'S COVE

GURNEY NORMAN: Allow me to flash back to the 1880s. At this place called Stone Creek, you go up a hollow to the southern base of Black Mountain.[1] My grandmother—Musick—was a Kirk, before she married. Her father owned hundreds of acres of the south slope of Black Mountain, with virgin timber and all coal rights. My grandmother was born on Black Mountain over the hill from Cranks Creek, in about 1880. And so by 1900 she was a teenage girl, growing up—we could say she was a little shepherd girl, one of her chores as a little girl was tending the sheep, she would go out and they lived a pure farming life. And she was the only daughter, she had three brothers, I think. And they lived in the forest, on Black Mountain. And, then her father sold the timber rights. And a logging company came, in 1905.

And what this meant was a crew of about twenty young stud loggers came, to cut down the forest, the original primeval forest with these trees. And they did it with hand tools, axes and saws. And they cut the trees, and they would get the logs into fifteen-foot lengths or something, and they had to build a little tram, it was called, which was like a wooden road, like a chute, going down the hill, and oxen would draw these logs to the chute and they would slide down to a sawmill at the entrance to this creek. And so one member of the logging crew was a young man named Rufus Musick. Rufus was about twenty-three years old. Powerful strong. And I think he had to compete with some of his other fellows to get the attention of the daughter of the owner of the land, who had sold the timbers. He did, and he married my grandmother. And they began their housekeeping right there, just down the creek a ways.

This story, told by one of Kentucky's most representative authors, is a poignant allegory for the transition from the golden pastoral age of "little shepherds" and "primeval forest" to the industrial age.[2] The sale of the timber and mineral rights was like a second fall, a loss of the original birthright to the land.

GURNEY NORMAN: When the logging was over, it was time for the coal companies to open the seam into Black Mountain. And my great-grandfather somewhere in there sold the mineral rights. And it's entirely likely that the purchaser was Franklin Delano Roosevelt—Junior. It's on record that he stayed in the hotel in Pennington Gap, Virginia. He was twenty-two years old, and he came down from the Hudson River representing his conglomerate family fortune, as a buyer. He was also surveying the family holdings.

In 1907, Warren Delano Jr. set up the "corporate mineral fiefdom" named Kentenia; his nephew Franklin Delano Roosevelt came to Lee and Harlan counties to survey and buy the land and the mineral rights. In a letter he wrote from Harlan to his wife, Eleanor, he wrote: "If you can imagine a succession of ridges, each fifteen hundred or so above the valleys, running up at a very precipitous angle and covered with marvelous trees and an undergrowth of rhododendrons and holly you can get a general idea of the country."[3]

GURNEY NORMAN: And in more recent years the scenes of all of this drama— including Miller's Cove, where my grandmother tended sheep, has all been strip-mined; two or three times. And the forces that turned Miller's Cove into Miller's Cove Energy Company owned by a Canadian conglomerate, are the same forces that destroyed my mother and my family—this tension from the farming life to the industrial life. And now, my mother's now eighty years old; and every six months I take her on a drive up the head of the creek to Miller's Cove. But there's this fence, a cyclone fence across with a guard, and we can't go past that. But we drive to the fence, and I always talk to the guard a few minutes, he's usually nice. But what's left is me and my eighty-year-old mother making these semiannual pilgrimages to the fence, is the limit now where we can go.

TREES INTO LUMBER

"Look around you," says James B. Goode, a distinguished poet from Harlan County. "I'm surrounded by it. I mean, I lived in nature. We ran in the hills, squirrel hunted, I could identify all the native trees by the time I was ten. I can tell you the difference between a red oak, and a white oak, and a pink oak and a chestnut oak and I can tell you a sourwood from a poplar, from a shag bark hickory to a sleek bark hickory."

Harlan's history and Kentucky's begin with the trees: George Burkhart's sycamore, or the trees "eight to fifteen feet in diameter [that] grew so close together that a man could barely squeeze between them," mythologized in the 1700s by future Kentucky governor Charles Scott.[4] In Blanton Forest, on Pine Mountain, "it is possible to walk among some of the same trees" that greeted the first settlers.[5] Blanton Forest was established as a nature reserve in 2001. "Because God created it," says high-school student Mary Beth Lee, "you want to preserve it."

JUDITH HENSLEY: Blanton Forest is a mixed-mesophytic old-growth forest here in Harlan County. There are only three like it in the world: twenty-five hundred acres of mixed-mesophytic old-growth temperate deciduous forest. It was under private ownership, and they had the discretion if they wanted to log it, to come in and clear-cut or do whatever. But once it was identified as the largest old-growth forest in the state of Kentucky and the thirteenth-largest old-growth forest east of the Mississippi, this state and different people realized, this is a treasure and we need to try to save it. Berea [College] led the campaign, but my students—sixth, seventh, eighth grade—have been active from the very beginning.

"Back when I was about fifteen, twenty years old, this whole country, the logs was old timber, had never been cut before" (*Ben Lewis*). In 1901, Secretary of Agriculture James Wilson wrote to the president: "These are the heaviest and most beautiful hardwood forests of the continent.... They contain many species of the first commercial value."[6] The tension between beauty and commercial value, trees as a cultural and spiritual resource and lumber as an economic resource, shapes the history of Appalachia.

RAY ELLIS: Right about the turn of the century, all there was in here, was logging. And they logged it out with steers and oxens and mules. My dad used to have a bunch of oxens he logged with, back before I can remember. I drove a team in the mountains when I was fourteen years old.

"They'd cut the timber down with axes and then they'd saw it with crosscut saws, and they used big horses to pull them in. Since back as I can remember they had them big old horses, some of them would weigh two thousand pounds a piece" (*Ben Lewis*). Logging began in Appalachia in the 1870s. First the loggers removed only the choicest and most accessible virgin timber; as tools and methods improved, they started making more intensive cuttings and penetrating into more remote areas.[7] Creeks and rivers were the only way of getting the logs to the sawmills: "They'd build what they call the splash dam, back the water up behind those logs, and then they'd tear it down, and floated them out" (*Ben Lewis*). "And they'd wash them down this creek, and to the river, and they'd take them down to Wasioto down at East Pineville. A fellow by the name of T. J. Asher, he had a big mill down there" (*Parris Burke*). Often logs were tied together into rafts that were floated down on the spring flows.[8]

After 1910, the mechanization of timber cutting and the removal process accentuated the environmental damage.[9] Rather than taking the timber to saw-mills downstream, bandmills were erected at the logging sites: "T. J. Asher, he built [a railroad] from Pineville up to what they call Teejay. They could ship [logs] out by rail; then, they mostly set their sawmills up, and cut their lumber up here" (*Parris Burke*). "It was dangerous work. Sometimes they'd get killed with them logs, trees fall back on them, kill them. They'd get them horses killed with logs, too. The horses would get snagged to some [tree] or another, then they'd have to kill the horse, you know, and snag them that way" (*Ben Lewis*). As logging reached further into the hills, timber had to be moved by other means.

> BEN LEWIS: When I first saw any logs took out, they took them out on a little engine. It'd take about six little cars loads at the time, they called them little trains, little engines, small gauge rails, wooden tracks, and they'd have about ten logs on a car, and one engine could pull six [cars]. And then in later years trucks was introduced. When I was about twenty years old, I guess, I started driving one of them log trucks. I drove them something like fifteen years, and hauled logs to the saw mill. They was just rotted out muddy roads, they couldn't hardly get cars over them.

Logging was the first important source of nonfarm employment. It paid cash wages to loggers, rail workers, and truckers and laid the ground for the first significant accumulation of capital, paving the way for outside investors, the railroad, and the coal boom. A protagonist in this process was Thomas Jefferson Asher, from Pineville: "T. J. Asher, before they had the railroads in, up this creek here, Yoakum Creek, he built a line about six or seven miles, to haul the logs and then dump them in the creek. He was one of the men that helped develop this country, he logged this whole country up. I mean the poplar, and virgin timber. T. J. Asher, he be a hero, 'cause he start the railroad up the Cumberland River up from Pineville, and then sold to the L&N, and he supervised the [rail]road in Harlan. Of course he owned thousands of acres of land in coal land, and he owned a big mine down there in Coxton" (*Ray Ellis*). After selling his timber company to a Michigan group, he established the Asher Coal Company with holdings in Harlan and Bell. In 1910, he brought the railroad to Harlan.

As profits grew and ownership passed to absentee owners, the forests were harvested with little concern for the environment. As the Rev. Dr. A. E. Brown, a Baptist preacher, pointed out, logging provided jobs but was "destroying the future...because the sides of the mountains have been denuded of their top soil and the bottom lands have been overflowed and swept away, thereby destroying their value for agricultural purposes." By 1930, the bulk of the forests outside the vast areas controlled by the federal government had been either clear-cut or logged.[10] "As the original forest stands were cut and logging shifted to the sparsest stands of second-growth timber, small portable mills took over part of the job of sawing up the forest material. These mills, using circular saws, were usually set up under temporary shelters to cut the available sawlogs from a tract of timber, then moved on to other tracts. Small mills are scattered, literally by the hundreds, throughout the Appalachian territory."[11]

Some local loggers retained some concern for their native forests. "My dad had a camp up Big Black Mountain at Lynch. He was very much aware of keeping the forest. He said that the United States had enough lumber that we would never be without if it's handled right (*Gladys Hoskins*). "My dad was a logger all his life but would never cut a tree but what he didn't plant another tree back. And I'd say a part of these trees is what he planted, back in the thirties and forties, early fifties" (*Annie Napier*). But contemporary industrial logging is ruthless: "Everybody is buying these big trucks and cutting everything. An older fellow who worked in the log woods told me, he says, 'They're taking everything, even the small trees; they cut them and grind up everything and then compress it to make a compressed wood'" (*Chester Napier*). Clear-cutting causes sedimentation in streams and rivers, damage to fish and wildlife, destruction of the landscape, and danger of fires and floods. "When you come down tomorrow look at that mountain over there, where they're logging it. And it's just ruining it. You can see the road back through where they've just tored it all to pieces. I don't think the bulldozers ought to be allowed in there. What they don't cut down they destroy it with the dozer track. And, we're gonna be in trouble, we're really gonna be in trouble again" (*Annie Napier*).

> RAY ELLIS: Right now, they're coming in and logging that whole country out up here, and, the first big flood we have, it'll ruin this country, it ain't nothing to hold the water back no more. They're cutting everything, I've seen them haul stuff out of there that's not bigger than [two to three inches]. The old logging, you build a road and take your mules and pull it in. Now they got them bulldozer and they go everywhere. They don't have no road, just pull it down and pull it down, and you got the whole country, you got it all tore up. Like now, they starting to, what they call, clear-cut logging. And if people don't get in now and start fighting it, it's gonna be worse than strip mining. Because there's nothing left to hold any of the dirt back. It'll be another flood.

"There is a real debate with me, as I get older. I have a company who sells mining equipment. And as I get older, the resources from an extraction economy, I really question the value. Our problem here, I mean Kentucky, and probably the United States, is that because we have so much land, there is no management to our natural resources. But our problem here is that so much of our property is owned by absentee ownership" (*Daniel Howard*). "Intermountain Coal and Lumber Company, they was out of Elkhorn, West Virginia. They owned nine-tenths of the land in here. Later on after they'd done all their logging, they sold to Hubert Land Company in Leslie County and then I believe Georgia Pacific got the land in Harlan County, and Georgia-Pacific I believe they was out of Canada" (*Ben Lewis*).[12] "In Benham, Lynch, all that property is owned by Arch [Coal] who has subleased it to Pocahontas. The state has spent a lot of money on developing a tourism-based economy, in that area, but the people up there are very upset because Pocahontas is going to come in and clear-cut, but they have no say. Arch is in St. Louis, Pocahontas is in Boston. They don't live here" (*Daniel Howard*).

ANNIE NAPIER: No, they don't live here. And it's fast money for them, it's fast money for a very few people. The bulldozer operator probably gets about fifty dollars an hour. Which that's good money for a man, you know? And then they have men in there cutting timbers with chain saws and, they don't get over six, seven dollars a hour. But the dozer man he always gets a lot because he's the one that pulls 'em out. And he's the one that destroys what's left. And, I don't think we ought to let it happen again. I don't know what to do about this here logging except just fight it. Get a bunch of people and fight it.

People don't respect the land anymore. And if you don't respect the land it's gonna fight back. It takes its toll, you know. That's what happened with the floods after the strip mining. And—the poor people, the old people, is the ones that's in the path of it, the ones that can't help theirself. And no way to put it back, you know.

BROAD FORM

JAMES HALL: Way back when I was going to school, I studied in grammar school, geography. It told about how coal formed, how coal was made. The dead trees and leaves and so forth. I wouldn't agree with that myself, that's the science. But I believe God made this coal when He made the world, that's my beliefs about it.

OTIS KING: The devils of coal mining thought about nothing. A way back yonder, they look ahead, and they [are] wise enough to have done things as made people worth multitudes of money. Big bunch of rich people come in here, and some of them got a whole big mountain of land for four or five dollars.

Shortly after the Civil War, a traveler reported from Appalachia: "We saw coal-mines all along the road, just sticking out of the mountains."[13] Most were mere holes in the ground, for local or family use; only toward the end of the century did coal mining develop as an industry. In 1880, British investors founded the town of Middlesboro, in Bell County; it "was supposed to be the Pittsburgh of the east, and it was named for Middlesboro, England and, it had English banking and backing to found it" (*Bill Raines*). Middlesboro never grew into the metropolis they envisioned, but coal became dominant in the region's economy and politics.[14]

In 1887, John C. Calhoun Mayo, a teacher from Paintsville, Pike County, began buying mineral rights all over eastern Kentucky. He would stop at homes and farms, offering the owners scarce hard currency in exchange for the right to mine the minerals underneath their land. Mayo's company and others like it collected rights to hundreds of thousands of acres and sold them to outside coal companies. In this way, they facilitated the industrialization of the mountains, enriched themselves, and delivered the region's economy and future to outside control.[15]

> BECKY SIMPSON: The way I see it happen when I was a kid, back to I was five years old: they get somebody that was well knowed, like a doctor, or a minister, and they would go to each house to get these deals worked up. So these people was, probably, saying, "Well this is a nice man, he is not going to lie to me." And they would sell their mineral rights to them.

From the vast extent of entitlements it granted to the mineral owners, the legal instrument designed by Mayo was known as the broad-form deed. While giving the owners the impression that they were getting a lot of money for minerals they could not use anyhow, it allowed owners of the mineral rights to access the ore by any means they chose, and to use and even destroy the surface and whatever was on it for any purpose "convenient or necessary" to the mining of coal, with no protection for the owners of the land.

> SID DOUGLASS (LAWYER): J. C. Mayo was hired as a purchasing agent by coal companies to buy mineral rights in eastern Kentucky. The companies decided that, rather than just obtaining a lease, they would obtain a deed for the mineral rights. A deed, in the United States is the basic instrument by which people own property, and, generally, you own what's called a fee simple interest. That is, you own what's on the surface of the land and everything underneath, and you own it to the world. The coal companies created a new type of deed that severed the title ownership between the surface rights and the mineral rights. The broad-form deeds gave them the absolute right to mine any coal, or get any gas out, any way that was feasible.

"In many instances the people from whom Mr. Mayo was purchasing this property from couldn't read or write and signed their deeds with an X. Mr. Mayo bought hundreds of acres of coal rights, worth millions and millions of dollars for just a song" (*Sid Douglass*). It wasn't only ignorance: selling mineral rights seemed a rational option for farmers burdened with increasing debt and mortgages on farms that could no longer support a growing population, or who wanted cash to buy more accessible or fertile land.[16]

"The broad-form deed was commonly used in eastern Kentucky," Sid Douglass explained. Yet, "amazingly, the broad-form deed was not used for Harlan County, Kentucky's second most coal-abundant county." Harlan Countians, however, also have plenty of stories to tell in which land and mineral rights were sold for a pittance.[17]

> OTIS KING: My mother, I believe, had a whole mountain of land, up there on Black Mountain, and she had a brother as crooked as a snake, and he got in with this lawyer, and he went round helping him get these people's

land. My mother got ninety-seven dollars, that was a big lot of money, for back then. Some of them got a dollar, and I know an old man that lived around the river down yonder, they was my first wife's close people, they promised them five dollars, and said they'd send it back, and never did send it.

BOB SIMPSON: They had 'em a piece of land to live on, but they knew nothing of the minerals under. And, all of these big mining [companies] they'd come right up to you and say, "I'll give you fifty dollars for your mineral rights—it ain't never gonna do you no good." Well, you don't know nothing about it in the first place, you don't know how the coal lays, you don't know what kind of mineral rocks are under there, it might be gas, it might be ore. And so they get them to sign the paper; they can have the land, all they want [is] the mineral. So, they went ahead and signed the deeds.

Buyers took advantage of the people's need and their lack of information, but also of the vagueness of ownership titles in postfrontier Appalachia.[18] It cost money to have the land surveyed, and the uncertainty of boundaries made for endless litigation, which played into the hands of investors with more money and political clout.[19] Becky Simpson's grandfather did not have a dollar and a half to pay for having his land surveyed and his property put on record, so "this land company went ahead and paid the fee, they took the land over, so he lost all he had."

LARRY HOLCOMB: From Highsplint to above Clover Darby, that belonged to my grandfather, and he leased it to the coal companies for a pittance of the real value. And there was a whole story about how, in the year before he signed the lease, he had to travel to the state capital to keep the coal company from stealing the land from him. And the records that he had paid taxes for a number of years had disappeared. It was like it was stolen from him.

In 1921, Kentucky's highest court ruled that the coal companies did not need the owners' consent in order to access the minerals underneath, but were only required to compensate the owners for buildings or improvements they damaged. This practice was declared unconstitutional in Kentucky in 1988. Until then, the rights of the companies regularly overruled those of the surface owners: the mountain farmers were second-class citizens whose rights were subjected to the feudal power of the "coal barons."

SID DOUGLASS: The advent of surface mining resulted in the coal companies going on the property, removing the surface earth to get down to the coal bed and removing that coal, and, in some instances, not even reclaiming what was there. A fellow might have a house or a barn or whatever, and the courts have ruled that the coal companies could go in there, tear their barn down, tear their fences down, destroy their well, and completely destroy the landowners' use of the surface.

BECKY SIMPSON: Say there was coal under my house and they want it, they can make me move my house so they can get the coal. I've knowed them to bulldoze the houses down over in Magoffin County. They bulldozed the house plumb down, left this old woman sitting outside, didn't have nothing. [They stripped] this Turner cemetery up with dozers; I used to wonder what on earth would be going through these people's mind, how can they drive up to a cemetery, and tear the cemeteries down and...all I could figure is, they see dollar signs and that was worth everything to them.

Some families didn't even remember that "way back, their daddies, their mothers, maybe, years ago, sold the mineral rights" (*Ben Lewis*) until the bull-dozers started tearing up their land. In 1956, the Kentucky Court of Appeals ruled that though strip mining could not have been contemplated when the deed was signed, the surface owner had no right to compensation for the damages it caused. In the 1960s, some courts recognized the surface owners' right to compensation, or held that the broad-form deed allowed extraction of minerals only by the means available at the time of its signing—only to be reversed by higher courts in often confusing and contradictory verdicts.[20] In the 1980s, a grassroots coalition, Kentuckians for the Commonwealth, campaigned, also in Harlan, for the abolition of the broad-form deed.[21] A 1984 state law that limited mining to methods that were in use when the deed was signed was struck down by the state supreme court; it took the 1988 constitutional referendum to restore the surface owners' rights.[22] It was a clear success for the rights of property, but with more mixed results for the environment—most of the land is owned by the coal companies and can be stripped anyhow.

OPENING UP THE COAL

BRYAN W. WHITFIELD (COAL OPERATOR): We came from Walker County, Alabama, where [my father] was in the coal business. He did prospecting here in the county in 1903. In 1907, he went to Straight Creek [Bell County] and developed the Left Fork Coal company, two mines there, ArJay and Glendon. He sold out to Continental Coal Company in 1911 and came to Harlan and developed the Clover Fork Coal Company, at Kitts, above Harlan. We bought this property from T. J. [Asher].[23]

"Coal barons still catch a lot of flak about their taking the money out of the country and riding roughshod over the area, and they did that, you know. But the roads in here and the railroads that were developed..." (*Dale Teeter*). "Local capitalists got in on the ground floor," wrote a *New York Times* reporter in 1938. "One of them was R. W. Creech, a patriarchal old gentleman with moustaches which spread a full eight-inches on either side of his nose. He had been a lumberman before the railroad came, floating his logs down the river. To him, his employees are like children, to be cared for and kept in order."[24]

> BRYAN WHITFIELD: Mr. Bob Creech, who was the brother-in-law of T. J. Asher and looked after his land and his timber for many years, developed the first big mine on Wallins Creek in 1911. And the second mine was White Star near Wilhoit. The third mine was Wisconsin Steel, Benham. International Harvester. The fourth mine was Clover Fork Coal Company, which was my father and uncle's operation, and they were ready to load coal when the railroad got there. We had sales agents in Cincinnati and Atlanta and I'd say 40 percent of it went north of the river and probably 60 to 70 percent south. [The leading operators] were Mr. Denver Cornett, was a native of Harlan County. His father was an early banker here in Harlan. Mr. R. C. Tway from Louisville and later on Pearl Bassham, in the thirties. I'm the last one that's living, I guess.

"The first load of coal that ever came out of this county, came in 1911 out of Trace Fork. There was five mines here; Henry Ford had a couple of mines here, and then Creech, big Creech coal mine" (*Lloyd Stokes*). By the end of the century, southern operators managed to capture a share of the industrial market in the Midwest and in the Great Lakes area; Kentucky entered the lake trade in 1909. Appalachian coal is of better quality, had lower labor costs, and was ideal for coking and steelmaking.[25] After 1910, as coal boomed in eastern Kentucky, railroads reached Bell and Harlan County. T. J. Asher brought a spur to Teejay, the mine village he built and, in baronial fashion, named after himself. In 1910, the railroad reached the county seat, which chose that occasion to change its name to Harlan.

Bob Creech, Bryan Whitfield, and Henry Ford represent three types of capitalists involved in the Harlan coal boom: local entrepreneurs who acted on their own or on behalf of outside investors; southern-born operators, from families that had lost money during the Civil War and saw the coal industry as an opportunity to rebuild the family wealth; and northern companies that started the so-called captive mines, whose production was entirely absorbed by their factories. In 1910, Wisconsin Steel Company, a subsidiary of Morgan–McCormick International Harvester, bought coal land and built a town at Benham, on Poor Fork: in 1917, U.S. Steel built Lynch, on Black Mountain; in 1920, Ford opened two mines at Banner Fork and built the town of Wallins.

> PARRIS BURKE: I guess Ford could be counted a captive mine. My dad moved here in the early part of fifteen [1915]. He moved out of Rockcastle County, to find employment. People was working full blast at the time and Henry

Ford, his company paid seven dollars a day, the rest of the companies paid less than five dollars a day. Henry Ford, he used to ride in here on a special coach, they'd bring a special train in for him.

In 1911, Harlan County counted three mines, producing 18,000 tons of coal annually, employing 170 men. By 1920, after the arrival of the railroads and the end of the war in Europe, Harlan was the leading coal county in eastern Kentucky, producing 30 percent of all the area's coal. In 1929, it had thirty mines, employing more than 10,000 miners, producing 15 million tons of coal. About half of the production was accounted for by the captive mines. The population rose from 10,566 in 1920 to 31,546 in 1920 and 64,557 in 1930: "If ten people were milling around the court house in Harlan in 1910 listening to 'Fiddlin' Alex's rendition of 'Sourwood Mountain' and if the increase in population chose to do the same, thirty-one people would be there by 1920 and sixty-four by 1930."[26]

DONALD HENSLEY: In 1920 Wallins was a great town, it was the first town in the county. They had a bank, they had three hotels and... They'd discovered coal in the county and, like I said, Henry Ford came in and opened up Number One and Number Two Banner [mines] and people were coming out of North Carolina, Virginia, Tennessee, other states. In other words this area was getting discovered. And they came in and, they got to work, they raised their families—and this was a booming town.

WHEELS

BRYAN WHITFIELD: I came in with the railroad in 1912. I remember the first train that came into the town of Harlan. There was people all over the place everywhere. Their locomotive number was 52. The train came to Baxter the year before and went to Benham. The line was built at Benham, and the train had been up eight or nine months on the road to Benham, the passenger train, before it came to Harlan.

"Used to, on Sundays, we would all go to church and then go over to see the train come in at the depot and that was a big occasion" (*Ed Cawood*). "I was small when the first train ran up through here. I remember my daddy, picking me up and carrying me, in the train. I can just barely remember that. At first when it run up, kind of, the first time I ever seen it, [I was scared]" (*Melinda Slusher*).

OTIS KING: I was a small boy, and I went to Kildav, that's as far as it went up in this hollow then. And people out at Pine Mountain, the first time a train come in there, they walked ten miles through them mountains, and come over there to see the train. I used to get up in the mountains and listen at it blow. Seemed like it was the lonesomest-sounding thing I ever hear in my life. Somebody told about one old woman coming across Pine

Mountain, coming to see that train, you know, and when it stopped it was making all that racket. She said, "Lord, have mercy! Children," she said, "go and get some bones or fodder and feed that thing—it's starving to death!"

WILL GENT: Used to, passenger trains come up through [Kildav], which they don't do no more now. [They] had them ol' wooden coal-burner jobs and steam engines. In summertime it'd be incorrigibly hot. And keep the window down and cinders and stuff'd be all in your hair and all in your face and you'd need a bath as soon as you got to where you were going. And a change of clothes, from the smoke smell.

"My daddy worked on the railroad, thirty-five cents an hour and raised fourteen of us. Kept us something to eat and clothes. He walked from over across these mountains in Virginia and worked for thirty-five cents an hour" (*Martha Napier*).The railroad moved people, supplies, coal, and jobs: the town of Loyall "was a neighborhood of railroad working families" (*Sid Douglass*). After all, indeed, "Life Is Like a Mountain Railroad."

PARRIS BURKE: When they first built [Twila], the creek was the only way you could get to and from. And the first car that went to Twila, it went up through the creek, through the rocks and boulders and everything. The fellow that took it up there, his name was Lee Sweete. And he was a merchant here in Wallins, and a coal miner. And Henry Ford, built this road, up Wallins Creek. It was built for a T-model or A-model Ford.

"Well, when miners were making fifty dollars a day, or more, everybody had a car" (*Ed Cawood*). "I built my first automobile myself out of a two-and-a-half-HP marine engine and wheelbarrow wheels in 1918 when I was sixteen years old and drove it from Kitts to Harlan. I swapped a shotgun for a two-and-a-half-horsepower marine engine and I made it out of wheelbarrow wheels. But I was able to drive it two miles to Harlan" (*Bryan Whitfield*). With the coal boom, modernity rushed into Harlan County, heralded by trains and the automobile. In spite of the poor roads, there were 73 motor vehicles in Harlan in 1922—and 475 in 1925. In 1924, the Harco Company automobile show was announced by such banner headlines as the "Greatest Event Ever in Harlan."[27] It was an exciting moment, as Harlan's historic isolation was breaking down. Among the new upper and middle classes, "quite a few people traveled. Every summer, some of your friends went to Europe" (*Ed Cawood*). Where Harlan's shopping mall now stands, there "used to be an airport, back in the early thirties: some people had planes and they flew in and out of here" (*Clyde Bennett*).

BRYAN WHITFIELD: I had the first airplane in Harlan County in 1923. In 1924, there was seven private-owned airplanes in the state of Kentucky and four of 'em in Harlan County. There wasn't any airports then, mister, they shipped airplanes by freight so they'd be sure to get there. I bought my plane the same time from the same man that Lindbergh bought his, 1923. Lindbergh said he paid six-fifty for his and I paid seven-fifty for mine. A JN4D2 Curtis.

PORTELLI: Why did you buy a plane? Just for pleasure?

WHITFIELD: Well, just young, and they had these surplus planes back in the twenties. We could buy a brand-new eight-cylinder airplane engine in a box, government sealed, for seventy dollars. There weren't any airports, nothing but big fields, where people graze cattle and raise hay. You picked these fields out and landed, and there was a crowd every time you landed. They'd let out school so the children could see the airplane. First airplane I ever saw landed out here in Harlan where the hospital is now.[28]

For the majority that did not own automobiles or airplanes, there was the VTC, Verda Transport Company, owned by Pearl Bassham's Harlan Wallins company and later by the Middleton family. Arthur Johnson remembers it in song: "I'm on my way to Cumberland—ridin' on the BTC / See my girl and hold her hand.../ Ridin' on the BTC / Tryin' to talk above the noise..."[29]

TOMMY SWEATT: The independence of the coal miners put trains out of business, put the local buses out of business. As soon as they could they bought cars. Soon as they bought cars, the local merchants started going out of business; there was no need for a store here in the middle of this little area. When people got their cars, they were able to travel on their own, more or less when they wanted to.

cars

Provided they *had* a car. Otherwise, once buses and trains are gone, what they are left with is "no transportation. Not unless you want to get a taxicab. We need buses back in Harlan County, again, we do" (*Sudie Crusenberry*). It was always hard to convince my university administration to reimburse travel expenses to Harlan because they could not believe that a county seat in the United States cannot be reached by any public conveyance and has no local transportation, and that I had to rent a car to get to and work there. Yet even the development strategies proposed by the Appalachian Regional Commission in the 1970s relied on the privately owned automobile and publicly built highway.[30]

Last time I counted, there were thirteen vehicles in various stages of decay in the Napiers' backyard. Poor people need to get as much mileage as possible from their cars, and to cannibalize the ones that no longer run for parts. The absence of public transportation may be one reason why, as journalist Calvin Trillin put it, "abandoned automobile hulks" are "the hardy roadside blossom of Eastern Kentucky."[31] And why one hears so many nostalgic stories of buses and trains:

JAMES L. TURNER: They had a little buses through Cranks Creek, and I'd catch that bus to come to town. It was run from Pennington to Harlan.

They didn't make about three or four trips, used to, a day. There was a fellow, he kind of run a taxi and he'd bring the mail, and we used to ride back to town with him. So, we used to have pretty good transportation that way, but—you can't get no transportation anywhere anymore.

ARTHUR JOHNSON: In the tri-city area, Cumberland, Benham, and Lynch—it was called Cumberland Coach Lines, and its station was in Cumberland, and it ran every twenty minutes during the week, and every fifteen minutes on Saturday, and every thirty minutes on Sunday. The same company had the transit buses, like Greyhound, that left here and went to Whitesburg, to Big Stone Gap, or Appalachia, Virginia, and to Pennington Gap, out beyond Harlan. And so we had good bus service, nice modern coaches. Blue buses with white tops, and they could sell you tickets anywhere, you could buy your Greyhound ticket right here to Chicago, or New York, or anyplace like that.

MOSSIE JOHNSON: There used to be a train, when I first come here, a passenger train, that come up in here and they called it, I believe they called it Ramona. And I rode it one time, after I had my baby we went to town one day and I rode it, and it cost one nickel. Then we had a little bus line up here that cost fifteen cents to go to town. [Now] if you [have] not got a car, you just hurting, if you don't have a neighbor or somebody that's got one.

Sister Mary Cummen regretted that "the poor cannot be Catholic in Harlan" because "they don't have transportation" to get to church in town. Or to the clinic: "Some people, even if they're willing to come here [Clover Fork Clinic in Evarts] and get taken care for, they don't have any way to get here. They live a half hour away and they'd have to pay somebody every time they come" (Dr. J. D. Miller). "Where we live at, getting out to a doctor, it's complicated, if you don't have a car. And when somebody gets sick, they call some of us at the [Cranks Creek Survival Center]. We run like a emergency hot line" (Annie Napier). Joan Robinett notes that democratic participation was hurt, as many citizens "were elderly and didn't have transportation" to meetings. Religion, health, democracy, even consumption patterns depend on transportation: "The numbers are real high of people that don't have cars, don't have telephones, that have no means of transportation. So they have to use whatever is in their community, and if that store wants to charge you four dollars for a gallon of milk, if you ain't got no car to drive thirty miles into town, you are going to pay four dollars for a gallon of milk" (Joan Robinett).

NOAH SURGENER: I was eighteen years old when we owned our first car. Skeeter, we called it. Thirty-one A-model. Yeah, we owned a lot of old cars, but that was the first one we ever owned. Well, a car's a good thing. You can do whatever you want to with a car, you know. They're a wonderful thing to have.

If not having a car imprisons, having one is a sign of success and of independent manhood. Perhaps the automobile is the last remnant of the famed Appalachian rugged independence. Or of another kind of dependence: "If you watch commercial television for long, you can see it trying to break down your sense [that] you can take care of yourself. It's like: if you want to survive, you need all these things. And so, what independence means is having this fast car, and what choice means is the choice of three kinds of carbonated beverages" (*Robert Gipe*).

On my tape of a service at Cranks Creek Pentecostal Church, the final words addressed to me are "Have a safe trip. Lots of drunks out tonight. Drive safely." In a religious culture that allegorizes life as the soul's journey to heaven, the automobile replaces the train also in symbolic and spiritual terms. Sermons and testimony often refer to the automobile, and God can work miracles on the road.

HIRAM DAY: Sometime back I had an old Ford truck. Me and my wife got down the road, and I'm sick some way, I don't know just what's bothering me, but sometimes I'll get bogged down and just fall asleep. And soon as I hit the highway, I lost control. I lost everything. I didn't even realize that I was alive, didn't hardly know nothing. I just fell asleep, laying on the wheel, and all of a sudden, I was right up under the rear wheels of a big truck. That's the first thing I noticed. He must have blowed his horn or something. I fell asleep. Well, now that's how quick death can get you. You can't stop it on your own. It's just God's will. I cut it right-handed all I had, and the tail end of my truck kind of edged into the bed a little. That was the only damage, but how easy, though, I could have lost a life. I'll tell you, God is real. He spares your life a lot of times. Bible says He makes a way where there seems to be none.

"Car wrecks [ruined my health]. Wrecks, mostly. Just wild, buddy, young and wild I reckon. But I thought I was enjoying it. I hit a truck, hit a coal truck. I'd got me a snort or two. I was drinking some, you know. That's what it boils down to" (*Henry Farmer*). "Drinking and driving don't pay, because I drank all that day, moon was shining that night, and I was gonna cross Clinch Mountain, and thank God I ran into a guard rail instead of some family, and cut my leg off" (*Sid Tibbs*). Inasmuch as "you can do whatever you want to with a car," it becomes an implicit symbol of free will. As in *The Great Gatsby*, being a bad driver is a sign of moral failure.[32] Every year, the Methodist church in Verda puts on a play, *Tours Through Hell*: "each part's got different scenes like, people on drugs, drinking, car wrecks..." To die in a car wreck is to "die without God; die without Jesus. Then they end up in Hell" (*Chester Clem*). Reckless driving, like snake handling, is another way of testing God's grace.

MARJORIE NAPIER: It seems like people here do not know how to drive; they just drive like maniacs. They think nothing about drinking a pint of moonshine and getting out there driving. They take the four-wheelers into the mountains where there's a cliff, to run over, just to see if they can get in there and can get back out. That's living on the edge. Just driving down the road without somebody else running over you; that's the chance you have to take.

"A late-night drive down the highway / Claimed an old friend of mine," sings Harlan songwriter Becky Ruth Brae.

BECKY RUTH BRAE: Becky and [Bob Simpson's] son got killed—Ricky. And when we were little, Ricky was always the daredevil. He was just a little wild child. We used to have this spot behind my grandma's house and there's this big tree and there's this big grapevine on it. And we used to go out there and swing on this grapevine with no ground underneath it, nothing but a cliff. I never will forget he would go out on that grapevine and he would say, "Look at me, Becky Ruth: I can fly." And when he died I said, "Yeah, honey, you can fly now." That's where the song came from:

> He can fly high, up there in the sky
> Way up in heaven, with all the angels on high
> And I find I'm looking forward
> To joining him someday
> Hand in hand we'll fly together
> Across the USA.[33]

A THRIVING PLACE

In March 1922, the *Harlan Enterprise* announced, "Radiophones for sale in Harlan." "A few of the very latest inventions fairly stagger our senses....Now comes Westinghouse and invents the Westing radio phone which permits one to sit in his or her home and distinctly hear oratory or music or noises in places hundreds, yea, thousands of miles distant....Truly the world is fast becoming localized." Harlan is excited about openness and progress, but worried about the loss of its own identity: "But this does not mean that races or nations are to lose their identity—that all bloods of the world become amalgamated. It is not well to be a fanatical dreamer."[34]

"They brought in the very finest entertainment on the trains. Traveling shows that normally just appeared in Louisville were booked for the black community and the white community. They brought in the biggest, the best-known jazz orchestras, and the performers of the day" (*Arthur Johnson*). "A large and enthusiastic audience greeted Signor Tino Pattiera at his first appearance in Lynch on the evening of Wednesday, February 22," reported the *Enterprise* in 1922. "This grand opera star was secured by the Croatian Club of Lynch at the cost of $1500.... This is the first time since the memory of man runneth not to the contrary that a grand opera star has ever given a concert in a mining town in the United States."[35]

NORMAN YARBROUGH: Of course, there was a couple of theaters in Harlan at that time, and when I was a kid, they'd have double features on Saturdays, and we could take a dime to get in each one of them, and maybe a dime to eat on, and for less than fifty cents we could have a big day on Saturday.[36]

"Since the railroad came to Harlan," G. C. Jones writes, "the people over these mountains started ordering more up-to-date farm machinery, such as hillside turning plows, hay rakes, and mowing machines, and some ordered scratch plows. They never heard of these things before the boom started moving in Harlan and money began flowing over the mountains for their farm produce and moonshine."[37] Harlan boasted a new hotel, clothing stores, restaurants, a Westinghouse appliances sales agency, and mining supply stores.[38] Some stores were owned by newcomers, Jews or immigrants: "Well, there was the Caruba grocery, they were Italian. And there's a Romano, right across this road, they had a novelty store, and a trucking business" (*Arthur Johnson*). "My grandfather was in the wholesale grocery business and came to Harlan in the 1920s. My father succeeded my grandfather in the wholesale grocery business in Harlan. All of my life, that I recall growing up, the wholesale grocery business was a very booming business, even in the fifties, when things were hard here" (*Sid Douglass*). The rising middle class changed the aspect of the town.

CHARLOTTE NOLAN: My father was a doctor; the lawyer two doors down, the banker two doors down, the woman two doors down worked in a bank. About six doors down, a cashier in a bank. Mr. Trent had his own service station. George Ward was secretary at the Harlan Coal Operators' Association. Two doors up, on the corner, was the sheriff. Across the street was the county judge. A merchant on the corner, a Jewish merchant who had three children. Then on up was Dr. Mahall, a dentist. This street was maple trees on both sides, it was a lovely, shaded street. Every house was owned by the family that lived in it. And they kept their yards, and a car would go by once in a while and we could play in the streets. We had a tennis court in the neighborhood.

GLADYS HOSKINS: When I first married [in the 1930s], my husband was in the dry cleaning business, and it seems unreal now to think that on Saturday nights we stayed open until eleven o'clock. Can you imagine that? They would come in on the weekends from all over the county. You've been around the county enough to see all the little roads up every little creek—and there would be an active mine there, and people would bring their dry cleaning in this Saturday and pick up what they brought last Saturday, and they would come into town and shop and go to the movie and have dinner, and the last thing they did was come by and pick up their clothes to take home. Business was booming, and it was a thriving place.

"In 1925 there was nothing unusual about the total blackness caused by the tall mountains surrounding the narrow valley in Harlan County to the native dwellers. There were no street lights. If any lights in the homes were on, they could not penetrate the darkness."[39] Yet "at night the town was full. Fifty-something operating coal mines at the peak of it. The restaurants and business places, they opened until late. They had buses back and forth to town, and they'd run early and late. Harlan was an open town" (*Dukey Jones*).

DONALD HENSLEY: And there used to be a lot of violence. Harlan County was a dry town, but down in Bell County, it was wet.[40] Right on the county line was a beer joint, you know, and every time we had an election there'd be three or four people killed. Arguing over elections, carry a gun... and there was always a lot of people killed in the mines.

Five subjects vied for space on the front page of the *Harlan Enterprise* in the early 1920s: shootouts, moonshine, mine accidents, baseball (in season), and the Kiwanis weekly lunch. In 1922, for example, hardly a week went by without a front-page killing or mine death.[41] Violence seems inextricably tied with the novelty and fever of the flush times: "We've had two or three people accidentally was shot at the depot in the station. You know, I told you that they all want the excitement on the Sunday afternoon" (*Ed Cawood*). By 1916, Harlan County had the second-highest murder rate in the United States, 63.5 per 100,000 population, second only to nearby Letcher County's 77.9.

BRYAN WHITFIELD: It was all new, and everybody used to go to Harlan on Saturday, get drunk and whatnot, have a big time. There was a lot of shooting till, I'd say about 1930. I mean just people shooting. There's two men buried right up here; chief of police killed them in Harlan and they killed him. They were bootlegging. December 11, I believe, [19]22. Yes sir. A lot of killing going on there.

Whitfield's memory is remarkably exact: the chief of police, Jim Pope, and two other men were killed in Cumberland while arresting two alleged bootleggers, according to the December 12, 1922, *Harlan Enterprise*. In one week: the revenge shooting of a deputy by George Lee at Wallins, and on the same date "Bloody Tragedy at White Star: Son in Law Kills Father in Law" (the victim's son later kills the murderer and says, "I'll take my supper now": he had tasted no food since the murder); a young man shoots his fifteen-year-old sweetheart at Ages; a twelve-year-old boy kills his neighbor. But life goes on: the Lynch Bulldogs win the Harlan County league baseball pennant.[42] In the 1920s, Harlan County's murder rate was the highest in the nation.[43]

LLOYD STOKES: [Wallins was] about the busiest place ever, for its size. Had two drugstores, they had the big bank; couple of poolrooms, big recreation center, they had two theaters, three real nice cafes, they had one extra nice, about the nicest one in the county. I couldn't describe it but they had a big dining room, tables and waitresses, they had it all. This used to be a pretty rough place, there was about four or five killed right around our doorway. They believed that an eye for an eye and a tooth for a tooth. "You killed my brother and now I'm going to kill you": that, that's the way it all worked out.

JAMES L. TURNER: They used to have them slot machines all over Harlan [in the 1930s]. Slot machines and beer. I'd come out over to Cranks Creek and sit around and drink beer all day and play them slot machines. Come down there with two or three dollars and go back home with nothing. And then they had a place over in Georgetown they called the Big House, and you could get anything to drink, dance or whatever you want to do over there. They had several places right down there, right on the bridges in Harlan. Black people was running it.

"You remember when they had it on the mountain, don't you? Yeah, beer joint, a bar, ever what you want to call it, a dance hall, a fighting place" (*Chester Napier*). By 1942, when Harlan County voted itself dry, it counted more than forty roadhouses, many running with political protection. Drunkenness and prostitution were rampant: during the war, the U.S. Public Health Service established a venereal disease clinic in Harlan County in order to ensure the healthy workforce needed for the maximum production of coal in the war effort.[44]

NORMAN YARBROUGH: Back before World War II, the county was wet, had whiskey, it was wild. There was an awful lot of vote buying. People passing out liquor and passing out money for votes. Yeah, back then, this county was filled up with slot machines, and the sheriff was taking a cut off of all of that. Back then, you'd get a liquor license to sell liquor, provided you sold food. So a man would get him a little old house or a little old store along the side of the road, and he would put an electronic nickelodeon in there, and a slot machine, and one of these little machines where you make hot dogs on it, and that was his food that he was selling, and then he sold beer and liquor, and then he had a room to the side, and he had a woman, or two women, or three women, depending on how popular that place was, that used the rooms on the side. And they called this a jenny barn. The jennies, you know, like the jenny, the cross between the horse and the mule. And he had one jenny, or he had five jennies, or whatever. So this is where the entertainment was.[45]

MOONSHINE AND AFTER

BOBBIE DAVIDSON: Grandpa, he came to Harlan when Harlan wasn't even settled. It wasn't even Harlan then, it belonged to Virginia. And he had four children, I believe. He made moonshine, he made saws, axes, he kept bees…Well, back then, that was normal. Everybody made moonshine, and it was just a thing that he did.

CHESTER NAPIER: Which, when I was a kid that was a way of life here. Making moonshine, I started helping Dad make it when I was six year old. And the first time I ever remember tasting moonshine, I couldn't have been over three to four years old. I was standing between my dad's legs, he was sitting in an old straight-back chair, and I was standing there, and he was giving it to me with a spoon. Everybody drank moonshine, when I was a kid. Even the preachers dranked it. They went from church to church, they carried a little bag with them and in that bag, most of them had them a little drink of moonshine.

In 1794, farmers from the Appalachian hills of Pennsylvania rebelled against a federal tax on distilled spirits. The so-called Whiskey Rebellion spread to the whole western frontier, including Kentucky.[46] The uprising was rooted in the resistance to taxation that had fueled the War of Independence and in the resentment of farmers living in faraway and isolated areas, for whom whiskey was the easiest and cheapest way of bringing to market the corn that they could not consume themselves.[47]

Corn whiskey was already being distilled in Kentucky in the 1780s; corn grew abundantly, and lime-filtered water was good for making liquor. In 1872, the federal government introduced a tax on whiskey production; mountain farmers refused to pay, and revenue agents began to seek out illegal stills and arrest violators.[48] "Moonshiners," however, were generally accepted and protected by their communities: "The mountaineer, about all he could grow was corn and he used his corn, sometime, to make moonshine, make whiskey. And it was considered his private business if he had some corn and wanted to make moonshine" (*Ed Cawood*).

CHESTER NAPIER: You'd like me to tell you how to make moonshine whiskey? Well, first you need oak barrels. Fifty-five-gallon oak barrels; drums, or whatever. You take plain corn meal, you put it in a sack—you already had it sprouted before; you grind it, you cook it. And you put it in a barrel, you let it ferment. And after you ferment, you put twenty-five pounds of sugar, you put it in hot water. Let it cool overnight, and after your sugar and everything's in there cools back down, you put a peck of malt corn. And then, it takes approximately a week to ferment, and what we call settling off.

"My grandfather used to make some. He never sold it or nothing. But it was medicine and what have you. What they did make it for was for like cold, flu, mix it in with other stuff, you know, together with ginger and what have you to make medicine" (*Will Gent*). "Make liquor. I mean it's hard work, but it's fun. You have to pack your meal, you have to pack your sugar to the mountains, you got to hide a place, find water" (*Martha Napier*). Martha Napier's old Cherokee face lit up, and she waxed almost lyrical when talking about an art handed down through generations of her family.[49]

> CHESTER NAPIER: Then when it works off, big old clear spots come. When it gets that way then you got to work it. You got to run it. You got to build your furnace, to put your still in. You wall it up with rocks and then you put your still down in there, you put your cap on top of that. Then you get flour and make it real tough and dab it up till no steam can't get out. If your steam gets out you won't make no liquor. Then you put your ignition rods into the barrel and fill it full of water, and put you a rod into where your liquor comes out in your jar. And when you build your fire, you can't build a too big of one, you just have to keep it slow till it gets to boiling, and when it gets to boiling all this here liquid goes back into the still, back into your thumping keg, back into your jar.

"My grandpa, he never was one to work a lot, you know. He loved his moonshine, and I think he got caught [making it] one time, and that pretty well weaned him. I have drank moonshine. It's powerful. Oh, it's smooth, it will go down so smooth, but once it goes down it's like somebody set a torch in your stomach" (*Donald Hensley*). "And it's a pleasure for me to make it. I love to do it. I love to drink it, too. I guess you can say I've drinked it all my life" (*Chester Napier*).

> MARTHA NAPIER: And when it gets done, then you've got to pack it out of the mountain. You got to pack your meal back and break it up and put it back in there to make another run. But it's hard packing it out of the mountains, that's a job making your own moonshine. Packing it out on your back and then you've got to bring it home. You've got to temper it down to the right temper, if you get it too low you'll ruin it, if you get it too high you ruin it. You've gotta get it just right. You'll get drunk making it. You watch your bubbles and when them bubbles got so big, then you stop, you've got to dip that all out. You've got to put it in your jar, and tighten it up, and then you've got to pack that all to the mountains and hide it again. And then when anybody wants to buy it, you got to go back and get it and pack it back. It's a lot of fun, it's a lot of work, but it's a lot of fun.

"We made free corn whiskey, we didn't fool with no sugared whiskey. And most of them used old tanks and things, dangerous to kill you to drink it like that. I come near dying on a drink made in that old tank" (*Fred Napier*). "We just had a funeral yesterday of a fella whose grandfather was a moonshiner and he also ran a store and he loved to drink. He got ahold of some poisoned moonshine, so when he was sick they thought he was going to die and his son said to him, 'Well, Pap, why in the world did you buy that old, cheap moonshine?' He said, 'Boy, it was a bargain.' He got it for a dollar a gallon" (*Ed Cawood*).

BILL LEE: [Sanctified Hill near Cumberland] was a rough place to live. A lot of bootlegging and moonshining. Federal people down there all the time trying to find them stills. You be out hunting and walk upon a still, they'd kill you. These hills were full of stills, they had their own wars about it. The old people now they've mellowed, but back during that time, if you made a mistake you died.

FRED NAPIER: The head revenue office man, [a] feller shot him. He'd catched a feller and sent him to the penitentiary. He got out, he [went to] the revenuer's house and shot him with a high-powered rifle and killed him. Ah, it was tough in them days, buddy. Most every man you seen nearly had two guns. A pistol and a .32 or .38 Winchester. There was a lot of killing and stuff going on, it was just a feud here and there where they would kill one another.

"Just as many people killed over that moonshine as there was [over union] organizing" (*Julia Cowans*). Tales about eluding or fighting revenuers are an integral part of the folklore of the Kentucky mountains, just as the stigma of the feuding and moonshining mountaineer is a part of the Appalachian stereotype. Indeed, moonshine was at times romanticized along with the feuds: an observer during the 1931–32 miners' strike wrote, "These are the men who, for generations, were known to the outside world only as feudists—rebels against the organized form of justice, and moonshiners in rebellion against the power of the State to tax them or to dictate to them."[50]

Even cinema ambiguously celebrates moonshiners as the epitome of the antiauthoritarian mountain character. In Arthur Ripley's *Thunder Road* (1958), Robert Mitchum plays a Korean war veteran running moonshine from Harlan to Memphis, fighting both the U.S. government and the big-city crime syndicate. The film and its soundtrack combine Appalachian cultural icons—moonshine, fast cars, God, and the devil—leading to a moralistic conclusion, a car wreck in which, as the theme song says, "The devil got the moonshine and the mountain boy that day."[51] No wonder the film (set in Harlan without coal mines, but also without "local color" and ragged poverty) was a hit in Appalachia, and the song reached number one in Harlan and Jellico.[52]

From the beginning, whiskey had always been made for one's own consumption as well as for sale. With the coal boom and Prohibition, commercial production became profitable and organized. Sill Leach recalls a man who flew his whiskey to Knoxville on a plane; one time he "loaded so heavy that they couldn't hardly get over Pine Mountain" and nearly killed himself. Most of the product, however, was hauled by more traditional means. G. C. Jones writes of taking sugar to the stills and carrying moonshine back by wagon over Pine Mountain, hiding it under loads of farm produce: "We made our trip in three days without any trouble. We brought the usual load back and carried it down into the cellar. We had six hundred gallons of the best moonshine that was ever made in the state of Kentucky.... We took enough sugar over the mountains to sweeten the whole county of Harlan." The sheriff, already on the coal companies' payroll for repressing the unions, was easily bought.[53]

> CHESTER NAPIER: I didn't start school till I's fourteen year old. That's when Dad was making whiskey, him and my cousin and his son-in-law. And I was on the lookout with the shotgun to shoot three warning shots if the revenuers was coming. So, the revenuers come. And I go to my spot, and I shot my three warning shots, but they was all asleep. So [the] revenuers, and some of the deputies, they walked up on 'em and waked 'em up. Told 'em, "You're under arrest." But in the meantime I had run and I'd shot at the revenuers, trying to kill the revenuers. I was just a kid, but I's using a shotgun. It was an old 1913 shotgun, J. Stevens, name of it, I still have it. And I shot the hard hat off of [a revenuer's] head. But they never did return fire at me. I guess they knowed I was just a kid. So they bringed Dad and [two other men], on out to the house. We was all tore up, afraid we was going to lose Dad. And I was hunting for some more shotgun shells. I was gonna kill 'em and hide 'em. And Dad he says, "It's all right, son, I'll be back tomorrow." So that kinda quieted me down. Sure enough, Dad was back the next day. Somebody went in with his bond and he come back. When they had his trial, they put him on what they call probation for four years, and that's when we moved out of the mountains, when I really started going to school. He come back and we started making moonshine again and selling it.

> CHARLOTTE NOLAN: There's two factions that keep Harlan wet, and that's the bootleggers and the preachers. We don't want bottles of liquor in the windows on display. It's kinda like putting your head in the sand and being an ostrich. If you keep it in the back room or out of the store windows where the children can't see it, maybe it doesn't exist. But, you see, we feel that if liquor is legalized then we'll have bars and people staggering around on the street coming outta the bar, and using foul language and all, and we just don't want bars in Harlan. You'd have women of the evening and men who like to tote pistols and shoot things up after they've had a few drinks.

Yet bootlegging and moonshine are such an integral part of the culture that local authorities are often involved or choose to ignore it. "Sheriff Blair, he was sheriff up till Prohibition. He knew the people that made the best whiskey across Pine Mountain. He gave my cousin A. F. Whitfield ten gallons of that good whiskey" (*Bryan Whitfield*).

> ARTHUR JOHNSON: We have one very famous bootlegger [in Cumberland], is she still in business, Mag Bailey? They get her once in a while and give her a front-page ad, and turn her loose and...everybody knows where Mag is located. One thing, most people involved with the court are her customers. Bring Maggie in the court, the lawyer would ask her if she was guilty of bootlegging, and she'd say "Well, your honor," or whatever, "there's no use for me to lie, you're setting there, you're one of my best customers and..." So pretty soon they just let the thing wear itself out. She supported some kids in college, and helped them to become lawyers, and politicians, and when they go to court, why they...[54]

"Well, poor folks, they tried to get a little extra money for Christmas or something, they'd make a run to a moonshine. I fooled around with it a little but I didn't do too much with it. I was too scared" (*Noah Surgener*). For blacklisted miners or for single mothers, whiskey could be a way to make a living: "I started bootlegging in the 1950s," a Harlan woman told sociologist Shaunna Scott, "so I could take better care of the boys. I didn't make moonshine. I sold bonded whiskey and beer. I bootlegged for eighteen years. Until the boys were raised, and then I quit. It kept me off welfare and I raised my three boys."[55]

Moonshine is not just a thing of the past; in recent times, however, it has been supplemented, often replaced, by more remunerative crops. "During World War II, down in Knox County, down Big Indian Creek down there, they grew marijuana for hemp, and made rope out of it. And now it scattered down the creek banks and things are growing wild down there. And they claim this part of the country is the best place in the world to grow pot. And, they'll grow maybe twenty foot tall" (*Parris Burke*).[56]

> ANNIE NAPIER: Out here we didn't know it was pot, we called it hemp. People raised it for the bark, they made boats out of it, and the government bought it for rope. They'd fix door hinges and cattle gates with it. In the old time they dried it. And if people couldn't get to sleep, they'd make them a tea from it. It was more like medicine.

As I drove toward Wallins Creek, I could hear a helicopter overhead. A young hitchhiker I had picked up explained, "They are looking for marijuana patches, ain't it?" According to federal agents, marijuana rather than tobacco is Kentucky's number one cash crop: Kentucky-grown marijuana sells for two to three times as much as the Mexican import.[57] "It just got to where they've laid a lot of the miners off, and a lot of the miners going back into the [moonshine] business. A lot of them are growing marijuana with their corn in the corn field. They said that Kentucky is about the second-largest-producing state now. They get in these remote areas, acres of corn, marijuana growing right between it" (*Bill Lee*).

"I ain't scared of pot. It's the owners with them shotguns. And then some of them puts guard dogs in the pot patches. Do you all grow pot over there?" (*Chester Napier*). Like old moonshiners, marijuana growers protect their crops by all means necessary. "Downstate you hear there was some planted like bombs around it, and they put shotguns in there with trip wires. And some of 'em got seriously hurt" (*Annie Napier*).

PARRIS BURKE: Where they grow this pot, they got rattlesnakes and copperheads turned loose in the patch. They might wear hip boots and things [to go in]. They also have razor blades put up about eye level that when the police goes in or anybody is around, it cuts in their eyes or face. And they got big booby traps like with nails in boards that be covered up with mud, or covered up with dirt that maybe they get in on it, with the vehicles, and cause it to have flats, you know, way back in the mountains.

6

A SPACE OF
THEIR OWN

FENCING IN

A conversation in Kildav, once known as Kitts and Kildow:

> PORTELLI: What kind of community is this?
> WILL GENT: Coal town. One of the original ones. Round 1910, 1917, I guess when it was put in. The houses up on the hill here they was put in in 1916, 1915? And the one here in the bottom was put in 'tween 1917 and 1918. The old coal mine seam up here, it run out, I reckon in 1932. When it worked out most of the people, they left.

"We had to have camps because there weren't any roads. If you wanted men, you had to house 'em. So that's the reason we built the camps" (*Bryan Whitfield, coal operator*). Harlan was distant from urban areas; coal is found in hard-to-reach places, and much of the workforce was brought in from outside. These conditions originated the so-called coal towns, coal camps, or company towns: enclosed settlements owned and ruled by the companies that built them. By 1925, at least two-thirds of the workforce in the Appalachian coal fields was living in company-owned towns. Harlan County counted no fewer than twenty-five camps; the last ones were dismissed in the early 1960s.[1] Some were for all intents and purposes slums, while others came to be known as model towns, but they were all under the absolute power of their owners, as though the sovereignty of the state and the rule of law stopped at the camp's gate.

> DELBERT JONES: In ways you had freedom, and in ways you didn't. Most of these camps had a private law, they was keeping the community peace and orderly.[2] Which, in one way it was good. A bunch of drunks start fighting, he come along, to keep peace and order. You actually need the law at times and at times you don't need it. Back in the organizing days—we called them gun thugs, back then—if they caught you talking union, they'd maybe have you killed or run out of town. They'd set your stuff out the side of the road, and, you'd have to move. And lots of times they'd black-ball you. Blackballing means, they wouldn't hire you nowhere in Harlan

County, you'd have to leave the county and go to West Virginia, some-where, and go to work. And they'd follow you, and get to you there. You just blackballed all over the country.

"Coal camps at that time were self-sufficient. [In Lynch] you had your doctor, and you paid a buck and a quarter a month, and you got free medical attention; we had a theater, they had a poolroom, a soda fountain, had a commissary, dry goods, and groceries, and everything. The school was right in the camp, and you could really stay in the camp and never go out, and get whatever you wanted" (*Norman Yarbrough, coal operator*). Employers furnished the basic needs and con-trolled all aspects of the miners' lives: "You didn't go nowhere. Like, over at Three Point, they put what you call commissaries; and you'd go buy all your stuff. They had a post office; they had a showhouse, the barber shop. You didn't need to go to Harlan for nothing" (*Becky Simpson*).

The camps were enclosed in tangible borders that set them off as separate spaces where the rights of property prevailed over the laws of the state and the citizens' rights. In the 1930s, steel ropes were used to lock the entrance gate at the Louellen coal camp owned by the Cornett-Lewis Coal Company on Clover Fork.[3] "They had a big post on each side, [where] you pulled off the highway and went over into the camp; they put a big cross tie on each side of the road, and they had a steel rope, stretched across there, and they kept a lock on it. And if you see any people come, you had to [alert] the watchmen, and they'd let you in and he'd lock it back" (*Lloyd Lefevre*). "They had guards to let you in and guards to let you out. Like a concentration camp or something. And we grew up under those conditions. You didn't get in that camp without permission and you didn't get *out* of that camp without permission" (*Julia Cowans*).

Union organizer George J. Titler also uses prison imagery in his description of Verda: "Across the highway a large tree towered by the road. Fifty-feet high in its branches was a tree house. This was no children's playground, however. It was a pillbox where the Harlan-Wallins gun thugs stationed themselves, like guards on a penitentiary wall, to guard the camp." The only access road to Verda was owned by the company.[4] Sill Leach remembered the machine guns on the Verda commissary's meat block and in the guardhouse. A fence around the model company town of Lynch was explicitly meant to keep union organizers out. Since Lynch was crossed by a public highway, the company could not lay a gate across it, but all strangers were escorted by company guards and requested to justify their presence or leave.[5]

In his testimony to the Senate Subcommittee on Violations of Free Speech and Rights of Labor (known as the La Follette Committee after its chairman), Louellen's manager, Robert E. Lawson, explained that the purpose of the rope and locks was not to keep union organizers out but to keep the miners in: to prevent employees indebted for goods bought on credit from the company store from leaving the camp before they paid up.[6] Lloyd Lefevre confirmed: "Mostly what they done that for, they was people that was going down to the commissary for furniture and stuff. Maybe one or two had sneaked out and moved out of the mines and they kept them with them. They did it to keep them from getting out with it."

"They had something like a pen, and somebody wasn't paying for their rent or for their bills, [the manager] he'd just tell [the guards], 'I want that man rid of,' you wouldn't see him no more" (*Bob Simpson*). Most camps had their own jails or pens. Preacher Marshall Musick testified (and Robert Lawson confirmed) that at Louellen "they had a place under the concrete steps of the office building that was called the jail.... It was used awhile to lock up United Mine Workers in. Often, men that became intoxicated were put in there temporarily until they were removed to Harlan County jail." "There were no toilet facilities," Titler noted, "because the town of Louellen had no sewer system."[7] The jail at Louellen was abandoned after 1937, but coal camps remained a law unto themselves.

> HAZEL KING: The company would have their own police department, and they called them deputy sheriffs; and the deputy sheriffs was the rule of the roost, that's the term we used, and they kindly made the people comply whether or not. And if you crossed the deputy sheriffs, why, you were in trouble. But if you were in good terms and did what was according to the company policy, I guess you were all right.

> BECKY SIMPSON: There's a colored woman, I forget her name, and her husband had pneumonia fever, and he couldn't get up to go to work, so they sent, they call them gun thugs over here, they stepped to the house and told him, said, "We need you in the mines today." And his wife, "He's so sick he can't work." So they beat him with their sticks, and he did get out of bed and go on to work. They wasn't only the black people that they was doing this to, they was doing the white people that too.

As Delbert Jones notes, company law had a double face. Many historians denounce the oppression, deprivation, and "concentration camp" image of the camps; others stress the sense of community and the services and benevolence of some companies.[8] The point, however, is not only the material living conditions but the violation of democracy: that so many "free" Americans had to abide a suspension of their citizenship, and that the federal and state governments not only countenanced this blatant violation of their avowed principles but often used their courts and their National Guard to help enforce it.

In 1925, the U.S. Coal Commission reported:

> The courts of the State [of West Virginia] have decided that the relation of landlord and tenant did not exist [in the coal camps], but that it was the relation of master and servant, and when the employment ceased the mine owner came to possession of the house.... The position of the miners in company-owned houses is anomalous. They are not tenants and have no more rights than a domestic servant who occupies a room in the household of the employer.[9]

The commission concluded that the conflict between the workers' right to organize and the rights of property "resembles the conflict between the definition in the Declaration of Independence concerning human rights and the then clearly constitutional right of human slavery." As a West Virginia miner's daughter said, "They paid him well enough and he didn't mind the work itself, but he often stated that a man couldn't call his soul his own in those communities."[10]

MAKING A LIVING

CHARLOTTE NOLAN: We were much impressed in the early days with Benham, International Harvester, and Lynch—United States Steel. They were painted nicely—they all lived in duplexes. [On the other hand,] I went into Kitts and, uh, it was dirty. All the houses painted the same color. Pretty drab, not many trees or flowers. It looked like people had thrown their cinders right out in the middle of the street.

In his history of Harlan County in the 1930s, John S. Hevener notes that Harlan County's company houses were generally better than those found in other Appalachian coal fields. The superiority was relative: "The typical company house...had a weatherboarded, regularly painted exterior. Interior walls and ceilings, though occasionally plastered, were usually finished with wallboard or wood. Each room was lighted by a single electric drop cord suspended from the ceiling. An outdoor hydrant, one for each six or eight families, supplied water. Toilet facilities consisted of an outdoor privy." Some of the camps "were primitive slums."[11]

In 1946, a U.S. Navy Bureau of Medicine report described housing and health in mining communities:

The state of disrepair at times runs beyond the power of verbal description or even of photographic illustration since neither words nor pictures can portray the atmosphere of abandoned dejection or reproduce the smells. Old, unpainted board-and-batten houses, batten gone or going and board fast following, roofs broken, porches staggering, steps sagging, a riot of rubbish and a medley of odors.

There is the ever present back-yard privy, with its foul stench—the most common sewage disposal plant in the coal fields. Many of these ill-smelling backhouses, perched beside roads, along alleys, and over streams leave their human waste exposed, permeate the air with nauseating odors, and spread disease and death.[12]

"Beauty / is a stranger / to the coal camps," wrote Don West, poet and organizer.[13] Tillman Cadle grew up in a coal camp on the Tennessee-Kentucky border in the 1910s: "They were just old shacks, you know, they wasn't insulated or anything, they had some old tin ceiling they'd seal 'em up with and put the ceiling across, and they'd cut 'em in four. For heat they'd have a grate, you could burn coal in; and for cookstoves they had old stoves that used coal. No inside plumbing, you had to go to the wellhouse to get your water, miners had to wash in the tub you used to wash clothes in." Not much had changed when Sudie Crusenberry lived at Brookside in the 1950s: "It didn't have no weather treating on it. It was rough boards strip-nailed over the cracks and fireplaces. No electricity; coal stove to cook on, washboard to wash on."

> PORTELLI: What was it like to make a home in these company houses?
> HAZEL LEONARD: A home? Well—it was okay, I mean, they arranged for you to use these houses and they took the pay out of your check, and...
> PORTELLI: Were they easy to keep clean?
> LEONARD: Oh yes—just a little four-room house, that's all it was, and it wasn't insulated or anything, they were awful cold in, but they, they was livable.
> PORTELLI: Did you have water in the house?
> LEONARD: No; no water in the house, had a pump. And then you burned coal. We had grates, you know what a grate is. We had one in two bedrooms, and then we had a cookstove, used to burn coal in it, you could stay pretty warm. 'Course you got plenty of coal. If you were out of coal they would bring it.
> PORTELLI: Did you pay for the coal?
> LEONARD: Huh-huh. It wasn't much.

Washing was an ordeal, particularly for women with large families, long without electricity and running water in the home; even in Lynch, soot penetrated everywhere. No wonder, as we saw in chapter 4, that it was God's own miracle that fixed the washing machine.

> HAZEL LEONARD: You had to wash the bank clothes, the work clothes; they'd be full of dust, and, you had to take 'em out, beat 'em on the wall or somewhere to beat out what you could; then your tub would be full of those fine settlings, you know, that come out of the clothes, and they'd be dingy, you couldn't get 'em clean again.
> When we first moved to Gano we lived next to the tipple and [soot] would just come right at it. And I was used to keeping my windows clean, I don't no more, but I'd go out in the evening and in the morning the coal dust would be back just like snow. And the porch, it'd be that thick on the porch, because that tipple shaking that coal, this cloud coming right toward your house.
> I'd rather lived under a clift than anywhere getting that dust. Couldn't open the doors, couldn't open the window, lock your house. But anyway, I moved out of there, and then we moved back to Clover Darby, and it was

clean. If you didn't live right under that tipple it was okay. The dust didn't come that way; it come the way the wind did, I guess, and it usually carried it in a certain direction.

Just like Delbert Jones's attitude toward the company "laws," the attitude toward living conditions in the camps is ambivalent and even contradictory. Hazel Leonard said that camp houses were easy to keep clean, and in the next breath described how hard it was. "They was livable"—and indeed, people did make a living in them.[14] Russell W. Lee of the Farm Service Administration photographed the substandard houses and drab camps, but also the families going to church in their Sunday clothes, the men getting ready to go hunting or to play cards, the children sitting in school or playing on the porch. "It was thriving, in the twenties, with coal, as the nation was thriving in the 1920s" (*Kate Blue*); the camps were crowded but full of "activities and people enjoying themselves" (*Will Gent*); "Three Point, Chevrolet, Crummies, they would have houses just sitting say three foot apart" (*Becky Simpson*); "Consolidated Coal Company built these houses in 1928 [at Closplint], and two families lived in these houses and every one of them was full, you couldn't find no empty houses. At that time there might have been two hundred families" (*Delbert Jones*).

Closeness was one of the virtues of the coal towns. A Harlan County miner's wife quoted in a 1980 government report remembered: "I really liked it in the coal camps. It was just one big family. All the houses were sort of close together. Everybody knew each other. If you had a problem, they had it. Everybody went to the same church. Everybody had the same occupation. We all had the same thing in common. Nobody considered themselves better than others because they all made the same. I think everybody just got along better." What she seemed to enjoy best, then, was the sense of equality—as long as one doesn't count management, operators, and guards.[15]

> JERRY JOHNSON: I kind of liked it. I mean I don't like a coal camp now, but when I was a child [in the 1950s] it was all union, and those miners, they drew good wages. And they had a nice store to hang around. But before the union it used to be terrible, if you didn't get your haircut at the company store they'd get rid of you, you know. This was Chevrolet, Kentucky, it had a strong union, and the union hall was in the coal camp, they had a school, they had a church, they had a commissary where you could go and get things, and the clean river you could go fishing, you could catch all the fish you wanted. I used to go swimming, you'd go ice skating. The river won't freeze anymore. The rivers are so polluted they won't freeze over no more.

Historian Crandall Shifflett points out that coal towns were indeed communities, with a social life revolving around such activities as sports, drinking, religion, visiting, and other leisure activities.[16] After all, people lived, drank, went fishing, and got married even in the worst of totalitarian societies. Sticking with each other was often a way of coping with undemocratic power relationships: "The companies exploited the people and then through that adversity the people were drawn together, you know, a sort of closeness" (*John Bledsoe*). Just as in Italian fascism, autocratic power provided amenities and order at the same time it abolished rights. Sports, religion, leisure, visiting rights were provided and regulated by the company. Whether out of goodwill or in order to generate allegiance and stabilize the workforce, some companies encouraged and promoted social activities and furnished a number of basic services, entertainment, some medical care, and religion. Hazel King, who lived next to the Louellen coal camp, recalled: "They had the church, they had different days for different religions, like the Protestant or the Catholics, they didn't restrict it to just one, which looking back it was a very nice thing. And, the school, I don't think we could have had a better school than we had in Louellen. The teachers were there to teach and you were there as students to learn, and you did."

"They that owned the company owned the churches. They paid their salaries. The preacher would go to the window and draw his pay just like the miners did" (*Hugh Cowans*). During a 1939 union drive at Benham, "the only minister (paid by the company) spoke in the only church in the community blasting the U.M.W.A."[17]

> JOHNNY JONES: That's the way they had control of the men [in Lynch]. Do it through the preacher. If you were a stranger that come in here and you wanted a house, you couldn't get no house, all filled up. You go over to the preacher, the preacher [would] go in to the superintendent and he would get that fixed. The preacher had power, he had a powerful stick to walk with. 'Course the company give it to him. And you didn't get no amateur preacher here, they gonna get a man that's got his degrees, the biggest majority was preachers from the big cities that's been educated.[18]

While company preachers are remembered mainly as purveyors of company ideology, more positive memories concern company-paid schools and doctors— often the only educational and health services available in underserved rural areas. Medical services were generally poor, and some doctors made huge profits out of the miners' health checks, yet many of them are remembered fondly.[19] Though her family did not live in a camp, Mossie Johnson was assisted in some of her sixteen deliveries by a company doctor: "Dr. Evans, he is a wonderful person, he is dead now. He sat up all night with me several times. And, these camp doctors, they work at the coal mines, and when they come to you, they stay as long as they had to be." "Old Doc [Rowan] had a office at the back of the commissary. And he done come out to the house and treat people if they was sick and did have no way into the office. He'd come out to the house, and if you didn't have money for his fees you could pay him with a chicken or a gallon of green beans or a bucket of potatoes" (*Annie Napier*). Harlan-Wallins at Verda charged married men $2.50 and single men $2.00 for the company doctor, and $1.00 for hospital services; they paid about 60 percent to the doctors and the hospital (which had to provide nursing services, equipment, and facilities out of that), and the rest was profit for the company. Sometimes, during strikes, operators would not permit company doctors to treat striking miners or their families.[20]

The companies provided goods and services, but not for free: Sudie Crusenberry could not go to school at Brookside because her father could not pay four dollars a month for it. Camp residents paid for rent and coal, and were docked for medical care, the school, and the church. "They had a big church in here [Louellen]. They didn't build it, though; the men built it. Cut 'em so much a month to build a church. The men paid for it, that worked here" (Lloyd Lefevre). After deductions for services and provisions bought at the company store, miners seldom saw real money. Often, all they could do was draw an advance in scrip (or "script")—a private currency issued by their employers. "You probably heard the song 'My soul is at the company store.' Well they had script, like Blue Diamond had their own money that they made for the people that worked for them. Then they could get credit at the company store" (Dallas Blue).[21] Scrip— "the finest bookkeeping there was" (Bryan Whitfield)—was ostensibly a credit system, in which miners received advances on the pay coming to them. It came at a price: Harlan-Wallins, for instance, charged 15 percent on each advance.[22] On payday, miners would often find themselves in debt to the company.

> HAZEL LEONARD: They didn't draw any paydays 'cause they didn't make much money and they'd spend it in the store. And, if you had any pay coming [beyond advances in scrip], you got cash. We never had one. We never had a payday. I didn't know anybody that did. Most everybody spent it in the store, you heared that song about the company store, "owe my soul to the company store"? Well, that's the way it was.

"They got it all back. They got back almost every dime you made" (Becky Simpson). "Well, we had to have a commissary because they had to trade there, that's the closest place to trade. If a man wanted to go buy or trade at the commissary, he drew scrip, he bought what he wanted and they gave him change" (Bryan Whitfield).

> JULIA COWANS: I was the oldest in the house. My mother would send me to the store, the grocery, and I never remember axing for but a dollar. One dollar. I've never gone to the window say two dollars, three, five dollars. But there would never be any money. Never be any money. Scrip. You did not leave off that company property, go to the next town to buy anything and bring it back in there. No, you didn't do that. And that kept the person, especially if you had a family of any size, that kept you in debt, all the time, you know, just stayed in debt. Work a lifetime and be in debt to the company.

"Always in debt. The poor old people had families, and they took what he made just to eat, and the few clothes you could buy. Now, that was before they got the union" (*Hazel Leonard*). "Yes, they run into debt. Times were hard then, mister, the Depression. There was no...this damnable aid, then. A man had to work for a living" (*Bryan Whitfield*). "The company store, some of them, would make more money than the mine. 'Cause the miner, he won't save any money, they spend it all" (*Ed Cawood*). According to Lawson, Cornett-Lewis made a profit of between 18 and 21 percent from its commissary at Louellen; between 1934 and 1937, the commissary at Verda generated a 170 percent profit. Prices in the camp commissaries were up to 20 percent higher than outside; operators systematically retrieved pay raises by hiking prices at the commissary. In the few cases in which miners had access to outside merchants who accepted scrip, they did so at a discount of up to 20 percent. Miners could be fired and evicted for shopping outside the camp.[23] As a superintendent told the miners at Kitts in 1931, "If you trade at Piggly Wiggly, you can get your job at Piggly Wiggly."[24] Hazel King's father owned a store outside the Louellen camp, and she said, "They didn't like to share their money or resources with anyone else; they liked to keep a captive audience with their miners. And the people had to be very careful about trading at our store, they'd come along at nighttime and trade, because they didn't want to be known to be spending their scrip [there]."

"Miners'd come out, with some scrip to buy groceries; if he couldn't get any scrip, if he began to grumble about it, a big thug walked up and tapped him on the shoulder—'Listen, if you don't like the way we're running this place here you better leave; if we hear you grumbling we'll take you to the slate dump and leave you'" (*Tillman Cadle*). Scrip and compulsory shopping at the company store were not universal, but prevailed in Harlan. In 1931, Black Mountain Coal Company wrote to their employee John Burton: "On checking our pay rolls and books in the store we find that you are not drawing very much scrip. This is evidence to us that you are trading with the independent stores.... We're furnishing your employment and pay you twice a month for your earned wages.... I am sure that things can be adjusted and you will give us one-hundred per cent of your trade." Another letter warned that the company hopes "we shall not be forced to discharge you for this cause." A woman whose husband was killed at work was allowed $3,000 compensation for her and her children, payable at $33 a month in goods at the company store.[25]

On the other hand, operators sometimes advanced credit during work stoppages and strikes. "When the coal miners were on strike Mr. Creech told his office staff that it was all right for a single man to charge one dollar per day and a family man could charge two dollars per day until the matter was settled. Now he's financing his own strike in a sense, but he was concerned" (*Bill Winters*). A work stoppage was no reason to lose the profit from the company store, and in most cases they would get their credit back when work resumed. "They would give you credit, they would carry you all through the strike, then you would get in debt, you would pay so much a month till you got out of debt. But they never did pressure you for the money. They could have got it any time they wanted" (*Lee Marsili*).

> BRYAN WHITFIELD: We shut down here for six months, during the bottom of the Depression. But we fed the men. We took the number of the members of the family and ordered bacon and white meat and the Red Cross gave flour and we furnished that through the six months. They lived in the houses, kept the lights on, burning electricity.
> PORTELLI: Did they pay you back?
> WHITFIELD: Yeah, they paid.

LITTLE NEW YORK

In 1948, a company publication proudly described the town of Benham, owned by Wisconsin Steel Company, a subsidiary of Morgan–McCormick International Harvester:

> *At Benham, when a miner ends his day's work, he goes home to a house built by Harvester. Water from Harvester's modern filtration quenches his thirst. His wife shops in a Harvester store. His children receive their education in a school built by Harvester. Should he fall sick, Harvester doctors in a Harvester hospital care for him. Even his Sunday worship is offered in a church provided by the Company.*[26]

Benham, Lynch, and Wallins Creek were the so-called captive mines, owned by International Harvester, United States Steel, and Ford Motor Company, respectively. Benham was completed in 1915, at the junction of Clover Fork and Poor Fork, shortly after the railroad reached the spot. Wallins Creek was established by Ford in 1920, then abandoned in 1931 after the vein was mined out. Further from Benham on Black Mountain, Lynch was established in 1917 and named after Thomas Lynch, first president of U.S. Steel subsidiary U.S. Coal and Coke Company. "An army of men was brought in to build homes, boarding houses, bathhouses, churches, a machine shop, a company store, and what was then the world's largest tipple."[27] By 1919, Lynch reached a population of ten thousand, including many blacks and foreign-born residents.[28]

Like many black miners in Lynch, Bernard Mimes was born in Alabama; he lived in New York as a child before he went to work in the Kentucky mines in 1942.

> BERNARD MIMES: It was a little much of a shock to come down here, but see, what I was intending to do was to go back. There was a lot of money to be made here. The place was owned by U.S. Steel, and they was shipping stuff all over the world, the United States was helping to build up the economy, selling a lot of steel. I guess this place had at least three

thousand and some men working here at that time. Before I went in the war it was five thousand.

In these model towns, the mother companies were less concerned with scraping every margin of profit from their employees than with the stabilization of the workforce, social peace, a regular supply of coal for their plants, and an outlet for their own production.[29] As Appalachian lawyer and social commentator Harry Caudill noted, Lynch was conceived as "an example of advanced corporate paternalism. Because there was enough coal to last more than a century, everything had to be durable. Labor peace and domestic contentment were essential for such a prolonged operation, so the town would have to be pleasant and the workmen happy. There would be no communism or radicalism at Lynch because there would be no need for them; in this worker's paradise, contentment, not agitation, would reign."[30]

"When U.S. Steel and International Harvester came in here, they were very benevolent companies. This city that was built here, Lynch, was supposed to have been a showcase for the rest of the world" (*Dale Teeter*). Although they "typified less than two percent of company towns in southern Appalachian coal fields and touched the lives of only a fraction of the mining population in the mountains," these model towns represented the best side of the coal town concept. As historian Ronald Eller notes, Lynch's excellent housing construction, advanced modern conveniences, well-planned streets, and parks produced a suburban atmosphere that made it very different from the ordinary coal camps.[31] The streets were lined with decent homes with orchards and gardens, plastered interiors, asbestos shingle roofs, and running water; company offices built of stone; a comfortable hotel; and, of course, separate white and black schools and segregated movie theaters.

Lynch and Benham were the closest thing Harlan had to an urban environment: "In the middle of little old mountains was just this little New York, literally built from the paper up, to be exactly what the company wanted it to be...a kind of cosmopolitan place [with] lots of different people doing different things from different cultural focuses" (*William H. Turner*).[32] Like urban working-class ghettoes, Lynch was a crowded multiethnic community: "This place here was mostly built on Hungarians, Mexicans, Italians, and the black people. It was people, people, people. You couldn't find a place to live, to room or nothing. It was just crowded" (*James Hall*).

MINNIE RANDOLPH: I used to have boarders and roomers to live here, and I raised children here, and my husband was working in the mines; and I kept boarders, men that was working in the mines that didn't have places, I cooked and fed them. Packed their bucket so they could go to work. I just always kept a house full of people. Because when they come in they didn't have enough houses. The men would come in, they'd get the job and then later on they'd send and get their wives from different places.

Lynch never slept. "I've seen the day that this town was just like New York City. Night and day, look to me whether anybody went to sleep. You could catch a party going on in every third house. If it wasn't nothing but a little party, a little card game. And that's what kept [it] alive" (*Johnny Jones*). The opera singer Tito Pattiera was not the only attraction that visited this little New York: "Cab Calloway and Glenn Miller used to come in here. There was a club, we called it the Lamplighter, it was a bunch of young men, all in our early twenties. We rigged that up and we put so much money with it, we had parties to raise money. Back in that time, you get up a thousand dollars, you could send and get a band to come in. We had one or two bands around here" (*Bernard Mimes*).

The making of Appalachian coal towns went through two phases: a frontier phase from 1880 to 1910, and a paternalistic one until their demise in midcentury.[33] However, since Harlan coal towns were established after 1910, both phases coexisted. Lynch was both a socially minded paternalistic project and a rowdy frontier town, "sitting at the last end of the mountain, and setting off from civilization in a way. And the biggest majority of them could get by with anything. There ain't been too good law enforcement back in this part of the country. They were just wild, that's why they call it bloody Harlan County, to tell you truth" (*Bernard Mimes*).

EARL TURNER: They tell me long time ago there used to be a lot of killing in Lynch. People used to gamble a whole lot and get drunk and kill one another. Other than that, I guess it's been as good as any other place, I guess. Some of these big cities, just about as many people just get killed regularly. You know, the United States is one of the most violent countries in the world. We kill more people here in one month than gets killed in the world by handguns, other than wars and things.

WILLETTA LEE: [My mother], she came on a Friday [in 1930]. She got here at night, somebody met her and took her to her room, said the first thing she remembered was the gunshots, and sleeping on the floor every Friday night and Saturday night and Sunday night. She didn't think she was gonna stay, but she ended up spending the rest of her life here. I can remember when I was seven or eight years old, which would be '57 or '58, I can remember standing upon Sanctified Hill watching people shoot each other down at the club we used to call the Bottom, and drag them off and you never hear any more about them.

According to Joseph P. Menefee, chief of Lynch's company police, ethnic and racial differences were the main cause of disturbances: "We have every nationality. We have got the southern Negro; we have got the native Kentuckian element and our native southern element. We have men in there from Illinois and Indiana. Our biggest trouble is maintaining order among them....They are clannish. In certain nationalities very much so...We find it among the

Kentuckians very much. It is true of the Virginians. It is true for the southern Negro."[34]

> CONNIE OWENS: There was a lot of division and not just between the so-called white and the Hungarians, and the black, but even within the black community. There was harmony on some issues, like when they would force things with the union, people were in the fight together, but even though you were in the fight for equality or whatever that fight was, they had fights among themselves for other reasons. And this is part of the reason that this community are still like that, they perpetrated those little things they used to divide.

Most coal towns were divided along class lines. In Wallins Creek, "one side they had real nice homes, they called that Silk Stocking Row; and on the other side [it] wasn't hardly as nice. They called that Cotton Stocking Row" (*Lloyd Stokes*). Management lived across from the miners' houses, often on higher ground; below, camps were often divided along ethnic lines, with separate "hunky towns" for immigrants and "nigger towns" for black people.[35] Lynch was no exception: "There was your contract people, and they pretty well stuck together, and then you had your salary people, and they pretty well stuck together. They didn't have any conflicts or anything like that, but they just didn't associate very much" (*Norman Yarbrough*).

Even Lynch, however, remained a closed community whose corporate owner ruled over all political and economic life. The bigger coal camps were established as incorporated cities, with their own mayor, town councils, schools, and police and fire departments, so that the operators could retain control over most of the property and school tax dollars and over the selection and activities of the town officials.[36]

> NORMAN YARBROUGH: At the time I went to Lynch, it was 1950, [the company] told me I had to run for the school board, so I served on the school board. It was pretty well a company-managed town. It was pretty well military regimented. Most of the people in U.S. Steel, up in the top positions, they'd come out of the army, and it was almost a military [ranking order]; almost a dictatorial leadership.

Companies began to divest themselves of coal camps after 1950, as rising maintenance costs and taxes made them less profitable.[37] In the late 1950s, Lynch's company houses were sold to the citizens. "The company don't own nothing now, we even own the houses now. The company lets us pay so much a month on these houses. I had a small house, I used to pay ten dollars and something a month" (*Bernard Mimes*). After the mines were mechanized and Lynch was privatized, many black and foreign workers, who didn't have the same allegiance to the mountains as native whites, moved on.[38] Yet they carried with them a sense of dignity and pride that they identified with their raising in a community that offered and demanded a great deal. As a newspaper put it, "the mountains breed their share of success": the sense of pride is embodied in an organization, the Eastern Kentucky Social Club, whose members meet annually in different cities to "celebrate their mountain experience."[39]

> EARL TURNER: Oh Lord God, they shut all the hand loaders down in '62. You was out of a job. You just had to go. They started putting in these Joy-loaders machines in the early sixties.
> PORTELLI: What happened to the people?
> TURNER: Well, 95 'cent of 'em gone. There's a lot of men stayed round here. My neighbor right here, he had a big family, he had no car, no way to travel or anything. Most of the blacks left. And the whites too. Most of the blacks went to Chicago, Detroit, Cleveland, Milwaukee. That's the reason we have these reunions every year. Gary, Indiana. A lot of guys worked for U.S. Steel transferred right from the coal mines to the steel mill.

A FATHERLY BOSS

"U.S. Steel, they had control of the land and they tried to control the people. They were here, they were in the community, and they did care about the community" (*Joe Scopa Jr.*). "They owned everything. They was Lord and God, to tell you the truth" (*Johnny Jones*). "And I'll tell you, there was a whole lot of blacks, older men been here since this place opened. And they believed in it [a] hundred percent, buddy. They just loved the U.S. Steel, they loved the way things was" (*Earl Turner*). The words *benevolent* and *benevolence* occur systematically in the accounts of former Lynch residents. The employers' main concerns were alcoholism, strikes, worker turnout, and safety: ultimately, ensuring the stability of a relatively satisfied workforce and preventing social conflict.[40] "Benevolence" might be either a result of some owners' conscience or a preventive response to the miners' implicit demand for rights and wages and to government pressures over health and living conditions: "The company didn't allow you to want for much. They did everything nice to keep the union out" (*James Hall*). According to a Ford company publication, "the Company, against its will, has been *forced* to adopt a paternalistic policy in all its mining camps" (italics added).[41]

There was a difference between the management of the captive mines, where impersonalness was the rule, and that of smaller, locally owned camps where power was embodied in figures that were half boss and half neighbor. For instance, Louellen's Robert E. Lawson was "a very likable person, and he knew every one, and all the children, and he was so interested in the beautification of Louellen. And he was always willing to assist 'em, especially in their interest of having flowers and everything and...I liked Mr. Lawson" (*Hazel King*).

JULIA COWANS: Some of the union miners, they fought him all the way, but they made a distinction between him as a person, and the company. My first husband, he, he drank a lot. And he'd leave home and go down to Harlan, and he'd be running out of money, he'd see Mr. Lawson riding down the street, stop him and get money from him. I've heard him tell that many times.

"Old Man" Lawson, or "Uncle Bob," as he was called, lived in the camp, shared in social activities, and taught Sunday school. Of course, he also owned company stock. Narrators strive to reconcile the contradiction between class power and personal relationships by means of implicit but systematic verbal strategies: in Lefevre's narrative, *he* (Lawson) gave credit to the miners, but *they* (the company) docked them afterward; *they* kept a "captive audience" with *their* miners, but *he* assisted them, *he* kept the camp clean, *he* gave them money (and *they* locked them up if they were drunk or unruly).

Lawson "was very fatherly-like" (*Hazel King*): paternalism is a father-to-son relationship, in which protective authority is held over immature menials for their own good. Management takes over the moral guidance of the community: Uncle Bob Lawson saw they kept the camp clean "whether they wanted to or not" (*Hazel King*) and held safety meetings "to caution the men about how to take care of theirselves in the mine, and be careful, and he'd give a little prize of some kind" (*Lloyd Lefevre*).[42] Lefevre remembered carrying many a dead man, crushed by motors or slate falls, out of the Louellen mine; Lawson's safety meetings, while useful, seemed to blame mine deaths and injuries on the miners' inability to take care of themselves. As in other domestic institutions, coal camp paternalism drew on a personal bond of affection (not necessarily feigned but always unequal) between the powerful and the powerless, barely covering the nakedness of exploitation and the totality of power. A Clover Fork miner said: "Pearl [Bassham, owner of Verda's Harlan-Wallins], he was a fine feller, but he didn't like the United Mine Workers. Just to talk to him he was just as fine a feller as you ever met. He'd hit me on one side and defend me on the other. But he had a lot of good men killed. In the organizing day, a lot of good men was helping get the union in and he had 'em killed. He ordered the thugs to kill 'em. He hired and they'd kill.[43] But he'd talk to you anywhere he'd meet ya, he'd stop and talk to you."

CHARLOTTE NOLAN: Pearl Bassham, he would buy his children a Ford car and they would drive it, and then when they were all through driving it, he would put it on a raffle. But he wouldn't say, "Do you wanna buy a chance?" He'd just deduct a dollar from their pay, then some Saturday they'd go out there and pick out a number and somebody'd win a Ford car that his kids had already driven the wheels off.[44] We went to school with [his] children. They were nice people. They were in church every time the doors opened. They gave plenty of money to the church and, certainly, they were folks and we knew them.

Sports could be a ground of community cohesion. "[Blacks and whites], we'd play all day football, basketball. Whites play the black, camp number five play number one, and number four play number two. Just got along fine. Otherwise, there was no integration during that time" (*James Hall*). Workers sometimes turned these activities to their own purposes. Black activist Bill Worthington recalled: "I was a good ballplayer so the companies were anxious to have me come and play. That way I stayed in touch with the union and always stayed active in the organizing. Since they recognized me as a ball player, I could walk into any camp anytime. I was never once bothered by the thugs."[45] Yet the main function of sports for the companies was to reinforce group identities and company allegiance as alternative to union solidarity. Companies created marching bands and hired ball players, gave them jobs outside the mine, and let them go if they didn't make the team.[46] "They had all them big-league players Ford company [had] to come in. And they'd have a big band there, it was just like going to a big-league game" (*Lloyd Stokes*). Of course, it didn't come free of charge. "The things that the company was doing for us, that was our money that they was taking and doing it. They was taking our money, having these big parades, pitching these big dances and shows, surplus money that comes off the poor man working" (*Johnny Jones*). Company benevolence stopped when, rather than accepting gifts, the miners began to claim rights. "When the UMWA began to organize in that area," Lynch native Bill Bosch remembered, "there were no more parades and there was no more candy and ice cream."[47]

Baseball was also a means to reinforce company allegiance and divide miners by inducing competition among the camps. "This competitiveness extended into social relations in general, so that hostility and mistrust characterized relationships among residents of the coal camps. Dating across community boundaries was discouraged."[48] Everything was an occasion for competition: in the camps for the prettiest yard, in the mines for who could dig the most coal, between camps on sports, schools, and company and town pride.

Tommy Sweatt: Lynch had a reputation for having a good football team, for having a good basketball team. And wherever the football team went, the band went, and wherever the band was, cheerleaders would be, and they'd be well-dressed, well-behaved parents, some carrying guns, most carrying a fifth or a pint—and if you were from Lynch you were either something special or something that was hated. And some of that still carries on. Guy was talking one day at work, and he said, "You folks in Lynch always did think you was better than anybody else." We was used to having things better, and expected it, you know.

"We can't get over basketball rivalries, or 'the people in Harlan are snoots and the people in Evarts, look down their nose at us,' or...you know" (*Daniel Howard*). "The people from Cumberland don't want to talk to the people in Harlan and the people in Harlan and Cumberland don't wanna talk to the people in Evarts and the people...That's because the companies and the little independent mines, each one was its own contained entity, and they didn't want the workers talking to each other about how their pay went or they wanted to keep these people isolated so that they could keep control" (*Theresa Osborne*).

Resentments can simmer for decades. Tensions between Lynch and Benham go back to the union wars between the UMW and Benham's Progressive Miners, in the 1930s and '40s. "My mother-in-law is hard-core Lynch, born and raised in Lynch and you know—'them Benham people are just scabs.' And I think, 'Well honey, that was fifty years ago,' but she still has that mentality. Her dad worked in the coal mines up Lynch, so the people that worked in Benham they were all scabs. They ain't probably even the same people that were here back then but that's what she says" (*Maxine Clay*). "Benham had women who had husbands to die, and they were still young enough to marry, but they still remembered the strife that there had been between the union and the non-union people. And one woman said, 'I like him, he's a nice fellow, but you know, I was married to a union man for twenty-five years, I can't settle for no scab now'" (*Tommy Sweatt*).

7

MINER'S LIFE

FORTY-TWO YEARS

"Forty-two years is a mighty long time," sings former coal miner Nimrod Workman, "to labor and toil inside a coal mine."[1] "My dad he was a coal miner, and he went in the coal mines when he was fourteen years old. And he retired out of coal mines until the end of his life and...my dad he was awful good at that; I mean he really knew how to pour that coal" (*Sill Leach*). "I started work in 1939 in the mines. I started at Creech Coal Company. I never will forget it, February 1939. I worked forty-two and a half years in the mines. That's what I was. That's my record" (*Parris Burke*). A miner's life is often summed up in one or two sentences: "[My husband] went in the mines when he was fourteen— well, he might not been signed up at the time, but that's when he started to work. So he was a coal miner until 1960 and then a big slate fall killed him" (*Mossie Johnson*). But the space between the alpha of early labor and the omega of retirement or death is filled with memories.

> REV. HUGH COWANS: Back in the thirties when I started in the coal mines I was nothing but a boy, I had not reached my thirteenth birthday, four-teenth birthday rather, because at that time they'd take you in at any age, there's some going in ten, eleven, twelve year old, but at that time they wasn't paying anything. I can remember many a time that I'd gone in the mines at five o'clock in the morning and I'd come out at one o'clock, the next day I still had to go back at five o'clock. And if I didn't go back, I didn't have a job. And you worked under all kinds of, uh, oppressive conditions, no organized labor, and they had gun thugs. That was in ordinance to keep the United Mine Workers *out*. And if you joined it, they would come in and beat your head and throw your family outdoors and throw you off the job and everything. I remember once on the job that they had my uncle to pull his britches down and they whipped 'im right before my face. In other words, it was just like slavery.

"I started when I was about twelve or fourteen years old" (*Henry D. Farmer*). "I always worked in the mines, forty-five years. When I went in the mine? I was fifteen. I never did go to school" (*Lloyd Lefevre*). "So I went to work in a truck

example of redundant quote

mine when I was twelve year old. And that was rough. If I hadn't went to work so young I may not of been in as bad of shape as I am now, because when you're that old you're not developed as a man, you know—the bones, the muscles, you still as a young boy" (*Delbert Jones*).

> TILLMAN CADLE: I started working in the mines at thirteen year old, I was just a kid. It was in 1915. They'd tell your father, they'd say, "Here, you got a boy big enough to be a-working in the mines"—you see, we only had six months of school at that time, then you had to loaf for six more months, before school started again. "Now," they'd say, "now that boy, he is just out here, loafing around, if he gets in trouble you'll feel bad about it, you ought to let him go to work in the mines where he'll be working and helping feed the family." You see, the reason they wanted these young boys to go to work at that age, these old men couldn't do [the] kind of work these boys could do, they was ready for the scrap heap.

Of course, it was illegal, so they would lie about their age, and the employers would pretend they didn't know. Initiation to coal mining took place under family tutelage, alongside a father, uncle, or older brother. Jim Garland recalled: "In 1919, at age thirteen, I too had entered the mines on my own word that I was sixteen. Since I only weighed ninety pounds at the time, anyone could have judged that I wasn't sixteen, but because my work went in on my brother's number (my tonnage was added to his), the company was willing to overlook the illegality. The worst part of it was that the coal company officials seemed to believe they were doing me and my folks a favor by allowing me to work."[2]

> TILLMAN CADLE: You see, they'd start you in as a trapper, unless, if your father was a coal loader they might let you work with your father. Or with some other old experienced miner. They called these boys that worked under old miners, they called them chalkeyes. You see, they had child labor laws at that time, but they had no way to enforce them. They wasn't supposed to let you go in there, but what they would do, if a boy loaded coal, they didn't give him his own check to put on cars. If he was working with his father, he'd load on his father's checks. So, if he got hurt or killed in the mines, the company would say, "We had no such boy on our payroll." The company could just say you had no business in there in the first place.

"I was born in 1917. I went in the mine in 1934, after my parents had died, and I had no other choice" (*James Hall*). Tillman Cadle's teacher insisted that he stay in school: "But you see, boys growing up in a mining camp, the only thing they could see, their older buddies, they might have a little money, a little better clothes and so on, and them always talking about the work in the mines, that was the only thing to look forward to, was working in the mines. Boy growing up, he didn't see nothing else." "People that grew up around the mines they usually have a store where all the miners hang out, and the kids hang out. And they let them. It's bred into you. Before you go you know what to expect. It's just like you've been there all your life if you listen to these old men talk. Well, I sat around and I listened to those old men talk. I listened, and I listened" (*Jerry Johnson*).

> PORTELLI: What was the impact, the first time you went down in the mine?
> TILLMAN CADLE: Well I, it'd be kind of hard to explain now. What these mines were like when I was a boy. I guess it was exciting for a while, but then you got accustomed to it, it got so it was a everyday experience where you didn't pay much attention to it at all.
> PORTELLI: What was exciting about it?
> CADLE: Well you see, you'd get in these what they called a mantrip, this motor runs in these mines, all you could see was this top, the ribs of the mountains, zipping along, you didn't know whether this motor was gon' jump track.... You might feel scary the first time, but eventually you get used to it, then you don't think nothing about it.

"Miner's life is like a sailor's," says an old union song, "Every day his life's in danger / Still he ventures being brave." "I was scared at first but I went," said J. C. Hall, who went in the mines with his father. If there is a trace of "fatalism" in the culture, it lies in the way a miner's life and working conditions were assumed to be all but inevitable. Yet many remember the damp, the darkness, the bad air, the lack of ventilation, the cramped space and awkward position: "It gets very spooky in there, buddy. People are afraid of dark, can't work in there. I worked in coal so low you couldn't turn over. And, when you're laying on your side and shovel all day, that's painful" (*James Wright*). "Shoveling that coal all day long, you come out, you was wet" (*Dallas Blue*). "It was dark, it's dark. All you have in there is a motor light; if you have a mule and a carbide light or a battery light, that's all the light you have. It's dark" (*Plennie Hall*). "Have you been in a cave? It's pretty much like that, except it's dark, it's black, it's cold ... it's not scary. It didn't bother me" (*Bobbie Davidson*).

edit

"A ten- or twelve-hour shift would kill you" (*Henry Farmer*). "If you was in thirty-six-inch coal, that's high coal for around here. As high as this table. That don't look like much, but there's a lot of room when you are down on your knees. See, you can crawl under that table good. But when you get down to twenty-five-inch coal, your back is rubbing the top and you have to crawl or stretch. I've got scars on my back from roof bolts, everybody does" (*Robert Wilson [name changed]*). "I never could work the low [coal]. I never, I couldn't stand it. I couldn't work on my knees. A lot of men got where their knees swolled up working on their knees. You gotta love that coal here in Harlan County. We had coal going up to four and five, six, seven foot. On top the mountain that coal averaged up between five and seven foot and eight" (*Earl Turner*).

JULIA COWANS: I was born and raised in Cardinal, Kentucky, down south, up in the mountains there—Bell County. The only life that I knew was coal mining. My father, grandfather, great-grandfather—they were all coal miners. And when I was growing up, the coal mining was just very bad. You didn't really live, you just existed, just existed. And I can remember many times when we were growing we didn't really see my mother's brother, my father. It'd be dark when they'd go to the mines, we'd be in bed by the time they'd come in and rest, and they'd be gone again, you know. And I can remember waking up sometimes during the night. Go in the kitchen, and I'd see my uncle laying asleep—on the floor. They wouldn't even pull off their bank clothes, their mining things. He'd be lying down there in front of the fireplace behind the cook stove, be laying there sleeping. And just get up, get some food, and go back.

"Oh, Lord, I remember that. Dad'd get up before we even leave for school, Dad would be gone. And, well, we didn't have much back then, but Dad always saved, you know, a cake or something or other, back in his dinner bucket, and me and the rest of my sisters run and meet him, we would fight over it. I can be thankful for one thing, that the Lord did let my daddy make it out of that big old hole. And some people's not that lucky. But I am" (*Melody Donegan [name changed]*). "Just scared to death, all the time. Just scared. And he never got home till after midnight. You know, they just didn't pay the men anything and they booted them around, made them do what they wanted to do, and...we got along pretty good, my husband worked on the tipple and he was a good worker, they never bothered him; but if you didn't work, they'd kick you out" (*Hazel Leonard*). To Melody Donegan, luck meant getting out alive; to Hazel Leonard, "getting along good" meant survival and staying out of trouble.

Not all managed to get used to the mine, and the most critical narratives come from those who did not stay long. Dallas Blue only spent six weeks in the mines in the late 1940s: "Boy, that's worst six weeks I've had in my life. I don't see how people work a lifetime in the coal mines. First, was going in that dungeon. You get in that car and you have to lay flat because of the mantrip. They let you off at your place, you go in, there would be rock falling, all overhead growling and crumbling. And the worst part, you'll have to drill your hole to shoot the coal down so that you could load it up. And then you were crawling through places. I've got a scar on my back now where—a piece of coal against the top—and I raised up and cut a place down my back."

ROBERT WILSON: It's a tough life, but you get used to it after a while and then you are kind of proud of it after you have done it for a while. I mean, you can ride up there right now in cold weather, it's just like laying down in that creek. Seven o'clock in the morning, mud, and come home froze, your [clothes] are froze. You go home and you eat, you done tired, you can't move after you've worked all day and it's all you can do to go home and wash if you are able and lay down, and most of the time you have got to get back up at five and do it again. It don't help your married life a bit, you know. Say you're given from five till nine, you see, you ain't in no mood for caring for anybody.

PICK AND SHOVEL DAYS

"When I went in [1942] they was hand loading. It was mostly physical work, you loaded coal with shovels, what we call hand loading. This was pick and shovel days. What I mean about pick and shovel, you had to pick the coal, and shovel it up in the car. And during that time if you didn't load no coal in the car, then you didn't get no pay. Now, it wasn't easy times in the mines in that pick and shovel. That was what I call backbreaking days. That was before the union" (*Bernard Mimes*). "My dad was using a pick and a shovel. My dad died when he was fifty-five. He got hurt up there at the mine, and he had black lung, he had emphysema, kidney problem, he had everything. He had an autopsy report on him, three pages long" (*Dale Teeter*).

EARL TURNER: Lord, I loaded forty tons of coal per shift—on piecework, yeah. But we got men beat that anywhere. I got a friend over in Virginia. During the war he averaged ninety days a seventy-five-ton day shift. A railroad car full a day. And he's a great big man. He worked hisself too hard. We had a big Swedish man, big blond man, had a big white moustache; and we had another man named Angelo Bernardo. He's an I-talian. Those men, I'm telling you the truth, I ain't never seen people who could shovel coal like that.

ARTHUR JOHNSON: In those old pick and shovel days, they were pretty tough men. I mean, the men's lifestyle, the way of working, the arms, the hands, the muscles, the big shoulders. Now what we would consider very hard work, those men could do with ease, because the kind of work they did at the mine, really developed, developed them. My father weighed two hundred pounds and he was five feet eight, and he could bounce a refrigerator on his back, you could walk under it. They were that kind of people.

"It wasn't all strength—a lot of skill. You know, you gotta pace yourself" (*Earl Turner*). Timing was essential also to the most physical aspects of labor: Dallas Blue noted that while he, as a greenhorn, found the shoveling too hard, "my uncle, it was just natural to him. He had the rhythm and everything. He would load two cars to my one-half." Until mechanization imposed a degree of industrial discipline, individual miners performed all the tasks of coal digging. Laboring on piece rate, they could be induced or forced to work themselves to death ("I've worked hard enough that you just lie down and puke. If you lay there too long, you are still fired anyway. That's how rough it is," *Robert Wilson*), but they could sometimes set their own pace when they felt they had made enough or quit when they couldn't go on any longer.[3]

> EARL TURNER: In those days, you had to do everything yourself. You had to lay your own track before cars could come in there on. You had to set your own timbers to keep yourself safe from the rock falling on ya. You had to drill your own holes to shoot the coal down. And it was a...a bare living. You had to keep the timbers set and crossbars. It all depends on the top. Sometimes you had a real bad top. The company furnished you great, big wooden crossbars to put across, big strainers just across the top. They keep the rocks [from] falling. Those timbers like to fall and kill you.

In the room-and-pillar system, miners worked in small parallel "rooms" set off from the main entry and connected to each other by "breakthroughs." The "pillars"—blocks of coal between the walls of the room and the breakthroughs—supported the roof. The first important task was securing the top with wooden supports. Then, at the coal face, work began by undercutting the coal seam: kneeling on kneepads or lying sideways, the miner would make a slit at the bottom of the seam, then use a hand-operated breast auger (later, an electric drill) to drill holes in the block of coal above the undercut. In those holes, he would then put charges of black powder, tamp them with paper cylinders filled with earth, move away, light the fuse, shout the warning cry of "fire in the hole," and wait for the explosion to shake the coal from the face. "When I went in there, they were shooting dynamite. You drill them holes and put dynamite, it would shake you to death just like a jackhammer. I almost got killed in there twice" (*Bill Lee*). "You drill a hole, maybe six inches to the back of the cut. And you tamp the holes two-thirds the length of the hole with incombustible material, rock and dust, clay, or water. And when you're shooting with pellet powder, now, some people think it's not dangerous. But a case of pellet powder, for a man that's trying to shoot in an open light is a dangerousest thing in the world. If you drop that light into this case of pellet powder, it will burn you into solid crust" (*Ben Campagnari*).

In the early days, undercutting was done by hand; later, cutting machines made the work easier but increased the dust and the noise ("if you're working close to them you can't hear nothing, for the noise of these machines," *Tillman Cadle*). After the 1940s, the wooden roof supports were replaced by steel roof bolts that were screwed onto the top: "Roof bolting is accomplished by drilling holes in the mine roof and inserting long bolts anchored in the roof by wedge or extension shields. Layers of roof strata, held together in a thick beam by the bolt, become self-supporting."[4] "First, you control your top. A roof bolter, he rolls up in this truck, stopping so many feet from the face, and you had a piece of metal to sound the roof to see whether it's solid or loose. If it sounded hollow that rock's loose. But if it's a good tough sound, well, it ain't no good top but it's a safe top. You survive there. Then you get your drills going and [stick the bolts in the roof]. Make sure it's tight enough 'cause if you leave it loose it will give" (*Johnny Jones*).

After the fumes from the explosion had cleared, the miners would shovel the coal onto cars and remove slate and refuse. The coal was then taken to the tipple, where it was washed or shaken clean of refuse and then taken to the cars waiting at the rail spurs. "My first mining, now, that was a pony mines. I had to shoot the coal, load the coal, and tram it out with a pony, you know, drive a pony outside, dump the car…oh man we had good ponies, the mining ponies, they're the [best]" (*Junior Deaton*). "I first started loading by hand, shoveling, you know. Load by hand and put it in a car. We had a little pony that would pull it outside or either we'd push it. That's my first coal mine" (*Delbert Jones*). Handed-down stories about the early days underline one fact: before the union, and before mules were replaced by motors, men were not the most precious beings in the mine.

redundant

HAZEL LEONARD: When they first started mining they used ponies, I mean, little donkeys or something small, you know. And—my husband didn't work in that kind of mine, but he heared this, that the boss would tell the men that drove ponies, "Take care of 'em now, that they don't get hurt. We can't replace them, you know, like we can men." But that was in the early 1900s, when mining first started.

DELBERT JONES: Back when they was organizing, when they had these mules in corners of mines, maybe a man'd get killed in the mine, they'd say, "Push him back in a gob, we'll get him this evening," but boy, watch that mule, don't get one of them killed. They thought more of a mule, you know, than they did of a man. 'Course, I didn't go through with that part, but I was told, you see, was that that happened. Back in the twenties, early thirties before the union, before they got organized here in Harlan County.

Once the coal was loaded, the work was not finished—but from now on, on the so-called cleanup system, it was all unpaid or "dead" work. Miners were expected to pick out slate and rocks from the trams, remove debris, and prepare their workplace for the next day. They received no pay for the time spent going from portal to face and back: "Dad would leave and go to work; until he put that first shovel in a car, that's when he would get paid. That's why they needed a union: to make sure the people get time to get to work, time to straighten their place up and everything, and then time to start shoveling the coal. All the work that they did prior to that and the travel time was the people's responsibility" (*Dallas Blue*).

The last job was the most dangerous: "robbing pillars," or "retreat mining." After an area is mined out, the pillars of coal that hold up the roof are pulled down, capturing the last fragments of usable coal and collapsing the roof as the men withdraw as fast as they can. "My daddy, he got that one job that I was talking about: they were going into the mines and taking the pillars out, robbing 'em, and they was taking all the track out, they were getting all the metal out, then they would rob the pillars coming back out towards the front—they would get everything and it was really dangerous" (*Mildred Shackleford*). Often the roof would collapse on top of the miners still engaged in the work. Coal operator Bryan Whitfield philosophically admits, "When you take the support out from under a [roof], it is going to come down sometime. I've had men killed, but, it's a terrible thing, but when you dig fifty million, forty million tons of coal, you've got to lose some." "In Harlan County, Kentucky, in the early 1930s, a phenomenon called 'bumps,' caused by irresponsible robbing of pillars emerged": pillars would be left standing in areas where coal was thin, while all those around them were removed, thus causing shifts in weight distribution and pressure and "a sudden violent expulsion of coal from one or more pillars accompanied by a loud report and earth tremors." A "bump" killed two men in Harlan County on April 9, 1932.[5]

> DONALD HENSLEY: My dad worked from [nineteen] thirteen to sixteen in Rose Hill, Virginia. And he, evidently he loved that type of work, and he worked twenty-eight years for Black Star Coal Company from nineteen and twenty-one to nineteen and forty-nine. And he worked for different mines, you know, through the years, but he loved his work. It was danger, there's people killed, but…he, he just loved that—he loved the production, he loved to do more than [the next man], he was a great worker, he worked all with his hands.

"It's a hard enough line of work, that if everybody's working good, you really turn out some production, everybody is happy" (*Robert Wilson*). "I was willing to work. And that's why today I can't stand a lazy person. A little work ain't never hurt nobody, you know" (*Hugh Cowans*). "I think coal mining, one skill that everybody has is to work together; even if I didn't like you, underground I like you. And you're my brother. No matter what kind of problems we had on the outside. Once we get inside we're brothers. You just have to depend on each other. You know what I mean?" (*Jerry Johnson*). The combination of physical strength, skill, sheer courage, endurance, and underground bonding generated a male culture in which men drew pride from the hardship of their work, the severity of their environment, their work and union ethics, the living they made for their families and themselves.

> BERNARD MIMES: Yeah, I feel proud about it, I feel proud about what I accomplished. If they don't take it from me I've got a good living made. I might had to work hard but I got something to back me up, I got a pretty good living. I've always had pretty good money, and I've bought just about anything I wanted. Just about any car I wanted I bought it. In the reach of a poor man.

Employers learned to take advantage of the miners' pride in their work, as well as of the culture's overall competitive drift and the men's passion for sports—encouraging, or forcing, them to compete to increase production. Thus, the pressure from the company hierarchy would meet a cultural disposition among the workers. One union worker recalled: "I would always think to myself, 'Let's try to beat that other shift. If they loaded 400 tons, let's get 450.' Shaunna Scott comments: "To Ernie, then, workers and their bosses functioned like an athletic team, in competition with other teams on the playing field of the market."[6]

EARL TURNER: You're lucky you didn't get killed. Did some dangerous things, some crazy things. Taking chances. Lot of miners did. Trying to...who could run more coal than anybody on the section, man, you know. "He got so-and-so many tons yesterday." Well, you know, try to beat, do more tomorrow. The company preached safety. I give U.S. Steel credit for it. And the boss was on you all day about working in a safe [way]. We was paid by the shift, you didn't make any more money if you loaded one car, a hundred cars. [So it was just] competition between the men. Everybody trying to show. And all the time the boss is getting a big bonus and we didn't know it. I guess that's a man's pride, I reckon, I don't know. I always take pride in any job I did.

"I've been in and around the mines all my life. I started taking my dad's and my granddad's lunch into the mines when I was six or seven years old. I've walked up to three miles each way just taking their dinner, then I went to working around the mines when I was twelve or thirteen. And, I put in twenty-seven years underground. I mean—mining's hard work. But, it's something that gets in your bones and you just can't get rid of it" (*James Wright*). "Well, I miss...I just miss everything about [mining]. It's a lot dangerous in the mines. Yes, roof bolting's a dangerous part of it, you know putting roof bolts, and I, I've done a lot of dangerous things, Lord He took care of me so. I think about it, think a lot about being back in there, but I know I can't hold up to what they want done. I miss it. I miss it, I miss working with people I've known and stuff" (*J. C. Hall*). Henry Farmer left the mines because he could not stand the hard work. But he could not shake what Merle Travis calls "the lure of the mine,"[7] and he went back: "It's different from any other job I've had. I just enjoyed it. Seemed like I was just anxious to get up in the morning and go. I was in good health then, you know. Yes, I enjoyed it. You meet so many different people, different guys, you'd see a new face just about every morning. And, that way, you get to meet a lot of people."

"My husband and my brother, one of the first things they say is if there is a rock fall you don't leave a man in there, you try to get them out, and if you see something the others didn't, about the top working, you let everybody else know. They're a really close group that way, both on and off the job" (*Donna Warren*). Solidarity is necessary both to safety and survival and as a way of reinforcing its manly, or even "macho," associations. Thus a new miner's incorporation into the team came by way of jokes and rituals that tested gender (such as "greasing," applying grease on the genital area and sprinkling it with rock dust) or familiarity with the job, its environment, its language.[8] James Hall was small for his sixteen years when he went into the mine in 1934: "The older guys would tell me, 'We got rats in here so big they gonna take you way back in the [tunnel] so far they can't hardly find you.' This was a tease [but it] kind of frightened me up." James Wright recalled a woman coal miner who was sent to get a spare tire for a continuous miner and "she was calling all over the county trying to find a spare tire."

> TOMMY SWEATT: The first thing that happened to me was, they expected me to understand their terminology. The walls in a coal mine are called "ribs." You have the "roof," the "ribs," and the "bottom"—not the floor, and the ceiling, and the sides. Sometimes you'd have to widen out a place; that was "shearing a rib." One thing a man did one time was, he told a man—it was his first week in—he said, "Go down to where them tools are, and bring me back a pair of rib shears." And the guy he went down, looking for a pair of rib shears. When the boss heard he didn't take it to be so funny, because that guy had wasted about an hour and a half of his work time, doing that. But people don't give you instruction in this kind of thing, they just laugh at you.

> ROBERT WILSON: It's a bunch of roughnecks. You're one of the roughest men a-living when you work in the mines, 'cause you are so used to slave driving. And you wrestle, play, you know, on your spare time. You get tough, is what it is. On your own time or like when you're going to work, riding in, they throw you out of the buggy into a water hole, or put grease in your hat, all kinds of good stuff. Capboarding—around here capboarding is the best thing for a new man. It's a capboard like you set timber with; jerk his pants off and just capboard him real good, you know. Or pull his clothes off and throw them on the beltline and run 'em outside. He knows what he's going to get, but everybody gets it. But I mean, it's just a matter of playing around. Most of the time they use a big rough guy, one of the roughest ones. You know, there's always somebody meaner in the crowd. They whoop you or wrestle ya, eat your lunch—that's the worst thing, and it's bad being in the coal mines all day and somebody eat your lunch. It ain't like you can jump to the store and get you something else to eat, you know.

DEATH AND THE MINES

> SUDIE CRUSENBERRY: I wonder how they're going to lie when judgment comes. Are they going to stand up and lie to God? I'm going to tell you, they will reap their dirt works away.

Amon "Cotton" Brock, fifty-one, of Closplint; Jimmy B. Lee, thirty-three, of Wallins Creek; Roy Middleton, thirty-five, of Evarts; George William Petra, forty-nine, of Kenvir; and Paris Thomas Jr., fifty-three, of Closplint: these are the names of men who were killed on May 20, 2006, in a coal dust explosion in the Kentucky Darby No. 1 mine at Holmes Mill, Harlan County.[9]

"Preliminary autopsy results released yesterday show that three of the miners died of carbon monoxide poisoning, and two were killed directly by the blast," probably caused by an accumulation of coal dust ignited by methane gas. "U.S. Mine Safety and Health Administration records show that the mine has been cited 47 times since April 2001 for not cleaning up coal dust and other combustible material, and for not properly maintaining or failing to properly apply crushed limestone—known as rock dust—to minimize the danger of coal-dust explosions."[10] Only three months earlier, an explosion at the Sago Mine in Upshur County, West Virginia, killed twelve men; another blast killed thirteen miners in Brookwood, Alabama, in 2001.[11] A roof fall caused by irresponsible robbing of pillars killed six men in Huntington, Utah, on August 7, 2007 (and three more died in the rescue effort). By then, the number of mine deaths amounted to seventy-one in twenty months.[12]

The series of disasters goes back through the years in Harlan and neighboring counties. Eight killed in an explosion in Kenvir in 1928, sixteen dead in Kettle Island (Bell County) in 1931: "They were sixteen men got killed at one time, had a big explosion in the mines, and they've had other explosions after that. I wasn't but fourteen and, I went up to the funeral home to see them, but I was real scared, and all I could see was this big row of coffins, with these men in it" (*Mossie Johnson*). In 1932 in Yancey, thirty-two dead, including five brothers; in 1943 in Three Point, near Cranks Creek, twelve dead: "Do you remember when that mine exploded at Three Point? The one they called Big Bertha, it's at Three Point holler. This was back in early forties, it exploded, it caught on fire and there was so many men that they never did even get out" (*Annie Napier*). At Fourmile (Bell County) in 1945, twenty-five dead: "I was pastoring a church one time in Fourmile. There was a mine explosion. Gas gathered in that, when it exploded, it brought the dust, and the dust and the gas together, you couldn't breathe it, and they died. I've preached some of the funerals" (*Thea Carter*). Thirty-eight dead in Hyden (Leslie County) in 1970.[13] "I have been assured," President Nixon proclaimed, "that Federal and State authorities are conducting a full investigation of this disaster.... Every appropriate step must and will be taken to identify the causes of this tragedy and to prevent future mining accidents."[14]

Explosions make dramatic news, but most mine deaths are caused by roof falls.[15] "One of the things caused me to quit mining [in the 1930s] was the danger. And then of course my oldest brother and my father both got killed in the mine. Slate fell on 'em, slate fall" (*Tillman Cadle*). In Evarts on December 9, 1984, a roof fall killed four miners. In 2005, Russell Cole and Brandon Wilder were killed in Harlan robbing pillars, a job for which they had not been trained.[16]

The official definition of a "disaster" is an incident resulting in the death of five or more people, but the vast majority of deaths in the mines take place under this radar. As is the case of Bud Morris, who bled to death after his legs were severed by an overloaded tram car in December 2005,[17] or the three men killed at Gray's Knob on June 3, 1981, when a continuous miner machine broke through a mine wall.[18]

> MOSSIE JOHNSON: Well, he went in, and he got on his machine. And he always tested the top first, so he tested the top and it seemed solid, and...then when he got his machine under the top, it fell down on him and the man with him said he lived about a minute. And all he said was, "Boys get this rock off of me." He always come in about two o'clock, but it's before two when one of the boys that was working with him come, and when he hollered, I know that's something wrong. So [we] let him come in the house and, and he...started to tell me, but he was hurt so bad hisself, because he really cared for him, and he finally told me. Well my oldest son, he jumped out of bed, he was nineteen at the time. He jumped out of the bed, run through the house and...all of us was in shock. So...it just made us numb at the time. And then the next day, [my husband's] daddy want me to go with him to pick out the casket, so when I went in the funeral home and [it] look like a big field full of caskets, I had to get out of there, so I took off running. And...then we had his, we had his funeral and I heard people say that there was more people at his funeral than any one funeral they had ever been at, because everybody liked him, he was a likeable person, he...took time to stop to talk to whoever, he...And he really had a big funeral. But all I could think about...was how much I needed him...all I could think about is, "I have to get away from here." So we went on the graveyard with him, but...it was the hardest thing I ever had to do in my life, to just watch them put him down in there. And that was thirty-three year ago coming, the thirtieth of this month.

"Verda, up there, they had one ambulance down there they called the Verda special. They had a man killed, just about every day in that mines. And sometime two and three hurt" (*Sill Leach*). "When I was going to grade school in Creech's, if there was an accident in the mine they always blew the siren. I can remember when we would hear it all the kids would be looking at each other wondering who is it they're bringing off the mountains...hurt, or something" (*Bill Winters*). "Every time an ambulance goes up the road, we call Mamaw—'Where's Derrick? Where's Marty? Where's everybody at? Are they at work? Is it one of our family members?' And even if it's not your family member, it's really no different because you still know the person. It's somebody else's family member that you've always knowed or you went to school with them or..." (*Donella Wynn*).

In seventy-five years after the beginning of the industry, at least thirteen hundred men were killed in Harlan County mines. A Harlan website lists forty-six mining deaths from 1980 to 1989.[19] I have not met one working-class person who did not suffer personal injury, lose a family member or a friend, or witness death or injury in the mines. "Well, yeah. We have accidents. I had one. My buddy was killed. He got killed. A rock fell on him. Yeah. It never hurt me. It scared me. It broke my nose a little bit, cut my eye up a little bit, just, you know, it killed him dead. That was in, let's see, I guess that was in '59 or '60" (*Henry Farmer*). "The only way to keep coal miners safe is not let 'em mine coal. That's the safest way. So I mean, what do you wanna do? You need the coal and people gonna work...and people gonna get killed. So I mean, that's the chance that you take" (*Chester Clem*). "You get hurt or killed, and that's it. You ain't any more than a dog" (*Sudie Crusenberry*).

> WILL GENT: Lady live down the street here on the end. Her husband was killed where the mine here was running. And it was on Christmas Eve. And him and his brother-in-law and another guy, they went in on Christmas Eve. Company wanted some holes drilled and some charges set off so they'd have some coal ready for after Christmas. They went in, anyway. Sunk the hole up, put the dynamite and stuff in. When he backed up, got into the high voltage wire and it barbecued him, roasted, killed him instantly. Like that. Two or three thousand volts, something like that it went though. That's 1956. And I hated that 'cause that family, the brothers and sisters, he was my pick of 'em.
>
> OMIE GENT: 'Bout a year ago out here —— got all hurt in the mines, his face and everything. They couldn't show him 'cause it was messed up so bad.
>
> WILL GENT: That's March 20 of this year. And I lost a good friend over there when they lost him. His brother took it quite hard, you know, his death. And he had a lot of friends, that attended the funeral. You couldn't get close to the casket, you know, people coming in, relatives and friends alike, friends he worked with.

"My father got killed in the mines, in 1953, December the thirty-first. He got caught in a cutting machine, it hit him twice: first time it caught his legs out, second time it cut him through his chest" (*James Wright*). "Anybody that's ever worked in the coal mines, they've got something, had a rock on 'em or broken arm or broken leg—rupture your back is the worst thing. I mean, you do all you can do, but you still get killed one way or the other, if it's bad enough. And round here, it's a living. If you miss a day's work, that's a week's grocery there, or something, see" (*Robert Simpson*). "My best friend got killed, in the mines, my grade school childhood friend, we grew up with, we went to the Scouts together, and all, and he got killed. Rock fall. He was a young fellow then and he would have been thirty, thirty years old, he had four children. One of them wasn't even walking. Anyway, he was killed" (*James B. Goode*).

The Federal Bureau of Mines was created in 1910 after the disaster that killed 362 men at Monongah, West Virginia (1907). It was a consultative organ, with no powers of enforcement. Mine deaths averaged sixteen hundred a year between 1906 and 1936; courts hardly ever found against the companies, ruling most accidents "acts of God."[20] After passage of the very weak 1941 Coal Mine Inspections and Investigations Act, the Federal Coal Mine Safety Act was passed in 1952; journalist Ben Franklin described it as "one of the great legislative mirages of all times."[21] It included preventive measures to guard against major disasters, but (until 1966) exempted small operations and allowed operators who knowingly owned dangerous electrical machinery or had ordered it before the act was passed to continue using it indefinitely. Meanwhile, miners kept dying by the hundreds (247 in 1964, 307 in 1968). A new Federal Coal Mine and Safety Act (1969) was passed in the wake of the 1968 disaster that killed seventy-eight men at the Mannington mine at Fairmont, West Virginia.[22] More legislation followed in 1977, 1999, and 2002. Enforcement, however, remained lax: the profit imperative in a highly competitive industry, the industry's political clout, the links between the industry and key government agencies, the decline of the unions, and the miners' need to make a living all converged in making controls erratic and sanctions very moderate at best.[23]

> ROBERT SIMPSON: I've had a buddy that's worked at different mines and get killed. He was wildcatting in that strike, the Pittston strike [Virginia, 1989]: all them men was union so they stepped out of the way, so they brought a wildcat crew in, see, and he got mashed up and killed. He was working in the strikers' place, see. A rock fell on him. [Replacing strikers], it's money. It pays better money. You have got to cross the lines and there's a chance of getting shot or something—you know, you was off fighting for a cause and here I am, I come in and take your job, the owner is making money while you all are out starving to death.

In the 1950s, safety programs run by the companies and the union at Louellen, Clover Fork, and Benham were among the winners and qualifiers in national safety contests.[24] The days in which a miner's death counted less than the loss of a mule were over, at least nominally; the union's keener awareness of safety issues and the fact that safety legislation, albeit weak, did exist helped put safety on the agenda. "Closplint, they had a good safety program when they got the union established. The company, they had a part in it. Consolidated Coal Company, that's a big company, and they didn't want fatalities, they didn't want no man get covered up by no coal or get killed" (*Delbert Jones*).

Human life and limb aside, accidents cost employers in terms of loss of equipment and work stoppages. Many of the safety programs duly emphasize safe practices at work but also end up blaming the miners' "carelessness" rather than the unsafe working conditions.²⁵ On one hand, management at U.S. Steel in Lynch "wanted you to work safe"; on the other, "all they cared about was black gold" (*Johnny Jones*). Delbert Jones described the first-aid procedures they were taught in safety drills, yet he concluded, "Only thing the coal operator wants from you is your labor. When you get disabled, or you get crippled up, they got no more use for you. According to the company, everything you do, if you get hurt or if you get killed, it's your fault. They lay them rules down there and they figure them rules controls you. And if you carry them out, nine times out of ten they will. But now, we had a lot of bosses that was trying to get promoted, you know, get ahead. Run more coal than the other boss, he will overlook those things. That's what causes the accident."

JAMES HALL: [I had a] hand smashed between two cars. It caught my hand right between there, just smashed it. This was on the eighth day on May in 1950. That happened around about eleven. That's one thing I can remember well. Just lucky I didn't get killed. A lot of men was getting killed during that time—brakemen, some motormen got killed. They was in too big of a hurry: "We got to get it, we got to get it, don't stop for this, and don't stop for that"...But when you get like that you can rest assured, something is going to happen. Long as you have a coal mine you're going to have an accident. Some men come out better than others, some is gonna get killed. After I got crippled, this hand crippled, three months' time, the doctors told me to go back. This happened in May, and I believe it was September, he told me, "Well, Hall, you're ready to go back to work now." I said I couldn't handle [my old] job with my [crippled] hand. When I refused to go back to my regular job they cut my compensation off. I had no other choice, I had to go back.

Even active union miners seem to be under a double bind: "We're protected by the UMW as far as safety. But I'm also one of them that like to see the company make money, and I'd do anything to get another block of coal as fast as I can get it, 'cause we need that on negotiating day for a new contract, you know. If you run a mine under safety conditions, to suit the UMW, it's going to cost money, extra money, a whole lot of money, but now that's what UMW is for—mostly safety, give us a good safe place to work" (*Junior Deaton*). Small operators claim that they could not survive if they abided by the union safety rules. "There's mines here that employ ten men, they couldn't stay in business if they had to meet the same standards that somebody [who] employs a hundred, two hundred, or five hundred, they just couldn't compete. And those people need jobs and they are mining coal [that] would never be mined otherwise. Their accident rate is not much more than in the large mines, which is probably worthwhile; otherwise they'll be on welfare" (*Clyde Bennett, coal operator*).

JULIA COWANS: And the coal operators, if that husband was killed in the mine, they had lawyers that would beat the widow out of her money. They would bury him and give her a few dollars, but beat the lady out of money that was rightfully hers and her children's. My stepfather was a coal miner. My mother had five children, me being the oldest, when he died. There were no human resources, no welfare, no nothing in Kentucky, that I know about, at that time. And we never got one dime, behind his death. My mother was sick when he died. I's a schoolgirl, fourteen years old. I had to come out of school and take care of my mother, my four sisters and brothers. And you know I wasn't trained for anything. All I knew was how to keep house, domestic, you know. And that's how I took care of my mother, my sisters and brothers—on my knees, scrubbing floors, climbing walls, just whatever I could do. And I worked all day long for one dollar. One dollar. I mean I worked all day long.

SID DOUGLASS: Another type of civil rights case is when a man alleges that he has been fired because he has complained of some safety violations. I have represented some men in cases where they complained of safety conditions and were fired. As a matter of fact, I'm representing a fellow right now. He received an electrical shock from a piece of electrical equipment that the company had altered; he knew about it, he tried to get his employer, the coal company, to get it fixed, but they didn't fix it. He finally received an electrical shock and survived. There was an investigation by a federal mine inspector. The coal company thought my client had caused the inspection. He hadn't, but he didn't lie to the inspectors when they interviewed him, so the company fired him.

Of course, "accidents" kept on happening. On March 9 and 11, 1976, two successive explosions killed twenty-six men at the Scotia Mine, at Ovenfork, in Letcher County, across Pine Mountain from Lynch and Cumberland. The first explosion killed nine men; six more were trapped in the mine and died from suffocation. Two days later, a second blast killed eleven members of a team that had gone into the mine to rescue the bodies. Many of the victims were from Harlan County. *Harlan Daily Enterprise* editor Ewell Balltrip covered the tragedy and talked to the families. He found "intertwined, complex attitudes of anger, horror, questions of why it all happened and how. Yet a degree of numbness prevailed, as it does when the greatest threat of going underground becomes a reality."

CHARLOTTE RHODES: I happened to live behind the railroad track over here, and I heared the sirens going, and there was just something inside me knew that something had happened. And then we got the news that the mines had blowed up, and I didn't get the news until later on that afternoon that he was in there. It was later on in the afternoon that I got the news, but as a matter of fact it was ten o'clock that night before I knew it for sure. We'll never know the whole truth of that or anything. I have the report that they came up with and stuff, I never even bothered to read it because I don't feel like everybody tells everything they know anyway. We had two daughters, one seven and one five at the time, and we just had to go on with our lives, you know, it was just an accident that happened and everything and we went on with our lives.

Speaking to the families, Balltrip wrote, "drains you....When you see something like that up close and you see the hurt that it causes the families and when you're standing there listening to recollections of the memories and listening to them talk about things that were that you know will never be again, it takes a lot out of you." Five days after the disaster, James Raymond Houston, age thirty-five, who had been working with the men killed in the first explosion, shot himself. "He had been depressed," said his wife. "He had been hearing voices of the dead miners."[26]

EWELL BALLTRIP: I think certainly the Scotia disaster had a tremendous impact because what happened there was the basic fear that everybody in the mines felt. And also, the basic fear of everybody who's on the other side of the mine, outside, waiting for the husband or the father to come out. That was the materialization of that fear, and it involved so many people that that fear was magnified so many times. In terms of what impact that event is going to have on these twenty-six families—that translates, you know, assuming that there are two children and a widow, remaining, you know, twenty-six times three, that's seventy-eight. You know, there're seventy-eight lives there that have been significantly altered in just a heartbeat by a blast running through a coal mine. You start thinking about that, and you start thinking, "What if it were me or my family?" And then at the end, thank God I don't have to work in a coal mine.

BLACK LUNG

PORTELLI: What would you say are the most common causes of death, from [your experience as a funeral home director]?
LEWIS BIANCHI: I guess heart attacks here are the most common. Heart attacks and black lung. A lot of black-lung deaths here. Black-lung-related deaths...
PORTELLI: Black-lung patients must be very hard to prepare...
BIANCHI: They're harder, yeah, harder to prepare.
PORTELLI: ...because they're wasted, aren't they?
BIANCHI: Most of them, yeah. A lot of times we have to restore them to normal by using tissue builder, or some type of filling. Wax, or mold, or something, to bring them back to normal, because a lot of time they get

real thin and emaciated, and, you know, sick over a period of long...long time, and they just go down to skin and bones. We do have to do a lot of work on those.

PORTELLI: So the only time they look healthy is after they're dead.

BIANCHI: A lot of times they look healthier after they die than they did before they die. Maybe ten years before they die, fifteen years, twenty years. A lot of times, I've had [relatives] come and say, "Oh, he look like he looked twenty-five years ago...thirty years ago...when we first got married...." You know, that poor old fellow got sick—worked and had black lung, couldn't breathe, died right out, you know.

"That rock dust, it's a terrible thing. I can tell you that. Especially on the roof bolter. Well, anybody that's in the mine, in a way it's bad on them. That's a chance he takes to be a coal miner" (*Johnny Jones*). One thinks of mines in terms of hard matter—rock, slate, coal—and sudden tragedies. But death in the mines comes also softly and slowly, in the form of progressive, gasping breathlessness caused by inhalation of rock and coal dust in the lungs. Specialists call it pneumoconiosis; miners call it "black lung."

"I run a motor all the time, sand and sand, and dust, motor wheels a burning, you breathe it. It just hits you. You can't hardly do nothing, you don't have enough wind to do nothing, you get tired right quick. It's in your lungs" (*Lloyd Lefevre*). "You never saw a mine, have you? Well, a mine is something like this, you compress the air in the mine. Most of the dust from that machine, cutting the coal makes a lot of dust. You have water, you have air, but you still gonna get dust and rock dust. You got to watch out for gas, and dust" (*Bernard Mimes*).

JAMES WRIGHT: One morning you get up and you can breathe good, the next morning you get up and can't breathe. I feel pretty good, as long as I'm sitting. But if I try to use any kind of energy at all, it's over—I can't breathe, and I start smothering, and—then after you got it for several years, why, you go to swelling; some people swells so big they just about busts, then on the other hand some people it dries up on the bones, you know. And my grandfather, he stood about six two, six three, and before he died, why, he just shriveled up to nothing. You ain't got no energy—you wake up in the morning, you lay there thinking what you're gonna do, you jump out of bed, you go arrrhhh—you better lay back down before you fall. And it's just that simple. You wanna do it, but you can't do it.

Miners' lung diseases had been observed since the early 1800s. However, company doctors refused to face a problem that would have challenged the operators' interests, and since usually the damage would not appear on X-rays and other machine-driven tests, the medical profession, increasingly dependent on technology rather than clinical observation, would not recognize it. Thus, black lung came to be redefined as "miner's asthma," an ordinary condition that need cause no worry. Doctors and operators even claimed that coal dust was good for the miners because it prevented tuberculosis: "In the old days doctors used to would tell you coal dust was good for you. You know, it was a company-paid doctor, you go to him and say, 'Doc, I'm spitting up coal dust.' 'Ah, that's good for you, that coal dust is medicine'" (*Johnny Jones*). Until 1968, only silicosis was recognized as a miners' occupational disease.[27]

> J. D. MILLER (PHYSICIAN): I've been here long enough now to take care of people who were having breathing problems but they weren't real bad. And over a period of years, maybe five years or ten, they progressed to the point of smothering to death. They could no longer get enough oxygen to…to live. We finally put them on home oxygen, a few of them we put on respirators, but most of them chose not do that because they knew it was a losing battle anyway, so we simply gave them more and more oxygen and tried to support them as much as we could, short of putting them on respirators.[28] Because once they got on respirators, they're afraid they'd be there forever. If somebody had gotten to the point that the only way they could live was on the respirator, most of them didn't want that for the rest of their life, and I'm not sure I can blame people for that. I wouldn't want my own existence to be, only if I was tied up to a machine.

A further obstacle to the recognition of black lung was the fact that the term covers different combinations of at least three types of impairments: tissue destruction, or pneumoconiosis; airway obstruction (associated with bronchitis and similar diseases); and oxygen deficiencies, caused by loss of the lungs' capability to transfer oxygen to the blood. The consequences are tragic in all cases: as a song says, "Pneumoconiosis, black lung blues / You got one, you got the other / Either way you lose."[29]

"The older you get the more badder you get. I felt I got it in my late forties, I'd worked in there since I was about eighteen years old, besides the three years I was in 'Nam. It just shortened my wind, you don't have the energy to do the things that you want. I don't see how no man can work in a mine over ten years and don't get some of it" (*Bernard Mimes*). "Well, the breathing when your lungs get covered up with dust, you see, that makes your breathing bad. You don't get no better when you got it, you just get worst and the older you get the worster it gets. The last five years my breathing has gotten to getting worser every day I live, see, and, they ain't no way they can get that off your lungs when it gets on there" (*Delbert Jones*).

> J. D. MILLER: What happens on these people with severe black lung is, the oxygen keeps getting less and less, but you can keep giving them more and more oxygen. So what happens is that their muscles finally wear out and they can no longer keep pulling it in. And so you put them on the

respirator to keep pushing it in there, you can keep them going a little longer. And I've had people on the respirators in the hospital for six weeks, or two months. That's their only existence. They can no longer talk because the tube goes through their voice box. They might be alert. They can write, write messages, but they can't talk because their voice box had the tube stuck through there.

"I believe if a fellow got black lung and all, he is entitled to [compensation], I think they deserve it and I think they should get it. You see, like it weakens your system down, to me it does, I mean it's whipping me down, so I just…I'm taking wheezing pills, and arthritis pills, and nerve pills, and sometimes I go to sleep in the night, I lay awake, and I can hardly go to sleep and I take a pill so I can go to sleep" (*J. C. Hall*). "Thousands of miners have died, and never received a dime. And are suffering the rest of their lives, you know. And people has been suppressed and oppressed and a lot of people give up hope, and a lot of people has in Harlan County, and if you stick out about any issue, you know, you're in hot water" (*Sid Tibbs*).

J. D. MILLER: Unfortunately, something that all of this does, getting a respiratory disease through your occupation, and then winning compensation because of your respiratory disease, one of the things that does is that a lot of people see that as a way of retiring. You…you want to get a respiratory disease, so you can draw that black lung and provide for your family after you retire. That's a very sad way to retire. Basically you have sold your health in exchange for a pension.

Technological progress and mechanization increase the amount of coal dust in the mines.[30] "On a good day, you can't see two foot in front of you, for the dust. And we've got to hold on to a cable, feel along the walls, to find out where you're going. All these machines has got water hoses to keep the dust down. But within thirty minutes that water mixes with the dust, it forms kind of like a concrete around, so it works no more" (*James Wright*). "Today, the government has safety regulations in regard to the maximum amount of exposure to dust in the mines, but still I hear stories from men who work in thick coal dust in the mines while working behind a continuous miner. This machine has a rotor on it with teeth, it chews the coal and it spews out just an enormous amount of dust. In the old days, obviously, there was a tremendous amount of dust in the air, but I don't think it put as much dust in the air as these continuous miners" (*Sid Douglass*)

Since the early 1950s, the UMW has provided health care for its members. But in the early 1960s, for financial reasons, the union canceled many of its provisions and introduced stricter eligibility requirements that deprived union miners of many health benefits.[31]

GRANNY HAGER: When the International took their [hospital] cards, I didn't know they'd took [my husband's]. I did know they'd knocked him out of his miner's retirement. One day, my husband got a real bad spell. My brother drove him to the Appalachian Hospital at Harlan, but as soon as I walked in, they told me he didn't have no hospital card. That was in May, and I had his union dues paid until October. They said there was nothing they could do for him with no hospital card and me not able to pay a fifty-dollar deposit. All we had to live on was a forty-eight-dollar Social Security check. We took him home. Doc Green said my husband had got so much of that rock dust and that old black coal dust in his lungs that it turned 'em like concrete. He said if we could take a hammer to 'em, it would be like breaking a saucer or a piece of dish. I sat right there by him for three weeks and watched him slowly die. If I'd had the money to put him in the hospital...if the union had still let him keep his hospital card...he might be alive today.

Granny Hager was to become one of leaders of the "roving pickets" and of the Black Lung Association in eastern Kentucky, which struggled against the loss of health care and for black-lung benefits. The BLA was funded in 1966 in West Virginia, after War on Poverty volunteer Craig Robinson and physicians Isadore E. Buff and Donald Rasmussen presented the Association of Disabled Miners and Widows with information on the work-related nature of black lung. By January 1969, miners were marching and demonstrating throughout West Virginia and in parts of eastern Kentucky. Hundreds marched in Pineville in January, and in February forty thousand West Virginia miners staged an unauthorized three-week walkout in support of state legislation for black lung compensation. Out of concern for the welfare of the industry, the union leadership, under president Tony Boyle, opposed the movement. In 1970, a wildcat strike in West Virginia culminated in a battle between reformers and Boyle supporters and in the arrest of the movement's leaders. But the black-lung movement fueled grassroots democratization in the union and would be one of the driving forces in the Miners for Democracy movement in the 1970s.

Rank-and-file pressure led to the passage of the Coal Mine Health and Safety Act, which officially recognized black lung as an occupational disease. "We got a black lung law, now. We fought for years and years, man, trying to get that thing through. Now every mine's got bit water pressure, big water holes. They wet that dust down. They got big exhaust fans right up in the face. It sucks all that dust into a great big container—it's not like it used to be. It's better" (*Earl Turner*.).

At least 365,000 miners had died from black lung before the act was passed. And more continued to die.[32] For years, black-lung claims had to be verified by a reluctant medical profession: in the first two years after the act was passed, 68 percent of claims by Kentucky miners were turned down. According to UMW president Cecil Robert, black lung "was supposed to be basically eradicated" by the new law, yet "miners who started work after the 1969 act are [still] getting black lung. That means either MSHA is not enforcing the safety standard or the standard is too lax.... It is more likely both."[33]

On March 9, 1981, as the Reagan administration cut eligibility for black-lung benefits, seven thousand coal miners marched in Washington to protest deaths from black lung, estimated to number more than four thousand annually. In 2007 the National Institute for Occupational Safety and Health announced that black lung had doubled nationwide over the past five years.[34] And miners still struggled with bureaucrats and doctors.

SUDIE CRUSENBERRY: See, they said I had to be—is it sixty-two?—before I could draw Social Security or go on the Medicare. That's the truth. I'll tell you, they gonna make sure you're sure dead. I believe with all my heart if you get anything, they'll have your grave dug and be a-taking you to the funeral. See, Grandpa smothered and died, and I never knowed of him getting anything but Social Security. That was all. You've got to be dead if you get anything, buddy.

And my daddy, he was smothering. And he went [to the office] and saw that man, about the black lung. And it went on for years, and Daddy hadn't got [compensation], he just got the Social Security. And then [the] company, they told us to move, and—our rent was paid, and so I told them I didn't have no money to rent no other house. And they said we had to go. Well, we had to hire a truck, open-bed, put what little we had in it. The little bitty house [we moved to]...part of the floor punchings was busted through. Part of the windows was out. Then Daddy come. He was smothering bad. Well, finally, Daddy's black lung [compensation] come, but the black...that coal dust was so bad that, you know, it wasn't any pleasure. When that man did bring that [check], Daddy was a-smothering down, he couldn't get no breath, you [saw tears] coming over his eyes.

I had to wade through [the flood to get him] to the hospital, and everybody a-looking, some maybe pass you by, they'd maybe frown, you know, if they was...you know, big people. [Just before Christmas] the doctor told me he was dying from the black lung, and I wanted Daddy so bad to come back, so he told me, "You can take him back," he said, "but your daddy is a-dying. Don't expect nothing." And so, three days, I never will forget it, before Christmas, Daddy was tucked back over there. And then he died.

8

IDENTITIES

WOMEN'S WORK, REVISITED

SUDIE CRUSENBERRY: Years ago, at one time, my husband's place fell in. He was working up in Coxton hollow in the mines, and his place fell in, so he came back to the house, and ... You know, in them days, them little mines where them ponies is worked, you either cleaned it up on your own, or you didn't have nowhere to work, no job. Well, we went down there on Sunday and geared the pony up, took some timbers in there. I went and helped him.

PORTELLI: You went inside the mine?

CRUSENBERRY: Yeah. But ... you know, [there] were no motors, or trips, it was a pony mines. Yeah, I've been in. 'Cause, I tell you, didn't have nothing to eat.

Women were involved in mining as wives and mothers in the coal camps; family laborers in small mines; union activists; temporary workers during both world wars; and, less commonly, mine operators.[1] All of these roles were played by women in Harlan County history. Coal mining wives worked hard to make a home in the camps, coping with fear for the men's lives, the consequences of injury and black lung, the anxiety of layoffs, evictions, and strikes, and the contradictions between their hard work and established gender roles.[2] "The man, he was the breadwinner, and women were very silent, but that changed during the union organizing" (Joan Robinett).

As Sudie Crusenberry reminds us, women also worked in and around the mines. Around 1928, Ethel Day Smith worked along with the rest of the family in her father's pony mine on Pine Mountain; in 1941, Ethel Dixon McCuiston went into the mine in Cumberland as a helper to her husband and stayed on the job fourteen years, while raising six children, keeping boarders, and working on the family farm.[3]

BOBBIE DAVIDSON: I started in '79. I worked in the mines for seven years. I was a nurse for nineteen years. And I have two children, and my husband and I got a divorce, and I wanted more for them than what I could give them as a nurse, so I went to the coal mines.

Women gained equal employment rights in the mines in the 1970s, in the wake of the civil rights struggle, the women's movement, and the Miners for Democracy movement, overcoming the reluctance of the union and the hostility of male co-workers. "Equal laws. It was mainly the women's movement. So when they forced them to hire so many women for so many men they hired, they didn't have any other choice. When we started working in the coal mines, we had to join the union. [The union] don't have a choice. They have to protect us. We've got just as much rights as the men. Brothers and sisters" (*Joyce Jones*). The first woman in a union mine was hired in 1973; in Harlan, the first may have been Judy Cornett, at Benham, in 1975.[4] Women went from 1 percent of the mining workforce in 1977 to 11.4 percent in 1979; although the percentage of women miners dwindled with the decline of the industry, they remain a presence today.[5]

> MILDRED SHACKLEFORD: I was twenty-five when I got married. I needed money when he and I split because I did have the two kids, and he didn't have any. My kids was two or three years old when we split up. And if you get 'em, you got to take care of 'em. And I couldn't see much of a way of doing it in Harlan County. I could have taught school, but I didn't like that because it was too much of an indoor-type job and I guess mining at that time was one of the [jobs] that paid the best in this country. And since this is where I was kind of stuck, that's what I wound up doing.

According to Harlan coal miner Brenda Brock, "It takes a certain breed of women to go underground. I think we're women who aren't satisfied with the role we've been out in all our lives."[6] The break with gender roles may be practical as much as ideological ("I just decided that I wanted the job, and that I wanted the money. I thought it was just as fair for the women to make it as it was for the men," *Joyce Jones*), but its consequences are radical. Harlan coal miner Linda Taylor noted: "I worked the same job that my husband works now; and I *know* what it's like. And I *know* that, when I worked it, I didn't just come home and collapse."[7] "When I first started underground, my husband, he gave me two weeks to stay under there. And here I am almost eleven years" (*Joyce Jones*).

"And another reason why I did it, because I don't mind getting into stuff and saying, 'Okay, let's see what we can do with this'" (*Mildred Shackleford*). Mining is hard work and has long been considered a "man's job": "See, all the jobs were called men's jobs, because there weren't any women. So they was a miner man, faceman, shuttle car man, belt man, all of these had *man* at the end because there were no women, and it's still that way. I was a faceman—we call it a faceperson, though" (*Joyce Jones*).

> MILDRED SHACKLEFORD: I have always been physical and I was always exceptionally strong. The first week they took bets that I wouldn't last the first day. Well, I had only been there three days and they put me in a

training program—you know what a jackhammer is? Like drills, they operate off of air and they drill holes that you put powder in and blast. The thing weighs ninety pounds and you pick it up, hold it up here, and you turn it and drill these holes, right? And so they took bets I wouldn't last another day. After two weeks they were taking bets I wouldn't last six months. And after six months, they quit.

Women were accused of stealing breadwinners' jobs for "cosmetics money."[8] "When we first started, the men did not like it; they didn't want it; we were even accused of taking the men's jobs away. They did not approve of us being in there, they didn't want us in there, they gave us a lot of trouble" (*Joyce Jones*). Women were denied both equality and difference. On one hand, they had to prove they were as physically able as the men, and at first were excluded from training and skilled jobs. "I did repair work, I mucked—the coal and the dirt, the rock and so on, that piles up, we'd have to clean it up, throw it on the belt and send it outside. With a shovel, right. I took care of the belt lines. [But now] I got my mine foreman's papers. I have a sister that ran the bolt machine. I have a girlfriend that ran the [continuous] miner" (*Bobbie Davidson*). On the other hand, "when we first started, the men didn't want us to have a separate bathhouse. They said we fought for the right to come in the mines underground to work as men, we ought to be made to bathe in the bathhouse" (*Joyce Jones*).

> MILDRED SHACKLEFORD: And when I first went to work there, they were scared to death. They told the superintendent that they would quit because some smart young fellow had told them that I have to take a shower with the men and change with the men, because that was the law—equality under the laws. They were ready to quit. There was a bunch of those older men that went in there and said, "We draw the line. When that woman comes in there and starts taking a shower with us, we are leaving."

Yet, as Joyce Jones recalls, when the women obtained a separate bathhouse at Lynch, "they cut a hole in it, trying to watch us undress." Beside "bathroom peepholes," the forms of harassment included rumors that tarnished their reputation, sexual comments, verbal abuse, unwanted advances, groping, and physical assault.[9] A half-joking, half-serious exchange in Lynch:

> IRWIN TURNER: I was in West Virginia, one year. The women's bathhouse, they had cut a hole in it. The boss was invading their privacy, and they sued him.[10]
> JOYCE JONES: You sue, because you've got harassment. It happened to all of us when we first started working. You had your snoops, trying to watch us undress.
> TURNER: In my opinion I don't think a lady should be in a coal mine.
> JONES: I think a lady should be anywhere she wants to be, anywhere she's qualified enough to. Not just in the coal mines, but anywhere else.

TURNER: Well, man, I don't want to hire no lady.

JONES: If he had a mine he would hire all women!

TURNER: I might say to somebody, "You look good, right? Hey, you look good.... I'll pick that bag for you, I'll hang your curtains for you if you give me a kiss...."

JONES: See? This is what we have to put up with.

"They put me with this repairman," said Brenda Brock, "who told the company he couldn't work with a hard-on." The presence of men and women in the same dark underground space is supposed to generate a sex-charged environment. Mining women, Shaunna Scott writes, "posed a double threat to miners' wives: They could either steal their husbands' jobs or steal their husbands."[11]

JOYCE JONES: First they called us troublemakers because a lot of the mens started to flirt, and so forth. A lot of the wives did not like their husbands working with the women. We was just there to mess around with their husbands. And the husbands became jealous because their wives were out there among a lot of men. On the job and off the job—with the woman out all night, day long, with all these men, you know, there's gossip gossip gossip, and you don't know what's going on, since you're under there and you don't know what to believe—it builds a lot of tension. But then you just had to have the determination to stick with it.

"Some of the old miners thought it was bad luck to have women underground" (*Bobbie Davidson*).[12] Folk beliefs and rituals mixed with harassment and boycott. Like most newcomers, women were the butt of practical jokes, with a keener edge. Hiding their tools, messing up their lunch boxes, and sending them on fool's errands were less ways of "making a miner" out of the women than attempts to scare them away. Mildred Shackleford recalls when some male coworkers set fire to a paper she was reading, or worked for hours dismantling the water pipes so that she couldn't wash her hands. Some rituals—"swatting with a capboard" (capboarding), "games that focus on the reproductive organs," "greasing"—are even less innocent.[13]

MILDRED SHACKLEFORD: They will pull your pants down and your underwear and they will paint you full of grease. And I told them, I said, "Now, fellas, we will draw the line at that. The first one that does something like that to me, I am going to take a piece of steel, when I get through beating on ya we will see if you can get out of here." They never tried to do that to me. And as far as I know, they have never tried to do that to any of the women. They don't talk dirty around me either.

"And as the years went by things got a lot easier, the men began to accept us staying, began to look at us as one of them, helping with out jobs even. When we went in there they wouldn't even pick up anything to help you with it; they said, 'You're here, you're making that kind of money, you axed for the job, you do the job'" (*Joyce Jones*). "Now I am tired to death of it and I would love to get into something else, but I can't do it yet. Now there is ten women that works there, and they do anything they want to and they are on any job. And nobody thinks too much about it anymore" (*Mildred Shackleford*).

> BOBBIE DAVIDSON: My son, he got out of school and went to work to the coal mines, and we were going to work one day, and he kind of laughed. I said, "Well, Keith, what's funny?" "Well," he said, "most boys follows the father's footsteps, and here I am, following my mother's."

IN ANOTHER COUNTRY

> BRYAN WHITFIELD: In the early days when the field was opening up, there just wasn't enough labor. And a lot of the Poles and Italians and Irish and Scots, all of 'em came over here. I used to work a lot of Italians.

> ARTHUR JOHNSON: I've been told, when Lynch was booming, the twenties and thirties, at the window at payday, they had five interpreters there to talk to at least five different nationalities. The Czechs, the Hungarians, the Italians, Polish, probably. By the next generation, their families understood English because they were going to the same schools, and the younger kids picked right up on it. And now, except for the five- and six-syllable names, you hardly know the difference.

> JANIS ROSS: I would ask [my father-in-law] often about what it was like where he lived in Italy and he said, "I lived in the mountains." He said, "Like here—not as green and not as pretty." And he told me that it was a hundred miles from Rome, in the mountains. He had a brick house, he was of Catholic religion, and it took ten days of travel, packing mules across the mountain to peddle or to do trading. And he told me he took a train, and it took about two hours to get to Naples. Giorgio La Vita, that was supposed to be his name. His mother remarried, his father had died, and there were three or four children, and he was the oldest, and she borrowed money for him to come to America. He was sixteen. He came with two uncles on the ship *Italia* and left Naples in April of 1905, and he sailed and he told me about the big fish [that] followed the boat, all the way to America.

"My dad came here in 1915. His brother came over and worked a year in the coal mines, then he went back and brought my dad and his brother back with him. From Montefiascone," near Rome (*Lee Marsili*). "Anyway, my father, when he was nineteen—he was born in 1919—he and my uncle and a double cousin, my uncle Frank and my double cousin Frank, my father came over here. He could speak just a little English" (*Joe Scopa Jr.*). "New coal mining companies were coming into our county," writes G. C. Jones. It seemed like a mine would open up and be producing coal overnight, and all the workers were strangers to these hills. A lot of them came from as far away as Italy, and I met a few who said they were from Scotland, Ireland, and England."[14]

In 1910, Harlan had nine residents of mixed or foreign parentage and foreign-born; in 1930 there were more than two thousand (1,374 mixed, 822 foreign), mostly in Lynch and Benham.[15] Appalachia had been importing immigrants since the beginning of the coal boom. No fewer than 3,162 Italians (the largest immigrant group) lived in four Appalachian mining counties in 1909; in West Virginia, one-fourth of all the foreign-born came from Italy.[16] In Harlan, by 1920 there were immigrants of twenty-one nationalities; Italians were second only to Hungarians (respectively, 233 and 320) at that time, but had become the largest immigrant group by 1924.[17]

> FRANK MAJORITY: My father came from Italy when he was fifteen years old—1902. In [the] early 1900s the United States was exploding with projects and there was a shortage of skilled labor. Stonemasons, bricklayers, coal mining engineers, coal loaders, experienced coal miners, and all that sort; and so, United States government sent hiring agents into all parts of Europe locating these skilled laborers to bring into eastern Kentucky, West Virginia, southwest Virginia, to operate and build the railroads. [My father] had some family members here already. And he came later, him and his brother.

> JANIS ROSS: So he landed in New York, and got misplaced, and separated from his uncles, and, he was waterboy on a railroad gang, and they were hauling logs in the southern United States. They laid track through West Virginia, there is a railroad trestle at Clinchport, Virginia, and it was a huge trestle for that day and time, and it must have been in 1907 or around then, and he helped build that trestle. And he talked about having starved to death, he was so hungry. He talked about the mules, falling off the mountainside. He was a relatively young man. He ended up mining in south West Virginia. And he met Mama Ross, she was fourteen years old, and he fell in love and she fell in love, and he took her on horseback all the way to Pike County, Kentucky, across the river, and they married.

"They would lease a train and have it meet one of the boats from Italy at Ellis Island. They'd load them on that train and bring them to Lynch and they'd put them in those boardinghouses, maybe two, three, four a room, fellows who had never been in the mines before" (*Norman Yarbrough*). "In 1903, the New York Society for the Protection of Italian Immigrants sent an agent to the region to investigate complaints of alleged maltreatment. [Later] the Italian ambassador to the United States complained to Secretary of State Elihu Root that his countrymen were being held against their will in West Virginia."[18] One hundred and seventeen Italians died in the first great mining disaster in 1884, at Pocahontas,

Virginia; 171 at Monongah, West Virginia, in 1907; 133 at Dawson, New Mexico, in 1913.[19]

FRANK MAJORITY: He [and his brother] landed in New York, and, when he got through immigration, they let him go out to the Grand Central Station, and then they neither one could talk any English, and they put tags on 'em where they were supposed to go—like cattle, you know. And they tagged them for West Virginia. That's where their kinfolks were. So they finally put 'em on the train and they sent them into West Virginia. So they were kinda late [at night] getting in. And they pulled into that station in that town, Beckley, I guess it was. And along the track, close by, they had a lot of coke ovens: they were right in the heart of the mine fields, and these coke ovens was burning this coal, to make coke. Well, it lit up the sky and my father, he had never seen anything like that—and when they got off the train, they got to looking at those ovens a little closer and they saw a big colored man with a steel bar all sweaty, no shirt on, he's pulling this coke out and he's sweaty, and they thought, "Well, we are in hell—and this is the devil." Yeah, he was scared. They were kids, you see, they hadn't seen anything like that, and you know, in a strange country, a strange town, nobody they knew.

Italian miners took part in the West Virginia strikes at Long Ton (1909), Paint Creek and Cabin Creek (1912), and Logan County and Blair Mountain (1921).[20] Giorgio La Vita came to Harlan around 1915, worked at Gray's Knob, then went to White Star because it was unionized. "He was a strong union man. I was looking at some papers, and there's a quotation there that says that he'd been a faithful union member for fifty-two years. This was 1952 that that document was written, he wasn't even in the United States in 1900, so there was some discrepancy, but he was always, as far as I know, UMWA" (*Janis Ross*).

"My mother's dad helped build the houses, he was a stonemason, a brickmason. They built the schoolhouse, the main office, the bathhouse, the hotel, and then they built the theater, it was all done by Italian masons" (*Lee Marsili*). Not all Italian immigrants worked in the mines: many were employed in construction, and most of the stone buildings in eastern Kentucky are their work. They don't look like anything to be found in Italy: the styles were influenced by the materials at hand and by local training. Stone work fell to Italians, Frank Majority claims, because "that whole story boils down to this: Italians were better at that work than the others, I mean, they liked the work better, they took pride in the work." "Some of them were trained here, but most of them were masons to start with. There were some darn good masons. There's some beautiful work done up there at Lynch" (*Norman Yarbrough*).

LEWIS BIANCHI: [My father] came when he was about eleven years old. I guess he left over there, you know, like young, adventurous people, looking for better, richer soils. He came with three other people, they were maybe cousins. And they came from Italy to New York, and around Jellico, Tennessee, I believe. And then, on up here, Harlan County. He was a stone-mason by trade, and he did a lot of stonework throughout Harlan County. He worked up at Lynch, then, after the jobs completed up there, he moved down to Harlan, and he worked in and out of the mines. He would work in the mines in the wintertime, and do stonemason work during the summer months.

"They've been all cousins, all them Italians was kin to each other" (*Ben Campagnari*). Bianchi's father came with his cousins; Joe Scopa Sr. had relatives in Lynch. Many came from the south (Joe Scopa Jr.'s father and grandfather from Calabria, Frank Majority's father from Campania), but not all: Campagnari's family was from Bologna, Bianchi's from Milan, Marsili's from Lazio. Often, they thought they would save money and go back: "My daddy came over here, I believe it was 1896," said Ben Campagnari; he ran a liquor store in New Jersey, worked on the railroads, "and he sent back eighteen thousand to his brother, to buy a piece of property, over there." He went back a couple of times, until the Depression forced him to sell the property to his brother at a loss. Joe Scopa Jr.'s father and grandfather "worked and sent their money back to my grandmother and my grandfather's brother. His intent was to get everybody on the farm [in Calabria] and everybody live there, and raise some cattle, maybe start a brick factory.... But World War II happened."

When Italy entered the war, Italian immigrants became enemy aliens. Joe Scopa Jr.'s father and grandfather were visited by the FBI; "he thought, maybe they would put the Italians in concentration camp, like the Japanese."[21] Frank Majority tells an emblematic story. The Italian stonemasons who built the Presbyterian church in Whitesburg had placed on the front of the building a stone that looked vaguely like a boot, the outline of Italy: "And then the war started. Mussolini got Italy in the war, and they all got mad at Mussolini and they said, 'Hell with him,' and they went and chopped that all up so it looked like it wasn't a boot. Then after they got rid of Mussolini they was kindly sorry they done that."[22]

Many, however, had already made their choice: "My cousins said they'd spent their youth slaving there on the farm and then they'd come to the United States and then slaved in the coal mines for their father to send money back, and they resented that" (*Joe Scopa Jr.*). A website lists foreign-born Harlan County residents who became U.S. citizens in 1928: two from Germany, one each from Bulgaria and from France, and six Italians: Froneca Bucca (Francesco Bocca?), Joseph Mirawhile (Giuseppe Mirabile?), Elisevo Mirslli (Eliseo Marsili), Joseph Lawrence (Giuseppe Lorenzi?), Rosario Trucia (?), and Joseph Emillo (Giuseppe Emilio).[23] Name changes became part of the assimilation process: Lewis Bianchi notes that his name is pronounced "'Bianki' over there [in Italy]," but he pronounces it "Bianchi" himself: "It means 'white.'" "And a lot of the people couldn't say Mongiardo [pronounced "Monjardo"], and they started calling him Majority because it was easier. So he got with some of the politicians and he was always kidding them—you know, saying, 'You got the Majority on our side'" (*Frank Majority*).[24]

> JOE SCOPA JR.: Everybody that was foreign was "hunk," that was their slang word. Hungarians. They didn't say "wop," but they lumped everybody together. And every day I would have a fight over that, and I always felt like, you know, they made you feel like a outsider—like you're from here, but not really. I wanted to get out of here, because everybody was too, too prejudiced.

"You'd go by the houses and they'd always have chickens hanging up. They plucked the feathers and hung 'em up a day or two before they eat 'em (*Bryan Whitfield*). "Mamaw said that they had to live in the I-talian camp [in West Virginia], and the women had ovens outdoors, large brick ovens, and they'd build the fires, and they'd bake Italian bread. She said you could smell it forever, even from a long distance away" (*Janis Ross*). Ben Campagnari's father ordered cheese and pasta in bulk; Eliseo Marsili bought cheese, olive oil, and grapes to make his own wine. "We used to drink a lot of wine at the house, we had wine with every meal. My mother, she could cook all the Italian dishes" (*Lee Marsili*). Some kept the crafts they came with: Eliseo Marsili was a barber, and his son remembers Italian tailors making suits for Lynch employees at the company store.

> LEE MARSILI: When they had a holiday they used to wear the costume, traditional clothes. When I was about nineteen, twenty years old I saw it change; I never did wear it. They had a funeral, they had these suits they put on, they had medals, they had kind of ribbons across their chest, they dressed up for that occasion. They had an Italian brass band, and I remember when I was a kid the family that lived above us they had two girls that played accordion. I remember we used to listen to that Italian brass band, they played Italian songs.

"My father, he only got a fourth-grade education, he could read in Italian but couldn't write, he could read English but he couldn't write. And he wouldn't teach us Italian because—I didn't find out about that until last year, that he really didn't speak good Italian" (*Joe Scopa Jr.*).[25] "My dad spoke Italian, Hungarian, and Portuguese. He couldn't speak English when he got over here, I think he said he learned to speak English in about three months. It was still broken English, but there were a lot of Italian families, it was easier for them to communicate with each other. My mom and dad, they spoke Italian in the house. They tried to teach to us, but I was too lazy to pick it up" (*Lee Marsili*). Most immigrants were men, and as they married local women there was even less incentive to teach Italian (or their regional variant of it) to their children. "My mother could not speak Italian and all the language [my father] spoke at home was the American language. Now, when he worked with his fellows who talked his language, spoke in Italian. And, every once in a while, when he'd get mad at some of us kids, he spoke in Italian" (*Lewis Bianchi*).

Ben Campagnari's maternal grandfather was so upset at his daughter marrying a "hunk" that he got the judge to destroy the wedding certificate: "And they didn't know that they wasn't married until nineteen and twenty-seven when they went to sell that property in Italy. Lots of old-timers, back then, they thought a foreigner was a snake in the grass, something you better not monkey with."

"And [in] some cases the religion gets to be a big thing. A Baptist girl married a Catholic, well oh gosh, this was terrible" (*Arthur Johnson*). "There was anti-Catholic sentiment in Harlan when I was growing up," said Sid Douglass, who was raised as a Catholic and whose mother was Catholic. "A schoolteacher in public grade school spent an inordinate amount of time in history class teaching the horrors of the Spanish Inquisition, and a Sunday school teacher in a local Protestant church told the children 'what sinful things the Catholics were doing worshiping Mary.' My mother told me stories about growing up in Middlesboro, in Bell County, when, as a child, she was bullied for being a Catholic, and of the experience of having a cross burned in front of her family's house by the Ku Klux Klan because they were Catholic."

There was no Catholic church until the Church of the Resurrection was built in 1923 in Lynch, with stones quarried by Italian stonecutters on Pine Mountain, adorned with slabs of marble imported from Italy.[26] These church-less Catholics arrived into an intensely churched land and married Protestant women, which generated complicated processes of conversion and syncretism. Immigrants often found it easier to take on whatever religion was at hand, possibly one not too different from theirs. Presbyterianism might seem like "watered-down espresso" (*Joe Scopa Jr.*) but served the purpose for some. Italians in Whitesburg attended services in the Presbyterian church they helped build, but "at heart they remained Catholics" (*Frank Majority*). "We're Presbyterians here," a lady told me in Whitesburg, "but when we are back in Italy, we are Catholics again."

WE NEVER HAD ANY TROUBLE

JULIA COWANS: My family were from Rome, Georgia. But they were brought from down there when they were babies. Back in those days, some of them come up here and didn't know what mining was, really. They were farmers—"What the heck is a mining camp?" But they were glad to make a little money even under those conditions, and they'd write back home, and then the coal operators would pay them to go back and bring other families up. I heared Reverend Cowans's father tell about how down South

you'd have to slip away from them farms. Sharecroppers, that's the word
the reverend uses. The Reverend Cowans's father says you never did get out
of debt. You'd work all the whole year, every year you *almost* came out of
debt.

African Americans came to Harlan with the earliest settlers; interracial marriages were not unheard of in Appalachia before the Civil War and in the early
stages of industrialization. While many former slaves left the region after emancipation, African American immigration accompanied the building of the railroads and the creation of the coal towns.[27] Most of them carried with them the
memories and attitudes of the rural South. Minnie Randolph, well into her
nineties, was intrigued that her words would be heard by strangers and preferred
not to share with a strange white person the details of her life. She did teach me,
however, how to talk in pig Latin.

MINNIE RANDOLPH: It's a white world. Because the white folks is the head
of everything ever since I've been a little bitty kid used to work on this
farm. That was "yes sir boss" and like that. 'Cause my real home is down
in Georgia, and it used to be tough down in Georgia. And the blacks they
had to work in the field for the white folks. Work all day long for probably
a dollar, a day. The black have to get up, and wash the white folks' clothes,
so when this story comes out in I-talian, I guess some of them Georgia
whites'll come up here and hang me! I used to work on the farm, I didn't
have no house, we lived in old shacks and things, my mom and dad, we
weren't able to buy nothing. 'Course my mom and dad have been dead a
long time.

PORTELLI: Were they sharecroppers?

RANDOLPH: Yeah, that was cotton patches and corn fields. Plowin' mules.
You've seen anybody plow a mule? I have plowed. Yes, I have. I was a girl.
I did that on the farm, after I married, down in Georgia. And I didn't mean
for all this to come out, but it doesn't matter I guess, I'll be dead when all
of that come out. You make sure [you let my grandson] Bill hear it,
someway.

The white folks got everything. Everything. So I know you gonna make
sure you say she said: "It's a white world." There's so much that I know
about the South, that whities do, you know. They was very mean and nasty
to blacks. There's not so much difference in it now, because whities, they
acts pretty nice with blacks, but they all don't mean it.[28]

Some of the founders of the mining industry in Harlan were descendants of
former southern slave-owning families. Bryan Whitfield was from the same generation as Minnie Randolph. He moved to Harlan in 1911 with his father, chaired
the Harlan County Coal Operators Association in the thirties, and claimed to
have been the last operator to sign with the union in the whole United States.

BRYAN WHITFIELD: My father worked colored labor at Kitts, and he quit in 1915 or '16. I had a couple of colored drivers, but I didn't use any colored labor in the mine.

PORTELLI: Why?

WHITFIELD: Mister, my family was from the Deep South. My grandmother inherited 138 slaves when her father died. She died the day they fired on Fort Sumter. One of my grandfathers had about 300 slaves; I've got invoices for 250 slaves, I've got the price of 500 slaves. What did you reckon the average was? Seven hundred dollars, seven hundred and some odd dollars.

At this point, Whitfield rose and took a bound book from a shelf. It was an inventory of his grandfather's slaves, for inheritance purposes ("[He] left his daughters twenty-five or thirty [slaves] apiece, but he'd already given 'em a plantation stocked with everything, including slaves"). As I skimmed through the columns listing names, ages, conditions, and monetary value, one entry caught my eye: "Big John, 35—ruptured." "That man was ruptured," Whitfield explained. "He wasn't worth much." I was reminded of the stories about mules being worth more than men in the mines, and glimpsed a connection between the feudal paternalism of the coal camp and the heritage of the "paternal institution." Like many old-time slave owners, Whitfield reminisced about a faithful black cook: "I loved that old nigger just as well as anybody I ever did...We got along with 'em, but they were slaves."

ED CAWOOD: Nearly all families had one black person maybe work for them, cook and so forth. And we had a woman here, was a [former] slave, Aunt Bess Turner, and when they'd have dinners or so forth, they'd have these black people come in and cook. Most of them are wonderful cooks, but they were all subservient, I'd say. Very polite, never had much trouble with them because they didn't mix, socially, at all.

CHARLOTTE NOLAN: It was very segregated but we depended on them. The black people were very proud of the white people they worked for. I want you to know that this is a quote: we grew up in a time when black people "knew their place," when black people knew they were "inferior" to white people and kept their distance. We grew up in a time before the civil rights movement and the "I have a dream" speech, when the black people lived in the ghetto called Georgetown across the river and the people who worked for you came in the back door and left by the back door, did not walk up and down this front sidewalk, they went down the alley.

"[In the 1940s] we were up in a place called Louellen. And going to Harlan, you go through two or three communities where blacks wasn't allowed to live" (*Julia Cowans*). Or to die: "They didn't even bury the colored people in the same cemetery with the white people. They buried 'em outside in a special cemetery, over here at Crummies—they called it the 'colored graveyard.'" (*Chester Napier*).

TILLMAN CADLE: When I was a kid [1910–20] they had signs in all those little communities, "Nigger don't let the sun set on you here." All over the coal fields. And if a black man come walking through with his knapsack on his back, bunch of boys would get after him and would start throwing rocks, and if he didn't run some of the old guys'd pick their rifle off the wall, shoot under his feet to make him run.

At Wallins, "back then what they called the black people, they lived up on the hill. And the white people lived down in the low part. They had them in two different camps" (*Nellie Leach*). At Mary Helen, "the colored people lived across the ridge, that's all they could live over; and they lived up on a hill. But it was nice—don't get me wrong—it was nice houses" (*Chester Clem*). The camps, however, were too crowded to allow for total separation, and blacks and whites shared the same conditions working underground.

JULIA COWANS: My great-grandmother ran a boardinghouse, and Lord, she kept as many white kids in our house. We slept with 'em as much as I did with my sisters and brothers. I was raised with 'em. We played together, we fought together. And you don't even be *aware* of this prejudice as a child till you become a certain age and the parents go to separating, you know. And I wadn't—wasn't aware of the prejudiced conditions till I was about twelve years old. That's when I knew a black girl didn't have as much right as a white girl.

HAZEL KING: I feel now, looking back at it, there was an awful lot of discrimination. The deputies were more aggressive toward those people if—they called it stepping out of line, and they did have a line to toe. The whites lived on one side of the railroad tracks and the blacks lived on the other side; and they kept pretty much to themselves and as long as the fights were within their own groups they didn't disturb too much; but if they crossed the boundaries then there was something said and done about it. I mean, we didn't know anything about segregation, and we didn't even know what the word meant: it was so set, I mean there was no ifs, no ands, no buts to it; just a line, you just accepted it.

Segregation also prevailed in the "captive," northern-owned towns. "When you left that bridge [at Benham], everything this way is black till you get to the next line. And everything the other way is white. And it's still that way. [Yet] we grew up in an atmosphere that was not as segregated as some of the other places because, I guess, the people who came from the North they didn't have the hang-ups those people in the South had" (*Constance Ellison*). "In Lynch, all of the adult males were coal miners. So those guys had personal relationships and bondages based on the fact that they would spend their days and nights underground and often time had to depend on each other for, just for their survival. So, there was a lot of comradery. [Yet] the neighborhoods were separated. It is hard to talk about separation when the town only had about five or six streets; but still, it was segregated" (*Porter G. Peeples*).

These clearly defined boundaries allow narrators to claim that "we never had any trouble." Ed Cawood recalled that they "never had much trouble" because "they didn't mix, socially"; in the next breath, he added that white people "would have them in their homes, they were just part of the family, some of them." This, however, was not really "mixing" because "polite" black people "knew their place" and minded their manners. Often, African Americans also negotiated social and physical space so as to avoid trouble ("I never had any kind of race problems" because "[I] stayed in my place," *James L. Turner*) or to assert autonomy and independence, as in Julia Cowans's grandmother's teaching: "There's gonna always be a line. So you stay on your side, let them stay on theirs." "This was white territory over here—black territory was over there. Wasn't no mix-up. No confusion, none whatever" (*Kate Blue*).

Space boundaries and rituals of avoidance are only a faint reflection of the undercurrents of racial feelings in the culture. "My grandfather used to tell us when we was kids: first came the white man, then came the Indian, then comes the blacks, and the last came the dogs. It was his idea of how life stacked up" (*Mildred Shackleford*). Although he often had black people stay in his house, Chester Napier couldn't bring himself to vote for Jesse Jackson or Barack Obama. "To this day, I know I'm still prejudiced. I can't help it," he admitted. "That's the way I've been raised."

> NELLIE LEACH: We was raised up and taught to be afraid of the colored. We were taught that they carried sharp straight razors and they would cut your throat. My mom always taught us to be afraid of them. And I was always afraid of them until I got grown, we got acquainted with colored people. I saw they were just like we were, [it was] just the color of their skin, that's all.

Jim Garland recalls a riot in Cary (Bell County), in 1923, after a white man was shot by a black man in an argument over a black woman: "Within a week, all the blacks in Cary had gone, leaving all that they owned behind....I don't think any blacks have lived there since the riot."[29] Trouble erupted when boundaries were blurred or violated, and there were countless ways in which black people could be considered in violation—if they joined the union, for one. But the most dramatic line was drawn at the intersection of "race" and sex. According to Earl Turner, "Most of those blacks coming that way back when they were building the railroads, after slavery time, they mixed in with whites and...you couldn't tell 'em from the white people. They were considered black people—but they were blue-eyed. A lot of that went back in these mountains, you know, these mountain towns. You meet some girls, honey, you couldn't tell 'em from white girls and boys, you couldn't tell 'em apart. Miscegenation, they was just mixing up. But you never hear nothing about it."[30] Yet "anytime that they wanted to bring trouble with the minorities, they'd use a black man and a white woman. I don't care how much this white man said he love you, he don't want that black man fooling with that white woman. And they know this. The Klan knows this" (*Julia Cowans*). Blues singer Iverson Minter Cook, aka Louisiana Red, told me about his father's death in Harlan County, possibly in Lynch, in 1941.

IVERSON MINTER COOK: We got a telegram, and it said Leroi Cook is dead. Well—I wasn't in Harlan; he was there. It's a coal-mining area. And he got killed, these Ku Kluck Klans. I was five years old. All I know, we got the telegram and, they had come to ask us where we'd bury the body. I remember precisely me, climbing on a chair, getting my granddaddy's shotgun...My grandmother told me that he went up on this hill, following his wife. His wife, she looked like she was white, but she wasn't. But [they thought he was with a white woman] and they ganged upon him. And knocked a hole in his head. I saw it, they had it covered up in the coffin. And they killed him. What you call a lynch mob.

MOSSIE JOHNSON: There is a colored camp, way down Straight Creek, almost Forks Creek. But one time there was a nigger, and he...done something to this girl up Forks, I don't know what he done to her, I think he killed her. And they hung him in the courthouse yard when my mother was twelve year old, because she said she went for the hanging. And that's something I can't understand, is why they have a big meeting, in a public place to hang a person. They didn't allow them up in Left Fork no more after, after they hung that nigger. They hung him in the courthouse yard.

Racial violence is endemic in newspaper reports of the 1920s and '30s.[31] From 1875 to 1900 there were at least 165 lynchings in Kentucky; two-thirds of the victims were black, the ratio increasing with the coming of railroads and coal mines. In 1919, a race riot in Corbin expelled all black people from the town: today, "Corbin is the only place I ever know was nigger free" (*Ray Ellis*).[32] The last "official" lynching took place in 1934, in Hazard (Perry County). A mob of nearly three hundred people took from the county jail twenty-year-old Rex Scott, charged with attempted murder after fighting with a white miner who had insulted him. His body was found riddled with bullets and hanging from a tree in Knott County.[33]

An undated picture in a supplement to the *Harlan Daily Enterprise* shows a Ku Klux Klan train departing from Clover Fork to Louisville; children are in the foreground.[34] Going into Wallins Creek, I noted a big graffiti scrawl—"Nigger lovers"—on the wall of a run-down building.

LLOYD STOKES: The Ku Klux Klan, they'd put on them big white things and burn crosses and that kind of stuff. There's a store right on the right there

as you come into town, there's some sign there yet from that Ku Klux Klan.
It's been there for years.

PORTELLI: What kind of people joined the Ku Klux Klan?

STOKES: Pretty nice people, most of them. That used to be against the black
people, you see. They just burned crosses and do this that and the other,
and wear them white clothes.

Mildred Shackleford recalls that Bill Worthington, a charismatic black union
miner, said that in the 1920s "the biggest thing they did was that somebody got
drunk and beat their wife up, then the Klan would go in and give 'im a beating
and tell him not to be bothering her anymore. And they kept a lot of laws in coal
camp towns, but they wasn't based upon doing bad things to black people."
Among the "nice people" that joined the Klan were union members and
preachers. "[Many] of them, that I knew that was Ku Kluxers, were preachers.
Preachers, they were all for it, and a lot of people was fooled by it, they didn't
know what the Ku Klux was. Ministers would make out that they was against
anything that was ungodly and that the Ku Klux was going to help straighten
things out" (Tillman Cadle).

> MILDRED SHACKLEFORD: The KKK, the last time they tried to make a come-
> back during the seventies, they called my mother up and asked her to join
> and she told them, if you will pardon my language, her exact words was
> that she was not a yellowed-bellied son of a bitch that had to dress up in
> a white sheet and go around and scare kids, and if that was all those peo-
> ple had to do, then by God they needed to take it someplace else.

In 1975, the KKK rallied in Verda to hear an address by Grand Imperial Dragon
David Duke. The local paper reported: "We arrived early to find burly Klansmen
dressed in their robes and hoods hard at work preparing a large cross soaked in
gasoline that would be ignited at the end of Duke's speech."[35] A few years before,
another murder had sanctioned another violation of the sexual (and class) line
of partition: "Around Bledsoe, across Pine Mountain. Black girl and a white
man. The community burned their home down" (Dallas Blue).

> KEVIN GREER: My cousin ———. They hung her up on Pine Mountain.
> They hung her up on Pine Mountain because she was with a white man.
> What happened is, she went with a well-known white gentleman from
> downtown—he was one of the upper class—and he must've felt alone,
> because he would come over all the time. They arrested her for prostitu-
> tion, but she never made it to the jail. And the next morning we get news
> that she was found hung and burnt. [It was in] '71—'72.

> JULIA COWANS: I lived down the hill and some families lived kind [of] up
> the hill. They didn't have no mother, but they had a father, these boys.
> And every day at noon them kids would come out from over at that school,

right up that hill, up to this house, white and black, girls and boys. You'd see 'em sneaking, going up there, to this house. Well, some of the white parents got ahold to it, and they started raising a whole lot of Cain. In fact, the daddy of two of the girls he got the police: "My girl's up here, in this house with these black boys. I want you to put them in jail." [The sheriff] said, "Now wait a minute. Have your girls cried rape? Was anybody raped? I sat and watched them come and you watched them come up to that hill and go to that house. I can't put anybody in jail."

The tragedy that might have followed was prevented also by the changed attitude of black people. Julia Cowans made it clear that the past was over: "I said, 'Ain't nobody gonna drag my son or my daughter out, like they have done and hang them or whatever.' I said, 'Have been a time that this happened, didn't nobody die but black.' I said, 'But, brother, you better believe that if they bury somebody black, they gonna bury somebody white.' I said, 'You'd better believe that.'"

"I didn't know the difference between black and white poor, we was all poor" (*Annie Napier*). "Well, being poor and being black is almost the same thing except just adding another point onto them" (*Becky Simpson*). "And I'm gonna tell you something else too. It wasn't only the black people that caught the devil during the time of the struggle of the coal mine, to organize. There were white people who went through hell too. But even the worst condition for the white man was better than the best for the black man" (*Julia Cowans*). During the union organizing days, killing black people was perceived as an ordinary occurrence.

FRED NAPIER: [When I was working in Virginia] they had a little trouble over the railroad, they sent in a bunch of them Alabama colored guys to work, get them much cheaper than they could the people here. And the section foreman, got up one morning, he said, "I'm gonna get rid of some of them niggers." And he killed eleven of them and made us throw them in the creek. I was working on the railroad, and throwed them in the river, eleven of them. He killed eleven of them and the rest of them got away before he got them. 'Cause he didn't want the work to be taken from the white men. They had signs that said "Read nigger and run." If they didn't run to get out of there, they'd kill them. They didn't allow no niggers to work, on account of the white men.

CHESTER NAPIER: When they was organizing the union here, my dad's cousin George Lee told me—well, I'll say the *n*-word what he called 'em. He said he killed he knowed thirty-five niggers.[36] That's colored people. See, they brought the colored people in here, shipped 'em in from the South, they bringed 'em in on trains to break the union and work in the mines. They was trying to organize a union. He said he would just kill 'em and throw 'em in the creek or whatever. He said it wasn't nothing after a thunderstorm, to see three or four colored people floating down the river. They didn't prosecute you for it back then. Nobody ever spent any time over killing 'em. They didn't count a colored person as nothing. I guess white people thought more of their dogs than they did the colored people. Uncle George Lee, he'd tell me them stories. I took it all to be the gospel truth. I don't know if it was or not.

While shared exploitation made for class unity, operators played on racial prejudice to divide the workers. Johnny Jones, who had been a union miner in Alabama before he moved to Kentucky, recalled the segregated union meetings in Tuscaloosa and the racial wage differentials: "You take this race hatred and stuff, all that sprung from the money man. They get betwixt you and me and make us distrust each other, and make people kill each other for a lousy dollar" (*Johnny Jones*). "They even brought a lot of men out of prison for strike breakers. In Bell County and Harlan County, they brought them out of prison, the worst criminals, killers. But some of 'em when they got here, find out about working conditions and what they brought them for, they went union. They took the miner's creed as brothers, and brother don't fight against brother" (*Julia Cowans*). Jerry Johnson recalled that Bill Worthington told him that his father used to ride the trains that carried "scabs" to Harlan County from the South, and "by the time they got to Harlan he had them organized, and soon as they got off the train they joined the struggle."

"When we is down there, all covered with coal dust, we is *all* black!" (*Bill Worthington*). The UMWA was the first labor union in the United States whose constitution includes a firm prohibition against racial, religious, or national discrimination.[37] However, "interracial cooperation began and ended at the mine entrance. Black and white miners would emerge side by side from the portal of Lynch Mine 31 at the end of a shift and then part ways to enter the washhouse by different doors to shower and change clothes in a building with a wall dividing blacks from whites." "Once the work day ended," Jim Garland writes, "blacks and whites were separated, living in different coal camps, attending different churches and schools."[38]

Inside, black miners were mostly confined to the less skilled and most dangerous jobs. "They'd take 'em in the deepest part, the dangerous part in there. They was expendable, you know," *Kevin Greer*. "At first they held jobs that the whites didn't care for. When they got more modern equipment, and you just shift levers and maybe change a little piece of steel that may have weighed less than five pounds, they had more whites that wanted those jobs" (*Tommy Sweatt*). Black skilled workers were systematically bypassed for promotion in favor of white men they might have trained themselves. Only in the 1970s did Earl Turner become the first black mine foreman in Harlan County. "Most of the boys you got was white boys, and it's pretty hard, pretty hard to work some of 'em. It went back to slavery time, I guess. Most mountain dudes couldn't think of a black man telling him what to do" (*Earl Turner*).

HUGH COWANS: My father, he's passed and gone now, told me, says, "You're crazy to go on those picket lines. You'll get killed." He said, "It's not going to benefit anybody but the white man." I says, "Well, I know it will benefit him more than it benefits me, but I see some good in that for you and I see some in it for me. In your old age, I see medical benefits, I see retirement, and everything. I know that it is discriminatory practice in it, but it's better than what we have working in these water holes and slave condition." And, sure enough, when he reached the age of retirement, he had medical benefits. He died drawing his pension.

MILDRED SHACKLEFORD: When the union was at its height in Harlan County, they had a lot of interrelationship between the blacks and the whites because you couldn't be accepted into the union if you were not willing to accept everybody. Bill Worthington used to tell me about softball games and stuff that he had with people down there. Thirty years ago, these black people, these white people were playing with each other and were eating together and sitting around together. They should keep that in mind and not forget it because that is one of the things that, it makes people stronger—to remember what they've had and hang on to it will make you a better, decent human being. Don't ever turn it loose and don't ever forget it. Because when you do, you lose something and Harlan County has lost a lot of it. So we are having to do it all over again.

STAND TOGETHER

HAZEL LEONARD: When I was born at Kitts the first strike in Harlan County was there. That was August 11, 1917. I heard my daddy talking, but I don't remember much he said, because he didn't stay there too long. I grew up at Wallins; I do remember when I started school there, and I remember my dad working in the mines, he ran a motor. And they had a big strike when we were there. The mine was owned by Henry Ford, and the name was Banner Fork, at Wallins Creek, you know where that is.

"In 1917 the United Mine Workers of America came into Harlan. There was a strike: the blacklist appeared for the first time in the Kentucky hills."[39] Founded in the 1890s, the UMWA had already fought epic battles in Appalachia, such as the strikes at Paint Creek and Cabin Creek in West Virginia in 1912–13. During World War I, the union began organizing in eastern Kentucky: "Kentucky and Tennessee and all these Appalachian regions, they never did get organized until 1917, about the time of the First World War. Well you see, when this war broke out, they knew there was going to be a big demand for coal. Then the union officials, they took advantage and come into that area, and began organizing. They knew that the coal companies would not put up a fight because they'd want [to] make quick dollars out of this wartime coal" (*Tillman Cadle*).

On June 10, 1917, twenty-five hundred miners gathered at the Harlan County courthouse square to hear a speech by UMW organizer William Turnblazer; about fifteen hundred joined the union. The operators refused to meet with them, and on August 11 they struck. The employers responded with violence: armed guards and scabs shot at the strikers at Benham; strike leader Luther Shipman was killed by a bullet in the back of his head. After two months, the strike ended in an arbitration mediated by the federal government, and the miners gained a wage increase, shorter hours, an elected checkweighman, and a grievance committee. By July 1918, all the mines in Harlan except Benham and Lynch were organized.[40]

> SAM REECE: Nineteen seventeen—that was when they had the trouble. We was loading coal, and you loaded coal by the car, thirty cents a car, and the cars'd hold from a ton to a ton and a half, and you pushed it and strained yourself to death. Thirty cents a car and there wasn't no such thing as hours, you got $1.71 for driving a mule, and sometimes it'd be eight p.m. before you got out of there. And they brought the state militia, hired all them thugs, they had thugs down here at Yellow Creek, and we finally had to leave and to get out and moved to Harlan County. [An organizer] come to us and said, "Sam, you better leave," say, "They are going to kill you." Said, "They gonna kill all of you." I said, "What about you?" Said, "Don't matter about me; I'm gonna take some of them with me."

As soon as the war was over, the operators "set in trying to break the union. When our contract would expire, then they'd start trying to run the mines without a contract, and trying to get in strike breakers to break the union" (*Tillman Cadle*).[41] The 1917 agreement bound the UMWA not to renegotiate the contract until the end of the war; however, when it expired in 1919, the peace treaty had not been signed yet and the war was not technically over. Meanwhile, the operators had been getting organized.

> BRYAN WHITFIELD: [The Harlan County Coal Operators Association] was formed because West Virginia and the other sections of the country had better freight rates than we did. I believe it was 1917, '19. We always had trouble with coal because we had unfavorable rates, freight rates. West Virginia, and Ohio and Indiana, they were close to the market, and we were further away. Just too much difference in the freight rates.
> PORTELLI: So you either had to run up the price or cut the cost of labor?
> WHITFIELD: Yeah, we cut the price of labor. Everybody did.

On November 1, 1919, the UMW called a national mine strike. In Harlan, the union managed to close all the mines except Benham and Lynch. The strike ended officially on November 11, when President Wilson obtained an injunction ordering the men back to work. John L. Lewis, the union's new, charismatic president, told the miners to go back to the mines: "I will not fight my government," he said, "the greatest government on earth."[42] The rank-and-file miners, however, stayed out until mid-December, when an arbitration by the newly created Bituminous Coal Commission awarded them shorter hours and a wage increase.

Harlan operators, however, refused to accept these terms, and as the strike went on they fired and evicted hundreds of union miners and their families. Violence flared again: two miners and a deputy sheriff were killed in a shootout at Ford's Banner Fork mine.[43] Miners were being starved into going back to work on the 1917 wage scale; the promised aid from the UMW had not materialized, and all attempts at arbitration had failed.[44] As coal demand and prices declined, wages and employment fell even more rapidly. "Such a condition naturally places a hardship on the laboring man," the *Harlan Enterprise* admitted. In 1922, the union struck again, but it was weakened by internal dissention, poor management, and inexperienced leadership, and the strike ended in defeat.[45]

TILLMAN CADLE: I guess this was round 1919. I was up in Harlan County, and they was a man, he had lost his leg in the mines, was on one of these peg legs they called it; but he still worked in the mines. We was on strike then. The miners they never pulled no picket lines or nothing like that. They just went out and pitched horseshoes or played cards and sat around and stayed away from the mines. These companies they was wanting to get trouble started and break the strike. Then they hired some of these gunmen; these gunmen, if they couldn't get some trouble started, they wouldn't have a job, you see. Their job depended on trouble. And so they kept prowling the roads; I could see them up and down the road with their big flashy guns and—there was this one-legged man and this neighbor had come over to talk with him. My God, they went in there, about ten of them, and shot that man down in cold blood right on the floor. And walked out. And when they arrested them the miners over the whole district began making up money to prosecute them. There was so much resentment against them murdering these men, you see, this one-legged man was a very religious man, I don't suppose he ever owed a gun in his life. So then one of these gunmen, his name was ———, took the rap on himself. And they gave him a life sentence. But they already had a pardon wrote up on him, he never did go to prison. See, I began to see then what justice was like.

In memory, all these strikes overlap and run together. Miners and their families remember less a series of discrete labor conflicts than a continuous state of war, marked by the violence of company guards, scabs, lockouts, evictions, the National Guard, and the blacklist ("My dad, he used to work around here for a union mine so they blackballed him, he had to go to Leslie County," *J. C. Hall*).

HAZEL LEONARD: I don't remember that strike at [Wallins]. I heard my dad talk about it, it seems real. They had a bad shootout there, it killed some people, an awful killing. I do remember him saying he saw his uncle being killed, Uncle Bud Taylor, he called him. They had machine guns, and they was just mowing the men down. The other side, the scabs. Probably the National Guard, I don't know. Could be company men, too. It certainly was war; it was war for a while. But they got their contract, it was probably the first one at that mine.

"It was rough, really rough, and there's several killed, there's five killed up here, in the hollow at one time. They had what the union people called them gun thugs. They [came] down and searched houses, without a search warrant or anything" (*Lloyd Stokes*). "Little Donald Noe, that was my daddy's aunt's boy, okay? He was killed over the union, you see. It was before I was ever born, when they was a-battling then. He was shot down at the courthouse steps, little Donald Noe, you know, which otherwise would have been my daddy's first cousin" (*Sudie Crusenberry*).

PLENNIE HALL: I holp organize Harlan County, and I seen a many good man die fighting for his rights, for his children to have a bite to eat. I was working when I was thirteen, and I got thirty-two cents a ton. I was awfully glad to get that much. I've got a whole lot of scars [from] bullets. It's too rough to think about now, I don't want to talk about it much now. It gets on your nerves, you old and went through all this stuff. It would be bloody war, you know. You had some awful good friends to get killed. The company's against you, seem like the whole world against you and there ain't nobody to help you. Seeing good friends die trying to make this thing good, it's too hard to think about. That's what burns you.

Miners, on the other hand, were learning to retaliate in kind. Sam Reece recalled that when carloads of company guards raided a union meeting, the miners chased them off with guns. Scabs were beaten at Yellow Creek, in Bell County; at Funde, a group of striking miners seized three scabs, and "with cowbells attached to their necks and hands tied behind their backs, these miners were 'ordered to run to the accompaniment of shots being fired.' They were then told to start down the railroad track and not return to work in the mines until a settlement was reached."[46] Another time, Sam Reece and a posse of armed union men disarmed two company guards who had beaten a union miner: "Then we put a cow bell on their wrist and every time the bell quit ringing they got their bottom kicked. Having gone a mile and a half to the line, and another bunch picked them up there. When we come to the big trestle, this other bunch, they got mean and they wanted to hang them at the trestle, and I said, "No, you ain't gonna do that." I wouldn't let them hang them. This was in the twenties."[47]

MILDRED SHACKLEFORD: My grandmother, Mom's mother, she used to tell us wonderful stories. Back in the twenties was one of the times they had one of the strikes and they brought in the state police to control the strikers. Have you heard some of this before? My grandmother told me this story, about this boardinghouse that was supposed to been at Highsplint or Closplint or someplace up in there. She was rooming with these two old women and they were highly displeased because [of] militia being in town, and they considered them scabs and scum of the earth and so forth. So I reckon for about two weeks straight they saved slops, if you know what I mean. There was outdoor bathrooms but at nighttime they had slop jars for people to use. So when they caught the troops coming by the window there one day, they just emptied all the slop as they walked by.

In his memoir, G. C. Jones writes about "people being killed, their women being raped [by the military], their homes being dynamited, burned and shot into...I could see men lying in ditches with the whole tops of their heads shot off. Men floating down Martin's Fork, bloated beyond recognition...deputies rolling bodies of striking miners over the edges of the road, watching them roll and slide into deep, dark wooded ravines." In an ambush, he writes, a roving union picket "riddled with bullets" fourteen state militiamen and three "thugs."[48]

Social conflict escalated to what amounted to a localized civil war in 1919–22 in West Virginia. Miners took up arms against the peculiar Appalachian combination of feudal oppression and capitalist exploitation, embodied in the reign of terror waged by the private agents contracted by the operators. "I've heared about that union war in West Virginia. The union mine workers was trying to organize that country and they had a lot of killings up there. One guy told me that he was in the National Guard and he said he had to stay six months up there, and he said there was killing nearly every day" (*Ben Lewis*).

JACK COLLEY: I grew up in Logan County, West Virginia; first union [battle] that I can recall about was 1919, or nineteen and twenty. The coal operators, they didn't want to have anything to do with the union. They had an agency, called it Baldwin Felts, that was located in Bluefield, West Virginia—so-called detectives, but what they were they were gun thugs, ex-gangsters, the rough element. These coal operators paid these fellows to do their dirty work. A fellow doing what they thought was not right according to the company, they'd go to his home, drag him out, kick him, and tell him to straighten up or get out. Many times he wouldn't straighten up, so they'd take him out of the house, load his things on wagon or a truck, and boot him out of the camp.

"Medieval West Virginia!" wrote the legendary union organizer Mother Jones: "With its tent colonies on the bleak hills? With its grim men and women? When I get to the other side, I shall tell God Almighty about West Virginia!"[49] In September 1919, a miners' march on the nonunion territory of Logan County was stopped by threats of army intervention and promises of an investigation into conditions. On May 19, 1920, in Matewan (Mingo County), a confrontation between the chief of police, Sid Hatfield, and a group of Baldwin-Felts guards that had come into town to evict striking miners' families from their company-owned homes resulted in the death of ten men, including Matewan's mayor, two bystanders, and seven Baldwin-Felts guards.[50]

> JEFF SALMAN (NAME CHANGED): That stuff over in West Virginia around Matewan had happened and they pretty much [started a] war, not only with the coal miners but the federal government. My dad was there, at fourteen, he was in the thick of it. His father had been killed in the mines. And one of the stories my grandmother told me was that in the middle of the night she'd hear this noise, this tat-tat-tat, and she's telling my grandfather, "I want to go across the mountains to my sister, I'm scared here." He said, "Hell woman, that's where the war's at." And the next morning there were seven dead people in that coal mining camp, that were dead and that had been assassinated for being scabs.

On July 21, 1921, Sid Hatfield, identified by then as a union supporter, was killed on his way to trial by company guards on the steps of the Matewan courthouse. Armed miners gathered and started marching into Mingo and Logan counties. Federal troops were called in. UMW leaders Fred Mooney and Frank Keeney, as well as Mother Jones herself, tried to stop the march, yet at the end of August ten thousand armed miners started toward Logan County and were met on Blair Mountain by company guards and deputy sheriffs. The battle resulted in at least thirty dead, from both sides. "There's a mountain that separates Madison County [and] Logan County, they call it Blair Mountain. And they had regular pitched battles out there, they had trenches, there was a lot of bloodshed. They used airplanes, they shot down [from] airplanes" (Jack Colley). The miners were actually bombed from planes hired by the operators and later, when federal troops were sent in to put an end to the strike, from those of the U.S. Army Air Service.

Some of the people involved in the West Virginia wars later found their way to Harlan County. Lawrence "Peggy" Dwyer, who had delivered guns to the marchers on Blair Mountain, was a UMW organizer there in the 1910s and the 1930s; Tillman Cadle identified one of Hatfield's murderers among the company spies at a miners' rally in Pineville in 1931.[51] Union miners never forgot the West Virginia wars: after Matewan and Blair Mountain, said Jeff Salman, "my dad stayed active in union organizing throughout his life. And that meant that if you was in Harlan and you were from our family you were union and damn you if you weren't."

The 1922 strike left Harlan County miners in a "terrible" condition: as UMW secretary Edward E. Reed noted, "Miners have worked but one day a week since the settlement of the strike." While claiming that "no real suffering exists in this field," even the *Harlan Enterprise* recognized that "it has been necessary for the miners to use economy."[52] Homeless and hungry families moved into barns and garages; milk cows were killed for meat. The UMW failed to deliver the promised relief, and the miners "agreed not to pay any more dues or not to belong to the United Mine Workers."[53] By 1924, the union had been virtually wiped out of Harlan County. "They said before we should have a meeting in Harlan County that the river would run blood" (*Sam Reece*). Organizing had to take place in secret: "[My husband] never got home till after midnight, they was always planning, you know, and having meetings and getting together" (*Hazel Leonard*). Cecil Cita, a UMWA organizer, testified years later:

> Lewis sent me to Harlan in 1922. When I got there I saw we could do nothing. They killed anyone who talked union. My wife and I stuck to the house we were staying in. One night we were sitting in the bay window. We were sitting in the dark when something crashed through the window. I struck a match. I found a big rock. A stick of dynamite was tied to it. . . . I sent my wife upstairs. I woke the woman who owned the house. She gave me her husband's gun. He was in jail for being a union man. I went back to the bay window. I sat in the dark with that gun in my hand. . . . Next morning I called Lewis. I asked him to take me out. "You can't do nothing in Harlan," I told Lewis.[54]

In March 1924, a few mines signed a UMW contract, on a scale "slightly lower than 1917 wages." In April, troops were called in "to suppress mine trouble" at Straight Creek: "The mine installed 15 guards with high-powered rifles. The State sent one machine gun company and one rifle company." According to Jim Garland, the company also brought in scabs, and prostitutes to entertain them; a group of miners raided the brothel and sent them off.[55] The only surviving union local, at Black Mountain, struck in March, when the contract expired. The company and the authorities responded by appointing company guards as deputy sheriffs, importing replacement workers, evicting dozens of union families, and keeping the mine open under the protection of high-powered rifles and machine guns. In September, the strike was lost, the local disbanded, and the men had to leave the county because no Harlan operation would hire them.[56]

"By the late 1920s the bituminous coal industry was a disaster area." In 1927, transport rates from the South and the Great Lakes were unified, and eastern Kentucky coal lost the edge that had kept it competitive. Production fell below the 1920 level; thousands of miners found only part-time work, making hardly enough to survive.[57] Caleb Powers, one of the organizers who came to Harlan in 1917, recalled that the UMW "died down here . . . about 1927. They kept cutting wages down until you couldn't make hardly anything at all."[58]

In 1929, Peggy Dwyer wrote to UMW's vice-president, Philip Murray: "After arriving here in Kentucky, I found that conditions was terrible. The men here in Bell County tell me they make from $5 to $7 dollars per week, it is not much better in Harlan County, and the men appeared to be whipped out and discouraged having lost all vim and spirit."[59] "They set in to break the union, and they finally did break it. At the time of the Great Depression, we didn't have no union at all" (*Tillman Cadle*). It would have to be rebuilt from scratch in the years to come.

9

NO NEUTRALS THERE

A GLASS BETWEEN US

"When the Depression hit, this company said for me to come, to take a job with them. It was Yancey in Harlan County. Then this mines got to working very slack, till they was only working one day a week" (*Tillman Cadle*). A skilled track-man, Cadle was allowed to work four or five days a week. But "my neighbor living in the next mining shack right by my side, when his one [working] day would come, I would have to give him food before he'd be able to go and work. They had no food to eat, and the man couldn't go in the mines to work but he had something to eat."

> MILDRED SHACKLEFORD: During the Depression, my grandmother kept the family alive by selling vegetables and stuff to coal camps. [She] would put it on her back and walk through the town and sell it. Daddy was four and five years old and he was out hoeing corn and beans and she would take the best stuff and sell it. Having that little piece of land made a lot of difference in what kind of lifestyle they had, how much food they had to eat. Made them richer, much richer than a lot of people in Harlan County.

In the spring of 1931, the Harlan coal industry was in trouble: the Depression was on, the winter had been mild, the coal demand from the industrial regions of the Great Lakes was slow. "People was just starving everywhere. They couldn't get no work, they got no money. [We had the farm so] it didn't hurt us. But we helped a lot of people though, all we could" (*Melinda Slusher*). "All over in the country, they'd help each other. They'd have a big farm, some of them, and they'd raise stock and help each other, and that's the way they lived" (*Lloyd Stokes*). On January 7, 1931, the local paper ran the headline "Future for Coal Business Bright According to Harlan County Coal Operators' Association."[1] On February 16, the same HCCOA announced a 10 percent wage cut.

> HAZEL KING: Food was scarce, jobs were even scarcer, and there was much plundering. If someone had a hog, pigs, cattle, chicken or what have you, you had to watch it very carefully, or it would disappear. I remember my mother telling about this one hog that disappeared and they trailed the blood to this man's home, and when they picked him up for stealing the

hog he just told them, "Yes, I've got it, my family was starving," and it was a question of either getting it or them starving.

TILLMAN CADLE: [We were] standing in front of a big store, I don't remember whether it was A&P or Kroger's, and I could see these hungry people looking at this food, through the window—couldn't buy it, didn't have no money. And I said, "Boys, we worked to make all that good food, and yet there's a piece of glass between us." And one day we was having a big mass meeting in Pineville, and there was a fellow, his name was Randalls, they called him the cussing preacher, he was a preacher but he could talk very violently sometime, and he was the last speaker at this meeting. And when he started to close his speech he said, "Well, I guess we'll all be gathering back here next weekend for another meeting," and they began clamoring out in the crowd, "What's the use to go home if you can't take any food to your family?" He asked, how many there was in that crowd, that didn't have any food in their homes for supper; and a whole gang of hands went up. He jumped down off of the steps, and he said: "Foller me." And he made a break for the A&P store; and by God, they was all follering him.

In the winter of 1931, stores were looted all over Bell and Harlan counties; between March and April, the *Enterprise* reported seven raids by "mobs" or "large crowds" on company or commercial stores.[2]

RAY ELLIS: They [broke into] the A&P store [in Evarts], they didn't have food to get through the winter, so they came with salt sacks—"Come in and get it boys." Same thing the next night. And my uncle, he run the IGA store here and he had to hire six or seven men to stay with it at night. You ought to seen that railroad, where they busted flour, discarded stuff—they had more than they could carry and they'd have to destroy some, it was all up and down the railroad.

TILLMAN CADLE: It scared the hell out of that man at the A&P store, and he began pleading with [preacher Randalls] to let him call the manager in Louisville. He said, "You call the manager and be damn sure you don't call no cops, we don't want to kill no cops." He called the manager in Louisville, and the manager told him, "You tell 'em that we're gonna give them some food, but tell 'em not to take it all from us, to let the others help too." The next weekend instead of having it in Pineville they had it in Middlesboro. And they had people a-going to all the stores and making out packages for the desperate people.

Harry and Bema Appleman, Harlan store owners, fed fifty children for free every day; since this was a way of helping strikers, they were indicted for "criminal syndicalism."[3] The Red Cross refused to help the miners, claiming that relief had to come from local sources, with local money (controlled by the operators).[4] And people went hungry.

"The principal food of the miners," Jim Garland testified, "is potatoes, beans and bacon—salt pork. Then, they make gravy. We call it 'bull dog gravy': a mixture of water, flour and grease, eaten with beans or with a 'water sandwich' (bread soaked in lard and water).'"[5] Sudy Gates, from Straight Creek, testified:

> The children are so cold, they turn blue. They try to go to school and try to learn but they have not got the energy to learn. . . . The wives here, you don't see a one that has sufficient clothes to go out in public. Their shoes is off their feet. They have them tied with strings. In the summer, if they happen to have a pair of shoes, they don't wear them, they save them for the cold winter. The kids they go around with no shoes and no food, do you wonder why we are losing children?[6]

On the left-hand fork of Straight Creek, Jim Garland reported, "at least 25 young children died with one disease, known as flux, during that spring and early summer. . . the doctors told me, that it was caused by eating one diet, and the lack of milk or such food as a baby should have. The way the disease works, it inflames their stomach and entrails, and they bleed." Conditions were not much better before the Depression: people in the coal camps had lived on beans, cornbread (usually without milk), and bulldog gravy. Milk was hard to find; in some camps malnutrition and diarrheal diseases (flux) killed as many as one person a day.[7] A state health officer told the Senate's Costigan Committee that the deaths from flux of children under two years of age numbered 56 in 1929, 91 in 1930, and 84 in 1931. Mortality rate of infants under one year oscillated between 86.6 per thousand births in 1929 and 87.2 in 1931.[8] Molly Jackson, union activist and midwife, remembered:

> I still hear hungry children cry. I held them in my arms and saw them die with the diseases of poverty—T.B., pellagra, and the bloody flux. I saw my own sister's fourteen-month-old baby starve to death for milk while the coal operators was riding around in fine cars with their wives and children all dressed up in diamonds and silk, paid for by the blood and sweat of the coal miners.[9]

On February 2, 1931, miner B. R. Gilbert wrote to UMW president John L. Lewis from Crummies Creek:

> DEAR BRO: This is an appeal to you for Help I haven't had a single days work since Black Mt. went down the operators of Harlan Co. wont let me work in or around the mines I have exhausted all my means I had saved when we had a job now I am at the mercy of the people I still preach unionism to every working man I see. . . .I really need some help I am humbly beggin you Bro Lewis, for help in some way. Please don't turn me down I have 2 little children and no Mother to them to help me if there is any way you can think of to help me you will always be remembered by me and make the hearts of those precious little kids glad.

Two weeks later, Lewis answered: "[I] am sorry indeed to know of the circumstances in which you find yourself. I am compelled, however, to advise you that under the laws governing the International Union there are no funds available for individual relief and it is, therefore, impossible for me to assist you. I trust you will be able to make other satisfactory arrangements to care for your needs."[10]

A WAR AGAINST STARVATION

"You could tell there was something in the air," recalled Chester Poore, who would spend ten years in jail for his alleged participation in the events that followed: "Evidently it had to be—not knowing where the next damn meal was coming from."[11] Two weeks after the wage cut, William J. Turnblazer, president of UMW District 19, and UMW vice president Philip Murray told a gathering of two thousand miners that the union was ready to come back. "The spirit of the miners in Harlan County," Turnblazer wrote to Lewis, "is just wonderful. I never saw a body of men who are making such a fight, notwithstanding they have been told that we could not extend any finance to them they continue to carry on."[12]

In fact, the union was actually asking *them* for money. "They wanted ten dollars initiation fee and nobody had ten dollars. Most of them couldn't get nothing to eat. So, they couldn't join the union if they'd wanted to" (*Tillman Cadle*). Jim Garland writes: "Anyone there, had he been any man at all, would have bought ten dollars worth of milk for his child before giving that money to any organization." However, hundreds did join: in some homes, "beds were sold in order to pay this dollar."[13]

The day after the meeting in Pineville, companies whose spies had reported the names of attending miners began to discharge and evict them. At Black Mountain, company guards threw women and children out of company homes and dumped their possessions into the road.[14] Most of the evicted miners and families moved to Evarts, "an independent town, the only place they was safe" (*Ray Ellis*). And they began to organize—"but it was the rank and file done this, they didn't have no leadership at all, only the rank-and-file leaders" (*Tillman Cadle*). W. B. Jones, a Black Mountain miner fired for attending the rally at Pineville, was chosen as local secretary; William Hightower, an illiterate seventy-seven-year-old miner who had been fired by Harlan-Wallins for union activity, was elected president.[15] Thousands of miners took the union oath and marched throughout the county, waving the American flag. By late April, the local had more than eight thousand members.[16]

> TILLMAN CADLE: When they started organizing, they'd have these big mass meetings on Saturdays. They'd have little meetings back at the mines where they worked, but these big mass meetings was held openly at the court house. Well, I was standing right by the side of W. B. Jones and he kind of turned to me and he says, "You watch my back, I can watch out

front." He thought they might have somebody slip around behind and shoot him in the back and get lost in the crowd, you see.

On April 13, the Ford mine at Wallins Creek closed. All of Harlan County was now in the grip of anger and unemployment. "You could talk with any of these [miners], and they'd say it wouldn't make any difference: if you struck, you starved; if you worked, you starved. It had come down to just a matter of starvation and war against starvation. It got to the point where I didn't consider it a strike, I considered it a war against starvation" (*Tillman Cadle*).

Everyone involved describes the 1931–41 period as a ten-year war. The *New York Times* reported: "Harlan resembles a scene of war. Fleets of automobiles parade the community, filled with guards and deputies armed with shotguns, machine guns and tear-gas bombs. Civil rights have been trampled on, arrests made on the flimsiest grounds and houses broken into without warrant." "I had not seen so many armaments of one sort or another, rifles, high-powered shotguns, and automatic revolvers and machine guns," reported writer Malcolm Cowley after a visit to Pineville in 1932, "since the French offensive in the fall of 1917."[17] Any history of those years may list fights, killings, and battles but must be read against the background of daily incidents that do not make it into the historical record: beatings, dynamiting, shootings, searches, evictions—and, always, hunger.

Murray testified later that Harlan operators "exact a tax from every ton of coal produced in that county to buy guns and munitions, tear-gas bombs, and put those instruments of warfare into the hands of irresponsible men, who float around the country killing and maiming people."[18] Technically, these men were deputy sheriffs; miners called them "thugs," armed guards, mostly paid by the operators, deputized by the sheriff to keep the miners in their place. "I've known 'em to have criminals pardoned out of these prisons and put a badge on 'em to be the law. Wasn't nothing but killers" (*Tillman Cadle*). Among the 169 deputies appointed by Sheriff J. H. Blair, 64 had been indicted for felonies, and 34 were convicted felons. Bill Randolph was facing his fourth murder charge in Kentucky when Harlan operators paid his bond and he became a guard at Three Point. In 1931, he killed Joe Chasteen, a union sympathizer. A Harlan miner's wife, asked what the law meant to her, replied: "The law is a gun thug in a big automobile."[19]

"They was just like Hitler's men, that's all it was. Guns, and good cars to drive, but wouldn't recognize the union, wouldn't feed the miners. They said they was deputy sheriffs; they wasn't deputy sheriffs, they was thugs, because they'd kill the men any time they wanted to" (*Florence Reece*). Certain names recur in the stories of "bloody Harlan" in the 1930s: Frank White, Lee Fleenor, George Lee— and Ben Unthank, who, as the Senate's La Follette Committee found, was on the HCCOA payroll and had received $8,000 for unaccounted expenses, possibly incurred in shooting and dynamiting union organizers.[20]

CHARLOTTE NOLAN: Ben Unthank was my friend's grandfather. Honey, Ben Unthank could've been Santa Claus. A rotund man, and his wife looked like the Queen of Sheba. She had a very regal bearing. They were Baptists, and he went to church every Sunday and donated very heavily to the Baptist church. Listen, they were lovely people. We thought they were fine and good upstanding people who were quite well-to-do. When we were grown we realized there was another side to them. [But there are] two sides to everybody.[21]

TILLMAN CADLE: Ben Unthank, he was the head gun man in Harlan County. He come to my house. He and two gun thugs and the chief of police from Middlesboro and the whole gang of them. They had a bench warrant for me, that I was charged with criminal syndicalism, and that they was to bring my body to the county court, dead or alive. Had their guns drawn, had shotguns and rifles and revolvers. You see, if they would have killed me, they'd have said I resisted arrest. Well, I wasn't at home when they come. They searched the house, for guns and for literature, and then they told my mother, "He need not be hiding from us; we'll find him and we'll shoot him just like he was a dog." She looked him right in the eye and she said, "You [filthy]-looking thing, you," she said, "maybe when you find him somebody else will do a little shooting too." I used to be considered one of the best marksmen in Kentucky.

And, of course, Sheriff J. H. Blair. "John Henry Blair? I knew him well. He was a strong man for the coal operators. He's very popular with that side—operators. That was his side, the operators, but he had some mighty good points" (*Ed Cawood*). "I did all in my power to aid the coal operators," Blair told a reporter. "There was no compromise when labor troubles swept the county and the 'Reds' came into Harlan County."[22]

BRYAN WHITFIELD: Who was the old sheriff that we all liked so well? Sheriff Blair. We thought he was a fine one. The union thought he was a sorry one. Man, you'd have to have been [there] back [then]. We had labor troubles from time to time. Of course there was people killed here from time to time. We didn't want to union. We didn't want somebody running our business. Blair was a good sheriff. Some [of his deputies] were pretty rough, but back in those days you had to be rough if you lasted very long.

"[Blair's] thugs came into our house several times at Molus while [my husband] Sam was run off [for organizing]," Florence Reece wrote: "They was in all of the rooms, in the boxes, and everything. They'd raise up the mattress and if they'd find a letter or a piece of paper, they'd take it....I felt that I just had to do something to help. The little children they'd have little legs and a big stomach. Some men staggered when they walked, they were so hungry. We were getting real low on everything. We didn't even have paper, so...I just jerked the calendar off the wall and sat down and wrote the words [of a song] on the back":[23] "They say in Harlan County there are no neutrals there / You'll either be a union man / or a thug for J. H. Blair. / Which side are you on? Which side are you on?"

"There was some mean people on both sides. This was not a cakewalk of thugs" (*Bill Winters*). Harlan's culture is one of sharp confrontations and pitched fights; thugs and deputy sheriffs were not the only ones with access to weapons and explosives. When they could, the miners retaliated: "I can show you a bullet hole in my house. Went clear through a desk, I found the bullet in a lampshade. And they'd come by and throw sticks of dynamite across the hedge over on your front yard" (*Bryan Whitfield*). "I had two uncles, they were part of security around the mines, and were shot at, one was shot up at Evarts, and one was shot some-place else" (*Daniel Howard*). On April 18, 1931, Deputy Sheriff Jess Pace was killed (and a miner wounded) in a gunfight at Evarts, where he was trying to arrest some men accused of beating a scab. The following week, a mine was dynamited at Shields, and sixteen vacant company homes were burned at Cawood.[24] Pickets of armed miners roved from to mine to mine: "They would tell nobody their names, see: called theirselves 'Jones boys,' that's what they called themselves. Everyone of them was a Jones. And man, they were rough on them fellows trying to scab, them Jones boys was" (*Lloyd Lefevre*).

In April, the UMW offered to give up the demand of union recognition and accept the nonunion shop. The operators refused.[25] On April 27, about fifty men opened fire on nonunion men from the undergrowth on the side of Black Mountain. Deputy sheriffs strafed the mountainside with automatic fire, but no casualties were reported on either side. "Hell, yes, I've issued orders to shoot to kill," Sheriff Blair said. "When ambushers fire on my men, they'll shoot back, and shoot to kill. That's what we use guns for here."[26] Afterward, Blair told the local paper that all was quiet, and no further trouble was expected.

EVARTS

"On Tuesday, May 5th, 1931," writes Harlan memoirist William D. Forester, "the continued pressure exploded. The expected confrontation between the striking or discharged miners and the deputy sheriffs became a reality....Four men were killed and many others were wounded in this fight that became nationally known as the 'Battle of Evarts.' It was charged that concealed miners and sympa-thizers ambushed a group of deputies on the out-skirts of Evarts, near the rail-road track...The dead were: Jim Daniels, a deputy sheriff, Otto Lee, a deputy sheriff, Howard Jones, store clerk...and Carl Richardson, alleged to have been in the mob of attackers."[27]

"My grandfather was sheriff of Black Mountain, and he died in a miners' strike. It's supposed to be in the history books. Daniels, Jim Daniels. Basically, he had his head blew off, they said, in a miners' strike. That's all I know; that's all that I was told as a child" (*Charlene Dalton*). The miners had congregated at the Evarts L&N depot when they heard that a truck carrying furniture for a nonunion worker was to pass through town, protected by deputy sheriffs, on its way to the Black Mountain camp at Verda. The town was rife with rumors: gun thugs were coming to Evarts to raid the town and rape the women.[28] "A little boy heard these thugs a-talking that they was gonna kill the miners when they come across that railroad there. This little boy told some of the people about it, and they beat them to the draw. They was there when they got there, they killed seven of them" (*Sam Reece*).

As the motorcade passed a narrow cut near the railroad depot, shots rang out. According to the version later accepted by the Kentucky courts, a volley hit the cars and killed two guards; Jim Daniels got out to fire back and was killed by a shot in the face. According to the miners' defense, the cars stopped after an isolated shot; Daniels got out and fired at the sniper, and only then did the other miners open fire on him.[29] "When Jim Daniels was killed at Evarts, I was standing ten foot of him when he was shot down, and the men was running over the riverbank going behind the crosstie piles; Bill Worthington said, 'Granny, why don't you go somewhere?' I said, 'You men took all the hiding places,' I said, 'I had no choice, I had to stand there!'" (*Granny Hager*).

Garfield McLain was at school that day at Kildav, and he remembered how the shooting scared all the children and teachers. They did not know what was happening and were sent to the basement to wait it out. Berenice Buckner said that her parents' neighbors came to seek refuge in their basement while it was going on. After the battle, Laura Blevins remembered, "me and my Dad went to Evarts and there were machine guns shooting all around these mountains...Me and my Dad went along that evening and we happened to see a piece of Jim Daniels' skull. We took a piece and buried it on the side of the road."[30]

> RAY ELLIS: I wasn't in the battle, I was just a boy, about eighteen, nineteen year old. These up there by the street went by, organized, the guns and all. Me and another boy was out there and [Al Benson], he [later] spent years in the penitentiary, he came up to me and that boy and he said, "You fellows ain't got no business here, you get home."[31] Well the night after that, oh man, it was a armed camp. They said the high sheriff sent word he was going to wipe this town off the map. Well, if he'd come, it would have been a battle.

Forty-three miners and organizers—including W. B. Jones, William Hightower, and Turnblazer, who were not even at the scene—were arrested; fifteen eventually faced trial for conspiracy and murder. Witnesses for the prosecution alleged that the day before the battle W. B. Jones had urged the miners to attack the deputies, saying, "Shoot to get meat, shoot their God damned heads off."[32] The trial was moved to rural Mt. Sterling, far from Harlan, its culture, and its conflicts. Defense counsel John M. Robsion wrote: "Scarcely one of our witnesses had any money with which to make the trip to Mt. Sterling and had no money to pay board or lodging...Furthermore, we were projected into a Bourbon community [that knows] little or nothing about organized labor and on the whole are unfriendly to organized labor."[33]

"When W. B. Jones and Hightower and all these people was being tried for that Evarts battle, I thought that we too would have some justice in the courts and all. I've never seen it" (*Tillman Cadle*). The Mt. Sterling paper editorialized that the "agitators" ought to be "shot at sunrise." "It is useless to send men and women of the stripe of the Harlan agitators to the penitentiary. They would be safer in a pine box six feet under ground." The prosecuting attorney claimed that there would be "bonfires of rejoicing in Moscow" if they were acquitted.[34] The court chose to believe the prosecution's witnesses. One of them later admitted that he lied, but it was defense witnesses who were systematically charged with perjury. Seven of the defendants received life sentences.[35]

In 1935, Governor Ruby Laffoon pardoned Hightower, William Hudson, and Elzie Phillips; W. B. Jones, Chester Poore, Albert Benson, and Jim Reynolds were pardoned in 1941 by Acting Governor Myers. By then, two of the three trial judges and forty-six out of forty-seven jury members still living said they considered the miners innocent; even Jim Daniels's wife favored a pardon. In Evarts, some people still believe that the wrong person was sent to jail. "But the man is so old now that really did the work, that I don't think that he would live through trial and get to the penitentiary" (*Granny Hager*). "I had [a] man to tell me at one time, that [Jim Daniels] had been killed by a black man" with a borrowed shotgun, "and the gun's owner got railroaded for that. According to this man, the man that did it was this black fellow. He never would tell me his name. He wouldn't tell me the name of anybody else that was involved in it" (*Mildred Shackleford*).

The multiplicity of versions leaves the factual reconstruction of the battle and its context uncertain. But the more enduring question is: what does the Battle of Evarts *mean*?

The conflict of meanings is implicit, for instance, in the body count. The official figure is four casualties: three deputies and one miner. However, both journalist John Ed Pearce and sociologist Shaunna Scott heard that several dead miners were buried secretly at night in order to shield their families from revenge. Sheriff Blair claimed that miners' casualties were many more than were reported. For the other side, Sam Reece claimed that the miners had killed seven deputies; his wife, Florence Reece, counted eleven—seven guards and four miners.[36]

This is the logic not of a civil conflict but of war—that is, of a conflict in which each side claims a military victory by swelling the number of the other side's casualties, rather than a moral victory by swelling their own. "When they have one of those battles, certain rules were just kind of forgotten. And, they played to win. At whatever costs" (*Arthur Johnson*). As in one great song of the Italian Resistance, *pietà l'è morta* (mercy is dead).

Or was it? John Ed Pearce reports that after the battle, miners allowed some of the deputies, including Sherman Percival, wounded sixteen times, to walk off to safety. In an act of mercy, Laura Blevins and her mother buried the remnants of Jim Daniels's skull. But other pieces of the same body become mementos of war: "And ——— was the one [who picked up] Mr. Daniels's head, and he picked up pieces of skull, and he showed my daddy in the courthouse, it had blood on it. He said, 'I'm gonna make me a watch from out of this.' And he was I-talian, see" (*Ben Campagnari*). This man may be the same "old miner" who reminisced, years later: "We went over after the fight and we was looking where he [Jim Daniels] fell at, and there was a piece of his skull...a kinda oblong piece...laying on the ground. They just shot it loose there and it peeled outta the skin...I picked it up and scraped the meat off of it, made a watch belt out of it. Took it to Middlesboro and sold it...Took in $50."[37]

The bones of Jim Daniels's head are a symbol of the tensions between mercy and hatred, pity and revenge, the battle and its memory. Memory, indeed, is the ultimate site of conflict. Union miners, guards, "scabs," and their descendants all lived in the same environment, and for a long time, "while the 'Battle of Evarts' is over, the divisions felt within the community continue to be felt."[38]

MILDRED SHACKLEFORD: They would tell you so-and-so did such-and-such, but they wouldn't tell you who so-and-so was. They would tell you what time they did it, the day, where they was standing at; they would never give you the names. And I asked some of them, "Are they dead?" They'd say, "Well, some of 'em are and some of 'em aren't." I said, "If I come back in a few years and they are all dead, would you tell me?" And they said, "No." I said, "Why not?" And they said, "Because that kind of stuff can carry on to their families. Let sleeping dogs lie."

In 2005, a lady in North Carolina e-mailed me to say that her maternal grandfather had been killed by J. H. Blair in Harlan County and that her mother was willing to be interviewed. As I made preparations for the trip, the e-mails stopped. The lady finally wrote that her mother was not up to it: the memory was too painful.

J. D. MILLER: You must realize that I'm an outsider. I have only been here for seventeen years. And people may not be as quick to share that with me as they would with themselves, but my sense is that there is a lot of memory, but people don't like to talk about it very much. Chester Poore was a patient of mine and told me that he was the only living convicted survivor of the Battle of Evarts. And I said, "Convicted of what?" and he said, "Why murder, of course!" Another man, who is deceased now, told me that he was sixteen years old, and that he was involved but he never was caught. He had a shotgun there, at the battle, and he went home, and hid his gun at the back of his piano. I said, "Why didn't you destroy your gun, throw it away, bury it?" He said, "Because it was a good gun, I didn't want to lose it." He said they searched his home, they couldn't find anything. His gun was behind the piano, and he left it there for years before he got it out and used it again. Because he didn't want anybody to ever associate him with that battle. Even when he told me, and often when people tell me things about that kind of stuff, it's in the examining room, with the door closed, and their voices drop and they almost whisper when they tell me about it. *cluster*

ROOSHIAN REDS

Two days after the battle, National Guardsmen in full combat gear marched into Harlan County. Two hundred miners greeted them in Evarts, waving the American flag. An officer commented: "These damned miners thought we came here to help them."[39]

The orders were "to establish and preserve and maintain peace" and "see that any man who wants to work and can get work to do be allowed to work, without intimidation or molestation to himself or his family."[40] "They sent the state police in here to cool it down. Well it crushed it, yes it did, it died" (*Ray Ellis*). Strike leaders were arrested, and nonunion men were escorted back into the mines. Men were arrested on charges of "criminal syndicalism" for urging miners to join the union; preacher Gill Green spent weeks in jail for saying that the sheriff was on the side of the operators. On May 24, Sheriff Blair's men teargassed a union meeting at the Harlan courthouse; on June 11, a deputy sheriff killed a union miner at Cawood.[41]

After a raid on the UMW local at Evarts, Sheriff Blair claimed to have found IWW literature and membership blanks. The Industrial Workers of the World were indeed present in Harlan: in April, IWW organizer Lee Lively had been president of the Evarts union local; and a charter issued to the Evarts branch of the IWW was later discovered in an organizer's house.[42] "All union organization work in eastern Kentucky was promptly branded 'Red' and propaganda and action to root out the 'Red menace' began" (*Tillman Cadle*). Deputies raided homes in search of IWW literature and copies of the *Daily Worker*; possession amounted to criminal syndicalism.

Nannie Powers, of Harlan, testified:

> It was about three o'clock in the afternoon, the best I remember. They came right on in my house and tore up everything, looked in all the drawers, tore up the mattresses, opened trunks, and messed up everything. And then one of them that was a-cussing around there said, "By God, we are going to take you to jail," and I asked him what I had done to go to jail and he said I never had to do nothing to go to jail. [They found] some Daily Worker paper and [membership] blanks.[43]

On June 20, IWW representative Tom Connors was beaten in Sheriff Blair's office, transported to the state line on top of Black Mountain, and ordered to walk down the road until, bleeding and dazed, he reached the next town in Virginia. By mid-June, the UMW concluded that strikes in Harlan County could not succeed, and refused to support any strike action or to assist strikers. Activist

Jim Garland explained: "They brought the militia and had the thugs, and finally the men went back at work—what we call breaking the strike. The strike was broke, the way we call it, because the men did not get anything to eat from the organization." After the defeat of the strike at Creech Coal in June, the UMW left Harlan County.[44] On July 23, the National Guard also left: the strike was over, justice was not restored, and peace was an illusion.

"Everybody wanted action. Nobody could wait much longer," miner and activist Bill Duncan testified. "I'd seen some copies of the *Daily Worker* and the *Southern Worker* and I kinda liked the way they talked. I held a speaking with some other men and we sat down and wrote the *Daily Worker* to ask for an organizer for us." Two days after the end of the strike, Dan Brooks, from the Communist-oriented National Miners Union (NMU), came to Harlan; he was joined later by Jessie Wakefield, from the International Labor Defense (ILD).[45]

In mid-July, Duncan and two dozen Harlan County miners attended a National Miners' Union meeting in Pittsburgh. "When these delegates come back to Kentucky and they told them about how things were so different in the National Miners Union from the United Mine Workers, that they was controlled from the bottom up instead of from the top down, then they started organizing into the National Miners Union" (*Tillman Cadle*). The NMU had split from the UMW after the failure of internal efforts for union democracy; it was part of the Trade Union Unity League, under the aegis of the Communist Party.[46] Local politicians and operators dubbed the Communists "outside agitators" dropped onto an unwitting local population; however, the fact that two dozen miners would travel to a dual union conference as far away as Pittsburgh suggests that the NMU was tapping a real need and a vein of native radicalism and dissatisfaction.[47] Within a few days after the Pittsburgh conference, the NMU received four thousand applications from Harlan County. On July 20, Bill Duncan's house was dynamited.

> DONALD HENSLEY: They were Communists that came in, and they would fight the companies, and the company didn't want it, they wanted all the profits, and everything. But they came in and...the men wanted...well, they wanted freedom. They were grasping for anything they could get a hold of. They needed help and a lot of them didn't realize what Communists were, you know.

"People out there were like that fellow, that said ninety percent of them wouldn't know communism from rheumatism" (*Tillman Cadle*). "If you had at this time said to a group of average mountain people 'I'm a Communist,'" Jim Garland wrote, "they more than likely would have answered 'I'm a Baptist' or 'I'm a Mason.'" According to Tillman Cadle, when Jim Garland was asked by the Senate committee if he was a Communist, he replied, "I don't know whether I am or not, but I'm sure as hell going try to find out." "In this country if you are hungry you are a red," a miner told a group of visiting churchmen, "and if you tell anybody you are hungry you are charged with criminal syndicalism."[48] Molly Jackson explained: "I've been framed up and accused of being a red, when I did not understand what they meant. I got all my progressive ideas from my hard tough struggles, and nowhere else." When Judge D. C. Jones asked coal miner Debs Moreland whether he knew that the NMU was affiliated with the Communists, he "replied that I had not been aware of it, but that if conditions in Harlan County would be improved by the Communists or any one else, I would throw my lot in with them."[49]

> TILLMAN CADLE: Anyone coming in from New York, or Chicago, or Ohio, anywhere like that, they called them outsiders. They come to the conclusion that anybody who would come all the way from New York to Kentucky to help out in this trouble, they would have to a be a Communist. So they got to calling everybody a Communist. Joe Weber, he was another young fellow, from Chicago. He was helping with the NMU. So—he made a speech, about outsiders. He [asked] some of us, who owned those mines; and it turned out that this British company owned most all that land,[50] and that all of these big coal companies, they was all from somewhere else, he got all this down, and the theme of his speech was, who are the outsiders? And he began naming this company, that company, the British company. Well, this was throwing too much light on them, so they issued a bench warrant for him to bring him in dead or alive. And they put a ten thousand dollar reward on his head, thinking they would murder him for that, you see.

Actually, whatever usefulness the NMU, the ILD, the National Committee for the Defense of Political Prisoners, or the American Civil Liberties Union had came from the fact that, as outsiders, they were able to expose conditions in Harlan to the rest of the nation and raise sympathy and relief. After the crisis in 1929, Communism in "the thirties wasn't such a bad thing" (*Mildred Shackleford*); yet in the early 1930s, the international Communist movement was at its most sectarian stage.[51] In the United States, as elsewhere, the leadership's ruthless persuasion that the party's historical mission took priority over everything else combined with the selfless dedication of the rank and file. The Communist Party may or may not have "exploited" Harlan for its own ends; one may wonder whether the activists who were harassed, beaten, expelled, arrested, and killed did it all out of cynicism.

On July 23, Allen Keedy, an Ohio socialist theological student, and Vincent Bilotta, a Harlan miner, were arrested as they brought food and clothes to a local family. That night, Jessie Wakefield's car was dynamited. Sheriff Blair hired twenty-five more deputies.[52] Wakefield was arrested on August 1, released, and rearrested a week later on charges of criminal syndicalism, along with Arthur Johnson (an ILD representative and theological student, accused of distributing an ACLU pamphlet on free speech). They spent six weeks in jail but were never brought to trial; they were released on the condition that they never return to

Harlan. Wakefield wrote: "The jailer told me, 'As long as you're a member of your organization and in Kentucky, you'll be in jail. What's more, we're going to put every member of your organization we can find in jail.' I told him the ILD was legal everywhere in the United States. He answered: 'Well, I'm the law here, and it ain't legal in Kentucky.'"[53]

The same day, Sheriff Blair led eleven deputies to the house of Harry Thornton, an African American miner who had attended NMU meetings. They beat him unconscious and jailed him for drunkenness. His brother-in-law McKinley Balden was taken to the Virginia border, handcuffed to a tree, and beaten.[54] The house of Jim Grace, a delegate to the Pittsburgh convention, was raided in search of radical literature; he escaped, was arrested with another organizer in Letcher County, and delivered to Harlan deputies, who took them to the county line on Black Mountain and beat them: "I made an escape into the darkness amid a hail of bullets and stones...I was bleeding so at the nose and my eyes were so bruised I could hardly see. In fact, I was only semi-conscious. I lay there about an hour before I was able to stand up." He made his way to the home of sympathizers in Middlesboro: "I was so weak, and my face so swollen, they did not recognize me."[55]

Arrests and charges of criminal syndicalism continued on an almost daily basis throughout August.[56] The press came in for special treatment: independent Appalachian journalist Bruce Crawford was taken to the county line and shot in the leg, Federated Press correspondent Boris Israel was abducted and wounded, and Israel's colleague Mrs. Harvey O'Conner was expelled. George Ward, secretary of the operators' association, commented that Crawford and Israel "may not be communists but we saw them talking to communists."[57]

Free speech, constitutional rights, and freedom of movement were not, however, the only things at stake. After all, this was not a strike, it was a war against starvation. The NMU knew that "you can't organize the people through their heads, you must organize them through their belly" (*Tillman Cadle*). The UMW expected starving miners to pay dues; the Red Cross refused to provide relief; and so the NMU did the most intolerable thing: it tried to feed them.

"I remember the soup kitchens—that's where people would go in and eat. I don't [know who set them up], 'less it was a...you know, union people, under cover" (*Parris Burke*). "There used to be one here at Wallins. I don't know who set this kitchen up—or who paid for the stuff they eat. It could have been the union, I don't know. I never was down there to it, but I know these people went down there and eat, and took soup home, to their children" (*Melinda Slusher*). "They had their soup kitchen right out here next to that Clear Fork's church. They had a big soup kitchen and organizing hall just out from that church. The National Mining did. Yeah, I grew up [hearing about it]" (*Larry Wilson*). "Somebody's told you about the soup kitchen? I can't think of who set that soup kitchen but, they had a soup kitchen, right down this street. I believe that was a...Communist thing" (*Lloyd Stokes*).

In August, the Evarts soup kitchen was dynamited. Shortly afterward, Findlay and Caleb Powers, guards at another kitchen, were arrested for "banding and confederating."[58] Debs Moreland, who operated the soup kitchen at Pansy, was arrested and held for a month; on his release, he reopened the kitchen, and was again arrested, beaten, and forced to leave the county. Deputy Lee Fleenor killed miner Joe Moore and NMU secretary Julius Baldwin at the Clover Fork soup kitchen. Elizabeth Baldwin testified:

> We were running the relief kitchen in the town when my husband was killed. All we knew he was killed for was because he was relief chairman of the kitchen. He was shot and killed the 30th of August, 1931, leaving me with four children to support, all under the age of 6 years old. Lee Fleenor and about 40 or 50 thugs come back in the house and said they was going to come in and search and see what the damn soup kitchen looked like.... Another lady, Mistress Holder, was there, and she asked [deputy sheriff] Joe Morris if he didn't have no sympathy for women and little children and he said no, he did not. That he would as soon blow them into hell as not.[59]

Lee Fleenor was acquitted on grounds of self-defense after five minutes' deliberation. Neither the victims' families nor any of the miners who witnessed the episode was called to testify.[60] By the end of October, the soup kitchens, their most important tool of resistance, had all been shut down.

The NMU's following was concentrated around the Harlan-Bell county line, where conditions were worst: Wallins Creek and Molus in Harlan, Straight Creek in Bell. In October, miners struck at ArJay, on Straight Creek; the company agreed to a checkweighman, a two-cent raise in pay, the eight-hour day, and extra payment for cleaning slate from coal.[61] However, when the company did not live up to the agreement, the miners struck again. "This time the strike was broke so what they gained was lost," Jim Garland testified before a congressional committee: "I was blacklisted just after this, though. During the week that we were not working, Theodore Dreiser and his committee came to Kentucky to investigate the conditions."[62]

The November 1931 visit of a delegation from the National Committee for the Defense of Political Prisoners, chaired by Theodore Dreiser and including such well-known writers as John Dos Passos, Samuel Ornitz, and Charles Rumford Walker, may be the most controversial episode in the Harlan story of 1931–32. Perhaps Dreiser was merely, as Appalachian playwright Jo Carson dubbed him, a "preacher with a horse to ride" who came to Harlan seeking to revive a flagging career or, as historian John Hevener suggests, to confirm his "prejudice" against American capitalism.[63] Or he might have been motivated by sympathy for the miners and anger for injustice. His committee held formal hearings in Harlan and Bell for two days before Dreiser was expelled and charged with crimes ranging from criminal syndicalism to adultery. "Who was that writer that came through here with women and everything else. You've heard that story, haven't you? He was down at the Continental Hotel at Pineville spending the night and he had some females with him and [Pineville journalist Herndon Evans] put toothpicks up on the door" (*Bryan Whitfield*). The toothpicks were still in place in the morning, which proved that Dreiser had spent the night with a woman.[64]

Dreiser's visit helped make America aware of what was happening in its very heart. The local power structure attempted to stir resentment against Dreiser and other "meddling" outsiders and "agitators" coming to slander Kentucky's name, and they did all they could to keep the miners from learning about the growing nationwide solidarity. Months after Dreiser had left Harlan, the *New York Times* wrote: "Terror continues to flourish in Harlan County, in the comfortable obscurity provided by a virtual censorship on news" enforced by "shooting and intimidation of reporters."[65] The treatment of visitors and observers in Harlan and Bell prompted an investigation by a subcommittee of the U.S. Senate Committee on Manufactures, chaired by Senator Edward P. Costigan. Though friendly to the miners, the committee conducted its hearings not in Harlan but in Washington, heard more outside observers than miners, and dealt more extensively with the violations of the visitors' civil rights, such as the framing of Theodore Dreiser, than with the miners' economic and political rights. Yet the violations of the outsiders' rights were a symptom of the denial of the miners' own political and constitutional rights—which in turn was functional to the denial of their economic demands and their human rights. Eventually, however, the Committee on Manufactures decided not to hold a full investigation.[66]

Dreiser and his partners may have violated the rules of fair and balanced reporting by drawing attention to Straight Creek and Wallins Creek rather than less desperate areas, and by listening to witnesses selected and prompted by local NMU activists. Yet the conditions to which they testified existed. They may not have been representative—other, perhaps, than in Emerson's sense of the word: representative not of the normal but the possible, of what power can do when threatened, and of the price that can be paid for resisting. Dreiser may have been opportunistic and prejudiced; one cannot, however, attribute to prejudice the fact that—as Hevener confirms—"in only three months during the fall of 1931, thirty-seven Straight Creek children died in the old midwife's [Molly Jackson] arms."[67]

ALL OF MY RIGHTS HAVE BEEN TAKEN AWAY

TILLMAN CADLE: When I went to New York, I got to talking about what we went through here, and about the role of the state; and some big professor, he come and collared me, and he said, "You have been talking about the role of the state, I was wondering what you had been reading about it." I said, "I didn't have to read it, mister: the damn thing fell and hit me right on top of the head."

By the end of 1931, hunger and powerlessness had all but broken the miners' resistance. Those who could went back to work, on whatever terms they could get. The NMU retained a base mainly among the blacklisted and unemployed miners around Wallins Creek, Molus, and Straight Creek. Overestimating their strength, the NMU miners voted to strike on January 1, 1932.[68]

The strike was doomed from the start. Only a few hundred working miners came out on strike, and the out-of-work miners who rallied around the NMU had no impact on the operation of the mines. The following of the NMU, however, still went beyond their numbers: up to fifteen hundred people marched and confronted police in mass demonstrations, and thousands turned to the NMU for relief. But the numbers dwindled as the union proved unable to help them, both because of its inherent weakness and because the authorities stopped all relief efforts.[69]

Within twenty-four hours, the Bell County court issued injunctions against strike activities on Straight Creek; all meetings in Harlan were stopped by Sheriff Blair's men. On January 4, Pineville police raided the NMU and ILD headquarters and arrested six women and three men—journalists, lawyers, and organizers. In court, prosecutor Walter Smith stated that they "ought to be lined alongside a wall, not waiting for the electric chair." A miner testified that he had been evicted by Harlan gun thugs and his baby had died of starvation; he was arrested in court.[70] The *Enterprise* editorialized: "We're just naturally not in the mood to have the Communists come in, some from Russia, some from Pittsburgh, some from the slums of the foreign-populated cities." On January 17, Joe Weber and Bill Duncan were arrested, taken to Lynch, and beaten.[71] "They thought they had murdered [Weber]; they beat him with clubs, and they left him by the side of the road, unconscious. Well, someone came along and found him, and picked him up and took him in, and he made his way someway to Knoxville after he regained his consciousness and then they brought him to my home and left him till he recuperated a little" (*Tillman Cadle*). Blair, however, denied everything.

Though the strike was losing momentum, it still made national news, and relief kept flowing into Harlan and Bell. On February 10, writer Waldo Frank and lawyer Allen Taub traveled to Pineville with a delegation including writers Malcolm Cowley, Edmund Wilson, and Mary Heaton Vorse, bringing supplies to the miners and their families. "Mary Heaton Vorse and the committee, they came to Kentucky, and they brought, best I remember, 'bout five small truckloads of food and one truckload of milk for the children. They [the local authorities] was not gonna permit them to distribute this food inside Pineville" (*Tillman Cadle*). The delegation's trucks were driven under police surveillance out of the town's limits; one truck laden with clothing was overturned.[72]

They were finally allowed to distribute the food, provided there were no speeches. But "when the trucks arrived, some young fellow in the crowd got upon the platform and was a-gonna welcome these people in with the food.

And as he began to talk one of these big gunmen jumped at him, was gonna grab him, and he jumped off the platform and got lost in the crowd. I never did know who he was, or anything. So then people on the committee, they began getting up and talking, and just as one would finish talking and start to step down, they would arrest him. And Harold Hickerson, he got up and he said, 'I went and fought in the First World War to make the world safe for democracy. And I've come back here to Kentucky, to find that all your rights have been taken away, you don't have any rights here in Kentucky anymore.' And so—they had an old song, 'Come on Mama and go my bail, take me out of this buggy jail'—they added a verse: 'Come on Mama and go my bail, take me out of this buggy jail, 'cause all of my rights been taken away'" (*Tillman Cadle*).

Hickerson was arrested on the spot, along with his fellow committee member Doris Parks. Waldo Frank and Allan Taub were taken to the Tennessee line, beaten, and told never to return. The police, the local press, and a UMW representative from Knoxville claimed that they had quarreled and beaten each other.[73]

The pattern was to be repeated throughout the spring, as church groups, students, and journalists were prevented from reaching Pineville and Harlan, or roughly expelled from Kentucky. Two hundred students from the National Student League were stopped at the Tennessee border and given the choice of posting $1,000 bond or going to jail. Most chose jail and were "escorted" back over the border, where, they claimed, they were beaten. A delegation from the Commonwealth Labor Training Institute of Mena, Arkansas, bearing relief and copies of the Bill of Rights, was stopped by Bell County police and handed over to Harlan officials, who took them into the woods at Black Mountain and whipped them. On the same day, an IWW attorney was abducted in Pineville, taken to Harlan, whipped, and threatened with death should he return. A delegation of ministers led by the theologian Reinhold Niebuhr was prevented from contacting local people and given a lecture in fundamentalist theology by Bell County authorities.[74]

On the day of Frank and Taub's visit, Harry Simms, a nineteen-year-old organizer for the NMU and the Young Communist League, was murdered in Barbourville, Knox County. Born Harry Hersch, from a Jewish family in Massachusetts, he was much respected by NMU miners and families. That day he was walking the railroad tracks from Barbourville to Pineville with his comrade Green Lawson to collect food from the relief committee. Near Brush Creek, two deputy sheriffs riding a handcar on the tracks caught up with them, and Arlan Miller, a guard at Bryan Whitfield's Jellico mine, shot Simms in the stomach.[75] "The National Miners Union, they was trying to organize. They was a Communist outfit. They came in and one of them was killed near our camp, Kayjay, in Knox County, and they took him to New York, put him on display for a week I think. I've forgotten his name—Simms, I believe" (*Bryan Whitfield*). Tillman Cadle testified: "They took him to the hospital, the hospital wouldn't take him in unless someone would make the payments good. They had to be sure they was gon' get paid or they would not take him in the hospital. Finally someone come along and agreed to make the payments good, they took him in, but he had practically bled to death by this time."[76]

> TILLMAN CADLE: When he died, you see, they knew the people was going to be awful angry to see them killing this young man in cold blood. So they was expecting maybe they'd stage a demonstration, maybe a big march on the town. So this town had declared martial law, had state troopers there. Then they informed the union that they would not turn his body over to more than a committee of three people; but they would not allow any funeral services. There'd be no walking, there'd be no talking. They could take his body, they could ship it out, and that was it.[77]

Harry Simms became a symbolic Communist and working-class martyr. Jim Garland and Tillman Cadle took his body to New York, where Garland eulogized him in front of thousands of sympathizers who filed by the casket at the Workers' Center. In September, after the strike was over and the NMU was gone from eastern Kentucky, the murderer was found slain. On his way back to Harlan, Jim Garland drew a moral:

> *Comrades we must vow today, this one thing we must do*
> *We must organize all the miners in the good old NMU*
> *And get a million volunteers into the YCL*
> *And sink this rotten system in the deepest pits of hell.*[78]

GOD, FLAGS, AND RED BLOOD

The day Harry Simms died, a group of Harlan miners returned from training sessions sponsored by the Communist Party in the North. "Fellow workers and citizens," wrote Findlay Donaldson, a miner and Holiness preacher, in a widely circulated statement, "the teachings of the Communist Party would destroy our religious beliefs, our government and our homes. In their teachings they demand their members to teach their children [that] there is no God; no Jesus, no Hereafter...I heard them in a mass meeting and a big demonstration while in Chicago denounce our government and our flag and our religion...The Communist Party believes in white and colored marrying each other and if you refuse for the negro men to keep company with your daughter you cannot be a friend to Soviet Russia."[79]

The day before, in court in Pineville, county attorney W. B. Smith had asked Doris Parks: "Do you believe in any form of religion?" Assuming that constitutional freedoms applied in Bell County, she replied: "I believe in the religion of the workers," that is, "the working class and their right to organize and to teach they can be led out of this oppression by the Communist Party." "And then he brought up the question of marriage. He says: 'You wouldn't want your daughter to marry a nigger, would you?' She said, 'I don't tell my daughter who she should marry'" (*Tillman Cadle*). "Once [Pineville journalist] Herndon Evans reproduced this statement in the *Pineville Sun* and called Doris Parks and the entire NMU atheistic," writes Jim Garland, "we lost more than half of our members." Ironically, while Doris Parks was being branded as unpatriotic and atheistic, hundreds of miners marched around the courthouse "singing hymns, carrying American flags, led by a fundamentalist preacher."[80]

Hunger, fear, the errors of the leadership, the naive illusions of many activists, and the sheer weight of the power relationship doomed the NMU strike.[81] But a deeper defeat took place on the cultural plane: as they lost the strike, miners also lost their reasons for it. A strike, a dramatic break with everyday practices and relationships, must be justified first of all in the strikers' own minds. In the face of unprecedented conditions, forced into unprecedented actions, lacking ideological alternatives, the miners attempted to legitimize their choices in terms of their traditional values and culture. But the same values and symbols were also claimed by the other side. The result was a fierce class struggle for the control of meanings, for the ownership and definition of the shared symbols of patriotism and religion—and race.

After the Battle of Evarts, the miners marched along with the National Guard carrying American flags. The Stars and Stripes was displayed at the head of all the miners' marches and motorcades—but also by the National Guard, the sheriffs, and the courts. While the miners were trying to legitimize their struggle by displaying their patriotism, the operators and the state were bent on proving that *they* were the real Americans. When the Evarts strikers came to trial, the prosecutor claimed that W. B. Jones "carried an American flag, but the red flag...was in his heart."[82] Some strikers thought that there was no contradiction there: "I remember —— who told stories about seeing miners buried maybe after the Battle of Evarts, said he remembered one had an American flag and a Red flag draped over his coffin" (*David Walls*).

The flag was the most visible symbol of a conflict over citizenship and rights. On reaching Pineville, Waldo Frank and his colleagues stated: "We insist upon our rights, our constitutional rights as American citizens" to distribute relief and to contact the striking miners. But after the beating they received at the state line, the deputies "poked fun at them about their constitutional rights; they would say to one before they beat him up, 'Maybe you'd like to get your attorney to give you an address on your constitutional rights.' Just making fun of the Constitution, you see" (*Tillman Cadle*).[83]

In April 1932, Arthur Garfield Hays of the ACLU wrote to Bell County attorney Walter B. Smith expressing concern for the violations of civil rights in Harlan and Bell. Smith answered: "The people of Bell County are fundamentalists in politics, religion, and social economies. They are perfectly satisfied with the government of the United States as it is now administered." They believe in freedom of the press and freedom of movement, but "do not approve the doctrines [of the ACLU], nor do they acknowledge that any man, or any such organization, or any group of persons representing it have any Constitutional rights in Bell County, that any person is bound to respect."[84]

In May 1932, a writer for the *New York Times* confirmed: "The rise and decline of the coal industry in Harlan and Bell County have not erased the religious and patriotic tenets of operators and miners."[85] The rulers and the ruled appear to share a cultural substratum of patriotism and religion in their "fundamentalist" mode. However, the same values and symbols were interpreted by the strikers in ways that went back to the country's very foundations. A miner told Dos Passos, "My grandpappy came to Kaintuck jes after he holp George Washington in the Revolutionary War." "I never felt the actuality of the American revolution so intensely," the writer commented. Mary Nick, a miner's daughter, age thirteen, sang: "We will all be united / We will march through the land / Then we will be free Americans / And get our full demands." "The National Miners Union," said Findlay Donaldson before his trip to Chicago, "stands for the principles that our forefathers fought for at Bunker Hill"—which meant revolution and struggle rather than law and order.[86] Donaldson preached:

I love the flag of the United States, I love the name of America, but I want to tell you what I hate. I hate the men that handles this country of ours... the miners of the State of Kentucky is today being worse mistreated than Slaves in Slave Times....You are denied every privilege that that United States gives you by unjust judges, [who] forbid us every privilege that the Constitution of the United States guarantees a man.

Some flirted with alternative symbols. Journalist Louis Stark reported that "a mountaineer of Anglo-Saxon lineage" had said in court that he'd rather live in Russia than in Harlan County. "If they won't let us march under the American flag," another said, "we'll march under the Red flag." Aunt Molly Jackson sang that the bosses' flag is "the old red white and blue / And ours is dipped in blood."[87]

Blood is another shared and contested symbol. According to Bell County attorney W. B. Smith, "One drop of pure Kentucky blood is worth more and is more sacred than an entire river of Communist blood"; Harlan County Judge D. C. Jones announced that he would "use the full power of my court to prevent these human rattlesnakes from injecting the virus of Communism into the veins of the American workingman." What they did not consider is that pure Kentucky blood is just naturally red: "I am a true American and can't be beat," proclaimed NMU local secretary Billy Meeks, "and I am a red-blooded one." Findlay Donaldson preached: "When you starve me down and deny me the food and raiment that is required to take care of my body and the little children that I claim to be the father of, I want to tell that you are putting Red Blood into me as sure as I live."[88]

"Red" blood evoked images of rednecks and red Indians: "They call us 'Rooshun Red Necks,'" one miner said. "I wonder why that is? My folks have been in Kentucky for five generations, but one of 'em was a Cherokee Indian. Maybe that's why I'm a Red." By casting themselves as pure red-blooded native Kentuckians, those "red Indian rednecks" turned the epithet into a badge of legitimacy. Aunt Molly Jackson sang: "I was raised in Kentucky / In Kentucky born and bred / And when I joined the union / They called me a Rooshian red."[89]

When Reinhold Niebuhr's delegation came to eastern Kentucky, a mine operator told them: "I am a good Christian and a member of the Christian church... but I would as soon tie a Communist in a sack and throw him into the river as do anything else I know." Religion was the other shared and contested signifier. While mainline churches denounced the strike, Niebuhr saw the miners as the hope for "a real proletarian religion."[90] Rural churches hosted union soup kitchens. "They were very religious, but they could be Communists and be very religious" (*Myles Horton*). Fundamentalists involved in the struggle included Findlay Donaldson, snake handler Harvey Valentine, Baptist pastor Frank Martin (jailed for criminal syndicalism), revival preacher Gill Green, and the "cussing preacher" Randalls.

Strike songs were based on hymn tunes; miners' "speakin's" wove the language of labor language with folk sermon imagery. Molly Jackson preached: "We have been under bondage for a long time but God is going to redeem his people. He is fixing a way and a plan for them to be redeemed from this bondage through this great organization." Findlay Donaldson preached:

> In the days when the Children of Israel was under bondage, when Moses went to lead them out and he came to the Red Sea and the Children got scared... and they thought they could not go through, they walked through dry-shod, and Pharaoh's host came on and the water closed up on them... We have the same opportunity presented to us, laboring men, by the National Miners Union to walk out as the Children of Israel did, and if we don't drown these Capitalists and this Capitalism, it is your own bad luck. You can't blame any one but yourself.

However, while the operators hardly entertained a doubt about their own righteousness, the miners were always in need of justification. The sense that their actions were both righteous and sinful can be heard between the lines. Findlay Donaldson explained:

> There is four things that the Nation and American people must [dis]like; that is, Degradation, Privation, Starvation, and Sin. If you put a man in privation you are driving him into sin, but if you give him something to live on, he can stand up to help the Christian world, but if you deprive him of food and raiment, you cause the man to commit in his heart, murder and robbery and stealing, and they have almost starved me.[91]

If Dreiser and Dos Passos, who heard him speak, had relied on their writer's ear rather than their ideological preconceptions, they might have realized that Donaldson not only "spoke like a hell-roaring evangelist," as Dos Passos put it, but *was* one. They might have understood that Donaldson obscurely tied his rebellion to a sense of sin: "Today, friends, I would not ask much to steal a good square meal, haven't had one in so long." To the visitors, this meant that he was challenging private property; to him, it meant that he was risking his soul.

"We learned very early that you cannot make people do something which they consider evil, a sin. You must know how people are, and what they believe in" (*Myles Horton*). Fascinated by the miners' courage and eloquence, the Communists and fellow-traveling liberals never really learned this lesson. On the other hand, the local elite knew the miners and shared some of their roots, language, and beliefs. Thus, when Donaldson and the others came back from their ill-conceived trip to Chicago, the power structure was ready to collect their affidavits and distribute them in thousands of copies.[92]

As long as they thought they could reconcile the strike to their beliefs, miners fought both repression and their own misgivings, but as the strike dwindled and they lost hope, the NMU's alien set of values became a threat to their souls. "Lean miners look levelly through solemn eyes and say, 'I couldn't deny my God,'" Malcolm Ross reported. "Religion in this case is on the side of the strike-breakers."[93] There is an unmistakable sense of relief in Donaldson's statement, as if he felt he had come in from the cold: "I feel at this time that the great capitalists and officials of this great nation of ours which I deem second to none, in some way will give relief and assistance to our poor starving humanity, which is now suffering in America." He had tried to take his life in his hands; now it was safely back in the hands of the capitalists. Which shows that "fatalism" is less an inherent trait of folk culture than an attitude actively created and enforced by power relationships.

Another cultural term was also, briefly, redefined by the strikers: race. The local politicians and operators seemed obsessed with the specter of racial equality and interracial marriages. W. B. Smith raised it in his interrogation of Doris Parks; a Middlesboro minister explained to the Kiwanis Club that Communism means "(1) hatred of God, (2) destruction of property, (3) social and racial equality and class hatred."[94] The same motif recurs in the affidavits of disaffected NMU members: H. L. Doan said that the Communists "believed and said in their meetings that they just as leave their girls to marry a negro as a white man, let the girls be pleased"; Harvey Collett reported that "they teach that there is no God, that a white woman is equal to a colored woman, that a negro has a right to marry a white woman." Black miners had been in the strike since the start. The NMU defied the taboo of social equality by insisting, if not on interracial marriages, at least on integrated soup kitchens. Whatever other errors they may have committed, one can hardly blame them for challenging this aspect of traditional culture.[95] Once again, at the peak of the strike white miners could overcome race antagonism in the name of class solidarity; on the verge of defeat, interclass harmony and race prejudice prevailed again, and all went back to normal.

The NMU departed from tradition in another way. As soon as it came into Harlan, Melvyn Levy wrote, the NMU called a meeting of miners and their wives. In the UMW, "women were not supposed to be informed of impending strikes nor the reason for them; and they resented it. In the National Miners Union conferences sit wives, daughters and sweethearts as well as miners."[96] When Molly Jackson sang "I am a union woman," the key word was *woman*: "You know these organizations that have been back that our husbands belonged to. It was all secret from their wives.... But this great and wonderful union has a woman's side as well as the man's. She can see it too, and they can discuss and she can help out, and I want each and every woman who wants to help her husband and children to join this wonderful union."[97]

A LONG WAYS FROM HARLAN

MYLES HORTON: It was hunger...hunger in the faces of the people, you know, gaunt-faced children and parents, people that you could see that they hadn't had enough to eat. A lifelessness. You know, this kind of-giving up; this kind of sense of no struggle left. No future. Organization was the only way to any kind of decent life and that had failed, so there's nothing. So there's a sense of despair. It was tragic, it was really tragic. It was the epitome of poverty and hopelessness. The kind of despair that you have when there's no hope. People with no hope will not do anything. And they weren't doing anything.

The strike was not defeated by the cultural class struggle, but the cultural class struggle defeated the spirit of the men and women. Miners could be heard saying that "the unions have made conditions in Harlan County a whole lot worse than they were...Then after they got us all out and blacklisted, they left us flat."[98] "When the union pulled out, some of the people resented it very much. 'Cause they hadn't any warning. And they thought it was just another sellout. To them it was the old UMW sellout; they didn't see any difference. Among the people I talked to—among the people who would talk—there was more resentment than defiance" (*Myles Horton*).

PORTELLI: Did you ever go back to work in Harlan or Bell?
TILLMAN CADLE: I never did go. I couldn't get a job, after all this trouble. Every time I'd go to a foreman trying to get a job, he'd start laughing and shaking his head, you see, keeping me from even asking.
PORTELLI: When did people begin to go back to work?
CADLE: Well, some began drifting back before others did, when they could get a job, but you see, for a long time there was no job anyhow, the mines, if they wasn't closed down completely they wasn't hiring anybody. There was nothing.
PORTELLI: How did people survive?

CADLE: Well, they's a lot of 'em didn't survive, if you believe me; they's a lot of them died. Lot of 'em left the coal fields. My brother, he left; he went to Michigan.

"There has been no trickle back to farm and mountain homes," the *New York Times* reported in May 1932. "Having no capital, the unemployed cannot move. Reports indicate that no farms are available in the broader valleys of Eastern Kentucky and across the State lines."[99]

MYLES HORTON: Then there was a lot of bitterness between neighbors, there was some rough stuff—both ways. People whose resentments are very strong; somebody'd scab, and they'd get work and their neighbors, or their cousins, or brothers—couldn't. A lot of people had gone back to work during the strike and there was a conflict between the scabs and the union members. That went on for a long time.

Communism's "frank advocacy of violence," Niebuhr reported, "creates a fear psychosis in the hearts of timid middle class people."[100] While the Communists justified violence ideologically, in practice the NMU's tenure marked the least bloody period in the Harlan struggle—at least on the miners' side. "After their arrival," the *New Republic* noted, "the miners went on being killed, but not a single gun-thug was killed in retaliation."[101] The NMU relied on organization, mass picketing, soup kitchens, and the appeal to solidarity rather than on gunfire. The Battle of Evarts was fought before the Communists came to Harlan; all later gunfights took place under the auspices of the UMW.

"Then the Communists left and the miners got their old Winchesters out of hiding. Some of the most notorious Harlan County killers have since that time been given quiet funerals."[102] The killing of Harry Simms's murderer in September 1932 was no isolated incident. On January 7, 1934, the *Knoxville News Sentinel Magazine* announced: "Harlan County Ends Its Bloodiest Year; 56 Shot to Death in 1933."[103] While the homicide rate in Harlan was the highest in the country at all times, much of this running massacre resulted from the "hard feelings" described by Myles Horton. In all the murders listed by the *News Sentinel*, the victims had been somehow involved in the repression of the strike: John Carnes, one of Blair's chief deputies, killed near a roadhouse on the Harlan-Pineville road; former city policeman Ike Pennington, at a chicken fight near Evarts; former deputy Byrd Fleenor (the father of Lee Fleenor, a deputy who killed three men in the 1931 conflict), near a roadhouse on the Pineville-Harlan road; deputy sheriff Joe Lee, killed in a political dispute.[104] Dillard Middleton, a deputy sheriff who had been involved in at least four killings, and Bradley Burkhart, an Evarts policeman who had testified against the miners charged with murder after the Battle of Evarts and had killed one of them, were shot at a gambling table. Hunston Johnson, nineteen years old, was killed by bullets aimed at a deputy sheriff seated near him.

"[Some] people were hanging on and tried to do something, about a union. It was still NMU" (*Myles Horton*). The Communist Party put Jim Garland in charge of keeping the core group together, but he had to leave when the Party proved unable to supply the promised financial support. He was replaced in 1935 by Don West, an organizer and Baptist minister. West went to work in a Bell County mine and managed to organize a strike, but he was discovered and arrested on charges of criminal syndicalism and "conspiring to overthrow the government by use of the churches." Local supporters paid his bail, but he had to leave the county—though not before he was beaten almost to death by thugs on Black Mountain.[105] Molly Jackson, Sarah Ogan, and Florence and Sam Reece were also forced into exile. Meanwhile, Harlan was trying hard to forget. "It was as if the condition for reemployment in the mines was a kind of voluntary amnesia" that "still exists in Harlan County" in the 1970s. "Most of those who joined the NMU in 1931 now bow their heads or avert their eyes when asked about the Communists.... Some even look away and say no group called the National Miners Union ever entered Kentucky."[106]

"All that bad stuff, they want to forget it" (*Sill Leach*). "Most of the old miners that I talked to [in the 1960s] did not want to identify themselves with that period or the National Miners Union. Most people would say they were around them but they wasn't directly involved. Except the ones who left the area at that time, people who stayed around were not inclined to talk much about it" (*David Walls*).

DARLENE WILSON: [My students], they've heard the term "bloody Harlan," but they don't really know where it comes from. We just passed the seventy-fifth year anniversary of the Battle of Evarts. And I wanted to do something around that, gathering people's memories...Nobody wanted to talk about it. Harlan became known forever as "bloody Harlan," but [textbooks say] nothing about the texture of history, the multiple levels of knowing that people have acquired through these experiences, and how they tell it to their children or grandchildren—how they share it in the union halls or in the hangouts, what's important to remember, and what isn't. The heroes of the struggle are gone, they're not in the pages of the official text.

A typical Appalachian landscape with thickly wooded hills and a valley farm. This photo shows what Black Mountain looked like before the town of Lynch was built on the site in 1917. *Southeast Kentucky Community and Technical College—Appalachian Archives—A111.16a.JPG*

Quilts adorn the beds in a traditional mountain home. Quilting was a creative expression of Appalachian women and a way of putting to use bits and pieces of discarded clothing and other material. *Kentuckiana Digital Library, Ford Photo Album Collection, 1890–1904: ford*

A funeral procession walks a mountain path. Appalachian culture's deep relationship with death has been expressed in intense rituals. *Kentuckiana Digital Library, R. C. Ballard Thruston Photograph Collection, 1880–1942: knt001177*

The congregation joins in the healing ritual of laying on of hands at the Pentecostal church at Lejunior. Religion in Appalachia is participatory and deeply emotional. *Kentuckiana Digital Library, Russell Lee Photographic Collection, 1979: 79pa103*

The town of Lynch was built by U.S. Steel in order to house the workers of the "captive" mine it owned on Black Mountain. Lynch was considered a "model" coal town, an advanced example of such coal towns in Appalachia. *Southeast Kentucky Community and Technical College—Appalachian Archives—A5234.3.JPG*

The No. 1 mine tipple at Benham, the coal town built and owned by International Harvester near Lynch. A tipple was the structure used for loading coal into railroad cars; the term later came to designate all the structures outside the underground mine. *Kentuckiana Digital Library, C. Frank Dunn Photographs Collection, 1900–1954, bulk 1920–1940: 1987ph2*

$2.00   I hereby assign to THE UNITED SUPPLY CO., Incorporated
TWO DOLLARS
out of wages owing to me, or that may become due to me by THE UNITED
STATES COAL & COKE CO., Incorporated.
Issued to _____ Check No. *1906*
By_____   **N⁰   6378B**
Power of Attorney
Witness_____ At Lynch, Ky., 6 — 19 9

Tokens called "scrip," usually redeemable only at the company store, were technically a form of advance payment to employees against future pay. In fact, miners hardly ever saw real money. *Coin courtesy of Jack W. Chapman; paper slip courtesy of Kentucky Coal Education, www.coaleducation.org*

Often brought in as replacement workers, and heavily discriminated against, African American miners joined the union and played an important role in the history of labor conflict in Harlan County. *Kentuckiana Digital Library, Russell Lee Photographic Collection, 1979: 79pa103*

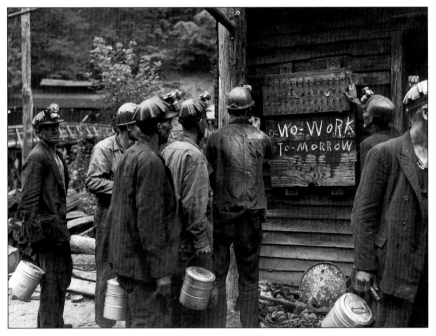

Miners at Lejunior bring in their "checks" (the medals with their identification number) after work and see the sign that there is no Saturday work. In times of crisis, such as the 1930s, miners often found themselves without sufficient work days to earn their families' livelihood. *Kentuckiana Digital Library, Russell Lee Photographic Collection, 1979: 79pa103*

Demonstrators march in Pineville, Bell Co., 1932. The 1931–32 strike in Harlan and Bell Counties drew national attention, also due to the role of the Communist-oriented National Miners' Union and of writers and intellectuals who traveled to Kentucky to investigate conditions. *University of Kentucky, Audio-Visual Archives, Herndon Evans Papers 82n1_38*

Striking miners block the road on Poor Fork in 1938 as members of the National Guard stand at the roadside. State troops were sent into Harlan County several times during the 1930s, to "keep the peace"—which to miners often meant "break the strike." *University of Kentucky, Audio-Visual Archives, Herndon Evans Papers 017*

Bolts anchored by wedge or extension shields are inserted in the mine roof to make it self-supporting, in a process known as roof bolting. Roof falls are the most common cause of death and injury in the mines. *Courtesy of Kentucky Coal Education, www.coaleducation.org*

Two miners are looking at "chock or shield type" roof supports that are utilized in longwall mining. The mechanization of mining, especially from the 1950s on, introduced new hazards at the work place and led to a sharp reduction in the labor force and mass migration from the coal fields. *Courtesy of the Utah Geological Survey*

Members of the United Mine Workers celebrate their victory after the signing of the contract at the Brookside mine. The 1973–74 strike against Duke Power Company became the subject of the award-winning documentary *Harlan County, U.S.A. Southeast Kentucky Technical and Community College, Appalachian Archives, Ewell Balltrip Collection*

An eastern Kentucky mountain after the top has been removed to extract the coal in the process known as "mountaintop removal." The truck on the mine road at the lower center of the photo gives an idea of the scale of the operation. Mountaintop removal has been the target of much criticism and opposition because of its destructive impact on the environment and on the lives of nearby communities. *Photo courtesy of Vivian Stockman / www. ohvec.org; flyover courtesy SouthWings.org*

Annie Napier at home, wearing the Cranks Creek Survival Center t-shirt. A mother and grandmother, and a wife to a disabled coal miner, Napier worked at many jobs, played music and told stories, helped organize community solidarity and resistance to strip mining, and is the most important voice in this book. *Author's collection*

Members of the Harlan community perform in the opening scene of *Higher Ground*, a Harlan County community play, in 2008. As unemployment, drugs, poverty, and loss of self-confidence threatened the community in Harlan, citizens rallied together in a cultural response that reinforced pride and solidarity. *Southeast Kentucky Community and Community College, Appalachian Archives*

10

GOD, GUNS, AND GUTS

TIMES OF HOPE, REIGN OF TERROR

PORTELLI: How did the union begin here?
DEBBIE SPICER: Fighting and shooting and everything else.

HUGH COWANS: And we were glad when John L. Lewis came along and God sent along the man, in '37, '38. I can recall [union organizers] George Titler, [William J.] Turnblazer, Virgil Hampton, Martin Hurd, all of these individuals. They came, and the first meeting we had was at Verda, Kentucky. That's where I worked. A fellow called Chester Smith, he had a large pasture out there and we built a flat for 'em and we had many speeches.

"Verda. That was one of the roughest places to organize in Harlan County" (*Delbert Jones*). "One night, they thought they was going to have a terrible battle here in Verda. Them scabs, had machine guns set up to shoot right into Verda, and kill union men. I knew it was there, because I lived right above them" (*Otis King*). Armed deputies and company officials systematically attacked miners on their way to union meetings in Verda. In one such incident, union preacher Marshall B. Musick was severely beaten; Carl E. Vogel, pastor of Harlan's Methodist church, denounced the incident to his middle-class congregation, and shortly afterward he was removed. "I'm glad you got out of there without a bullet in you," his bishop told him.[1]

HUGH COWANS: And we would go and try to get individuals to sign a check-off slip. That was in ordinance to set up a local. And you'd crawl, in men's places, on my knees and beg them to sign [up with the union]. And they would cuss me out. But eventually we were able to set up locals, at different mines, and, you know, they used force, and we had to use some force, too. But, we were victorious after.

Like Verda, all of Harlan County was again a battleground from 1933 to at least 1941. Between 1932 and 1935, coal production in Harlan had more than doubled. Lower labor costs made up for higher freight rates due to Harlan's distance from Great Lakes markets, but frustrated the New Deal's effort to stabilize coal prices and regulate competition. Some operators even complained to John L. Lewis about the unfair competition of Harlan operators whose miners worked longer hours and days for the same wages. "If the situation is allowed to continue," Lewis wrote back, it would cause a return to "the old cut-throat competition practiced by the industry for the past fifty years."[2]

Yet things looked more hopeful in 1933. Sheriff Blair was no longer in office, and a "reform" slate that included Elmon Middleton as county attorney, Theodore Middleton as sheriff, and Morris Saylor as county judge had won the election.[3] As part of Roosevelt's New Deal, Clause 7a of the 1933 National Industrial Recovery Act (NIRA) sanctioned the workers' right to organize and bargain collectively through unions of their choice. The NIRA code for the coal industry guaranteed a higher minimum wage, the eight-hour day and five-day week, the miners' right to designate their own checkweighman, the abolition of scrip and child labor, company check-off of union dues, and grievance procedures. Many owners and operators welcomed federal intervention as a means to revive their industry but resisted the changes in labor relations; on the other hand, word went around among the miners that "the President wants you to join the union."[4] In the summer of 1933, UMW organizer Lawrence "Peggy" Dwyer held rallies in Harlan and Pineville; five thousand miners signed up for the union and more than forty UMW locals were established in Harlan County.[5]

In October, after a three-week strike, the Harlan County Coal Operators Association (with the exception of the Whitfield family mines and the "captive" mines at Lynch and Benham), under federal pressure, accepted the terms of the Central Appalachian Agreement based on the NIRA code for the bituminous mining industry. The success, however, was short-lived: the NIRA lacked the powers of enforcement, and it could be ignored with impunity. In Harlan, Sheriff Middleton and Judge Saylor reneged on their promises and entered into business partnerships with the operators. (When asked by Senator La Follette to explain why his income was so much above his sheriff's salary, Middleton replied, "I am just as puzzled about it as the senator is.") Middleton rehired most of J. H. Blair's deputies and added others from his own social circle and family members.[6]

In the summer of 1933, Peggy Dwyer was shot at twice by the operator's security head, Ben Unthank and his deputies; twice his house was dynamited. In the following winter and fall, deputy sheriffs and company guards several times attacked the hotels where union representatives were staying and raided union offices, arresting organizers or forcing them out of the county. The house of Peggy Dwyer's replacement, William Clontz, was "fired into and shot up with high-powered rifles and bullets," one barely missing his son's head.[7]

William Clontz was no "outside agitator." A coal miner and a Methodist minister, he had lived in Harlan since 1920. Other preachers, including Missionary Baptist Marshall Musick, Matt Hollars of the Church of God, and Presbyterian Matt Bunch, were on the front line. Their conservative theology and morality proved that there was nothing alien or subversive about the union and that God could be counted on the side of the workers, especially when His representatives were working miners themselves (and, like Reverend Matt Bunch, packed a gun along with their Bible). "See, people love preachers. And the preachers have a weight with the people. The sinner people had a-fit for them preachers, 'cause they knowed they lived good" (*Debbie Spicer*).[8]

One of Debbie Spicer's neighbors was Holiness preacher Benjamin Harrison Moses, pastor of the Black Bottom Baptist Church. Born in Whitley County in 1890, Moses had gone into the mines at fourteen and joined the UMW at seventeen. In 1932, he was fired and blacklisted for refusing to work on Sunday. Called to pastor the church at Black Bottom, he opened it to meetings in support of political reform and the union. In 1933, two attempts to blow up his church were very near misses.[9]

> DEBBIE SPICER: I'll tell you another incident, too. They met at the old church house over there. And they blowed it up. They was having union meetings, so you can take it for granted [who] did it. Brother Moses lived up there. And they put dynamite to it. And that dynamite burned up pretty close and went out. You can't destroy a child of God as long as the Lord's got something for him to do. They didn't do nothing with Daniel, they put him in the lions' den but the lions wouldn't eat him, they just laid down. And they throwed the Hebrew children in the fiery furnace and it didn't burn them a bit. Didn't even singe the hair on their head. It didn't blow Brother Moses up. Brother Moses was a real man of God.

Warned that there were threats on his life, Reverend Moses moved to Kenvir. A few days later, the church was destroyed by a bomb.[10]

The God-fearing, patriotic UMW, then, met with the same violence, Red-baiting, and charges of "outside-ness" as the atheistic, Communist NMU: perhaps Communism had not been the real issue after all. In 1935, when Governor Laffoon sent a committee headed by National Guard general Henry H. Denhardt to investigate conditions in Harlan, local authorities told them that the county would be more peaceful if radicals, agitators, and "Reds" were kept out. On the other hand, the UMW used much more incendiary talk than the Communists: organizer Sam Caddy offered the governor "a division of coal miners that would march into Harlan County and place the American flag over the sheriff's office"; district president William Turnblazer claimed that only he was able to stop the miners from making "the Cumberland river run red with blood."[11] As late as 1986, a slogan on a cap proudly worn by an old coal miner in Lynch read, "God, Guts and Guns Made the UMWA."

In a 1934 memorandum to the Labor Relations Board, John L. Lewis denounced "an organized and desperate attempt on the part of the coal operators of Harlan County Kentucky to defeat the purpose of the National Industrial Recovery Act [by means of] brutal beatings, ambuscades, dynamiting, kidnapping, shooting into cars upon public highways and into private homes by hired gun-men of the coal operators of Harlan County, acting under authority of deputy sheriff commissions."[12] General Denhardt's committee concluded that in Harlan "There exists a virtual reign of terror . . . a monster-like reign of oppression, whose tentacles reached into the very foundation of the social structure . . . It appears that the principal cause of existing conditions in Harlan County is the desire of the mine operators to amass for themselves fortunes through the oppression of their laborers, which they do through the Sheriff's office."[13] In 1937, the National Labor Relations Board found that "one of the major functions of the [Harlan County Coal Operators] Association is to exert the combined power of the coal operators of Harlan County against the organization of the mine employees, and to interfere with, restrain, and coerce the workers in the mines of Harlan County in the exercise of their right to self-organization."[14]

"Old Man" Lawson's Cornett-Lewis mine at Louellen and the U.S. Steel town of Lynch were exemplary cases. In 1933, Cornett-Lewis signed a contract with the union, and three hundred men joined it. But a year later the company abolished the union checkweighman, evicted all union activists, and compelled the remaining miners to work longer hours. About a hundred men struck in soli-darity; deputy sheriffs went from house to house, forcing them back to work at gunpoint.[15] A few days later, John L. Smith, a black union miner, was kidnapped in Louellen by deputy sheriffs in the presence of Robert Lawson, taken to Black Mountain, whipped, and left for dead.[16] When miners voted on union represen-tation, Lawson required them to sign their names to their ballot slips—of course, the vote was overwhelmingly against the union. Miners also voted, under Lawson's supervision, to reject the right to elect their own checkweighman. Cornett-Lewis didn't sign another contract until 1938.[17]

At Lynch, the UMW was confronted with a full-fledged military structure, funded and trained by U.S. Steel's private police organization, under orders from chief Joseph R. Menefee. In view of the UMW drives of 1933 and 1935, the Lynch police department spent more than a thousand dollars on tear gas and weapons.[18] The union fought back: "Naturally don't nobody want to bear the blame when it comes to the shooting, but it's both sides. There was some regular bushwhackers. They'd tell you, 'Don't go to 32 mine of a morning: there's gonna be a few men standing around, and if you go in there some of them gonna kill you'" (*Johnny Jones*).

> JAMES HALL: Everybody was sitting on the edge: you didn't know what was going to happen next. They were trying to set the union up. Men used to go back in this garage, my father was in the group. They said they had a cow club, that they went across this mountain to buy a cow, and they'd bring it back and divide the meat. But they were trying to organize a union. If the company caught you trying to organize a union, you wouldn't have no more job here. They would take you to the line: "Don't step back over in Lynch." And you didn't come back.

The company police stopped and harassed anyone who came to Lynch and expelled those who could not justify their presence: "I remember my mother, her sister used to come and visit us, and when she would get out of the train a policeman would follow her to see what she was doing. They would follow her to my dad's house and they would come in and ask who they were, how long they were going to stay" (*Lee Marsili*). George Titler writes about a deputy sheriff known as Preacher Johnson, "a big, ugly, sandy-haired fellow who looked something like a gorilla... Many a man was beaten up and kicked around in the Lynch camp by this so-called preacher." Harry Caudill recalls a guard known as "Thuggie," who was executed in revenge years later.[19] Black miners were told that if the company went union they would be taken off the skilled and better-paid jobs and their places would be taken by white men, that all the union wanted was their money, and that strikes and starvation would result if they joined. U.S. Steel also played the paternalism card by establishing an alternative company union, the Union of Lynch Employees.[20]

> EARL TURNER: When I came here in the thirties, they had what they called a ULE. It was just a company union. It wasn't no benefits or nothing at all. And I'll tell you, there was a whole lot of blacks, older men been here since this place opened. And they believed in it [a] hundred percent. They just loved U.S. Steel, they loved the way things was. And they jumped on me. They was gonna whup [me]. I got my shotgun one night. Man, I was about to kill people. You mess with me, I'm gonna kill you, buddy. I told 'em, "You see, we gonna get you all; you gonna join the union. You gonna be a union man if you work here." And one Sunday, I signed thirteen of them up.

By the time NIRA expired in 1935, only Black Mountain was union. Union membership had dwindled, labor rights and civil rights were nonexistent, and miners were left to wonder if, indeed, "a 'new deal' had come to the coal fields."[21]

OTHER BATTLES

> PORTELLI: Was your husband in the Battle of Evarts?
> DEBBIE SPICER: No. I knowed one of the men pretty good that got killed; but I didn't hear much about that.
> HAZEL KING: It was about politics, it wasn't about the union.

In Harlan, blood was spilled not just in union battles. For Debbie Spicer and Hazel King, the Battle of Evarts was not the clash of miners and deputies of May 5, 1932, but the shootout that took place on August 3, 1933, two days before the Republican primary—the only vote that really counted at the time in Harlan ("Use to, Republicans run this county, you couldn't even vote if you're not a

Republican. Your vote didn't amount to anything," *Ed Cawood*). Reform candidate Theodore Middleton and his brother Clarence caught some of J. H. Blair's men stuffing the ballot box with votes for the "courthouse gang," and in the shootout that followed, one of Blair's men was killed and two wounded. The county seemed to be on the brink of civil war, as hundreds of armed men converged on the county seat. In the following weeks, Governor Laffoon twice deployed the National Guard to oversee the election and keep the peace. Yet on election day three men were wounded in a battle at Tway and one was killed at Wallins Creek.[22]

> THEA CARTER: A place they call Layman, on election day, they got into it over the election, there was about five or six of them killed. I guess it was in the thirties. It's because they was drinking too much. Somebody [was giving out] liquor in order to get somebody to vote for him. And too many of them got to drinking a little heavy and they got in them brawls and when it was all wound up a bunch of them killed.

> RAY ELLIS: On election day the money and liquor flowed. Everybody buying votes and giving them a drink of liquor, a pint of liquor. I bought a few votes in my life: you'd hand them three dollars and they'd go vote. Then you'd give them a pint of liquor...Very little of it I've done, but I have done it. I handed out a little liquor, and handed out a few dollars. The first thing you know, they're shooting at each other. You'd have killings and things like that on election days. I remember an awful good friend got killed once, over nothing. They had been friends for years, and then they got into it, and shooting started.

"Back before World War Two, see, this county was filled up with slot machines, and the sheriff was taking a cut off of all of that—he got his cut off of the prostitution, he got his cut off of the slot machine, he got his cut off the liquor, the sheriff, and the judge" (*Norman Yarbrough*). In 1937, *Time* reported that Thomas R. Middleton "served five months for bootlegging before he was elected High Sheriff of Harlan County in 1934. Member of one of the section's largest families, Sheriff Middleton once had a distant cousin named Elmon Middleton who was prosecuting attorney of Harlan County and started a crusade for miners' rights. Two years ago Cousin Elmon stepped on his automobile starter, went up in confetti, flesh and dynamite." "Elmon married a cousin of mine. They wired his car, blew him up. He was the county attorney and this had nothing to do with coal mines. The people that killed him were interested in the slot machines" (*Ed Cawood*).[23]

Harlan had been solidly Republican since the Civil War; though the Democrats began to gain some ground thanks to the New Deal, the two-party system remained little more than a fiction. In both parties, the local chairman was an official of the HCCOA anyway.[24]

EWELL BALLTRIP: In the twenties, especially in the thirties and up into the forties, politics and the affairs of government were things that most people didn't have much control over. When we had the coal camps, the miner was dependent upon the company for everything. As long as a family or a miner did what the company wanted, there were no problems. [But] if the miner voted for a candidate who was not in line with the operator, the operator would know about it [and] it was not uncommon for the operator to fire the miner. I mean, poll watchers had a way of figuring out who was voting for whom, there were illegal voting tactics.

BILL WINTERS: A friend of our family was involved in the election. And what he did, he was voting people himself. My dad had passed on and this guy he votes my dad too. Of course they caught that man. There was a family there that owned a mule and they told a story that he had voted the mule. He stayed out of jail, somehow. And I remember one time down in Wallins Creek, the Democrats were paying a dollar for vote. The Republicans had some money so they were paying two dollars.

"The managers of the mines, they'd tell you how to vote. And they voted people had been dead for years, and mules and everything. It was rough, back in those days" (Lloyd Lefevre). Elections were invalidated for irregularities in 1931 and 1937; in 1935, the National Guard came in to oversee the Republican primaries, and in 1942 forty-four county officials were convicted of fraud in the U.S. senatorial election. At Mary Helen in 1937, the company clerk cast all the votes in his precinct and threw away the voters' real ballots. At Klondike, near Highsplint, three election officials (all UMW members) and a company guard were killed over the attempt to steal a ballot box.[25] At Molus, Sheriff Theodore Middleton ran a "chain ballot" in the company commissary.[26]

"We have always been ruled by the Coal Association to a certain extent, because that's where the money is" (Hazel King). Since the Civil War and the industrial revolution, and to some extent up to recent times, clientelism, corruption, and familism have been tools of political domination, as the people who controlled jobs also dominated politics and used the political system for personal gain and power.[27]

JEFF TIPTON: It's just pure power. Poverty is so high here, you got a person on food stamps, and you got a person on unemployment, don't have a job, living in poverty. Here comes a guy, the bag man, "We want you to vote for such-and-such candidate, we'll give you fifty dollars." That's a lot of money to them, it's a lot of money to me! And then, they have people in the polls, that watches, and the person goes in and votes right, and when he leaves they'll pop him fifty dollars.

Election billboards in Appalachia display only the candidates' names, without any indication of what programs or ideas they stand for. I asked *Enterprise* editor Ewell Balltrip what politics means in Harlan: "I guess, just the way the system works. Boy, I'll tell you, you're making me think. Politics in this context means that people are employing certain methods to achieve the end that they desire." In interviews, Anne Napier and Joan Robinett told me that politics in Harlan is based on "lies" and "corruption"; they may generalize unduly and be overly pessimistic, but they have ample experience of local politics.

"They say, 'Let's get this man in, because he will help us over here and he will help us get this road straightened out, this creek drained.' So this is the way politics works. It's part of our heritage and in America too. Support the politician who is closer to where we live" (*Arthur Johnson*). "Traditionally, the patriarch of the family would put the word out that he thought that his clan ought to vote for candidate B and all the members of that family would just vote for candidate B. Because Granddaddy said to. And I think that still happens today [1986], but I think there is not as strong an attachment to Granddaddy's wishes as it was twenty years ago" (*Ewell Balltrip*).

> JOAN ROBINETT: When I was campaigning for county judge [in the 1980s] and I would door-to-door across the county, I met this one fellow, and he said the best way to win the election here in Harlan County, he said, "You buy it off on the inside first." I learned later that buying it off on the inside [means] you pay your poll workers first, and then you pay people to come in and vote for you. I met this fellow, up on Yoakum Creek. And he said, "I'll set this precinct up for you. I get your voters lined up," he said "but you're going to have to bring some money." And he said, "Bring me a brown paper sack, just put small bills in it. I'm going to need some election whiskey and some vino." I didn't know what vino was. But I found out later it's a two-dollar bottle of wine. And he said: "I'll get your hollows lined up and there'll be a hundred dollars per car, you know, driver." And he said: "Now, if you don't, you won't carry this precinct." And I said: "I won't carry it then. Because I don't believe in doing that." His family had always worked the area, they had always been election workers, and that's something that I learned, that people that buy and sell votes are not really bad people. They are not all crooks, and they are not all corrupt. It's something that's been handed down from generation to generation, and it's a way of life.

THE KILLER SHOT

SILL LEACH: In the thirties, I guess it was, what they call spinal meningitis broke out through that part of the country. We lived up on the hill there. You could see the other houses down here and I'd see them carry three and

four people out of the house that would be dead, from that spinal meningitis. And they had the hospital full of people, and they had them in the
courthouse, laying around, laying on cots. It killed a lot of people.

Seventy-five people died from spinal meningitis in Harlan County in 1936–
37.[28] "It was a trying time. I remember spalingitis...whether that's what it was. I
don't if it was correct to call it that. And then there was a lot of liver disease that
came about—an epidemic of yellow jaundice. It seemed like every kid in the
coal mine camp got it. I woke up one morning and I had it. My eyes were all
yellow" (*Bill Winters*).

SILL LEACH: They had outdoor toilets, didn't have no bathroom like they
got now, you know. They didn't have good water supply either. You had to
go pump your water [from] springs, creeks, and at that time the hogs and
cattle they run out, maybe up above the spring, maybe an old hog would
die, or a cow'd die or something and [be dumped into the creek]. During
that time, hogs, a lot of them died with they call cholera. I don't know
whether [the epidemic] could have developed from that or what, but
anyway they had no bathrooms, it was all outside toilets.

In 1913, a sanitary commission found that 42.3 percent of the individuals sam-
pled in the county were infected with hookworm; tuberculosis and trachoma
were also widespread. Meningitis was not unknown, and the infant death rate
was appalling.[29] Influenza hit Harlan in 1919 and came back in 1931—though even
more people at the time died from pellagra and flux—and took its toll especially
among children. With hardly any medical facilities available, the prevalent cure
was Vicks salve. In the mid-thirties, sewage was still regularly dumped in the
rivers, and flies and rats were rampant.[30] "They didn't have screens over the windows and flies come, in the summer and..." (*Nellie Leach*).

SILL LEACH: Then, they come along with this spinal tap, what you call the
spinal tap. [If diagnosed for meningitis], they given them a shot in their
spine, and a lot of people got kind of upset, 'cause they didn't know what
it was, and, some of them would die after they give them that, and they
thought maybe that was what killed them. But anyway, me and my sister
went into a house where this child had died. And they had the house
quarantined. We went to school with this child and we went to see him,
and that's how come we've catched that. And then they had what they call
the killer shot. Two doctors had to be there when they give that shot. So
they called [the doctor] from Highsplint and this doctor at Kitts and they
give me that shot. Dad he come and told me, "Son," he said, "they're
going give you a shot they call the killer shot." He said, "In fifteen minutes, you will be getting better, or you'll die within fifteen minutes." So I
said, "Well Dad, it looks like I'm going to die anyhow." I was real small,
you know. "Just let them go ahead and give it to me." So they did and

Mother she said she quit hearing me breathe, and she thought I had died. But what happened, that stuff that was in my throat had just left, I guess.

"They quarantined everything. Couldn't be over two on the street together. They're two or three guys out in the street, they break it up" (*Ray Ellis*). Churches and schools were closed; all meetings, including the union's, were banned. As Reverend Musick noted, however, certain places stayed open: "And while all the doors of our sacred meeting places were closed, the doors were wide open for all the roadhouses and beer gardens that were owned and controlled by Mr. Middleton and his friends...We thought that we should have a right to meet and sing and pray and preach if Middleton's folks could sing and dance with a packed hall, six or seven nights out of each week."[31]

> PORTELLI: You remember a meningitis epidemic in the thirties?
> DUKEY JONES (FUNERAL DIRECTOR): Yeah. Mr. Anderson had the contract to haul all of them. He had the funeral home at the hardware store on Common Avenue, did the embalming up on the third floor. He always said, "Put your white coat on, son, your gloves, let's go." Handle them and bury them. Different ages, babies and everything. They didn't have a lot of funerals either. They dug the graves and buried [as fast as they could].

IN THE NAME OF JOHN L. LEWIS

The union started another campaign in 1935, after the enactment of the National Labor Relations Act (Wagner Act), and again in 1937 after it was upheld by the Supreme Court. The act excluded company unions, blacklists, yellow dog contracts, and discriminatory antiunion practices.[32] The HCCOA reacted by giving free rein—as well as money and weapons—to Ben Unthank and his cohorts. On July 7, 1935, a miners' rally to celebrate the passing of the Wagner Act was attacked and dispersed by deputy sheriffs in what came to be known as the "second Battle of Evarts." In August, union activist Howard Williams was kidnapped from his house, taken to the county line, and ordered never to return to Harlan (he did, and was arrested and jailed). Once again, the National Guard returned to Harlan.[33]

After the November election, Albert B. "Happy" Chandler replaced Ruby Laffoon as governor. The union had supported his rival Thomas Rhea in the Democratic primary but endorsed him in the general election. However, Chandler immediately cleared Sheriff Theodore Middleton of all charges and ended his predecessors' efforts to enforce some degree of rule of law in Harlan.[34] Antiunion violence flared again: organizer "Tick" Arnett and his co-workers were tear-gassed in the Harlan hotel, and two of their cars were dynamited; later, Arnett was shot at on the road from Black Mountain to Harlan; in February, organizer Thomas Ferguson was critically wounded in an ambush near Verda.[35]

On February 9, while the Reverend Marshall Musick was visiting Ferguson in the Pineville hospital, gun thugs fired into his home and killed his son Bennett. A miner and a Baptist minister, Musick had lived and worked at Louellen for twenty years. He had been a union field worker and had served as union check-weighman. Many times he was beaten, arrested, shot at, threatened.[36] "I knowed Preacher Musick. I knowed his family well, I lived by 'em. You're talking about the one his son got killed? He was a good preacher and had a wonderful family. His wife was with me when [my daughter] was born" (*Debbie Spicer*). "Musick was one of our neighbors. They had a garden right in front of our home, on the hillside. And one of the boys that we knew so well and had seen as a teenager, working in his garden, was killed. They said that some men, gun thugs, was in the cars, and they shot into the window and the young boy was the one that was hit" (*Hazel King*). "Mr. Musick was out that night and the thugs thought he was home. Or they didn't care who they killed. They shot through the window, and killed his son. Eighteen-year-old boy; was sitting at the table, doing his home-work. Mr. Musick, he wasn't home that night. They meant to kill him, but they killed his son" (*Hazel Leonard*).

"We were all in the living room, me and the three boys, setting around the fireplace, and the daughter was ironing at the ironing board just behind us, cleaning up just between us and the radio, when the shooting began on that side of the house," Mallie Musick told the La Follette Committee. "The first shot that I heard...I thought for a second it was something exploded in the grate. I was setting in front of the grate, and I looked down, and by that time there was another one." They went into the bedroom for cover and found Bennett lying on the floor. He was fifteen years old; he had already worked in the mines for a year, and had joined the union.[37]

We did not know he was dead until Pauline—she just fell to the floor and crawled into the dresser and then she said, "Be quiet, Mama." And we hushed for two or three seconds, or two or three minutes maybe, then the shooting stopped, and I thought—well, I said, "are any of you shot?" And the baby boy said, "I am shot in the arm," and Pauline said, "I am not shot," and Virgil went behind the door, the fourteen-year-old boy got behind the door and two bullets went in just above his head. He just scattered down behind the door that stood open just a little, and I took Bennett by the shoulder. I was right over him and I thought my leg was bleeding...And I shook Bennett, and he was dead. We did not have a light in the room, and Pauline and I just drug him to the door where the light shined in from the living room and seen he was dead. She unbuttoned the clothes and felt his chest, and he was already dead.[38]

After Bennett Musick's murder, a subcommittee of the U.S. Senate Committee on Education and Labor, chaired by Senator Robert La Follette, investigated what was termed "Violations of Free Speech and the Rights of Labor" in Harlan County. For the first time, the federal authorities were assuming that the rights of labor were civil rights that the government ought to protect. FBI agents were sent into Harlan County to seek evidence of a conspiracy to violate the miners' rights. The purpose was not only to restore the rule of law in the county but also to break the resistance and unfair competition of the "coal barons" who had frustrated the government's effort to stabilize markets and labor relations.[39]

Twenty-two companies, twenty-four operators, and Sheriff Middleton, along with twenty-two of his deputies, were brought to trial for violating the 1870 Civil Rights Act.[40]

BRYAN WHITFIELD: Mister, I went through that trial and we got a hung jury. A hundred and one of us were indicted under an old Civil War act, wanted to protect the niggers...The main thing was we wouldn't sign with the union. That was the whole damn trouble. John L. Lewis had given Mr. Roosevelt five hundred thousand toward reelection and in my opinion, Mr. Roosevelt was trying to pay him back. We polished the benches down there for a number of weeks; we got a hung jury. The lawyers, after the trial they said that the government would drop it if we'd sign with the union. Several of the old men—old man Bob Creech, Mr. Tway, and several others—said, "We are just too old to go through this again. We are going to sign."[41]

Though legally inconclusive, the trial did change labor relations in Harlan. The Kentucky legislature put an end to the company-paid deputy sheriff system; in September 1938, the majority of the operators (with the exception of the captive mines of Lynch and Benham) signed the current national contract. For the first time almost all the workforce in Harlan was covered.[42] But peace did not last long. In April 1939, the contract expired, and the UMWA called a national strike for the union shop; all the mines in Harlan were shut down. Spirits were high, wrote George Titler to Lewis: "Each day a parade starts somewhere in the county and marches to Harlan with banners and flags and they usually have a string band to furnish the music for the parade"—yet "we have about fifteen hundred men in Harlan County and about eight hundred in Bell County who are practically destitute." This time, however, the miners could not be starved into submission: the union provided some relief and posted bond against evictions, and food and supplies also came in from the Works Progress Administration.[43]

Attempts to reopen the mines at Clover Fork and Kentucky Cardinal were thwarted by mass demonstrations and pickets. "Hordes of union miners," writes G. C. Jones, swept through the coal camps, setting fire to buildings, running strikebreakers and deputies out, and destroying the property of operators who had worked them at starvation wages. Railroad bridges were dynamited—in some cases, Jones claims, by the companies themselves in order to blame the union.[44] Miners who refused to join the union were singled out for punishment.

SILL LEACH: If you didn't join the union, they would put a cowbell on you and throw you in the river. They jumped Dad up one day, he was waiting for the bus, and told Dad they was going to put a cowbell on him and throw him in the river. He said, "You're not going to do no such thing either." Well, so Dad got a rock and he conked this fellow on the head with this rock. About that time the bus [came] so Dad jumped on the bus and he was gone and left that guy laying there. But they didn't get to throw him in the river.

According to a National Guard report, the strikers' "favorite past-time…was to catch some worker or a member of his family alone by himself and to throw him into the creek with the baptismal ceremony, 'We baptize you in the name of the Father and of the Son and of John L. Lewis.'" The strikers would "parade in force to each mine along their route and by threats and jeers…intimidate those who might desire to go back to work." Pickets would "hang around the mining camp all night and keep the men who went to work and their family awake the entire night and in fear for their safety. They would scratch on windows, throw rocks against the doors and through the windows, throw bunches of fire crackers on the porches and under the houses, and fire pistols around the houses." In a speech on May 1, 1939, Governor Chandler proclaimed: "During the last few weeks miners have been thrown into the river. Miners and public officials have been beaten and bruised and miners have been baptized in the name of John L. Lewis and the CIO, and many workers have been intimidated by representatives of the union. This is not peaceful picketing."[45] By mid-May, most Appalachian operators had signed union contracts. Only Harlan County held out. On May 15, Chandler sent in the National Guard.

"[They came] to keep peace in the family. Miners were striking and we was trying to operate and couldn't. [The purpose] was to keep them open. [The miners] always thought it was against them. Of course, the National Guard was to keep law and order" (*Bryan Whitfield*). The troops were quartered on the property of the Whitfields and other mine companies.[46] "We lived at Shields. That's where they had the big strike in '39. And they brought the National Guard in. It was really scary. I could look out and see the guards behind trees and over the tipples. What they did was guard the nonunion people, and let them go on to work. That's all they did" (*Hazel Leonard*).

LEWIS BIANCHI: I was in junior high school. They called us all down to the auditorium and said, "The militia's coming in. Gonna be a lot of killing. We're going to dismiss school. All you children go to the riverbank, and go home." And, of course, as soon as we got out, we went to see what the militia looked like. It was like a little army had moved in there, you know.

GLADYS HOSKINS: Yes, I can remember seeing the National Guard march down Main Street. And—this might sound terrible to say, but somehow it was a little bit exciting. When I think about it now, I can just see myself standing there on the street and seeing them go by, and—I guess I just felt, "Gee, this is exciting. Look, what's going on here." And I didn't take it as seriously as I should have and as all the people involved took it, you know.

The *London* (Kentucky) *News* reported: "[At Kitts] I found troops manning machine guns on the bridge and another on the roof of the company store. Others had automatic rifles. Movement of pickets was confined between the rails of the Louisville and Nashville Railroad...Any attempts by pickets or bystanders to step outside the rails was promptly thwarted by the guards." "Like Hitler seizing Czechoslavakia [*sic*]," the paper editorialized, "the Governor thrust into Harlan County hundreds of mystified Guardsmen, bristling with automatic rifles and machine guns, [with] order to 'shoot to kill'....In Germany and Italy, labor questions are settled by armed suppression of the workers. In America the people through their legislatures and courts have established the enduring, democratic method of collective bargaining which must not be destroyed."[47] "Happy Chandler done told us he's goin' to run Harlan town," sang Hazard miner-musician George Davis; but if he sent the National Guard in to protect the strikebreakers, "the undertakers will be busy a-puttin' on some brand-new shrouds."[48]

> BEN CAMPAGNARI: And then we went to Kitts one time to picket. And when we got to Kitts and we got on the hill, here come the state police, two of them, and said, "Now boys," he said, "we are not against the union. We just want you to not tear up none of the company property, peaceful picketing." And this colored fellow, "Well," he said, "maybe it's all right, but," he said, "just think about some of them that's in here, they had no breakfast yet." And the National Guards was standing in this little alley that some of them women up there, their husbands belonged to the union. And I don't see how we kept that poor old soldier, that guard, for not shooting that woman. She [threw] scalding water right out on him. He stood up like that, and the captain told him no. But lots of the National Guards wouldn't have done anything anyway because half of them was from the area, see, brothers having to fight against their own people. They wouldn't have done much anyway.

On the Kitts bridge, the *London News* article continued, "several United Mine Workers fraternized with the guards." An eighteen-year-old Guardsman said: "I'd rather be on the picket line, because that's where I belong—with the workingman." Another, also eighteen, from Harlan, had a brother on the picket line; he refused the coffee and cigarettes served to the troops by the order of A. F. Whitfield: "The coffee don't taste so good and I won't smoke the cigarettes. My brother's one of the Jones boys" (the roving pickets). An aged miner told

Guardsmen, "We ain't got nothing against you boys....You don't mean us no harm and we don't mean you any. If we wanted trouble us miners have rifles too, and we can shoot. There are 12,000 of us and only five hundred of you."

HUGH COWANS: I can remember right there in Cardinal, when Governor Chandler, Happy Chandler, sent those tin horns in there to guard what they call scabs, in the mines. I faced the machine guns, that morning. A line of machine guns, the National Guard's there. And, you see, we had a woman's local in Cardinal, Kentucky. And their son was manning over the machine guns. And we sent for them. And they came down the road with clubs in their hands singing "Amazing Grace" and all those spiritual songs. And one woman looked up from singing her song and she—"What you doing up there?" And she got him off that machine gun that was sitting on that boulder. And that's when we broke through. She said, "You're not gonna fight *me*." We organized that place, too.

PORTELLI: I heard you met your wife on the picket line.

HUGH COWANS: But she was on the company side then. She was throwing rocks at me. We had gone to this mine where they lived, in Cardinal, Kentucky. And we had told the people to stop working because we were out trying to get a contract, and they was just about the ones that was working...

JULIA COWANS: See, they were ignorant of the fact of being united, what this union would do. Whatever the company officials said, that was the law: "If you let this union in here, you're not gonna have a job, you and your family gonna have to get off, you know." So the men were frightened. They had their families and they couldn't afford to be thrown out, with no work or nothing. And we would stand and see all those pickets coming, it scared us to death. We knew they were coming to stop the men from working. That's all we knew about it. And we'd be little kids at that time, and so I used to get a bunch of kids and we'd line up and get us a pile of rocks and we'd start throwing rocks at 'em, you know.

HUGH COWANS: But when they find out all this benefit that was for them, they was willing to fight for it. But before they got organized, Harlan County blood ran like water. Many a man lost their lives. And oh, they were slaughtered like hogs.

Letters poured into the governor's office, arguing passionately for or against the sending of the National Guard. Citizens from Bell County wrote that "75% of the miners are willing to work, if they can get protection"; as if in reply, a letter from Clover Fork pointed out that they were indeed willing to work, but not without a contract. Several letters from union members reiterated the revolutionary demand: "We want representation in our government." From a union representative: "Is Harlan County part of the United States or Germany? Does your office represent the coal operators or the 20,000 miners of Harlan County,

Kentucky?" From out of state: "I greatly admire your courage in daring to act in opposition to that foreigner, John L. Lewis and his loyal backers, the President of our United States and the New Dealers"; "It is your duty to arrest and imprison John L. Lewis and any others who come into your state to inject themselves in the coal strike." A letter from Chicago suggested sending all nonresidents found on the pickets to the penitentiary; Chandler found the suggestion "excellent." Mrs. A. D. Barbour, a Kentuckian living in Lansing, Michigan, warned: "There has been enough blood shed in those mountains, you will have to answer to God for every man that is hurt—you will pay through eternity."[49]

EARL TURNER: Some places you never did get organized. Some men [were] just venom. They stood against it. I went on a picket line up to Yancey, Kentucky, above Harlan. It was rough there then. And we'd left [Lynch] about one o'clock that night. I had a little ole 32-20 automatic pistol. In about fifty cars, old cars back then. We loaded up at the union hall. We were gonna go up and organize that mines up in that hollow. And went about four o'clock that morning, three o'clock. And they could have killed us that night. They was waiting on us, up a little narrow road, just like a pig path. And, buddy, they'd poured like two bushels of roofing tacks, roofing nails, all over the highway. Punctured those tires, and the first four or five cars stopped, had the whole caravan held up, 'bout seventy-five cars, I guess. And we were hemmed up right between two mountains. If they'd been in the woods shooting they could [have] killed every one of us. And we finally got them flats fixed, changed tires, got on up at the hollow, and went on that mountain where the mine is, way up on that mountain. And [our] guys saw them coming off out of the night shift— you talk about whipping jokers' tails. I 'member a man named Camel Johnson. He grabbed a white fella there and he whupped him good, buddy. You gonna join the union or else. They finally got that place organized. But in the sixties they went back the other way.

By the beginning of July, organizer George Titler writes, the situation seemed stalled: the National Guard was protecting nonstrikers, and only Creech had signed the union contract. At the Mahan-Ellison Coal Company mine, a $4,000 cutting machine was dynamited. A few days later, pickets attempted to stop nonunion workers from entering the mine at Stanfill under the protection of the National Guard. Shots were fired—each side said the other had fired first— and a union miner, Dock Caldwell, was killed. Another, Daniel Noe, died three days later from his wounds. A National Guard officer and a soldier were wounded.[50] The National Guard lined up the pickets and marched them under the gun nine miles to jail in Harlan. Titler was also arrested, taken to Harlan, held for four days with 221 other prisoners, charged with "sedition, forcible rebellion and armed attack on a National guardsman," and released on bond. On July 15, union miner Bill Roberts was killed at Stanfill (in self-defense, according to the police; according to others, in a drunken brawl) by a non-union man.[51]

Meanwhile, the UMW and the Harlan operators had reached a compromise: there would be no formal recognition of the union shop, but the right to strike and the union's role as bargaining agent for all Harlan County mines were guaranteed. "Things are quieting down slowly," Titler wrote to John L. Lewis. But while much changed, some things stayed the same: "Most of these miners' families are about as naked as Jay Birds."[52]

One place that became organized, but not by the UMW, was the International Harvester mine at Benham, where the company union chose to affiliate with the Progressive Mine Workers of America, a smaller organization based mainly in Illinois.[53] After Lynch signed with the UMW in 1937, the rivalry between the two adjacent company towns developed into an antagonism that peaked in an all-out battle in 1941.

> JOHNNY JONES: I was right here when they was organizing this place and Benham. They had a pretty hard time, a lot of trouble down the road, a lot of people got killed. It was a lot of shooting going on in Lynch during that time, but it was the Benham fellows shooting. It's two or three got killed down in there, one young boy got killed right on the highway, opened his door and somebody shot him. And then they found one [body] up on the mountain, they didn't know who killed him because the woods was full of both sides.

> JAMES HALL: The bullets were coming across the line. That's during the time they were trying to organize Benham, and Benham never was organized into the UMWA. They set up a union of their own. The company furnished all them men down there guns, they had machine guns, they had rifles. I know one of my friends got killed. Lived in Benham, we played football against each other. He come out one of those little houses down there with a rifle in his hand, and, see, they was shooting from mountain to mountain. They was all over the mountain. Somebody shot him, I don't know who shot him, but he was killed.

"DADDY JOHN" LEWIS

"We were glad," said the Reverend Hugh Cowans, "when John L. Lewis came along and God sent along the man, in '37, '38."

> LLOYD LEFEVRE: We had a hard time getting it [the union] in, but we finally got it. We wouldn't have it though if it hadn't been for the President, and John L. Lewis. They worked together on that. I heared President Roosevelt making a speech one time, he said he was a worker hisself and he wouldn't work for nobody he had [not] hisself agreed to work with. That's when we got it in.

Samuel Boggs, from Closplint, sang:

> *Then along came a man, brave as any lion*
> *He called us together and asked to join.*
> *Long as we may live we'll love "Daddy John"*
> *For the many good things that he has done.*[54]

John L. Lewis and the union, then, were "sent" or "came along" or "came in": the union was not built by the miners, but existed outside and independently of them. The heroes of the struggle are John L. Lewis and Franklin Delano Roosevelt. "The President wants you to join the union": somehow, the miners' greatest act of self-assertion, joining the union, sounds like another act of obedience. The paternalism of the union continues or replaces the paternalism of the coal camps.

Preacher Musick told the La Follette Committee that in Louellen in 1934 the strikers were "*made* to put on their work clothes [and were] *driven* to the main hoists, where they *were loaded* up and *taken* to the mines" (italics added). Lawson, in turn, claimed that the men were forced to strike by the union, which had sent organizers to knock on miners' doors at night to tell them not to go to work the next day.[55] In both versions, rather than free agents, miners appear as passive objects of contention between two forces, either benevolent or malevolent, but both endowed with power over them. They don't do things; they are *made to* do them. Thus, the rise of the union means less providing the miners with power of their own than placing them under the aegis of another protective institution, to the point that the UMWA took on some of the paternalistic functions of the company.[56] The dependence inherited from the company town continued in the union shop, from "Old Man" Lawson to "Daddy John" L. Lewis. On occasion, the two paternalistic powers might interact, and one could be accessed through the other:

> BRYAN WHITFIELD: I remember one time we had a man that belonged to the union, from the beginning. But he was a good coal miner and just as honest and straight as could be, and whenever we had labor trouble he just got out of the way. Well, I had to write John L. Lewis one time when he put in for a pension. I don't know [why], he couldn't get it. So I wrote John L. Lewis and told him he was turning down one of his own best men, and he got his pension.

"John L. Lewis, he was probably one of the greatest union organizers and leaders of all time" (*Mickey Messer*). "I've got his picture hanging there, and I've got another one, if I get another frame, I'm going to manage to put it up, too" (*Sudie Crusenberry*). Just as company power became humanized and personalized in the figures of Robert Lawson, Pearl Bassham, and Old Man Creech, the benevolent power of the union is embodied in John L. Lewis. "He has stopped them working us twelve hours a day," sang Samuel Boggs; never mind that it was the workers' bodies on the picket line, their courage, their endurance, even their violence that changed conditions in Harlan County.

The larger-than-life image of John L. Lewis, especially in the epic days of the early CIO; his untrammeled, autocratic power over the organization; the accentuated personalization of American politics; the association with the popular image of President Roosevelt—all these factors meshed with the miners' own culture, their religion ("learning to lean"), and their company-town experience to shape a projective identification with the leader. This attitude was reinforced when the union brought welfare, relief, services, and opportunities unthinkable only a few years before. "I am so grateful for the Welfare Fund," wrote a Wallins Creek miner in 1948: "I will be for John L. Lewis 'til my dying day and stand for the union and my rights. Bless him, he has stopped the starving here in my home as well as kept others from starving." A miner from Highsplint, in the same issue of the *UMW Journal*:

> I certainly wish to express my most sincere appreciation and thanks to Mr. Lewis for making it possible for me and mine to have a swell time each year on my ten days' vacation and $100. For, having spent approximately 25 years in the coal mines and having worked for as little as 28 cents per ton, I think it is something to be mighty thankful for.[57]

In all the letters published by the *Journal*, miners never seem to say that it was *they* who put an end to starvation in Harlan County, made John L. Lewis the president of a powerful union, and were paying his salary. Indeed, there is a vicarious sense of pride in being represented by a wealthy power figure that can impress, and even hobnob with, the other side: "Old Thomas Moses [president of Lynch's U.S. Coke and Coal Company] and John L. Lewis was buddies and they didn't depend on the little one-horse owners, here; they went to Pittsburgh and worked out the thing, and that just kept down the trouble" (*Johnny Jones*).

> BRYAN WHITFIELD: Well, John L. Lewis, he had a tough reputation. If he'd run for president, I'd have voted for him because he could get what he wanted. A big man. One of the most gracious men I ever saw in my life. He was the most powerful man in the United States, wasn't he?

Letters and interviews evince the virtues of the subaltern: trust, faithfulness, gratitude. Cover after cover of the *Journal* (at least three in 1948) show miners or widows receiving checks from Lewis or other union officials, or Lewis signing or handing out relief or pension checks.[58] The amount of the checks is often prominently indicated; headlines remind members of how much their welfare payments are costing the union treasure, as if these were gifts rather than hard-won rights. In telling continuity between company and union paternalism, a photograph shows union officials in Lynch dressed as Santa Claus, handing fruit and candy to the miners' children.[59]

"God sent along the man," says Hugh Cowans; and again, "The Lord bless[ed] us, as I said, with John L." A Baptist preacher, Reverend Cowans wouldn't take the Lord's name in vain. Nor are miners who are very serious about their religion entirely tongue-in-cheek when they engage in the "sacrilegious" act of baptizing scabs "in the name of the father, the son, and John L. Lewis." Of course, we must not take too literally what amounts to worship of the leader figure. But the religious imagery is there all along: "These miners, he was their savior, he brought them out of darkness" (*Donald Hensley*).

Lewis's image shades imperceptibly into myth, imagination, and prayer. A spate of letters from Bell County in 1940–41 evince a folk belief that Lewis can be approached for personal contributions. Lee Jim Rossie, from Hulm, Bell County, begs Lewis for "your old castaway pants and shirts for my Boys. Mr. Lewis my wife can fix them so we can send them to school." Joe Spine, from Pineville, asks for "your old pants shoes coats hats for my kids."[60] "There was a brother here that said for me to write you and you would help me some" (Roy Fly, from Hulm). Just as in contemporary urban legends, the writers say they heard of this from unnamed secondhand sources:[61] "A Brother from Cardinal, Ky. told me that if I would write to you he told me that you send him a $5.00 Bill" (Jim Rossie); "I have a friend in Pineville that told me that you helped him out one time...the brother in Pineville told me to write you that you would send me some kind of help and told me that you sent him 5,00 Dollars to help him out brother" (Gary Brint, Newsdale).

Miners appealed to Lewis over the heads of their district officers, only to be referred back to them. Tillie Smithers, from Verda: "I am a widow and got 3 children to support and my husband got killed he was the President of the Yancy Local at death he was giving out aid for the miners when he was shot and killed and Im not able to work my children is small...my husband was Leslie Smithers got killed June 9, 1938." "I am sorry to learn of your unfortunate circumstances," Lewis answered; "I would suggest that you discuss your condition with the District Officers."[62]

George Titler concluded his autobiography, published during some of the UMW's most troubled times, with some ominous "Fatherly advice: 'It is not wise to attack the name of the Legendary John L. Lewis among the coal miners of America.'" More and more, "standing for the union" came to mean unquestioning support for its autocracy, an inbred attitude of dependence, an impulse to defend the union from real or supposed enemies, and the branding of all criticism and dissent as treason. In these attitudes lie the seeds of disaster and tragedy.[63]

CRUMMIES, APRIL 15, 1941

FLORENCE REECE: Was it 1938 or 1941 when the sheriff's deputy mounted a machine gun on the counter in the company store and shot down nine miners as they entered the door? Oh yeah, 1941.

Frances "Granny" Hager had been in the Battle of Evarts and remembered it well. Yet when historian Mike Mullins asked her, "What was the roughest place over there that you can remember? Roughest time you had here in organizing?" she said: "Let's see, I'll think the name of the place—Crummies Creek." Her interviewer couldn't place the episode. Likewise, when Florence Reece referred to Crummies Creek, the interviewer commented that even veterans could not recall what she was talking about.[64]

> GRANNY HAGER: Crummies Creek. Now, there was killing there and I can't tell you just how many that were killed. You see, I used to have all of that down, but it got washed away so many times, and burned out. I don't know all that did happen, but they really had a battle up there. I think there was five killed. They wanted the scabs to go on to work and they wanted to run the union men away, you see. And that is what started the battle. Now that was the roughest place we had in Harlan County.

History books and coeval media discuss the Battle of Evarts in detail; the equally dramatic Battle of Crummies is all but ignored. On the other hand, while the local memory of Evarts is suppressed and fragmented, the local memory of Crummies was vivid and long-lasting. I had no problem placing Florence Reece's and Granny Hager's reference: the abandoned company store at Crummies used to stand by the road from Harlan to Cranks Creek, where I stayed with the Napiers, and often, as we drove by, someone would mention the battle. But then the building was razed, a new road passed it by, and the site of memory was lost.

> GURNEY NORMAN: Each time I went by, it would be called to my memory. At some place I had heard stories of what had happened along that stretch of road, and I realized that every stretch of road is marked with blood. There isn't a curve that doesn't have a story, and that's why I like to drive these roads, is to have the stories return to my own thinking. I remember the commissary at Crummies always as a place that had this power of history and big events that took place there.

Crummies may have been easier to remember because it was more recent and less ideologically problematic; its absence from history may depend on the patterns of periodization and closure of much historical writing. "The thirties" is often taken too literally. Both John Hevener's history and William D. Forester's memoir end with the signing of the contracts in 1939: "striking a new balance of power," "let's stop right here, while it's nice and peaceful."[65] It makes narrative sense for a story that begins with a battle to end with some kind of peace; forget that miners had very little power and peace after 1939 anyway. As for the media, they are more interested in beginnings than in continuities. Evarts alerted the nation to the shocking discovery of class struggle in its own midst; by the time

Crummies took place, attention had shifted, war was looming, and a union shootout in the mountains was no longer about capitalists and workers in the class struggle but about "hillbillies" killing one another, as they just naturally will. The battle was not considered serious enough to send in the National Guard, nor was there a major trial (and no court records). All we have is the stories.

On April 1, 1941, the nation's mines were on strike over the operators' refusal to sign contracts with the union. On April 14, 1941, union pickets invaded Mary Helen. A mine superintendent was beaten unconscious; a night watchman, Earl Jones, was killed. "There's two or three people got killed up here, before my time. I remember my grandpa talking about [it]. His brother kept on working when the union was trying to get him not to work, so...they beat him up pretty bad (*Chester Clem*). The next day, the union descended upon nearby Crummies.[66]

> PLENNIE HALL: The day before the battle, I went into the office and I told Mr. Johnson, "Mr. Johnson," I says, "won't you sign the union? It would be good for everybody, to be satisfied with everything." And he said, "Hell no"; he wouldn't [sign] under no circumstances. And the next day, the union come up there to stop them from working.

> BECKY SIMPSON: Six years old. Me and my mother always walked from Cranks Creek to Crummies to the commissary [with] my dad's paycheck. They had a bunch of pickets up at the commissary. Me and her went into the commissary, and this big bald-headed guy, they called him Big Jim Black Hair, he was a big ball league player, he told my mother, "What're you doing here with this child today? Get what little you're going to and get this child back out, there's gon' be trouble today." As we was leaving the commissary, they was rolling up these big machine guns, that they could open up the double doors and shoot out. So me and Mommy is walking back up the mountain, we heared the shooting start. And they just mowed the men down.

The victims were union men Virgil Hampton, Oscar Goodlin, Charles Ruth, and Ed Tye. According to George Titler, they had gone into the Crummies company store to get a drink of water and were mowed down by company guard Bill Lewis, who had placed a machine gun on the store's meat block (Lewis himself was killed four months later).[67] The *Harlan Daily Enterprise* editorialized: "A few days ago a bunch of men invaded the commissary at Crummies Creek Coal Co., and four of them were carried out dead, and others, wounded. There were other dead which have never been admitted. A known leader of the men said the men were shot down when they entered the store to get a Coca-Cola apiece. Do I believe that? NO!...The only thirst the leaders of these men had was the thirst for the blood of someone not paying dues to the union."[68]

HAZEL LEONARD: In the morning the men, they'd all meet at a certain spot [to organize the pickets]. My husband was a rustler; he just went around through the camps, woked everybody up that morning. And he was scheduled to go to Crummies. And they was having some problems at Highsplint so they sent him to Highsplint. That's how he missed that; or he'd been in that too. And all of them carried guns, the union men carried guns: they had to, because they had to protect themselves, you know. And, when they got to Crummies, it was just like a army there.

Some details, like the machine gun on the meat counter, stand out in all the stories. Others are more uncertain: Did Lewis fire before or after the men entered the store? Did they really want a Coke? How many were on the picket? Were they armed? Was all the shooting on one side? Were there more casualties? If so, on which side, and how many?

BEN CAMPAGNARI: There was about five hundred that was on that march. We was all up there and the cars was parked around the commissary, all the way to the wood. Anyhow, the union had this van, with a loudspeaker. Virgil Hampton, he was talking over the loudspeaker. They said, "They closed the commissary." He said, "Let them close that damn scabby commissary, we don't want any of it no way." And part of our men was in there.

"And so some of the men went on in the store, not knowing that they had it set up, they'd just start firing on them. And when they got in there, they just started shooting the union men" (*Hazel Leonard*). "Then the machine guns started shooting, out from the top, upstairs, and it's cutting streaks of that pavement up, it looked like a big twisted tobacco. And, there was four that got killed there, see" (*Ben Campagnari*).

PLENNIE HALL: And there was a Hampton boy; he is related to these Hamptons that lives down here. There was three men killed, trying to save his life. He got shot in the leg, up in this thigh here, he was trying to get a bandage around it, keeping him from bleeding to death, and the machine gun upstairs in the office in the commissary [kept firing]. Never did know how many was killed at that time. One of them bullets hit me, and I don', know where it came from. It was a machine gun bullet; it was a .45 machine, upstairs. Were you ever in any kind of battle or anything? Never? If [they] ever begin a machine gun fire, you might as well lay there because if you move, or try to get up or get away, you're hurt, killed or shot. It's hard to think about, how times were pretty rough at that time.

BEN CAMPAGNARI: Now, we were running, and we had a pegleg man. You wouldn't believe it. Going down that railroad track, and he's hitting about four ties at a time; and he outrun half of the people that had good legs, and we was all a-running because they was cutting down with the machine gun, or trying to. It's lucky that more [didn't] get killed, you see. Virgil Hampton, and Tye, I can't think of the other two names. And one of the thugs was killed, but they would never tell his name. And I said: "If I ever go on a picket line, again, I'll go with protection." We died just like ducks. Peaceful picketing! One fellow went back to his car, he had a high-powered rifle, [placed] it over the crossing, and boy when you'd seen that thing fire, you could see them bricks a-flying out there. He was hitting that commissary, but he wasn't hitting that window where the machine gun was set up. They had it set up on meat blocks.

HAZEL LEONARD: The biggest battle happened in the basement. The store manager or maybe the butcher—anyway, he had a machine gun on the block where they chop meat. And he's the one turned that gun loose on these men that walked in first. And then when he did that—the rest of them was ready. They knew this battle was coming; and they was ready for it. All the union men went in there too, and they just wiped them [thugs] out. They just started killing—when it cooled down enough they could close the doors, you know, they did. I don't know how many they killed; we'll never know 'cause they didn't let it out.

MEEDIA JONES: [My husband and his brothers] was up on the mountain in the road up there, in a ditch. But they was close enough that they could see some of the thugs getting killed, and one of them was begging for help. He was shot and laying and I guess there was people who would have went and help him but they was afraid to show theirselves, that if they did they'd get shot or something. My husband was very upset when he came back that night. He had nightmares, you know, to think that things could be that rough.

Just as after the Battle of Evarts, the body count was a matter of debate. Neither side would admit to military defeat and let it rest. The union probably hid some of its casualties, the company never acknowledged any, and the killings went on in retaliation and vengeance in the days and months to come.

PLENNIE HALL: Three weeks later I was over there getting a payday, and there was a drainpipe runs down there, and somebody crawled in that drainpipe and that died, and the dogs pulled out some of his bones. There never was no more said about it. I wondered about who that could have been, or where they were from.

HAZEL LEONARD: And, that night, the thugs that lived, they carried all their dead men out of there and hauled them to the top of Crummies mountain, and burned them up. There was a place there, that they called the Halfway House, it was just a dive, you know, just for men to drink and hang out at. And they sold booze and everything, you know what I mean. So they hauled all these people out there, that had got killed that night—the thugs. They hauled them up that mountain to that place and then they burned it. They burned them up.[69]

Bill Lewis, who manned the machine gun in the commissary at Crummies, was killed four months later by a young man named William Deane. When asked why he did it, Deane said he was trying to win a medal.[70]

HAZEL LEONARD: And then some women from out west started investigating, wanting to know what'd become of their husbands, they didn't come back home and they never got any word. They don't know what happened to this day. Their husbands never made it back home, but they got killed and burned up, up on that mountain. 'Cause they'd hired guns, they told me, from out west, to come here to do this. One reason I know so much about this, my aunt's husband was one of the thugs. He was a police in Evarts, everybody knew him. They run him out of Harlan. They told him they never wanted to see him here again. And she told me.

Two weeks after the Battle of Crummies, another gunfight took place at Fork Ridge, on the Tennessee border, in Bell County. "The little mines over there called Fork Ridge. They worked all during the strike, nonunion. One morning, we heard it on the radio: three Fork Ridge leaders—I knowed them, all three—got killed this morning" (*James Belew*). The dead were three company officials and a union miner.[71] Shortly afterward, nearly all the operators signed the contract.

BRYAN WHITFIELD: I'm the last man in Harlan County to sign a union contract. I believe it was 1944. I was the last man and the reason, you see, I lived in the camp. I had 165 houses around here at Brookside. I knew my men and they knew me. And we didn't have any troubles like that. I had 404 men here and only four that belonged to the union. And then the war came on, and the contract was up. The union had most of the coal mines in Harlan County. There were a few of us not union—till practically into the war, when we had a general strike and the pickets wouldn't let us start up. They'd move five hundred, a thousand men down here just to take over the tipple and every damn thing and we couldn't start. The war was on. And the government put pressure on [the operators], said, "You've got to start that coal mine." So, reluctantly, my cousin, Ed Whitfield and I, went to Washington. And when we got to Washington, I said, "Be darned if I am going to be the first of the two." So when we got on to John L. Lewis's office ready to sign, I said, "I've got to go to the restroom." So my cousin had to sign first, and I had to sign second. So I guess I'm the last one of the old ones to ever sign a union contract.

11

HARLAN ON
OUR MINDS

LONG WAY TO HARLAN

Well, where were they? Goddamn, who knew? Way off in Perry County some-where, close to the Harlan County line. When you got close to Harlan County you were close to the Virginia line. And when you were in Virginia, you were in a state that ended at the ocean. Think of that. The Atlantic Ocean, just on beyond those hills there.[1]

As this passage from Gurney Norman's story "Night Ride" suggests, Harlan is both a real place and an elusive place of the imagination. Gurney Norman's character stands at its border but looks beyond, as if the ground of Harlan had no power to retain his imagination but only to set it in motion and project it further away.

Harlan on our minds is always part of a travel narrative: in Walter Tevis's *Man Who Fell to Earth*, the title character also "flew over Harlan, Kentucky, a drab city sprawled loosely in the foothills, and then over vast barren fields and into a valley."[2] John Cougar Mellencamp sings, "I've been to Harlan County / And I've been to Paris, Texas, and I've spent some time in Rome." Harlan is a place one flies over, leaves (Seldom Scene, "Leaving Harlan"), returns to (Kate and Anna McGarrigle's "Going Back to Harlan," or the country standard "Shady Grove": "Shady Grove, my little miss / I'm going back to Harlan"), or misses (Merle Haggard, "Sidewalks of Chicago"). Even staying is steeped in the idea of leaving (Darrell Scott, "You'll Never Leave Harlan Alive").[3]

One is always "a long way from Harlan, a long way from Hazard"—as in Merle Travis's "Nine-Pound Hammer"—but never really there. "I sang 'Nine Pound Hammer,' the other night," notes Harlan County musician Arthur Johnson, "which was written by Merle Travis, but Merle Travis is from western Kentucky. He mentions Harlan and Hazard, but he says he'd never been to Harlan and Hazard, he just knew where they were, or that they were in existence some place."[4]

Harlan County of the mind is a often a dark, complex place. In *Poems out of Harlan County*, Vivian Shipley molds Harlan memories into tormented poems of illness, problematic motherhood, death, nightmares. Remembering an aunt who burned shoes to keep snakes away and chopped copperheads that had crawled into the cabin, she adds that her analyst has suggested that she "work snakes into poems." In this new sort of snake handling, Harlan is a metaphor for the untamed, "primitive" side of the psyche—a "dark and bloody ground" indeed. On the other hand, to the McGarrigles, who are Canadian, Harlan is a place of nature and childhood, a synecdoche of a dreamed South, resonant with fiddle tunes and Child ballads. In Steve Earle's "Harlan Man," one of the few songs not about coming or going ("Born in east Kentucky and here I'll stay"), references to coal mining, black lung, religion, and family add up to a monument to the quintessential American workingman: "I'm a Harlan man / Never catch me whinin' 'cause I ain't that kind."[5]

Sometimes the material Harlan and the imagined one have barely heard of each other.

> GEORGE ELLA LYON: I wanted to be a folksinger in Greenwich Village, and I wrote songs, every political thing that happened I had a song; but I didn't know how to do this. I knew I couldn't just go and set myself down on Bleecker Street and expect something to happen. I started getting *Sing Out!* and through *Sing Out!* I started writing to people in Ireland and Switzerland, and I found out partly through them that I was a folk. It took me a while to make the connection between the music I was interested in and the place I was from.

On Bleecker Street or Washington Square, George Ella Lyon might have heard Harlan County songs played by people for whom Harlan County was "in existence in some place," mainly of the mind. After all, the American folk music revival began in the 1930s with a bunch of Harlan County exiles.

HUNGRY RAGGED BLUES

The moment Theodore Dreiser heard Molly Jackson sing her "Kentucky Miners' Hungry Ragged Blues" on Straight Creek marks the beginning of the modern folk music revival: the urban awareness, tinged with progressive or radical overtones, of the alternative presence and oppositional potential of rural folk music. Harlan was proof that folk music was not a remnant from the past but a contemporary expression of America's modernity. Modernization and the mining industry had been dumped upon Harlan wholesale, so quickly that there had been no time to forget the expressive powers of oral tradition. The result was an unusual dialogue of traditional gospel and ballad tunes ("Lay the Lilies Low," "Precious Memories," "Jack Munroe") with contemporary and radical words and themes ("Which Side Are You On?" "Dreadful Memories," "Join the NMU").[6] The beauty of the music and the voices and the passionate intensity of the words made Harlan an example of tradition as an ongoing process rather than passive transmission of artifacts. The idea of authenticity was couched no longer in a supposed uncontaminated purity of the folk but in the living experience of the social protagonists. Molly Jackson's move to New York in December 1931 was the beginning of a cultural exchange that brought folklorists such as Alan Lomax and Mary Elizabeth Barnicle to Kentucky and taught the new urban activist musicians the songs of Harlan and Bell.

TILLMAN CADLE: Have you met Pete Seeger? I met him when he was just a boy. You know that song, "Which Side Are You On?" I took that to him. The Reeces, they was living in Harlan County in 1931. When they left Kentucky, I didn't know where they had gone to and what had become of them. Then Sam one day he came over to see me in Middlesboro and told me he'd found some people he wanted us to talk with. I went over and I stayed two or three days with 'em and—and one evening, after supper he told his two oldest daughters, "Why don't you girls sing that song for Tillman?" And they did, that was the first time I'd ever heard it. One of the girls got a writing tablet and wrote the words out for me. And, when I went to New York, when I saw Pete I told him, "I've got a new song for you Pete, I believe it'll make a hit if you'll sing it." Of course it's to an old melody that most everybody knew, so they started singing and it wasn't long till someone thought it should be recorded. Well, he come to me and asked if he could record it. I said, "You will have to get in contact with the Reeces." And I gave him their address and he got in touch with them and they told him yes, that he could record it. And one of the last cards I have from him was when Florence died and he wrote me a card, and said he learned so much from people like her and me.

"Yeah, I remember that song: 'Which side are you on brother? Which side are you on?' I remember the song now that you've refreshed my memory" (*Bill Winters*). "I know an old woman, she's the one that made the song 'Which Side Are You On?' I never sawed her. I heared another woman singing it, lives up at Dartmont, I can't think of her name. She sung it in the picket lines [during the 1973–74 Brookside strike]" (*Otis King*). Florence Reece's song became an international workers' anthem, yet few remember it in Harlan. "They still sing that song at all the rallies, when you have the KFTC [Kentuckians for the Commonwealth] meetings. Now, when they're talking on 'Which Side Are You On?' what do you think they really mean? Sometimes it's not union or scab. Sometimes it's the black people singing about what's happening to them. Sometimes it's women. You're choosing the side when there's an issue out there" (*Hazel King*).[7]

Born Mary Magdalene Garland in 1880 in Clay County, Aunt Molly Jackson lost her father, a husband, and a son to the coal mines.[8] She wrote "Hungry Ragged Blues" after seeing her sister's children go hungry and barefoot: "The tops of their little feet was busted open from the cold wind and you could track them down from the blood running down between their toes....So I sat down at the dining room table and with the pains in my heart from the condition as I often do I composed a song of the condition of the people which is the only kind of a song that is a folk song. This is what the folk composes out of their really lives, out of their sorrows, out of their happiness and all." "This is what a folk song realy is," she wrote later in her idiosyncratic spelling: "the folks composes there own songs about there own lives an there home folks that live around them."[9]

Forced to stay in New York by a crippling accident and the blacklist, she became a powerful voice for the union movement, speaking and singing all over the United States. "She lives in New York City now," Woody Guthrie wrote, "over on the east side. In the slums and tenements. Where filth and starvation and disease is just as bad, only thicker, than anywheres in Kentucky...She's still one of the nation's best ballad singers and can say for herself, 'I can sing all day and all night every day for a month, and never sing the same song twice.'"[10] "Aunt Molly's style of singing," folklorist Alan Lomax observed, "marks a peak of the wild, strident, highly emotional manner of eastern Kentucky....Her songs of protest can only be matched by those of Woody Guthrie, but they were more passionate than his, and they cut deeper."[11] Music historian D. K. Wilgus writes: "By most standards Aunt Molly never had a good voice. She was not a good singer—merely a great one; Aunt Molly's singing contained the essence of Appalachian tradition; to the uninitiated an Aunt Molly Jackson performance is frightening. The beauty and truth lie *behind* rather than *in* the performances." She served the cause of the working class, was sometimes used as a tool, but learned to use her visibility to be heard and recognized as a creative artist, constructing and reinventing herself through creative and sometimes self-aggrandizing storytelling.[12]

She never forgot that she was an exile: "I'm nine hundred miles away from home," she sang, "I love coal miners, I do." She died, poor and almost forgotten, in Sacramento, in 1960. Only a few family and friends attended her funeral; her few possessions were quickly disposed of. The loose pieces of paper on which she had written her songs were thrown away with the trash.[13]

Molly Jackson's half brother Jim Garland joined her in New York in 1935. He worked at a variety of jobs, and though he retained his radical ideas he later became dissatisfied with the "intellectual hassles" and the "all feathers and no meat" of the Communist Party. So he moved into folk music, collaborating with folklorist Mary Elizabeth Barnicle. In 1936, Barnicle went to Kentucky with Tillman Cadle and heard about Molly's half sister Sarah Ogan. As Cadle recalled, "When we went to see Sarah, it was too pitiful a sight to ask her to sing, and Barnacle took the whole family back to New York with her. The old shack they lived in was all torn apart and holes in it. I'm sure you heard her songs describe it. Well her songs is the truth. She didn't have to make anything up."[14] She sang:

I hate the capitalist system, I'll tell you the reason why
They caused me so much suffering, and my dearest friends to die.
Oh yes I guess you wonder, what they have done to me
I'm going to tell you mister, my husband had TB.
Brought on by hard work and low wages, and not enough to eat
Going ragged and hungry, no shoes on his feet.[15]

"The reason that [Molly] composed her songs," Sarah Ogan explained, "was to focus attention on the plight of the miners at the time. I composed mine because they were the truth about my own life and other people's at the time that I left there."[16] Ogan's songs are outspoken and radical but never ideological: when she sings about capitalism, she sings about her lived experience of the system, not a political abstraction: "I am a coal miner's wife, I'm sure I wish you well," she sang. "Let's sink this capitalist system in the darkest pits of hell."[17]

"I heard her voice thin, high, and in her nose, with the old outdoors and down the mountain sound in it," Woody Guthrie wrote: "Singing out to her skies had made her voice a thin one, but with that unknown gift of carrying up and out to the several directions. Singing to us as she had sung into the rifle fire of Sheriff Blair's deputies, Sarah Ogan got the house of people to keep so still that the cat licking his hair sounded like a broomstick rubbed against a washtub."[18]

Her songs are argumentative and impassioned pleas, aching dialogues, efforts to understand and to educate ("Perhaps dear friends you wondering what the miners eat and wear / This question I will try to answer for I'm sure that it is fair"). They often start on an elegiac tone of memory, sorrow, and loss: "I am a girl of constant sorrow, I've seen trouble all my days. / I bid farewell to old Kentucky, the state where I was born and raised." But they end in a denunciation of injustice and a call to rebellion: "What can we do about it / To these men of power and might? / Well, I'll tell you, Mister Capitalist / We are going to fight, fight, fight."[19]

Sarah Ogan and Jim Garland were "rediscovered" in the topical revival of the 1960s, and they appeared at the 1963 Newport Folk Festival.[20] Their songs, as well as Molly Jackson's and Florence Reece's, were performed by musicians of all generations, from Pete Seeger to Uncle Tupelo, from Woody Guthrie to Hazel Dickens, Barbara Dane, Billy Bragg, and Natalie Merchant. This small group of exiles helped etch Harlan County into the nation's conscience and imagination. Yet theirs was the remembered, reimagined Harlan County of the exiled, the uprooted, the blacklisted: distance enhances, as in bold relief, the stark realities of injustice and struggle and Harlan's symbolic meaning as a place of memory. The complexity of social background and of the ambiguities of everyday experience were left to the voices of those who stayed and struggled to survive, sometimes to forget.

COME ALL YOU COAL MINERS

In April 1931, Walter Garland, a twenty-eight-year-old miner from Straight Creek, the father of seven children, told a reporter: "I got a job near Harlan working two days a week...I could only make enough to pay my board, so I quit. Me and some other boys at Wallins are trying to get up a string band and try to get a job as radio entertainers."[21] In Harlan, music was often literally a way of living. There is much music *about* Harlan, but the place itself is also brimming with music. I have hardly entered a house or a church that didn't have musical instruments in it. "Nighttimes, when we got our work done, and it would be dark, we'd eat supper and then we'd play music—sitting around the fireplace. Daddy played the banjo, he never did sing. And sometimes it would go on to wee hours of the morning" (*Annie Napier*). "As we was growin' up, we didn't have Nintendo or Atari, stuff like that. We just played music, so we sung up and down all our lives" (*Chester Clem*).

While the New York exiles were constructing the symbolic Harlan, local musicians chronicled events and conditions, with less radicalism and more humor. One need only look at the songs folklorist George Korson collected in and around Harlan in 1940: Joe Glancy's "Mule Skinnin' Blues" and "Coal Loading Blues" ("Hurry up driver, give me two on a trip / My wife's gone to the store for to draw some script"), Richard Lawson's "Coal Buckin' Misery" ("Back in the days when we had to scab / Worked two for one, had to hold our gab"), George Davis's "The Spirit of '39" and "Harlan County Blues" ("You didn't need to be drunk, they said / To get throwed in the can / The only thing you needed to be / Was just a union man"). Mary Elizabeth Barnacle and Tillman Cadle gathered a wealth of music around Cumberland Gap, including Findlay Donaldson's hymns, ballads ("The House Carpenter"), and topical songs ("Come All You Hardy Miners," "Hard Times," "Miner's Farewell").[22]

TILLMAN CADLE: Miners would sing in the mines when they were working; motormen particularly. And the way they used to sing around the mines, particularly labor songs, they'd get together at someone's home and sing that way. I've even heard some of those Holiness ministers sing songs, at rallies and things. Have you seen this book, *Coal Dust on the Fiddle*? Well now, there's one of my father's old friends in that book. He used to write songs, and he used to sing his own songs at union meetings. His name was Dave E. Robb, and I heard him sing when I was just a little kid. He got involved in a strike down in [Ludlow] Colorado and got put in jail, they put him in an old cell that was wet and he lost his voice.[23]

PARRIS BURKE: Alfred Hunt, lived up here at Twila. He wrote songs all the time. And I remember he wrote that song, "Sixteen Tons." Of course he never got credit for it. I remember [another] song he wrote: "The coal I load, and the cars I pushed, I wear my fingernails into the quick, I am a coal-loading daddy with a coal-loading blues." He never got paid for "Sixteen Tons," of course.

Alfred Hunt was not the only one who claimed authorship of Merle Travis's classic.[24] Whatever the merits of the case, the popularity of the song indicates how attuned Harlan was to the world of radio, recordings, and, later, television.[25] "Lots of people didn't have a radio. And we'd go to somebody's house that had one, and sometimes, I have known thirty-five, forty people being in the house listening to the Grand Ole Opry; all sitting out in the yard, on the porch, listening to the radio" (*Becky Simpson*).

ANNIE NAPIER: We had a battery radio. And the only time we listened to that, we listened to the Grand Ole Opry, on Saturday night. And then after [my parents] started going to church the only time we listened, for the news, and on Sunday mornin' for the preaching. Otherwise we couldn't afford the battery—which was about a dollar. And we conserved that energy for when we needed it.

BECKY SIMPSON: Me and Bobby got a television, I guess in 1958. Which was against my mommy's religion to watch one. So it was awful scary to have one in the house, that she would see in passing. Cowboys and Indians was on. And Mommy asked Bobby one day, said, "Bobby, what is that thing a-doing, what's that thing doing now?" And he says, "Well Mommy, you won't never believe it but I've had to turn it out." And she says, "What in the world happened to all them? All them Indians is dead?"

"It started in the church, when I was about twelve years old, learning how to play the guitar, and then in church playing gospel music, that's what we cut our teeth on" (*Sid Tibbs*). Before I met them, I heard Hugh and Julia Cowans, on a Highlander Center video, sing a spiritual that is also a song of resistance, "How I Got Over." I remember black congregations singing "Just a Closer Walk with Thee" in Lynch, or "Learning to Lean" at Pride Terrace. Or Chester and Megan Clem playing bluegrass gospel in their mobile home ("I'd rather be in a big dark grave / And know that my poor soul was saved / Than to live in this world in a house of gold") and leading the choir at Verda Methodist Church. And evenings at the Cranks Creek Survival Center, Becky Simpson, Annie Napier, Hiram and Junior Day, Becky Ruth Brae, and Judy Surgener sang gospel songs, and "Foggy Mountain Top" or "Rocky Top, Tennessee."

ARTHUR JOHNSON: They have a church here in Cumberland established 1834, and they don't use musical instruments. They thought it was a sin to play the fiddle or the banjo, and if a person became a member of their congregation, they asked them to put the fiddle and banjo away. A fiddle was often called the "devil's box."

There were no such strictures in the Holiness churches: "The Bible says make a joyful noise unto the Lord.[26] They beat a tambourine, they slap their hands, the play piano, they play guitar, they play a banjo, they play a mandolin, they play a fiddle, just far as they want to play" (*Debbie Spicer*). I was moved by Hiram Day and his son Junior singing hope ("I Can Almost See the Lights of Home") to the tiny congregation in Cranks Creek Holiness Church,[27] by Ed Hanson belting out "Fire in My Bones" in Wallins Creek, by Jamie Daniels in Cranks Creek Pentecostal Church pounding a gospel piano that was a living reminder of the Holiness roots of rock and roll. "The Pentecostal Church, they have a lot of this modern rock-type gospel, where you have a lot of volume, a lot of percussion, a lot of the drum sets, very expensive instruments. They watch it on the television, and they buy tapes and records and listen and then play it to the best of their ability" (*Arthur Johnson*). "They are really emotional, that's why I love gospel. And I guess that's why I love country, because you can really put your emotions into it, something that's going to put a little chill up on your arm" (*Becky Ruth Brae*).

"You got musicians in these hollers just as good as any studio musicians in Nashville" (*Chester Clem*). Becky Ruth Brae tried to make a music career in Nashville: "[But] you have to be a part that they can sell, you've got to be something that people is going to be willing to put their money into. I kind of felt really strange because, it's like they were having to make me over, doing my hair, and my makeup and I ain't never had nothing like that done." Becky Ruth Brae is a fine singer and songwriter but couldn't be converted into a commodity. In her songs, the country themes of family and love are steeped in a poignant sense of working-class life ("I don't need all the things you're working for / All I need is to have you more with me") and of death looming in the landscape:

> Coal mines, coal mines, you've claimed too many lives
> Taken too many fathers from their children and wives
> Oh, ain't you never gonna be satisfied
> And stop taking our men from the midst of our lives?[28]

Arthur Johnson is another versatile Harlan County musician. A blind man, he worked as a piano tuner ("the well-to-do families had pianos, coal miners didn't have them"), a music store clerk, a radio artist ("I learned something by Schumann, and something of Beethoven, but you want pop music, so I [learned] some of the popular tunes of the day, and a country tune, or a religious song"). On his porch in Cumberland, he played old-time standards ("Wreck of the Old 97"), Carter Family and Merle Travis classics ("Keep on the Sunny Side," "Dark as a Dungeon"), gospel songs ("Amazing Grace," "Sweet Bye and Bye"), ballads ("Three Nights Drunk"), and a delightful song about courting girls on the old Harlan County buses.

I met Arthur Johnson at a Kentuckians for the Commonwealth meeting in Harlan in 1989. The topical song tradition in Harlan has not vanished: at the same meeting I met young songwriter Kenny Rosenbaum, and recorded him a few days later singing songs about the big corporations, pollution, and strip mining, just over the Bell County line near Molus, where Florence Reece wrote "Which Side Are You On?"

In 2003, Dorothy Myles, from Lynch, wrote a powerful song describing the families that stood at the mine gate as the men who lost their lives in those mines were being brought out one by one. During the 1978 Jericol strike, Mary Beth Layne, of the Lexington women's bluegrass group Reel World String Band, joined the women's support group and wrote "The Battle of Jericol": "Bless the fathers, bless the brothers, bless the sons who pass their time / Standin', sittin', waitin' upon the picket line." Reel World's Beverly Futtrell celebrated Cranks Creek's survival and resistance after the 1976 flood: "Something's rising up on Cranks Creek / And it won't be the waters next time." In 1974, Si Kahn sang about the death of Lawrence Jones, killed during the Brookside strike: "The night is cold as iron, you can feel it in your bones / It settles like a shroud upon the grave of Lawrence Jones / The graveyard shift is walking from the bathhouse to the mine / 'Cause there's one man dead on that Harlan County line."[29]

No wonder that Barbara Kopple's documentary on the Brookside strike, *Harlan County, U.S.A.*, is intensely narrated through music and song, including new verses to "Which Side Are You On?" and a moving scene of Florence Reece singing it in Evarts. The film ends with Hazel Dickens's anthem to struggle and endurance:

> *United we stand we stand, divided we fall*
> *For every dime they give us a battle must be fought*
> *So working people use your power, the key to liberty*
> *Don't support that rich man's style of luxury*
> *And there ain't no way they'll ever keep us down.*[30]

WRITING THE MINES

Literature, as well as music, has described and reimagined Harlan ever since (as described in chapter 9) Theodore Dreiser and other writers came to Harlan in November 1931 to help the miners—but also, as some suggested, in search of new sources of inspiration.[31] Waldo Frank, Malcolm Cowley, Edmund Wilson, and Mary Heaton Vorse used their Harlan experience in rather undistinguished later works. The only one who did not turn the visit into literary material was Dreiser: his only output was the book *Harlan Miners Speak* (1932), a fascinating and disappointing collection of contributions from members of the committee, minutes from the hearings conducted in Harlan, and reports of meetings and "speakin's." Some of the pieces are informative, others problematic (such as the rehashing of Appalachian stereotypes in Lester Cohen's opening contribution). Miners and coal camp women, however, do speak for themselves: the first voice in the book is Molly Jackson's "Kentucky Miners' Wives Ragged Hungry Blues."[32]

Since then, Dreiser and his colleagues have been the object of much criticism, especially from Appalachian authors. For example, Jo Carson's brilliant and vitriolic play about the 1931–32 strike, *Preacher with a Horse to Ride*, portrays a Dreiser more concerned with his own writer's block than the plight of the miners, exploitative of women, reluctant to give to charity, opportunistic: "Kentucky is such a story that this nation will fall to its knees and weep. And I can write it."[33]

Indeed, the public circumstances in which the Dreiser committee's meetings were held, and Dreiser's effort to provide an aura of "objectivity" by imitating the rehearsed question-and-answer method of judicial proceedings, combined to reduce many witnesses' voices to short factual statements. However, these proceedings have long remained the only text in which these voices were heard at all. And in Dos Passos's report on the "Free Speech Speakin's," Molly Jackson, Sudy Gates, and Findlay Donaldson do express themselves in the fullness of their eloquence and power.[34]

Dos Passos is the most interesting example of literary use of the Harlan County experience. In his 1938 novel *Adventures of a Young Man*, the hero, Glenn Spotswood, works as an organizer for a Communist-oriented union in Harlan County but realizes that the somewhat stereotypical party bosses are more interested in propaganda than in helping the miners: to them, the murder of two miners is only an opportunity for a mass funeral for two working-class martyrs. Glenn joins the International Brigades in Spain, is accused of being a Trotskyite, and is sent to his death on a mission ordered by the party.[35] *Adventures of a Young Man* marks a departure from the literary experiments of *Manhattan Transfer* and *U.S.A.* Apparently, as Dos Passos was becoming disenchanted with the Left, he also began to drift back toward more conventional forms of the novel.

Mary Lee Settle's *Choices* (1995) can be read as a response to *Adventures of a Young Man*. Southern belle Melinda Kregg travels to Pineville in 1931 to work with the Red Cross. She soon realizes which side the Red Cross is on, is appalled by the conditions of the miners' families, and witnesses Dreiser's and Dos Passos's arrogance and the insensitive stupidity of (stereotyped) opportunistic Communists who (albeit "for the wrong reasons") are, however, "the only people doing anything in this poor sick country of ours."[36] She falls in love with a young activist, patterned after Harry Simms, and leaves Kentucky after he is murdered by company guards.

In Settle's broad and gendered perspective, the lives and subjectivity of everyday individuals are much more important than a polemic about "Reds" or "outsiders." In Kentucky, Melinda loses her "innocence" and breaks with her aristocratic family. The Kentucky mine "war" is placed in a worldwide context of twentieth-century wars, as Melinda survives the war in Spain, goes on to exile in France, air raids in World War II London, the cold war, and the civil rights movement in Mississippi, then dies on an Italian island.

James Sherburne's *Stand Like Men* (1973) also represents Dreiser's visit as farce; yet the reconstruction of the events of 1931–32, based on oral histories and the recollections of struggle veterans, is well documented, and the character of NMU organizer Mike Rogoff relatively nuanced. In the end, the local rank-and-file leader Breck Hord tells a returning UMW organizer: "I won't fault the NMU, Mr. Sizemore. I worked for it, and I believed in what we done, and I reckon I'll be proud I was a member for the rest of my days." As Sherburne explains, the book is a reply to the "voluntary collective amnesia" that covers those events.[37]

The struggles of the 1930s remain the dominant story about Harlan. For instance, in Kurt Vonnegut's *Jailbird*, a speaker who had left Cambridge to work as a miner and organizer in Harlan raises funds for a union that "was then run by communists. It is run by gangsters now." In fact, most literary mentions of Harlan are about strife and conflict rather than everyday work and community. In Lee Smith's *Fair and Tender Ladies*, the two mentions of Harlan are both about strikes (including, apparently, the Battle of Crummies), and the hero of Elmore Leonard's *Pronto* derives from his Harlan County upbringing the hard-boiled endurance that enables him to face death without flinching: "I've worked deep mines and wildcat mines, I've worked for strip operators, and I've sat out over a year on strike and seen company thugs shoot up the miners that spoke out."[38]

Harlan as metaphor of deadly conflict and strife received further treatment in Robert Schenkkan's 1992 Pulitzer Prize–winning play, *The Kentucky Cycle*, which follows three eastern Kentucky families from pioneer days to the War on Poverty in a thinly disguised Harlan County. Schenkkan meant to make Appalachia a metaphor for America, based on the myth of the frontier; however, these "good intentions" are defeated by the play's historical inaccuracies and primitivistic stereotypes. According to Gurney Norman, Schenkkan belittles the history of struggle and resistance in the mountains, and portrays mountain people as passive victims who have brought about their own fate by stupidity, greed, and shiftlessness. Schenkkan's Kentuckians are genetically locked into an essentialist and hopeless cycle of violence and passivity, greed and fatalism, cunning and gullibility. In the end, rather than America's metaphor, Appalachia comes across as a land apart, America's other all over again.[39]

The last thing on the mind of most authors who write about Harlan seems to be writing itself. On the other hand, writing and language are precisely what the work of two representative Harlan-born authors, George Ella Lyon and James B. Goode, is primarily about. "As far as writing goes," says Lyon, "being from the mountains was a real advantage because I grew up with people who loved to talk and tell their stories, who cared about language."

GEORGE ELLA LYON: All the attention I had seen paid to the mountains came from the outside. And wanted to make changes, missionary kinds of changes, not internal kinds of things. I was at the point of writing my dissertation [and] I had taken a lot of creative writing classes, so I tried to see if they would let me write a book of stories and poems about the mountains as a dissertation. Well, of course they wouldn't. But it was important to me, I thought that was a literary worthwhile thing to do.

Sense of place, Lyon argues, is predicated on the sound of the language. "To sound urban when you're rural, to sound English when you're American, white when you're black, male when you're female, bluegrass when you're Appalachian" is the literary equivalent of "the telephone computer which tells us 'the number is'" or the synthetic voice in the Atlanta airport that warns, "You are entering the people mover. There will be no food or drink beyond this point."[40] Language draws its nourishing power from difference, place, and gender. Lyon's perhaps most mature work, the play *Braids*, is not about strikes and manliness but about mother-daughter relationships and family narratives.

> GEORGE ELLA LYON: One time I was sitting down to write and I couldn't get started and I was looking at my hands and I looked at my rings and this ring [is] my grandmother's wedding ring and I got to thinking about how I was married to my grandmothers and I wrote a poem about it, "Rings," because it was so powerful to me to think of having worn rings and these rings having gone through their lives. As I grow older I feel less and less of an individual, I feel more connected, and I feel there's a deeper knowledge which we share somewhere beneath our consciousness. I feel that this is a powerful source for me of writing stories that have been told to me and the people I grew up with, their personalities, their voices, their ways of being in the world, and my grandmothers will be talking to me forever.

Both Lyon and Goode dabbled with the meters and forms of oral tradition and the ballad genre (Goode's "Ballad of the Harlan County Criminal Justice System" is a devastating and singable political satire), yet theirs is a more modern sensibility. Goode's books have been recognized as "the most important collections of coal-related verse written by any individual in the modern era."[41] Yet he started out with more cosmopolitan models.

> JAMES B. GOODE: Well, originally, I suppose I was motivated like most young poets are, to explore as much as I could about the medium. For the first few years I just played with images. I was toying with sounds, just toying with the words, and the way they juxtaposed and the way they're put together. And, if somebody asked me what my form was all about, I'd say, "It's a bastardization of T. S. Eliot and Robert Frost...." I'm with the generation of Lawrence Ferlinghetti and Allen Ginsberg—e. e. cummings was somebody I studied, quite a bit.

At first Goode's imagery came from the environment: "I knew my plants, the images, and, was very sensitive to the moods. Then, I turned to coal mining, as an agenda."

JAMES B. GOODE: I think the thing that triggered it was the series of explosions that occurred, beginning in Mannington and ending up in Scotia. When the Scotia explosion occurred, I lost three high school classmates. I was already working on a book on coal mining but that was the catalyst, and then in 1978, my best friend got killed, in the mines. So, the agenda was to talk about mining, talk about its impact on the people, and get inside the coal miner's head, sort of figuring out what was going on there, and, explore, for the outside world, what mining was all about.

Death in the mines is an overarching theme in Goode's *Poets of Darkness*. But it is rendered through a vivid attention to the everyday sounds of places where people live, gather, and talk—taverns, roadhouses, churches. Goode's poetry has a realistic dimension ("I do praise the miner for his internal fortitude and his strength, and what he had to put up with") but also a symbolic, metaphysical undercurrent: the true "poets of darkness" are the miners themselves, who dig deep into the bones of the world and might "tell us what it means to see into aeons / where no man has seen."[42]

BLOODY AND/OR DUMB

ANNIE NAPIER: I'm a hillbilly.

PORTELLI: Well, what is a hillbilly?

NAPIER: I don't really know what a hillbilly is. They call 'em a backwoods person. But I ain't a backwoods person 'cause I've been in thirty-eight states. And Canada.[43]

GLADYS HOSKINS: I can remember going to California and we were in a restaurant in San Francisco, and George Ella was just little. She was only three. It was '52 then, when we got TV, but the woman who owned the restaurant came over, and she said, "You have such nice, well-behaved children." And I said, "Well, they're very tired. We've come a long way." And she said, "And where are you from?" And we said, "Harlan, Kentucky." And she just sat down, and she said, "Oh, have you ever seen any television?" And, of course, we said, "Yes." And she said, "Well, have you ever seen a 3-D movie?" And we said, "Yes." But, see, that was the idea people have of Kentucky.

Harlan Countians can be tourists as well as migrants. But in both capacities, wherever they go, they are faced with an image of themselves out of movies, books, and comic strips, caught at the crossing of two stereotypes: "dumb hillbilly" and "bloody Harlan."

WILL GENT: When I say I'm from Kentucky, I know they's gonna ask me, "Well, what's the county?" When I'd say Harlan County, they'd say, "Oh, bloody Harlan, huh?" I couldn't understand, why they called it that.

JUDITH HENSLEY: I was in third grade, and I was starting a new school [in Chicago Heights] and my mom had dressed me in all new clothes and, you know, everything about me was totally acceptable. But when the teacher read where I came from, [she] said, "Just another dumb hillbilly." That's what she said in front of me. Well, instead of believing that I was a dumb hillbilly, I determined that I would prove to her that I was anything but dumb. I might be a hillbilly, whatever that meant, but I wasn't dumb.

The temptation is at times to ride this stereotype. Ewell Balltrip recalls a local politician who "felt that we should capitalize on this bloody Harlan image; and he erected a huge billboard, said 'Welcome to Bloody Harlan,' painted in bright red letters and the blood was, like dripping out of the lettering in 'Bloody Harlan,' and had a character in one the corners dressed like a stereotypical hillbilly, with a beard, the overalls, carrying a shotgun, barefooted, he had this old raggedy hat. And a lot of the folks took offense to that and compelled him to remove that billboard." Judging from the souvenirs and T-shirts in Harlan's shops and motels, however, this strategy is still in fashion.[44]

In much popular imagination, the "bloody" and the "dumb" combine: as critic J. W. Williamson observes, the hillbilly monster and the hillbilly fool come from the same territory of the imagination.[45] The roots of this attitude are to be found in the most problematic Appalachian stereotype: inbreeding and incest, and what it means in terms of the relationship of nature and culture.[46] In Henry Kuttner's story "Pile of Trouble" (1948), incest and inbreeding turn a family of hillbillies into immortal mutants. True "living anachronisms," they speak "Elizabethan English" and are building an atomic pile underneath the house. In another, late-1950s science fiction story, incest and intermarriage have turned a family of hillbillies into a new breed of mutants whose dialect is neither quaint nor picturesque, but only a sign of their inability to express themselves like human beings. In a thinly veiled metaphor, Bob Leman's science fiction story "The Pilgrimage of Clifford M." (1984) is about an Appalachian vampire raised as a human being, who goes home again to find and reject his family and dies along with them rather than live with them and commit incest with his own mother.[47]

Inasmuch as prohibition of incest is supposed to be the one rule that exists in all human cultures, its (imagined) practice literally drives "hillbillies" out of the human race and into an uneasy relationship with nature. One need only think of James Dickey's *Deliverance* (1970) to glimpse what Appalachian "nature" can mean to the suburban individual thrown into sudden contact with it. In a number of films—John Boorman's 1972 film version of *Deliverance*, Stan Wilson's *Pumpkinhead* (1988), Sam Raimi's *The Evil Dead* (1983)—the mountains themselves are the monster, and nature is an alien and ambiguous entity that attacks, destroys, or contaminates urban violators.[48]

The "bloody" takes second place to different degrees of the "dumb" in television programs such as *The Andy Griffith Show*, *The Dukes of Hazzard*, *Hee Haw*, and *The Beverly Hillbillies*, which highlight the rural rather than the coal-mining dimension of Appalachia. *The Beverly Hillbillies* (CBS, 1962–71), about a poor mountain family who become rich when oil is found on their land and who then transplant themselves to Beverly Hills with ludicrous consequences, was for a while the most popular TV show in the United States. In 2002, when CBS hit on the idea of turning the series into a reality show—moving a real "back-woods" Appalachian family into a California mansion—the Letcher County–based Rural Strategies Organization launched a national campaign that succeeded in stopping the project.[49] On the other hand, some Appalachian critics have recognized a degree of ambivalence in the hillbilly image. Sandra Ballard notes that the comic hillbilly is often a variant of the Shakespearean fool and in his simplicity is often the bearer of the more positive values; J. W. Williamson points out that the American hillbilly often stands in opposition to the ethics of capitalism and to free market ideology.[50]

The best-known image of the "dumb" Appalachian hillbilly, of course, is Li'l Abner, Al Capp's cartoon character. Charlotte Nolan, who worked with the grassroots Barter Theater in Abingdon, Virginia, played his partner Daisy Mae in a theatrical version that toured the United States and was welcomed enthusiastically, she says, by Kentucky migrants all over the country.

CHARLOTTE NOLAN: Of course, lots of people think that we ought to resent it, but actually that cartoon was politically astute; it was satire, good satire. Al Capp dealt with issues, made fun of the people in Washington, and he had something to say. I, personally, was never insulted by it. It was exaggerated, of course; I mean, satire has to be exaggerated. What I don't like are the blue bib overhauls, big, long beard—judge, rifle, barefooted, dumb, stupid *Dukes of Hazzard*. They are the ones that are insulting, they really show us up to be really stupid.

Al Capp's Dogpatch debuted in the 1930s as "a morality tale" in which the simplicity of his hillbillies is a comment on the duplicity, greed, and stupidity of the rich outsiders who try to manipulate and deceive them. However, in time this critical approach was lost as Dogpatch turned gradually into a demeaning fantasy world inhabited by weird, grotesque, and sexually charged characters.[51]

CHARLOTTE NOLAN: Actually, Dogpatch was a victim. Because the mountain person is wide-eyed and naive, he can be flattered out of anything—and that's what the surveyors did years ago. They came and cajoled them, and for a pittance, they bought those mineral rights. And it's not that he's dumb—intellectually dumb. It's just that you have no knowledge of some things. That doesn't mean you're dumb. And mountain people have been exploited by a number of people. The paper pulp companies exploit us by cutting down our trees and haul out our logs and leave us here to be flood-prone—and they're not even here!

12

EXODUS

TO WAR AND BACK

EARL TURNER: My brother Hobart got killed in the service. He got killed in Italy, in the Po Valley, and I named my son after him 'cause I wanted to keep that name going. My daddy liked Hobart, and he was the baby boy. And we lost him, for nothing, but fighting. I never did believe in fighting the war—especially the way the boys were treated after they came home.

"And the war came and, everybody was going to help win the war, and I decided I'd help win the war rather than finish high school, so I dropped out in my senior year and I joined the army auxiliary corps" (*Hazel King*). "The Appalachian character [is] fiercely patriotic. These people, the people who settled Appalachia were the dregs of society from England and Scotland and Ireland; and they were the people who were waving the flag of glory, when the Declaration of Independence was signed. Boy, it's simply the patriotic thing to do to join the armed forces, to serve your country" (*Ewell Balltrip*). Don Whitehead, a celebrated Harlan-born journalist, admitted that he was "scared at times" during the war, "but I was trained for it. I grew up in Harlan."[1]

NORMAN YARBROUGH: There was an awful lot of boys from here went—the fellows I was raised up with, I don't guess there's a half a dozen of them that didn't go to the service, even though they could have got exempt because they were working in the mines. I was in the Eighth Air Force. I volunteered. I always thought I would like to fly, and I enjoyed it. I didn't make it as a pilot so I went on as a gunner, running B-24s. We flew out of England, we flew all over Germany, and we made a couple of missions to Munich— trying to kill Adolf Hitler. And the last one, we went to Weimar, which was where the Germans was building their jet fighters and their jet rockets. We were the lead plane, and got hit in a number one engine, and it caught on fire, and we went on and bombed, and when we came off the bomb run, we were twenty-one thousand feet, and we dived down to four thousand feet and put out the fire. And we came back out of Germany at four thousand feet by ourselves. We were on the D-Day bombing trip. The troops went in at six o'clock, and we hit the beaches about ten minutes to six.

Ernie Mynatt, from Knox County, was at Omaha Beach: "The little old town I grew up in had about six hundred people in it. And most of the guys that I ran around with in that town are dead, were killed. They were called up, and it was because we were a bunch of ignorant hillbillies who didn't know how to do anything but shoot a rifle. From the beach, you know where the water slushes up on the beach, the white, it's not white, it's red. For maybe ten yards, twenty yards. I had that blood all over my clothes, it soaked in my britches and everything, and it was stiff as a board. And it was my buddies, it was their blood, it wasn't mine."[2]

> BERNARD MIMES: I was working in the mines about six months when they called me to the service. I was eighteen years old. I landed in Africa. We fit in the desert. We left there and went to Sicily. I saw a lot of it. The people that I met there were really nice people. I kind of hated to leave, but we went up the coast to the Mediterranean Sea. We invaded southern France, I think it was Marseilles or some other little place, it was a summer resort. Then we went on up through Paris. When I quit I was in Hamburg, Germany.

The Reverend Gary Page's father was stationed in Naples: "He was there when Mt. Vesuvius had a small eruption. He brought a dagger back that was made from the lava. I've got it somewhere put up." Brigadier General Edwin Howard, who was Harlan-born, landed at Salerno, took part in battles at Fiumefreddo and Anzio, and was decorated by the U.S. and Italian governments. Sixteen Harlan County soldiers were killed on the Italian front.[3]

Harlan Countians also served on other fronts. Basil Collins was wounded during the Bataan Death March "and literally carried a friend on his back for two days that was dead and he didn't know it" (*Alicia Thomas*).

> MILDRED SHACKLEFORD: He was in the Bataan Death March, and he was one of the few people that survived that, when the Japanese took over some of the islands in the South Seas and MacArthur, he left, and left those American soldiers on the island. There was five or six hundred of 'em at the time, I believe, and the Japanese captured 'em. They was something like two or three years, and by the time MacArthur came back, there was very few of 'em survived it. But this guy was one of the few people that had survived, that two or three years of just pure hell. And a lot of 'em died of starvation and beating to death, their eyes were gouged out, and all sorts of stuff.

Later, when Basil Collins was the head of the company guards during the Brookside strike, this history made him feared and respected. "I remember Daddy telling me, 'You need to be very careful of that man 'cause he would not hesitate to kill you.' But as a person, Dad had a lot of respect for him—because of the fact that he survived the war, because, you know, he fought for his country" (*Mildred Shackleford*); even in the strike, Collins "was still fighting for what he thought was right" (*Alicia Thomas*).[4]

Just as in southern Italy, military service has been a way for many Harlan Countians to get away from limited opportunities, see the world, fly airplanes. "I married before I [joined] the army, in '42. I went to Germany and Amsterdam, Belgium, Holland, Norway. I went in France from Dover to Germany" (*Ray Ellis*). "I was sent to Florida in basic training. And from there I took some medical training and I went overseas to Australia and New Guinea" (*Hazel King*). "I served at the 101st Airborne Division, Europe, and I stayed almost forty-five months in the service. I got a big thrill, when I went in the Eighty-second Division and they made an airborne division out of you. And I joined the paratroopers, went to Fort Benning, Georgia, and went to school down there. I made five jumps, but I almost refused on my first jump—and that, that was the thrill of my life" (*Parris Burke*).

HUGH COWANS: Going on forward, I had many things to happen to me. I'd go into the service. That's why I'm blind now. I got hurt in the Philippines. I had been inspecting crews to planes to unload 'em or freight. And I was going in one night, and the Japanese come over and laid a direct hit on the airstrip which turned the jeep over, threw me out. I had a concussion and ribs fractured and everything. One man killed, the other one's leg cut off. I had these, skin rash, that you get in the jungle that had broke out on me. And there in the jungle I had contact with tuberculosis. I had to stay in a sanatorium for six long months.

"Corp. Willis Lee Brock, 27, of Harlan, who had been in the army for only five months has been killed in Germany, reported the War Department. Corp. Brock, grandson of Attorney W. A. Brock, Harlan and son of the late Earl Brock, had been overseas only a few weeks. He spent a furlough in Harlan a few months ago. He was a former employee of the Clover Fork Coal Company at Kitts. His mother is Mrs. Betty Sellers and lives in Wells, Ky.," noted the *Harlan Daily Enterprise*. "Pfc. Robert W. Creech, of the U.S. Marine Corps and son of Mr. and Mrs. Henry C. Creech, Pine Mountain was killed in action recently in the Pacific. Private Creech, a grandson of the late William Creech whose land founded Pine Mountain Settlement School had been in the service for two years. He was a former employee of the Enterprise Publishing Company." "Pfc. Beecher Howard, son of Mr. and Mrs. M. J. Howard, Cawood, was killed in action in France, August 12. Private Howard, who entered the Army in 1943 met death after returning to duty following recovery from a wound suffered in France in April. He had spent some time in an army hospital. He was a timber truck driver, and received schooling in Hall Radio School before entering the service. He is the grandson of Morgan Middleton of Kildav" (October 1, 1944).[5]

GLADYS HOSKINS: We lost a lot of boys during the war. We had several who were prisoners for a long time. My oldest brother was in the war, and he was in the Battle of the Bulge, and, you know, everybody had somebody close to them in the war. It was terrible, when you look back on it, to think of all the lives that were lost and changed and ruined during that war. Of course, you [in Italy] know that even more because we, at least, didn't fight right here, which we should be grateful for.

"During the war I think most of the people had it pretty good, you know. Because their sons were in the army and the soldiers would send their wages to Mom and Dad at home or to the wife and the kids" (*Mildred Shackelford*). "There was a big demand for coal, and the county was booming, everybody had jobs, everybody made good money. A lot of the younger fellows were drafted, and a lot of the older fellows that worked in the mines got deferments to help mine coal" (*Lewis Bianchi*). The government enforced a union no-strike pledge and pressured employers to sign union contracts so that wartime production would not be hindered by labor conflict; the high demand for coal spurred a boom in small, locally owned, nonunion truck mines.

Miners died on the home front, too, as their rights and safety took second place to the imperative needs of wartime production.[6] Resentment against the wartime no-strike pledge resulted in scattered wildcat strikes and walkouts, until in April 1943 the union called a national strike for contract renewal. On May 1, the government seized control of the mines (as it did again in 1945 and 1947). "And then, they froze labor. You couldn't go from one mine to the other, you had to get a release. They raised the flags, make like we was working under government" (*Ben Campagnari*). Eventually, however, the union won its demand for portal-to-portal pay: miners would no longer be paid only for the time they spent at the coal face, but for all the time they spent inside the mine.[7]

JERRY JOHNSON: In World War II, the U.S. government, they brought the U.S. marshals to try to drive [the striking miners] out. My father was in that. There was two thousand of them arrested, and they marched them to the mines. From Yancey, all the way to Harlan. Which is about ten miles. And when they got to Harlan, somebody jumped on top of a car and started shooting with a .45 pistol. And everybody started running and they all switched coats, switched shirts and hats and went home.

"They rationed everything. Gas, and lard, and meat, everything. It'd affect you on a lot of stuff, like coffee, you know. Sugar. I've known Mammy to make burnt-meal coffee. She'd put meal on the stove and scorch it, brown it, put water in it, and it made pretty good coffee" (*Noah Surgener*). "Shoes was kind of scarce; I think you got two coupons a year for shoes or something. That's where the fake leather and the synthetics came in, because I guess they used real leathern stuff for the war efforts and everything, so what I call the fake shoes came in, they wasn't made of anything that would last. And sugar was rationed, meat—yeah, we had coupons, I wish I'd kept some of those little old books. But most people had their hogs and their chickens and stuff. Those that had them wasn't as bad as the ones that lived in the camps—we raised a garden, and we never went hungry" (*Meedia Jones*).[8]

"During the war, my husband was called, and he went to Camp Blanding in Florida, and then he was out of the army. And so for a while he worked in Ypsilanti, Michigan, where they were making bombers. I guess in a way that it was good for all business. Because, for one thing, so many women went to work. Of course we didn't have the factories for women to work in, but many of them would leave and go places to work. They'd go to Louisville or Cincinnati or someplace and, and go to work" (*Gladys Hoskins*). Omie Gent followed her father and other relatives to Detroit: "She run a freight elevator, and they'd load that elevator up with wings or planes, whatever they was working on and send it down to another assembly area to do their part on it and back, all over the building. And she had a whole school of things [to do], she had to punch buttons, you know, labor room, whatever" (*Will Gent*).

"When I came back [from the war], all these big mines were booming. Used to be a mine up in this holler here, it had fifteen hundred men on the payroll" (*Ray Ellis*). Yet wars never really end. William D. Forester lists forty-three Harlan men killed in Korea. And the consequences of war live on in the bodies and souls of the survivors. "And my boy, he went to Korea, and when he come back, there was something wrong with him. He was in the hospital there, and I...I know of some boys, they come back, don't live a long time" (*Otis King*)

> HUGH COWANS: I come out of the army. Didn't report no injuries because I's figured that if I had it on my discharge I wouldn't get a decent job. I go back into the coal mine and work for ten long years. But sometime I would be able and sometime I wouldn't. And I had not accepted my calling to the ministry. But eventually the Lord bear down so heavy. And the doctors always did predict I'd lose my sight. I just backed my automobile in the driveway—that was '60—and woke up the next morning blind as a bat. But the Lord had been good to me. He brought us thus far.

GREAT EXPECTATIONS

> GURNEY NORMAN: My grandfather, he never moved more than fifty miles away from Miller's Cove. Three big mines were opened in the seam up there—Monarch, VIC, and another one called Darby. And around these mountains grew coal camps, with commissaries, the whole thing. And my grandfather commuted every day to his job. But he also preferred to own land; he wanted farming land. See, he always had twenty acres of land.

Anyhow, he was a worker every day of his life. Got up at three o'clock in the morning and he rode in the back of his truck and came home.

And then after World War II his sons came home from the war [and] opened a coal mine. If this is Harlan County here, then right here is Black Mountain; and this is Cranks Creek. And on the south side is a creek called Ely's Creek. You probably drove from Cranks Creek over into Virginia? You passed through Stone Creek, a little community: that's where my grandfather worked underground, all of his working life. After the war, the boys came home, his three sons, all came home. They had saved a lot of money, mainly combat pay. So suddenly they had some money, some capital, and they opened a coal mine, and it was a pony mine, on Ely's Creek. And so this coal seam is Black Mountain coal. Due south of Cranks Creek, there's the same coal seam coming from the South.

Let's say they had ten thousand dollars each. Put that together—my grandfather really knew coal, he knew how to do it. So they went back to Ely's Creek which is closer even to the Harlan County line, to Stone Creek. And, opened a pony mine in 1946, and they opened it with hand labor. I've got my uncle to write an article, about the opening of a pony mine, and it's about how they drill to find the exact seam with a hand drill, and all the workers [use] pick and shovel, and dynamite, and ponies. They built a tipple, they hired three or four men locally, and they ran a classic pony mine.

'Course, nonunion. In sentiment and in spirit all my uncles would have been liberal kind of guys. But any veteran coming home after World War II, there was one thing that everybody had in mind and you were invited to do this, which was to get rich. And it didn't matter how you got rich, the point was to get rich. And it was their chance to get rich. And they made quite a bit of money for three years. They had a truck—I used to hang around up there with the ponies, I'd crawl on the tipple, I rode in the truck with my uncle to carry the coal to the railhead. They never incorporated their business, they never paid taxes, they didn't even keep books. It was all cash. And they kept the cash in money belts. And one of the uncles finally got married, his wife was a good bookkeeper, and she insisted finally on systematizing this; but only after a couple of years. The first two or three years were truly like the Wild West.

So they were veterans; they were home from the wars; not married; making money, and not one of them was twenty-eight years old yet. And their only sobering [influence] was their father who understood business. But they were wild, and what they wanted to do was to go to nightclubs. So every day, every workday, my grandfather and these three men, these three uncles, would get up at four o'clock in the morning, get in the coal truck and drive to Black Mountain, at Ely's Creek. And work all day. Then they would come home at night. The mine on Ely's Creek became a central point of reference for the whole family, over the years. On Saturday night, though, they would clean up, and they would take a hose and clean the truck, spray the inside, the seats, the back, and use it to go courting. And there was a nightclub, it was called the Nigger Head, and you go there, and you take five thousand dollars in your money belt, and you had hair oil on your head, you know, I remember how their hair would just like shine with this oil—and they had their idea of fancy clothes for Saturday night. And of course they wanted women; but what they were also doing was fighting a lot, it was an uproar all the time.

The thing that killed it all was the strike of 1949. John L. Lewis, UMWA, came in with a major organizing effort, to organize all the small mines. And so there was a violent confrontation, when my uncles insisted on running their coal in the face of the strike. And I was in the truck one time: I made the one run with them, and my uncle had this .38 special revolver, and they had an automatic shotgun sawed off—and I used to shoot these guns; they used to let me shoot them. I was in the truck one day, and they rode from the Harlan County line, on to Pennington, was almost shoulder to shoulder with men; hundreds and hundreds of men. And my uncle had to come out of Ely's Creek and drive past them to go to the railhead. And I remember he got his pistol out and put it in his lap, and everybody was jeering and throwing rocks and things like this. But we weren't stopped. But I was very impressed by the drama of this, you know. And then one day a group of pickets, two carloads of union boys came down to picket the entrance to the mine, and one of my uncles was in this truck and he had this loaded with coal—he drove the truck down and rammed it into these cars, full of people, and they were banged up. And then my uncles were charged for I guess attempted manslaughter or mayhem or something, but there was a big court trial; and they were acquitted. But it broke them financially. And this was '49; by 1950 it was pretty much gone. But this whole drama happened right there in that stretch of road between the Harlan County line and Pennington Gap, seven miles. And it's right at the same place where my grandmother was born. By 1952 or '[5]3 they were completely out of this business.[9]

MODERN TIMES

EARL TURNER: In 1946 was the first time John L. Lewis got us talking about trying to get a miner's vacation every year. And the papers, all these old *Harlan Daily Enterprise*, talking about whoever heard tell of trying to give a coal miner a vacation? Whoever thought he'd bring it up? Well, he got that contract signed, they give us two weeks' vacation. We thought we had something, but you know what the vacation paid us? Two dollar a day. That's the best he could do. But see, now they got their regular wages plus the wages for every day of vacation. If you work on your birthday you get paid double time. We got eleven holidays in the contract. You used to work on Christmas Eve. Now you don't, you get paid for Christmas Eve and Christmas Day. You get paid for New Year's Day, you get paid for Thanksgiving, you get paid for Easter, Fourth of July. And Labor Day, all the holidays right down the line.

When the union struck on April 1, 1946, John L. Lewis raised a new demand: a royalty for every ton of coal extracted, to finance a miners' health and retirement plan. This was the first time the union had made demands concerning matters outside the workplace. The request was rejected, the strike continued, and once again the government seized the mines. However, when the contract was signed in July, it did include a five-cent-per-ton royalty toward the health and retirement plan. In 1949, Lewis and the UMW were heavily fined for violating a back-to-work injunction, but the new contract increased royalties and benefits for the miners.

These were rough times, and fierce battles were fought all over the county. "His name was John Ydelelnoski, he was a company policeman, he got killed in front of the big store [in Lynch]. They was coming here, trying to organize the store employees, they got in a gun battle...I remember two policemen getting killed in the bathhouse over there. You could see where the bullets had hit on those bricks. Nobody was ever indicted over it" (*Lee Marsili*).

But times were changing. Competition from oil, increased energy efficiency, and the shift to alternative fuels for home use and for the railroads were eroding the market for coal. Even in Harlan, by 1951 gas and oil prevailed in domestic uses even in coal operators' homes.[10]

NORMAN YARBROUGH: John L. Lewis knew what was coming. He was a smart man. He didn't have a lot of scruples and a lot of principles, but he was smart enough to know that mines had to modernize if they were going to stay in business. And he always said he would rather have a small, high-paid workforce than a large, low-paid workforce. And [the miners], they resisted, but they really didn't fight it. The men at that time were so enthralled with his leadership, they didn't question anything. Lewis could have told them to jump off a bluff, and 75 percent of the people would have gone and jumped off, there was no two ways about it. They did what he said.

Lewis had long believed that the future of the industry lay in mechanization, consolidation, and stabilization of competition: doing away with small marginal outfits, encouraging capital-intensive investments, accepting a drastic reduction of the workforce.[11] This strategy was embodied in the 1950 agreement between the UMW and the Bituminous Coal Operators' Association (BCOA), negotiated with Consolidation Coal ("Consol") president George Love and U.S. Steel's

Harry Moses. The pact amounted to an alliance between the union and the large coal interests. The UMW gave up labor conflict and accepted a steep reduction of the workforce; in exchange, the union obtained higher wages, benefits, and the payment of royalties into the health, welfare, and pension fund for what remained of its membership.[12]

The union and the operators had now a shared interest in the constant flow of production: the more coal mined, the more royalties into the union's chest. From 1952 to 1971, the UMW authorized no strikes against BCOA companies and never demanded a royalty raise.[13] The control of the huge sums of money generated by the royalties increased autocracy and corruption in the union's top ranks. Gradually, the main concern of the union became the preservation of its own financial assets rather than the well-being of its members. The UMW controlled the National Bank of Washington, through which it loaned, often at no interest, large sums of money to coal companies to help them modernize; it invested in coal companies and even (briefly and disastrously) in the ownership of coal mines.[14]

> JERRY JOHNSON: Now, we've got a bank in Washington. Why in the hell do we need an office in Washington—he needs to live down here with us. And another thing he should do—a president of the union shouldn't make no more money than a coal miner. Because you will not fight for somebody unless you're in the same boat with them.

Mechanization changed radically the work in the mines. "I started running a Joy loader, about 1948. It was made by Joy Manufacturing Company. It's a big machine load coals. You had to blast the coal down with the powder, the cutaway machine shook it, then the shoe'd pick it up and dump it in the cars, haul it, put it on the belt. I run one of these machines two or three years, then they got the continuous miners in" (*Earl Turner*). The continuous mining machine eliminated drilling and blasting, as it tore the coal from the seam, scooped it up, and loaded it in a continuous sequence with very limited human intervention.[15] "I was the first black man ever to run a continuous miner. It's a huge big machine. It's got a buncha big wheels on the head of it. It's got what you call carbide bits in it. And you go into the face of the coal and the big wheel just chews the coal up, and runs it back over the belt, right back into the shuttle car" (*Earl Turner*).

The ultimate technological development is the longwall miner.[16] "They come out of Germany. The man from Germany stayed here about two years, set that longwall up. That's the most amazing thing to run. It's got about sixteen, eighteen big big jacks. They must be a hundred-ton jacks, I reckon. It's all hydraulic. And you got big steel shields on 'em, and they pivot like this on big legs. And that hold that roof up: those big machines, mash a button, the big jacks support the roof and the men can be more safer. It's a modern way of running coal. And that big machine goes in there on the back side of this big block of coal, cut out about thirty-six inches of coal. And that coal be falling right back on a pan. And the cut's coming right back, just like that. Oh, it's a mighty sight. They'll take nine men and right now they can produce ten, twelve thousand tons of coal. It's amazing. That's why you don't need no men. It's getting more modern every day. There're no more picks and shovels. There ain't no hard work like there used to be. The guys in the mine, they got it made. It's easy work. In these modern mines" (*Earl Turner*).

"These modern times, in some ways it was [better] and in some wasn't. The dust is a lot worse. [But] it isn't as backbreaking" (*James Wright*). As they move through the seams and bite into the coal face, machines liberate much explosive methane and grind an immense amount of dust, increasing the risk of black lung and explosions.[17] "[The longwall]'s got two big augers. That's what kills so many people. You've got to walk so close to an auger, like me to you. The only light you that you've got is what's on your head: battery light, lasts about ten or twelve hours. You can't move, see nothing. It's just naturally dark" (*Earl Turner*).

In the wake of postwar prosperity, Harlan memoirist William D. Forester writes, "Harlan was choking to death with traffic." Population was at its peak and a great future seemed at hand for the county: "Some of us were as blind as a bat in the sun."[18] "We mechanized Lynch; it was all off-track loading, and belts, and modern equipment. When I left Lynch, we'd come down from about thirty-one hundred to about eleven hundred people" (*Norman Yarbrough*).

Between 1950 and 1960, 350,000 miners, 60 percent of the workforce, lost their jobs. More than 1.5 million people, almost one-fifth of the population, left Appalachia between 1950 and 1960; 600,000 more followed them in the next decade. The population of Harlan County dropped from 71,751 in 1950 to 50,765 in 1960 and 34,789 in 1980: Harlan ranked 119th out of 120 Kentucky counties in negative population trends. In 1954, average annual earnings in Harlan were $844, against a national average of $1,800.[19]

> PORTELLI: When did you begin to feel that something was happening to the community?
> GLADYS HOSKINS: I really don't know exactly. But, see, it would just be such a gradual thing—you mentioned Louellen: that was Cornett-Lewis Coal Company, and just suddenly it's gone. And—you say, "Oh, gee, this is terrible. Cornett-Lewis is closing," and you'd just accept it and say, "Gee, I'm sorry." And then—time passes and everything, and then somebody says, "Oh, you know, I think Threepoint's closing." Well, this is another really bad thing, and you're really sorry, and—but, you see, it didn't happen like, one morning you get up and all these things are just gone.

In May 1952, Southern Harlan Mining at Lenarue closed; Riveridge Collieries, Black Mountain, and Southern Mining cut production and the workforce. In 1957, Pearl Bassham closed Harlan-Wallins; Kitts closed in 1957, Mary Helen and Louellen in 1958. U.S. Steel at Lynch dropped from almost 8,000 workers to fewer than 1,700 by 1960. "We were gradually cutting down in the fifties. I'd say from 350 and down to about 60 people, maybe 75. There were a lot of coal companies in this county that shut down and never went back to work. And I'm probably the only one in this county, with the same ownership today; from 1960, everybody else has sold out and quit" (*Clyde Bennett*). By 1954, five thousand Harlan County residents were receiving surplus food from the Kentucky Department of Agriculture.[20]

> GLADYS HOSKINS: I can look back and, it's like—you know, you don't realize that, "Well, I lost this friend two years ago, and three years ago another one, and then maybe I go a long time and, and I've lost another good, dependable friend that I loved," and suddenly you look around— and it's sort of that way with this county. It was a gradual thing—a little like growing old, every day you are getting older and everything, but you're just not knowing it, you know. But Harlan has had an unusual kind of history, I think.

By the end of the 1950s, as mines closed and the workforce was cut, coal camps had become unnecessary. Companies had retrieved whatever investment they had made in their construction and were now raking in the miners' savings by dangling before them the American dream of home ownership. By the early 1960s, houses in Benham and Lynch were being sold for a few hundred dollars each.[21] "The company don't own nothing now, we own the houses now. The company lets us pay so much a month on these houses. I had a small house, I used to pay ten dollars and something a month" (*Bernard Mimes*). Since the companies retained ownership of the land, the new owners were often compelled to remove their houses from company property and reassemble them elsewhere. In Louellen, "they sold them houses out; people [had to] tear 'em down and move 'em. [The company] just had a lease on that ground, and if they left the houses, they'd have to turn them back in to the land company" (*Lloyd Lefevre*).

> WILL GENT: I's telling Mom the other day, I'd like to know the third of what this house, you know, [if] had thoughts—the people's come through, and lived in it, and, the history, the things it seen over the years. Floods, fires, disasters, whatever. And it could fill a book half full, probably. When they started selling 'em all off, most of 'em went in the fifties. But they sold the rest of 'em off in the early part of 1960s and by mid-sixties; they individually owned now. Only thing that's left is the name and the memory of 'em.

A BETTER LIFE

> JERRY JOHNSON: What happened to the coal industry back in those days was, they sold the oil so cheap that the coal companies couldn't compete.

The oil companies only had a little bitty hole in the ground, there was no labor involved, no labor. They pumped the oil out, they ran the coal out of business. At that time there was only one place to go. You could go to Detroit. There was a boom, so everybody went to Detroit.

RAY ELLIS: I was born here [in Evarts], the year 1911. I growed up here, except four year in the army. And, outside of that, I have been here all my life. Of course I've lived in Dayton, Ohio, and I lived in Chicago awhile. And I worked two year on that H-bomb plant in South Carolina, the Savannah River plant, and I worked for U.S. Steel and I worked for General Motors, I worked for Chrysler Motors, worked for Dupont and I worked in Louisville awhile and Wichita, I worked for the Pennsylvania Railroad a while, and all over the country. The rest of the time I've been here.

CHARLENE DALTON: I'm from Black Mountain, Harlan, Kentucky. I left there, I guess maybe I was six years old [1954]. There was no work, and my dad moved us to Tennessee, where he worked at a Stauffer's Dairy. Then we moved back to another part of Kentucky; now I can't recall where that was. And then back to Tennessee again. We were moving back and forth a lot, because of the jobs, things like that. When we moved from Tennessee to Cincinnati, we moved in one car, seven people, in a white car that smoked, and we all five kids in the backseat and Mom and Dad in the front; and everything [we] owned was packed right there, and that's the way we moved. And we ran out of gas right across the Kentucky and the Cincinnati Bridge, and my dad had to sell pop bottles in one of the little folding chairs to get us across the bridge to Cincinnati. And, I can laugh about it now, but really it was a horrifying experience for me, because I was embarrassed, running out of gas and we was going to the big city.

"My father started working in the coal mines when he was twelve years old and when he married my mom he decided that he didn't want to raise his family with the shadow of the coal mines always on his mind. He had been in some near fatal accidents, and he decided that the auto industry was safer and a better way to raise his family than the coal mines" (*Judith Hensley*). Migration was the consequence of poverty and unemployment, on one hand, and of the opening up of new horizons, on the other. The mine was no longer the inevitable fate of miners' children: "Harlan County—that is where I grew up—most of the parents wanted their kids to leave 'cause they didn't want us to have to work in the coal mines. A better life was an opportunity to work for Ford, Chrysler, Chevrolet, in Cleveland, Detroit, Chicago. And that was the desires and wishes of our parents: that you finish high school, and then that you move on" (*Porter G. Peeples*). "I had too many kinfolk killed in the mine. I went to Detroit and become a longshoreman, for over five years. We moved back down here in 1978 and I hasn't been back to Michigan since" (*Will Gent*).

CHESTER NAPIER: And then my oldest brother he got married, so he goes to work in the mines; and then one of the guys got electrocuted in the mines where he was working, so he quit the mines, he goes to Chicago. And my oldest sister she go to Chicago; then Dad and me, we kind of got into a tuffle. He told me the house wasn't big enough for both of us and one of us had to go. So I got me a ride into Chicago. Hitchhiked. I mean, I's seventeen when I left and went to Illinois. Fifty-nine. I had thirty-five cent in my pocket when I got there. And no experience to say of. Didn't even have a birth certificate. And it was kind of, you know, hard for me to find a job on my own. I didn't know how to get around.

JERRY JOHNSON: I've been in Chicago. I was sixteen years old. I never had seen buildings like that. And I kept walking down the street looking up at those buildings and walking into those light poles and hurting my head. I worked for those daily paychecks. You'd go and line up, somebody'd look you in the eye, pay twelve dollars a day. I'd do whatever. Cleaning up basements, whatever.

CHESTER NAPIER: Finally I found out this place where you could go buy a job, you know, pay for it. So I went and bought a job. I borrowed twenty-five dollar to pay down; I borrowed part of it from my brother, part from somebody else. Minimum wage was a dollar and a quarter an hour. The first job I ever had in Chicago, I paid I believe it was $45, cost me for my job. It was a plastic factory. Like I said, a dollar and a quarter an hour was what I was making. But I got ten, twelve hours of work a day. I made it pretty good till the weekend, then I'd get drunk, gambling, most time Monday morning I'd have to borrow money to go to work on. But I really thought I was enjoying myself, then I found out I wasn't. I guess we married in '61. I married her one day and took her to Chicago next day. It was still warm here in the country. She just had a light jacket on. We got out there in Chicago. And it's November, and it's cold in Chicago. She almost froze to death.[22]

In 1957, the *Chicago Tribune* denounced the "strange breed of people pouring into Chicago by the truckload...like a plague of locusts."[23] A year later, *Harper's* proclaimed under the headline "The Hillbillies Invade Chicago": "These farmers, miners, and mechanics from the mountains and meadows of the mid-South— with their fecund wives and numerous children—are, in a sense, the prototype of what the 'superior' American should be, white Protestants of early American, Anglo-Saxon stock: but on the streets of Chicago they seem to be the American gone berserk....Clannish, proud, disorderly, untamed to urban ways, these country cousins confound all notions of racial, religious, and cultural purity. [Their children's] habits—with respect to such matters as incest and statutory rape—are clearly at variance with urban legal requirements and parents fail to appreciate the interest authorities take in their sex life." Yet the article admitted that migrants faced overcrowding, lack of police protection and an abundance of police repression, job discrimination, and poor housing.[24]

BILL WINTERS: There was a lot of resentment. The only time when we felt welcomed is if we was going in to purchase a pair of work shoes, work pants, work shirt. But outside that—we weren't Ypsilanti people. I've always felt that I was never accepted for many years because I was from the South.

ROBERT SIMPSON: I went to Detroit for a couple of weeks. Got in, we took a bus, downtown Detroit, and that's the first big city I've ever been in. Got out there and got a cab, trying to talk to the guy, be sociable, and they've got a big old bulletproof thing, you couldn't understand nothing he said. When I first got there, I clumb out on the street and had my pistol, everybody here carries a gun. So I had my pistol in my pocket and they started warning me about it, said they would take it away from me. Which that's why you're wearing one, so nobody would mess with you. That's back in the young days though. You ain't got a lot of sense when you're young.

ANNIE NAPIER: They called us hillbillies. I never met nobody up there that's not prejudiced against hillbillies. But now, they was the colored, and the Mexicans hated the colored. Puerto Ricans hated both of them, and they each hated them. I had friends in all of them, including blacks.[25]

CHESTER NAPIER: The colored was really hostile against us from the South. [Where I] worked, we had some Polacks. Polish, oughta call 'em. But it was mostly hillbillies and Italians. And the Italian people, they was really good to me. They tried to feed me and fatten me up.

JUDITH HENSLEY: When you are from one culture and transplanted into another, like Chicago—at that time it was called the great melting pot of the world, and there were so many interesting people and so many interesting cultures represented there: German, Italian, Italian was very dominant in that area, Polish, just lots of different people. It made me wonder about who I was and where I'd come from, because many of my friends' parents didn't even speak English. So, I think it built in me a curiosity about why my parents were the way they were and why we had certain traditions and certain values that weren't like the people that lived around us.

ANNIE NAPIER: We went to Chicago. We lived up there about nine years. But I hated it. The work, you could always find good work up there. But after Martin Luther King got killed, there was a lot of violence, and the schools got so bad. They, I guess you'd call it integrated. They transported the colored kids into the white schools and the white kids into the colored schools, and it got to be a mess. I'd just had surgery and I didn't feel good, and Petey was sick and I had to walk Shirley to school to keep the neighborhood kids from beating the crap out of 'em. They'd come out of the alley and just beat the daylights out of them kids. You was afraid to leave the kids in the classroom, 'cause they'd throw bricks through the schoolhouse windows. And I got up and told Chester one morning, I said, "I'm going home." It was right before Christmas.

Will Gent felt hurt when people labeled him with the "bloody Harlan" stereotype, "till I got older and realized, when the union was being organized, that's how come it got that name. Then I understood. It didn't bother me no more." One thing Kentucky migrants brought with them was their union consciousness and their memory of struggle. Bill Winter's family had not been coal miners in Harlan, but he had absorbed the union spirit there and joined the United Auto Workers. "Oh, yeah, we joined the union. If you didn't join the union, you didn't work. I walked the picket line some because I really believed in the union then" (*Chester Napier*).

ED SADLOWSKI: I mean, "Which Side Are You On?" ... "They Say in Harlan County" ... I remember the guys in the steel mills that was from there— "I'm from Harlan County, I was born in Harlan County"—and I remember guys telling me they could hear the rattle of machine guns when they were kids, with the battles there. In labor history, you know, books were just full of Harlan County, and I had one story after another told by people that were actually there.

Many Appalachian migrants still thought of the mountains as home. For years, the "hillbilly" cars driving south and back on the weekends lined the routes between Chicago, Detroit, Cincinnati, and Kentucky. "Mommy was here, and my daddy was here, and Chester's parents lives up Smith. We come home every two or three weeks. Sometimes I come home every week in the summertime. I'd just drive down here on Friday and leave back out on Sunday. I got this reputation for long-distance driving, so everybody that lived down here, they'd come over and ask me to come and help them drive" (*Annie Napier*). "I lived in the southeast side of the city right off the Route 41, the federal road there that goes from Milwaukee, Wisconsin, all the way down to Florida. When there were strikes in the mills in Chicago, you could see all the cars turning around and going back south, and when times were good you could see the cars coming the other way" (*Ed Sadlowski*). Many just couldn't take it and went back for good.[26]

PORTELLI: What was it like in Michigan?
WILL GENT: Cold. The people. The people more so than the weather. Sometimes you get to feeling which ones was the coldest, the weather or the people.

"I couldn't hardly take the city [New York]. The city is the thing that is really rough. You take all these big cities and things, just drugs, prostitution, and all that stuff" (*Bernard Mimes*). "I never did like the city. I've lived in Louisville, Chicago, and Dayton, I don't like it. You ain't got no friends. In Dayton, Ohio, I lived across the hall for eleven months before somebody [said] 'How de do'" (*Ray Ellis*). "I went to Columbus, Ohio, and it got to snowing on me there; caught me a freight and come back right here. And I ain't left since" (*Johnny Jones*).

> JERRY JOHNSON: Hillbillies are homesick people. When they get to Chicago they're homesick, they're always playing that sad music, "I wanna go home, I wanna go home,"[27] first thing you know they're drunk. Everybody that leaves the mountains wants to come back. The only reason they left is to make a living.

"I was a boy from the sticks, city life didn't agree with me. I got laid off and I came back home, I was happy here in the fields, and I settled back down here" (*Donald Hensley*). Migrants missed the protective aura of the mountains and the perhaps romanticized closeness of social relations. "I missed the friendly people. Up here you knowed everybody, everybody knowed you. When I was growing up I knowed every man in town, and I was kin to two-thirds of them" (*Ray Ellis*). "[In Chicago] It was different. It was just that I loved these hills. People here are safer; it's dangerous anywhere you live, but people here they see you walking down the street, they know you, they protect you" (*Nancy Mayer*).

Many, willing or not, ended up staying. Family ties (Appalachian migration was mostly a chain process), the pressure of prejudice and poverty, and the difficulty of adjusting to urban environments resulted in the growth of Appalachian enclaves, as in Cincinnati's Over the Rhine neighborhood.[28]

> CHARLENE DALTON: We got to Cincinnati, we went to my grandmother and stayed with them until we could find an apartment. We'd never lived in an apartment; that was a big deal. Lived with her for about a month until my father got a job at First Covenant Presbyterian Church. And my grandfather worked there also. My mother worked at a bakery on Vine Street and Over the Rhine. Now, you got to understand, Over the Rhine is a rough place, okay, there was riots. Yeah, similar to what's going on right now, but a lots worse, at least that's the way I've seen it, maybe that it's in a teenager's eyes, I don't know; I was scared to death.[29] I felt I was somewhere where nobody wanted me to be, and I felt fear. We moved up to East Clifton which is another poor part of Clifton, and, I recall, my mom was sitting out in the yard, and my sister was there; my brother was across the street, I had one child at that time, and all of a sudden, it is like from midair, there was people on the roof—Guardsmen, I forget what you call them; they had rifles and stuff, on my roof where we lived, and marching up the street and

rifles was drew, and guns was drew. I thought we was gonna die, I mean as simple as that. But we survived it.

JEFF SALMAN (NAME CHANGED): We lived on Pendleton Street [in Over the Rhine] for quite a while. Now I'm going to tell you the truth, okay, my dad beat on my mother, and they was a lot of drinking on both their behalves and the neighborhood, all the local bars and stuff kind of lent itself to that. So she filed for divorce and got custody of us kids, but he came up to her apartment, and beat her up so bad that I didn't see my mother again for four years, five years. She just left, basically to save her life. Later on I found out that she was hiding from him over the top of where my grandmother lived, in an attic with her broke jaw and eyes that could barely see.

I wanted to get out of the house pretty bad. About fifteen years old, I quit school and left. Immediately, got a girl knocked up, and being from Harlan, we marry them when we do that, whether we like them or not. I had some crazy idea that if you got them pregnant you did what you were supposed to do, which I know now is part of that culture I came from. So, she's a little hillbilly girl and I'm a little hillbilly boy and we had babies bing, bing, bing. We had three children die and that was a pretty big mess for me, personally.

PORTELLI: Did you ever go hungry?
CHARLENE DALTON: Yeah, we did. I don't want to say hungry, but we didn't have supper at times, and my dad would leave and he'd come back and he'd have a bag of food, from churches and stuff. He went out begging and, it takes a lot from any person, not just because they're Appalachian, to have to ask. It takes that pride away; it strips you of everything. And Appalachian people, you know, are proud people. We never questioned where it had come from; we'd just eat it.

JEFF SALMAN: So here I had no education, and I started working, at this bread pan company where we glazed the bread pans. I worked there a year or so. Then I worked at the public library as a janitor for a while, but, that's when the first baby died, and I quit that job, and we went to Indiana and that was a mess and we came back and, then sometime after that, I worked at a little company for about five years, but I ended up splitting up with the first wife during that period. I started drinking real heavy and using drugs, so I was pretty messed up for a good long while. I would have periods of not being so messed up, and I would work, try to get my life together, building my life up and tearing it down. I met a girl and we got married, we had no children and we stayed married for fifteen years. And quite frankly my alcoholism killed that. And I got sober in '89 and I was going to AA, and some guy says, "Would you want to work with me Saturday?" He was an electrician and I went and did some work and he liked what he saw and he said, "Why don't you come and work for me and I'll send you to school." And I went through all four years of the apprenticeship, and have been working the electrical trade ever since. I get to teach the third year in that apprenticeship now.

CHARLENE DALTON: A lot of people that come to Cincinnati, including my parents, worked low-wage jobs; what they could get. They're proud people; they don't want to go on welfare. But you was pushed from one culture into another culture; I call it shock, shock probation, shock whatever you want to call it. It was very hard to make that adjustment, especially as kids. Now that I'm older, I know that for my mom and dad probably it had to be a bigger adjustment than what I had to make because it was the pride thing. And I think it stripped my dad of his pride. I see a lot of Appalachian men that's alcoholics, and I think again it's because of the self-esteem and the fifty thousand questions asked when they have to belittle themselves. Welfare strips people; they break up homes whether it's meant to be that way or not. And when you strip a man of his pride, or a woman, you make them feel like they're nothing and once they get to that level it's hard to get back up to do something with yourself. And I've been blessed, that I can run a school, that I can talk about the culture, that I can be who I am.

"I still love the country, and there is a piece of me that thinks of Harlan as home. It wasn't all terrible memories—when my grandmother, my mother, and her sisters would quilt out in the side yard, and I still think of that as a very cool thing. The songs and stories, when I hear songs about the miners and stuff, I knew we had a struggle, and my family along with other families played a big part, in bringing some justice to the working class people and that, I know that, first hand" (Jeff Salman). "Baptist churches—yeah, there are some churches that changed through the years but the style of religion from Harlan County—some still feel that going to church here on Sunday in some of those churches is the same as being back in Kentucky. There's bluegrass in some of the taverns. Every year there's a Kentucky-Michigan Festival. It's just an all-day party: drink, dance, everybody who can play plays" (Bill Winters).

JERRY JOHNSON: When my brothers left Harlan, they had shopping bags, and they left hitchhiking. They went up there and they got jobs, they came back and they had suitcases. They'd rub you on the head and give you a quarter. They had clean shirts when they came back. And then they went away. And they came back in about a year—a new car. Then they'd rub you on the head and give you a dollar. And then their voices changed, they didn't know how to talk anymore. They said "cah," "got a new cah." And then, they got too good to eat with us anymore. They thought we were nasty people—my own brothers. They used to say us was garbage. So they quit coming to see us. And they quit rubbing you on the head and giving you the dollar. Began to be ashamed of us.

"Southern [people] they went to get jobs in the city, like Ford, Chrysler, and places, and made Detroit their home. And stayed there and they had kids, and their kids had kids" (*Will Gent*). "The mountains breed their share of success," proclaimed the *Lexington Herald*, listing the African American doctors, lawyers, professors, and other middle-class figures who moved north from the Tri-City area of Harlan County. "We have reunions all over this country. The black people from anywhere around here, southeast Kentucky, meet together. Thousands of people come and they meet from California to Detroit or Chicago. Every year on Labor Day weekend. And it's a big thing. Million-dollar thing, you know. They call it the East Kentucky Social Club" (*Constance Ellison*). African Americans are not the only successful migrants: "I've received the key to the city, which is the biggest honor that Cincinnati can bestow on you. One of our big council people, he's Appalachian; Bishop ———, he's Appalachian. Once you start searching, you can find many famous people who are Appalachian" (*Charlene Dalton*).

> BILL WINTERS: I left in 1947. I had some friends who came to the Detroit area, found jobs. I just got married in 1947 so I thought it was time for me to do something and I had an opportunity to get a ride into Detroit. So we left. There were many Kentuckians in this area. It's been quite a trip here. Just getting acquainted with people, knowing how the system works, what's available to you. Learning people, finding a job, trying to live in a community—amazing.
>
> I worked in a automotive supplier plant, then I worked in the state highway department. Later, I worked at General Motors in a warehouse and I became a union representative, later I became president at my local, UAW Local 157 in Romulus. [Then I] got involved in politics, so in 1968 I ran for a county commissioner. I was elected—three terms. Then I ran for township supervisor. I was elected one term. I was defeated the following election. But I had a good experience in it.
>
> PORTELLI: Did you ever think of moving back?
>
> BILL WINTERS: Probably through the years...I was never very serious about it. Early on I would go, "Yeah, get out of here." Never went, never happened. I guess just getting into the community; and accepting the school, accepting or liking the education, those kind of things. As time went by, with the jobs and everything, I just felt this is where I needed to be. My oldest daughter was born in Harlan. The others were born here.

HEALTH CARE BY THE TON

"There wouldn't be a hospital in Appalachia if it hadn't been for the United Mine Workers" (*Jeff Tipton*). "After they got the union here, they built a big hospital—free medical, and free anything, if you couldn't it [get] here they'd send you where you could do it, and it was paid. And the miners got pensions, give them a pension which it never would be there before" (*Ray Ellis*). "John L. Lewis built a hospital. It was a good hospital when we had it. It ain't much now" (*Debbie Spicer*).

> JUNIOR DEATON: That was best thing about the UMWA, that hospital card. Paid for everything, no exceptions. We started, let's see, 1946. In order to be eligible to draw a mine worker's pension you had to have twenty years in the mines, out of the last thirty, and you had to be working on or before May the twenty-ninth, 1946. So by late forties everybody had a hospital card, and they built this hospital, which we would never had a decent hospital in this county, if it hadn't been for the UMW.

The most progressive result of the new union strategy was the creation of advanced health care services in the world's only industrialized nation that has no comprehensive health care system. In 1956, the union opened ten hospitals in Appalachia, including one in Harlan, bringing quality medical care to a historically underserved area.[30]

> MOSSIE JOHNSON: [John L. Lewis] he's one of my real protégés. I love that man, because he helped us so much. When Charlie died, they didn't have to give me but a thousand dollars. But they paid all my debts off and they gave me fifteen hundred dollars, and we got two hundred and fifty-five from social security at that time. And all them things that they didn't have to do for me, they done. I was afraid measles was going to kill the baby. So I had to set and hold him, I was so scared he'd die. And them men would come down to my father-in-law's house. They treated me awful nice, they give me all that extra money, paid all my debts off for me and set me free on that part. So, I think the union is the most wonderful thing they are, because if our union goes down, everybody is going to go down with it.

> BOBBIE DAVIDSON: We had the best specialists anywhere in the nation. Patients that were injured in the mines, paraplegics, paralyzed, we had them that stayed there all their lives. We had wards for them. Then nursing was nursing. You did what you needed to medically for the patients. Then you would go in and you'd sit down with them, you'd talk to them, you'd read to them, you'd play cards with them...I've even brought beer in to them. But then, it was a lot different than it is now. Then you treated the patient as a complete person, not just as a diagnosis.

Of course, the union was attacked for practicing "socialized medicine"; indeed, at the height of the McCarthy era, Lewis "was willing to hire medical radicals in the teeth of McCarthyism because of their professional ability and willingness to work with a militant labor union."[31] Their idealism, however, conflicted with the politics of business unionism. The Welfare and Retirement Fund was essentially a private service reserved for members of an organization for which finances soon took priority over service. Royalties depended on production and productivity, so the Fund was itself subject to the ups and down of the mining industry. As royalties dwindled, it began almost immediately to reduce its services, turning gradually from the project of a comprehensive health system to what was basically little more than a health insurance plan.[32]

In 1953, the UMW announced that members were required to have worked twenty years exclusively in union mines in order to be eligible to receive health and pension benefits; later, it specified that those years had to have been served in the thirty years immediately prior to retirement,[33] that one had to retire from a union mine, that all benefits were lost if they worked even temporarily in a nonunion mine or had been unemployed for a year, and that there would be no compensation paid to miners whose employers did not pay the per-ton royalty. In 1954, the union cut all benefits to widows and disabled miners. In 1956, pleading financial difficulties, it discontinued medical assistance to miners who were going to college or undergoing retraining.[34]

> J. D. MILLER: United Mine Workers probably tried to overdo it a little bit and be a little too fancy—number one. Number two: the coal industry has always been a boom-and-bust industry and so it went into a kind of a bust. Not too long after they had got everything going, they didn't have money to keep it going. Payment for health care was tied to the tons of coal produced, and if you weren't producing tons of coal, then ...

This contradiction accentuated conflicts of interest within the union's leadership. While the service-oriented progressive medical staff worked to create a model health care system, sociologist Curtis Selzer writes, the union leadership "turned the Fund into a carnival of financial jugglers, pickpockets, and sideshow sharpies." The contradiction between service to the miners and enrichment of the Fund caused it to both offer and deny care and hope; thousands of medical cards were canceled at the same time as the UMW extended interest-free loans to coal companies and invested in mining companies and stock.[35] In 1962, the union announced that it was selling its hospitals. "So they went bankrupt, and the hospital was actually closed for a little while. Then, a private corporation bought them out. It still stayed nonprofit but it became a private corporation and they called themselves Appalachian Regional Hospitals, and now they've changed their title to Appalachian Regional Health Care" (J. D. Miller).

> JERRY JOHNSON: When we lost our hospital cards, that was the worst that hurt the union in Harlan. Even some of the old men that were great union leaders, when the union tried to come around again, they said, "The hell with you, you took my hospital card when I was a kid." I remember them taking our hospital cards, too. I remember when you'd go to the doctor and he'd say your card's not good. I'm still smart enough to know that you're better off sticking together with a group of people who are not so great, than you are by yourself. [But] that was awful, selling those hospitals.[36]

ROVING PICKETS

GURNEY NORMAN: In about '62, Tony Boyle of the United Mine Workers, his administration, they canceled the medical cards of hundreds and thousands of loyal union men. The issue was total disenfranchisement of all those middle-aged miners. And so suddenly these guys were just totally pissed at the union, at the coal industry, at everybody. And they began, in effect, to riot. And they would have wildcat pickets. They were not employed, so they would convene, sometimes in groups of three and four hundred and would go to this mine and picket all day, just shut it down. And the next day they'd be sixty miles away, shut another mine down. So they were called the roving pickets. There was a lot of violence that came out of that; you didn't always know who did it, burned tipples down, blew up cars and railroad bridges and that kind of thing.

The policy of class collaboration inaugurated by the UMW-BCCOA agreement stabilized the large, capital-intensive mining operations, but it did not bring social peace to Appalachia. In 1951–53, a strike in Clay and Leslie counties was reported in the *United Mine Workers Journal* in terms reminiscent of the "reign of terror" in 1930s Harlan, including mass incriminations, dynamitings, ambushes, and attacks on union activists—who in turn did not refrain from hitting back.[37] Lewis's main concern was the persistence of and increase in small, nonunion truck mines that competed with the BCOA companies by paying lower wages. By the late 1950s, a majority of Harlan miners outside Lynch and Benham had no alternative but to accept employment in this kind of mine, often under archaic working conditions ("In 1953, '54, I went to [work] the mines that sells their coal to Brookside. Now that was a pony mines. I had to load the coal, shoot the coal, load the coal, and tram it out. I got a dollar a car," *Junior Deaton*). In 1959, the *Journal* noted that five thousand working miners (mostly working part-time) were supposed to earn enough to support a population of more than fifty thousand.[38] Nonunion "dog holes" took up a large share of the market by selling coal at prices lower than those offered by the larger, unionized companies. They were often the only alternative available to desperate unemployed miners, so the union's hold in eastern Kentucky was seriously challenged.[39]

CLYDE BENNETT (MINE OPERATOR): We had to make a decision. Our natural conditions, our roof and bottom conditions weren't as good, maybe our organization wasn't as good, but—they had the big contracts and we had small contracts; big contracts generally pay more than small contracts...[we couldn't] compete. We lost everything we had, practically—until we went nonunion.

Throughout the 1950s, Lewis repeatedly called for the U.S. government to stop buying coal from "scab operators."[40] In 1953, BCOA president Harry Moses actually criticized the union for not organizing the small mines. Thus, when the union struck in 1959, its aim was less to improve members' wages and conditions than to protect its own economic power and that of the BCOA. It is no surprise that in 1969 a federal jury in Lexington found the United Mine Workers and major coal companies guilty of a "conspiracy" to create a monopoly in the coal industry.[41]

The 1959 strike turned into an all-out guerrilla war. Roving pickets went from mine to mine to stop the men from working, by strong-arm tactics if necessary. Mines and equipment were blown out; in Harlan, the strike extended to dozens of large and small operations. Two mine operators were killed in Virginia and Tennessee.[42] A young woman from Hazard remembered:

I would be asleep at night and wake up to the sound of dynamite charges blowing dozers and trucks half way to heaven. Sometimes we would count four or five separate charges going off in one night. [One night] as we got to the point in the road where the creek bottom widened and the L and N trestle crossed the creek, a volley of gun shots barked from ahead of us at the trestle. Bullets flew all around us, screaming into the pavement at our feet, both sides and over our heads.[43]

JUNIOR DEATON: [That was] about as the roughest time it's ever been in [Harlan] county. We've had a few truck turnovers and things like that.[44] I have been accused, you wouldn't believe it, every time a stick of dynamite went off around here, every time somebody got shot at or something. You had a tipple [blown up] right down here in Ages; that was in the sixties, somewhere, '64 strike: somebody blowed it all to [bits]. It was setting right across the railroad from here, right across the street—they accused me of that. My uncle owned a house up here, had a scab living in it, and, they got dynamited; [they] laid that on me. Early [one] night, me and my wife setting there watching TV, and the bullets started flying. They shot five shots, one come through the door, hit one wall, glanced over to another wall and fell right in front of us, just like that movie we was watching was coming alive, buddy. They shot up the whole town, Brookside. Well, I was accused of being in that. And I'll tell you something else. It's true that union men does a whole lot of it. I mean, we'd say at the time, "That's the company doing, they'll blow this and that up and lay it on the union"; well, they will do that sometime.

Junior Deaton recalled other incidents from those times: a boss's car blown up (a man "went down and wired that up with dynamite, just blowed it all to hell. And nobody never did know who that was. Well, that was one of our...good old union man, buddy"), the electricity lines to the Brookside mine destroyed ("this fellow [that did it], he can't even read and write, but buddy, he is brave, he is a good strong union man. He wired them poles up, he told me how many sticks of dynamite he put on. Now, I might approve of things like that, but, I will be no part of that. It's important to me, to have enough sense to not get into something that will get you into the penitentiary").

DELBERT JONES: The last roving picket was '58, '59, somewhere in there. We was out for a contract and they was trying to run us off the picket line. And they done a lot of shooting at us early in the morning down there. We wanted decent contracts, decent wages, and they refused, they refused everything we'd demand. And finally, you know, they never did sign. Went nonunion and they still that way.

Again, as in 1939, Governor Chandler sent the National Guard to eastern Kentucky, to enforce the "right to work" and prevent union "outrages"—"an unnecessary action," the union claimed, "forced upon him by a barrage of operator propaganda and misleading acts of pseudoviolence staged by operators."[45]

"Let's go back to that '59 strike. Your union is not always on your side 100 percent like you think they would be. Now, let's go back to 1959. We was on strike, and, after some time, they managed to meet with our district officials, and work out a contract, what I call a sweetheart contract" (Junior Deaton). A "sweetheart" or "yellow dog" contract is the miners' label for a compromise in which the union agrees to exempt employers from parts of the national contract as long as they retain a nominal contract relationship and pay royalties.[46] Deaton complained: "I got me a letter right back from Tony Boyle, and it said, we was going to lose that mines, and it's better to give in a few ways there, and wind up with a bunch of men under the UMW contract. But I always thought our motto was 'No Backward Step,' and I thought that was a backward step."

JOHNNY WOODWARD: There was an agreement, but there was little pockets of localized union activities that just refused to go along with the sweetheart contract, as they called it—they really called it the yellow dog. They felt like they'd been sold out. There was a lot of resistance, a lot of resistance to that. My dad had a lot of union activity, and he was on a blackball list for a long time. Most of the people who resisted have left, they didn't have any choices. The sweetheart contract, or the yellow dog contract, lasted here until the early nineteen seventies.

"The roving pickets was sometime between '59 and '64" (Junior Deaton). In memory, there is hardly a break between the strikes and roving pickets of 1959, the rank-and-file rebellion of 1962–63, and the strike of 1964. However, while '59 and '64 were promoted by the union, the second wave of roving pickets was a spontaneous movement that the UMW refused to recognize.

After the union cut medical benefits and closed its hospitals, thousands of miners whose employers had signed a sweetheart contract with the UMW felt betrayed: they had believed that at least they and their families would receive medical care, but found it was not so. There was bitterness and anger in Harlan and throughout eastern Kentucky, and even talk of dynamiting the hospitals if they were closed.[47] As winter came, motorcades of hundreds of miners went from pit to pit, led by such charismatic rank-and-file leaders as Perry County's

Berman Gibson, Everett Tharpe, and Granny Hager, closing down nonunion mines and those that were not paying into the health fund.

GRANNY HAGER: We'd meet down at Allais [Perry County] Union Hall, we'd go out, and picket a mines. We have had as high as forty car and motorcades, and them all loaded. And then we'd go to [another] mine and when we'd come back we'd have a meeting at the union hall. The next morning, they'd be about fourteen, from fifteen to sixteen carloads of patrols lined up right along beside of the highway where we come out from the union hall; and they did their best to cut in between us. They was right there, a-waiting for us to come out of the driveway; and I got where I knowed somebody was tipping 'em off from our side because they knowed where we was going. And I said, "If I find out who he is," I said, "the men ain't gonna have to bother him: us women are gonna beat you up; we take him right out and tie a rock around his neck and pitch him off over that bridge and dare anybody to go [bring] him to the ground." That man didn't set there five minutes, he got up, he never was back in the union hall, and he never went on the picket line with us no more.

"They talk about violence," Berman Gibson told a meeting, "let 'em hire all the gun thugs they want. We shut 'em down, and we'll keep 'em shut down till we get a union contract, and if they try to run nonunion coal over us there'll be blood on the roads!"[48] The movement's core was in Perry County, but it did spread to other counties. In Harlan—where only Lynch, Glenbrook, and Brookside were paying royalties, and truck mine operators claimed that they employed more than eight times as many men as union mines—motorcades roved from mine to mine in November 1962.

JOE SCOPA SR.: I'd leave about three, four, five in the morning. And I'd go to Cumberland, pick up somebody, and they'd follow me anywhere I'd go. We'd get together up at Harlan Hospital, in that parking lot down there, then what we'd do, each mine that these people had a complaint, "We want that mine shut down today." And we'd shut it down. Then the miners that worked in that mine they'd join us. Each one, each mine we went, them people would join.

However, he recalled, "we didn't agree to combine people from Harlan County and the other counties. We come to the conclusion it was a little bit too—on the rough side, I'd say. You got to keep to the law, okay? I was one of the committee, and we figured you'd get in too heavy and, you ain't got no chance. All they've got to do is call the National Guard in, if things get too far out of hand, and that's it." Even so, the roving pickets in Harlan were stopped by an injunction at the end of November 1962.[49]

The roving pickets made Appalachia news again. "Unemployment is ordinarily a dull subject, but violence titillates everyone, and I imagine it was this aspect of the Hazard situation that drew so many of us reporters—like vultures circling in on the wounded town—to what had previously been an unknown place."[50] As in the 1930s, the idea of class struggle attracted radical political groups, such as the Progressive Labor Party: "They want[ed] to believe that the revolution has broken out....They came down into Kentucky to bring arms to the miners. And they ran into the contradictions of the place, which is that even though these people were dispossessed and disenfranchised and are in a local uprising, they're totally loyal Americans. And so they didn't welcome these radicals too well" (*Gurney Norman*). Not all local people eschewed the sympathy of the "outside agitators." Clara Sullivan, a coal miner's wife from Perry County, wrote to the *Progressive Labor Journal*:

> *The operators have beautiful homes, Cadillacs and aeroplanes to enjoy, and our homes (camp houses, by the way) look like barns.... The operators wouldn't go in a mine for fifty dollars a day. I've seen my husband come home from work with his clothes frozen to his body from working in the water. I have sat down to a table where we didn't have anything to eat but wild greens picked from the mountain side.*[51]

Malvina Reynolds and Pete Seeger turned this letter into an eloquent protest song.[52] Folk and topical singers were among the sympathizers who came to eastern Kentucky in 1963 and went back to write songs such as Phil Ochs's "Hazard, Kentucky" ("Well, minin' is a hazard in Hazard, Kentucky"), Eric Andersen's "The Blind Fiddler" ("I lost my eyes in the Harlan pits in the year of '56"), Tom Paxton's "High Sheriff of Hazard" ("He's a mine owner too, you know which side *he's* on").[53] Even Bob Dylan came to Hazard, bringing used clothes for the miners in the winter of 1964; the visit was not a success.[54]

JOE SCOPA SR.: We got the impression from the District 19 people, see, they told us, "We're with you 100 percent." Then when the mines shut down, they denied everything. That's the reason I say that the district people, the field workers and the organizers, they're the ones that destroyed the union. They and the coal operators. [The miners] they'd feel betrayed—but they wouldn't say nothing.

Disowned by the union, the movement was beset by police harassment, injunctions, restraining orders, arrests, and "gun thugs." As a reporter, Gurney Norman joined one of the pickets' last night rides, from Hazard to Letcher County.

GURNEY NORMAN: So we go into the night and it was dark and there was a mountain that this road went over, it's called Sand Lick—but I was far back enough in the caravan to have a long view, and I just marveled at this long string of automobile headlights and taillights winding over this mountain on this switchback road. It was beautiful. Anyhow, we got on the other side of Sand Lick Mountain and arrived at the entrance of South

East coal mine. It must have been seventy-five to a hundred former miners, disabled miners, family members, some women, and a few young ones. The state police were out in force, there were at least twenty cops; I just remember how young they were. And they were all armed with shotguns. And the pickets were standing near the entrance to the mine, and just as day began to break the employees of the coal mine were coming to work. And as they drove up, there seemed to be this instinctive kind of surge, of all the pickets, toward the entrance as if to block it. And I remember this: these were automatic shotguns, you know; and I remember twenty shotguns going *tsch!* as they chambered shogun shells and pointed these shotguns at us. And what they did was push the pickets back to create a avenue for these scab workers, to enter the mine. We stood here and there was no stopping them. But at one point there was one of the roving picket group that—I don't know if he picked up a rock, or cursed, but the police arrested him, and dragged him roughly to a police car. Again, the large group of pickets surged again—but those were loaded guns the police were pointing at us. And it amounted to a demonstration, it did not impede the workings of this mine. And so, muttering and grumbling, cursing some, the miners wandered to their vehicles and the crowd started breaking up. And I will venture to say that this was the last ride of the roving pickets.

On January 8, 1964, however, Berman Gibson led a contingent of coal miners to Washington to picket the White House.

BERMAN GIBSON: Johnson won't meet with us. He wouldn't talk to us. We picketed the White House. They came back the next morning and said, "What do you intend to do?" I said, "We're gonna stay here and picket until he does say he will meet us." Well wasn't till an hour after that we see the guards come over and said, "Gibson, get you four or five men and make a committee and come up. We'll let you meet him." So we went up. They searched us and everything, you know, taking us in.[55]

The Johnson administration was just then preparing to launch the War on Poverty. George Reedy, the president's press secretary, met with the miners and suggested a change in strategy: "'Look, you've got to quit burning bridges and dynamiting things and you have to go home, incorporate yourselves, rent an office, print up some letterhead stationery, and be legitimate, because we're going to create the Office of Economic Opportunity. And what this means is that we're going to funnel federal funds for community development through community action groups. And what we want is for you to be legitimate so that we can work with you.' So these guys came back and opened an office and it was called the Appalachian Committee for Full Employment" (*Gurney Norman*).

Wildcat strikes continued throughout the sixties. The strike in 1964–65 was as bitterly fought as ever: "I used to be on the picket line too; then finally I got tired of picketing because they paid me [only] twenty dollars a week vouchers, and I started going back to work, and they called us scab and all that. They blowed my car up once, put the dynamite on the top of the transmission, blow the car up" (*J. C. Hall*). It ended in defeat and disenchantment. "I guess it just broke the union," said Ray Ellis, who never got a job in the mines again. Most union contracts were lost, and many blacklisted and jobless workers were forced to leave the area. "In '64, there was quite a few of us that worked at Brookside that were on the picket lines, but this number dwindled in a few months. I had to leave myself. I stayed on the picket line that long. But we lost it; we lost that union in sixty-five" (*Junior Deaton*). Brookside wouldn't be organized again until 1974.

CLYDE BENNETT: We were union from 1941 to 1964. We've been nonunion since 1964. We [were] at the point of going completely out of business, we're almost completely broke. And we offered the union a deal which they wouldn't take, to give our men a raise and quit paying part of the health and welfare, and they wouldn't agree to it. And we told our men that we're going to have to quit if they didn't sign the contract, and we started back nonunion. Most of them didn't like it, but we had no choice. A lot of operators shut down. Us and a couple of others didn't shut down. We were union one day and nonunion the next.

13

THE OTHER AMERICA

WAR ON POVERTY

GURNEY NORMAN: The Appalachia angle begins in the Kennedy campaign in 1960 when Hubert Humphrey is the favorite, Lyndon Johnson is the favorite, and Kennedy is just this kind of dark horse, but Kennedy picks up steam, and he defeats Hubert Humphrey and LBJ in the West Virginia primary. And Robert Kennedy was his campaign manager and spent a lot of time in West Virginia and met those coal miners, these old UMW guys, and these people turned it around, and that's where Kennedy picked up his momentum that took him all the way.

JOHNNY WOODWARD: When I was a high school kid, I joined the VISTAs [Volunteers in Service to America], which I guess for that time was a radical bunch; we decided that when [Robert] Kennedy came down the path of [his] trek across Appalachia and its poverty-ridden communities, we were gonna go over [in Neon] and protest. I was standing there with a little brown bag over my head, I had a couple of little eye holes cut in it, and we had our little signs, protesting our economic conditions and our education systems, and Robert Kennedy walked up and stuck his hand up to me, said, "Son, tell me your problem." It took everybody by surprise. And I finally collected myself and, we sat down in the lobby and talked. And he wanted to know what the problems were, how he could help, where we were from and we had a good, long talk.[1]

The sixties are often identified with Berkeley or Columbia, Paris or Prague, but the era also had an impact in supposedly isolated and "invisible" peripheries. Indeed, one of the harbingers of the sixties was the discovery of Appalachian poverty in affluent America during John Kennedy's 1960 primary campaign.[2] In 1963, the Kennedy administration created the President's Appalachian Regional Commission. The following year, in Inez, Kentucky, Lyndon Johnson proclaimed: "I have called for a national war on poverty. Our objective: total victory." And in 1965, Congress passed the Economic Opportunity Act, a key element of the War on Poverty, and established the Office of Economic Opportunity (OEO).

When the roving pickets returned from their 1964 meeting in Washington to form the Appalachian Committee for Full Employment (ACFE), a class war of the poor turned into a War on Poverty based on what sociologist and former volunteer David Walls later described as "a consensus model of community development." *Community* and *consensus* can be misleading words when the community is split by inequalities in power, wealth, and status: as Ronald Eller notes, the War on Poverty in Appalachia became an effort to eliminate poverty without dealing with its institutional and economic causes.[3]

However, the OEO's call for "maximum feasible participation of the poor" and ACFE's background in the roving pickets were a clear threat to the power structure and to the political machines, which saw the poverty programs as a challenge to their vested interests and the status quo. On the other hand, the same powers also saw government intervention as an opportunity to establish themselves as mediators, turning federal programs into patronage mechanisms, often through the locally administered and OEO-funded Community Action Programs (CAPs).

> GURNEY NORMAN: By summer of '64 this kind of infatuation with grass-roots finally had begun to wane. There was a deadline to get your grant proposal in for the first money from the Office of Economic Opportunity to go directly to the people, represented by the successor organization to the roving pickets. And then [as the deadline neared] the Democratic Party in Kentucky suddenly woke up, and they said, "What do you mean, millions of dollars are coming from a Democratic Congress and administration to Kentucky and it's not coming to us?" And then the machine kicks in, so in the end the project submitting a grant proposal for a million dollars, was carried through by the [Perry] county attorney, and other courthouse officials. But by this time far more powerful people in national politics were putting their hands in to get this largesse, and so at the last minute, just one day before the Kentuckians put in their proposal, Mayor Daley of Chicago got *his* proposal in, of course not to fight poverty but just to create programs to reinforce his power.

In Easter week of 1964, the Appalachian Committee for Full Employment and the radical Students for a Democratic Society (SDS) jointly sponsored a conference in Hazard. ACFE hoped to attract student volunteers to help with organizing work; SDS envisioned an alliance between unemployed whites and the civil rights movement.[4]

> GURNEY NORMAN: The town filled up with these radical-looking kind of kids. Part of the style in those days was the women would wear jeans with these big boots up to the knee almost, and some of them had fur hats and, you know, the style was that you didn't bother to try to ingratiate yourself with anybody. One time everybody was eating in this restaurant, it was

like the whole bunch of kids over here, and some of the businessmen were over there, and they were outraged that these people were over here not knowing their place, you see. And I was eating with these people and this businessman was very worried about me and he had no idea how much fun I was having. He called me aside as we were going out and he says, "Watch 'em, Gurney," he says, "be careful," he says. "I know who those people are in college," he says: "they're *art* majors."

ACFE did not long survive the transformation into a channel for federal funds and the struggle with local officials and coal operators over their control: by the mid-1960s "it played itself out. The out-of-state radicals got tired and left, went back to school or something. The local people were exhausted. They put up a candidate for sheriff [Bernie Gibson], lost, and that spent the energy. And the government's poverty program began to pay these men a dollar an hour for make-work. And suddenly these men who had two or three years before been burning bridges, accepted a government subsidy for, essentially, for make-work" (*Gurney Norman*). By 1965, the OEO funding stopped, and ACFE ended.

However, the roving pickets had put eastern Kentucky back on the map at a time when America was in ferment. The Berea-based Council of the Southern Mountains created a group called Appalachian Volunteers (AV) and sent them into the most depressed areas. At first, they were mostly local college students with a culture-of-poverty orientation and a concept of "Appalachians helping Appalachians" through education, school renovation, and improvements in the curriculum. Their first meeting was held at Pine Mountain Settlement School; their first action was the painting of a run-down rural school in Harlan County in the winter of 1964.[5]

"AV began as a project from some students from Berea College going out to work in very poor communities, and they would help repaint these old school-houses and they collected books, they even did a national book drive called Books for Appalachia. It was essentially a one-year volunteer program on the model of the Peace Corps" (*David Walls*). By 1965–66, the Appalachian Volunteers were cooperating with VISTA, a new organization created in the framework of the War on Poverty on the pattern of the Peace Corps.[6]

These programs brought into Appalachia committed volunteers (and, later, some paid staff) from other parts of the country with experience in the student movement, the Mississippi Freedom Summer, and the Peace Corps. Appalachia became one of the issues and places in which members of the activist generation of the 1960s could invest their passion for change. David Walls, who came from the Free Speech Movement at Berkeley, recalled: "My first awareness of the Appalachian area developed while I was a student at the University of California at Berkeley. I think, in 1962, I read two books that were very important to me. One was Michael Harrington's *The Other America*, which was a general introduction to poverty in America. And, secondly, and maybe more powerfully, Harry Caudill's book *Night Comes to the Cumberlands.*"[7]

On the other hand, as more young Appalachians began to attend college, they in turn became attuned to the new spirit of the times. Gurney Norman got a scholarship to Stanford, joined the psychedelic culture, and returned to write about the utopian convergence of his two "countercultures," California and Appalachia.[8] George Ella Lyon recalled: "I went to college and it was wonderful. I found friends and people interested in writing and teachers I could really talk to. There was a march after the invasion of Cambodia, there was a moratorium where we read the names of everybody killed in the war and stopped classes. There was a group of us who picketed barbershops because they wouldn't cut black people's hair in Danville."

JAMES B. GOODE: [The University of Kentucky at Lexington] was full of unrest, full of drugs... I remember Timothy Leary coming and the police had the house surrounded, they were doing LSD; I remember at UK they burned the ROTC building down. The governor brought the National Guard, they brought in antiaircraft guns, antitank guns. And we couldn't reconcile that—what were they gonna shoot? I remember participating in occupying the administration building at UK. That was a period of a lot of anxiety and unrest. I decided that I was going to come back, and that, whatever talent I had, no matter how limited it might be, I was going to invest it back in the culture from which I came.

JANIS ROSS: Like so many people of that time, the sixties, I was influenced by John F. Kennedy. By '65 we had the Great Society, we had the great influx of people into the Appalachian area, VISTA volunteers, Appalachian Volunteers. I didn't feel like I was one of those that needed to be helped. But I thought, "I can help them help others." I was interested to find something on a part-time basis. And the job that became available, at day care centers here in the county, was special funding for a pilot project from the Office of Economic Opportunity. I applied, I got the job, and began to work. We had to find our own students, or children for the center, and they were chosen from those who were economically depressed. We only had a few children, less than thirty per center; but they operated in the county for about four years. Some of the [children] had tremendous health problems. Parasites; worms; some had hearing difficulties, speech difficulties. Many of their fathers were unemployed; none of the women were employed, other than in the home.

"So the AV started as this very do-good, simple program of college students working weekends. [But] as they began to see the deeper poverty in the communities I think they came to see that the problems were more involved with local politics and corruption than they first thought, so the new staff had a much more radical notion of social change, and as they moved in[to] the coalfield areas [they] quickly radicalized" (*David Walls*). The initial culture-of-poverty approach, focused on bringing the supposedly backward Appalachian people into the mainstream of American life, was superseded by an "internal colonialism" theory that saw Appalachia's problems as related less to the shortcomings of mountain culture than to the workings of national and local power. The new approach sought solutions less in a strategy of uplift than in a movement for social justice.[9]

> LOWELL WAGNER: I'm originally from Virginia. I came to Harlan County in 1968. I worked for Appalachian Volunteers, which was a group that was involved in environmental issues, welfare reform, better medical care, community issues. I'd just gotten out of the Peace Corps, and I felt a real kinship between this part of the United States and the Third World culture that I experienced in the Peace Corps. There was a lot more personal relations, things were slower, people seemed more interested in how they related to one another. Those were the things that attracted me, and just the physical beauty of the place. If you look at it politically, from a colonial standpoint, you have these huge mines. You had huge logging operations and other entities that were controlled from outside. So I think they were colonial, in that local people had no control or no say; and, those organizations didn't just run their company, they ran the schools and the government and everything. So I guess in that way, I would think of it as somewhat of a Third World state.

> JOHNNY WOODWARD: We're really a part of a Third World country, here in Appalachia. We have a lot of natural resources. We have an abundance of coal, highest-grade coal in the world, we have an abundance of timber, hardwood that's sought after the world over. We have an abundance of natural gas, we have oil, but we don't use any of that here. We ship it all out. We export everything we have. And there's a term called the "brain drain." We're graduating some of the most intelligent kids in the world, right here out of Southeast Community College, but as soon as they clear our doors, they also clear our county, and, in many instances, they even leave the state. So, we're exporting all of our natural resources, and our most important ones are our kids.

At first the volunteers were welcomed. "The people were so sympathetic, and they were so warm and friendly, and they cooked a big meal for us, I don't think I've ever eaten such a big meal" (*Liz Blum*). "The nurses and social workers like myself, physical therapists, we'd go into the home, and they sort of took us in as part of their family. You were out there to take care of them, but they wanted to take care of you" (*Lowell Wagner*). However, some Harlan residents also saw them as the new face of the old-time missionaries and social workers who had been coming to Appalachia since the end of the 1800s. The initial semiofficial guide to the region for the volunteers was Jack Weller's *Yesterday's People*, which explained poverty mostly by the cultural "difference" of these contemporary ancestors.[10] "It really is strange to see some young girl or boy from Brooklyn or Queens or somewhere who would come here, and they would sit and tell me about, 'I went up such and such a creek, and I talked to John Doe, and he just needs to get out of there and go to the city and learn what the real world is like.' And I'd say, 'Well, you know, John Doe is sitting at that hollow trying to eke out an existence on that little plot of land, might know more about the real world, honey, than you do.' But, so many of them came with a superior attitude, and that's never good, wherever you are, and particularly here" (*Gladys Hoskins*).

Don West, union organizer, poet, and Baptist minister, wrote: "The southern mountains have been missionarized, researched, studied, surveyed, romanticized, dramatized, hillbillyized, Dogpatched and povertyized." The average "poverty warrior," like the missionaries, he argued, was not concerned with "how they related to the mountains but how the mountains related to them and their notions." In a bitter poem, he attacked the "missionaries...soul savers...folksy ballad hunters" that carried out "a revolt in patterns / counter culture counter revolutionary / counter poor people!"[11]

> MYLES HORTON: There was a lot of resentment if they went in knowing everything, that kind of thing. What we'd do, we'd get hold of some of these people, say, "If you wanna work here, find out what they want you to do and work quietly, and remember: you're different, they're not different. You're the odd person. You're the freak, they aren't." Some of them were very useful; but most of 'em had all the solution to the problems that people didn't have, the problems that they wanted to solve for 'em. It was a mixed situation.

In 1966, the Appalachian Volunteers separated from the Council of Southern Mountains and became an independent, action-oriented organization. "There were a lot of people with pretty good intentions, but they were sort of living out their dream of what the world ought to be, and they might have been using local people, taking advantage of them to carry out their mission of change. But a lot of them made real good relations, and created long-term relationships. On the other hand, some of them had a lot of ego to fill" (*Lowell Wagner*).

> MILDRED SHACKLEFORD: We had kids from California and they would come and they would have dope or whatever, and they would have a good time and they would get out and buy quilts off of old ladies for two dollars apiece or five dollars and they would take them back home and they'd laugh about what a good deal they got. I remember this one kid that was after guitars. And there is a famous brand name of guitar that people like Hank Snow used and there were people in Harlan that had got it years

before when the price had not been too awful high. And this guy ran around and I bet he bought five or six of those guitars and he was getting them for thirty or forty dollars apiece, and they were really worth five, six, seven hundred dollars. And he was running around driving a little MG and he was getting two, three hundred dollars a week from his folks out in California and he was getting pay salary by the AVs. And one of the guys that he bought one of those guitars from was living in a three-room shack and he had a little ole $130 pension from Social Security.

The sexual revolution was in full swing and, as in the 1930s, some of the problems came from different notions of lifestyles and sexuality. "Many of the people were very young, this was for most of them after college their first real significant life experience, and it was intense and the emotional and sexual relationships among the staff and the volunteers and the VISTAs were very intense. These were people who, while not hippies, were certainly more liberal in their lifestyles than others, many of the staff had affairs with some of the volunteers. Of course it was used against the AV by the people who were unfriendly, or whose interests were challenged by the organizing done by the AVs and the poor local communities they worked with" (*David Walls*).[12]

"I agreed with their criticisms of what was going on here, what was happening environmentally, criticizing the power structure, but I wasn't sure in the long run if that was the best thing for local people, because they're the ones that had to stay and live here. I think they probably did a lot to raise the consciousness of some of the people here, but on the other hand, I think most of those people pretty well understood themselves. Nobody had to point it out to them" (*Lowell Wagner*). Some AV fieldworkers, however, were able to learn from the mountaineers: "I felt like I was radicalized or politicized or whatever by the people who lived in the mountains themselves," one volunteer recalled.[13]

"They wanted changes and wanted them right now," says Harlan journalist Ewell Balltrip, but "they did not understand the people that lived here. They certainly did not understand the political system that was here." David Walls recalls his shock at the discovery of an "entrenched political machine that was very corrupted and controlled people through the distribution of jobs. They managed to have an elaborate system of patronage, not just with teachers, but more importantly with jobs for bus drivers and cooks and janitors in the school, and this was probably, given the decline of the coal industry, the major single employer in Harlan County."[14]

The volunteers' activity in Harlan County was hardly subversive: a community program of literary readings and crafts lessons at Verda, a tutoring program and a "charm school" for girls at Evarts, knitting classes for girls and mountain hikes for boys at Jones Creek. However, these programs ignored or bypassed the local Community Action Program, which was supervised by the county superintendent, and this, plus the fact that the Verda program was interracial, was enough to make a stir. The AVs became more confrontational as they began to organize against strip mining and campaigned unsuccessfully for an alternative candidate for school superintendent.[15]

Throughout Appalachia, the AVs were subjected to the same charges as the National Miners Union in the 1930s: being outsiders, racial integrationists, atheists. In 1967, in Pike County, former AVs Joe and Karen Mulloy and Southern Conference Education Fund (SCEF) workers Alan and Margaret McSurely were arrested, investigated by the Kentucky Un-American Activities Committee, and charged with sedition and attempting to overthrow the government of Pike County by campaigning against strip mining. SCEF representatives Carl and Anne Braden, who had never even set foot in Pike County, also were indicted. Rumors had it that Russian tanks were headed for Pikeville. Although the Kentucky sedition law was later declared unconstitutional, Governor Breathitt and the Office of Economic Opportunity cut all the grants to the AV. Many former volunteers continued to live and work in the area, but this was the end of the group as an organized presence in Appalachia.[16]

The Kentucky Un-American Activities Committee held hearings in Pikeville on supposed subversive activities in the local college. Though none of the charges was sustained in court, the difficulties and divisions they caused (culminating in the suspension of OEO grants) were a major cause of the 1970 demise of the Appalachian Volunteers.[17]

"They were considered to be Communists, radicals, trying to overthrow the status quo. They came to Evarts and signed up a little place, and they were threatened, they were physically abused, their houses were shot into, the windows were broken out...A lot of them would be caught out driving and they would run them off the road into the ditches. The reason they did that was because they had these kids here starting to think. Starting to read material other than what we had been handed out in the classroom" (*Johnny Woodward*). Some local young people were intrigued, sought them out, and began to entertain a different view of the volunteers, and of themselves. "In two summers of my college time I worked for the *Harlan Daily Enterprise*. And one year I got to interview some community action people, some VISTA people. My parents, my mother in particular, there was a lot of fear about this. And I was not encouraged to be too friendly with these people and, I went up to Cumberland to do an interview and then we sat around and played and sang and had a good time" (*George Ella Lyon*).

MILDRED SHACKLEFORD: I got involved in them because I thought they had something different to offer and I wasn't too sophisticated at that time. I was about sixteen or seventeen years old. I was reading a lot. I was finding out different things. The involvement in Vietnam—I was finding out a little bit of it and I found out that, what the United States was doing in that country, wasn't something that I could respect; and I hadn't thought [of] looking at Harlan County in the same way that I looked at Vietnam.

That's one thing I did learn from those people pretty quickly: that in a way, we were more like the people in Vietnam than [like] the people in the rest of the country.

JOHNNY WOODWARD: When we were told that these people were Communists trying to come in here and overthrow the government, we had a meeting with 'em. There's like thirty kids there that had really got involved in a lot of social and I guess political movements and we said, "Look, if you're Communists, tell us now. We believe in what you're doing, but if you're Communists that's not the direction that we're headed. If that's your bag, your thing, then you'll have to go in that direction without us." And they emphatically denied anything having to do with any Communism whatsoever. And we stayed a pretty close-knit bunch, until they were forced to leave.

MILDRED SHACKLEFORD: Harlan County at that time, the school board was the political power, they were the ones that had the most pull, they had everything under their thumb. One of the first things that I can remember we got involved in was trying to get the principal to close up a hole in one of the bathrooms. It was an old building and it had never been maintained very well, and the seventh and eighth grade building had already been condemned two or three years in a row and was considered unsafe. So they was trying to get the principal to patch a hole that was letting raw sewage leak out into the schoolyard. And they had this little paper, *Clover Fork Newsletter*, and they published an article about the bathroom, pictures of it, and the principal was threatening to expel them.

The school board refused to hear the students' grievances and had them thrown out by the police. They arranged a meeting with a group of parents, and Johnny Woodward recalls that the volunteers warned them to avoid antagonizing them. However, when one parent who was a school board member attacked them all as "a bunch of long-haired dope-smoking Communists," some responded with "a few irrational statements; the parents simply got up and walked out. And then things deteriorated and those folk [the volunteers] had to leave" (*Johnny Woodward*).

EWELL BALLTRIP: Yes, the war on poverty was lost. Poverty won, we still have it, and I think we always will have it. It goes beyond Kennedy's Camelot to think that you could eradicate poverty. But did the War on Poverty improve this area? Yes; I think it did tremendously improve this area. I think it gave some people means through which they could secure a better education: in terms of public facilities, public buildings, and highways, things along that line, we received things that we never would have received. The War on Poverty focused a tremendous amount of attention on this segment of the world. Things happened that really did work for the betterment of the community.

By 1970, as the War on Poverty drew to its end and the Appalachian Volunteer program closed down, the population of Harlan County had dropped to 37,370. In a U.S. Department of Agriculture ranking, Harlan ranked 2,934th out of 3,097 U.S. counties in "socio-economic status," 2,929th in health, 2,765th in "family status," and 2,022th in "alienation."[18] One of the young people who had gone to meet Kennedy at Neon, with paper sacks over their heads, was a student from Evarts named Tom Duff.[19] He was also the one who was expelled for taking and publishing the pictures of the leaking bathroom.

> JOHNNY WOODWARD: We had a couple of fellows in our group who had to leave Harlan. They had to leave because...we started our own press, we'd write our own articles, we'd go and take pictures of all the things we wanted to improve. But there was one fellow whose name was Tommy Duff, he was very, very active; very radical. He believed very strongly in whatever we did. He believed very strongly in trying to improve his own community. And he had to leave Harlan County. He realized he couldn't come back, and he was a very high-strung fellow, and he ended up committing suicide. I think it was probably related to him having to leave and not be able to come back.

CIVIL RIGHTS

> MILDRED SHACKLEFORD: I remember the first day that black kids came and all [the] white kids was already seated in the classroom, there was four rows of seats and the white kids were in the first three rows and there was one row of seats left and all these black kids come in and they just went down that row there and sat one right after another. And every white kid in there was a-staring trying to figure out what it was, you know, that made 'em so different. Why was everybody sitting there with abated breath to see what was going to happen when the black kids come into that classroom. Of course, nothing happened. Sat there and looked at each other and looked at each other and after two or three weeks, the ones that was aiming to make friends made friends, the ones that had picked up too much of the hate and stuff that they couldn't tolerate it, just stayed away from 'em. And things worked out fairly good. They left each other alone and I'd say the black kids'd probably felt better to a certain extent staying in their own school. They was shy. They wasn't too much in the way of getting out there and taking a baseball bat and beating people over the head and saying, "I want my liberties. Give me my rights." No, they were more along the line of sitting back and making sure somebody didn't hurt 'em. Because it was dangerous to be doing any of that—even in Harlan County.

"When this integration started, you better believe was just as many blacks against integration as whites. 'Cause I didn't wanna go to school with 'em, didn't want my children going to school with 'em. Let them go to they school and they go to theirs, see" (*Julia Cowans*). Constance Ellison, a teacher at Rosenwald, a historically black school, also feared that integrating into a larger school at Cumberland would "take away our little closeness. But when I got there it wasn't like that. I tell you the first day the children there just wiped that out. They were just like my children here, and I felt just as close to them and I loved them and they loved me." She recalls that "every black teacher was given a job"; however, that didn't last long, and soon she was the only black teacher left in Cumberland. "Most [black teachers] left the county and got jobs elsewhere. Some of our teachers, before they would be subjected to [demotion], left. This area was really raped of the black leadership when they integrated the city schools" (*Nancy Johnson*).[20]

> WILLETTA LEE: When we integrated we lost a great value. We lost the people that loved us, the people that cared about us to teach us. We were taught to respect our elders, we didn't sass, we didn't talk back. You had respect for your teachers, because they cared about you. Before the schools were integrated, our teachers pushed us to go and do and learn. I feel after integration, the teachers that we had didn't care. When I went to school it was all black. We were always pushed to do and be something. They would teach us even if you were gonna be a garbageman, you be the best garbageman you can be. If you can't learn to do anything but haul garbage, you be the best garbageman you can be. Always excel at what you're doing. And we weren't taught that after integration.

Lynch-born sociologist William Turner wrote that between 1960 and 1963 all the "colored schools" in eastern Kentucky were closed. An ironic consequence of integration was a sharp drop in the percentage of black students who went on to college.[21]

> MILDRED SHACKLEFORD: Our senior year in high school we had this teacher who was supposed to be teaching a class called the History of the Colored Man. And he lived in Cumberland, which you know that Harlan is a dry county, Cumberland is a city that's wet. And, whenever we would rake up enough money to get it, he would bring us a fifth of bourbon back to class. And we was sitting in there one day. The boys was in the back having a card game, gambling for money, we were sitting up front talking to the teacher and there was two or three black kids sitting up there with us and we was all drinking bourbon and having a good ole time and these three black kids got up and left. And I reached over and got one of 'em's glass and said, "Pour me a shot of that." And [the teacher] grabbed it up and he wiped it out and he said, "You don't want to drink after them niggers."

And it just hit me. I said, "I didn't know you was prejudiced. Don't you find it slightly ironic that you feel the way you do and you are teaching this class?"[22]

LINDA HAIRSTON: We were like sitting on the side, blacks were sitting on one side, whites on the other side. We didn't like white people, I guess white people didn't like me. And we had a big fat principal over at the Lynch high school that hated black kids, and created a lot of problems. I think it was '68 or '69. He hated blacks. And there was no way you could tell your parents this man really hated blacks because he would get in front of them and...but behind their backs he would do things to black kids—"Why don't you mop that thing?...You're dumb...You people!" I hate that. That's an expression, don't ever say that to me because I hate it. "You people!" Why, who "you people"? Who are "you people"? "You colored people." I told the principal one time, I said, "Colored people? When I was born I was black," I said, "and my mother raised me, I was black; when I go out in the sun, I'm black; when I die I'm gon' be black. You white: you born red, when you're in the sun you turn pink, when you die you gonna be gray...What do you mean colored? I'm black! But you change colors, you know."

"Most of the black people here, we had a few establishments where we'd go if we wanted to go out, you know; but there was segregation" (*Tommy Sweatt*). Given the absence of a plantation culture and the presence of the union, Harlan's experience of segregation had been less harsh than elsewhere in the South. In Lynch, "you could go in the store and get what you wanted," but the bathhouses in the mines were segregated (*Bernard Mimes*). Willetta Lee was proud that "I can never remember riding on the back of the bus. My grandmother, she never sat on the back of the bus." Her husband, Bill Lee, however, had different memories: "I remember people doing that. There were places [in Cumberland] that we could go, you could buy hamburgers as long as you were outside, but if you come inside they wouldn't serve you. You've got stores here today, you can go in there and be shopping, say you have to use the rest room, they'll lie and tell you they don't have a rest room you can use. I've been in stores and be waiting to be served, some of their friends come up, they'll wait on them, and I leave. 'Cause I can go somewhere else and spend my money."

LINDA HAIRSTON: I was twelve, I got slapped at a drugstore downtown, and my father almost went to jail for that 'cause this white man slapped me because I was sitting on the barstool and blacks weren't supposed to sit on the barstool. And I never forgot it. I could remember times when my mother said, "You can't go in that bathroom, you've got to go around here and use it on the ground," and I was determined that I was going.

"Every child that could sponsor himself with fifty cents for registration proudly wore his NAACP lapel button" (*Tommy Sweatt*). There had been a NAACP chapter in Harlan since the 1950s, and it staged sit-ins at some of the stores, with mixed results. "We got to sit in at the drugstore, and we did get some things done. Any victory was considered pretty big at that time, because there just weren't any. The NAACP were more the nonviolent, they were following Dr. King and other leaders. They went through a lot of changes with us, training us, how to behave when we were in certain places, to whom to speak and if to speak at all, when we're going to do a sit-in, kinds of things" (*Connie Owens*).

> TOMMY SWEATT: We had our own sit-ins, demonstrations, things like that. We had a minister come in, named Matthew Peckway. Matthew Peckway came to Lynch in the fall of 1963. I was a freshman in high school. He had been in marches, rubbed elbows and talked with the late Dr. Martin Luther King, Dr. Ralph Abernathy, a group like that. When he came here, all the civil rights struggle, with sit-ins, bus boycotts, hoses and police dogs, Lester Maddox with his ax handle down in Georgia and George Wallace and that kind of stuff, it was all over the news.

> JULIA COWANS: We joined the Equal Rights Congress but we got a lot of opposition, even from blacks 'cause they were afraid and they said that we, Reverend Cowans and I, would get them killed, and we'd gotten up a lot of mornings and we found Klan leaflets that had been thrown in our yard. But that didn't stop us. I believe God just really took care of us. There's been times when they wanted us dead. They could've had us killed. It's a lot of white people that just really don't go for this stuff, you know? And, when we lived in Harlan, we had white friends that kept us informed as to what the movement would be against the blacks. But I think it's just the hand of God that kept us so many times.

"And they were calling me 'Martin Luther King of the coal field.' I don't have those qualifications and, see, Martin Luther King's philosophy and my philosophies are very much different. See, Martin Luther King's philosophy was nonviolent. Now I'm for nonviolence up to a point. I'm a minister, but you see, I think you gotta fight for some things, you know. I might be wrong in my saying, but I just have to be me" (*Hugh Cowans*). "I was at college, when Dr. King was murdered. And I was one of those people, who was like, 'Okay, I understand the nonviolence thing,' I didn't have a problem with that because I didn't like physical fighting. But it was so cool to me, watching the Panthers, and I listened to Angela Davis—it didn't really matter, as long as I was in the fight" (*Connie Owens*).

> EARL TURNER: You remember them two black boys at the Olympics in Mexico when they held that black-gloved fist up?[23] Well, the same year's playing a football game right in November. Tony, my son, was class

president. And it was real cold that night. I guess a couple thousand people over there. And they played the national anthem. Everybody didn't get up and stand. And Tony didn't stand. And [the superintendent] called him in his office the next day. He said, "You being the class president, you supposed to stood up and salute your [flag]." He told Tony, "You oughta be in Mississippi, in a cotton patch picking cotton." And [Tony] told 'im, he said, "No, *you* ought be in Vietnam with a bullet up your ass."

Though integration entailed serious losses to the community, yet "integration was good for the children, because I think it gave them a feeling of worth" (*Constance Ellison*). Even Julia Cowans was proud that her daughter was the first black girl who ever made the sorority and became a cheerleader. "I was the first black person that worked for the Bureau of Highways" (*Linda Hairston*). Hairston was also the first black person hired at a big drugstore in Cumberland: "We do a lot of business here," she told the managers, "there is no black faces, we need some black, here, blood, we're people too, you know." In 1964, Bernard Mimes recalled, the partition wall in the Lynch mine bathhouse went down; shortly afterward, following a series of discrimination suits, Earl Turner became the first black foreman at U.S. Steel. And yet—

> TOMMY SWEATT: Right now, as far as racism goes, it's just as alive, but it's shaded very very subtly. There are so few blacks actually in the coal mine, and the relationship is more or less casual, very polite, even to the point of social interaction. Among the older people the terminology, the racial slurs and things, are very much a part of their conversation, back at home; but when they come out they're very polite. [But] you can just about read 'em. You can tell the way they're thinking. And I know a lot of guys that have a little bit of that prejudice, and after they get 'em a couple of beers, get 'em a couple of shots of Jack Daniel's, [they start telling jokes and] one of them is [sure] to be about blacks. And they start poking this kind of humor and stuff at you.

In 2006, black people were estimated at no more than 2.5 percent of Harlan's population.[24] Many migrated after the decline of the coal industry; those who stayed saw many of their communities eradicated and scattered. "You know, Georgetown was the first black community. And—then they ran us off, they destroyed this black neighborhood, 'cause it was too close to town—they ran us to Clovertown—well, we were still too close. We stayed there for a while and they said that that area was a flood zone. So, they had them moved from there [too]" (*Kevin Greer*).[25] In 2008, the vote for Barack Obama in Harlan County was less than 28 percent.[26]

> HUGH COWANS: To make a good minister, you got to bring things to people's remembrance. I remember now that when we worked on the farm you had to go to the man—the plantation owner—and you have to get

meat and meal until your crop come, and then sometime what you'd gotten from him would give out but the corn wouldn't be hard enough, you had to shell it off and put it on the house and let the sun dry it and take it to the mill. And sometimes it was so green the man wouldn't even let you grind it. And I just remind them of the old buildings we used to live in which are modernized now. I don't forget what the Lord hath wrought. See, a lot of people now are like the children of Israel, when God had brought them out of Egypt. Just as soon as they got in the jungle, they went to drumming against Moses. So we have a tendency to forget, and the word of God is like a two-edged sword: it cuts coming and going. And right now we have individuals that will speak ill against Martin Luther King, both white and black. I remember that if it don't be for Martin Luther King, it would not have been where a Negro could have a decent job in this town.

WE WERE POOR BUT...

ANNIE NAPIER: I think a lot of people is ashamed of the way they was raised. But under the circumstances, the older people did the best they could. We didn't have good clothes to wear. We wore patches on our britches 'cause we had to. Now you buy patches, they're designer jeans. We lived almost two miles from the school. Mammy always said we didn't have good clothes to wear and good shoes, and it getting cold in the wintertime we didn't have coats or nothing, and she didn't send us.[27]

MELODY DONEGAN (NAME CHANGED): When I went to school, we didn't have much and people made fun of me. They made fun of my clothes, and I was one of them persons that didn't like for nobody to make fun of me. I didn't have much, and, it was all I had. A little old pair of Levi's, something or other like that, someone had given them to us. You know, I was proud of that. Mom, Dad, they'd tell me not to fight, but that would hurt me when people would make fun of me, and—I made it to the ninth grade, two or three weeks of the ninth grade, and I got kicked out. For fighting.

MILDRED SHACKLEFORD: If we took our lunch to school, we had to take ham and biscuits, you know, homemade, and stuff like that. And we were looked down upon because of that. There were even times when my sister and I took buttermilk and cornbread in a glass jar in a brown paper bag to school and there was one other family at that time that went to school that was poorer than my sister and I. And they brought lunch in a tin pail, like miners used to take. And they had soup beans in it with a piece of cornbread on top of it. And people would make fun of 'em ... But they wouldn't make fun of me and my sister because I was the meanest, toughest child at that school.

Appalachia is not the only place where school lunches and clothes are a fighting matter and a sign of status and class. A steelworker from Terni, Italy, recalled: "I saw the other boys eating their bread with butter and jam, and to us it seemed something extra, and we used to take it from them!"[28] There is a difference, however: Italian memories of poverty are dominated by anger, Appalachian narratives by shame. The narrators from Terni were angry because they were poor; Mildred Shackleford and Melody Donegan were angry because the poor were shamed. "I never had too much respect for the social system because I had always figured it was just so unfair that these little kids sitting here just as sweet as they could be—everybody was making fun of 'em because they was eating buttermilk and cornbread and soup beans...I never did have much respect for a kind of system that always picked out weaker people or people they think is just a little bit different" (*Mildred Shackleford*)

In Italian narratives poverty is associated mainly with social class and with unequal distribution of power and wealth; in Shackleford's and Donegan's, it is associated with identity, difference, and exclusion. Influenced by Marxism and Catholicism, Italian culture has perceived poverty as a source of class conscious-ness and social rebellion and/or austerity and virtue; the Calvinist element in American culture perceives it rather as a sign of personal and spiritual failure. Italian narrators often base their self-esteem on having struggled against economic hardship and social injustice; in Appalachia, dignity is often asserted by downplaying hardship or balancing it against other, positive elements. "We was poor in that way, but...we wasn't poor in enough food to eat. We ate really well; we had a four-room house that had pine floors and pine walls; we burned coal" (*Mildred Shackleford*). Many narrators insist that they never *felt* poor: "We were poor, but we were never poor in spirit" (*Myles Horton*); "People was good to each other. They loved each other, they shared with each other, they took care of each other when they're sick" (*Debbie Spicer*).

Because poverty is related to shame, the response is an emphasis on pride: pride in having survived hardship, in being a hard worker, in the self-sufficiency and warmth of the family. *Growing Up Hard in Harlan County*, the title of the autobiography of Harlan county native G. C. Jones, refers not just to growing up in difficult conditions but also to *becoming* hard by gaining strength of charac-ter—yet also learning tenderness from hardship.[29] "We growed up hard. But I guess we really learned the value of growing up that most people never know. And that's love. We all worked together, we played together, we cried together, and we still do" (*Annie Napier*).

JOHNNY WOODWARD: There's a friend of mine who has a very profound statement about growing up in a coal camp and being a poor kid. He says he was happy as he could be when he was a kid. Didn't have any worry, didn't have any problems—he was poor; didn't know he was poor. And he said that all his life he would overhear conversations, from his own cousins, talking about "them poor sons of a bitches down there." And didn't know until he was sixteen years old that he was the poor sons of a bitches they was talking about. And he said that just depressed him beyond no means, and that he really didn't know it was a bad shape he was in until somebody told him.

What "depressed" Woodward's friend was not the experience of scarcity but the stigma attached to being poor. "We didn't know what the rest of the world was like. We didn't have anything to compare ourselves to" (*Johnny Woodward*). In a sense, subjective awareness of poverty in Appalachia is a consequence of modernization. While mechanization, unemployment, environmental damage, and the demise of self-sufficient agriculture were eroding the region's economic basis, migration and television offered glimpses of other standards of living, and exposed the "poor" to the gaze of outsiders who took it for granted that, in the land of opportunity, they were poor only because there was something wrong with them. The "poor dumb hillbillies" are poor because they are dumb, and dumb because they are hillbillies.

> ROBERT SIMPSON: I was watching something on TV the other night, they had a thing 'bout over in Floyd County [Kentucky], on NBC. And they had all the bigger folks, the governors and all that, they was putting it down and they were showing just like poor people is. You go in these little hollers, they ask why they don't leave. I mean it's family, you know, you here trying to make a living and if you go to a city, you are just about as worse up there with no education.

This particular television program was received as an insult all over Kentucky in 1989. This resentment, and the sometimes violent hostility it generates, is to some extent the consequence of a cognitive difference.[30] Often, local media and public opinion see the fact of calling attention to poverty as a way of labeling Appalachians as somewhat damaged and inferior, and respond by pointing out that not all Appalachians are poor (and that poverty also exists elsewhere), and therefore there is nothing inherently wrong with being Appalachian.[31] To sympathetic (and sometimes paternalistic) observers who do not tend to blame poverty on the character of the poor, however, the fact that not all Appalachians are poor only heightens the sense of injustice. The VISTA workers and Appalachian Volunteers were shocked precisely by the discovery of stark "differences in power between the people in poor communities [and] the power of the companies. That was a shock: to see that much poverty in an industrial community, that had a few [model] towns like Lynch, or Benham, but to see the rest of Harlan County outside of the cities of Harlan in such a dismal shape, with such a poor educational system and poor health care for people" (*David Walls*).

This attitude shaped the reception of possibly well-intentioned programs in the 1960s, such as the CBS News documentaries *Depressed Area U.S.A.* and *Christmas in Appalachia*. With sensationalist overtones, both exposed the worst images they could find of conditions in eastern Kentucky; both, however, also included criticism of local politics and an assertion of the responsibility of the local officials and operators, which caused those in power to become increasingly worried about how the region, and their role, were being represented. Barbara Kopple's *Harlan County, U.S.A.* (1977) met with the same criticism: "I was able to see how frustrated the, the well-to-do people were, they didn't want TV cameras taking pictures of all this stuff. And, in many instances, I would have to agree with them that the TV cameras found the very worst things to take pictures of" (*J. D. Miller*).When I first visited Harlan County in 1973, I could see that not all of it was the "very worst." But I saw enough to be reminded of the slums where I had been organizing in the "very worst" places in Rome. I knew my hometown was not all like that, that it also possessed golden churches and beautiful palaces—but those riches made the existence of poverty even more offensive.[32]

Just as in the 1930s, the upper classes manipulate to their advantage the feeling that social criticism is a way of "putting down" the people. Rather than drawing attention to inequality and injustice, the presence of wealth in a poor region is parlayed as a way of redeeming it from the spiritual and biological stigma of intrinsic inferiority. Thus, the insistence on a better representation of the region results in asking that it be represented by its "better" people, hiding class differences under a veneer of spurious cultural homogeneity. Again, members of the power structure evoke identity traits they may share with the poor in order to hide the economic and political gap that separates them.

> ROBERT SIMPSON: Well, after the show, they had a panel that comes on there. You know, people that's well-off and you know they don't care. They didn't have a poor person, to back up what they was saying. They was talking 'bout, "Yeah, we're doing something for this and something for that...."

The insult is compounded by the fact that, by describing what they are "doing for" the poor, the well-off dismiss what the poor and the underprivileged are doing for themselves. Forget maximum feasible participation; the poor are objects, not subjects, of political action. This attitude also informs the relationship with the welfare system. "It's charity," says Robert Simpson, and "a working man's got his pride," yet it's also "a big help"—a help, however, that does not come from a reciprocal relationship with equals and neighbors but is doled out by an impersonal bureaucracy that implies that if you need help, you are somehow defective.

In 1989, Annie Napier introduced me to her young neighbor Melody Donegan. At one point, Melody told us that food stamp recipients were required to attend vocational training classes in order to remain eligible. Since she had no transportation and was illiterate, Melody feared she might lose her benefits. Annie Napier suggested that she apply anyway; transportation could be arranged with neighbors or by the Survival Center. But Melody had so little faith in herself that she was reluctant to admit that she would like to try. While external difficulties could be dealt with, inner ones were harder to overcome.

> ANNIE NAPIER: You can do it. You're older now; you're more sensible. About flying off the handle when they make fun of you. We'll get you anything you need to go to school. You'll be as big as anybody.
> MELODY DONEGAN: Good Lord... Me, I always got down on my old knees and I always prayed the Lord—"I need you to help me with this, or to do this for me."
> NAPIER: See, just be yourself. Go ahead and do it.
> DONEGAN: I don't think people'd like me if I was myself.

Melody Donegan's low self-esteem was geared to an image of "flying off the handle" that was, in turn, caused by people making fun of her—first for being poor, and then for losing control because she was made fun of. Her anger began as a rebellion against shame, but she lacked the cultural means to perceive her rage as a defense of her pride and dignity rather than as evidence of personal pathology. Being "herself" meant responding with anger to humiliation, and being humiliated for being angry.[33]

> MELODY DONEGAN: I would just like, you know—for something, just halfway decent. I ain't used to nothing fancy. Just something, you know, when you lay down at night, you're warm, you just might have a blanket on you, instead of having three or four blankets. You might think I'm crazy but this is God's truth. I'd just like to have enough money to get me a halfway decent home; and pay my light bill, my TV bill, and buy my [quilt] patterns and clothe me and Johnny, because I'm blessed with furniture. It might not look like much to other people, but it's enough to me.

Last I heard, Melody didn't make it to school, and her house is still cold in the winter.

READIN,' 'RITIN', AND 'RALITY

On my first visit to Harlan, I was thrilled to hear Hiram Day at the Cranks Creek Survival Center sing one of my favorite hymns, "Life Is Like a Mountain Railroad." Afterward, I asked him if he knew the union version, "Miner's Lifeguard." He did not, so I wrote the words on a page from my notebook and handed it to him. He stuck it in his shirt pocket without comment. Later, his half sister Annie Napier explained that he could not read and had never worked in a union mine. I had not expected to find illiteracy in the wealthy and advanced United States. Nor did I realize how steep the price for it could be.

ANNIE NAPIER: When Hiram went to work with this man, they got him to sign a paper saying he was part owner, like 3 percent. But it was just enough to clear [the owner] of having to pay any kind of workmen's compensation. Hiram had to pay his own taxes out of it, Social Security, state tax, federal tax, had to provide his own health insurance, just like he was an owner in the mine. And then when Hiram got hurt, in 1980, when he got mashed up in the mine, he couldn't draw workmen's compensation 'cause he wasn't covered by it. And he didn't draw nothing, I mean absolutely nothing. He didn't never get 3 percent of what that man was making either. [If he had known how to read] he would have never signed them papers for 3 percent of the mine ownership. So they're signing away their rights.

Rather than a relic of the past, functional illiteracy in Appalachia is also a result of modernization. It is both an effect and a cause of poverty and of the stigma placed upon its people. Psychiatrist David H. Loof thought he found a high incidence of "school phobia" in Appalachia's children and explained it in terms of pathological aspects of their culture: "overly dependent personality disorders" and "symbiotic psychosis" created by "over-affectionate and over-indulgent family background." At no time did he contemplate the possibility that the children's experience in school may also be a factor.[34]

When I met her in 1988, at an adult literacy center in Harlan, twenty-two-year-old Nancy Mayer (name changed) was functionally illiterate. She described herself as "a nervous-type person" and answered my questions in monosyllables. But when I asked whether her nervousness had to do with her school experiences, she waxed eloquent.

NANCY MAYER: Oh, I can really put you down in school. The schools that I went to—they didn't care. And I know there's too many kids in school and I know the teachers can't take time and show you each and one what we're gonna do. But they don't try. See, I quit because I didn't like the way the teachers was doing. Because the other kids didn't want to learn, so—they're not learning, why should I? I can remember this teacher: I walk in, he gives us one assignment to do. And my paper was half done. He doesn't even look at it; he just puts an A on it and says, "Don't worry about it." I barely knew how to read, and I got up to the ninth grade. I would bring my report cards home and they would be A's and B's. And it's shocking, I wanted to read so bad, they just didn't wanna teach. And I just, I got mad and I walked home and I told my mama, "I'm not going back." She remembers this as clear as day, because she dropped her sheets. I explained to her what was happening. She said, "It's up to you. I can't force you to go." And, I just never bothered going back. I always wanted to and I regret quitting, but— why should I go to a school that don't teach me nothing? And I never went back.

Nancy's face lit up when she talked about the literacy program: "And then I came here—God, I loved it here! It felt so good to pick up a book and try to read it now. And it just feels good to...to learn." Her motivation was both economic ("I'm getting tired of eating hamburgers") and psychological ("I have a niece, and she walks up to me one day: 'Read me this.' And it hurt me so bad because I couldn't read it"). She wanted to read her Bible, but also "love stories. And news—but mostly love stories. They used to be read to me, I'd sit there and—but now I'm trying to read them myself. I wrote a letter the other day myself—it was wonderful to write this letter, then reread it."

A beautiful, modern consolidated high school now sits by the highway halfway between Harlan and Cumberland. Education has come a long way from the days of the one-room schools—their loss regretted because of the close relationships they encouraged and because they were the heart of small communities, but their passing also welcomed because of the dilapidated conditions, the often inadequately trained teachers, the system of patronage and political control, and the lack of equipment and books. Yet the price of generations of substandard education is still being paid.

In 1980, the Appalachian Regional Commission found that functional illiteracy in Appalachia stood at 46 percent, compared with a national rate of 20 percent. In 1989, Sister Mary Cullen, who ran the literacy program Nancy participated in, estimated that although progress had been made, up to three-quarters of the unemployed in Harlan were functionally illiterate.[35]

Among the reasons usually listed for this situation were the dismal quality of the schools in underfinanced school systems, the tendency of good teachers to leave the region, and the increasingly depressed condition of the economy. Young people were expected to go to work in the mines, which did not require much formal education. On the other hand, mountain children, especially from poor families, are often assumed to be mentally inferior, unwilling and unable to learn.[36] When Nancy walked home from school for good, none of the authorities that were supposed to enforce her compulsory education bothered to do anything about it.

Neither did her mother. Education does not always rank very high in the priorities of mountain families. "Getting above one's raising" is a serious infraction in a culture based on equality and solidarity. "A lot of parents, they feel for kids to get smarter than them, they're in trouble. They don't care about education that much" (Jerry Johnson).

There are exceptions and counterefforts. Schools, grassroots groups, and government agencies have created excellent projects, and most families that can afford it support their children's education. Pine Mountain Settlement School and Southeast Kentucky Community and Technical College have raised the quality of education in the area. Harlan County schools have been noted for excellence in sports and other activities: the Harlan school boys' choir and the Musettes (a girls' choir) performed in Washington, D.C., and abroad.[37]

SISTER MARY CUMMEN: I think the younger people that we've met have better basics and are better able to continue their education than the people in their forties, fifties, sixties. But being literate means to be able to get a job and to carry on with your daily life. So I don't think that the level is enough yet to make them employable. And as each year goes by that level of education goes higher and higher, technology gets more and more sophisticated, so it's going to be very difficult to get a job.

In literate cultures, those who do not possess the alphabet are assumed to possess no language at all. For a time, the reading difficulties of black ghetto children were explained in terms of "verbal deprivation"; psychiatrist David H. Loof likewise describes "school-phobic" Appalachian children and their parents as "nonverbal," sitting silently through the interviews and showing "disturbing feelings." As linguist William Labov has explained in another context, these feelings may be caused precisely by the interview—like Nancy, those functional illiterates who are nervous when interrogated can be quite verbal when speaking on their own terms.[38]

Indeed, the concept of illiteracy makes sense only in societies endowed with writing. In nonliterate cultures, no one is illiterate—no one is defined by the absence of what does not exist. If we define literacy as consciousness "of oneself as a user of language" in all its forms, then Harlan is endowed with a high degree of "oral literacy."[39] Children are reared in a tradition of oral skills and storytelling: "I can remember sitting around, when we were younger, and them talking about being on picket lines, organizing, and, that was mostly what we talked about, sitting round the table after supper and all" (Bessie Lou Cornett).[40] The church educates its members in verbal skills through preaching, testifying, and singing; many "illiterate hillbillies" are highly proficient in one or more musical instruments: Hiram Day is no exception. In fact, the power of oral culture in Harlan can be gauged precisely by its ability to absorb and influence writing, as shown by the influence of orality in the work of local historians and memoirists.[41]

What happens to this love for and proficiency in the uses of language and in musical arts when they come in contact with literacy, as embodied in specific practices and institutions?

We have seen what school did to Nancy Mayer; Melody Donegan, in turn, had to deal with a welfare bureaucracy based on the power and mystery of writing in its most abstract and inaccessible form. The advantage of writing is that it allows for neutral, institutional, technical communication; in an oral culture, however, communication means being immersed in a web of direct personal relationships. The poor and the illiterate face the impersonality of the modern state without enjoying the equal rights that are supposed to go with it. Nancy Mayer resented teachers who "do not care," who do not "take time" to "show you each and one." Melody Donegan fantasized about learning to read and getting a job in the welfare system so that she could humanize and personalize it: "And when a poor person come up to me, I could look at 'em, say, 'Yeah, I know how you feel there.' And if I couldn't help them, and they didn't have no money, I'd say, 'Well, I'll take care of it myself.'" In a way, Melody imagined herself on both sides of the desk: the person she imagined helping was also herself.

Jerry Johnson had been a leader of the Brookside strike in 1973–74. When I interviewed him in 1988, he said he could not read or write.

> JERRY JOHNSON: I was about twelve years old and, I went in there and helped my father load coal after school. With a little bitty shovel. And he got a dollar and a quarter a car. I'd rather have been in school. I'd rather have got an education. That is the reason that my kids are gonna get an education. I didn't learn how to read and write because my family couldn't afford it. The reason my family couldn't afford it, is because the union dropped away about that time.

The difference between Jerry Johnson's story and those of Melody Donegan and Nancy Mayer is that he evinced no humiliating sense of personal failure and rejection. He knew the social causes behind his illiteracy and felt that age, work, and time were in the way of his learning to read now, but the most important obstacle was his unwillingness to appear as a needy, disadvantaged person: "I was the president of my [union] local, and I won almost every case; but I didn't have to read the contract. I presented them with the fact that we were the ones that mined the coal [and] unhappy miners don't dig no coal. And we'd settle our grievances. And when we couldn't do that, then I'd get somebody to help me." Indeed, Jerry Johnson had a great deal of pride in the oral literacy that he learned in the union, in the workplace, in the community. His children's education was not a challenge to his pride because book learning and his own knowledge of "survival" were equally important.

> JERRY JOHNSON: I want my kids to get an education. Now, I don't have none. I have an education in survival. I can teach my kids how to survive. My kids can pick and eat every food there is in these mountains. I don't expect them to raise their families like that. All I would like for my kids to do is, have an education and then they can read whatever the hell they want to.

These three stories suggest that literacy and illiteracy ought to be conceived more in terms of an interrelationship rather than an opposition.

Because writing enjoys a higher cultural and social status and prestige, those who are alphabetically illiterate may also end up losing much of what we have called oral literacy: once writing is available, people who may be verbally proficient *become* illiterate—and therefore "defective." Hiram Day, an accomplished musician and church deacon, was an active participant in the culture of his community but was crushed by his inability to read a contract. The combined effect of the institutions of literacy—school, welfare, the mining industry—is to deepen the sense of shame of a whole social environment, and to disrupt and depreciate the cultural capital that had allowed individuals and groups to cope with the hardships of their lives.

SCARS ON THE MOUNTAINS

In October 1986 I was staying at Chester and Annie Napier's. One evening after dinner, I started helping with the dishes. But no matter how hard I scrubbed, the yellow and black stains would not go away. Finally their daughter Marjorie told me: "It's no use—it's in the water."

> MARJORIE NAPIER: Yeah, it settles on everything, you can't get your clothes clean, you can't get your dishes clean; you can get the grease off, but you can't get the yellow stains off because that is settled in. You don't necessarily work in the mines here to get black lung or lung cancer. You just have to be in the area and breathe it. We had perfect water, and they were strip-mining on the Virginia side, and they blasted so hard it busted our water tables. Now the water turns our clothes orange. We have to bring our drinking water in.

In coal fields with high sulfur content, as in much of eastern Kentucky, the "gob pile" of mining waste, containing sulfur, iron, and low-grade coal, can self-ignite and burn for years, causing further air pollution, while acid mine water kills all life in the streams.[42]

> PORTELLI: So this beautiful color in the water comes from pollution.
> NOAH SURGENER: You mean red water? Yeah, that's acid and iron. Iron water's red; acid water's clear but it turns a white, milkish look, as it sets over a while and a skin comes over it, and...it's kind of nasty-looking. Well, now, this ain't caused by strip mining, here, this is caused by deep mining. But strip mines flood the whole country; strip mines ruined Cranks Creek and just about ruined Harlan County. We didn't have no floods like we have now. And they just took these mountaintops and things off and it's ruined everything.

In surface, or strip, mining, the coal vein is reached by removing the surface rather than digging from underground. After the surface is bulldozed or blasted away, the uprooted vegetation and the topsoil ("overburden") are pushed aside into a pile, which (especially in steep and high-rain areas such as eastern Kentucky) tends to slide into the valley below, burying houses, fields, and trees, polluting rivers, and causing floods. A mine inspector reported on a Harlan County strip site: "When we reached the bench it looked like the aftermath of

Hiroshima. Spoil was piled up helter-skelter. Massive broken highwalls loomed above. Deep pits of acid water littered the landscape like pockmarks...and the rain only made it worse. It was the mother of all slides, at least 200 feet across and 800 feet down the slope, directly into Clover Fork. It was one of those slides where you could actually see material moving down the slope. What really bothered me was the amount of spoil and rocks still to come. It was an impending disaster—like the Sword of Damocles."[43]

Until 1940, strip mining accounted for a small portion of production, but its impact grew during and after World War II: by 1960, it accounted for 29 percent. The process was authorized in Kentucky in 1955; it grew dramatically after the Tennessee Valley Authority (TVA)—pressed by growing demands for cheap electricity and by the cold-war needs of the uranium enrichment plants at Oak Ridge and Paducah—began to buy massive quantities of surface-mined, nonunion coal, and actually purchased mining rights to vast areas in eastern Kentucky and eastern Tennessee. Ironically, an agency that had been created to conserve the soil contributed both directly and indirectly to the destruction of the mountains.[44]

In Kentucky, efforts to control strip mining and limit the impact of the broad-form deed had been perfunctory at best. By the mid-seventies, after the 1973 oil crisis, more than half of Kentucky coal came from strip mines—mostly from small, nonunion truck mines, operating with small-scale machinery, little capital investment, and narrow margins of profit.[45]

> HAZEL KING: I love the mountains. I have someone come in here and say, "This is so isolated, you're down in a hole." I say, "It may be isolated to you, but it's privacy to me." And this hole is a protective, it's like a retreat to the womb in a sense—I get rather sentimental when I talk about this. Rather than being closed in, I feel enclosed with the comfort of it. And I'm very prejudiced toward my mountains. And when they come with their strip mining, to destroy it—it's too much [*crying*].

> ANNIE NAPIER: I hate strip mining. I hate anything that destroys the land. I growed up with strip mining, it's scary. When we lived up in the hollow they stripped in front of the house. I must have been about seven or eight years old. And you'd wake up a morning to this gosh awful screeching and rocks coming off that mountain and, they stripped trees and all, you know, right over the hill, sometimes rocks would jump plumb over in our yard. And I was terrified, I'll be honest with you, I growed up terrified.

"I just adore, I just love the mountains, I feel safe here in this community and I just couldn't live nowhere else" (*Crystal Vanover*). In a culture rich with a deep sense of place and attachment to nature, to wildlife, and to the landscape, the destruction of the mountains is an emotional as well as environmental and human disaster: "They stripped Noe holler where I was borned and raised. And it was pitiful. We used the spring in the mountain for a refrigerator, you'd take your milk up there, your butter, anything that you wanna keep, and saved it in the spring. When they strip-mined them mountains, it all just washed in, there's no water left at all" (*Becky Simpson*).

> OTIS KING: I'll tell you what I've seen. I've seen this. They come to a graveyard and they had them bulldozers, buddy, coming through there. And they come to that graveyard, and there's a grave they had to move. And they told that bulldozer to push it over the hill. He just stepped out of the bulldozer, he said, "I won't do it." There's a fellow, just like a scab'll do. He said, "I'll put it over." And he jumped up in that bulldozer and pushed it over.

The scars on Granny Hager's body come to mind when looking at the marks of strip mining on the mountainsides. Reclamation inspector Aaron Warren spoke of a "scarred" landscape; an anti-strip-mining activist in Knott County said that "looking at the strip mining sites in the wintertime was a scar that you couldn't forget." After seeing eastern Kentucky from the air, the writer and environmentalist Wendell Berry wrote: "This industrial vandalism can be compared only with the desert badlands of the west. The damage has no human scale... It is a domestic Vietnam."[46]

> HAZEL KING: In the early seventies, I had seen some obvious signs of the muddy water in the rivers, and they said, "If you think that's bad you ought to see this particular place where this lady lived." And then I went to this place at Day's Creek, up Clover Fork, and this man that assisted her in her garden, he took me up to show where the mountain was just oozing down the mountainside into her garden area. And it was the only land that was available to have a garden, and it was just destroying the place.

"[It's] like a thunder—you get thunder rolling, now that's how that was and the whole river filled up full of logs and rocks, blocked this river—they about cleaned up Harlan County, buddy, this strip mining did. They destroyed houses in this county, they come here to my house, sunk my well, they destroyed the holler. The whole mountain fell in—that whole mountain broke all to pieces" (*Delbert Jones*). "They have this one little creek called Mule Creek that they were using for drinking water, laundry, everything. Well, the bastards come in to strip-mine, they began to clear-cut log and they've destroyed the stream. It's full of mud. So, here they are, twenty miles back in the mountains, and no water, no source of water whatsoever, none. Their wells are dry, the creek's full of mud, all the minnows, any kind of aquatic life, or anything that was there, it's dead, gone" (*Joan Robinett*).

> MELODY DONEGAN: When we first moved up there it was a beautiful place, and the house was real good and warm, and we had plenty of water. And when they got up there strip-mining and dynamiting it, it sunk them wells

and it destroyed the house. We never did have nothing since. They lit that [dynamite] off, it just shook the whole earth. Then, when they done that, the water turned bad. And if it rains or something, that mud just keeps coming down. And that makes me mad, you know, because I know what that place was, before they done that.

It did not happen without a fight. Throughout eastern Kentucky, and most notably around Clear Creek in Knott County, bulldozers were dynamited and gunfire exchanged between residents and strip miners in what amounted to guerrilla warfare. Otis King remembers: "We was fighting strip mines. I went in way back in Pine Mountain, and way back in Floyd County, and Knott County. We went up in the worst time there ever was, boy, it was raining, and the mud-diest time there ever was." As they reached the strip site and began taking pic-tures, "I come to find out, boy, they was up on that hill with high-powered rifles on us."[47] In 1965, on Clear Creek, Knott County, "Uncle" Dan Gibson, an eighty-year-old Baptist preacher, faced the bulldozers of a TVA supplier that were pre-paring to strip his grandson's land (who at the time was fighting for democracy in Vietnam), and held back deputy sheriffs at gunpoint.

OTIS KING: You ever hear of Gibson? Dan Gibson? He took a .22 rifle, over there, and man, he was the meanest man I've ever seen. He was an old fel-low. He got behind a big rock, with that .22 rifle, and he held them off. He had that .22 rifle, loaded full ... shot sixteen times, I think. Buddy, he, he stood them off. He backed right up and sat down right up against that big rock, and buddy, they didn't go get him, either.

Gibson was eventually arrested. His neighbors gathered on his land to save it from the bulldozers and surrounded the Hindman county jail until he was released. A few weeks later, a rally in Hindman created the Appalachian Group to Save the Land and People (AGSLP).[48] Dan Gibson was only one among sev-eral folk heroes of civil resistance to strip mining in eastern Kentucky. In November 1965, after several members of the AGSLP were arrested in Knott County for interfering with surface mining operations, widow Ollie Combs and her two sons sat down in front of a bulldozer that was about to destroy their home. On June 29, 1967, Jink Ray, an Island Creek, Pike County, farmer, stopped the bulldozers with the help of his neighbors, the Appalachian Volunteers, and the AGLSP, until—under pressure from the AV—the company's mining permit was revoked by the state. In August 1968, four unidentified men tied up the guards on a Round Mountain Coal Company strip site in Leslie County and blew up a giant diesel shovel, a D9 bulldozer, an auger, a conveyor belt, three Hi-Lifts, a truck, three generators, and one jeep.[49]

The photograph of Widow Combs being bodily carried off from her own land by deputy sheriffs shocked the nation. Governor Breathitt was moved to introduce new legislation to limit the use of the broad-form deed and to regulate strip mining—which, however, failed to pass the Kentucky House of Representatives.[50]

The reaction was quick and devastating: the Pikeville subversion trial of the Mulloys and McSurelys that destroyed the Appalachian Volunteers was only one aspect of the repression of organized opposition to strip mining. The struggle went on, but the odds were uneven. In January 1972, a group of women from the Eastern Kentucky Welfare Rights Organization occupied a strip site at Trace Fork, Knott County, for fifteen hours, until they were driven out with violence and threats; later the same year, citizens of Floyd County shut down a local strip operation.[51] In Cranks Creek, Melody Donegan recalls: "My mom went up there with the shotgun, and she told that man [to] stop it, or she was going to stop him. Well, that didn't do no good. And so it just destroyed it. We had [the operator] in court, but they told us that a poor person couldn't sue a big man. That's what they told my mom." "Back here in the mountains, from the time you're born and learn to talk, people will tell you you can't fight a coal company and win. You might as well just roll over and play dead" (*Annie Napier*).

> CHESTER NAPIER: [In] '75 they was gonna strip [my place]. I owned the surface rights, but I didn't own the mineral rights. So I come in from work, and they'd moved their equipment in, gonna start the next morning. So next morning I go down and I park my car across the road, and I blocked the road, and I asked 'em what the hell they think was going on. "We're gonna start stripping today." I said, "I don't think so. From where my line starts down there to where my line ends up here is private. You see that sign there said No Trespassing." And then I said, "I'll tell you what. I'm going on to work. But when I come in from work today I don't wanna see no equipment up here. I got a brand-new .30-30 hanging up 'ere on the wall, and I tell ya, you can replace that piece of machinery with money, but a good operator is hard to replace because when he sticks that dozer blade in my property I'm gonna brain him offa there. Deep mining I didn't mind," I said, "but when it comes to strip mining I don't want it, and I'm gonna fight it." In '75, I finally sold. 'Cause I talked to a lawyer, and I talked to some judges, and they all told me the same thing. You can't fight it.

"And there was nothing they could do about it," said Hazel King, referring to the destruction of the garden in Day's Creek. "And I couldn't believe that you couldn't do anything about something, after all this is a free world, free country, as we always use the terminology, so somebody must be in authority somewhere, that could do it." In 1955 and 1967, Kentucky courts upheld the mineral rights owners' power to extract the mineral by whatever means they saw fit under the old broad-form deed, with no compensation to the surface owner. In the 1970s, new challenges were brought to the system as groups such as Save Our Cumberland Mountains and the Appalachian Alliance continued to oppose strip mining, denounced absentee (and untaxed) ownership of land and mineral resources, and promoted the formation of the Kentuckians for the Commonwealth coalition.[52]

"We're still fighting it," said Annie Napier. With her sister Becky, she started attending strip mine hearings. "For a long time there wasn't a soul that went but me and her 'cause they thought, you know, we couldn't do nothing. It wasn't worth the fight. Nobody'd listen to us no way. And, come to find out they did listen to us. You've got four or five lawyers, and you got two hillbilly women sits there that knows more than they do. I've heard them say that: 'Let's call this quits as soon as we can 'cause they, they're more up to date than we are.' [Most people here] feel intimidated by somebody with a big fancy suit on and necktie. But I've never met nobody I was intimidated by."

"We had heard rumors," Hazel King recalled, "that there would be federal regulations that would control the stripping. The federal government, they were going to pass regulations. Kentucky really responded. They came out with some tremendous regulations. They said, 'We will have the best regulations, and we'll be a model for the rest of the nation.' And on paper, they were. But, in actuality, it was destruction." Actions got mired in bureaucracy; the state "did not enforce their own regulations."

In 1974 and 1975, federal bills regulating the environmental impact of strip mining were opposed by the UMW, which was concerned about the loss of jobs and royalties, and vetoed by President Gerald Ford. A compromise Surface Mining Control and Regulation Act was finally signed into law by President Jimmy Carter in 1977. Operators were to be required "to go back to AOC— approximate original contour. It means when you get the coal out then you put the material back where you excavated from to the approximate original contour of the land. And that had to be seeded, mulched, and if it had forest then you had to put back a certain species of trees. [There had to be] ponds, treating the water, cut down acid and, and manganese, and keep the [sulfur content] in the water at an acceptable level" (*Aaron Warren, mine inspector*). The act left enforcement mainly to the states, provided exemptions for small operators, and left gaping loopholes for the more radical and damaging technology of mountaintop removal. However, in cases of noncompliance and imminent harm, mine inspectors were authorized to issue cessation-of-work orders.[53]

The first such order was issued in Harlan County, after a complaint filed by Hazel King on Clover Fork: "I was with one of the parties that called for an inspection of a site that had been damaged and this whole community, it's called Georgetown on the map but it's called Wynntown locally—they had damage by blasting, the water had been destroyed, and rocks had been thrown over the community, the mountainside was coming into the Clover Fork river. And we formed an organization, Concerned Citizens for Water" (*Hazel King*).[54]

Reclamation leaves much to be desired. "Reclamation," writes Mary Beth Bingman, one of the women who occupied Trace Fork in 1972, "isn't enforced. It's just a name. It's a pacifying name to the people. It's a, it's—nothing."[55] "You can't tear these mountains up, they're what, sixty degrees? and put them back the way they was once was. Anybody with common sense knows you can't tear up a steep hill and [restore it], it will eventually come off" (*Meedia Jones*). Operators claim that reclamation results in tillable land and pasture for cattle raising. However, "these mountains are too steep, and I don't think you'll find any cattle grazing, you may find a few in some spots where it's not too steep, but on Clover Fork, the land is too steep for the cattle now. They have a few hogs, and hogs make more trouble than they're worth. So, I think it's just a camouflage" (*Hazel King*).

Camouflage is a good word: huge tracts of eastern Kentucky are now covered with kudzu vines, an invasive plant used as camouflage by the U.S. armed forces in the South Pacific during World War II. Kudzu seemed the fastest way of covering the strip mine scars on the mountain sides—until it became an environmental problem itself.

In 1988, after a referendum promoted by Kentuckians for the Commonwealth, the state constitution was amended, making it illegal to strip land without the surface owner's consent and without compensation. This success, however, only protected locally owned land; in the huge tracts owned by the companies themselves, strip mining continues to this day in even more destructive forms, as environment becomes the new battlefield for the struggle for survival in Harlan and Appalachia.

14

DEMOCRACY AND
THE MINES

MINERS FOR DEMOCRACY

On November 20, 1968, in Farmington, West Virginia, an explosion at the Consolidation Coal Company's Mannington 9 mine killed seventy-eight men. The next day, UMW president Tony Boyle praised Consol as "one of the best companies as far as cooperation and safety are concerned" and explained that "as long as we mine coal, there is always this imminent danger."[1]

John L. Lewis retired as UMW president in 1960; he was succeeded by Thomas Kennedy and, in 1963, by Tony Boyle. "John L. Lewis had made sure that he had nobody that would contest him. So, when he was gone, there was a void. Tony Boyle was the only man. A little man in a big job" (*Norman Yarbrough*). Boyle assumed that he would just step into the same role of authority and the same structures of power that had been firmly institutionalized under Lewis.[2] However, he lacked his predecessor's charisma, and presided over a union plagued by corruption, nepotism, and patronage, in which all opposition and dissent were intimidated and treated as treason.

In 1969, Jock Yablonski, president of UMW District 5 in Pennsylvania, ran against Boyle on a reform platform. The election was marred by threats, irregularities, and lies: Yablonski was described as an "enemy" paid by coal operators, in cahoots with "totalitarian liberals," who would take away miners' pensions and "deliver the union to outside forces." As sociologist John Gaventa notes, forty years of unquestioning obedience to the union leadership ensured that these allegations would be believed by the membership.[3] In the end, Boyle prevailed. District 19, which includes Harlan, voted heavily in his favor: "Yablonski was supposed to come—he never did come into this district—too dangerous" (*Joe Scopa Sr.*). A few weeks later, Yablonski, his wife, and his daughter were murdered in their Clarksdale, Pennsylvania, home.[4]

Federal courts found that Boyle had misused union funds in his campaign and ordered a repeat election. This time the opposition candidate was West Virginia miner Arnold Miller, president of the Black Lung Association, who was supported by Miners for Democracy (MFD), a coalition of rank-and-file groups.[5]

When MFD opened its campaign with a rally at the site of the Battle of Evarts, in June 1972, Granny Hager was one of the speakers.

GRANNY HAGER: People say to me, "Well, Granny, why are you out working and doing this when you've got no kids, nobody but yourself?" I said, "Yeah, but there're old people, who needs their miners' retirement pension, there're old people who needs their Social Security, there're fathers who has died and left their little children, they need their black lung. And if I can help one person that really needs it to get something to live on, buddy I think it's worth all these here forty years that I've been on the job."

I told them at Evarts at the kickoff rally: if I could see the union mine workers back here strong, Arnold Miller elected, and the United Mine Workers organized, then I'd be willing to die. [If] I could see just see Kentucky organized, that would be the happiest moment of my life.

This time, Arnold Miller won; however, Harlan's District 19 again voted for Boyle. "District 19 was loyal to Tony Boyle—because in the days before the Miners for Democracy movement the UMW president installed in positions of leadership people who would support him. It was sort of a self-perpetuating organization" (*Ewell Balltrip*). In 1972, the district president was still William J. Turnblazer, who had been appointed by Lewis fifty years earlier. In 1933, Lewis had overridden a vote to remove him while the opposition was Red-baited and threatened with expulsion. At the 1964 UMWA convention, a "wrecking crew" of hard-hatted District 19 "white hats" silenced and physically assaulted anti-Boyle speakers. ("They called us the wrecking crew, the goon squad, everything else," recalled Junior Deaton, who was one of the "white hats." "We had a fight. We had a battle that first day. And it was because some anti-Boyle people [were] just there to sort of wreck the convention. And we seen to it they didn't.")[6]

JOE SCOPA SR.: District 19 [officials] sent word for me, advised me, to leave the district. I told him, "No way, I'll stay here." My wife had been threatened because I was campaigning for Yablonski, and then after I was campaigning for Miller. They tried to run me out of the district, the only reason because I tried to disclose the crooked work that was done.

When Miller did come to Harlan County, Scopa adds, "we told everybody he was going to stay at my house, one night, but he didn't—we made arrangements to take him to Big Stone Gap [Virginia]. We formed a convoy and we escorted him to Big Stone Gap, to a hotel. It was too dangerous to [be] in this state." "Where leadership was not to be questioned and exit was not a choice," writes Gaventa, "then loyalty was the only response possible."[7] As membership declined (from twenty thousand in 1940 to three thousand in 1964) and its composition changed (to a prevalence of pensioners), the appointed leadership of District 19 felt threatened by all dissent, and reacted according to its ingrained history of violence and repression: "Yablonski. Yeah, I heard it came from this district. Somebody killed this fellow, didn't they? Somebody shot him and killed him. That's because he was gon' be the president and Tony Boyle..." (*Irwin Turner*).

The Yablonskis were murdered by three Appalachian migrants recruited and paid by a retired miners' local from LaFollette, Tennessee, across the border from Harlan and Bell. The orders came from organizer Albert Pass. Like District 19 officers Albert Prater and Silous Huddleston, who helped recruit the killers, Pass had been involved in earlier acts of violence against dissenters and nonunion operators. It was proved that Turnblazer knew about the plan, and ultimately the orders were traced to Boyle: "Tony Boyle was coming to Harlan, made his speech at a rally, and a woman went in carrying a sign—'Wash your bloody hands Tony Boyle'" (*Granny Hager*). In 1974, Boyle was convicted of murder and sentenced to life in prison.[8]

"Power was the cause of that. When you got a good high-paying job, and election time comes and you still want that job, you do anything, to keep it" (*Delbert Jones*). "Tony Boyle became embroiled in killing off his competition. The people [that] did that, they represented the union, and in Lynch I dealt with them time and time again. These were outlaws, these people were criminals. They had no principle, no concern for anything" (*Norman Yarbrough*). The memory of the Yablonski murders haunts Harlan County like a ghost: everybody has heard about it, but nobody gets down to specifics; it's always hearsay or secondhand. "We have one guy who was a former district officer at the union, and we talked about him being the bag man—on something that happened a long time ago where a guy was actually killed—they say that the money for that came out of this district. I kept hearing about it; it got a lot of play on the local television stations" (*Tommy Sweatt*). "Yeah, I know about all of them, the local people that were involved in hiring the [killers]. From what I understand, a lot of people in Harlan and Bell County had something to do with it, no question about that, but the deal was hatched up in Washington. Just some people in the union, you know, that was afraid they was going to lose power, and they done it. And Tony Boyle was right behind it. It was hard to believe, that your union brother would do something like that" (*Mickey Messer*).

Resentment toward the district leadership had been mounting in Harlan ever since the 1964 strike, because the miners felt that they had been let down.[9] "We come up to organize Brookside and these people at Brookside, they called me one day and said, 'Joe, if you wanna organize Brookside you'd better keep these [district] field workers out of here. Don't let 'em, not even come around us. Because we've got no use for those people'" (*Joe Scopa Sr.*). When Turnblazer approached Junior Deaton about organizing the Brookside mine, Deaton asked him to "send me a man that I could trust, a man that nobody knew, that was not connected to District 19. If your name or Albert Pass or any of the rest of them is brought up, there ain't no way in hell these fellows'll sign a card, because they have no confidence in District 19 no more."

"The miners have now found a voice," Bill Worthington said after Miller's victory: "The union spirit will come back. The union will be great again."[10] However, Miller's efforts to return the union to its membership met with mixed feelings and achieved mixed results. It was not easy to overcome half a century of authoritarian paternalism. "Miller," says Delbert Jones, "I'll give him credit for the black lung. That's the only thing I give him credit for. He was the one that started letting the miners decide what they want. One way it helped, another way it hurt, when you let the rank and file speak. That causes a split, and you start splitting up, you get division amongst the members. John L. Lewis, we let him make our decisions for us whether it be good or whether it be bad." The enthusiasm generated by Miners for Democracy waned as divisions among the leadership, opposition from the former Boyle camp, and the difficulty of running a union in complicated times took their toll. Many reforms were gradually repealed or diluted. In 1978, the longest strike in UMW history ended in a disappointing compromise over the health fund and a failure to retain the locals' right to strike over grievances. Shortly afterward, isolated and ill, Miller resigned.[11]

DEMOCRACY AT BROOKSIDE

PORTELLI: Why did it get so rough?
JACK WRIGHT: Well, I don't know. I guess it's just the companies making all that money, they won't give us nothing. These big people want to make all the money and just let the poor man root hog or die.

When I first visited Harlan, in September 1973, "Brookside on Strike" signs dotted the winding roads up Clover Fork. The company houses at the Eastover company village at Brookside reminded me of the shacks of Rome's slums.[12] "There is no running water," another observer wrote; "an outdoor spigot serves each row of houses. The water comes from a well owned by the mining company. Apparently, the pipes are rusty, as the quality of the water is very poor. Privies line what was once a beautiful creek, but which is now an open sewer." In 1973, a health inspection found the camp's water "highly contaminated with fecal bacteria."[13]

The Brookside camp and mine belonged to Norman Yarbrough's Eastover Coal Company, a wholly owned subsidiary of Duke Power Company. Eastover also owned another camp and mine on Clover Fork, at Highsplint. Duke bought the mine through Eastover in 1970; within five days, without consulting the workers, it signed a contract with the Southern Labor Union (SLU). It granted higher wages, but medical benefits, pension, job security, and safety guarantees were inadequate or nonexistent. Miners complained about the danger of roof falls, flooding, dangerous machinery, ceaseless pressure to increase the pace of work, absence of the legally required safety committee, and an accident rate two to three times the national average.[14]

In June 1973, Brookside miners voted to join the United Mine Workers, while those at Highsplint chose to stay with the SLU. UMW supporters were fired and evicted, and contract negotiations at Brookside soon broke down.[15] "We wasn't after more money as we was after better benefits: better medical, dental...[and portal-to-portal pay]. And the company would always reject" (*James Wright*).[16] "The company did recognize the UMW as the bargaining agent, which led to another question, which was: will this company accept the standard United Mine Workers of America contract? And until a particular point in the strike the answer was no" (*Ewell Balltrip*). "I didn't have any objections to [the UMW] but I didn't intend to sign the national contract because we couldn't live with it. We couldn't exist under the national contract [as it stood] at that time" (*Norman Yarbrough*). By the end of June, Brookside was on strike. It would last fourteen months, making national news and working-class history.

> NORMAN YARBROUGH: The union had just gone through getting rid of Tony Boyle. They had gone through this killing up here in Pennsylvania, and they had gone through democracy, which...they're going away from it now. They elect a plain old coal miner out of West Virginia, and he decided that Brookside was going to be his cornerstone, that he was going to run over Brookside and then the rest of the county would, just like dominos, would fall into place.

Actually, District 19, still in the throes of the Yablonski affair, recognized the strike only reluctantly.[17] Yet the national attention still focused on the miners' union, the reform spirit of the new administration, and the mythic power of the Harlan County name, as well as Duke Power's national visibility, made it impossible for the new leadership not to take up the challenge. The union pledged financial support to the miners, and by mid-August Miller paid his first visit to Brookside. Willingly or not, the strike had become a test case.[18]

Soon the conflict between the company and the Brookside miners was complicated by the tension between Brookside and Highsplint. "In the beginning Brookside made the mistake of going up there and raising hell with Highsplint [where they were still] under Southern Labor Union contract, and tried to get them in the UMW. Now, you had more men up there that was for the UMW than that wasn't. But they was so much harassment went on by our Brookside miners, it caused those men to go against the UMW" (*Junior Deaton*). "We [at Highsplint] just worked, we worked and they called us scab and all. 'Cause I believe in working and making a living for your family. I didn't believe in unions, I lived in the camp and they'd stop everybody coming across the bridge, they'd call us scabs and company sucks and they'd say if UMW win over us, then they'll get rid of us, and so we kept on working. I'd get four or five flats every time I go across the bridge, where they set the tacks, some nails" (*J. C. Hall*). "For over a week they wouldn't let anybody come out of that camp. So finally [the Highsplint miners] got together, and they had pickaxes, handles. And they cleaned that bridge off up there. But the company had nothing to do with that. I knew it was going to happen, but I didn't stop it" (*Norman Yarbrough*).

LARRY HOLCOMB: My aunt was having an emergency surgery so my mother and dad walked down to be with her, and they got caught in one of the road-blocks. And the roadblock that he was stopped at was a roadblock by a com-peting union, really a company union, the Southern Labor. And, anyway, he told me, "There was one point when I could see the guns of the guys down here, and I knew they were all over the mountains. I knew there wasn't a big rock that didn't have a man with a gun pointed in our direction."

At the beginning of September 1973, "the coal company went to court and got various restraining orders, contempt orders, and injunctions that limited the number of pickets that could be on the picket line, and other orders to keep the public roads clear" (*Sid Douglass*). The orders came from Special Judge F. Byrd Hogg, who had also been in the coal business. "I know him well and know him to be an honest, fair jurist, but the problem that we've had in the judiciary in eastern Kentucky is that some of the judges have also been in the coal business, and, as a result of that, miners felt like they couldn't go to the courts and get justice. [So] they'd turn to violence" (*Sid Douglass*). The state police were called in to keep the peace, "and of course the state police took the position that they were there to enforce the orders of the court, and to keep the public highway open. The union saw the position of the state police as being one of trying to bust the strike" (*Ewell Balltrip*). Under police protection, Eastover tried to break the union pickets and brought in replacement workers and armed escorts.[19]

JAMES WRIGHT: And we wasn't even allowed to have a gun. Even in a vehicle. I'm not saying they wasn't there, but we weren't supposed to have them. Now, we got ambushed above Cumberland one time. And all we was doing was holding up signs. We'd talk to the truckers as they'd come by; we'd just ask them, if they'd been pulling ten loads a day, pull nine; pull eight. Slow down, you know. And they opened up on us, and went to shooting, and they shot one of the men; and by the time the state [police] pulled them over, there were no weapons to be found nowhere. They give 'em plenty of time to get rid of 'em.

The miners occasionally retaliated: "We got dynamites out here in the yard, and me and my wife sitting in there got knocked off of the couch.... Windows rattling and everything. I think they were trying to scare me" (*Norman Yarbrough*). To stop the trucks, miners used the same weapon that Italian Resistance fighters had used in Rome to stop German convoys on the road to Anzio and Cassino: "Take two pieces of metal about that long, and bend them and weld them together, I don't care how you throw one, it'll always lay with a point up. When a truck goes over it, it ain't going far. We'd stick 'em over the toes of our shoes, walk up to the [trucks and kick their tires]" (*James Wright*). Harlan miners called them "bobjacks."[20]

> JAMES WRIGHT: I've seen people hiding in bushes, and trucks go by, they'd jump out, hang on the rear end, pull all the plugs out of 'em, turn loose the axle. I've seen them stick taters on the barrels of the guns, hide in bushes, shoot holes in radiators; and I've seen 'em hide in the bushes and shoot out transformers. Jump on the trucks and pull the drivers right out of 'em when they thought they would run [through the picket line].

The injunctions were repealed by another judge in January, but from the beginning they contained a loophole: they applied to the miners, not to their wives and families. So at the end of September, the women stepped in.

> BESSIE LOU CORNETT: *We kind of organized ourselves and got to talking to each other about how these scabs were crossing the picket line. The first week of the strike, the miners—you know, our husbands, sons, our fathers—were able to stop the scabs, but then Duke Power got an injunction limiting the miners to three pickets on an entrance. So, with two entrances at Brookside, this was six miners, and as many as seventy-five scabs were crossing every day, they were taking shifts and the scabs were spitting on them and cussing them and calling them names, and they would come home and they'd be talking about taking their shotguns down to the picket line, how they were going to stop the scabs and that was the only way to do it.*
>
> *We wanted to be able to help the men stop the scabs and get a contract without all that violence. And so what we did was we talked to each other. We had a march and said, "Why don't we just go down to the picket line ourselves. We can stop the scabs. The court don't have an injunction against us." So that's what we did.*[21]

"When Brookside come out on strike, Daddy tried to go [to the picket line], and he began to smother down [with black lung]. So we brought him home, I hooked Daddy's oxygen up, and I went back because, you know, we wanted the union, because [we needed] hospitalization, retirement, and my daddy would need it real bad on account of that black lung. So I went back, and that's when I began to lay down in the road" (*Sudie Crusenberry*). The women's primary tactic was passive resistance; however, not all their actions would meet strict definitions of nonviolence. "We didn't stop them by asking them not to cross the picket line. We whipped them with switches and with whatever we had.... As it turned out, several women were arrested—my sister, my mother, and a couple of other women. But the scabs were stopped" (*Bessie Lou Cornett*). In October, nine men and seven women (with their children), fined for violating the injunction and for contempt of court, committed themselves voluntarily to prison, but were released; in May 1974, eleven people, including several women, were sentenced to sixty days in jail for contempt of court.[22]

JENNY SAYLOR: My aunt [Lois Scott] was involved in that. She was a good woman. She carried a gun in her bosom.[23] And she whipped 'em with a switch and she called 'em yellow-bellied scabs. Is that right, am I saying it right? My mom was also on the picket line, several of my cousins were there, they were all there. I remember my mother and everybody getting up real early and leaving and not coming home until late in the evening and telling about all the things that had happened, the shootings, the switches, and laying down in the middle of the road.

"And Lois Scott, she wasn't afraid of nothing, and she was meaner than seven devils" (*Otis King*).[24] The Brookside women weren't everyone's idea of ladylike behavior: "I happen to know one of the women, and I couldn't believe that she was out there doing that" (*Gladys Hoskins*). "There's been some conduct that I would hope that U.S. women wouldn't have to resort to" (*Norman Yarbrough*). "Yarbrough says he wouldn't let his wife go on a picket line," Lois Scott retorted. "Well naturally, because he owns her. Because she is not a woman on her own." Part of the women's motives in joining the struggle, as Sally Maggard has shown, was devotion to their husbands ("I guess I done it because I loved him so much," one woman said)—which does not mean that there were no negative attitudes among the men.[25]

Yet "we could have never got a contract at Brookside, if it had not been for the women. Well, a scab is something that will run over a union man and not feel bad about it. He will cross that picket line. But a woman ... he can't do nothing, really. Women were able to do the things that men can't do and get by with. State police are reluctant to use their weapons, their sticks and things on women" (*Junior Deaton*). After he was hit with switches and sticks as he tried to remove women from the picket line, state police captain James Cromer explained: "The women are a problem. You just don't hit a woman in Harlan County." This may have been due to traditional male attitudes toward the "weaker sex"—but also to the fact that there was no weakness in these ladies.[26]

JAMES WRIGHT: The women, they played a big part at Brookside commissary. We's standing there one day and a bunch [of scabs] come off the mountain, come into Coxton. [One of the women], she had a board, buddy, a good six foot long, she had nails drove sticking out of that board. And this ole dude heading for his car at the commissary—she caught him, it give me cold shivers just thinking about it.

"Churches from all around, the Church of God, Pentecostal, and the Baptists, they begin to [help] miners, getting stuff, and cooking hot meals, you know, and bringing them in and serving and all" (*Sudie Crusenberry*). "I preached one [sermon] on Jesus Christ on the Brookside strike line, just turned loose and preached on Jesus Christ. And a lot of them come and told me, 'That's the best sermon I ever hear preached in my life'" (*Otis King*). Workers from other mines came in to help; even some Highsplint miners refused to cross the picket lines.[27] Sudie Crusenberry noted in her scrapbook some of the women's strike songs: "'You can't be union if your light don't shine'—yeah, we sung that on Brookside picket line." Lois Scott remembered: "'You take a scab and you kill it and you put it on the skillet / And you fry him up a golden brown. / That's union cooking and it's mighty nice.' We made one up, 'You ain't woman enough to take my man....'" This particular song is based on Loretta Lynn's country hit; others are reminiscent of the union song tradition, like the Almanac Singers' "Casey Jones, the Union Scab" or Joe Hill's "Scissor Bill." Sudie Crusenberry had one about a scab who thinks he is going to heaven because "I have never grumbled, I have never struck, never messed with the union truck." St. Peter, however, sends him right down to hell—but "even a devil can't stand the smell of a cooking scab on a griddle in hell." So they send him "back to your master on earth and tell that they don't even want a scab in hell."[28]

"They brought some [scabs from] outside, and they had security guards, you know, from outside, and some lived around. They hired all the old gun thugs that was there in the thirties and the forties that were living, all the old thugs. I had a few guys that I was raised up with, that went scabbing, I ain't spoke to them since. I don't speak to them, don't want them to speak to me. I don't talk with scabs. Scum of the earth" (*Mickey Messer*).

> J. D. MILLER: Two people who worked in our business office at that time, one woman came from a long family of UMW people, the other one came from a family that had not been UMW, even though they were a poor class [of] people. And they were best of friends. And during the Brookside strike, they were being so angry with each other, [that] the administrator, he finally just had to say, "In order to get our work done, we are not going to talk about the Brookside strike, or the UMWA at the clinic at all, that's just off-limits. We just don't talk about that here." And when they quit talking, they got along better with each other.

"The time of the Brookside strike, I had a drugstore here. [Company guard chief] Basil Collins was one of my customers at the drugstore, the Whitfields were one of my customers, [another neighbor] was on the union side, so I had customers on both sides, and I had people that are still friends of mine on both sides" (*Daniel Howard*). "I had some family members that were company [and some] who were union and were trying to go union—and that's probably why people won't open up and talk as much about it, because they got family and friends on both sides" (*Preston McLain*). Mildred Shackleford, a staunch pro-union activist, recalls her father's respect for Basil Collins's war record and concludes: "It makes you look at people in a different light [than] just being that dirty, rotten scab on the other side, as opposed to us good people here on the right side and everything."

DONELLA WYNN: My papaw, he was what they called a scab. When my mom was five, they lived at Highsplint, where a lot of the strike went on. And my papaw, he decided he was going to work. And Mom tells me they would have to lie on the floor because people would shoot through the windows; and [they] would have to sneak across the trestle of a morning to get to school. And they would have to land helicopters and bring them food, because they couldn't get out. My uncle, a lot of great-uncles, they were on the union side. Yes, I had family on both sides. So if you get all of our family together today, there are still arguments, if you mention union. My papaw he thought that what he was doing was right and they felt what they were doing were right.

ALICIA THOMAS: My father, he was a thug. He didn't talk much about it, but I can remember my mom, she would tell stories like, he would leave for work and she wouldn't know if he'd be home a week from now or two days, you know. He would take what he needed and he'd go up in the mines and he'd stay, and the only things he'll say about it today is, "I had four kids at home and a wife to take care of and standing on a picket line wasn't going to put food in their mouths." So he'll tell you, he thinks the union is a good thing as far as the benefits and things that they offered and brought here, but he had a family to feed and he was going to feed them and he packed a gun and he shot over people's heads, you know, but that was going both ways, they were shooting and blocking the roads and trying to keep them from going to work and so they fought back and they went to work. I mean my dad, he's a Christian man and we were always raised in church, and he's not going to pack a gun unless he feels his own life is in danger.

The strike, however, had a limited impact on Duke's operation: only 4 to 5 percent of its coal supply came from the Harlan County mines. Thus the UMW decided to bring the struggle before the media and national public opinion. "They really put their campaign against Duke, they didn't put it against Eastover. And a public utility can't stand up under that kind of pressure" (*Norman Yarbrough*). The UMW brought the public relations offensive to Duke's home state of North Carolina (where the company was seeking a rate increase at the same time as it was fighting the strike in Harlan); miners picketed the New York Stock Exchange, urging union pension funds not to buy Duke stock. At a stockholders meeting, Brookside miner Bill Doan addressed Duke's president, Carl Horn: "I tell you, we in Harlan County, all our life we been kicked around. We been put in jail, we been shot at, we got dynamite thrown at us, and then you don't want us to have nothing. Well I tell you, Mr. Horn, I'm going to be standing right there on the picket line, looking at you just as long as it takes."[29]

In October, director Barbara Kopple and a film crew came to Harlan, with union approval, to make a film about the strike. The film was also a way of indirectly influencing events in Harlan: as Kopple said, "The scabs and gun thugs weren't going to commit murder in living color." "It probably helped a lot, in some situations. It may have saved lives, you know, by them being there filming" (*Mickey Messer*). The filmmakers joined the strikers on the picket line, lived with them and their families, took the same risks.³⁰ As film critic Peter Biskind wrote, "The film's power comes from Kopple's intimate involvement with the people she filmed, the risks she took, the places—jails, courtrooms, stockholder's meetings—into which she forced her camera. Its strength lies not in its beauty, not even in its politics, but in the moral authority that is inscribed in every frame."³¹

"It wasn't about objectivity," says Barbara Kopple.³² "I think that's important to make that distinction when you're talking about *Harlan County, U.S.A.*: the filmmakers made no pretense of being objective. They said, 'We're pro-union, this is a story about the union, and this is the way it was from our point of view.' And you can't argue with film; I mean, what you saw actually did take place. Pictures don't lie" (*Ewell Balltrip*). The film met with the usual objections: it did not show the best aspects of the county, and it fell short of fair and balanced reporting. "There were primarily two opposing views of the movie. People who sympathized with the miners saw it as patriotic, and people who sympathized with the coal operators saw it as propaganda. The truth is, it was a one-sided film. Except, what you saw was not acting. What you saw in that film actually happened. Those gunshots that you heard, you know, in that film, that was real" (*Sid Douglass*). Some criticism also came from cultural difference. "I think that there was some resentment toward that film crew, among the local people. I think that there was some resentment of their appearance. We're still talking early seventies when if your hair was down below your ears you were a dirty filthy hippy" (*Ewell Balltrip*).

As the strike gained visibility, Brookside drew sympathizers and supporters, attracted also by Harlan's historical fame. Faith Holsdorf, a civil rights activist, came from West Virginia to the final strike mass meeting: "It was very intense and I had this sense of history. My parents were not Communists but my mother [was] a good liberal, so I'd heard about the fights, the strikes in the coal fields in the thirties and had a tremendous sense of excitement." "We had a lot of Communists here in the seventies. The only thing, they weren't real people. They would look you right in the eye, when they had something to say, and it looked like your eyes bounced right back in your head. And I will say, they had some good ideals and we used them. I didn't belong to any of those parties, don't get me wrong. I'd just as soon'd have joined the church. Snake handlers. They were about as fanatic as the snake handlers" (*Jerry Johnson*). Yet Jerry Johnson and Bessie Lou Cornett were repeatedly Red-baited. "We put out a paper called *Harlan County Labor News*, and mentioned something about strip mining, that we didn't like strip mining, and they said I was a Communist again. So right now I'm Red-baited. It makes you feel bad that people turn against you just over a little word" (*Jerry Johnson*).³³

MILDRED SHACKLEFORD: People have always went to Harlan County and they have always told people what to do and how to do it and when to do it. And, oh, how I resented people that showed up during that strike that was from outside! There was some idiot that was carrying a gun and was from California or some place and he must of come for the sole purpose of feeling like a great big old cowboy. [He dropped his gun in a super-market and might have killed somebody.] And I stood there thinking, every time something happens in Harlan County, this is what we have to put up with—idiots who think that they are going to get involved in I don't know what, whatever it is they are dreaming of or whatever it is they are looking for.

Relationships between local people and outsiders, however, were more articulated: there were marriages between local miners, outsiders, filmmakers (one of the Brookside women "ended up marrying one of the men that came in from Chicago, I'm not sure if he was a Communist or what but she ended up marrying and moving to California," *Jenny Saylor*). At the end of our inter-view, as I thanked Lois Scott and Hazel King and told them how much it meant to me, they said that it had been a "learning" and "strengthening" experience for them, too, and compared it to the solidarity that came in during the strike. "You know, Hazel," said Lois Scott, "when we would be so depressed on that picket line, it'd take somebody like him to come around. And to show us they really cared. Man, then we were..." "Rejuvenated," Hazel King suggested. And Lois: "Yeah. It was like, well, that would give you strength to fight some more."

In July 1974, Eastover fired many of the strikers and served eviction notices to eight Brookside families. On July 7, pickets blocked the Highsplint mine; on July 11, retired miner Minard Turner was shot by a strikebreaker, and gun thugs opened fire on rescuers who were taking him to the hospital. Shots were fired into the home of union activist Jerry Johnson and local president Mickey Messer. The state police escorted strikebreakers back into the Highsplint mine, allowing it to resume production by the first week of August. On August 12, as scabs broke through the picket line under cover of gunfire, Bill Worthington was attacked by a gun thug, and a pistol stuck in his stomach. In the film one can hear a guard shout, "Kill that nigger," and Lois Scott's reply, "That nigger is a better man than you'll ever be."[34]

SUDIE CRUSENBERRY: That's the day they shot at us. And I lay down flat on the ground until one of the men from Highsplint stuck a barrel of a pistol into Bill Worthington's chest. I run up trying to get the gun, to keep him from killing him, and my daughter Nora went to the back of Bill Worthington and said, "Now, I'll knock it out of your hand." And [the thug] says to me, he said, "Well, 'ere she does it," he said, "I'll kill him." And I said, "Well, if it's knocked out of your hand, believe me, brother, you ain't going to get that gun to fire at nobody." And so we got him that way, but we got to looking, and here come [other scabs with] ball bats, sticks. Well, you might battle a one, but you can't battle with a dozen like that. They was a-kicking, they was a-fighting us with sticks, and others are shooting…

BARBARA KOPPLE: It was really dark, and we were all sitting like sitting ducks there, and suddenly the scabs went through and then the thugs started shooting tracer bullets that lit up the mountainside … the gun thugs then came across and I felt that I had to be there first, so [in the film] you sort of see my hair and my headphones moving forward; and so the gun thugs came and just knocked me down, and knocked Anne [Lewis] down, and they started kicking me, but I had a Nagra, which was my recording machine that was on my chest and so when they kicked it I didn't feel anything, and then I had a long fish pole with a mike at the end of it, and so I just started swinging that at them. But it was very scary … But it was a scene that shook us all up and we realized that the strike was going to change, the strike was going around another corner, the strike was gonna get more violent and possibly somebody could be killed.[35]

The next day, strikers and scabs and troopers faced each other for hours with cocked guns across the line at Shields.

MILDRED SHACKLEFORD: There was one day that I was up there on the picket line, and everybody I know was up there. My uncle was up there. He was armed to the teeth. My mother was up there with her pistol in her pocketbook and she was armed to the teeth. And, you know, just everybody milling around on the side of the railroad tracks, and they'd park their cars across the road to keep the scabs from coming across. And I had some kinfolks on the other side, that was over there messing around with the scabs, which I wasn't too proud of, but I guess they didn't have much choice 'cause they were foreman for one of the mines. And the guy that was really doing the most threatening, the most intimidating, was one of the superintendents up there. And Daddy told us about him: he was in the Bataan march, and he was one of the few people that survived that. I remember Daddy telling me, "You need to be very careful of that man," 'cause he was dangerous. He would not hesitate to kill you.

Afterwards, I was sitting on that car that was parked across the road, and that old guy came up there and got so close and he told us, he said, "Move the car." And we said, "No, we are not moving the car." And he said again, "Move the car." And we said, "No." And he yanked his pistols out and he cocked 'em and when he did that, then everybody was sitting on the other side, they cocked their pistols, and I thought: "Uh-oh, we are getting ready to have a big shootout here." And he stood there for a minute and he finally turned around and walked back. And Mom was sitting in the car behind me and she looked up and said, "Ain't got a thing to worry about, I had this pistol pointed at him the whole time. If he had shot you, I would of shot him." That sure would have done me a lot of good, wouldn't it?

Meanwhile, Duke's Carl Horn and UMW's Arnold Miller had been talking. The issues remained the application to Eastover of certain clauses of the national contract, and the company's insistence on a no-strike clause. On August 23, Arnold Miller spoke to a mass meeting of more than four thousand people who had come to Harlan from all over the coalfields. The next day, union miner Lawrence Jones was killed on Jones Creek by company supervisor Bill Bruner.

"I was standing ten foot from him. And [Bruner's] truck pulled up, and Jones walked over to the truck, and when he did they just shot him. They shot him and pulled out. For no reason. And, to the best of my knowledge, that night there was nobody had a weapon. I'm pretty sure if they had they'd have used it" (*James Wright*). "Of course, it was union-related, it was a company boss that killed him, you know. Shot in the head with a shotgun. It was two or three miles from the picket line, but it was still a company boss that shot him. He was a union man, they killed him" (*Mickey Messer*). "Everybody's got a different story," Junior Deaton said.[36] According to one that Lois Scott heard from an eyewitness, a bunch of people were sitting around drinking, and Lawrence Jones reluctantly accepted a beer.

> Lois Scott: He didn't even finish the beer and Bill Bruner drove up; when he drove past one of them boys made a sign at him. Fingered him or something. And he just pulled in ahead of them and jumped out with that shotgun and he aimed and [the boy] stuck his hands up and said, "Now Bill, we don't want no trouble." And he pointed the gun right at Lawrence and said, "You're the son of a bitch I want," and he shot a double-ought buckshot right through the head. And then he turned around where the boy was at, and the boy ran behind that truck that was sitting there, and he shot like five buckshot in that fender. And they started shooting at him. One of them got him through the tail bone, the flesh part of it.
>
> That evening at seven o'clock they called me and told me to come down, that Lawrence Jones had been shot.

"Bill Bruner was tried for murder in Harlan Circuit Court, and he was acquitted on the grounds of self-defense. I would say it certainly was true that he could make a case of self-defense" (*Sid Douglass*)—especially after a key prosecution witness changed his statement in court. But beyond the different narratives, the meaning of the event lies in the crude image of Lawrence Jones's brain spilled on the asphalt in the film, and in the intensity of emotions that followed his death. Lawrence Jones had a sixteen-year-old wife and a five-month-old baby. Lois Scott sat in the hospital with the young woman and Jones's mother:

Lois Scott: And she started telling me that she knew that her boy would get killed. [His mother] said her mother and daddy had been union and she was union all of her life. And she said she told her brother's boys to be union but she had one of them that was a scab. She was saying all these things that was hurting her, and she knew that Lawrence was dead.

And when I went in there, they had him on this [stretcher]. They had his head all taped up and you could see his heart going up and down. But he was as white as that sheet. There wasn't any blood in him at all. But they kept saying that he was alive, the doctors and all. We found out later that they just kept him alive long enough to keep down the trouble.

Ewell Balltrip: The night that occurred I was at the hospital when they brought the miner in. Lawrence Dean Jones. I remember the name very well. That night, out at the hospital, what I saw was a very mixed bag of emotions. On one side I saw anger; extreme anger. Some of the miners who were there, the union miners, the first thing that was in their mind was revenge. And I saw that. I saw fear, in some people: fear that what had been a very tense confrontation up to that point, that confrontation could escalate into a little war, on Clover Fork. I saw that fear. I saw the, the, just the hurt of the family. I saw the emotion of hurt and pain that they were experiencing, from having their husband and their son and their brother, you know, laying in that room, quite simply dying. I saw apprehension from other people wondering what was going to happen next. I recall a fellow name of Barney Aaronson, he was Arnold Miller's right-hand man, basically, in the Brookside strike. And I walked over and I talked to him, briefly, and best that I recall that evening Barney was afraid. He had a fear about what would be the next step after this miner was shot and ultimately dead. That evening they had some fairly tense moments up on Clover Fork.

"We wanted to [go after the killer]. We wanted to. And the president, and the vice president, and a bunch of preachers come in. And, they talked to us, and told us to give it twenty-four to forty-eight hours and think about it. 'Cause there was no need of no more bloodshed, 'cause it's not gonna help. But they were a mad bunch of men" (*James Wright*). In a tense meeting, documented in *Harlan County, U.S.A.*, as the union organizers announce that the company and the union are talking, one man rises: "Looks to me like the best for us is to try to get old Yarbrough and old Basil Collins. They're the leaders, and they's some way that they can be got.... I tell everybody, take the shelter and let the lead go." And an older man responds: "The contract is what we're fighting for; that's what Lawrence Jones died for, to get a contract. But I told his family, it was for a good cause. And what I said, why can't it be somebody like me just about spent anyhow, but it took a young man's life, to bring this thing, the government, the union and the operators together. If this shooting hadn't happened, probably there mightn't have been a meeting, to negotiate a contract. But every contract that we've ever got has been hard, we've had to fight for it. I've been around bloodshed back yonder in the thirties, blood all around me, where men died right around my feet for a contract. And I think if ever we did hold our peace, let's try to hold it tonight. The price has been paid for it."

As Hazel Dickens sang, "We've got a contract in our hands, signed with the blood of working men."[37] The death of Lawrence Jones tilted the moral balance of the conflict. "That's what settled the strike. The company didn't want more publicity; so they went ahead and signed the contract. And that was the end of it" (*James Wright*). "And I'm convinced that the death of Lawrence Dean Jones led to the settlement of that strike. That quite simply the company was told to sign that contract, and move on with the business of mining coal with people working" (*Ewell Balltrip*). "And the irony of that case is that the killing of a United Mine Worker by a coal company employee resulted in public pressure being brought on the coal company to settle a contract with the union" (*Sid Douglass*).

MICKEY MESSER: We had a lot better working conditions. The company changed a little bit on about safety, we got a raise in pay, and we got good hospitalization and job protection and...some vacation, and some holiday pay, and...just different things. Got about fifteen dollars a day wage increase, and...job security and hospitalization was the main thing for me. That's what I was really fighting for.

Although these were significant gains, the union also had to accept the no-strike clause: "I guess everybody was about starved out from being on strike, they was just happy to get back to work. [Conditions were better] for a while. Then it went back to the same, ask you to bend [safety] rules, and break rules" (*James Wright*). "We actually believed," said Darrell Deaton, vice president of the Brookside UMW local, "that once the Brookside mine fell that all the other mines in Harlan County would just capitulate and wave the white flag, but like some other domino theories this didn't seem to be true. In fact in some ways the victory had the opposite effect. It stiffened the resolve of the coal operators."[38] Along with their traditional practices of repression and corruption, the operators used sophisticated public relations techniques: they bought ads, mobilized communities, offered higher wages than the union rate (but with no comparable benefits). As a consequence, the union lost some important mines in Harlan County.[39]

JAMES WRIGHT: Number one, they sold the mine, then they shut it down for one year, then opened it up under another name. And we still sat on the picket line for a while, but they told everybody to break it up and go home, or they'd never work again in Harlan County. And the majority of 'em went home. There was three hundred and fifty-some men worked at Brookside, and Trumka, the president of the union, told us if we could get as much as one-third of the men on the picket line he would give us two hundred dollars a week, a medical card, and an extra hundred for gas and stuff. But the most we ever had was twenty-four. Because they told the boys, if they didn't get out of the picket line, they'd never work again in Harlan County.

SUDIE CRUSENBERRY: Now, my son-in-law can't get a job nowhere, here in Harlan County. He had to go down to the lower end of Kentucky at Peabody's.
PORTELLI: You mean he's blacklisted?
CRUSENBERRY: Well, I feel that, and believe it. Of course, you know... ain't nobody can [prove it].

NORMAN YARBROUGH: These fellows that make a big issue that we had a blacklist, we would blacklist these people so they couldn't get a job anywhere. There *was* a blacklist, but they done it to themselves. When they publicized themselves, and what kind of trouble they were causing, nobody else would hire them, so they made their own blacklist. I never in my lifetime ever told anybody not to hire anybody because they'd cause you trouble.[40]

There were other prices to be paid. Bessie Lou Cornett was accused of being a Communist (during the strike she had "stated her opposition to fascism") and of being friends with "niggers." "They gave my cousins—[Lois Scott's] daughters—hard times. You know how people spread gossip and lies and that kind of thing. Beth's marriage broke up" (*Carla Jo Barrett*). Even the Ku Klux Klan reared its head: it held rallies and raids, burned crosses, harassed and intimidated union sympathizers.[41]

SUDIE CRUSENBERRY: I even have the Ku Klux a-fighting me. They burn a cross at my neighbor's gate, wanted to stick one in mine. I lay round that porch, waiting for them to come, 'cause I'm going to tell you something: I'm not going to sit and let them burn the house up, with my kids little. And then I got them letters from the Ku Klux said they was coming to kill the whole family, and I said, "No, they ain't. They might get me. But, they might be got, too. I'm not going to just sit [there] and let somebody burn me or something." I've worked like a dog in my life. I have. I've worked like men in my life. Now, I've got scars from bullets hitting them gravels and them gravels taking a bounce, you know, and hit your legs. They were there a-laughing and rejoicing, and I said, "One more scream, I'm going to run my fist down your neck, and that'll do it. Then, if I get killed, I died for something. I didn't die for nothing."

The Brookside mine was closed after the strike ("We reopened, but we never was able to come anywhere close to being a productive mine. They closed it down, and got out," *Norman Yarbrough*). The camp was demolished and the mine sold to a local nonunion operator.

> DARLENE WILSON: The story of Brookside is told in the recommended textbook on the history of Kentucky; it has a very small mention, though. And it's not the way Grandma who stood on the picket line tells the story, okay? Many [students] have never seen Barbara Kopple's *Harlan County U.S.A.* So I show that in class. The ones who know because Granny was there, or Aunt so-and-so was there—you see 'em kind of unfold, and sit up a little straighter and say, "Yeah, I knew about that, my grandma used to talk about it." When they see that their life experience is relevant to somebody, it validates their experience. The other kids who didn't know are kind of like, "Wow! I didn't know!"

DEMOCRACY AT JERICOL

The momentum of the Miners for Democracy movement and the Brookside strike continued throughout the 1970s. In the fall of 1977, the UMW struck for a new contract. It was the longest strike in the union's history, lasting more than a hundred days.[42] After it was over, however, the Jericol Coal Company mine at Glenbrook in Harlan County refused to sign the contract, and its workers stayed out: "The last strike we had was at Jericol for a contract. They come out for contract in '77, and they never did sign up no more. There was a lot of violence there, I guess it was on both sides, but we lost that mine" (*Delbert Jones*). As in Brookside, the strike culminated in a death, but this time it was on the other side.

> SID DOUGLASS (FORMER HARLAN CIRCUIT COURT JUDGE): We had a coal mine strike at Glenbrook, Kentucky, when I was on the bench, during which nonunion employees of the coal company were riding back and forth to work on a company-operated school bus. Someone shot at the bus, and a nonunion employee was killed. That resulted in the strike being broken in favor of the coal company. The union really lost ground as a result of this act of violence.

The conflict centered around the company's practice of escorting nonunion workers across the strikers' pickets and roadblocks. "They'd put about thirty carloads of polices up and down this road, to guard the workers to and from work, the ones breaking the strike. And you'd go up there and try to stop 'em, the police, they'd knock your brains out. Same way [as] at Brookside" (*Delbert Jones*). Rather than riding in trucks and motorcades as at Brookside, however, the strikebreakers were transported in an armored former Harlan County school bus, which traveled along the roads at the same time as the regular school buses. "And that caused a tremendous uproar. The union sympathizers said the company was cowardly, trying to hide behind school buses to get their men to work" (*Sid Douglass*).

> JAMES WRIGHT: They welded five-inch steel all over the school bus. And they were paying a hundred dollars a day, to anybody that would work. As much as two hundred dollars. They picked you up at home and took you back home. They had steel all around the bus and a gap about [two inches] wide, that's all the driver had to see outside.

Families were afraid to send their children to school, fearing the real school buses might be mistaken for the strikebreakers'. "We the parents of Harlan County," a group of Clover Fork families wrote President Carter, "recognize your peace-making ability with foreign countries, while we here at home have to put up with armored buses on the same road at the same time our children travel to school."[43]

> SID DOUGLASS: The company came back and said, "This is a free country, there's no law saying we can't transport our workers in a school bus." I ended up just trying to keep the parties from killing each other. I ordered both sides not to be around each other with firearms. And that caused all kinds of objections based upon the Second Amendment to the Constitution of the United States concerning the right to bear arms. Many of the men on both sides were armed with guns, which, in such an emotionally charged situation, made it very dangerous for all involved. I ordered the UMWA pickets and the nonunion miners not to be in possession of guns when they confronted each other as the nonunion miners crossed the UMWA picket line going to work. I ordered the state police to monitor the order at the picket line, and to arrest anyone at the picket line with a gun and take them to jail. The guns disappeared, at least during this confrontation.

> DANIEL HOWARD: I've seen the [strikers], where they throw those slipjacks, what they call jacksnipes, you know, to ruin tires; I've seen [strikebreakers] leave out of here and Jericol [in] a little armored truck [sitting] in the back because there were constant sniper fire. Yes, it was. If you feel that you're right and you feel that you're making a living for your family, and you crawl in the back of a coal truck that's lined with steel and you got little peep holes to ensure your safety and coming across where they got you blocked, you have a tendency to get a little angry sometimes. And sometimes they go over the line a little bit, I know one boy that was driving a company truck, and he incidentally tried to run over some, probably did. But, you have to understand he felt provoked too.

Strikers used dynamite ("We took out some transformers one night," one of them recalled). The other side used fire: in February 1979, a church building used as a strike meeting place was burned to the ground. Both sides used guns. On March 16, 1979, "replacement worker" Odus Griffith Jr. was killed by a shot fired by a sniper at a company vehicle.[44]

"You know, a man got killed but they never did know who done it—but he did get killed" (*Delbert Jones*). As in Brookside, the killing became a moral issue, tilting the balances of right and wrong—which explains why union people insist that the shooter's identity remains unknown, or try to blame the company: "Yeah, a scab got killed. How did it happen? Well, we figured the company hired somebody to kill the scab, see?" (*Mickey Messer*).

> SID DOUGLASS: After the school bus was ambushed and a nonunion miner was murdered, there was just an outrage—on both sides, it turned out. Both sides said, "If you're gonna disarm us, they'll slaughter us. We have a right to carry guns!" That was one of the most difficult decisions that I ever had to make.... After this bus had been shot into and people the court had ordered be disarmed came back into court and said, "We want the right to carry firearms. If we're shot at, we wanna be able to defend ourselves." I still imposed the orders that they couldn't carry firearms on the picket line. At that point. I ordered the state police to protect and escort the non-union convoy to the mine.
>
> MICKEY MESSER: State police was all over the place. Of course, they'd say that they were keeping the road open, but hell, there wasn't nobody on the damn road. They was just escorting them. They called it law and order, and they'd go home and get them scabs and bring them home. They called it "troublesome area," you know. They send all them state police to guard them scabs to work.

Just as at Brookside, the side that had suffered death had the moral upper hand. Gradually, the strike dissolved and miners returned to work. Somehow the material, the moral, and the spiritual merge in the meaning of the strike and its defeat.

> DELBERT JONES: Serve the Lord first. Whatever you need, He'll give it to you. He is always on your side.
> PORTELLI: Which side was He on during the Jericol strike?
> JONES: You must be on God's side, you must not drift away from Him, He doesn't drift from you; you drift from Him, if your mind isn't clear and pure.
> HAZEL KING: You mean the company was cleaner than the miners?
> JONES: Well, when the children of Israel was in bondage, they were in bondage for a long time, until God sent them a leader, Moses. Now if we had had a leader we wouldn't have lost that strike. We was out twenty-seven

months and we damned ourselves. We damned ourselves by not sacrificing. Not sacrificing. I mean, go without a meal—walk instead of riding about in them cars; skip a meal, go without for a few days. But we were depending on those two hundred dollars a week, and when the money ran out the men ran out.

DEMOCRACY AT ARCH

I went back to Harlan County in 1986. William Turner, whom I had met at the University of Kentucky in Lexington, arranged for me to stay with his parents, Naomi and Earl Turner, in Lynch. When I arrived, the mine was in the process of being sold to Arch Minerals, a wholly owned subsidiary of St. Louis–based Ashland Oil Company. It was a huge change for a community that had felt secure in the double paternalism of U.S. Steel and the UMW: "These guys called it Uncle Steel: Uncle Steel will always be here, and the union will stand up for us no matter what you do. And when Arch was gonna buy it, it was, 'Oh well, we're gonna be one big family, and they're gonna come in and care about us trying to help the community.' And I was right there, telling people—Arch were away from here, they were strippers, they weren't underground" (*Joe Scopa Jr.*). In less than five years, Arch was to become one of Kentucky's fastest-growing coal companies, operating mines in Harlan, Letcher, Knott, Breathitt, Pike, and Lee counties.

> CONNIE OWENS: Arch, before they came they told us: "Look, we're in business to mine coal for profit. We're not in the people business, we are not coming to be your friend. We don't wanna be your big brother, we just wanna make some money."

> JOE SCOPA JR.: That night at the stroke of midnight, when Arch took over, and we scratched and painted over everything had U.S. Steel on it, because Arch, they wanted to get rid of everything that had U.S. Steel, and then they said they wanted to get rid of all the employees, the salaried people that had been U.S. Steel, and you had these people coming in—good people, but they lived in Virginia instead of here, and people here kind of resented it, all the guys that was bosses, they'd been in the union, and they'd come up through the ranks. But Arch, they started replacing everybody, and they had these young engineers that come in, and when they wanted to get rid of somebody they'd walk in, tell the guy to clean his desk out, and security would stand there and wait for him to clean it.

On my first Sunday in Lynch, I attended church with the Turners. The Reverend Frederick Brown, a pastor and the chief of Cumberland police, preached that "there is talk about a strike. But we can't afford a strike." But conflict was on people's minds. There was talk about the union-busting firm

Arch was said to be bringing in. Even mild-mannered retired teacher Henrietta Sweatt was ready: "They say there might be a strike, and I said, if there is one, somebody better talk to Arch Mineral, and tell 'em they're fooling with the wrong people. These mountain people know what a strike means; these people are union men, pure-dee honest-to-God union men. We've been through some terrible strikes here. Where you couldn't hardly get to the store for guns upon the mountain were shooting and all that going on. But they stuck by their guns, and I believe they're gonna do it this time. Because they say they wanna bring some other men to work, take all the seniority away from them, so they're not gonna stand for that." A few days later I talked to Tommy Sweatt, a Methodist preacher and a coal miner.

> TOMMY SWEATT: These mountain people can be as forgiving and loving as anybody you ever seen; they can also carry a grudge for a long time. 'Cause just as you see them easy-rider rifle racks on the trucks going down the road, they got fishing rods on them where they just go to the park, maybe cast a few times and if they don't catch a trout they don't worry—they could just as easily have an M14 or an M16, .30-06, or one of those 460's where you've got a thing this long. You use that thing to shoot big mountain sheep, go elk hunting, shoot stuff that's so far away you have to put salt on your bullets to preserve your meat till you get to it. And they'll put on camouflage or bush-fighting stuff, and they'll go in the hills. They'll tell you right quick, "I'm not gonna let anybody take my [job], ain't nobody gonna walk over me."

Arch had too much experience to force a showdown. The change was radical but gradual. Arch started hiring new employees on a nonunion or temporary basis and gradually easing out the older workforce—"some of them two months before they would have their twenty years for their union pensions. Of course, there was resistance; but this didn't take place in a couple of months, this took place over years. And they were always laying off some people, calling back others, they worked maybe a week, and be laid off. It was just awful" (*Connie Owens*).

> TOMMY SWEATT (INT. 1986): Since they have taken over these mines, we're working with slimmer crews and we're actually mining more coal per man than we ever have. And now, they're going about it another way. They're going to cut out a bunch of benefits and stuff that we've gained through the union, over the years, very slyly, they're trying to change from a union operation to a nonunion operation. And that's not only gonna hurt us all down the road, but is going to hurt the guys that have already retired and are drawing pensions off of that company.

> JOE SCOPA JR. (INT. 2005): There was one guy, he got on the mantrip, he was getting ready to go underground and they went and told him to clean

everything out and he had to leave. Arch was real, real kind of ruthless, it didn't make any difference if it wasn't right or wrong, it was their idea. It seemed that Arch didn't think about the future, they just wanted there and now. The geologists and the engineers would try to tell them, what's gonna happen above the top seam, or the below seam when we do this and that, and what's gonna happen when this coal reserve over here [is mined out]? They just wanted to get this stuff. The same thing with people. One example was the electrical engineer, whose father worked here, he went to college, got a degree in electronics, and when the power lines would go out, on weekends, on Sundays, sun or rain, he'd go out and see to the power lines—they didn't care about that. They laid him off. Just like that. And he lost his job.

Arch systematically tried to pit white-collar workers against the underground miners. "They would send us salaries underground, when they would do the longwall move, because they didn't totally trust the union people. And then later on when they struck [in 1989] they sent us underground, at first to do cleanups and things like that. They would take us from the main office [to] the mine down here, with school buses, or we would do a caravan of cars to go across the picket lines" (*Joe Scopa Jr.*).

CONNIE OWENS: One time [the strikers] came up and surrounded the building and they weren't going to let any of us out, until certain demands were met, or at least they were heard and someone had responded. I saw people under their desks, just [scared]—and I wasn't afraid 'cause I always lived among my people, and listened to them, and talked to them; I didn't have the nonrelationship that a lot of the supervisors had. So they were lying on the floor, and they had rental security in there, for extra patrol and all this, and threats of bombs at the mine operations; I should have been afraid, but it was all just so comical to me. So it went for several days like that. Reverend Brown, he was part of the security group, and—they were wearing camouflage and stuff and going to these different locations, and the union guys called them the mutant midget Ninja turtles—'cause, you know, they looked like Terminators or something.

JOE SCOPA JR.: I remember on the second day, in the morning we'd have a meeting before we went underground, and they told us, "Okay, you guys be prepared to be barricaded underground." They had put two rows of empty coal cars in front of the mines, and they had bought some bullet-proof—whatever, and they were gonna put it around the power station, and they said, "We've bought all these cots so you can sleep and live underground." They hired all these security people, and they would go up in the mountains and they'd keep an eye, with binoculars, on what was going on. And we heard these stories where some union guys went up, snuck up on 'em, and took their guns away from 'em. So, you got the people who are working on a salary, okay: you got clerks, the accountants, the clerks from supply, you got us, the surveyors, the engineers, the drafts-men, and they send us underground. So we said, "We can do it, it'll be fun, we get to run the motors, we get to move the scoops," and stuff like that. But when they started talking about barricading, a couple of bosses stood up, they said, "We don't think this is right, you're taking things too far." And they said, "We don't care. You and everybody in this room can leave, and we'll get somebody else to do the job."

The 1989 strike at Arch—the last unionized deep mine in the county—was the swan song of the union in Harlan mines. "They made some major concessions, at the national level. Then, then they made some local agreement, where they agreed to allow the company exemptions from parts of the contract" (*Connie Owens*). Slowly the union was eased out of Lynch, its last stronghold in Harlan County. "My brother had started working in the mines [at Arch] and he would belong to the union, but when the mines started closing down that's when the union sort of went out" (*Jenny Saylor*). In order to keep a foothold in Harlan, the UMW started organizing school and hospital employees instead of miners. In the nation's memory and imagination, Harlan remains identified with the unions and labor conflict; but the struggle that began in 1917 is over, and lost. There have been scattered labor controversies (such as a hospital workers' strike in 2007), but at least one generation has grown up in Harlan for whom the union has little meaning.[45] Yet the struggle is not over—it has only moved to other grounds.

15

STAYING ALIVE

NOT JUST A WORD

> Lois Scott: My older daughter died from lupus when she was thirty years old. And I think that was one of the reasons I threw myself into [the Brookside strike]. My daughter was gonna die, and I lived with that every minute. But if I could become so involved that that didn't stay on my mind constantly, then I could survive.

"If you think about the way we growed up, actually, it was a miracle that we survived. Before you're ever two years old, you've already beat the odds of survival" (*Annie Napier*). I learned on my first day at the Cranks Creek Survival Center that in Harlan survival is not a metaphor—"not just a word," as Annie Napier explained.

"When the unions was trying to get into existence, I guess you would call it a struggle to survive" (*Frederick Brown*)—and "a lot of 'em didn't survive, if you believe me" (*Tillman Cadle*). Jerry Johnson taught his children "an education for survival." Basil Collins survived the Bataan Death March. Will Gent and Timothy Lewis survived Vietnam ("If you survived it without getting hit you're a veteran") and Iraq. "I've survived a lot," says Tammy Haywood: her husband's murder, breast cancer, raising children as a single mother. "Yes, I am tough. But I think that's from being raised here."

Survival may indeed be a metaphor—economic ("[We] need a little bit of diversity here, economically, in order to survive," *Johnny Woodward*), political ("We're still in the survival mode," *Daniel Howard, mayor*), social ("It's surviving, being able to maintain your mental health as well as your physical health," *Carla Jo Barrett, social worker*), cultural (in Cincinnati, "[I] survived [in] a culture that I did not understand," *Charlene Dalton*).

> Portelli: So, the key word here is survival.
> Marjorie Napier (nurse): Exactly! The cancer rate in this county is probably higher than any other place in the state. We don't know why; we can't get anybody to come in here and do the studies. We're just a bunch of dumb hillbillies, they don't care if we die or not. Women have a higher rate of cervical and breast cancer here than anywhere else in the state. Why

is that? Is it something in the area? Is it from the coal mining? Is it because we burn coal all the time? From the water that we have mined so much?

After the coal camps closed and the company doctors retired, "really there was no care available in this area" (J. D. Miller). It was only in 1970, with support from the Appalachian Regional Commission and the University of Kentucky, that Dr. David Steinman started the Clover Fork Clinic in Evarts—billed as "a community controlled clinic" with "a team approach to health care."[1] "I came in 1973, after the clinic was already going. I wanted to work in an underserved area—in the U.S. there are plenty of doctors competing for lucrative jobs in big cities, and I didn't have any great desire to be one of those people" (J. D. Miller).[2]

DONNA WARREN: People die a lot. Back years ago it was nothing for a woman to have ten or twelve kids and only have three or four of them live to adulthood, and parents if they didn't get killed in the mines they died early from diseases and lack of medical care because you either couldn't get to a hospital or you couldn't afford to go, and then a lot of the people wouldn't seek medical help because of their religious beliefs.

MELODY DONEGAN (NAME CHANGED): The hospital over there, if you ain't got a medical or insurance or money, they turn you away. And if me and Johnny get sick, we can't go to the doctor, because we ain't got no medical card, no money, or no insurance.[3]

TAMMY HAYWOOD: We are probably the richest country in the world. I have a hard time understanding why any child in this country is without health care, why any child in this country should go to bed hungry, why anybody should do without heat. The other day I was watching on the Discovery Channel and—I can't remember what country it is—but everyone has health care. And it's not a rich country. See, that just boggles my mind.

Because so many doctors in Harlan County are from abroad (they are required to serve two years in an underserved area in order to get a visa), some residents feel that "maybe they don't understand our culture" (Carla Jo Barrett) and Harlan is getting inferior care. "A lot of these doctors were coming to Harlan, putting in their two years, and then leaving. Yet, some foreign doctors have become endeared to the local people, and stayed on" (J. D. Miller).[4] For example, Dr. Albino Nunes, born in the Philippines, has been practicing in Harlan since 1971.

ALBINO NUNES: If you see the resume of a lot of these doctors, a lot of them have advanced studies, like cardiology, surgery...American doctors like to go to the big cities, they don't like to go to the boondocks. The foreigner can adjust easily with the poor people, because they know hardship. Because they are born in a country where you live for survival, no luxury, you only live for survival.

PORTELLI: People use the word *survival* a lot around here.

NUNES: Because it's a Third World country, they call it now.

Mental health is also in jeopardy.[5] "When I got here, I was so overwhelmed with the amount of emotional problems, that I really had difficulty coping with it. I've always thought that it probably was just because people felt totally powerless and helpless to do anything for themselves. People feel like they have no control over what's happening to them. And after a while, how can you help but get depressed when you feel that way" (*J. D. Miller*).

Older miners complained of "nerves being run down" because of "bad air" and "hard work."[6] "And sometimes you have one of them days where small things come closing in on ya, and you feel like grabbing your hair and pulling it out" (*Will Gent*). "People kill theirself mostly, people kills theirself. There's a guy down here on the foot of this mountain killed hisself this other day" (*Henry Farmer*). "We have had suicide, in our patients, and we have, every week, violence of a spouse toward a spouse, sometimes to a child. But I think we often don't understand the root of where the man's violence comes from, which is his feeling of…total lack of worth, and feeling of guilt. So the man takes out his anger toward the person who makes him feel guilty—for not being able to provide for her. And, it's a misdirected anger, but it's still there" (*J. D. Miller*).

Death, says Annie Napier, "is another part of survival." Betty Cole's one grandchild was killed by a truck; her husband died from a heart attack and black lung; "and then my uncle died, and it was no time until his wife died." "My brother, he got killed over thirty-five cents playing poker on Jones Creek. I had two older brothers, and one of them died with leukemia, and that one got shot, and then my sister-in-law [died] from drinking, alcoholic, cirrhosis of the liver, I guess they call it" (*J. C. Hall*).

> ANNIE NAPIER: Chester's brother died last September with cancer, and then Liddie liked to cut her foot off in October, and she don't believe in a doctor, so she didn't even go have it stitched up. She liked to bled to death. And then Johnny died. And then in May, Uncle Charles got killed in that car wreck, and one of my cousins died at the same time. [One] thinks a lot about death and dying. It's because every day you hear somebody has gotten killed in mine, disaster, or car wreck, or shot and killed. It's—it's a everyday, day-to-day basis.

Eastern Kentucky, historian Richard J. Callahan writes, is "haunted by the ghosts of coal mining…The dead are present in their absence, haunting the landscape and drawing attention—by the manner of their deaths—to the very everyday matters of work, even as they provoke awareness of *something else.*" A disabled miner and union organizer says that "the attitude about death here is much better than it is in most other places I've been. There is always a realization of death here."[7] "I think there is a lot of understanding of death as something that God has decided when you are going to die, and you just die then. Oftentimes, I'll be taking care of someone in the hospital, and I didn't really expect them to die but they died, and the family response will usually be, 'Well, it was God's time.' So it's kind of a fatalism, like there is nothing we can do about it: it's out of our control" (*J. D. Miller*).

> CHARLOTTE NOLAN: And I'll tell you other things that are interesting here in the mountains. Burial traditions. The tradition is that you bring the body to the house, and you have sort of a wake. Nobody goes to bed, nobody gets undressed. You sit up three nights from the time the body is brought home until they take it to the church, and sometimes they have the preaching right there at the house until they take it to the cemetery for burial. And it gives relatives a chance to get here from Detroit. Or Ohio, or wherever it is. Some people, who die from being bitten by a snake, they'll bury the snake with them. Put it right there with 'em, yes sir.

Until the mid-1900s, the dead were buried mostly in family graveyards. "They got just a head stone and a foot stone. They carved their names and the dates of the death on them rocks, little flat rocks sticking up. There's one on the head of this holler, it's all rocks, old people years ago. It's cut in the rock, when they died, when they was born" (*Ben Lewis*). Modernization changed the culture of death: the dead no longer lie among family and ancestors but are buried in public cemeteries in "individual little spaces: here is Grandma, over there is Grandpa, and all these strangers are in between, and so it fragments your emotional experience" (*Gurney Norman*).[8] "By the early sixties," Norman explains, "cemeteries had become a business. And the graveyards came to be called gardens. Rest havens. The things are operated like a mass production facility, and all stones are uniform, and all must be level to the ground, you know why? Efficiency of lawn mowing." Burial societies, union burial plans, and family insurance help pay for the rising cost of death. Funeral home owner Dukey Jones admits, "It's a business, it's very competitive."

"A lot of situations you run into funerals for killing and things like that. Personal friends of the family, boys in the penitentiary, bring them back for funerals, police are out with them and they'd be handcuffed and things like that. And then, labor trouble, down through the years. Pickets, and gun shooting, coal strikes and all that stuff" (*Dukey Jones*). "It was either Crummies or Yancey where these men were all killed at the same time—in some sort of a labor battle, and when they had them at the funeral home, I heard people say that it was horrible to see seven men lying there who'd been killed like that" (*Gladys Hoskins*).

> LEWIS BIANCHI: [After the body is embalmed] the next step, you put the clothing on. Most time you'd like to get a long sleeve and something that

fits up tight around the neck. A lot of times, people have had shots in their arm, or glucose, or something of that nature, so it's discolored. But we can use regular clothing, or a special-type burial clothes that is the same as street clothes, except it snaps in the back, which makes it easier to dress. After they're dressed, the casket's opened up for visitation. Sometimes, they take them back to the family home [or] to a church. A lot of times they have preaching and singing. I've had several funerals where they handle snakes.[9]

Sometimes the casket stays closed. This is what was done with the "invisible" casualties of the Iraq war, or the bodies that came home from Vietnam. "We buried a lot of them, all closed caskets. It's against the law, you can't see them. We would have the funeral, then they'd have a military service. Later [I would] put them in a casket [with] a glass top, but it's frosted; and [some] I've taken out and put them in a different casket, but that was between me and the family" (*Dukey Jones*).

JUNGLES AND DESERTS

TONY SWEATT: After high school in [1988] I joined the army. [I was] petrified of the coal mines and my granddad didn't want none of us going in it, so I joined the army.

MARJORIE NAPIER: I signed up voluntarily while Desert Storm was going on. I was young; I was healthy; I felt it was my duty to go.

CRYSTAL VANOVER: A bunch of my son's friends volunteered about a month ago, and they wanted my son to volunteer and I told him, "No, don't you volunteer, don't go."
PORTELLI: Did they think it would be a job?
CRYSTAL VANOVER: That, and the money. In this town, money means a lot for these kids because they don't have nothing to do here.

PRESTON MCLAIN: We have a young man that my wife taught in school, and he just received the Silver Star for bravery. Reading the commendation, is typical of what a honored Harlan boy would do. He risked his life and saved quite a few other lives. I think we have two Medals of Honor from this county. Here they're proud: their young men and women go away and serve and they're glad when they return home. They treat them like heroes before they go; when they come home there's a lot of respect.

Whenever America goes to war, Harlan is bedecked with yellow ribbons and "Support the Troops" bumper stickers. Harlan men fought in the Civil War, served in the world wars, in Korea, and in Vietnam. Yet "even these Appalachian folks who are extremely patriotic, they had some severe questions, about Vietnam" (*Ewell Balltrip*). "It was a mixed-up war; a lot of good men and women died fighting for what we thought we were trained to do, ending up being more politics than anything else. I'm not saying it was done in vain, it just wasn't done the right way" (*Preston McLain*).

> WILL GENT: I went in '62, was fourteen years old. I lied about my age. But Uncle Sam wasn't too choosy to question us about it, you know. [I reen-listed] seven times, pulled eighteen months ever time. The B company, 3rd Platoon. Special Forces, or Green Berets. Wounded several times. Two girls, one was about seven, the other one about nine. Spun me around, and the second one throwed a hand grenade and the fragment hit me in the back and when I straightened back up, the first girl shot again, hit me right in the breast. And some of my buddies got them. I didn't know they was kids. That aggravated me to death for ever so long.[10]

> PRESTON McLAIN: The civilian population is what I felt sorry for: they were taking the brunt from the Americans and the North Vietnamese as well. I've seen a lot of stuff that a sixteen- or eighteen-year-old young man should never see. Beautiful country. Along the coastline it looked like downtown Miami: with the palm trees, the greenery and the shrubs, the beautiful flowers, the animals and so forth. There was some very nice peo-ple: very dedicated people. The culture is deep into religion and it was interesting, but I didn't get to do that much seeing...if you go out in a mission, on a helicopter, to fly over Vietnam looks like you're going over a vacation resort, and, all of a sudden, it would explode. That destroyed a lot of ecosystem and the country was badly damaged inside and out.

Annie Napier warned me that Will Gent would not talk about Vietnam in front of his mother, because it hurt her nerves. She sat with us in the interview, so I asked him only if he'd been in the military, he said no, and I left it at that. Later I came back to take pictures. He met me alone on the porch, and, sitting in my car under driving rain and thunder, he began his tale—a war story, and an old-fashioned Harlan County snake tall tale.

> WILL GENT: They sent us out to disrupt their communications, take out [as] many of the officers that we could, but we had to avoid a fight till we got to our objective. We saw a small patrol come by and we found something to hide behind so we wouldn't bump into 'em. And I thought was a tree that fell, and I laid down behind it. And I's laying there, it started wiggling—I turned around: big old snake, it turned its head around, it was looking me right in the face. I couldn't afford to get up 'cause the enemy if it had a-spied me, we woulda had to fight and ruin our mission. And that's the worst scare I ever got. I'd rather face a hundred Cong by myself [than] that one snake with a whole platoon.

"I left many friends over there, and I'd like to leave it just like that" (*Preston McLain*). "I think Vietnam people that were really there don't talk about it 'cause there wasn't nothing to talk about. That's what my dad said: anytime you meet a guy and he's talking Vietnam, nine times out of ten he's blowing hot air" (*Tony Sweatt*).

WILL GENT: [Our mission was to] take care of sentries, take 'em out quietly as possible. Use camouflage clothes. Barefooted. We took out the enemy, killed 'em. How many I killed I lost count. After the first few kills, it gets a little easier. It don't get real to loving it. But it gets easier to pull the trigger. Slash one's throat or whatever, you know. And you just turn everything off. Stay alive. Do your job to the best of your capability and the way you was trained for it.
PORTELLI: Did they use to take pieces of the enemy's body?
GENT: Pretty well. Yeah, I did. It's several incidents where we captured some prisoners and done interrogation. They cut 'im, trimmed 'im. Took a knife, cut his balls, pulled 'em out, hit him in the gut, and made him swallow. Cut the ears off. And cut their ribs from the backbone, pulled 'em right out the meat. And them alive. Torture, heavy, that I've done. But I didn't like it none, though. Many time when I got home I'd have nightmares about it. What Hitler did was nothing to what I seen in Vietnam go on. Cruelty. The Vietcong'd get little girls, take 'em off in the nests with 'em and cut their throats. [Americans] didn't really mess with the women, you know, sexually. If they didn't want to, they'd slap 'em around a little bit and then force theirselves on 'em. A lot of times they'd [be] willing, for a few dollars. 'Cause it's poor country, had lots of brothers and sisters, family. I was quite bitter when I come back, for what I had seen. And had done. It's what's making me shake right now.

I never checked on Will Gent's story. There are a couple of contradictions, but it conveys an anguish that has a credibility of its own.[11]

"I thought we had learned a lesson in Vietnam, but I don't know if we have" (*Preston McLain*). Tony Sweatt left the military before he had to go to Iraq: "I didn't agree with that war and I figured if the president can wake up and he wants to start a war, then, you know, that's not for me." Marjorie Napier's unit didn't get to go to Iraq, but she saw its consequences: "I was treating the people as they came back. They would have skin diseases; they were having a lot of problems from the medications that they had taken over there. There's been a lot of cancers that they can't really explain; children are being born with a lot of problems that they can't explain. It's just like Agent Orange years ago."

JOAN ROBINETT: During the Gulf War, we had people in our citizens' group that was gung ho—"bomb them, bomb them," you know—and then we had other people that said, "Well, maybe we shouldn't." We supported the troops because I had family, in there—I supported them, didn't want them to be there, but I did not support the war. I felt like that we stuck our nose in where we didn't belong, and I think the U.S. does that a lot, and we got to quit doing that. But that's something that you just didn't talk about here, publicly.

And then it was September 11. "I think everyone felt the same sense of shock, disbelief. We all absorbed an amazing amount of bad energy over that period, we all exuded our own pain. People were just standing around in knots crying" (*Darlene Wilson*). "September 11 was really good, for a moment. People forget how much we have in common—we all are feeling the same thing, the same way; we need to come together, and deal with this pain, this anger—this betrayal. And—it almost lasted a week" (*Connie Owens*).

"I don't understand why the people flew them planes and killed all the Americans in this American place" (*Crystal Vanover*). "I think with Afghanistan, people were willing to accept the rationale that Osama bin Laden and his organization had claimed responsibility. They felt it was justified to go after him" (*Darlene Wilson*). "I wasn't for it but whenever the troops had to go somewhere I would support them. I was for going over there quick and back out, [getting] bin Laden, Saddam Hussein, all of them terrorists' groups" (*Larry Williamson*).

TIMOTHY LEWIS: I was in Iraq in 2003, and I'm part of a reserve tank company out of Fort Knox, Kentucky. In January 2003 we were activated for active duty. It took us about a month to float to Kuwait. And once we got to Kuwait, we were there for about a month, to get acclimated to the climate and everything, 'cause it started to get really hot. We came back in July 2003, so it was six months, total time.

"I don't know that we need to be over there. I support our troops. And I think Bush had his own agenda. I don't think it was the mass destruction weapons. I think it's mainly oil" (*Jane Perkins*). I remember the amazement and disbelief in people's eyes when I reminded them that Saddam Hussein was not involved in September 11. The explanations for the war echoed the dominant public discourse: self-defense ("If we didn't go over there, they would be over here. I don't want them coming over here taking our freedom away from us," *Crystal Vanover*), weapons of mass destruction (weapons that Tony Sweatt said "weren't there," but which, according to Timothy Lewis, must have existed: "I never saw a weapon of mass destruction. [But] the deserts of Iraq are vast. Maybe they moved it out, maybe they dismantled it on their own. I don't know—that's above my pay grade"), overthrowing a dictator ("Hussein was doing some bad things and, I don't know...," *Jenny Saylor*). "I don't know" was a frequent refrain; interchangeable rationales suggested mixed feelings ("I think that in a way they should've went over there and then I don't," *Crystal Vanover*).

TIMOTHY LEWIS: It was March 21 or 22, 2003, when we crossed into Iraq, and we proceeded north to the city of El Nassiriya and we first started seeing some action.[12] An army maintenance convoy had [been] ambushed in El Nassiriya, got split up, and we put our company tanks between the soldiers that were injured and the Iraqi insurgents that were attacking them. We bailed them out, and got them medevacked, got medical assistance, they flew them out in helicopters. And we proceeded north into the city, then you could see the rest of the convoy, and they were just butchered. There was one fuel truck that was burning right by the side of the road, we could feel the heat coming out as we passed it. So that's when we really started seeing some of the destruction.

Many in Harlan found it hard to feel compassion for Iraqi deaths and to recognize any logic but pure evil behind 9/11 and Iraqi insurgency. "It hurts me to hear about these kids, putting bombs on and getting on a bus or something to kill people, I just can't understand it" (*Jenny Saylor*). It was always "yes, but…": "You never want to kill innocents, but at the same time there was people jumping out with a sneak attack or throwing grenades and running away" (*Larry Williamson*). "Well, I understand that [Iraqis are also dying], but you've got to understand what they've done to us" (*Crystal Vanover*).

TIMOTHY LEWIS: There were situations that, the outcome wasn't the outcome I wished would have happened for civilians, for whatever personnel. You don't want anyone to get hurt or anyone to die, but—you do what you have to do to survive. You have those orders come down, and you have to follow your orders. And you have to do what you have to do to make sure that your buddies survive because you expect them to do that for you. And some of the stuff that we had to do, yes, it does bother me. And if someone says that the things that they had to do in war doesn't bother them, then I think they're not telling the truth. Because the things that happened in war, they're so—they're so unnatural. You see a lot of devastation, and a lot of death, and a lot of sadness especially for civilians, it's something that unnatural that it's hard to get used to it.

"I don't think civilians should be targeted," says Timothy Lewis. "We're Americans, that's what makes us different than other countries." The United States shares with all Western nations a history of civilian massacres and an attitude of denial. Italian war crimes in Ethiopia and in the Balkans are missing from our textbooks. Just as Italians are taught that we were an especially *brava gente*, good-hearted folk bringing civilization to the savages,[13] many Americans believe that they are a moral nation bringing democracy to the oppressed. Thus, the only deaths that count as the war drags on are American deaths. "I feel it's bad and a lot of our people are dying and I would like for them to hurry up and get it over with or pull our men out and come on home" (*Jenny Saylor*).

CRYSTAL VANOVER: I just wish our boys wasn't over there because there's so many has got killed, and they're babies, like my son-in-law—he was old enough to go over there and kill but he wasn't old enough to go into a bar and drink or even buy cigarettes. My daughter, they got married in February, he had to leave in April. He was over there for a year, and there was times when we didn't even know where he was at and my daughter, she would not leave the TV, every day we'd sit and [listen] if someone got killed or something. He had a really rough time when he come out of there moving into the society again. They flew him to San Diego, California, to a psych ward. He stayed there for almost six months. He just couldn't cope with what all he had to see over there and what he had to do. He never told me anything, he told my daughter some things, but I'd rather not say. He's doing better and that's the reason I just wish all of our boys would come home.

Doubts are hard to formulate and to voice publicly. "Iraq, a great deal more questioning by Joe on the street, [but] you'll never see a letter challenging President Bush in the *Harlan Daily Enterprise*" (*Darlene Wilson*). "Who did they poll? They didn't ask me. We don't know who they're asking, but they're not asking us" (*Connie Owens*). "And now they've got Home Front Security. It's scary how much freedom are we gonna lose, to be secure" (*Joe Scopa Jr.*). "I think that there is this racist issue, because they're less then lily white" (*Theresa Osborne*). "Brown people are in possession of resources and that shouldn't be, so we have to take it. Now all we have is people dying every day. On both sides" (*Connie Owens*).

TIMOTHY LEWIS: Sometimes bombs go off course, sometimes the wrong people get killed. We actually had to engage in killing some civilians, in my company. And they were Iraqi soldiers that had gotten into taxicabs, and they are charging at us. But yet, there was women and children, families, that had got in those cars. I did not trust anyone. There was a woman with two children and was hanging clothes out to dry, and she pulled out an RPG [rocket-propelled grenade] and hit an MV that was part of the convoy that was behind us. So, everyone was a threat.[14]

ANGEL HOLT: I think we did something first, and that's why they came over here. I don't know a whole lot about it, I'm not a news person. I was upset about 9/11 and I understand the retaliation but I just kind of felt like, I don't know, we just should have minded our own business, I mean that's their country, we got ours to run, everything is not perfect here in the United States.

TIMOTHY LEWIS: But, right in the middle, my platoon got stuck in Nassirya, a man came out of his house, he was gonna go pray, and he had both of his children, he was holding their hand, and bullets were flying, so this man actually walked up and was kissing Marines' arms, thanking, thanking God that they were there.

ACTS OF GOD AND MEN

On December 15, 1972, a huge mud slide forced the African American community of Sanctified Hill in Cumberland to evacuate their homes.

WILLETTA LEE: We kept hearing this noise, and we thought it was our furnace kicking off and on. In essence, the hill was beginning to slide and our basement had started to sink down into the earth. Other people had noticed where the trees were moving away from their homes, the foundations were pulling away from the houses. They were having floodings in different areas, and they finally found out that there was a big boulder under the hill that was moving and everyone had to evacuate the hill.

For years, the black community of Sanctified Hill had warned in vain that such a mud slide might happen. As soon as it did, insurance companies immediately labeled it as an "act of God." As one resident said, it may have been "partly the responsibility of the Lord," but it was also "partly the responsibility of the city."[15] "It had been declared a disaster area, but they weren't getting any help from the government. So my mother, Mattye Knight, and a few residents formed a board and they had assistance from people from Atlanta, Georgia, Washington, D.C., that were concerned and filled in to help them to get to Washington. They met with the president and his aides, with the help of the Lord they were able after a few years to get this thing established" (*Willetta Lee*).

"This thing" is a model community, tellingly named Pride Terrace, built with federal funding on land leased from the University of Kentucky in Cumberland.[16] It was not the first nor the last time that communities struggled to survive when the earth and the waters moved in Harlan County and Appalachia. In 1972, a flash flood caused by the collapse of a Pittston mine slag heap at Buffalo Creek, West Virginia, left 125 dead and 5,000 homeless. In Harlan, where the Cumberland River reached flood levels twenty-four times between 1947 and 1977, the worst came in 1963 and 1977.[17]

ROBERT SIMPSON: I lived in Wallins when I was first married. We had an old shack we lived in and that morning the water was down the street, people had their horses and cows tied up, this side of the water. We got into Harlan and man, I'll tell you, it was a good ten foot, above anything. And it took me six and a half hours to go from Harlan to Wallins. That's about an eight- or nine-mile trip. Over here, it took cars plumb down in the field, washing everything out. We lost everything, lost our car, lost my job on account of the flood.

"The damage was in the millions of dollars. Homes were destroyed, businesses were destroyed. Devastating—that's the only word for it; devastating, catastrophic" (*Ewell Balltrip*). "One thing that they can't never pay you for is when they destroy your peace of mind. It'd start raining, I'd walk the floor" (*Annie Napier*). "People had literally lost their lives' work, when their home was destroyed; they'd lost letters from their mother and father who are now dead, a picture of a child who died in infancy, you know, very emotional items" (*Ewell Balltrip*).

> CHARLOTTE NOLAN: That first flood in 1963, May the twelfth, I can't forget it. My mother had a heart attack that night—and a year later my mother was not alive. I've always figured that my mother didn't drown in that flood, but floods have taken lives anyway. My mother was of the age that the things she lost in the flood in her cedar chest, her baby books, locks of hair that she had cut from the heads of her children, many years ago. And nobody can repay you for those things. And so, the older people found it difficult to pitch in and to start all over again. I know the man right behind me said, that night, "I'll never live through this. I'll just never live through it." And he didn't. One woman, down in Loyall, shot herself. She just couldn't face it again.[18]

In April 1977, another flood killed three people and left hundreds homeless. "It took the bridge and all out down here, honey. If you look close you can tell where the flood waters went. In this house. I believe they have to be a-stripping and a-causing it, like I told Governor Carroll right to his face" (*Sudie Crusenberry*). Governor Julian Carroll claimed that the flood was caused mainly by "farming, housing development, and the wind, which scatters soil."[19] "Some people say it was strip mining that caused that flood of '77. Mining perhaps contributed to it, but I think it's just the geography of the area. You cannot take six inches of rain, in less than twenty-four hours, in a mountainous area where the hillsides are extremely steep and the valleys are extremely narrow, and not have a flood" (*Ewell Balltrip*).

According to a report by Science in the Public Interest, however, the impact of surface mining—destruction of vegetation, increased runoff rates, loosening of the soil, high sedimentation—was "responsible for at least $4 million of the damage." "The initial despair and feeling of helplessness," the report continues, "soon disappeared as work began with shovels and brooms to clean up the homes and salvage what they could. The spirit of the mountain people...shone brightly in the flood's aftermath." In Cranks Creek, however, where the flood hit again in October and in November, "the response of the people was anger and frustration."[20] The primary cause of the flood was that the silt dams that were supposed to retain and filter the water from the strip site at the head of the hollow overflowed, and it all washed down the valley.

> ANNIE NAPIER: Anytime that you have a coal seam, you have water. So where they stripped it off and leveled the mountain down, this whole thing will fill up with water, and from time to time it busts, and you get all these trees and rocks and mud and car bodies, refrigerator bodies, bulldozer parts, everything's down into the creek bed, and the river don't have nowhere to go but out and that night it really wiped out Cranks Creek. There was thirty-seven homes damaged up there. My cousin's house was completely washed away. And Walt Reimer's house, it was sitting on the edge of the riverbank, and that logjam caught it. It tore his house all to pieces, in early morning hours, and he died that morning in the hospital. He never knew about his house. It would have killed him anyway if he had knowed about it.

"They said, 'Well, it's the big hand of God...' No! God didn't own that Caterpillar, he didn't tell that man there, 'Get up there and rip the mountains off.' He made them!" (*Sudie Crusenberry*). "We went to this big meeting and this [government] man got up and he said, 'Don't you think that was an act of God?' And I said, 'The rain was an act of God, but God didn't set that bulldozer on the side of that mountain and tear it all to hell either'" (*Annie Napier*).

In spite of stereotypes of fatalism and passivity, Appalachia is the scene of many strong citizens' movements for social, economic, and environmental justice.[21] A response to the disaster was the creation of groups including Martin County's Flood Preparation Group and the Clover Fork Organization to Protect the Environment.

"I had organized an anti-strip-mining group here in Clover Fork, called COPE, Clover Fork Organization to Protect the Environment, and we had such lofty goals that we were going to shut down all strip mining in the whole Clover Fork area. People from Clover Fork came, but people like Annie Napier and Becky Simpson heard about it and they would drive over here and attend our meetings too" (*J. D. Miller*). After contacts with some Lexington groups, COPE took on also other issues, such as the fact that coalfield counties hardly received any tax money from the immense wealth that was extracted from their soil: "You know that the tax on mine minerals was a tenth of a cent per hundred dollars evaluation, which meant there was no tax, basically. And we tried to challenge the assessment on property, we tried to get legislation passed, we took it all the way to the State Supreme Court, finally, and won. And during that time there was a lot of push to organize Kentuckians for the Commonwealth, there were people in other counties that were doing similar kinds of things and, so we actually had the first organizing meeting of Kentuckians for the Commonwealth in the basement of our house."[22]

In Cranks Creek, the Survival Center was set up to seek prevention and reparations. "I thought the least thing was to call the operators, that they would pay and, reimburse people for things they'd lost, make those responsible pay, or at least get some compensation" (*Becky Simpson*).

ANNIE NAPIER: Nobody knew what to do, how to go about nothing. They'd never been in that situation before. We'd never heared of reclamation or anything. And [we] started going to meetings and getting some information we should of knowed years ago, and the first thing they developed here was a flood control project. [People] didn't know they had any rights. It was just like, "I don't have no rights to say nothing about a coal company." See, you grow up with it. Nobody's ever fought a coal company and won. It took a long time to convince people that they had rights, just like everybody else, and somebody should be responsible for destroying their homes.[23]

"So we finally got a hearing, and sixteen families got $155,000. That was the first time in history that people got paid from a strip miner" (*Bob Simpson*). A floodwall now stands between downtown Harlan and the river. "Many people say it's ruined our town, they say it boxes them in and so forth. I worked really hard in this Chamber of Commerce to get some flood control. The Corps of Engineers, they've cut through the mountains and changed the road and displaced so many people. But now people are going to actually feel safe" (*Gladys Hoskins*).

Safety remains relative. In Coxton and Ages, a multimillion-dollar project to "to make this a model community so it wouldn't flood out every ten years" was never completed (*Dallas Blue*).[24] In 1981, a sludge pond owned by Eastover Coal collapsed at the head of Ages Creek: "That sludge pond was inspected, and they said it was in good shape. Broke the next day. That's when it killed Nelie Woolum" (*James Wright*). "Ages? There was a lady there, had been complaining about the conditions, and they didn't respond and the debris that came of that holler covered the roads, the houses, and she was covered, her whole home was covered with this sludge and they had to take bulldozers and remove the debris from where she had lived" (*Hazel King*).

Floods caused by stripping and mountaintop removal are still killing people and destroying homes and rivers in Appalachia. On October 11, 2000, in a disaster at least twenty times larger than the *Exxon Valdez* oil spill (but ignored by the media), a mine pond in Martin County collapsed, polluting rivers with coal slurry, rocks, and chemicals. Martin County Coal Company claimed that the event "was the direct, sole and proximate result of an act of God, the occurrence of which was not within the control of Martin County Coal." But as Appalachian environmental activist Larry Wilson commented, "God should have known better."[25]

POISONING THE EARTH AND THE WATER

ANNIE NAPIER: I mean, here we have to fight for basic things, you know, that we have to have for survival, like water, I mean, God gave us water, and He gave us air, and He gave us soil, and here, you know, we have to fight for this stuff. It's ours anyway!

JOAN ROBINETT: This side, along the Cumberland, is in the flood plain area and in '77 everything was underwater. After that flood, people continued to raise vegetables along the flood plain. In March of 1989 the State Division of Water came through a community called Dayhoit and they were testing public water systems for organic compounds. So they came in to the Holiday Mobile Home Park, which was about sixty-five mobile homes, and they tested the drinking water well, and it was found to be contaminated with vinyl chloride and trichlorophene.

National Electric Coil, a mining machinery repair plant, had been operating near Dayhoit since 1950. The trichloroethylene they used to clean machinery released carcinogenic chemicals (including polychlorinated biphenyls or PCBs, dichloromethane, and vinyl chloride) and heavy metals (mercury, lead, cadmium, and chromium). The mixture was burned in open barrels, releasing dioxins into the air, and dumped on the banks and into the waters of the Cumberland River. The state inspection found amounts of vinyl chloride and PCB that were 148 and 50 times higher, respectively, than the federally allowed maximum. The authorities, however, claimed there was no proof that the high rate of cancer in the area was related to these agents.[26]

JOAN ROBINETT: The EPA told the people, "Don't drink your water, don't water your gardens, your lawns, don't wash your car, don't do laundry, don't take a shower, but you are going to be okay, your chances of getting cancer are slim. Just don't do anything with your drinking water." And then we began to notice a lot of health problems within these children, especially in the mobile home park. Constant flus, viruses, diarrheas, colds. And mainly it was the mothers, when they began to realize, "This is not really common; these kids shouldn't be this sick. There's got to be a reason." Everybody had their garden on the riverbanks, and everybody eats vegetables from these gardens. Everybody eats fish from this river. All these kids are swimming. They have been baptized in it. And you go through family pictures and it's their first bicycle ride, their first tent, and here you are sitting next to this polluted site and had no idea, nobody had any idea. I can remember [my son's] sandbox two feet from this site, and they found dioxins there; his first swing set was here, it's eat up with lead in the soil.

In 1988, I drove into Larry Wilson's front yard in Yellow Creek, Bell County. He warned me not to get out of the car until he came to get me: "My dogs don't like strangers." They have reasons not to. Larry Wilson had been organizing to stop the contamination of Yellow Creek by waste from a local tannery: "We have 4.8 times the leukemia rate of the nation. We have like ten times the miscarriage rate, something similar in overall cancer rate and liver damage, kidney damage, birth defects, still births, problems in pregnancy, and we trace that directly to the chemical contamination." In 1980, Wilson started the Yellow Creek Concerned Citizens—and trouble, violence, and Red-baiting began. "Have you been shot at today? Have you had rocks thrown your way?" sang Bell County songwriter Kenneth Rosenbaum: "I want good water, it's the worst thing I've said / You don't have to kill me, if I drink it I'm dead."[27]

> LARRY WILSON: The brake lines on [my wife's] car was cut, our watchdog was poisoned, and then we got a telephone call saying, "What happened to your dog is going to happen to you, if you don't keep your mouth shut." One night, they fired a shotgun in the pickup truck I was driving. We were with a television crew filming the lagoon system at the tannery when we were shot, they got that one on film. You get audited by the IRS, you get taps on your telephone, you get followed around by the police. I've been fired from three jobs. I was told by a local politician, "We will see to it that you never again work in this county. Your family will starve or you will move." That's what happens to you in the hills, in the land of the free and the home of the brave, where we are politically free and where we have freedom of speech. We are free to practice it, if we will take what follows.[28]

Larry Wilson did not move and managed to support his family with help from the Highlander Center and "by taking my pickup truck and buying vegetables on credit, and going around knocking on doors, 'Do you want to buy an apple, do you want to buy an orange today?'" Yellow Creek Concerned Citizens was finally able to get a seepage treatment plant that improved the water quality somewhat, and to make the company pay for some of the damage. The group became a nationwide example of grassroots mobilization for the environment. Dayhoit's Concerned Citizens Against Toxic Waste was another.

> JOAN ROBINETT: So then, in '89, the neighbors and we began to talk. I called Hazel King, and I called Larry Wilson, and the people said: "We got to organize a citizens group, the government's not going to tell us how long we have been drinking this stuff, what our kids have been playing in, nobody is going to tell us. We got to do something. They poison their families and they are not getting away with it. We are going to find out what they have done, how bad it is, and they are going to pay, with whatever it takes, whatever we can do, within the law." So we organized a citizen group with community people, and people in the mobile home park, and plant workers, who had been very helpful, because they had worked in this stuff all these years [and] had the same health problems [as] the children. Actually, plant workers have had a lot more cancer deaths than we have seen in the community.[29]

Joan Robinett and her group went through much the same as the citizens of Yellow Creek: "I've been run off the road twice. We've had two cocker spaniels poisoned. My husband gets harassed at work. I don't travel at night anymore by myself." Children were affected: Larry Wilson's son was excluded from his high school football team, and Joan Robinett's son's bicycle was vandalized twice. "You get labeled as a troublemaker. Just because you ask a single question, or because you find out that you have the right to these answers. You get so angry. Your whole life changes, the way you look at things, your attitude…And you don't do it by choice. It's survival, you have to do it. I mean, it's live or die. It's just a matter of survival."

The concerned citizens of Dayhoit had to face the company's political and economic power, the authorities' inefficiency, inertia, and complicity, the lack of adequate counsel. "We found a lot of fear, fear of job loss and repercussions. And we have to deal with this dumb-hillbilly syndrome, and I mean, we're hill-billies, but we are not dumb. The people aren't dumb here, but they're kind-hearted. And they get taken advantage of easily" (*Joan Robinett*). As one member of the group recalled, "At the meetings, the people from EPA would accuse us of being too emotional. I told them, 'Let all of your family members and friends die around you and see if you don't get emotional.'" A Yellow Creek resident said, "We really are a Third World state—Appalachia."[30]

> JOAN ROBINETT: We community folks, we go into meetings all the time about different things, and agencies pull us into the table with the impres-sion that we all have equal say, that we are equals, okay? And I've done it many, many times knowing full well that when I go in that room I'm gonna walk out and just raise hell, okay? That one more time I've been the token citizen. It's like, "You can come to our table but you can't eat our food." We learned early on, the burden of proof is on the community. Your well is sunk from coal mining—you go in and turn your faucet on and you have no water, no well water—and we [must] prove that it's mine related. "It's an act of God": yeah, God decided that He's not gonna put any water in this well anymore.

In 1992, EPA declared Dayhoit a Superfund site, "which means it's one of the most contaminated sites in the U.S. and it's supposed to take top priority and they are supposed to, quote, 'clean it up' and all they do is just move the pollution from one place to the next" (*Joan Robinett*). Five thousand tons of soil excavated from Dayhoit were trucked to Emal, Alabama, and stored next to a poor African American community. As pumps drained the contaminated wells, they spread carcinogens in the air.[31]

BEHEADING THE MOUNTAINS

> BILL RAINES: [I took a trip] back to Middlesboro. I hadn't been down for like fifteen years. I was raised on the side of this mountain, had a house there, and I used to play on this mountain all the time, and we would play

cowboy and Indians and, you know, I mean, the mountain is gone. They actually blew the top of the mountain off. Tears actually came to my eyes, I mean, it just wasn't there. It's just a hole, a hole in the mountains. And I don't, I don't see how they can do it—not legally, I don't see how they can do it morally; that's God's creation, you know.

Over the last few years, I took several drives across the Kentucky line, over Black Mountain. This is how environmental writers Silas House and Jason Howard describe the landscape I saw there: "After dozens of stomach-churning curves, a small sign announces that the Virginia state line has been crossed. And suddenly, everything changes. Now there is a moonscape below, a barren wasteland of dirt and exposed rocks and yellow bulldozers. From near the summit of Black Mountain can be seen a mountaintop removal site that stretches itself brazenly above the town of Appalachia, Virginia, and it looks like a scar on the face of the earth."[32]

CARLA JO BARRETT: I happened to go across Big Black Mountain and hadn't been across there in a long time. I came around a curve and it looked like I had been in a war-torn area. It looked like craters; it looked like a bomb had gone off. And I almost wrecked my car. Because I was in a curve and I literally had to stop my car and look; it was just the pictures that you see of Iraq, you know, after they've bombed. And I cried. Because I hadn't been over there since that happened. And it's just completely destroyed.

The 1977 Surface Mining Control and Reclamation Act required restoration of strip sites to their original contours, but allowed for variations if the resulting land can be used for residential, commercial, or industrial development. This loophole allows the mining industry to claim that by removing the tops of the mountains they are creating in mountainous Appalachia the flat land supposedly needed to create development and jobs. Strip mining destroyed the sides of the mountains; in mountaintop removal, a whole mountain can be blown up to reach a relatively thin seam of coal. The overburden, or "waste," is pushed into the valleys below, and is neatly redefined as "valley fills."[33] With unconscious tautological irony, the president of the Kentucky Coal Association claims: "To imply that we're flattening Appalachia is so untrue. We're creating level land for Appalachia." According to the president of the National Mining Association, "People have used these sites to build high schools and golf courses....Some of the sites are so beautifully reclaimed, many people can't tell the difference."[34]

In the space of a decade, hundreds of peaks were flattened across Appalachia, thousands of tons of debris were dumped into the valleys, and hundreds of miles of mountain streams were buried. Most of the resulting "flat land" remains unused, while mechanization has resulted in the loss of tens of thousands of jobs.[35]

"Rivers used to run deep here, now they are shallow" (*Carla Jo Barrett*). Since blasting away the mountaintop is less expensive than using earth removal machinery, explosions and "flyrocks" threaten nearby homes and villages. In Inman, Virginia, on August 20, 2004, a boulder weighing half a ton crashed through a trailer and killed three-year-old Jeremy Davidson.[36] At a meeting in Harlan in 2007, Larry Easterling, from McRoberts, Letcher County, took the floor:

> *These blasts shake every home in the hollow.... The barren landscape has caused it to flood five times within a period of three months in our hollow and makes our water unsafe to drink. But what [angers] me most is they say it's an "act of God." Did you know that? I didn't know that the acts of God started right here in McRoberts, Kentucky.... I'm a mountain man and I hunt.... And I was ready to take my shotgun and pop holes in every piece of equipment they had [until Kentuckians for the Commonwealth] made me see that violence was not the way to go.*[37]

During the George W. Bush administration, U.S. officials simply reclassified the debris resulting from mountaintop removal from objectionable "waste" to legally acceptable "fill," thus legalizing the practice of dumping debris into streambeds. At the end of his second term, Bush proposed relaxing the rule that forbids mining less than one hundred feet from streams; the Kentucky House Natural Resources Committee approved the change with a one-vote majority.[38] Getting as much coal as possible by any means necessary is supposed to be a way of increasing the country's energy autonomy without cutting its high level of energy consumption; thus, a further incentive to mountaintop removal is the plan to turn coal into synthetic liquid fuel. Though the economic and environmental consequences of this operation are uncertain, "coals to liquid" and "synfuels" are touted as the region's future, overriding all concerns and alternatives and furthering the as yet doubtful search for "clean coal."[39] Thus, while opposition to the practice grows, the industry is responding with aggressive mobilization, pitting jobs and miners against the environment.[40]

"They take some of these beautiful mountains, I think they're beautiful, and they'll push the whole top of them off, to get down to the first seam of coal" (*James Wright*). A region that looks at tourism and culture as economic and social resources promotes the destruction of memory, history, and the landscape (but also attracts "disaster tourism," in which visitors tour destroyed mountaintop sites).[41]

In 1998, Arch Mineral obtained a permit to strip the top of Black Mountain, the highest peak in Kentucky and a place of great natural beauty. Judith Hensley, who was teaching junior high in Wallins, was approached by some of her students.

JUDITH HENSLEY: Did you know they're ready to blast the top off Black Mountain? And I did know, but it was their—the students'—choice; and so they decided that they wanted to get together and see what they could do to try to help save Black Mountain. Since they had the passion for the knowledge and the desire to try to make a difference, then I was more than happy to support them, and that's how the whole thing started.

"It became a statewide effort to protect the statewide treasure—our highest point" (*Robert Gipe*). "And that was a lot like the civil rights struggle. Things happen—but things don't really happen, until the children are involved" (*Connie Owens*). The children wrote letters to the Office of Surface Mining and went to Frankfort to deliver them. They sat down at the base of the mountain and did research on the Internet, "and Hazel King paid for a helicopter to take me up so I could videotape and take photographs of what was going on" (*Judith Hensley*). Other schools and community groups all over the state, including Kentuckians for the Commonwealth, joined in. "There were basically only two sides: either you want it to be mined—and they were looking at people being employed, in an occupation they knew—or they have to do it someplace else, because this place is sacred to us as a people. And while I like for people to be employed, I don't like for people to look at their job as their identity, 'cause we're always much more than that—so I lined up on the side where my heart was" (*Connie Owens*).

JUDITH HENSLEY: The children's parents actually told them, "You can't do this! Coal companies are never going to listen to a bunch of children." I had students tell me that there had been representatives from the coal mines where their fathers worked who came to their house and threatened them, "If I see your child's face in the news again, if I see any quotes from your child in the newspapers or on television, you will lose your job!" I have no proof, but they told me. It took a tremendous amount of courage, but the amazing thing was that as the parents saw that the media was involved, and that their children appeared before the legislative research commission, and they were on television, then the parents began to take pride in their child's accomplishment. So, in a way the parents vicariously gained a voice that they had never had, because their children were willing to take a stand.

And the other important point that sometimes gets left out, is that we did have a few children who—because of the job situation and because of their family stand—were opposed to saving the mountain—"If it makes jobs for two or three years for my family then it's worth blowing the mountain up." We made sure that their work was honored as much as that of the [others]. In a way they were heroes of another kind, because they were willing to stand up to their peers.

"Once the children got involved, the battle was won—for the time being" (*Connie Owens*). In the end, the state bought the mining rights from Arch, which ended up making money out of the deal anyway.[42] No mining would be allowed above 3,800 feet. "We were sort of successful in that the state bought the land and protected the highest points from mining, but it didn't protect it from logging, and, actually, closed [it], so that it became less accessible to people than it was before. So, it was hard to feel great about it when the company got paid almost ten millions on the taxpayers' dollars, and it's not likely to be a park or anything that belongs to the people at any time" (*Robert Gipe*).

> JUDITH HENSLEY: [Saving Black Mountain] does have a spiritual meaning to me because I think we are given the charge of stewardship over the earth and all forms of life on the earth. God gave man dominion but He didn't give him the right to destroy. Harlan County has been known because of the mining wars, and the bad publicity has abounded. And these children have a passion about wanting to be remembered for something good, to change the way the world looks at Harlan County. I think they gained a sense of worth, a sense of the citizens' right to an opinion, they gained a respect for themselves. And I think they realized that there is something unique about Harlan County and that they as citizens of the county and descendants in this county should be proud of where they came from, and not ashamed.[43]

ALTERNATIVES

In 1980, historian Paul F. Taylor took his labor history classes to Harlan County. They found that most of the young miners, who came from UMW families, were not interested in the union. Brookside was closed, Highsplint was nonunion, the landscape was dotted with rusty and falling tipples.[44] "You got a whole younger generation, very few of them went into the mines at all. They have the family member of the union but they don't have personal experience with the union" (*Roy Silver*).

Harlan's population increased slightly after the 1973 oil crisis but slid back in the 1980s. The vagaries of the energy market resulted in a seesaw of slumps and ephemeral "boomlets" (*Roy Silver*), but the trend remained negative. By 1997, Harlan's population was down to 40,400, with a 16 percent jobless rate; by 2007, it was 31,065, with 29.3 percent living below the official poverty line and a high percentage of the middle-aged and the elderly (39.1 percent of the population was over age forty-five) and women (52.1 percent).[45]

> DARLENE WILSON: Outmigration has resulted in a feminization of our communities. You have four times the level of female-headed households in eastern Kentucky that you have in the rest of the nation. You have more females and more children living in poverty. Women are the placekeepers, the caregivers for ailing, aging parents, and for the children. The women

stay here and take care of the kids when men go off and try to find work, and send money back home.

Since the onset of the War on Poverty, it was clear that eastern Kentucky needed to diversify its coal-based economy. The Appalachian Regional Commission felt that the region needed to be broken out of its supposed geographic and cultural isolation and brought into mainstream America. Actually, mainstream America, the absentee owner of most of the region's land and resources, was part of the problem.[46]

"I think there ought to be something on the order of Michelangelo's *David* in the rotunda of the county courthouse for all the wealth that's flowed *out* of Harlan County" (*Sid Douglass*). For decades, the profits of the companies that extracted Kentucky's natural wealth generated hardly any tax revenues for the state and the counties involved. A coal severance tax was passed in 1972; however, according to Kentuckians for the Commonwealth, the counties received only a fraction of the 50 percent that was supposed to be returned to them by the state. "In 1993 alone, there was over $16 million taken out of Harlan County in coal severance tax. And where in the hell is that money? Well, that money is divvied up in Frankfort, and it's not coming back to Harlan County" (*Joan Robinett*). Kentucky's legislature has found ways of using tax severance money to indirectly subsidize the coal companies, such as requiring counties to use it to maintain "coal haul" roads, or funding research on the conversion of coal to liquid fuel.[47]

Hundreds of millions were spent in eastern Kentucky on highways and infrastructure; tax breaks and incentives were offered to bring industry to Harlan. None of this, however, generated the expected economic diversification. At best, what came in were small furniture, apparel, and food plants—declining industries themselves, with low wage standards and no commitment to the area. Four of the seven companies that received subsidies closed or never opened.[48] "As soon as those tax incentives are gone you'll see these people pulling up and going someplace else. We've had one that's been a success. That was Tailbank, they make a very good, moderate-price upholstery, sofa, sleeper sofas, chairs, and do a wonderful job. Call centers, we have one company who has been very successful. That's a sweatshop. It's there still, but the turnover is just unbelievable, and that's not how you develop a community" (*Daniel Howard*). "Southeastern Kentucky Rehabilitati[on] Industr[ies], they make chemical weapon suits for the military, so as long as there's a war going on they're going to have a big demand for their product" (*Roy Silver*). "Southeastern Kentucky Rehabilitation Industries. They hire 30 percent disabilities. I thought that would be a good job, but, they started me out below minimum. It was not a union thing. My boss was complaining 'cause I wasn't doing things to his standards. But he didn't realize the pain that I was in. So I just said, 'Forget this.' Five sixty-five an hour is not worth it" (*Jebediah Caldwell*).

One reason for the relative feminization of the population is that many new jobs (chain stores, fast-food places) tend to employ women. "Pizza Hut. That's one of the few places in Harlan County that you can work now. They'll let you work thirty-six hours a week, but they won't let you work a forty-hour week because then they have to pay unemployment insurance" (*Mildred Shackleford*). Sherry Napier had been working thirty-five hours a week at Pizza Hut, without insurance, below minimum wage ("you're supposed to make it up in tips"), when I talked to her: "I've been called everything but a milkman [by customers] and had Cokes poured on me and everything, just 'cause their pizzas wasn't made right. Have to grit your teeth, grin, go out back and cuss, and come back in. I ain't going to stay at Pizza Hut forever. Ain't nothing here to do. And the only thing for a woman to do is Kmart or Kroger's or something."

Another form of diversification and survival in times of crisis has been the retrieval of old-time, preindustrial practices: selling snakes to churches ("We'd be on the strike [at Brookside]—had to make a dollar or two some way. I'd go chasing a few snakes. They were paying ten dollars a foot," *James Wright*), swapping guns ("A lot of times my dad dealing in guns is what made us have a good Christmas," *Donella Wynn*), raising and selling fighting roosters ("People come to the house, and they'll buy chickens off of us and that helps us out. If it wasn't for chickens, we wouldn't have a whole lot of money," *Donella Wynn*). And crafts: "The coal mines is about gone. So everybody is starting out in wood-working or whatever it takes to make a living" (*Robert Simpson*).

> SID TIBBS: We have started the Appalachian Heritage Yard Sale to reach out to artisans in the mountains. And there's hundreds and hundreds. Ladies up in the holler making quilts; people carving, blacksmithing, chair makers. And we're trying to keep it alive, pass it on down to the next generation. Gathering ginseng in Appalachia is a cultural thing. Now, you get about $300 a pound, for dried ginseng. And when it goes through ten different hands, time it gets to the Orient, you get $1,800, $2,000 a pound. So what we want to do is set up a cooperative, it would be a good supplementary income for people here in the mountains.

One night in 2007, to my surprise, I could not find a motel room in Harlan County: a nationwide ATV convention had claimed all available spaces. Tourism had long been perceived as another alternative to the coal industry.[49] Harlan possesses much natural beauty, from Kingdom Come Park to Martins Fork Lake, and there have been attempts to bank even on the "bloody" heritage. But what put Harlan on the national tourist map was the discovery that the abandoned mine roads were perfect for all-terrain vehicles. Local groups such as Mountain Crawlers and Ridge Runners have grown to attract riders from all over the United States and even from abroad. In July 2008, 1,136 ATVs joined in one parade in Harlan County, setting a Guinness-certified world record.[50]

PRESTON MCLAIN: The beauty about our mountains is the beauty itself. They come and see the scenery; they want to get away from Disney World and so forth; and they want to get back to nature with the family. We got families with children who stay a week and camp on the mountain, they enjoy the town; they enjoy the way they're treated. These trails we ride on, they were built eighty or ninety years ago with coal and logging companies. So, we don't have to disturb the environment, we just have to maintain the trails that are there. That's the beauty of it: we play on our toys.[51]

"In some ways, the place is better off now than it's ever been before. Most of the people own their own homes, they have transportation, and they have what we call the modern conveniences, the washers and dryers. And they couldn't do without TV it seems" (*Hazel King*). Economic woes did not keep Harlan from acquiring the crust of commercial modernization that homogenizes many American peripheries. In 1989, the Louisville *Courier-Journal* cited as an example of local entrepreneurship the Harlan Village Mall, built by coal operator Clyde Bennett, on what used to be a large farm outside of town.[52]

GEORGE ELLA LYON: It seems as though the malls, and the fast food, and so forth are another kind of imperialism—the materialization and the com-mercialization of all the things that we needed to have in Harlan. You should have seen what that valley was like. It was gorgeous. There were houses, there were pastures, like a sea of green. You came out of the down-town, that's all tight together, dark and close, and it really opened up, it was wonderful. And what did they do? They've got one of the largest concrete parking lots in the world at that mall.

"[There's] a very exclusive ladies' shop. Coattails is a very exclusive chil-dren's. Then we have Magic Mart, Kmart; we have Belt-Simpson, which is a fairly selective clothing store. We have, of course, drugstores. We have a drugstore here in the mall, then we also have another one over in the physi-cian's building" (*Bobbie Davidson*). Though junk food and merchandise add to Harlan's health and nutrition problems, there are signs of an implicit "cultural resistance" (*Robert Gipe*) to the idea of fast food and shopping. Harlan can bend the logic of modernity: convenience stores or gas stations become storytelling venues, people socialize leisurely in "fast" food places (I did several long interviews in McDonald's). Even air-conditioned Walmart can serve as a substitute town square.

Rick Moore, who ran the mall's record store ("I sell pop, rock, country and gospel—and rap. There's a lot of people, that listens to rap around here"), noted another function for that huge parking lot: "People, on the weekends, they just come out here and they ride around and around in circles, in the mall parking lot. That's about all there is to do around here, unless you go to a nightclub or something, and you gotta be old enough to do that." Twenty years later, when the mall was all but deserted, parking lots were still the only available public space. "Anybody that can drive goes down to Walmart parking lot or to the movie theater [lot]" (*Megan Clem*). "Since there's not a lot of stuff to do—as far as teenagers, the Walmart parking lot is a big deal" (*Donella Wynn*).

For twenty years I heard the same refrain from young people: "Ain't nothing to do." "Ain't nothing around Wallins. About the only thing you can do is get drunk every now and then" (*Lowell Hanson*). "There is nothing to do around here. We got a bowling alley and that's it. And an arcade. Like pinball games and a pool table and a few electronic games. We got a lounge. Usually packed down. The party people go there. Besides, people stay away from it because there's usually fights, there's always a fight at the lounge" (*Marjorie Napier*). "Only thing we got right now is the Eagle's. It's a dance club in Cumberland everybody goes to get drunk and show their butts and dance. I go Wednesday nights. That's the only night I get off. Any other time, I get up, I go to work, I come home, and I go to bed. Exciting life" (*Sherry Napier*). "It's nothing to do around here. We used to have a bowling alley at one time, and it went away" (*Angel Holts*). "We had a skating rink, but they shut it down. Honey, if I ever win the lotto there's going to be a place here for these kids" (*Crystal Vanover*).

KILLING THE PAIN

> ANDREW SMITH (NAME CHANGED): I was a runaway at twelve and a half year old. I ran away because from about the age five, up until the age twelve I was being physically and sexually and mentally abused. And...I lived on the road. Didn't have no money or nothing. I found out, that things that I was being made to do, at home, I could do it on the road and get money for it. So I did it, to survive. I'd stay in the bridges overnight, or I would run into somebody that wanted to have a good time and we'd go to a motel or something. And, the baddest part, every time, I would go right back into the same situation that I was running away from. I guess I just missed the abuse and stuff. That's like...the only way I know how to relate; I knew people cared about me when they abused me. After that, I started OD'ing. The first two times, I OD'ed on aspirin. I mixed 170 aspirins in a glass of water and drunk it straight down. I'm on Zoloft which is an antidepressant, Stelazine which is an antipsychotic, I'm on codeine to stop the shakes from the Stelazine. I've used marijuana, LSD, cocaine, just about every kind of drug there is now except smoke crack, I ain't done that. I have nightmares. I see a lot of stuff from my past, the things I've had to do to live. And then, I guess I feel guilty, maybe it was my fault, maybe when I was little I done something to cause all this. I don't know.

When I first came to Harlan, drugs did not seem to be a major concern: "Here, we are on the fringe of the Bible Belt, people tend to have a code of ethics, and, more likely to be antidrug," James B. Goode explained. The young people at the Harlan mall agreed that "there's some around here, but I don't think it's as bad as a lot of big cities. I haven't heard nothing—anything—about [crack]" (*Rick Moore*). Yet Frederick Brown, a preacher and the Cumberland chief of police, had a different perception:

> FREDERICK BROWN: They made one big drug raid, it was the twenty-sixth of September [1986]. Marijuana, PCP, cocaine—these are the main drugs that are on the streets now. Valiums hit the street a lot here; Procaine and Quaaludes, these things. Medication that's taken for back illness, for terminally ill people, people will get them from their doctor and they'll abuse them, sometimes forging prescriptions, and they'll take and sell 'em on the streets. They'll take marijuana and lace it down with [pills], we had a lot of people flipping out when they first started experimenting with this—they was thinking they was smoking a little harmless marijuana, in fact it had all this morphine in it and it started going directly to the brain.

As the abuse of prescription pills suggests, drugs were less a matter of tradition or counterculture than a response to psychic and economic depression. For three generations, Harlan had fought what amounted to a class struggle. By the mid-1980s, it was clear who had won, who had lost, and who was left to deal with the wreckage.[53]

> MARJORIE NAPIER (INT. 1989): A majority of the teenagers are on drugs. A lot of their parents are unemployed, the pressure is high and they go out and get drunk to sort of get away from all that. There is nothing to do around here. So—"Hey, let's go get drunk, let's go get stoned." One of my friends every time I see him he is—fried. A friend of mine died [from] crack. She used to... she sold her clothes, her jewels...

A 2008 report found a higher rate of abuse of prescription drugs in Appalachia than in the rest of the nation, especially among young people and in the coal counties. As the mountain counties of eastern Kentucky were flooded with narcotics and prescription pills, the media labeled the region as the nation's "prescription painkiller capital." OxyContin (street name "oxycotton"), a powerful painkiller introduced in 1996 by Purdue Pharma, was dubbed "hillbilly heroin." I have heard several people in Harlan County make the claim (which Purdue staunchly denies) that Appalachia was intentionally singled out as a test market.[54]

> DARLENE WILSON: Appalachia, with all of its coal-mining-related injuries and black lung and whatnot, they'd seen it as a prime marketplace. Because you have so much acute medical conditions, so many people who suffer debilitating pain, and for whom life's been one long series of painful

experiences.[55] The lightweight medicines and the lesser painkillers can't do it anymore, can't take care of the pain. So you had a lot of this drug being prescribed here legally and it was being pushed by the pharmaceutical company.

"When taken in pill form, as intended, OxyContin is a slow-release narcotic prescribed for pain caused by cancer, severe arthritis, sickle cell disease, and nerve damage."[56] "If you take it orally, the way it's supposed to be taken, it'll divide out over the hours. But they're not taking it that way; they melt it down and inject it into their veins to get an immediate really, really bad high" (*Marjorie Napier*). "Nothing can bring you down," a user said. "You don't have to think about nothing. All your troubles go away. You just feel like everything is lifted off your shoulders."[57] It's "like a candy, that everybody loves" (*Dorothy Harrison [name changed]*).

> DARLENE WILSON: It's the most seductive thing I've ever encountered. It's in your soul. Sex is better with it. Everything's enhanced, everything is pleasant. The sky is going to be blue all the time. You're lifted into a state of euphoria, you feel that life is sweet. It's very easy to become disconnected from everything. You can appear to be normal. I sat in meetings and smiled pleasantly at people, and didn't appear to be out of my head but I was. So it's the disconnect from reality that allows one not just to not feel pain but not feel deeply anything. People will sell their children's clothes, sell everything they own, steal from their parents. People will do things for this drug that they would not ever do for any other kind of substance. It takes hold of one emotionally, physically, and spiritually. It replaces all the other things you may have had faith in or relied upon—it becomes like your new God.

OxyContin addiction can sometimes begin with a single use. Used in ways other than prescribed, and in conjunction with other drugs, it can be deadly. Figures are difficult to pin down, as many estimates are based on impressionistic evidence. In 2003, a federal advisory panel claimed that OxyContin was responsible for 500 to 1,000 deaths a year; from 2000 to 2002, drug-related deaths in Kentucky were estimated at 1,300. In 2000, Harlan County sheriff Steve Duff counted at least eight OxyContin-related deaths; in 2004, the toll was eleven overdose deaths, caused by methadone, oxycodone, Xanax, or hydrocodone—not counting traffic deaths caused by driving under the influence of drugs.[58] "A boy told me one time—he had went to rehab, and got off drugs—he said: 'You see old drunks walking around on the streets; you see old potheads walking around on the street. But you don't see an old pillhead, you know, because they die'" (*Donella Wynn*).

In 1996, Dorothy Harrison's husband was prescribed OxyContin after surgery following a mining accident.

DOROTHY HARRISON (NAME CHANGED): So that began the nightmare of hell for me. It changes people; it changes them into a person that you never knew before. A caring person turns into somebody that they don't care if you're on this earth. Monsters. He used to be a caring father, a caring husband. And it just turned him into an evil person. He was probably in a lot of pain, in the beginnings of crippling rheumatoid arthritis. At first he was taking it by mouth, how you're supposed to take it. Within six months he started snorting it. He had to keep taking more and more and when he tried to come down off them, his bones would ache so bad—because, it's their bones. And they feel like they're having withdrawals and flulike symptoms. That's why so many of them overdose. And they mix with Xanax, so—the Xanax and the OxyContin is deadly together. That and Xanax and methadone. Deadly.

"There's not hardly been a family in this town that's hasn't been touched by it. We have kids that their parents were drug addicts before they were born" (*Jenny Saylor*). "There has been the downturn in population, with that loss of jobs: people have left; their children have left; we have been left with an element who has been on welfare subsistence. They have no initiative to move; they have no initiative to get a job. So these people are hooked" (*Daniel Howard*). "People who don't get up in the morning with purpose in their life—like a fish floundering out of water on the bank gasping for air—enter into this void where there is so much pain and so much confusion and a lack of a sense of personal purpose that they try to dull the pain" (*Judith Hensley*).

Darlene Wilson was prescribed OxyContin by three doctors after she had surgery for a broken wrist.

DARLENE WILSON: So I was getting a huge quantity of it. I didn't shoot it up, I wasn't snorting it. I was breaking them in half, chewing them up. Taking half of one in the morning, the other half three or four hours later, another half—you know...And I was smiling and not realizing just how addicted I was becoming. And then one day they just quit giving me the prescriptions—and so when I ran out it took about a week, and I was in the full throes of withdrawal. Hallucinations, tremors and convulsions and sweating and inability to sleep, panic attacks, anxiety attacks, physical problems. You don't tend to eat very much while you're doing it, you don't feel hungry for anything except another pill, so a lot of people are finding that they're doing serious damage to their health while they're addicted to it. And then I turned to alcohol, because it was cheap and free. Then I found people who could get me some [pills] and I'd drink on top of them.

"My dad had his leg crushed in the mines, he's had problems with his back, he has to take heavy painkillers, and he has to lock his medication up because we've had people come in and take stuff from our house and some of it has been his medications" (*Danielle Burke*). "I'll never forget the first day that he got his Oxys. We wasn't home five minutes, people were calling asking [to] buy them. I know somebody from the pharmacy had to tell them that he had bought the pills there. [Then] he started selling things out of my home, or he was giving them to somebody for money. He told me they were stolen" (*Dorothy Harrison*). "I almost would say I had a perfect marriage. I never was talked down to. Always was told I could do anything I wanted do, be whatever I wanted to be. Anyway, he got hurt in the mines, and had back operations and they put him on OxyContin and on October 19, 2000, his friend murdered him [to steal his pills]" (*Tammy Haywood*).

> DARLENE WILSON: It didn't take long for a very interesting social phenomenon to occur where Grandpa was getting it for his cancer— grandson says, "Grandpa, I can make you some money on those." Grandpa doesn't have his black lung yet, couldn't get a disability; now he's dying of cancer and needs the money. So he keeps half of his prescription and gives the other half to his grandson to sell. Grandson gets busted; Grandpa feels devastated because he has contributed to it.

Between 2003 and 2007 the *Harlan Daily Enterprise* ran more than two hundred front-page drug-related headlines. Drugs were found in mines, in the jail, near schools, in cars after routine traffic stops; police raids yielded dozens of arrests.[59] Pharmacies were burglarized: in 2007, two burglaries in Cumberland netted almost $80,000 worth of stolen narcotics. In 2003, a Harlan doctor was sentenced to twenty years in prison for prescribing drugs without a legitimate medical purpose. "That was the one, behind the mall in Harlan, before they turned the power on to his office he had people lined up for the prescriptions for OxyContins, and for years people knew that if you wanted a certain kind of drug there was a certain doctor you could go to" (*Roy Silver*). "There were a couple of places that were real prescription mills—you'd see a doctor for less than thirty seconds or less than three minutes, and all you'd have to say is 'I'm in pain' wink wink. There were a few doctors who were writing literally thousands of prescriptions a week" (*Darlene Wilson*). A doctor, charged with prescribing pills in exchange for cash or sex, was caught before he managed to escape to the Cayman Islands. Another was arrested in 2009, with his partner, for prescribing OxyContin, methadone, and other drugs to hundreds of clients, knowing they were not for personal use.[60]

"In the beginning, they probably experiment with drugs because of peer pressure and boredom. Our culture has changed from a couple of generations ago, where children had chores, and responsibilities that filled up their time until they became an adult. Now there is this huge gap between say twelve and eighteen or nineteen years of age, where they have money that they didn't have to earn, they have cars that they didn't have to work and pay for, and they have no constructive way to be challenged or to fill up that time" (*Judith Hensley*). "I talked to a girl a couple of weeks ago. She was clearly suffering, from anxiety and depression. And instead of dealing with the problems that was causing it, she says, 'I need to go to the doctor and get some pills.' It's a mind-set. A lot of parents are taking their teenage kids—'You need to go see the doctor. He'll give you some nerve pills.' Instead of saying, 'What's your problem and let's work through it'" (*Carla Jo Barrett*). "And I talked to a girl I went to school with; a real good girl. And this is somebody you would never in a million years would dream would ever do anything like that, and she told me, she said—she said, 'You wouldn't believe the things that I have done to get a pill.' She said—she said, 'I am ashamed of myself, but I still do it. And it's bad'" (*Jane Perkins*).

"The street price on it now, is like two dollars a gram; you get a bottle of pills of fifty, you can make thousands of dollars. Kids try to sell it and then they get hooked on it and then they start stealing from their family and neighbors. In class when this first started, I'd ask how many know someone that is involved in this, you'd get maybe 10, 15 percent of the class; now it's not unusual to get the whole class to say that they know someone who's impacted" (*Roy Silver*). The college's Listening Project found people who were selling pills to pay their bills. "We can't understand how to respond to drug abuse until we understand its roots in our economic situation" (*Joan Robinett*).[61]

DOROTHY HARRISON: Things had been missing from my home. My rings were gone. I don't think nobody stole them, I believe, you know, he was selling things. He was making twenty-six hundred dollars a month and it was gone just like that. No bills paid or nothing else. I went to pick up my check at school one week and my check was for eleven dollars. And I said, "Something's wrong. I mean, y'all give me the wrong check." And they said no, that they were garnishing my wages because he was not paying the bills. He was taking his money and blowing it and snorting it and whatever. So I was so angry at my husband; I went home early—and there he was with a bunch of whores. And a bunch of men from the neighborhood, snorting pills off my counter. And I was so angry—and my blood pressure was up, too, because all these things was just hitting me—then I shot at him. And that was the last thing I remember. I've shot guns all my life and I never aimed at nobody. Never. [But] I'm a very good shooter. And especially with that .38. But, you know, my daughter, she had jerked my arm up and was holding it. And that's what brought me to.

In 2005, in the woods on top of Stone Mountain, Chester Napier showed me the remains of a methamphetamine lab that had burned down. "I think they're going into other types of drugs. Like cocaine and meth. Meth is starting to increase. As OxyContin use goes down, the others go up" (*Carla Jo Barrett*). "Oxys now it's a little harder to get a hold of than maybe a year ago. Meth's moving on up into this area. I mean, a lot of people will get addicted and they'll just grab anything they can, whether it's a Lortab or a Xanax, anything" (*Donella Wynn*). "I have friends that do drugs and they will take different pills—OxyContin, Lortabs, Percocet, Darvocet, and they will put 'em in a line and they call 'em totem poling" (*Maxine Clay*). In the first months of 2005, methadone, oxycodone, Xanax, and hydrocodone had already claimed three lives in Harlan County.[62]

> BONNIE THOMAS: I was nineteen, a single mother; I lived in South Carolina, and was fresh out of an abusive relationship. I didn't have any meaning in my life, and just didn't have any will to live. A girl that lived above me introduced me to crystal meth, which I call the monster because that's what it will make you, and I did it for about two years. Then I met my husband and I quit because he was a good guy and he brought a little bit of meaning to my life. We got married and within a year I was pregnant with my twins. After I had them, I got really depressed and things got bad again. The same lady came back into my life and I started using again. It was the only relief I knew and at that point the monster had me. It was just a downward spiral from there. Within six months I gave up my husband and kids, gave up my house, gave up everything I had, and moved into a little trailer park and dealt with my guilt and shame by using even more. I lost everybody and everything. I went with that for about two years and when I woke up one morning in the woods beat up, naked, and had no clue what had happened to me, that was enough. I had reached a turning point. I told God, "If You can get me up off this ground and get me to Kentucky with my kids, I will do better, I will get some purpose, some meaning in my life." And that's what I have done. With God's help I found that meaning and purpose in my life; it was within me the whole time, I just didn't realize it.

ON HIGHER GROUND

> CONNIE OWENS: And part of that is, and that's I think blood on our hands, that before this came, we maybe didn't do enough, to make sure they knew their value as people, as creatures. Just the basest of levels. We failed.

> DOROTHY HARRISON: [My husband] always told me I would never make anything of myself and I was no good. I got tired of that life, and I went on to college, and it opened my eyes to a lot of different things.

The wounds of class are deeper than broken backs and broken lungs. They sink into the soul and erode people's sense of themselves and of their environment. Perhaps not much can be done at this time about economics, politics, power. But the struggle to stay alive, perhaps to fight another day, begins with the healing of the wounds in the soul, the recovery of the people's and the culture's sense of self-esteem.

> ALICIA THOMAS: I started drug use at about fifteen or sixteen, I started smoking marijuana and taking the nerve pills, pain pills, drinking, had a car wreck, killed someone and went to prison at age eighteen and when I got out I chose to go to Lexington and to another rehab center and they helped me get a job, get an apartment, I was staying clean. [Then] I got in a bad relationship, he was a drug user, so out of fear of relapsing I chose to come home and got enrolled in [college] and I graduate in December and I plan to be a certified alcohol and drug abuse counselor.

An important change I have seen over the years in Harlan is the development of what, for lack of a better term, we might call a small but committed group of organic intellectuals, coming out of citizens' groups or Southeast Kentucky Community and Technical College in Cumberland. Increasingly, the college and its Appalachian Center have become a resource in the search for a personal and cultural identity, a trade, and a way to cope with hard times.

> ROBERT GIPE: In the spring of 2002, we [at Southeast Appalachian Center] got a request for proposals from the Rockefeller Foundation [on] how to use the arts to address a tough community issue. One of our assets was storytelling ability, creativity—and our education system had so marginalized people's need to express themselves and to be creative that this is something that we could address. Another thing was that we thought that we could deal with something that had to do with the arts. [This way] we could fly beneath the radar of the power structure, you know. Not just gathering stories, but gathering people together.

The project, known as PACT (Partnership Affirming Community Transformation), drew on the community's own resources and skills: photography ("Almost everyone had had his hands-on experience with photography"), performance ("And every Friday, in some of the little schools, people had to get up, say a poem or sing a song, recite a speech"), crafts. "And the other thing was to address the lack of public art, which of course gets you into the lack of public space" (*Robert Gipe*).

> DANIELLE BURKE: We had [an] age range from two to ninety-two that were involved in the photo project, and we gave them disposable cameras and we told them to take pictures of what they would like to change about Harlan County and what they would like to see stay the same. We got back some really beautiful pictures and then some pictures of trash and things like that.

Donella Wynn: The first year we took pictures of stuff that we liked and stuff that we thought was real important here in Evarts. We went down behind Dairy Hut, and there was a lot of garbage on the riverbank and a lot of the students took pictures of that. Just because they didn't like that. Because, you know, it's really pretty down there but people had damaged it. There was like a waterfall that we took some pictures of and people had spray-painted on it, on the rocks. So, that's what a lot of people took pictures of, that they didn't like.

Theresa Osborne: If we want to tell the story of Harlan County through photography and tile and the play you can't have just all bright and happy cheery things because that's not being truthful and you have beautiful things side by side with really bad things.

Danielle Burke: I know of these two pictures that everybody that saw these two pictures the impact was just kind of like, "Whoa!" One picture was of a picture of Jesus and the other picture was of pills and a syringe and money and a gun laying on a couch and they were put side by side, and that was a very powerful thing.

The photography project (and the beautiful tile mural that grew out of it, now on permanent display at the college) relied on the visual imagination of the younger generation. In turn, the Listening Project, coordinated by Joan Robinett, focused on the storytelling skills of Harlan's anecdotal society, and—as all oral history should—on changing the interviewers through the experience of listening. "We started talking about, what gives your life power and meaning? They started talking about family gatherings and relationships and get-togethers and singings and homecomings and all the things that really didn't have anything to do with the economics of the place and more about the people and relationships" (Theresa Osborne).

Jane Perkins: We went out and picked people. Like the two ladies I picked, I thought they were interesting. One was blind and she had a lot of interesting things to tell. And then the other one, I know she was in with the coal strike and stuff, which she didn't really talk that much about it. She mainly went into ghost stories. I loved it. We talked to all kinds of people, young people, old people, coal miners, stories about growing up, what molded you into the person you are, the things that helped you raise your kids and what are the morals and stuff that you need to pass on to the kids. It's a way of bringing people together, helping each learn about each other, and to know that there are people out there that cares. I think it gives you a better sense of where you're from. A little bit more pride in your county. Because people did work really hard back in the old days to get you where you're at, and people forget that.

"It gives us a little pride, it's let us show off where we're from, before we got pushed aside and, ridiculed and give a bad name" (*Donella Wynn*). "I met with people that had been through things that I had been through—drug abuse in the home and having to deal with it and work and trying to keep them out of jail and trying to get them in rehab...That opened my eyes to a whole lot of different things and they would tell me things that I already knew but I just did not want to believe" (*Dorothy Harrison*). "Even though what I had been through was bad, it's always something worser with somebody else, so I consider myself very lucky that I didn't lose my mind and I could help deal with their problems instead of just focusing on mine" (*Tammy Haywood*). As Joan Robinett put it: "Our lives here have been steeped in the tragedy and problems of a community long exploited from within and without. We've been disempowered far too long. But we are stubborn and the Listening Project has helped us mobilize our stubbornness into determination and new possibilities."[63]

The stories became the foundations of a community play, called *Higher Ground*. Written by Jo Carson, an Appalachian playwright with a genius for making poetry and theater out of everyday speech, directed by Jerry Stropnicky, choreographed by Kevin Iega Jeff, the play opened at the college in October 2005 with a cast of more than a hundred, and was seen by more than three thousand people locally in 2005 and 2006.[64] As the *Harlan Daily Enterprise* wrote, "*Higher Ground* celebrates the strengths of Harlan County while looking at how these strengths can be used to help the county cope with its current challenges such as drug abuse."[65] The performances showcased the extraordinary narrative, theatrical, and musical talent to be found among the everyday people of Harlan. *Higher Ground* and the 2009 PACT production, *Playing with Fire*, offered an example of self-expression and cooperation to a community that had been fragmented and silenced. "The cast's energy, diversity, awareness of one another onstage, and joy in one another's company provided perhaps the play's greatest impact," reported Robert Gipe.[66] After being written and sung about in so many ways, Harlan was speaking and singing in its own voice.

Higher Ground refers to the memory of the floods, when people sought "higher ground" from the waters, but it is also a metaphor for the flood of drugs, "the medicine floating around" Harlan County.[67] Two of the most memorable scenes are the arrest of a pill-mongering doctor and the much acclaimed "dance of the zombies":

> *I've got a pain, I've got a pain,*
> *I've got a pain in my hip,*
> *in my back, in my neck...*
> *in my soul.*
> *And I'm searching for a cure*
> *to take my pain away.*

Other scenes focus on the lessons of personal responsibility to be drawn from the stories (in one, a father gives a car to his son—who then realizes that the only way he'll get it to run is by learning how to fix it himself).[68] Understandably, *Higher Ground* stays away from controversial themes—politics, the coal industry, the environment. What is does is more basic: it reconstructs the people's and the community's faith in themselves, which is the prerequisite to being able to stand up to all these things.

> ROBERT GIPE: It took us a hundred years to get into this, then it'll take a hundred years to get out. Maybe not even the seed has been planted, but the ground has been turned. America, the people who get the most frustrated and cynical about [it], they're great believers. And to me, that's what America was supposed to be—even though some people might end up with more money and [things]—that we were all trying to build a country that truly believed in democracy and the right [for] everybody to participate, and so, I feel like for the last three years we've done our part in the hundred-year struggle.

> TAMMY HAYWOOD: So here I was with a fourteen-year-old daughter and was nothing but a daddy's girl and I had lost everything. So I thought I was going to lose my mind. And my friend said, "Go to school." I had been out of school for twenty years and didn't care a lot about school, as a teenager. I went and signed up and got in college. Met a lot of different people, made a lot of friends. And we got in the Appalachians class and we started to talk about what things we'd like to see different. And I thought, we'll change the county, then we'll work on the country, then we'll change the world.

People I Owe

I have heard a storm of words [around] me, enough to write several hundred songs and that many books. I know that these words are not my own private property. . . . I borrowed them from you, the same as I walked through the high winds and borrowed enough air to keep me moving. . . . Your works and my works held hands and they never did separate. . . . The only story that I have tried to write has been you. . . . You are the poet and your everyday talk is our best poem by our best poet. . . . I am no more, nor less, than your clerk that writes it down, like a debt always owed and partly paid. This book is a book of debt and part payment.

—Woody Guthrie, *People I Owe*

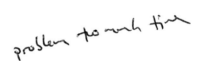

<u>It has taken me almost twenty years to complete this</u> book, and it has taken the help of hundreds of people to be able to even think of writing it. More than 150 are the ones whose words make up these pages and who are listed in the narrators page that follows. Many others, however, contributed by making it possible for me to hear their voices.

To begin with, the people who brought me to Harlan and to Kentucky: Barbara Dane, who first taught me the Harlan County songs and aroused my passion; David Walls, who first took me and my wife, Mariella Eboli, there (and Frank Casale, who connected us), and then John Stephenson and Ramona Lumpkin, who arranged for me to be the first international James Still Fellow at the University of Kentucky's Appalachian Center. John Stephenson was crucial in establishing a faculty exchange program between the University of Kentucky and my university in Rome; though badly underfinanced, the program has managed to stay alive all these years and create contacts and friendships across the waters.

Then, the people who gave me hospitality and in whose homes I stayed. The Napier family—the unforgettable Annie, her husband, Chester, their daughters, Sherry and Marjorie, and their grandchildren, Duke, Scooter, and Deirdre, are my

Kentucky family and kinfolks. They fed me, sheltered me, guided me, introduced to people, and told me endless stories over the years. For years, Annie would drop everything and drive around with me to do interviews, which she enjoyed at least as much as I did. And I was moved by the example of Annie's half sister, Becky Simpson, her husband, Bob, and their Cranks Creek Survival Center.

I first came into Harlan County via Lynch, when William H. Turner, then at the University of Kentucky, arranged for me to stay with his parents, Naomi and Earl, and to meet his brother, Irwin, his grandmother Minnie Randolph, and his neighbors in Lynch. All these years, Bill Turner has been an inspiration (and an early source of precious contacts also outside Lynch), and his family an example of wisdom and warmth.

My other "Kentucky home" was provided by my personal guru, Gurney Norman, and Nyoka Hawkins. For years, my trips to Kentucky began and ended with long talks into the night with Gurney and Nyoka. Gurney also drove me around Harlan and Hazard, lent me his car to get to Harlan the first couple of years (Debbie Bays also gave me the use of her pickup truck, later on), and his concept of an immaterial but living and breathing "Kentucky Folk School" connecting Lexington, Harlan, and the community of academics, activists, and students in Rome has kept us together all these years.

Mariella and I spent a few memorable nights at Don West's Appalachian Folklife Center, where he tested our authenticity by getting us to help him round up the cows and explained to us the many layers of meaning in Appalachian "fundamentalist" religion.

I stayed with the UMW's Joanne Delaplaine in Washington, and she made it possible for me to consult the union's archives; with Mike Henson in Cincinnati, where he arranged interviews with Harlan migrants in Lower Price Hill and other parts of the city; with Joan Robinett and Andy Jones in Harlan (and they helped me with interviews on Pine Mountain). And Linda Eklund, my New York sister, who listened to my endless stories, gave me a roof many a time on my way to Harlan and back, and a friendship I have treasured for many decades now.

I wish to devote a special thought and recollection to Hazel King, the fantastic Harlan County lady who almost single-handedly took up the fight to protect her beloved mountains. Hazel recognized the value of what I was trying to do, and took time to come along with me to some of the most important interviews in this book, including with her neighbors in Louellen and Black Bottom, and some of the protagonists of the Brookside mine strike. When I was on the road, she always called to make sure I arrived safely where I was going.

I also received support and guidance from many institutions—always, through the personalized goodwill and passion of individual people. First of all, of course, the Appalachian Studies Center at the University of Kentucky, my Appalachia "alma mater," as it were. After John Stephenson, I was welcomed and helped by Ronald Eller, and then by Herb Reid, Joanna Badagliacco, Evelyn

Knight, Dwight Billings, Alan De Young, and many more. My most important research resource has been Special Collections at the University of Kentucky's Margaret E. King Library, and the wonderful people I met there who opened their files and papers, the remarkable oral history collection, the photography fund: Anne (Campbell) Ritchie, Kate Black, Terry Birdwhistell, Doug Boyd, Jason Flahardy (thanks to Betsy Brinson, the first twenty years of my Harlan County tapes are now in their archives). At Southeastern Community and Technical College, in Cumberland, Harlan County, I found a community of committed teachers and researchers: James B. Goode, who introduced me to their oral history collection, and, more recently, the essential Bob Gipe, and Theresa Osborne, Connie Owens, and Larry LaFollette (at least one visit, and one set of interviews, was funded through Southeast's PACT project).

Two of my dream institutions are in Appalachia, and I was lucky enough to get to know them firsthand. First, the Highlander Center for Social Research, where Myles Horton, Helen Lewis, John Gaventa, Sue Thrasher, and Guy and Candie Carawan (who introduced me to Hugh and Julia Cowans and to the Cranks Creek Survival Center) gave us hospitality, talked to us for hours, opened their library and tapes, and provided a model for creative and democratic education. And then Appalshop—I've said publicly that Appalshop is what I hope the Circolo Gianni Bosio, the organization I founded in Rome, will be when it grows up, and I mean it: a cultural experience deeply rooted in and committed to a specific community, but capable of making film, music, and history with a worldwide appeal. Mimi Pickering and Dee Davis (also at Rural Strategies) were my primary contacts, friends, and hosts; and along with them many others, from Elizabeth Barret to Herb Smith, Andy Garrison, Josephine Richardson, Anne Lewis, Rich Kirby, and more. Through John Stephenson and Loyal Jones, I was able to access the Appalachian Archive at Berea College. Ned Irwin, at East Tennessee University, gave me access to old recordings of the Garland clan and Tillman Cadle, which I did not use in the book but which helped me gain a closer understanding of those people and those times. And perhaps the most precious of all, Mary Marshall Clark (and Ronald Grele, her predecessor as director of the Columbia University Oral History Office): their Summer Institute has been my home base in the United States for years and years, and they have offered stimulating intellectual and political environment, a warm friendship, a lot of good advice, and another home. Mary Marshall and Ron have been constantly supportive of my Harlan County project: they brought Annie Napier to New York, where her eloquence and humor stunned the Summer Institute fellows; provided the stimulus and the support for *I Can Almost See the Lights of Home*, the "essay in sound" I co-produced with Charles Hardy III after he challenged me to use sound rather than just writing as a way of bringing oral history to an audience; and they also helped generously with transcriptions (talking of transcription, I would like to thank and acknowledge Glenna Richardson and Patty Smith in Lexington, Angel Holt in Harlan, and

Nathanial Peterson Moore in Rome, who transcribed the tapes I was not up to doing myself).

And then there is the Italian side. Agostino Lombardo, chair of the English and American Literature Department at the University of Rome "La Sapienza," was broadminded enough to understand that we could stretch an academic definition of "literature" to include oral history, music, and human solidarity. When no other sources were available, the department has contributed to travel expenses to Harlan. Most importantly, through Professor Lombardo's support (and to the university's Theater Department), I was able to get the university to fund three Appalachian conferences that allowed us to bring to Rome representative of Highlander and Appalshop, and artists, writers, scholars, and organizers including James Still, Hazel Dickens, Jo Carson, Gurney Norman, John Stephenson, Bill Turner, Guy and Candie Carawan, Ed Cabbell, Linda Parris Bailey, Gail Story, and—most precious of all—once again Annie Napier. A small grant from the National Research Council supported the first conference, but they were all made possible by the passion and hard work of my colleagues Annalucia Accardo, Cristina Mattiello, Anna Scannavini, and all the students and graduate students who for years fluctuated around our Appalachian Project.

All this came to fruition thanks to Oxford University Press. My thanks go to Rob Perks, who first made the connection; to Nancy Toff, to whose sympathetic editing I owe the fact that my huge manuscript achieved a manageable size without losing any of its meaning and form (and, indeed, gaining much in clarity and purpose); and to Sonia Tycko and Joellyn Ausanka: I couldn't imagine more helpful, patient, and able co-workers than they have been throughout the final stages of the project.

And finally: the Hinze family started it all by taking me in for a year as a foreign exchange student in Los Angeles half a century ago, in 1960.

The Narrators

INTERVIEWS

The list below indicates for each person year of birth, type of employment, and place and date of the interview(s). In some cases some information was not collected at the time of the interview and is missing. I indicate for all individuals either the work in which they have been employed for the most important part of their lives or the job they were working at the time of the interview. When no employment is indicated, in the case of women, this means that all their life work was carried out in the home. Where noted, names have been changed for privacy or other reasons. Unless otherwise indicated, all interviewees were born or living in Harlan County and all the interviews were carried out in Harlan County by the author. The list includes a few people whose interviews, for various reasons (such as faulty recording at times), were not directly quoted in the text but contributed to its general background anyhow and ought to be recognized. This list includes narrators who were not interviewed by me but to whose tape or original transcript I had access; it does not include the narrators I from published sources, which are always specified in the notes.

Quotes from the narrators are credited in two ways: at the beginning, in the case of long, separate and indented quotes (the type I describe in the introduction as _arias_); after the quote, italicized and in parentheses, in the case of shorter quotes mounted in running paragraphs in which several voices, including at times my own, are heard (what I describe in the introduction as _chorales_). When I thought it would help the reader place the quotations in historical time, I have inserted the interviewee's year of birth or the date of the interview.

This list also includes the names of a few people whose interviews were carried out by other researchers. In all cases I had access either to the original tape or to the full transcript. I list the names of the interviewers and, where appropriate, the archive.

Ewell Balltrip, 1950, journalist, *Harlan Daily Enterprise*, Harlan, July 16, 1987
Carla Jo Barrett, 1965, training specialist, Kentucky Transitional Assistance Program, October 21, 2008
James Belew, 1916, coal miner, union organizer, Wallins Creek, August 28, 1991

Clyde Bennett, 1930, coal operator, Harlan, December 26, 1989

Lewis Bianchi, 1924, funeral home owner, Evarts, November 3, 1990

Jeff Bittner, 1971, Harlan, October 24, 1988

John Bledsoe, coal mine inspector, Harlan, October 25, 1988

Dallas Blue, 1925, truck driver, Coxton, October 29, 1988

Kate Blue, 1909, Coxton, October 29, 1988

Elizabeth Blum, 1941 (Norwich, Vermont), former VISTA worker, Delta
flight 740 New York–Rome, October 19, 1996

Becky Ruth Brae, 1958, musician, songwriter, Cranks, December 23, 1989,
September 28, 1997

Frederick Brown, 1943, Baptist minister, Cumberland chief of police,
Cumberland, October 7, 1986

Danielle Burke, 1982, student, Cumberland, June 13, 2005

Parris Burke, 1919, coal miner, Wallins Creek, August 25, 1991

Tillman Cadle, 1902, coal miner, NMU organizer, Townsend, Tennessee,
July 25, 1987, November 20, 1989

Lottie Caldwell, 1906, farmer, Chapel-Laurel Creek, August 27, 1991

Jebediah Caldwell, 1978, unemployed, Harlan, July 2, 2001

John Caldwell, 1901, logger, farmer, Chapel-Laurel Creek, August 27, 1991

Ben Campagnari, 1917, coal miner, Harlan Sunshine, October 28, 1988

Thea Carter, 1916, Pentecostal preacher, Laurel Hill (Bell Co.), August 26,
1991

Ed Cawood, 1906, banker, Harlan, October 27, 1988

Maxine Clay, 1967, Cumberland, June 13, 2008

Chester Clem, 1956, coal miner, musician, Lenarue, September 6, 2006

Megan Clem, 1981, student, musician, Lenarue, September 6, 2006

Betty Cole, 1931, Cawood, December 24, 1989

Jack Colley, 1913 (Logan Co., West Virginia), insurance agent, October
29, 1988

Iverson Minter Cook (aka Louisiana Red), 1932 (Vicksburg,
Mississippi), musician, December 27, 1988, Rome, Italy

Hugh Cowans, 1920 (Cardinal, Bell Co.), coal miner, Baptist preacher,
union organizer, Lexington, September 28, 1983

Julia Cowans, 1925 (Cardinal, Bell Co.), Lexington, September 28, 1983,
August 18, 1988

Sudie Crusenberry, 1934, union activist, Brookside, November 23, 1989

Mary Cummen (Minnesota), Franciscan sister, Harlan, October 24, 1988

Hiram Day, coal miner, August 28, 1991, July 7, 1997

Bobbie Davidson, 1938, coal miner, nurse, Harlan, November 2, 1990

Junior Deaton, 1927, coal miner, merchant, union organizer, Ages,
August 25, 1991

Melody Donegan [name changed], 1965, Cranks Creek, October 23, 1989

Sid Douglass, 1941, lawyer, Loyall, July 13, 1987

Ray Ellis, 1911, coal miner, Evarts, September 9, 1993

Constance Ellison, 1925, teacher, Benham, March 23, 1999 (interviewed by Betsy Brinson, Kentucky Civil Rights Oral History Project)

Henry Farmer, 1935, coal miner, Cranks Creek, November 1, 1990

Omie Gent, 1918, factory worker, Kildav, October 18, 1996

Will Gent, 1948, miner, longshoreman, Kildav, October 18, 1996

Robert Gipe, 1963, college teacher, writer, Harlan, September 4, 2006

James B. Goode, 1948, writer, college teacher, Benham, October 27, 1988

Kevin Greer, 1960, carpenter, Harlan, September 4, 2006

Frances "Granny" Hager, midwife, union activist, Hazard (Perry Co.), September 11, 1973; Lothair (Perry Co.), March 31, 1973, March 28, 1978, interviewed by Mike Mullins, Appalachian Oral History Project, Alice Lloyd College

Linda Hairston, 1954, salesperson, Lynch, October 8, 1986

Dorothy Harrison [name changed], 1956, teacher, Cawood, June 14, 2005

Judith Hensley, 1951, teacher, Harlan, July 1, 2001

Clarissa Hoff, 1966, Cawood, June 14, 2005

Larry Holcomb, 1945, social worker, Cincinnati, Ohio, July 3, 2001

Faith Holsdorf, 1943 (New York), teacher, Youngstown, Ohio, May 19, 2001

Angel Holt, 1978, medical assistant, Rosspoint, June 16, 2005

Myles Horton, 1912, founder, Highlander Center for Social Research, New Market, Tennessee, September 23, 1983, July 16, 1987

Gladys Hoskins, 1922, secretary, Harlan Chamber of Commerce, Harlan, October 16, 1996

Daniel E. Howard, 1946, merchant, mayor of Harlan, Harlan, July 2, 2001

Arthur Johnson, 1928, musician, Cumberland, October 23, 1988, October 16, 1996

Jerry Johnson, 1945, coal miner, Wise, Virginia, July 18, 1987

Mossie Johnson, 1918, Straight Creek (Bell Co.), October 11, 1993

Nancy Johnson, 1931, teacher, March 19, 1999, Harlan (interviewed by Betsy Brinson, Kentucky Civil Rights Oral History Project)

Delbert Jones 1930, coal miner, Closplint, October 24, 1988

Dukey Jones, 1917, funeral home owner, Harlan, November 3, 1990

Johnny Jones, 1909, coal miner, Lynch, October 8, 1986

Joyce Jones, 1951, coal miner, Lynch, October 8, 1986

Meedia Jones, 1921, Highsplint, October 24, 1989

Hazel King, 1919, retired military, Highsplint, October 24, 1988, October 28, 1988

Otis King, 1982, preacher, coal miner, Jones Creek, December 23, 1989

Sill Leach, 1925, coal miner, Wallins Creek, August 25, 1991

Nellie Leach, Wallins Creek, August 25, 1991

Bill Lee, 1944, coal miner, Cumberland/Pride Terrace, October 7, 1986

Mary Beth Lee, 1991, student, Harlan, June 16, 2005

Willetta Lee, 1959, housing development manager, Cumberland/Pride Terrace, October 7, 1986

Lloyd Lefevre, 1913, coal miner, Louellen, July 19, 1987

Hazel Leonard, 1917, Black Bottom, October 28, 1988

Ben Lewis, 1919, logger, farmer, Big Laurel/Greasy Creek, August 27, 1991

Timothy Lewis, 1978, maintenance worker, Iraq War veteran, Cumberland, June 15, 2005

George Ella Lyon, 1949, writer, college teacher, musician, Lexington, July 15, 1987 (interviewed by Annalucia Accardo), November 2, 1988

Frank Majority, 1918, stonemason, Whitesburg (Letcher Co.), October 21, 1988

Lee Marsili, 1928, mine foreman, Lynch, July 19, 1987

Nancy Mayer [name changed], 1966, Harlan, October 24, 1988

Preston McLain, 1951, telephone company employee, Evarts, September 5, 2006

Mickey Messer, coal miner, then horse farm employee, Nicholasville (Fayette Co.), November 3, 1988

J. D. Miller, doctor, Evarts/Clover Fork Clinic, October 31, 1990

Bernard Mimes, 1925, coal miner, Lynch, October 10, 1986

Rick Moore, 1967, music store owner, Harlan, October 28, 1990

Annie Napier, 1942, school bus driver, Cranks Creek, July 10, 1986, July 17, 1987, October 23, 1988, December 25, 1989, November 3, 1990, November 23, 1991, October 11, 1993, October 16, 1996, October 20, 1996, June 4, 2005; Rome, Italy, January, 19, 1989, January, 23, 1989

Chester Napier, 1941, truck driver, Cranks Creek, July 17, 1987, October 23, 1988, December 25, 1989, October 11, 1993, October 15, 1996

Deirdre "Dee Dee" Napier, 1987, student, Cranks Creek, June 16, 1996

Duke Napier, 1980, factory worker, Cranks Creek, June 16, 2007

Fred Napier, 1899, logger, coal miner, Smith, July 12, 1986

Marjorie "Petey" Napier, 1969, nurse, city police worker, December 28, 1989, November 3, 1990, July 1, 2001

Martha Napier, 1914, Smith, July 12, 1986

Sherry Napier, 1973, waitress, Harlan, November 3, 1990

Charlotte Nolan, 1928, actress, writer, teacher, Harlan, October 26, 1988

Mary Esther Nolan, store employee, October 26, 1988

Gurney Norman, 1936 (Lee Co., Virginia), writer, college teacher, New York, September 27, 1987 (interviewed by Ronald Grele; Columbia Oral History Office Archive); Lexington, November 11, 1996, October 15, 2009

Albino Nunes, 1933 (Philippines), doctor, Harlan, September 6, 2006

Donna Nunes, Harlan, September 6, 2006

Theresa Osborne, 1956, college teacher, Cumberland, June 13, 2005

Constance Owens, 1951, coal company employee, church administrator, Cumberland, June 13, 2005; Lynch, June 15, 2005

Gary Page, 1966, Pentecostal preacher, coal miner, Cranks, October 20, 2008

Porter Peeples, teacher, Lynch, 1999 (interviewed by Betsy Brinson, Kentucky Civil Rights Oral History Project)

Jane Perkins, 1965, Evarts, June 15, 2006

Bill Raines, 1959 (Bell Co.), social worker, Cincinnati, Ohio, July 3, 2001

Minnie Randolph, 1894 (Alabama), Lynch, October 3, 1986

Florence Reece, 1900, union activist, New Market, Tennessee, August 31, 1968 (interviewed by Myles Horton)

Sam Reece, 1900, coal miner, union activist, New Market, Tennessee, August 31, 1968 (interviewed by Myles Horton)

Bobby Reynolds, 1954, unemployed, Wallins, November 10, 1993

Charlotte Rhodes, restaurant owner, Cumberland, June 14, 2005

Joan Robinett, 1945, teacher, environmental activist, Dayhoit, November 9, 1993; Benham, October 16, 1996

Mary Rogers, 1915, educator, Pine Mountain Settlement School, August 27, 1991

Burton Rogers, 1915, educator, Pine Mountain Settlement School, August 27, 1991

Kenneth Rosenbaum, musician, Pineville (Bell Co.), October 25, 1988

Janis Ross, 1938, city employee, Rio Vista, October 29, 1988

Ed Sadlowski, 1938 (Chicago, Illinois), union organizer, Youngstown, Ohio, May 15, 2001

Jeff Salman [name changed], 1951, electrician, Cincinnati, Ohio, July 3, 2001

Jenny Saylor, 1957 (Baltimore, Maryland), June 16, 2005

Joe Scopa Jr., 1951, coal company employee, art teacher, June 5, 2005

Joe Scopa Sr., coal miner, union organizer, Tots, June 16, 1987, and August 19, 1987 (interviewed by Doug Cantrell, University of Kentucky, Margaret E. King Library, Louie B. Nunn Center for Oral History, Coal Miners Oral History Project)

Lois Scott, 1928, store owner, union activist, Dione, October 28, 1988

Mildred Shackleford, 1950, zinc miner, poet, New Market, Tennessee, November 2, 1990

Roy Silver, 1959 (New York), college teacher, Cumberland, June 16, 2005

Bob Simpson, 1936, farmer, miner, community activist, Cranks Creek Survival Center, October 6, 1986

Bud Simpson, 1917, Wallins Creek, August 28, 1991

Jimmie Simpson, Wallins Creek, August 28, 1991

Rebecca "Becky" Simpson, 1939, community activist, Cranks Creek
Survival Center, October 6, 1986, November 8, 1993

Robert Simpson, 1958, coal miner, crafts artist, Cranks Creek, December
27, 1989

Melinda Slusher, 1906, Wallins, August 25, 1991

Andrew Smith [name changed], 1956, Cranks Creek, November 8, 1993

Debbie Spicer, 1907, Louellen, October 28, 1988

Lloyd Stokes, 1901, barber, Wallins Creek, August 26, 1991

Lydia Surgener, 1926, Holiness preacher, store owner, Pennington Gap
(Lee Co., Virginia), July 7, 1986 and October 16, 1996; Cranks,
September 27, 1997

Noah Surgener, 1928, businessman, Cawood, November 1, 1990

Henrietta Sweatt, 1898, teacher, Lynch, October 16, 1986

Tommy Sweatt, 1948, Methodist minister, coal miner, Lynch, October 7, 1986

Tony Sweatt, 1970, construction worker, Cumberland, June 17, 2005

Dale Teeter, mine inspector, Harlan, October 25, 1988

Alicia Thomas, 1970, student, Cumberland, June 17, 2005

Bonnie Thomas, 1979, student, Cumberland, June 17, 2005

Leonard Thompson, coal miner, Evarts, September 9, 1993

Sid Tibbs, 1954, coal miner, crafts artist, Baxter/Pine Mountain, June 30,
2001

Jeff Tipton, union organizer, coal miner, Harlan, October 24, 1988

Earl Turner, 1916, mine foreman, Lynch, October 5, 1986

Irwin Turner, 1940, coal miner, October 8, 1986

James L. Turner, 1924 preacher, post office worker, Harlan, November 9, 1993

Crystal Vanover, 1960, medical assistant, Rosspoint, June 16, 2005

Lowell Wagner, 1941 (Jackson Co., Virginia), agricultural agent, Benham,
October 16, 1996

David Walls, 1942 (Chicago, Illinois), college teacher, former VISTA
volunteer, Rome, Italy, July 18, 1992

Aaron Warren, union organizer, Harlan, October 24, 1988

Donna Warren, Harlan, July 6, 2005

Bryan Whitfield, 1901 (Alabama), coal operator, Brookside, February 9,
1989 (interviewed by Henry Mayer, University of Kentucky, Margaret E.
King Library, Louie B. Nunn Center for Oral History), November 1,
1990

Larry Williamson, 1991 (Delaware), student, Harlan, June 16, 2005

Darlene Wilson, 1952 (Wise Co., Virginia), college teacher, Cumberland,
July 3, 2003

Janice Wilson [name changed], 1972, student, Cumberland, October 7, 1986

Larry Wilson, 1940, environmental activist, Yellow Creek (Bell Co.),
October 30, 1988

Robert Wilson [name changed], coal miner, Cranks Creek, 1990
Bill Winters, 1927, factory worker, Ypsilanti, Michigan, March 17, 2001
Johnny Woodward, 1951, college teacher, Cumberland, November 1, 1990
James Wright, 1944, miner, crafts artist, Baxter/Pine Mountain, June 30, 2001
Donella Wynn, 1987, student, Evarts, June 15, 2007
Norman Yarbrough, 1922, coal operator, Brookside, November 2, 1990

EVENTS

Cawood Holiness Church, Cawood, June 15, 2009, the Reverend Jerry
  Collins, pastor
Cranks Holiness Church, Cranks, October 27, 1988
Cranks Creek Survival Center, music sessions: July 7, 1987 (Hiram Day,
  Junior Day, Annie Napier, Becky Simpson); October 16, 1996 (Hiram
  Day, Junior Day, Becky Ruth Brae, Annie Napier, Mike Henson)
Cranks Holiness Church, Cranks, July 17, 1987, October 27, 1988, Lydia
  Surgener, preacher
Cranks Pentecostal Church, Cranks, October 19, 2008, October 20,
  2008, the Reverend Gary Pace, pastor; Patricia Pace, Cynthia Wilson,
  Jamie Daniels (on October 20), piano; Gary Pace, Kenny Ledford, Carl
  Daniels, Cynthia Wilson, Michelle Ledford, Patricia Pace (singers); Ida
  Colegrove (guitar)
First Baptist Church, Cumberland, October 10, 1986, the Reverend
  Baxter [name changed], pastor
First Pentecostal Church, Wallins, August 25, 1991, the Reverend Ed
  Houston, pastor
First Southern Missionary Baptist Church, Verda, October 28, 2008, the
  Reverend Danny McQuarry, preaching; Chester and Megan Clem
  leading the choir, Danny Hairston, piano
Harlan Village Mall, Harlan, December 26, 1989, conversation with
  teenagers: Boyd (1976), George (1972), Jazzy (1973), unidentified (1972)
Jenson Pentecostal Church, Straight Creek (Bell Co.), June 18, 2007, the
  Reverend William Roberts [name changed]
Kentuckians for the Commonwealth meeting, Harlan, July 17, 1987,
  anti-broad-form-deed meeting: Mary Jane Adams, Gurney Campbell,
  speaking; Arthur Johnson, Jane Sapp, Guy and Candie Carawan,
  Kenneth Rosenbaum, music
Macedonia Baptist Church, Cumberland, October 5, 1986, Lee Brown,
  preacher
Mill Creek Holiness Church, Cranks, September 27, 1997, Lydia
  Surgener, preacher

Molus Pentecostal Church, Molus, August 25, 1991, the Reverend Ray Stepp, pastor

Mount Sinai Baptist Church, Lynch, June 15, 2005, prayer service

Pittston mine strike, Castlewood, Virginia, December 17, 1989, Harold Dutton, Duran Dutton, Peggy Dutton, Tommy Mead, strike stories and songs

Riverside House of Prayer, Pennington Gap (Lee Co., Virginia), October 16, 1996, Lydia Surgener, preaching; Hiram and Junior Day, music

Southeast Community and Technical College, Cumberland, June 16, 2007, rehearsals for *Higher Ground*

Notes

Harlan County, 1964–2009

1. Florence Reece, "Which Side Are You On?" Copyright (Renewed) by StormKing Music, Inc. Used by Permission. Performed by the Almanac Singers, *Which Side Are You On? The Best of the Almanac Singers*, Rev-Ola Records, CR-REV 182; performed by Florence Reece, *They'll Never Keep Us Down: Women's Coal Mining Songs*, Rounder 4012. I first heard the song on a French LP reprint of the original Folkways album, *Chants des Syndicats Américains*, Chant du Monde FWX-M-55285. John Henry Blair was sheriff of Harlan County at the time the song was written. On the background and history of the songs mentioned in this introduction, see chapters 9 and 11. See also Florence Reece, *Against the Current* (Knoxville, TN: Florence Reece, 1981); Florence Reece, "They Say Them Child Brides Don't Last," in Kathy Kahn, *Hillbilly Women* (Garden City, NY: Doubleday, 1973); "Which Side Are You On? An Interview with Florence Reece," *Mountain Life and Work*, March 1972.

2. Aunt Molly Jackson, "Join the CIO," *Aunt Molly Jackson: Library of Congress Recordings*, Rounder 1002. See also New Lost City Ramblers, *Songs from the Depression*, Folkways FW 05264. On Molly Jackson, see "Aunt Molly Jackson Memorial Issue," ed. Archie Green, *Kentucky Folklore Record* 7, 4 (Oct.-Dec. 1961); Shelly Romalis, *Pistol Packin' Mama: Aunt Molly Jackson and the Politics of Folksong* (Urbana: University of Illinois Press, 1999). When the song was first composed in 1931, its title and refrain were "Join the NMU," referring to the Communist-led National Miners' Union.

3. Jim Garland, "The Ballad of Harry Simms," in Jim Garland, *Welcome the Traveler Home: Jim Garland's Story of the Kentucky Mountains*, ed. Julia S. Ardery (Lexington: University Press of Kentucky, 1983), 71. For variants of the song and its history, see Jim Garland, "The Murder of Harry Simms," *Newport Broadside*, Vanguard VSD-79144 (I heard it on an Austrian reprint, Amadeo AVRS 9162); Garland, *Welcome the Traveler Home*, 169–71; Mary Elizabeth Barnicle, "Harry Simms: The Story Behind This American Ballad," notes to the Folkways record *American Industrial Ballads*, Folkways FH 5251.

4. Sarah Ogan Gunning, "I Hate the Capitalist System," *Girl of Constant Sorrow*, Folk Legacy CD-26, and *Silver Dagger*, Rounder Records 0051. My original recording of Barbara Dane's performance is in *L'America della contestazione*, ed. Ferdinando Pellegrini and Alessandro Portelli, Dischi del Sole 179/81/CL; Dane also includes it in her LP *I Hate the Capitalist System*, Paredon P-1014. Barbara Dane has long-standing family ties to Harlan: "My father's mother, Hattie Turley…was born in Harlan or nearby.…She died, probably in childbirth, about 1905, when my dad, Gilbert Spillman, was about three years old. She would have been married then to Herbert M. Spillman. That's all I've been able to find out" (e-mail message to the author, June 25, 2009).

5. Annalucia Accardo, Cristina Mattiello, Alessandro Portelli, and Anna Scannavini, eds., *Un'altra America. Letteratura e cultura degli Appalachi meridionali* (Rome: Bulzoni, 1991).

6. Alessandro Portelli, "Between Sanctified Hill and Pride Terrace: Urban Ideals and Rural Working-Class Experience in Black Communities in Harlan County, Kentucky," *Storia Americana* 7, 2 (1990): 51–63.

7. See Alessandro Portelli, "Tryin' to Gather a Little Knowledge," in *The Battle of Valle Giulia: Oral History and the Art of Dialogue* (Madison: University of Wisconsin Press, 1997), 55–71.

Actually, Enoxy Coal, a joint venture of the Rome-based, state-owned energy conglomerate ENI (Ente Nazionale Idrocarburi) and Occidental Petroleum, owned for some time four mines in West Virginia and eastern Kentucky. In 1988, Enoxy refused to sign the UMW contract, used the professional paramilitary outfit Asset Protection Team to repress a miners' strike, and even blocked access to the local airport: "Coal Company Limits Access to Airport," *Lexington Herald-Leader*, May 7, 1988; according to the Whitesburg, Kentucky, *Mountain Eagle*, the airport had been turned into something not unlike a military base (April 27, 1988). On September 1, 1988, union miners demonstrated in Washington in front of the Italian embassy: Alessandro Portelli, "Le squadracce dell'ENI. Sceriffi, campi minati e filo spinato nelle miniere americane Enoxy," *Il Manifesto*, November 16, 1988.

8. See Alessandro Portelli, "There's Gonna Always Be a Line," in *The Battle of Valle Giulia*, 24–39; see also Ms. Cowans's profile, based on my interviews with her, in Catherine Fosl and Tracy E. K'Meyer, eds., *Freedom on the Border: An Oral History of the Civil Rights Movement in Kentucky* (Lexington: University Press of Kentucky, 2009), 177–85.

9. Charles Hardy III and Alessandro Portelli, *I Can Almost See the Lights of Home*, electronic publication in *Journal for MultiMedia History*, 2 (1999), http://www.albany.edu/jmmh/vol2no1/lights.html.

10. William Faulkner points out that an overly didactic transcription of the vernacular "is confusing to people who have never heard that speech," while those who are familiar with it "would know how it sounds" no matter how it was spelled; quoted in *Faulkner in the University*, ed. Frederick L. Gwynn and Joseph L. Blotner (New York: Random House, 1965), 181. For a similar point, see Cleanth Brooks, *The Language of the American South* (Athens: University of Georgia Press, 1975), 37–38.

11. Anita Puckett notes that the final *g* is never used in Appalachian speech, and therefore the apostrophe would suggest the "loss" of a sound that in fact was never there; *Seldom Ask, Never Tell: Labor and Discourse in Appalachia* (New York: Oxford University Press, 2000), xiv–xv. In fact, the majority of interviewees oscillated between a sounded or an absent final *g*, and often in-between, slurred sounds—a signal of a cultural location somewhere between pure vernacular and standard English. For an Italian analogy, see my "Dividing the World: Sound and Space in Cultural Transition," in *The Death of Luigi Trastulli and Other Stories: Form and Meaning in Oral History* (Albany, NY: State University of New York Press, 1991), 81–98.

12. See my "The Death of Luigi Trastulli: Memory and the Event," in *The Death of Luigi Trastulli*, 1–27.

13. See chapter 1, note 5.

14. An edited version of the interview, with changed name, is "Non vedevamo sconosciuti, allora. La vita di Maud Jenkins," ed. A. Portelli, *Acoma: Rivista Internazionale di Studi Nordamericani* 27 (Summer-Fall 2003): 4–13.

Chapter 1: The Bear and the Sycamore Tree

1. John Egerton, *Generations: An American Family* (Lexington: University Press of Kentucky, 1983), 21. *Generations* is the story of the Burnam-Ledford family, reconstructed from the memory of Curtis Burnam and his family.

2. George Washington's legendary Christmas crossing was over the Delaware, not the Potomac. David Hackett Fischer, *Washington's Crossing* (New York: Oxford University Press, 2004).

3. "The Burkharts of Harlan Are Descendants of George," *Harlan's Heritage III* (supplement to *Harlan Daily Enterprise*), February 28, 1986, 40–41.

4. Kentucky became a state in 1792.

5. "John Shell," unsigned biographical sketch in the possession of the family of Bobbie Davidson of Bledsoe, Kentucky. According to this document, John Shell produced a document showing he had paid taxes in 1809. Since taxpayers were supposed to be at least twenty-one, that was supposed to prove that he had been born in 1788. On the other hand, the first mention of his name in the Harlan County tax records is in 1844: http://

appalachianhistory.blogspot.com/2008/07/worlds-oldest-man-kentuckian-john-shell. html. His death in 1922 was reported by the *New York Times*: "Oldest Man in World Is Buried in Kentucky," July 11, 1922. Mabel Collins, "John Shell: A Man with Memories," *Harlan Daily Enterprise*, September 15, 1975, reports conflicting stories, giving his age anywhere from 112 to 133. See also Harry M. Caudill, *Night Comes to the Cumberlands* (Boston: Little, Brown, 1963), 255.

6. Eugene H. Rainey, *Historical Resumé of Evarts*, Evarts, The Community Church, Black Mountain Academy, presented at the Fiftieth Anniversary Celebration, November 8–9, 1942, 4.

7. Harvey B. Fuson, "History of Harlan County, Kentucky: Some Chapters," typescript, Margaret E. King Library, Special Collections, University of Kentucky, Lexington, 4, 5.

8. Elmon Middleton, *Harlan County, Kentucky* (Big Laurel, VA: James Taylor Adams and James Taylor Adams II, 1934), 11; "Sam Howard Was First Settler of Harlan County About 1790," *Harlan's Heritage V*, February 27, 1988, 27.

9. "Pioneer Lives in the Old Sycamore Tree," *Harlan's Heritage V*, February 27, 1988.

10. John Lawson, *History of North Carolina* (1714), quoted in Daniel Hoffman, *Form and Fable in American Fiction* (New York: Oxford University Press, 1961), 17; Otis K. Rice, *Frontier Kentucky* (Lexington: University Press of Kentucky, 1975), 20.

11. Mabel Green Condon, *A History of Harlan County* (Nashville, TN: Parthenon, 1962), 48–49.

12. Rainey, *Historical Resumé of Evarts*, 4.

13. Condon, *A History of Harlan County*, 33.

14. Richard B. Drake, *A History of Appalachia* (Lexington: University Press of Kentucky, 2001), 49–50; Lowell H. Harrison and James C. Klotter, *A New History of Kentucky* (Lexington: University Press of Kentucky, 1997), 11–13. On Daniel Boone, see Richard Slotkin, *Regeneration Through Violence* (Middletown, CT: Wesleyan University Press, 1973), 278–92 and passim. The event is commemorated in an iconic American painting: "Daniel Boone Escorting Settlers Through Cumberland Gap," by George Caleb Bingham (1851–52).

15. Fuson, *History of Harlan County*, 6–7.

16. Elijah H. Criswell, "Lewis and Clark: Linguistic Pioneers," *University of Missouri Studies* 15, 2 (April 1, 1940). On the naming of coal towns after owners and management, see Crandall Shifflett, *Coaltowns: Life, Work, and Culture in Company Towns of Southern Appalachia, 1880–1960* (Knoxville: University of Tennessee Press, 1991), 34.

17. "John Shell" (see note 5).

18. A tradition relates that a Virginian named Joseph Martin, seeking land for a syndicate that included Patrick Henry, found clover growing along a stream and left behind two names—Martin's Fork and Clover Fork. Henry M. Caudill, *Theirs Be the Power: The Moguls of Eastern Kentucky* (Urbana: University of Illinois Press, 1983), 86.

19. George Rogers Clark (1752–1818) was the leader of the Kentucky militia in the Revolutionary War. See Harrison and Klotter, *A New History of Kentucky*, 31–47.

20. Ellen Churchill Semple, "The Anglo-Saxons of the Kentucky Mountains: A Study in Anthropogeography," *Bulletin of the American Geographical Society* 42, 8 (1910): 1–34. On Indian ancestry, see Caudill, *Night Comes to the Cumberlands*, 14–16.

21. The Appalachian region derives its name from the Apalachee nation, who inhabited northern Florida and southern Georgia. Robin C. Brown, *Florida's First People* (Sarasota, FL: Pineapple Press, 1994).

22. Wilma A. Dunaway, *The First American Frontier: Transition to Capitalism in Southern Appalachia, 1700–1860* (Chapel Hill: University of North Carolina Press, 1996), 25, 43.

23. For instance, John F. Day, *Bloody Ground* (Lexington: University Press of Kentucky, 1981 [1941]); Lester Cohen, "Bloody Ground," in Theodore Dreiser, ed., *Harlan Miners Speak: Report of Terrorism in the Kentucky Coal Fields* (New York: Da Capo Press, 1970 [1932]), 9. Joe Grushecky's song "Dark and Bloody Ground" is a terse but accurate rendition of events in eastern Kentucky history; it can be found on *American Babylon*, Razor and Tie Music, 1995.

24. Middleton, *Harlan County, Kentucky*, 18–20.

25. The chronology of Fred Napier's narrative is questionable: he was born in 1899, and by that time there was no organized Cherokee presence in Harlan. It does, however, evoke

the Cherokee's adoption of white ways—Christianity, writing, a constitution, even slavery.

26. Jenny Ferguson, post on http://historical-mulngeon.blogspot.com/2008/08/quadrule-indians-harlan-county-ky, July 27, 2008 (in a response, a Cherokee descendant claimed that the Quadrules never existed: ibid., January 10, 2009); Middleton, *Harlan County, Kentucky*, 18–20.

27. See "New Perspectives on the Cherokees," special issue of *Appalachian Journal* 2, 4 (Summer 1975)

28. Egerton, *Generations*, 21–22.

29. Thomas Bangs Thorpe, "The Big Bear of Arkansas" (1841), in Kenneth S. Lynn, *The Comic Tradition in America* (New York: Doubleday, 1958), 246–55; Anna Scannavini, "Bear Facts and Bear Stories in *Go Down Moses*," in A. Clericuzio et al., eds., *Telling the Stories of America* (Rome: Nuova Arnica, 2000), 280–88.

30. See the folktale "We Killed a Bear," collected on Pine Mountain by Leonard Roberts, in *Sang Branch Settlers: Folksongs and Tales of a Kentucky Mountain Family* (Austin: University of Texas Press, 1974), 288–89.

31. Sid Tibbs served as an officer in the Kentucky Coalition to Carry Concealed, which lobbied for the right to carry concealed weapons; see http://www.kc3.com/pdf/APR_2006_Newsletter.pdf. Some of his handmade knives can be seen on http://www.xdtalk.com/gallery/showphoto.php?photo=83&si=ACP.

32. Bears have been growing in number in Harlan County recently, to the point that they have become a nuisance to some of the residents: *Harlan Daily Enterprise*, June 23 and 24, 2004, September 13, 2005, March 15, 2006, September 3, 2007, and June 7, 2007. For a girl killed by a bear, see *Harlan Daily Enterprise*, April 15, 2006.

33. I know Chester Napier almost certainly didn't mean it, but I found it impossible to resist the biblical overtones in a story about a snake and an apple tree in the garden—and the man killing the snake in the absence of the woman.

34. On snake handling in churches, see chapter 4.

35. Originally, the tipple was the place where the mine cars were tipped and emptied of their coal. The term is still used in that sense, although now it is more generally applied to the surface structures of a mine, including the preparation plant and loading tracks. See http://www.irs.gov/businesses/small/article/0,,id=139342,00.html#t.

36. Another narrative with mythic overtones: the same story is told (and portrayed in classical art) about Hercules, who as a baby strangled the snakes Hera had placed in his crib to kill him. See http://www.metmuseum.org/toah/works-of-art/2006.453.

37. Condon, *History of Harlan County*, 68.

38. "White Creature Walks Through the Rooms of the House" is one of the ghost stories collected in Harlan County by Lynwood Montell, in *Ghosts Across Kentucky* (Lexington: University Press of Kentucky, 2000). Montell lists several Harlan County ghost stories: headless ghosts, ghosts of little children who died a violent dead, bloody handprints. Leonard Roberts, *South from Hell-fer-Sartin: Kentucky Mountain Folklore Tales* (Lexington: University Press of Kentucky, 1988 [1955]) includes a number of ghost stories from Harlan County. See also Lynwood Montell, *Haunted Houses and Family Ghosts of Kentucky* (Lexington: University Press of Kentucky, 2001); Lee and Joy Pennington, "Two Tales from Bloody Harlan," *Appalachian Journal* 1, 2 (Spring 1973): 139–41.

39. What is known as the "Battle of Crummies" took place in April 1941. There were indeed five men killed, but the weapon was a machine gun, and the man who fired it was later killed in retaliation; see chapter 10.

40. Donna Warren told about living in a house that was haunted by the ghost of a little child who had died in it twenty years before ("she got sick one winter and her folks didn't believe in doctors, and she died"). The ghost disappeared after a hidden closet containing the child's clothes and toys was found and its contents disposed of.

41. I have used the song's correct title here; it was referred to by the Napiers as "Taking Mary Home," which is a quote from the Bible (Matthew 1:20). There is, however, another country-western song by the title "Taking Mary Home." See John Harold Brunvand, *The Vanishing Hitchhiker: American Urban Legends and Their Meanings* (New York: W. W.

Norton, 1981), 49–55; Roberts, *South from Hell-fer-Sartin*, 190 ("Spirit of the Wreck"); Cesare Bermani, *Il bambino è servito. Leggende metropolitane in Italia* (Bari: Dedalo, 1991), 51–111.

42. Montell, *Ghosts Across Kentucky*, 187–88.

43. Franco Moretti, *The Modern Epic: The World-System from Goethe to García Márquez* (London: Verso, 1996).

44. A "blue baby" is a newborn that appears cyanotic from lack of oxygen, generally due to heart problems.

Chapter 2: Of Hardship and Love

1. On the Hensley Settlement, see Bill Peterson, *Coal Town Revisited: An Appalachian Notebook* (Chicago: Henry Regnery, 1972), 113–22.

2. See the census data in Shaunna L. Scott, *Two Sides to Everything: The Cultural Construction of Class Consciousness in Harlan County, Kentucky* (Albany: State University of New York Press, 1995), 5, table 1.1.

3. John W. Hevener, *Which Side Are You On? The Harlan County Coal Miners, 1931–39* (Urbana: University of Illinois Press, 2002 [1978]), 1.

4. "The Harlan County Feud," *New York Times*, October 28, 1889.

5. G. C. Jones, *Growing Up Hard in Harlan County* (Lexington: University Press of Kentucky, 1985), 1.

6. Darrell Scott, "You'll Never Leave Harlan Alive" (2004), in *Music of Coal: Mining Songs from the Appalachian Coalfields*, produced by Jack Wright, Lonesome Records, 2007; also recorded by Patti Loveless on *Mountain Soul*, Epic EK 85651, 2005.

7. Thomas R. Shannon, "The Economy of Appalachia," in Grace Toney Edwards, JoAnn Aust Asbury, and Ricky L. Cox, eds., *A Handbook to Appalachia: An Introduction to the Region* (Knoxville: University of Tennessee Press, 2006), 67–84.

8. Dwight B. Billings and Kathleen M. Blee, *The Road to Poverty: The Making of Wealth and Hardship in Appalachia* (New York: Cambridge University Press, 2000), 323.

9. Poke is a wild green found all over Appalachia. When picked early in spring (later it can be poisonous), it is used for a salad. Since the 1970s, the Poke Sallit Festival has been a favorite event in Harlan.

10. On ways in which rural women provide and preserve food, see John Van Willigen and Anne Van Willigen, *Food and Everyday Life* (Lexington: University Press of Kentucky, 2006), 139, 192, 194.

11. Vivian Shipley, "Wrap It in Cellophane," *Poems out of Harlan County* (Greenfield Center, NY: Greenfield Review Press, 1989), 47–49. Planting by the signs consists in matching zodiac signs to the moon's phases and planting in the "fruitful" signs. Cancer is said to be the most fruitful sign, Leo the most barren. Aboveground crops should be planted when the moon is waxing, root crops in the third quarter in a waning moon; *Harlan County Almanac*, 1991, 13–14. According to Richard J. Callahan, planting by the signs is based on the belief in correspondences between the natural world and God's cosmic design; Callahan, *Work and Faith in the Kentucky Coal Fields: Subject to Dust* (Bloomington: Indiana University Press, 2008), 32–33.

12. Ronald D. Eller, *Miners, Millhands, and Mountaineers: Industrialization of the Appalachian South, 1880–1930* (Knoxville: University of Tennessee Press, 1982), 11, 39, 64; Robert S. Weise, *Grasping at Independence: Debts, Male Authority, and Mineral Rights in Appalachian Kentucky, 1850–1915* (Knoxville: University of Tennessee Press, 2001), 228ff.; Paul Salstrom, *Appalachia's Path to Dependency: Rethinking a Region's Economic History, 1730–1940* (Lexington: University Press of Kentucky, 1997), 42.

13. Dunaway, *The First American Frontier. Transition to Capitalism in Southern Appalachia, 1700–1860* (Chapel Hill: University of North Carolina Press, 1996), 76–77, 87ff.; Mary Beth Pudup, "Social Class and Economic Development in Southeast Kentucky, 1820–1880," in Robert D. Mitchell, ed., *Appalachian Frontiers: Settlement, Society, and Development in the Preindustrial Era* (Lexington: University Press of Kentucky, 1991), 235–60; Harry M. Caudill, *Night Comes to the Cumberlands* (Boston: Little, Brown, 1963), 81–82.

14. Billings and Lee, *The Road to Poverty*, 323; Salstrom, *Appalachia's Path to Dependency*, 42.

15. Jim Garland, *Welcome the Traveler Home: Jim Garland's Story of the Kentucky Mountains*, ed. Julia S. Ardery (Lexington: University Press of Kentucky, 1983), 1.

16. Appalachian Land Ownership Task Force, *Who Owns Appalachia? Land Ownership and Its Impact* (Lexington: University Press of Kentucky, 1983), 91; "The Passing of the Family Farm," in *Appalachia in the Eighties: A Time for Action* (Berea, KY: Appalachian Alliance, 1982).

17. From a news report quoted in James S. Brown, "The Family Behind the Migrant," *Mountain Life and Work*, September 1968; Robert Coles, *Migrants, Sharecroppers, Mountaineers* (Boston: Little, Brown, 1971), 500.

18. Scott, *Two Sides to Everything*, 110, 5, 172. See also Thomas A. Arcury and Julia D. Porter, "Household Composition in Appalachian Kentucky in 1900," *Journal of Family History* 10, 2 (1985): 183–95.

19. Early sociologists blamed intermarriage on Appalachian "backwardness." A late but influential trace of this approach in an otherwise admirable book is in Caudill's classic *Night Comes to the Cumberlands*.

20. On early marriage as a coal mining tradition, see Carol A. B. Giesen, *Coal Miners' Wives: Portraits of Endurance* (Lexington: University Press of Kentucky, 1995), 22.

21. Julia Cowans had one other child from her second marriage, at the age of forty-four.

22. Thomas A. Arcury, "Industrialization and Household and Family Life Course Characteristics: Appalachian Kentucky Young Adults in 1880 and 1910," *Journal of Family History* 15, 3 (1990): 285–312.

23. Jim Daniels was one of the deputy sheriffs killed in the "Battle of Evarts," between deputies and miners, on May 5, 1931. See chapter 9 and Hevener, *Which Side Are You On*, 43–44.

24. "Sex in these marriages is often a dismal affair. The wife is taught not to enjoy it, the husband is taught that he is not to engage in foreplay and neither seem to connect love or emotions with sexual activity." Harvey L. Gochros, "Sex and Marriage in Rural Appalachia," in Frank S. Riddell, ed., *Appalachia: Its People, Heritage and Problems* (Dubuque, IA: Kendall/Hunt, 1974), 76–84.

25. Marat Moore, *Women in the Mines: Stories of Life and Work* (New York: Twayne, 1996).

26. Scott, *Two Sides to Everything*, 3.

27. A sugar tit is a piece of cloth soaked with sugar water.

28. For lists of home remedies, see John F. Day, *Bloody Ground* (Lexington: University Press of Kentucky, 1981 [1941]), 272–77.

29. Dolly Parton, "Coat of Many Colors," *Coat of Many Colors*, RCA LP 4603.

30. David H. Loof, *Appalachia's Children: The Challenge of Mental Health* (Lexington: University Press of Kentucky, 1971), 33.

31. Katherine Pettit, the founder of the Hindman Settlement School, noted the "rough and brutal...treatment of children": David E. Whisnant, *All That Is Native and Fine: The Politics of Culture in an American Region* (Chapel Hill: University of North Carolina Press, 1983), 46.

32. Scott, *Two Sides to Everything*.

Chapter 3: Wars and Peace

1. Sojourner Memorial Calendar, a feature of the Eastern Kentucky Social Club, Lynch Kentucky, 1983. The child might have been America Ledford, born a slave to Aley Ledford, listed in the Harlan phone directory in 1880. See John Egerton, *Generations: An American Family* (Lexington: University Press of Kentucky, 1983), 103.

2. Ellen Church Semple, "The Anglo-Saxons of the Kentucky Mountains: A Study in Anthropogeography," *Geographical Journal* 17 (June 1901): 588–623, in W. K. McNeil, *Appalachian Images in Folk and Popular Culture* (Knoxville: University of Tennessee Press, 1995), 145–74; William H. Turner, "Introduction," in William H. Turner and Edward J. Cabbell, eds., *Blacks in Appalachia* (Lexington: University Press of Kentucky, 1985), xvii; Otis K. Rice, *Frontier Kentucky* (Lexington: University Press of Kentucky, 1993 [1975]), 59, 75.

3. Wilma A. Dunaway, *Slavery in the American Mountain South* (Cambridge: Cambridge University Press, 2003).

4. In Appalachian Kentucky, 14 percent of the families owned slaves, as opposed to the state's 31 percent slaveholding rate overall. Wilma A. Dunaway, *The First American Frontier: Transition to Capitalism in Southern Appalachia, 1700–1860* (Chapel Hill: University of North Carolina Press, 1996), 79. See also Mary Beth Pudup, "Social Class and Economic Development in Southeast Kentucky, 1820–1880," in Robert D. Mitchell, ed., *Appalachian Frontiers: Settlement, Society, and Development in the Preindustrial Era* (Lexington: University Press of Kentucky, 1991), 235–60; James B. Murphy, "Slavery and Freedom in Appalachia: Kentucky as a Demographic Case Study," *Kentucky Historical Society Register* 80 (Spring 1982): 151–69.

5. Earl Turner was not related to the Cranks Creek Turners.

6. Egerton, *Generations*, 24.

7. Harvey B. Fuson, "History of Harlan County, Kentucky: Some Chapters," typescript, Margaret E. King Library, Special Collections, University of Kentucky Libraries, Lexington, 8–9.

8. Dunaway, *Slavery in the American Mountain South*, 201–3.

9. Egerton, *Generations*, 24, 76. Because Kentucky was a slave-owning state that did not secede in the Civil War, the Emancipation Proclamation did not apply to it; slavery was abolished in Kentucky only with the passing of the Thirteenth Amendment in 1865. See Catherine Fosl and Tracy E. K'Meyer, *Freedom on the Border: An Oral History of the Civil Rights Movement in Kentucky* (Lexington: University Press of Kentucky, 2009), 2.

10. Mabel Green Condon, *A History of Harlan County* (Nashvile: Parthenon, 1962), 75, 77.

11. Nat Turner led a slave rebellion in 1831 in Southampton County, Virginia. See Kenneth S. Greenberg, ed., *Nat Turner: A Slave Rebellion in History and Memory* (New York: Oxford University Press, 2003).

12. Holly Timm, "Keeping the Homes Fires Burning: Civil War in Southeast Kentucky," http://rootsweb.com/~seky/civilwar/homefire/homefire2.html.

13. Elmon Middleton, *Harlan County* (Big Laurel, VA: James Taylor Adams and James Taylor Adams II, 1934), 27–30; Timm, "Keeping the Homes Fires Burning."

14. "History of the Town of Mount Pleasant," *Harlan's Heritage III*, February 28, 1986, 3–13.

15. Ibid.

16. Narcissa Middleton, wife of William Middleton, quoted in John Ed Pearce, *Days of Darkness: The Feuds of Eastern Kentucky* (Lexington: University Press of Kentucky, 1994), 13; "Feuds of Harlan County," http://freepages.genealogy.rootsweb.com/~bloodhound/feudsofharlancoky.html.

17. Timm, "Keeping the Homes Fires Burning."

18. See chapter 1.

19. "Devil Jim Turner Outlaw of Harlan County," http://www.rootsweb.com/~kyharlan/index.html.

20. Theodore Dreiser, *Sister Carrie* (New York: Penguin, 1986 [1900]), 354.

21. "The Harlan County Feud All the Result of a Drunk. A Faction War That Has Cost Many Lives and Still Disgraces the State of Kentucky," *New York Times*, October 28, 1899.

22. *New York Times*, November 10, 1878, quoted in James C. Klotter, "Feuds in Appalachia: An Overview," *Filson Club Quarterly* 56 (1982): 290–317; John F. Day, *Bloody Ground* (Lexington: University Press of Kentucky, 1981 [1941]), 117. For a novel about the Howard-Turner feud, see T. C. Ballou, *A Cumberland Vendetta, or the Howard-Turner Feud* (1906). For film, see J. W. Williamson, *Hillbillyland: What the Movies Did to the Mountains and What the Mountains Did to the Movies* (Chapel Hill: University of North Carolina Press, 1995).

23. As Dwight B. Billings and Kathleen M. Blee note, violent community conflict was widespread in the post-Reconstruction South, but also in the West and the industrial and urban North. See their "Where 'Bloodshed Is a Pastime': Mountain Feuds and Appalachian Stereotyping," in Dwight B. Billings, Gurney Norman, and Katherine Ledford, eds., *Confronting Appalachian Stereotypes: Back Talk from an American Region* (Lexington: University of Kentucky Press, 1999), 119–37. Among the most notable feuds were the Hill-Evans feud in Garrard County (1820–53), the French-Eversole war in Hazard (Perry County, 1881), the Baker-White feud (Clay County, 1899), the Hargis-Marcum-

Cockrell-Callahan conflict in what came to be labeled as "Bloody Breathitt" County (starting in 1899), and the "Rowan County War" (1884–87).

24. Altina L. Waller, *Feud: Hatfields, McCoys, and Social Change in Appalachia, 1860–1900* (Chapel Hill: University of North Carolina Press, 1998).

25. John E. Kleber, *The Kentucky Encyclopaedia* (Lexington: University Press of Kentucky, 1992); "The Kentucky Feuds," http://fixit24.tripod.com/feud.html. According to Pearce, *Days of Darkness*, 12–14, one source of resentment was that Alice Howard, accused by the Turners of selling whiskey to their alcoholic father, was offended when they "spoke roughly" to her.

26. Klotter, "Feuds in Appalachia"; "The Howard-Turner Feud"; *New York Times*, September 17, 1889; "Feuds of Harlan County."

27. Pearce, *Days of Darkness*, 17.

28. "Feuds of Harlan County."

29. "Kentucky Vendetta," *Herald Dispatch* [Decatur, IL], July 27, 1896; "A Drunken Quarrel Ends in a Tragedy," *Los Angeles Times*, June 29, 1888, both reported in "The Howard-Turner Feud."

30. On the Cawood-Day feud, see Egerton, *Generations*, 65.

31. "Belligerent State over the Whisky Question," *New York Times*, July 24, 1888.

32. *New York Times*, October 22, 1889. As in other Harlan County battles, each side has a different body count: Howard sympathizers report no casualties on their side and six dead or wounded in Judge Lewis's posse (Pearce, *Days of Darkness*, 21).

33. L. E. Tupper, "The Story of a Kentucky Feud," *Independent*, 1892, reproduced in "The Howard-Turner Feud."

34. This is probably why Ed Cawood dates the feud at 1895.

35. http://boards.ancestry.com/localities.northam.usa.states.kentucky.counties.harlan/6037.1.1.1.1.1.1.1.1/mb.ashx.

36. *Berea Quarterly*, quoted in Dwight B. Billings and Kathleen M. Blee, *The Road to Poverty: The Making of Wealth and Hardship in Appalachia* (New York: Cambridge University Press, 2000), 311.

37. Blee and Billings, "Where 'Bloodshed Is a Pastime,'" 119–37.

38. L. E. Tupper, "The South: A Trip to Harlan County, KY.," *The American Missionary* 46, 9 (Sept. 1892), http://dlxs2.library.cornell.edu/a/amis/amis.1892.html.

39. See W. D. Weatherford, ed., *Religion in the Highlands: Native Churches and Missionary Enterprises in the Southern Appalachian Area* (New York: Poligraphic Company of America, 1993); Loyal Jones, "Old Time Baptists and Mainline Christianity," in J. W. Williams, ed., *An Appalachian Symposium* (Boone, NC: Appalachian State University Press, 1977), 120–30.

40. Egerton, *Generations*, 33, 82; Condon, *A History of Harlan County*, 28; William W. Harney, *The Mountain People of Kentucky: An Account of Present Conditions with the Attitude of the People Toward Improvement* (Cincinnati: Robert Clarke, 1906), 134–35.

41. David Whisnant, *All That Is Native and Fine: The Politics of Culture in an American Region* (Chapel Hill: University of North Carolina Press, 1983), 251, 257; Arnold J. Toynbee, *A Study of History* (New York: Oxford University Press, 1946), 149; Henry D. Shapiro, *Appalachia on Our Mind* (Chapel Hill: University of North Carolina Press, 1979), 15–21, 32–58, 65ff. See also Deborah Vansau McCauley, *Appalachian Mountain Religion: A History* (Urbana: University of Illinois Press, 1995), 397–98; Helen Matthew Lewis, Sue Easterling Kobak, and Linda Johnson, "Family, Religion, and Colonialism in Central Appalachia: Bury My Rifle at Big Stone Gap," in H. Lewis, L. Johnson, and Donald Askins, eds., *Colonialism in Modern America: The Appalachian Case* (Boone, NC: Appalachian Consortium Press, 1978), 113–39.

42. Semple, "The Anglo-Saxons of the Kentucky Mountains."

43. Will Wallace Harney, "A Strange Land and Peculiar People," *Lippincott Magazine*, 1873, in McNeil, ed., *Appalachian Images*, 429–38; John Esten Cooke, "Owlet," *Harper's Magazine*, July 1878, 161; Katherine Ledford, "A Landscape and a People Set Apart: Narratives of Exploration and Travel in Early Appalachia," in Billings, Norman, and Ledford, eds., *Confronting Appalachan Stereotypes*, 47–66; William Goodell Frost, "Our Contemporary Ancestors in the Southern Mountains," *Atlantic Monthly*, March 1899, 311–19; Allan W. Batteau, *The Invention of Appalachia* (Tucson: University of Arizona Press, 1990); Alessandro Portelli, "Appalachia as Science Fiction," *Appalachian Journal* 16, 1 (Fall 1988): 32–43.

44. Ledford, "A Landscape and a People Set Apart"; Ben Alice Owens, "Folk Speech of the Cumberlands," *American Speech* 7 (1931): 89–95; Lester Cohen, "Bloody Ground," in Theodore Dreiser, ed., *Harlan Miners Speak: Report on Terrorism in the Kentucky Coal Fields* (New York: Da Capo Press, 1970 [1932]), 18.

45. Semple, "The Anglo-Saxons of the Kentucky Mountains."

46. *The Pine Mountain School 1913–1980* (Pine Mountain, KY: Pine Mountain Settlement School, 1980), 9.

47. Whisnant, *All That Is Native and Fine*, 17–101.

48. Ibid., 201; on crafts, see Shapiro, *Appalachia on Our Mind*, 218–27, and Jane S. Becker, *Selling Tradition: Appalachia and the Construction of an American Folk 1930–1940* (Chapel Hill: University of North Carolina Press, 1998); for the ballad canon, see Francis James Child, *The English and Scottish Popular Ballads* (New York: Dover, 1965 [1882–98]).

49. Cecil Sharp, *English Folk Songs from the Southern Appalachians* (London: Oxford University Press/Humphrey Milford, 1932 [1917]), xxv. On Sharp and ballad collecting, see Whisnant, *All That Is Native and Fine*, 51–57, 110–26; Benjamin Filene, *Romancing the Folk: Public Memory and American Roots Music* (Chapel Hill: University of North Carolina Press, 2000), 20–26.

50. Whisnant, *All That Is Native and Fine*, 56; Shapiro, *Appalachia on Our Mind*, 249–56. On the dulcimer, see R. Gerald Alvery, *Dulcimer Maker: The Craft of Homer Ledford* (Lexington: University Press of Kentucky, 2003).

51. Shelly Romalis, *Pistol Packin' Mama: Aunt Molly Jackson and the Politics of Folksong* (Urbana: University of Illinois Press, 1999), 62; Jim Garland, *Welcome the Traveler Home: Jim Garland's Story of the Kentucky Mountains*, ed. Julia S. Ardery (Lexington: University Press of Kentucky, 1983), 57, 174; Leonard Roberts, *Sang Branch Settlers: Folksongs and Tales of a Kentucky Mountain Family* (Austin: University of Texas Press, 1974), 100–10.

52. Also known as "Life's Railway to Heaven," the song was copyrighted by M. E. Abbey and Charles D. Tillman in 1890. Some of the verses may have been written earlier by the Mormon poet Eliza R. Snow.

53. Semple, "The Anglo-Saxons of the Kentucky Mountains." On contemporary quilting, see "Year of the Quilt," *Harlan Daily Enterprise*, January 29, 2005.

54. Cratis Williams, "Dialect and Speech," in Nellie McNeil and Joyce Squibb, eds., *A Southern Appalachian Reader* (Boone, NC: Appalachian Consortium Press, 1989), 31. On Appalachian English, see Cratis Williams, "Appalachian Speech," *North Carolina Historical Review* 55, 2 (April 1978): 174–79; Walt Wolfram and Donna Christian, *Appalachian Speech* (Arlington, VA: Center for Applied Linguistics, 1976). For a critique of the "Shakespearean English" myth, see Michael Montgomery, "In the Appalachians They Speak Like Shakespeare," in *Myths in Linguistics*, ed. Laurie Bauer and Peter Trudgill (New York: Penguin, 1998), 66–76.

55. See the "Appalachian Accents" issue of *Now and Then: The Appalachian Magazine* 17, 2 (Summer 2000); Donna Christian, Walt Wolfram, and Nanjo Dube, *Variation and Change in Geographically Isolated Speech Communities: Appalachian English and Ozark English* (Tuscaloosa: University of Alabama Press, 1988). Linguist Linda M. Blanton points out that many of the traits identified with Appalachian English are shared with other forms of nonstandard English throughout the United States, and that *social* variants, rather than regional ones, exist within Appalachia itself. See her "Southern Appalachia: Social Considerations of Speech," in Joyce Lee Dillard, ed., *Toward a Social History of American English* (Berlin: Mouton, 1985), 73–90.

56. See Charlotte Nolan, "Harlanese Is a Separate Language," *Harlan Daily Enterprise*, February 8, 2006; also, *Ah Has Spoken from the Heart*, a collection of Nolan's columns from the *Harlan Daily Enterprise*, http://www.harlanonline.net/charlottenolan.

57. Fuson, *History of Harlan County*, 5, 6, 8.

Chapter 4: These Signs Shall Follow Them

1. Thomas R. Ford, "The Passing of Provincialism," in Thomas R. Ford, ed., *The Southern Appalachian Region: A Survey* (Lexington: University Press of Kentucky, 1967), 9–34; John B.

Boles, *The Great Revival, 1787–1805: The Origins of the Southern Evangelical Mind* (Lexington: University Press of Kentucky, 1972).

2. Earl D. C. Brewer, "Religion and the Churches," in Ford, ed., *The Southern Appalachian Region*, 20–18; Deborah Vansau McCauley, *Appalachian Mountain Religion: A History* (Urbana: University of Illinois Press, 1995), 13, 15, and passim; Melinda Bollar Wagner, "Religion in Appalachia," in Grace Toney Edwards, JoAnn Aust Asbury, and Ricky L. Cox, eds., *A Handbook to Appalachia: An Introduction to the Region* (Knoxville: University of Tennessee Press, 2006), 181–97; Richard J. Callahan, *Work and Faith in the Kentucky Coal Fields: Subject to Dust* (Bloomington: Indiana University Press, 2008), 25. Much of McCauley's fieldwork in Harlan was carried out with people and churches that are also part of this book, such as Lydia Surgener and the Cranks Pentecostal Church; see *Appalachian Mountain Religion*, 59–62, 72–74, 195–98, and Charles Hardy III and Alessandro Portelli, eds., "I Can Almost See the Lights of Home," *Journal for MultiMedia History* 2, 1 (1999), www.albany.edu/jmmh/vol2no1/lights.html.

3. John 3:3–6.

4. Steve Robrahn, "Satan Surfaces in Kentucky (Again)," Associated Press, September 19, 1988, reports on rumors about Satan worshipers in eastern Kentucky said to be looking for blond, blue-eyed children to kill in a sacrifice before Halloween. That summer, a black-clad photographer was taking pictures of schoolchildren in Estil County, and rumors that that she was photographing prospective devil-worship victims were so pervasive that she had to leave the state; "Artist Called Devil Worshiper," [Whitesburg] *Mountain Eagle*, October 5, 1988; "Devil Worshipers Exist Only in Rumor, Police Says," *Mountain Eagle*, September 14, 1988. See also Ray Ellis, *Raising the Devil: Satanism, New Religions, and the Media* (Lexington: University Press of Kentucky, 2002).

5. Corinthians 11:14–15.

6. Luke 3:16.

7. Luke 12:7; Matthew 10:29–30.

8. Ecclesiastes 1:9.

9. The U.S. Constitution (written in 1789, not 1776) sanctions separation of church and state.

10. Marjorie Napier may be mistaking the Ten Commandments for the ten amendments that make up the Bill of Rights. The motto "In God we trust" was adopted for the dollar bill in 1908.

11. Hiram Day is speaking in church and addresses the preacher, his half sister Lydia Surgener, whom he calls Liddy.

12. Jonathan Edwards, "Sinners in the Hands of an Angry God," preached at Enfield, CT, July 8, 1741.

13. For a comparative discussion, see my "Sfere del sacro. Tra Vallepietra e Harlan County, Kentucky," in *Storie orali. Racconto, immaginazione, dialogo* (Rome: Donzelli, 2007), 341–47.

14. McCauley, *Appalachian Mountain Religion*, 314.

15. Jimmy Morrow with Ralph W. Hood, *Handling Serpents: Pastor Jimmy Morrow's Narrative History of His Appalachian Jesus' Name Tradition* (Macon, GA: Mercer University Press, 2005), 16–29. Hensley died of snakebite in 1955 at seventy-eight; for an account of his life and work, see Thomas Burton, *Serpent Handling Believers* (Knoxville: University of Tennessee Press, 1993), 41–60, 149–58. Hensley's presence on Pine Mountain in 1919 is recalled by Morrow, 74–76, but not mentioned in Burton.

16. The movement evolved around the turn of the century from the Holiness movement: Burton, *Serpent-Handling Believers*, 5. "There's basically two different denominations that handle serpents. One is the Jesus Only. They believe that God the Father is God the Son; they don't believe in a Trinity godhead. And then there are the Trinity people, the Pentecostal" (*Rev. Gary Page*). On the difference between Trinity and Jesus Only, see Burton, *Serpent-Handling Believers*, 20–21; on Jesus Only believers, see Morrow, *Handling Serpents*. See also David L. Kimbrough, *Taking Up Serpents: Snake Handlers of Eastern Kentucky* (Chapel Hill: University of North Carolina Press, 1995).

17. John F. Day, *Bloody Ground* (Lexington: University Press of Kentucky, 1981 [1941]), 9–10. On legislation on snake handling, see Burton, *Serpent-Handling Believers*, 74–85. Harlan possessed the highest concentration of serpent-handling churches in the region: Nathan

S. Gerrard, "Churches of the Stationary Poor in Southern Appalachia," in Frank S. Riddell, ed., *Appalachia: Its People, Heritage and Problems* (Dubuque, IA: Kendall/Hunt, 1974), 92–106.

18. Day, *Bloody Ground*, 1–14; Steven M. Kane, "Ritual Possession in a Southern Appalachian Religious Sect," *Journal of American Folklore* 87 (1974): 246, 293–302. Bertolt T. Schwarz notes that the snakes are also in a "cataleptic" state akin to "hypnosis": "Ordeal by Serpents, Fire and Strychnine: A Study of Some Provocative Psychosomatic Phenomena," *Psychiatric Quarterly* 34 (July 1960): 405–29, cited in W. K. McNeil, *Appalachian Images in Folk and Popular Culture* (Knoxville: University of Tennessee Press, 1995), 285–305.

19. A minister named Ernest W. Short, forty-one, died of snakebite at Ages in 1989; Linda Fee, "Minister Dies After Being Bitten by Snake in Ages Church Service," *Harlan Daily Enterprise*, January 31, 1989. According to the same article, the Reverend Gerald Fleenor, who had been bitten by a snake in November 1988 ("Snake Bites Preacher," *Washington Post*, November 22, 1988), recovered after reluctantly accepting hospitalization. Snakebite is not necessarily deadly, as the effect depends on such factors as the snake's age, size, and type (copperheads are less dangerous than rattlesnakes); see Stephen M. Kane, "Holy-Ghost People: The Snake Handlers of Southern Appalachia," *Appalachian Journal* 1, 4 (Spring 1974): 255–62. On deaths and survivals from snakebite, see Morrow, *Handling Serpents*, 75–84, 116–26. In Harlan County, Morrow cites the deaths of Erin Long in the 1970s; Daril A. Collins, twenty-three, in Arjay; and preacher Kale Saylor in Bledsoe in 1997 (ibid., 78, 121–22). A Harlan County funeral director told Morrow (*Handling Serpents*, 125) that he had performed funerals for about ten snake-handling victims in forty years. Two deaths were reported in 1944, and for one, George Hensley was indicted for murder; see *Chicago Tribune*, September 20 and 24, 1944.

20. See Morrow, *Handling Serpents*, 125. For images of serpent handling, strychnine, anointing with oil, and fire handling at the Church of Jesus Christ in Baxter, see Burton, *Serpent-Handling Believers*, 15–16, 129, 179.

21. Alfonso M. Di Nola, *Gli aspetti magico-religiosi di una cultura subalterna italiana* (Turin: Boringhieri, 1976).

22. Mary Lee Daugherty, "Serpent-Handling as Sacrament," in John D. Photiadis, ed., *Religion in Appalachia: Theological, Social and Psychological Dimensions and Correlations* (Morgantown: West Virginia University Center for Extension and Continuing Education, 1978), 103–11. Bertolt E. Schwarz, "Ordeal by Serpents," associates serpent handling with experiences of "narrow escapes from torture and death." According to Nathan Gerrard, serpent handling "helps soften the inevitability of poor health, illness, and death"; "The Serpent-Handling Religions of West Virginia," *Trans-Action* 5 (1988): 22–28 (quoted in Burton, *Serpent-Handling Believers*, 130). As Burton notes (131–33), these interpretations (as well as Freudian ones) are neither exhaustive nor incompatible with the complexity of a spiritual experience.

23. Thessalonians 3:6–12.

24. Jim Garland, *Welcome the Traveler Home: Jim Garland's Story of the Kentucky Mountains*, ed. Julia S. Ardery (Lexington: University Press of Kentucky, 1983), 80–88, 145; Carletta A. Bush, "Faith, Power, and Conflict: Miner Preachers and the United Mine Workers of America in the Harlan County Mine Wars, 1931–1939," Ph.D. dissertation, University of West Virginia, Morgantown, 2006. See also chapter 10.

25. Reinhold Niebuhr, "Religion and the Class War in Kentucky," *Christian Century*, May 25, 1932, 637–39.

26. Shaunna L. Scott, *Two Sides to Everything: The Cultural Construction of Class Consciousness in Harlan County, Kentucky* (Albany: State University of New York Press, 1995), 190, 177.

27. David Corbin, *Life, Work, and Rebellion in the Coal Fields: The Southern West Virginia Miners, 1880–1922* (Urbana: University of Illinois Press, 1981), 150.

28. Luke 13:3–4.

29. George J. Titler, *Hell in Harlan* (Beckley, WV: B.J. Printers, 1972), 94; "Violations of Free Speech and Rights of Labor," hearings before a Subcommittee of the Committee on Education and Labor, Harlan, KY, and Washington, DC, U.S. Senate, 75th Congress, April 1936 and April–May 1937, Part 10, 3612.

Chapter 5: Flush Times and Rough Times

1. Stone Creek is in Lee County, Virginia, across the line from Harlan, on the other side of Black Mountain. Gurney Norman points out that the vein of coal that his family mined is the same vein that ends in Cranks Creek, in Harlan County: a good metaphor for deep connections.

2. As in the classic Appalachian novel, John Fox Jr.'s *The Little Shepherd of Kingdom Come* (1903), set in Harlan County.

3. Roosevelt is remembered as a friendly "young collegiate fellow who wore a turtle-neck sweater with a large H [for Harvard]." Historian Mabel Condon writes: "My father had a frame country-style store on the courthouse square and on cool mornings the men sat around a pot-bellied stove and spit on the hot stove. The sizzling noise this made on the stove fascinated young F.D.R. and soon he was sizzling louder than the old-timers": *A History of Harlan County* (Nashville: Parthenon, 1962), 12. Roosevelt's letter, dated June 15, 1908, is reprinted in Harry M. Caudill, *Theirs Be the Power: The Moguls of Eastern Kentucky* (Urbana: University of Illinois Press, 1983), 88-89.

4. Lowell H. Harrison and James C. Klotter, *A New History of Kentucky* (Lexington: University Press of Kentucky, 1997), 5-6. On forests in Appalachia, see Erik Reece, *Lost Mountain: A Year in the Vanishing Wilderness* (New York: Riverhead Books, 2006), 32-34.

5. http://www.ket.org/kentuckylife/100s/kylife102.html.

6. Quoted in Ronald D. Eller, *Miners, Millhands, and Mountaineers: Industrialization of the Appalachian South, 1880-1930* (Knoxville: University of Tennessee Press, 1982), 87.

7. H. A. Gibbard, "Extractive Industries and Forestry," in Thomas R. Ford, *The Southern Appalachian Region: A Survey* (Lexington: University Press of Kentucky, 1967).

8. Eller, *Miners, Millhands, and Mountaineers*, 90.

9. David L. Rouse and L. Sue Green-Pitt, "Natural Resources and Environment of Appalachia," in Grace Toney Edwards, JoAnn Aust Asbury, and Ricky L. Cox, eds., *A Handbook to Appalachia: An Introduction to the Region* (Knoxville: University of Tennessee Press, 2006), 53-63.

10. Eller, *Miners, Millhands, and Mountaineers*, 89, 111; David Corbin, *Life, Work and Rebellion in the Coal Fields: The Southern West Virginia Miners, 1880-1922* (Urbana: University of Illinois Press, 1981), 6; Gibbard, "Extractive Industries and Forestry"; Rouse and Green-Pit, "Natural Resources and Environment."

11. Gibbard, "Extractive Industries and Forestry."

12. Georgia-Pacific is a pulp and paper company based in Atlanta; Georgia-Pacific Canada is one of its affiliates.

13. Harrison and Klotter, *A New History of Kentucky*, 307.

14. John Gaventa, *Power and Powerlessness: Rebellion and Quiescence in an Appalachian Valley* (Urbana: University of Illinois Press, 1980).

15. Harrison and Klotter, *A New History of Kentucky*, 284. See also Harry M. Caudill's chapter "The Strange Rise of John C. C. Mayo" in *Theirs Be the Power*, 57-66; Eller, *Miners, Millhands, and Mountaineers*, 63; John Gaventa, "Coal and Theft," in Helen Lewis, Linda Johnson, and Donald Askins, eds., *Colonialism in Modern America: The Appalachian Case* (Boone, NC: Appalachian Consortium Press, 1978), 141-59; Warren Wright, "The Big Steal," in Lewis, Johnson, and Askins, eds., *Colonialism in Modern America*, 161-75.

16. Robert S. Weise, *Grasping at Independence: Debt, Male Authority, and Mineral Rights in Appalachian Kentucky, 1850-1915* (Knoxville: University of Tennessee Press, 2001), 270.

17. See Shaunna L. Scott, *Two Sides to Everything: The Cultural Construction of Class Consciousness in Harlan County, Kentucky* (Albany: State University of New York Press, 1994), 229n.

18. "A lot of the old deeds are in this shaky, illegible handwritten English. A deed's description is supposed to close, it's supposed to go from one place to another and go back to the beginning. In a lot of these old deeds, not only do they not close, but the descriptions are not plotted to permanent markers. In one of the greatest ones that I've seen, part of the property description read, 'from the edge of a creek to a rock to a snow bank.' Pretty good in the wintertime, but not so great when spring comes and the snow melts!" (*Sid Douglass*).

19. Harrison and Klotter, *A New History of Kentucky*, 284; John Egerton, *Generations: An American Family* (Lexington: University Press of Kentucky, 1983), 51.

20. Chad Montrie, *Save the Land and People: A History of Opposition to Surface Mining in Appalachia* (Chapel Hill: University of North Carolina Press, 2003), 67–68, 82–83; "Broad-Form Deeds in Kentucky: A Chronology," in *Balancing the Scales*, Kentuckians for the Commonwealth, October 20, 1988, 2–3. The coal industry claimed that restricting extraction to means available in the early twentieth century meant going back to child labor; see *Kentucky Coal Journal: The Monthly Newspaper of the Coal Industry*, November 14, 1988, 1.

21. According to Shaunna L. Scott, Harlan Countians "played a major role" in the anti-broad-form-deed movement in the 1980s. I attended a big rally in Harlan in 1986.

22. Melanie Zuercher, ed., *Making History: The First Ten Years of the KTFC* (Prestonburg: Kentuckians for the Commonwealth, 1991), 67–86.

23. On Bryan Whitfield, see Paul Nyden, *The Coal Miners' Struggle in Eastern Kentucky* (Huntington, WV: Appalachian Movement Press, 1972), 4.

24. F. Raymond Daniel, "Behind the Conflict in 'Bloody Harlan,'" *New York Times*, June 26, 1938. Union organizer George J. Titler names R. W. Creech as one of the few Harlan County operators he regarded as "decent human beings": Titler, *Hell in Harlan* (Beckley, WV: B. J. Printers, 1972), 42.

25. Eller, *Miners, Millhands, and Mountaineers*, 129.

26. Thomas N. Bethell, "Foreword," in Jim Garland, *Welcome the Traveler Home: Jim Garland's Story of the Kentucky Mountains*, ed. Julia S. Ardery (Lexington: University Press of Kentucky, 1983), xx; Eller, *Miners, Millhands, and Mountaineers*, 148–49; William D. Forester, *Before We Forget: Harlan County 1920 Through 1930* (Harlan, KY: William D. Forester, 1983), 2.

27. Forester, *Before We Forget*, 20; *Harlan Enterprise*, April 25 and May 2, 1924.

28. See a photograph of Bryan Whitfield and his plane in *Harlan's Heritage V*, February 27, 1988, 51.

29. Courtesy of Arthur Johnson Johnson changed the acronym to avoid legal consequences.

30. Ronald Eller, *Uneven Ground: Appalachia Since 1945* (Lexington: University Press of Kentucky, 2008), 185.

31. Calvin Trillin, "The Logical Things, Costwise," *New Yorker*, December 29, 1969, in David S. Walls and John B. Stephenson, eds., *Appalachia in the Sixties: Decade of Reawakening* (Lexington: University Press of Kentucky, 1972), 109–19.

32. F. Scott Fitzgerald, *The Great Gatsby* (1925), in *The Fitzgerald Reader*, ed. Arthur Mizener (New York: Charles Scribner's Sons, 1963), 147–48.

33. Becky Ruth Brae, "I Can Fly," in Charles Hardy III and Alessandro Portelli, eds., "I Can Almost See the Lights of Home," *Journal for MultiMedia History* 2, 1 (1999), www.albany.edu/jmmh/vol2no1/lights.html. Courtesy of Becky Ruth Brae.

34. *Harlan Enterprise*, March 10, 1922.

35. Ibid., March 3, 1922.

36. See Forester, *Before We Forget*, 68–69.

37. G. C. Jones, *Growing Up Hard in Harlan County* (Lexington: University Press of Kentucky, 1985), 2.

38. Forester, *Before We Forget*, 20; *Harlan Enterprise*, March 10, 1922.

39. Sylvia F. Warfield, "Love Is the Tie That Binds: Memories of the Early Black Mountain Community," *Harlan's Heritage VI*, February 28, 1991.

40. After the end of Prohibition, Harlan remained wet until 1942.

41. Jess Blanton was sentenced to fourteen years for the murder of James Britton, age eighteen, over damage to his car (January 27, 1922); one miner was killed in a slate fall at Kentenia; two died in a slate fall at Louellen (February 24, 1922); two deputies were shot at Kitts, Melcroft (April 14, 1922); Will Coleman, a black man, was killed by a white boy at Loyall (April 28, 1922); "Homicide at Liggets," "Accidental Shot Kills Small Boy," "Samp Standford Killed at Verda" (May 19 and 26, 1922); Pete Gulley died of a gunshot wound; Jim Lee was killed by a deputy sheriff (June 2, 1922); Sheriff Floyd Ball and two deputies were shot on the road to Pineville (July 7, 1922); Lee Swanson and Jeff Napier were killed in two separate incidents at Cawood (August 10 and 15, 1922).

42. *Harlan Enterprise*, July 7, 14, and 21, September 1, 1922.

43. Robert M. Ireland, "Violence," in James C. Klotter, ed., *Our Kentucky: A Study of the Bluegrass State* (Lexington: University Press of Kentucky, 2000).

44. Paul Frederick Cressey, "Social Disorganization and Reorganization in Harlan County, Kentucky," *American Sociological Review* 14, 3 (June 1949): 389–93.

45. See John F. Day, *Bloody Ground* (Lexington: University Press of Kentucky, 1981 [1941]), 132–47.

46. Thomas B. Slaughter, *The Whiskey Rebellion: Frontier Epilogue to the American Revolution* (New York: Oxford University Press, 1988); Mary K. Bonsteel Tachau, "The Whiskey Rebellion in Kentucky: A Forgotten Episode of Civil Disobedience," *Journal of the Early Republic* 2, 3 (Autumn 1982): 239–59.

47. Lisa Kirk, "Easier to Moonshine than to Ship Corn," *Harlan's Heritage III*, February 28, 1986, 16.

48. Jess Carr, *The Second Oldest Profession: An Informal History of Moonshining in America* (Englewood Cliffs, NJ: Prentice-Hall, 1972), 16; Harrison and Klotter, *A New History of Kentucky*, 252; Forester, *Before We Forget*, 58–68; Bruce Stewart, "Attacking 'Red-Legged Grasshoppers': Moonshiners, Violence, and the Politics of Federal Liquor Taxation in Western North Carolina 1865–1876," *Appalachian Journal* 32, 1 (Fall 2004): 26–48; Elvin Hatch, "The Margins of Civilization: Progressives and Moonshiners in the Late 19th-Century Mountain South," *Appalachian Journal* 32, 1 (Fall 2004): 68–99.

49. For a description of whiskey-making, see Ray Renzi and Leo Downing, "A Touch of Mountain Dew: The Art and History of Whiskey-Making in North Georgia," in *The Many Faces of Appalachia*, Proceedings of the Seventh Annual Appalachian Studies Conference (Boone, NC: Appalachian Consortium Press, 1985), 196–203.

50. Melvyn P. Levy, "Class War in Kentucky," in Theodore Dreiser, ed., *Harlan Miners Speak: Report of Terrorism in the Kentucky Coal Fields* (New York: Da Capo Press, 1970 [1932]), 21.

51. "Ballad of Thunder Road," by Don Raye and Robert Mitchum, recorded by Robert Mitchum, from *Thunder Road*, 1958, directed by Arthur Ripley, starring Robert Mitchum.

52. See http://www.univie.ac.at/Anglistik/easyrider/data/Thunderr.htm. As Harrison and Klotter point out, Kentucky as the "land of feuds and moonshine" was a major theme in dozens of Hollywood movies—many directed by Kentuckian D. W. Griffith (*A New History of Kentucky*, 342). On *Thunder Road*, see J. W. Williamson, *Hillbillyland: What the Movies Did to the Mountains and What the Mountains Did to the Movies* (Chapel Hill: University of North Carolina Press, 1995), 126–41.

53. Jones, *Growing Up Hard in Harlan County*, 94–95; see also 15–17.

54. On Maggie Bailey and bootlegging, see "Bootlegging Is Accepted Way of Life Here," May 31, 1972; "Booming Liquor Traffic Is a Leading County 'Industry,'" June 7, 1972; "Another Moonshine Craze Hits Region," December 27, 2003, all in *Harlan Daily Enterprise*.

55. Hobert E. Carts, "Blacklisted Miners Tried Bootlegging," *Harlan's Heritage V*, February 27, 1988, 5; Randall Norris and Jean-Philippe Cyprès, *Women of Coal* (Lexington: University Press of Kentucky, 1996).

56. "Another Moonshine Craze Hits Region," December 27, 2003, and "Moonshine and Marijuana Turn Up at Raid," December 30, 2004, both in *Harlan Daily Enterprise*.

57. Tom Lasseter and Bill Estep, "Just Growing Marijuana," *Lexington Herald-Leader*, January 29, 2003. See also "Marijuana Use Increases Sharply," June 29, 1973; "Two Charged with Marijuana Cultivation; Plants Destroyed," August 26, 1991; "Marijuana Found in Mine," October 14, 2003; "Marijuana, Moonshine Turn Up at Raid," December 30, 2004, all in *Harlan Daily Enterprise*. Arrests for possession of marijuana together with other drugs are reported frequently in recent years: *Harlan Daily Enterprise*, November 19, 2004.

Chapter 6: A Space of Their Own

1. Crandall Shifflett, *Coal Towns: Life, Work, and Culture in Company Towns of Southern Appalachia, 1880–1960* (Knoxville: University of Tennessee Press, 1991), 3–4; Harry M. Caudill, *Night Comes to the Cumberlands* (Boston: Little, Brown, 1963), 108; John Gaventa,

Power and Powerlessness: Rebellion and Quiescence in an Appalachian Valley (Urbana: University of Illinois Press, 1980), 84–96.

2. As is often the case with vernacular working-class American English, "law" means "police."

3. Testimony of Marshall A. Musick, "Violations of Free Speech and Rights of Labor," hearings before the Subcommittee of the Committee on Education and Labor, Harlan, KY, and Washington, DC, U.S. Senate, 75th Congress, April 1936 and April-May 1937 (henceforth "La Follette Committee"), 3452ff. See also my "Patterns of Paternalism," in *The Death of Luigi Trastulli and Other Stories: Form and Meaning in Oral History* (Albany: State University of New York Press, 1991), 195–215.

4. George J. Titler, *Hell in Harlan* (Beckley, WV: B.J. Printers, 1972), 48–49.

5. Testimony of James A. Westmoreland, union organizer, La Follette Committee, 3824ff.; Jim Garland, *Welcome the Traveler Home: Jim Garland's Story of the Kentucky Mountains*, ed. Julia S. Ardery (Lexington: University Press of Kentucky, 1983), 135. See also Caudill, *Night Comes to the Cumberlands* 194; on U.S. Steel's "unalterabl[e]" opposition to unions, see Caudill, *The Mountain, the Miner, and the Lord, and Other Tales from a Country Law Office* (Lexington: University Press of Kentucky, 1980), 27.

6. Testimony of Robert E. Lawson, La Follette Committee, 3833.

7. Titler, *Hell in Harlan*, 48. Drunkenness was often a pretext to arrest union organizers or sympathizers: see testimony of J. W. Freeman, in Theodore Dreiser, ed., *Harlan Miners Speak: Report on Terrorism in the Kentucky Coal Fields* (New York: Da Capo Press, 1970 [1932]), 201.

8. Shifflett, *Coal Towns*; David Corbin, *Life, Work and Rebellion in the Coal Fields: The Southern West Virginia Miners, 1880–1922* (Urbana: University of Illinois Press, 1981), 61–86, 117–27; Ronald D. Eller, *Miners, Millhands and Mountaineers: Industrialization of the Appalachian South, 1880–1930* (Knoxville: University of Tennessee Press, 1982), 181–98.

9. *Report of the United States Coal Commission on Civil Liberties in the Coal Fields* (Washington, DC: Government Printing Office, 1925), 169.

10. *Report of the Coal Commission*, 176; Corbin, *Life, Work, and Rebellion*, 32.

11. John Hevener, *Which Side Are You On? The Harlan County Coal Miners, 1931–39* (Urbana: University of Illinois Press, 2002 [1978]), 19.

12. U.S. Coal Mines Administration, *A Medical Survey of the Bituminous Coal Industry*, Washington, D.C., 1947 (Boone Report), quoted in Brit Hume, *Death and the Mines: Rebellion and Murder in the United Mine Workers* (New York: Grossman, 1971), 104–13.

13. Don West, "Harlan County Portraits," *No Lonesome Road: Selected Prose and Poems*, ed. George Brosy and Jeff Biggers (Urbana: University of Illinois Press, 2004), 109–10.

14. James B. Goode, "Coal Camps in Appalachia: How They Shaped the Present," *Up from the Mines* (Ashland, KY: Jesse Stuart Foundation, 1993), 135–42.

15. *The American Coal Miner: A Report on Community and Living in the Coal Fields: The President's Commission on Coal, John D Rockefeller IV, Chairman* (Rockefeller Report), Washington, DC, 1980, 33.

16. Shifflett, *Coal Towns*, 3.

17. Sam Caddy to John L. Lewis, August 7, 1937, UMWA Correspondence Files.

18. According to Lynch native William H. Turner in "Race: The Ignored Dimension of the Colonial Analogy as Applied to Powerlessness and Exploitation in Appalachia," *Western Journal of Black Studies* 7, 1 (Spring 1983), 10–20, black churches in coal towns retained some degree of autonomy.

19. Helen Lewis, "Fatalism or the Coal Industry?" in Frank S. Riddell, ed., *Appalachia: Its People, Heritage and Problems* (Dubuque, IA: Kendall/Hunt, 1974), 221–38. In 1947, District 19 president Abe Vales told the *United Mine Workers Journal* that often, and particularly in Harlan County, doctors were stockholders in the coal mines or in the land companies, and getting rid of doctors disliked by miners was hard: *United Mine Workers Journal*, August 14, 1947. See also Ivana Krajnovic, *From Company Doctors to Managed Care: The United Mine Workers' Noble Experiment* (Ithaca, NY: Cornell University Press, 1997), 18–22.

20. Testimony of Lindsay Baker, La Follette Committee, 4465ff. Baker broke his jaw in the mine; the company doctor gave him some pills to "rinse his mouth." It was a month before he could get an X-ray at the Pineville hospital, at his own expense.

21. The reference is to Merle Travis, *Sixteen Tons*: "St. Peter don't you call me, 'cause I can't go / I owe my soul to the company store," *Folk Songs of the Hills* (1947), Capitol Vintage LC 0249.

22. Testimony of Lindsay Baker and Jasper Clouse, La Follette Committee, 4465, 4475.

23. Testimony of Robert E. Lawson, La Follette Committee, 3833ff.; Hevener, *Which Side Are You On*, 22; Corbin, *Work, Life and Rebellion*, 32; Shaunna L. Scott, *Two Sides to Everything: The Cultural Construction of Class Consciousness in Harlan County, Kentucky* (Albany: State University of New York Press, 1995), 15.

24. Testimony of Jim Garland, U.S. Senate, Committee on Manufactures, "Conditions in Coal Fields in Harlan and Bell Counties, Kentucky" (1932) (henceforth Costigan Committee), 17–18.

25. Melvyn P. Levy, "Class War in Kentucky," in Dreiser, ed., *Harlan Miners Speak*, 30. On script, see Shifflett, *Coal Towns*, 179–89.

26. "Harvester Town: Black Diamonds from Kentucky Hills," *Coal Mines: Benham* 5, 3 (1948): 15–16, quoted in Thomas E. Wagner and Philip J. Obermiller, *African American Miners and Migrants: The Eastern Kentucky Social Club* (Urbana: University of Illinois Press, 2005), 72.

27. Andy Mead, "Memories Draw Generations Back to Lynch," in "Blacks in Appalachia," special issue of *Appalachian Heritage* 19, 4 (Fall 1991): 20–22.

28. Ronald Eller, *Miners, Millhands, and Mountaineers*, 147.

29. According to Norman Yarbrough, the captive coal towns "were what amounts to a stepchild, really. The steel people...primarily, what they were interested in was it was an outlet for steel."

30. Harry M. Caudill, *Theirs Be the Power: The Moguls of Eastern Kentucky* (Urbana: University of Illinois Press, 1983), 95, 96.

31. Eller, *Miners, Millhands, and Mountaineers*, 190.

32. William H. Turner, interview in *Long Journey Home*, an Appalshop (Whitesburg, KY) film by Elizabeth Barret and Herb E. Smith, 1987.

33. Shifflett, *Coal Towns*, 48.

34. Testimony of Joseph R. Menefee, La Follette Committee, 3959.

35. William D. Forester, *Before We Forget: Harlan County 1920 Through 1930 with Background Dating Further in Time* (Harlan, KY: William D. Forester, 1983), 9. On the racial structuring of the space at Benham, see Scott, *Two Sides to Everything*, 14.

36. James B. Goode, "Lynch: A Coal Legacy," *The 1991 Harlan County Almanac*, Harlan County Chapter of Kentuckians for the Commonwealth, 5; Caudill, *Night Comes to the Cumberlands*, 112, 100.

37. *The American Coal Miner* (Rockefeller Report), 345. At the time of the report, 30 percent of Appalachian coal miners were living in mobile homes; ibid., 45.

38. Goode, "Lynch: A Coal Legacy."

39. Bob Hill, "Black Home in Appalachia," Louisville *Courier-Journal Sunday Magazine*, June 28, 1987, 6–14; Bob Hill, "Just Who Is Bernie Bickerstaff?" Louisville *Courier-Journal Sunday Magazine*, January 27, 1991; Wagner and Obermiller, *African American Miners and Migrants*, 44–46.

40. Harry M. Moses, general superintendent for U.S. Coal and Coke Co., controlled by U.S. Steel, testified in the 1930s that at the time his company found it convenient not to incorporate Lynch. The company owned all the property, including the church and the school, and paid all the taxes. No miners were included on the school board. All regulations were issued by U.S. Coal. The town was policed by deputies and county patrolmen paid by the company. La Follette Committee, 3942ff.

41. *The Ford Industries: Facts about the Ford Motor Company and Its Subsidiaries*, Ford Motor Company, Detroit, 1924, 75. I thank Roy Silver for pointing out this source.

42. See "Here's a Safety Story for All Mines to Copy," *United Mine Workers Journal*, July 15, 1951.

43. See testimony of Jasper Clouse on the killing of Lloyd Clouse by Harlan-Wallins company guards at Verda in April 1937, La Follette Committee, 4476ff.

44. Pearl Bassham claimed that raffle tickets were bought voluntarily, but he admitted that "I could not be able to sell the tickets, sir, if I did not have the mine" (La Follette Committee, 4487ff.). Company employee Bill C. "Thug" Johnson testified that he would pressure the men into buying the tickets but was in turn pressured to sell the tickets if he wanted to keep his job (4509ff.). The company made up to 50 percent profit on each car raffled off.

45. Bill Worthington, quoted in Kennet Warren Mirvis, "An American Portrait: A Phenomenological Analysis of the Appalachian Coal-Producing Counties," Ph.D. dissertation, Boston University, School of Education, 1981, 218.

46. Wagner and Obermiller, eds., African American Miners and Migrants, 29, 61.

47. William Bosch, interviewed by Thomas Wagner, May 31, 2003, in Wagner and Obermiller, eds., African American Miners and Migrants, 44.

48. Sherry Cable, "From Fussin' to Organizing: Individual and Collective Resistance at Yellow Creek," in Stephen L. Fisher, ed., Fighting Back in Appalachia: Traditions of Resistance and Change (Philadelphia: Temple University Press, 1993), 69–83.

Chapter 7: Miner's Life

1. Nimrod Workman, "Both Lungs Is Broke Down," Come All You Coal Miners, Rounder Records 4005.

2. Jim Garland, Welcome the Traveler Home: Jim Garland's Story of the Kentucky Mountains, ed. Julia S. Ardery (Lexington: University Press of Kentucky, 1983), 89.

3. Keith Dix, What's a Coal Miner to Do? The Mechanization of Coal Mining (Pittsburgh: University of Pittsburgh Press, 1988), 12–14, 199–210.

4. United Mine Workers Journal, November 15, 1950, 19.

5. Crandall Shifflett, Coal Towns: Life, Work, and Culture in Company Towns of Southern Appalachia, 1880–1960 (Knoxville: University of Tennessee Press, 1991), 103–4.

6. Shaunna L. Scott, Two Sides to Everything: The Cultural Construction of Class Consciousness in Harlan County, Kentucky (Albany: State University of New York Press, 1995), 137. See my "Sports, Work and Politics in an Industrial Town," in The Death of Luigi Trastulli and Other Stories: Form and Meaning in Oral History (Albany: State of New York University Press, 1991), 138–60.

7. Merle Travis, "Dark as a Dungeon," Folk Songs of the Hills (1947), Capitol Vintage LC 0249.

8. Charles Vaught and David L. Smith, "Incorporation and Mechanical Solidarity in an Underground Mine," Sociology of Work and Occupations 7, 2 (May 1980): 159–87.

9. James R. Carroll and R. G. Dunlop, "Coal Dust Suspected in Blast: Mine's Operator Had 3 Related Fines Just This Month," Louisville Courier-Journal, May 22, 2006.

10. Ibid.; "The Widows of Harlan County," CBS News, March 11, 2007, http://www.cbsnews.com/stories/2007/03/08/60minutes/main2547001.shtml. On dust as a cause of explosions, see Brit Hume, Death and the Mines: Rebellion and Murder in the UMW (New York: Grossman, 1971), 7. Crushed limestone dust helps prevent explosions but contributes to the miners' lung diseases.

11. "Historical Data on Mine Disasters in the United States," Mine Safety and Health Administration, http://www.msha.gov/MSHAINFO/FactSheets/MSHAFCT8.HTM; see also the United States Mine Rescue Association website (http://www.usmra.com/saxsewell/historical.htm). These sources list 623 coal mine disasters from 1875 to 2006. The worst disasters occurred at Monongah, West Virginia (1907, 362 killed), Dawson, New Mexico (1913, 263 killed), and Cherry, Illinois (1909, 259 killed). Ninety-four men were killed in explosions in Kentucky from 1970 to 2006, including twenty-six at the Scotia mine in Letcher County in 1976 and thirty-eight at Hyden, Leslie County, in 1970.

12. John Cheever, "Two for the Money," Lexington Herald-Leader, October 20, 2006: Kathy Still, "UMWA President Lays Recent Mining Deaths at the Feet of the Bush Administration," Bristol (Tenn.) Herald Courier, September 16, 2007.

13. "Historical Coal Mine Accidents in the United States 1839–1976," http://members.aol.com/_ht_a/tcook79370.

14. http://www.presidency.ucsb.edu/ws/index.php?pid=2873.

15. Between 1921 and 1948, 16,702 fatalities (54.9 percent of the total) were caused by roof falls, as opposed to 4,053 (13.3 percent) caused by explosions; Dix, *What's a Coal Miner to Do*, 101, table 6. Ronald D. Eller, *Miners, Millhands, and Mountaineers: Industrialization of the Appalachian South, 1880–1930* (Knoxville: University of Tennessee Press, 1982), 179, notes that out of 48,000 mine deaths between 1906 and 1935, only 16 percent were caused by explosions; the rest occurred in the course of ordinary activity, such as haulage and, especially, roof falls. Out of 254 mining casualties in Kentucky in 1946 and 1947, 169 were caused by roof falls (*United Mine Workers Journal*, February 15, 1947, March 1, 1948).

16. Testimony of Tony Oppergard, general counsel to Kentucky's mine safety agency, to U.S. Committee of Education and Labor, hearing on "Protecting the Health and Safety of America's Mine Workers," March 28, 2007, http://bulk.resource.org/gpo.gov/hearings/110h/34100.

17. Testimony of Tony Oppergard. Morris's death was due also to the absence of medical facilities at the mine; Ken Ward, "Disasters Get the Headlines, But Most Miners Killed on the Job Die Alone," *Charleston Gazette*, November 5, 2006, http://www.reclaimdemocracy.org/articles/2006/miners_die_laws_violated.php.

18. http://www.rootsweb.com/~kyharlan/minersdeaths1980_1989.html.

19. Scott, *Two Sides to Everything*, 200; http://www.rootsweb.com/~kyharlan/minersdeaths1980_1989.html.

20. Eller, *Miners, Millhands, and Mountaineers*, 179.

21. Ben A. Franklin, "The Scandal of Death and Injury in the Mines," *New York Times*, March 30, 1969, in David S. Walls and John B. Stephenson, eds., *Appalachia in the Sixties: Decade of Reawakening* (Lexington: University Press of Kentucky, 1972), 92–108.

22. Bennet M. Judkins, "The People's Respirator: Coalition Building and the Black Lung Association," in Stephen L. Fisher, ed., *Fighting Back in Appalachia: Traditions of Resistance and Change* (Philadelphia: Temple University Press, 1993), 224–44.

23. Franklin, "The Scandal of Death and Injury in the Mines"; Hume, *Death in the Mines*, 9; Barbara Ellen Smith, *Digging Our Own Graves: Coal Miners and the Struggle over Black Lung Disease* (Philadelphia: Temple University Press, 1987), 127–35: Judkins, "The People's Respirator"; John Cheever, "Two for the Money."

24. "Here's a Safety Story for All Mines to Copy," *United Mine Workers Journal*, July 15, 1951; see also November 1, 1949, January 21, 1950, July 15, 1951, and October 15, 1954.

25. Dix, *What's a Coal Miner to Do*, 95–97. Tony Oppergard's testimony concludes that while industry spokespeople insist that most accidents are caused by the carelessness of coal miners, what is needed is increased mine inspections and strict enforcement of the Mine Act, rather than "the Bush Administration's fairy-tale emphasis on 'compliance assistance.'"

26. *Harlan County Heritage*, XVII, March 30, 2002.

27. Smith, *Digging Our Own Graves*, 3–30, 153.

28. "A respirator is a device which actually pushes the air into your lungs, so you have a tube in your throat and the respirator pushes the air through that tube in your lungs so that you can get enough. It basically does the work that your muscles would normally do when you take a breath" (J. D. Miller).

29. Smith, *Digging Our Own Graves*, 29; Goins Brothers, *Black Lung Blues*, REM 45-449.

30. Henry N. Doyle, "The Impact of Changing Technology on the Health Problems in Coal Mining Industry," *Papers and Proceeding of the National Conference on Medicine and the Federal Coal Mine Health and Safety Act of 1969* (Washington, DC: U.S. Government Printing Office, 1970), 195–97.

31. See chapter 11, para. 5 in this book; *The American Coal Miner: A Report on Community and Living in the Coal Fields: The President's Commission on Coal, John D Rockefeller IV, Chairman* (Rockefeller Report), Washington, DC, 1980; Jeanne M. Rasmussen, "In the Outside Lookin' In," *Mountain Life and Work*, September 1969, in Walls and Stephenson, eds., *Appalachia in the Sixties*, 176–83.

32. Judkins, "The People's Respirator"; Smith, *Digging Our Own Graves*, 109–10, 114–26; Richard A. Couto, "Appalachian Innovation in Health Care," in Alan Batteau, ed., *Appalachia and America: Autonomy and Regional Dependence* (Lexington: University Press of Kentucky, 1983), 168–88.

33. Kathy Still, "UMWA President Lays Recent Mining Deaths at the Feet of the Bush Administration"; James Branscome, *Annihilating the Hillbilly: The Appalachians Struggle with America's Institutions* (Huntington, WV: Appalachian Movement Press, [1972]).

34. Judkins, "The People's Respirator"; Still, "UMWA President Lays Recent Mining Deaths at the Feet of the Bush Administration." According to some estimates, miners still die from black lung at the rate of three a day; see Jeff Biggers, "Tip of Iceberg of Massey's Titanic Violations," www.huffingtonpost.com/jeff-biggers/tip-of-iceberg-of-masseys_b_529846. html, posted April 8, 2010.

Chapter 8: Identities

1. Marat Moore, *Women in the Mines: Stories of Life and Work* (New York: Twayne, 1996), 3.

2. Carol A. B. Giesen, *Coal Miners' Wives: Portraits of Endurance* (Lexington: University Press of Kentucky, 1995).

3. Ethel Day Smith, Evarts, 1913, and Ethel Dixon McCuiston, Benham, 1918, interviews in Moore, *Women in the Mines*, 27–31, 39–43.

4. Brandon Sergent, "Women Miners Overcame Superstitions, Misconceptions," *Harlan County Heritage*, XVIII, March 31, 2003, 6.

5. Moore, *Women in the Mines*, xxvi–li; Suzanne E. Tallichet, *Daughters of the Mountain: Women Coal Miners in Central Appalachia* (University Park: Pennsylvania State University Press, 2006).

6. Moore, *Women in the Mines*, 143.

7. Shaunna L. Scott, *Two Sides to Everything: The Cultural Construction of Class Consciousness in Harlan County, Kentucky* (Albany: State University of New York Press, 1995), 89.

8. Moore, *Women in the Mines*, xxxi.

9. Carletta Savage, "Regendering Coal: Female Miners and Male Supervisors," *Appalachian Journal* 27, 3 (Spring 2000): 232–48; Sue Thrasher, "Coal Employment Project," *Southern Exposure* (Winter 1981), 48–50; Suzanne E. Tallichet, "Gendered Relations in the Mines and the Sexual Division of Labor Underground," paper presented at the 8th World Congress Meetings of the International Rural Sociology Association, Pennsylvania State University, August 11–16, 1992.

10. See Tallichet, *Daughters of the Mountain*, 65–78.

11. Brenda Brock interview, in Moore, *Women in the Mines*, 146, 143; Tallichet, *Daughters of the Mountain*, 44–60; Scott, *Two Sides to Everything*, 90.

12. Sergent, "Women Miners Overcame Superstitions"; David A. Corbin, *Life, Work and Rebellion in the Coal Fields: The Southern West Virginia Miners, 1880–1922* (Urbana: University of Illinois Press, 1981), 65; George Korson, *Coal Dust on the Fiddle* (Philadelphia: University of Pennsylvania Press, 1943), 210–11.

13. Charles Vaught and David L. Smith, "Incorporation and Mechanical Solidarity in an Underground Mine," *Sociology of Work and Occupations* 7, 2 (May 1980): 159–87.

14. G. C. Jones, *Growing Up Hard in Harlan County* (Lexington: University Press of Kentucky, 1985), 31.

15. Scott, *Two Sides to Everything*, 13.

16. Ronald L. Lewis, "Beyond Isolation and Homogeneity: Diversity and the History of Appalachia," in Dwight B. Billings, Gurney Norman, and Katherine Ledford, eds., *Confronting Appalachian Stereotypes: Back Talk from an American Region* (Lexington: University Press of Kentucky, 1999), 21–43; John C. Belcher, "Population Growth and Characteristics," in Thomas R. Ford, ed., *The Southern Appalachian Region: A Survey* (Lexington: University Press of Kentucky, 1967), 37–53.

17. Doug Cantrell, "Immigrants and Community in Harlan County, 1910–1930," in Doug Cantrell et al., eds., *Kentucky Through the Centuries: A Collection of Documents and Essays* (Dubuque, IA: Kendall/Hunt, 2005), 201–17.

18. Crandall Shifflett, *Coal Towns: Life, Work, and Culture in Company Towns of Southern Appalachia, 1880–1960* (Knoxville: University of Tennessee Press, 1991), 66–75; Ronald D. Eller, *Miners, Millhands, and Mountaineers: Industrialization of the Appalachian South, 1880–1930* (Knoxville: University of Tennessee Press, 1982), 173–74; Kenneth R. Bailey, "A Temptation to Lawlessness: Peonage in West Virginia, 1903–1908," *West Virginia History* 50 (1991): 25–45.

19. AA. VV., *Monongah, 1907: una tragedia dimenticata* (Rome: Ministero Affari Esteri), 2007.

20. Fred A. Barkey, "Stepping into the Southern West Virginia Mine Wars: Italians of the Upper Kanawha Valley and the Long Ton Coal Strike of 1909," http://www.marshall.edu/csega/research/minewars.pdf; Fred Mooney, *Struggle in the Coal Fields: The Autobiography of Fred Mooney*, ed. J. W. Hess (Morgantown: West Virginia University Library, 1967); Corbin, *Life, Work, and Rebellion in the Coal Fields*, ch. 8.

21. Lawrence Di Stasi, *Una Storia Segreta: The Secret History of Italian American Evacuation and Internment During World War II* (Berkeley, CA: Heyday Books, 2004).

22. According to another version, it wasn't the Italian stonemasons who broke the stone, but the act was prompted by local "prominent citizens." William T. Cornett, "A Poet in Stone," Whitesburg *Mountain Eagle*, August 3, 1988.

23. http://www.rootsweb.com/~kyharlan/index.html.

24. Harry M. Caudill, *The Mountain, the Miner, and the Lord, and Other Tales from a Country Law Office* (Lexington: University Press of Kentucky, 1980), 109–21. Caudill, however, gets Majority's first name wrong—the feminine Francesca instead of the masculine Francesco.

25. What he means is that his father, like most people from a rural or working-class background at the time, spoke a regional dialect rather than the standard Italian of school and media.

26. Cantrell, "Immigrants and Community."

27. Ronald L. Lewis, *Black Coal Miners in America: Race, Class, and Community Conflict, 1790–1980* (Lexington: University Press of Kentucky, 1977), 124. The African American population in the Kentucky coal region grew from 5,814 in 1860 to 15,692 in 1920.

28. On Minnie Randolph, see her grandson William H. Turner's sketch, "Even at 100 Granny Still Has the Stuff," *Lexington Herald-Leader*, August 28, 1994. "Granny's stuff consists of customs, values, songs, stories, dances, sayings, jokes, techniques, information, beliefs, superstition, prejudices, tastes, and attitude."

29. Jim Garland, *Welcome the Traveler Home: Jim Garland's Story of the Kentucky Mountains*, ed. Julia S. Ardery (Lexington: University Press of Kentucky, 1983), 114.

30. According to Dwight B. Billings and Kathleen M. Blee, *The Road to Poverty: The Making of Wealth and Hardship in Appalachia* (New York: Cambridge University Press, 2000), 214, interracial marriages were not unknown before the Civil War in nearby Clay County.

31. For a barely avoided lynching, see *Harlan Daily Enterprise*, February 29, 1932.

32. James C. Klotter, *Kentucky: Portrait in Paradox, 1900–1950* (Louisville: Kentucky Historical Society, 1996), 68; Walter C. Rucker and James N. Upton, *Encyclopedia of American Race Riots* (Santa Barbara, CA: Greenwood, 2007), 550, 557; W. Fitzhugh Brundage, *Racial Violence, Lynchings, and Modernization in the Mountain South* (Urbana: University of Illinois Press, 1993), 302–16; John C. Inscoe, ed., *Appalachians and Race: The Mountain South from Slavery to Segregation* (Lexington: University Press of Kentucky, 2001), 302–16.

33. "Lynching era was 'the American holocaust,'" *Lexington Herald-Leader*, June 13, 2005.

34. *Harlan Heritage*, VI, February 28, 1991.

35. *Harlan Heritage*, XVI, March 30, 2003.

36. George Lee was one of the most notorious deputy sheriffs, or "thugs," who shot, beat, and harassed union miners in the 1930s. See John W. Hevener, *Which Side Are You On? The Harlan County Coal Miners, 1931–39* (Urbana: University of Illinois Press, 2002 [1977]), 99, 108–11, 140–42, and passim.

37. "A Brief History of the UMWA," *United Mine Workers Journal*, August 15, 1957, 12–19; Bill Worthington quoted in Linda Ann Ewen, *Which Side Are You On? The Brookside Mine Strike in Harlan County, Kentucky, 1973–1974* (New York: Vanguard, 1979), 41. See also Herbert G. Gutman, "The Negro and the United Mine Workers of America," in Julius Jacobson, ed., *The Negro and the American Labor Movement* (Garden City, NY: Anchor Books, 1968).

38. Thomas E. Wagner and Philip J. Obermiller, *African American Miners and Migrants: The Eastern Kentucky Social Club* (Urbana: University of Illinois Press, 2005), 44–46; Garland, *Welcome the Traveler Home*, 114.

39. Melvyn Levy, "Class War in Kentucky," in Theodore Dreiser, ed., *Harlan Miners Speak* (New York: Da Capo Press, 1970 [1932]), 23–24. Hazel Leonard's memory is accurate: see George J. Titler, *Hell in Harlan* (Beckley, WV: B. J. Printers, 1972), 8.

40. Hevener, *Which Side Are You On*, 6.

41. "During the war the operators were forced by the Fuel Administration to sign wage agreements with the United Mine Workers, but they did not recognize that body, and after the war the agreement was never renewed": statement by Howard E. Evanson, president, Clover Splint Coal Co., Conditions in Coal Fields in Harlan and Bell Counties, Kentucky: Hearings Before a Subcommittee of the Committee on Manufactures, U.S. Senate (Costigan Committee), 1932, 203.

42. Saul Alinsky, *John L. Lewis: An Unauthorized Biography* (New York: G. P. Putnam's Sons, 1949), 19.

43. "Union Man," letter to the *United Mine Workers Journal*; "Harlan County, Ky., Gunmen Shoot Down Coal Miners," *United Mine Workers Journal*, May 1, 1920.

44. Frank Walters, International board member, to John L. Lewis, November 16, 1921, UMWA correspondence files, 1921–22.

45. Frank Walters to John L. Lewis, November 16, 1921; *Harlan Enterprise*, January 13, March 10, March 17, 1922; Hevener, *Which Side Are You On*, 7–8.

46. Alan Banks, "Miners Talk Back: Labor Activism in Southeastern Kentucky in 1922," in Billings, Norman, and Ledford, eds., *Confronting Appalachian Stereotypes*, 215–27, 223.

47. This ritual would later be refined by dumping scabs into the creeks and "baptizing them in the name of the Lord and John L. Lewis." See University of Kentucky Library, Special Collections, Albert B. Chandler Collection, First Gubernatorial Series, State Correspondence, box 54; Archie Green, *Wobblies, Pile Butts, and Other Heroes: Laborlore Explorations* (Urbana: University of Illinois Press, 1993), 34ff.; Titler, *Hell in Harlan*, 182.

48. Jones, *Growing Up Hard in Harlan County*, 48. Jones's chronology and factual details are sometimes uncertain. Apparently he places these incidents around 1927.

49. Mother Jones, *The Autobiography of Mother Jones* (Chicago: Kerr, 1990 [1925]), 235.

50. Robert Shogan, *The Battle of Blair Mountain: The Story of America's Largest Labor Uprising* (Boulder, CO: Westview, 2004), 23–26, 114–17; Howard B. Lee, *Bloodletting in Appalachia* (Morgantown: West Virginia University, 1969), 51–64. On the background of the Matewan Massacre, see Rebecca J. Bailey, *Matewan Before the Massacre* (Morgantown: West Virginia University Press, 2008). John Sayles's film *Matewan* (1987) is based on these events.

51. On Dwyer, see Lee, *Bloodletting in Appalachia*, 97, 199. Titler, *Hell in Harlan*, 79–80, names two former Baldwin-Felts agents among the "thugs" who harassed union meetings near the Harlan-Wallins Verda camp in 1934.

52. *Harlan Enterprise*, September 29, 1922.

53. Statement of Elzie Smith, miner, Costigan Committee, 105–6.

54. Quoted in Art Shields, *On the Battle-lines* (New York: International Publishers, 1987), 143; William D. Forester, *Before We Forget: Harlan County 1920 Through 1930* (Harlan: William D. Forester, 1983), 93 (he has the name as George Cecil).

55. *Harlan Enterprise*, March 14 and April 7, 1924; Garland, *Welcome the Traveler Home*, 113 (Garland remembers the date as 1923).

56. Forester, *Before We Forget*, 91; Titler, *Hell in Harlan*, 13–14.

57. Melvyn Dubofsky and Warren Van Tine, *John L. Lewis: A Biography* (New York: Quadrangle/ New York Times Book Company, 1977), 100.

58. Testimony in Levy, "Class War in Kentucky," in Dreiser et al., *Harlan Miners Speak*, 131.

59. Dwyer to Philip Murray, May 3, 1929, UMWA correspondence files, 1929–30.

Chapter 9: No Neutrals There

1. John Hevener, *Which Side Are You On? The Harlan County Coal Miners, 1931–39* (Urbana: University of Illinois Press, 2002 [1978]), 33; *Harlan Daily Enterprise*, January 7, 1931.

2. *Harlan Daily Enterprise*, March 4 and April 30, 1931.

3. Louis Stark, "In the Blighted Realm of the Miners," *New York Times Magazine*, October 11, 1931, 9; George Korson, *Coal Dust on the Fiddle: Songs and Stories of the Bituminous Industry*

(Philadelphia: University of Pennsylvania Press, 1943), 296. Section 1148-1 of the Kentucky code defined "criminal syndicalism" as "the act of committing, aiding or counseling crime, physical violence, arson, destruction of property, intimidation, terrorism, or other unlawful acts or methods, as a means of accomplishing political ends, or as a means of bringing about political revolution."

4. *New York Times*, April 7, 1931; *New Republic*, December 16, 1931; Hevener, *Which Side Are You On*, 37–38; *Harlan Daily Enterprise*, May 9, 1931.

5. Statement of James Garland, U.S. Senate, Committee on Manufactures, "Conditions in Coal Fields in Harlan and Bell Counties, Kentucky" (1932) (henceforth Costigan Committee), 7.

6. In Theodore Dreiser, ed., *Harlan Miners Speak* (New York: Da Capo Press, 1970 [1932]), 291.

7. Kenneth Warren Mirvis, "A Phenomenological Analysis of the Appalachian Coal-Producing Counties," Ph.D. dissertation, Boston University, School of Education, 1981, 119.

8. Statement of Arthur T. McCormack, Kentucky state health officer, Costigan Committee, 157.

9. Quoted in John Greenway, *American Folk Songs of Protest* (New York: Octagon Books, 1977 [1953]), 258.

10. B. R. Gilbert to John L. Lewis, February 2, 1931; John L. Lewis to B. R. Gilbert, Feb 16, 1931, UMWA Correspondence Files (henceforth UMWCF).

11. Quoted in Bill Bishop, "1931: The Battle of Evarts," in "Here Come a Wind: Southern Labor on the Move," special issue of *Southern Exposure* 4, 1–2 (Spring-Summer 1976), 92–101.

12. *United Mine Workers Journal*, March 15, 1931, quoted in Hevener, *Which Side Are You On*, 34; Turnblazer to Lewis, March 27, 1931, UMWCF.

13. Jim Garland, *Welcome the Traveler Home: Jim Garland's Story of the Kentucky Mountains*, ed. Julia S. Ardery (Lexington: University Press of Kentucky, 1983), 140; statements of Melvyn Levy (secretary, National Association for the Defense of Political Prisoners), and James Garland, Costigan Committee, 31, 7.

14. Hevener, *Which Side Are You On*, 33–34; Paul Taylor, *Bloody Harlan: The United Mine Workers of America in Harlan County, Kentucky, 1931–1941* (New York: University Press of America, 1990), 13. Taylor's description of the Black Mountain evictions is based on his interviews with miners in the 1950s.

15. Hevener, *Which Side Are You On*, 36.

16. Bishop, "1931: The Battle of Evarts"; Hevener, *Which Side Are You On*, 36–37.

17. "Harlan Coal Fields Face Civil War; Kentucky County Is an Armed Camp," *New York Times*, September 28, 1931; *New York Times*, March 19, 1932; Sterling D. Spero and Jacob Broches Arnoff, "War in the Kentucky Mountains," *American Mercury*, February 1932, 226–33; statement of Malcolm Cowley, Costigan Committee, 59.

18. Testimony of Philip Murray, "Violations of Free Speech and Rights of Labor," hearings before a Subcommittee of the Committee on Education and Labor, Harlan, KY, and Washington, DC, U.S. Senate, 75th Congress, April 1936 and April-May 1937 (henceforth "La Follette Committee"), Part 10, 3443.

19. Jerold S. Auerbach, *Labor and Liberty: The La Follette Committee and the New Deal* (Indianapolis: Bobbs-Merrill, 1966), 117–18; Hevener, *Which Side Are You On*, 39–40; Arnold Johnson, "The Lawlessness of the Law," in Dreiser, ed., *Harlan Miners Speak*, 61; statement of Melvyn P. Levy, Costigan Committee, 35n; Harry Gannes, *Kentucky Miners' Fight* (New York: Workers' International Relief, 1932), 6, 17.

20. *Time*, May 3, 1937, summarizing reports from the La Follette Committee.

21. George Titler notes that in his later years Unthank was "living quietly in Harlan, trying to atone for his sins as a Deacon in the Baptist Church"; *Hell in Harlan* (Beckley, WV: B. J. Printers, 1972), 204.

22. Louisville *Courier-Journal*, March 27, 1932, quoted in Hevener, *Which Side Are You On*, 39–40.

23. Quoted in Loyal Jones, "Florence Reece, *Against the Current*," *Appalachian Journal* 12, 1 (Fall 1984): 68–72 (review of Reece's self-published 1981 book).

24. *Harlan Daily Enterprise*, April 19 and 24, 1931; Taylor, *Bloody Harlan*, 16; Titler, *Hell in Harlan*, 22.

25. Hevener, *Which Side Are You On*, 48.

26. *Harlan Daily Enterprise*, April 28, 1931; Taylor, *Bloody Harlan*, 16; Hevener, *Which Side Are You On*, 41, quoting Blair from *Knoxville News-Sentinel*, April 29, 1931.

27. William D. Forester, *Harlan County: The Turbulent Thirties* (Harlan, KY: William D. Forester, 1986), 9. The killed miner's name was actually Carl Richmond. Taylor, *Bloody Harlan*, 18.

28. Titler, *Hell in Harlan*, 24.

29. Attempts at reconstruction are in Hevener, *Which Side Are You On*, 43-45; Taylor, *Bloody Harlan*, 17-18.

30. Evarts High School Humanities Class 1987-88, *Taproots: A History of Cloverfork, Harlan County, Kentucky*, ed. Phyllis A. Middleton and Linda R. Wilson (Evarts, KY: Shoestring Press, 1988), 96-97.

31. Al Benson was assistant police chief in Evarts, and a member of the Evarts union local.

32. Hevener, *Which Side Are You On*, 43; Taylor, *Bloody Harlan*, 21-22.

33. John M. Robsion to J. L. Lewis, December 14, 1931, UMWCF.

34. Gannes, *Kentucky Miners' Fight*, 13; Kentucky Miners' Defense, *Bloody Harlan: The Story of Four Miners Serving Life for Daring to Organize a Union—Daring to Strike—Daring to Picket* (New York: Kentucky Miners' Defense, 1937); John Ed Pearce, column, Louisville *Courier-Journal*, October 6, 1985.

35. Hevener, *Which Side Are You On*, 72ff.; Taylor, *Bloody Harlan*, 20-25, 43.

36. John Ed Pearce, column, Louisville *Courier-Journal*, October 6, 1985; Shaunna L. Scott, *Two Sides to Everything: The Cultural Construction of Class Consciousness in Harlan County, Kentucky* (Albany: State University of New York Press, 1995), 296; Forester, *Harlan County: The Turbulent Thirties*, 10. Bill Peterson heard the same story in Evarts; see his *Coaltown Revisited: An Appalachian Notebook* (Chicago: Henry Regnery, 1972), 26; Florence Reece, "They Say Them Child Brides Don't Last," interview in Kathy Kahn, *Hillbilly Women* (Garden City, NY: Doubleday, 1973), 31.

37. John Ed Pearce, column, Louisville *Courier-Journal*, October 6, 1985.

38. Evarts High School, *Taproots*, 97.

39. *Harlan Daily Enterprise*, May 8, 1931; American Civil Liberties Union (ACLU), *The Kentucky Miners' Struggle: The Record of a Year of Lawless Violence* (New York: ACLU, 1932), 6.

40. Colonel Daniel M. Carrel, officer in command of the National Guard dispatched to Harlan, Costigan Committee, 113.

41. ACLU, *Kentucky Miners' Struggle*, 6; *Harlan Daily Enterprise*, May 24, 1931.

42. Hevener, *Which Side Are You On*, 45-46, 37; Taylor, *Bloody Harlan*, 26.

43. Dreiser, ed., *Harlan Miners Speak*, 161-62.

44. ACLU, *Kentucky Miners' Struggle*, 7; Charles Rumford Walker, "Organizing a Union in Kentucky," in Dreiser, ed., *Harlan Miners Speak*, 45: Titler, *Hell in Harlan*, 36; statement of James Garland, Costigan Committee, 7.

45. Melvyn P. Levy, "Class War in Kentucky," in Dresier, ed., *Harlan Miners Speak*, 34; Walker, "Organizing a Union in Kentucky," 45-46.

46. Theodore Draper, "Communists and Miners 1928-1933," *Dissent*, Spring 1972, 371-92.

47. Some Harlan miners had attended the 1928 "Save the Union" convention that tried in vain to oppose John L. Lewis's autocratic rule. According to Tillman Cadle, many Harlan miners had much sympathy for Socialist leader Eugene Debs.

48. Statement of Reinhold Niebuhr, Costigan Committee, 90; see also Reinhold Niebuhr, "Religion and the Class War in Kentucky," *Christian Century*, May 28, 1932, 637-39.

49. Debs Moreland, Harlan County miner, affidavit, November 4, 1931, in Dreiser, ed., *Harlan Miners Speak*, 97; Aunt Molly Jackson, quoted in Greenway, *American Folksongs of Protest*, 261-62.

50. John Gaventa, *Power and Powerlessness: Rebellion and Quiescence in an Appalachian Valley* (Urbana: University of Illinois Press, 1980), 47-83.

51. Draper, "Communists and Miners."

52. ACLU, *Kentucky Miners' Struggle*, 7; Titler, *Hell in Harlan*, 38.

53. Jesse Wakefield, "Dynamite and Harlan County Jail," in Dreiser, ed., *Harlan Miners Speak*, 69–74.

54. ACLU, *Kentucky Miners' Struggle*, 7, 9.

55. Jim Grace affidavit, November 4, 1931, in Dreiser, ed., *Harlan Miners Speak*, 96. For a similar story, see Debs Moreland affidavit, 98–100.

56. Walker, "Organizing a Union in Kentucky," in Dreiser, ed., *Harlan Miners Speak*, 47.

57. Bruce Crawford, "Harlan County and the Press," in Dreiser, ed., *Harlan Miners Speak*, 75–80; statement of Melvyn P. Levy, Costigan Committee, 29; Hevener, *Which Side Are You On*, 58–59; Gaventa, *Power and Powerlessness*, 106.

58. Titler, *Hell in Harlan*, 39.

59. Testimony of Elizabeth Baldwin, Costigan Committee, 101–4.

60. Hevener, *Which Side Are You On*, 61.

61. A checkweighman is a miner delegated by his co-workers to verify that the weight of the coal loaded by each miner is accounted correctly.

62. Testimony of James Garland, *Costigan Committee*, 10–11.

63. Jo Carson, "Preacher with a Horse to Ride" (1993), in Valetta Anderson and Kathie deNobriga, eds., *Alternate Roots: Plays from the Southern Theater* (Portsmouth, NH: Heinemann, 1994); Hevener, *Which Side Are You On*, 64–66.

64. Herndon J. Evans, "The Truth About the Dreiser Case," University of Kentucky, Margaret E. King Library, Special Collections, Herndon Evans Papers (henceforth "Evans Papers"), box 1, folder 1.

65. *New York Times*, March 19, 1932; Hevener, *Which Side Are You On*, 58–59.

66. Gaventa, *Power and Powerlessness*, 106–9, 116; Hevener, *Which Side Are You On*, 87.

67. Hevener, *Which Side Are You On*, 63–70.

68. Draper, "Communists and Miners."

69. Hevener, *Which Side Are You On*, 81. Hevener (71–72) notes that after the Dreiser committee's visit, local groups distributed food and relief work to thousands of Harlan residents. Yet one ought make a distinction between handing out belated charity and recognizing rights.

70. Vern Smith, "From Behind Kentucky Bars," in *Harlan and Bell Kentucky 1931–32: The National Miner's Union as Reported at the Time in the Labor Defender* (Huntington, WV: Appalachian Movement Press, 1972).

71. *Harlan Daily Enterprise*, January 10 and 19, 1932.

72. Hevener, *Which Side Are You On*, 82.

73. Waldo Frank to the Costigan Committee, Washington, DC, February 12, 1932, in Dreiser, ed., *Harlan Miners Speak*, 321; *Harlan Daily Enterprise*, February 11 and 17, 1932.

74. Hevener, *Which Side Are You On*, 85–86; *Harlan Daily Enterprise*, March 19 and 27, April 11, 1932.

75. Hevener, *Which Side Are You On*, 79; Jim Garland testimony, Costigan Committee, 13–16.

76. Polly Boyden, "We Blame Rockefeller and Morgan," *Labor Defender*, March 1944, 45, in *Harlan and Bell Kentucky 1931–32* (n.p.).

77. *New York Times*, February 18, 1932, September 13, 1932.

78. Garland later changed the last verse to "and travel through this country and Harry's story tell"; however, both versions are included in his autobiography, *Welcome the Traveler Home*, 169–71. Jim Garland sings the later version in *Newport Broadside: Topical Songs at the Newport Folk Festival*, Vanguard VSD-79144 (1963); Pete Seeger sings the original verse in *Dangerous Songs?* Columbia CL 2503. See also Archie Green, *Only a Miner: Studies in Recorded Coal Mining Songs* (Urbana: University of Illinois Press, 1972), 420–22, and Mary Elizabeth Barnicle, "Harry Simms: The Story Behind This American Ballad," notes to *Songs of Struggle and Protest, 1930–1950*, Folkways FH 5233, 3–4. Courtesy of Folk-Legacy Records, Inc., www.folk-legacy.com.

79. "Miners Expose Reds," Evans Papers, box 1, folder 4.

80. Gaventa, *Power and Powerlessness*, 116; Garland, *Welcome the Traveler Home*, 58.

81. The Communist press and the Party's secretary, William Foster, admitted to a lack of communication between party leadership and the strikers, a failure of local organization, and an inability to bring closure to the strike: William Z. Foster, "The Coal Strike," *The Communist* 10, 7 (July 1931): 595–600; "Next Step in the Coal Strike," *The Communist* 10, 9

(August 1931): 703–5; S. Willner, "Some Lessons of the Last Miners' Strike," *The Communist* 11, 1 (January 1932): 27–46. Jack Stachel, "Lessons of Two Recent Strikes," *The Communist* 11, 6 (June 1932), noted that "our comrades were swayed by the sentiments of the unemployed and blacklisted miners" when they called the strike on January 1, and "there was no mass response among the employed miners."

82. Kentucky Miners' Defense, *Bloody Harlan*; Hevener, *Which Side Are You On*, 74.

83. Dreiser, ed., *Harlan Miners Speak*, 315; "The Week," *New Republic*, February 24, 1932.

84. Walter B. Smith to Arthur Garfield Hays, April 16, 1932, in Evans Papers, box 1, folder 6. The letter went on to state: "To Bell County you and your self-appointed committee are just one more nauseating smell; we have had several. First there was Dreiser, and we almost lost our appetites; then came Frank Borich (NMU) and we completely lost it. We regained some strength, however, by the time Waldo Frank and his aides arrived, enough to gently but firmly vomit them across the border; and we have vomited twice since. We might say that our capacity for vomiting is not exhausted when our stomachs are assailed by bad odors." After a court hearing in London, federal judge A. M. J. Cochran found the ACLU guilty of "invading" the coal fields area—as if they were not citizens of the same country as Kentucky—and violating people's "right of freedom from annoying, uninvited, pestering investigations": Taylor, *Bloody Harlan*, 30.

85. Joe Green, "Poverty Back of Mining Turmoil," *New York Times*, May 8, 1932.

86. Charles R. Walker, "'Red' Blood in Kentucky: Why 100% Americans Turn Communist," *Forum*, January 1932, 18–23; John Dos Passos, "The Free Speech Speakin's," in Dreiser, ed., *Harlan Miners Speak*, 295–96; transcripts of Findlay Donaldson and Mary Nick's speech and song are in Evans Papers, box 4, folder 27.

87. Louis Stark, "In the Blighted Realm of the Miners," *New Times Magazine*, October 11, 1931; Walker, "'Red' Blood in Kentucky." Molly Jackson sings "Join the CIO" (originally "Join the NMU") in *Aunt Molly Jackson: Library of Congress Recordings*, Rounder 1002.

88. W. B. Smith, quoted in Gaventa, *Power and Powerlessness*, 110; D. C. Jones, "Additional Instructions to Bell County Grand Jury by Judge D. C. Jones, Judge of the Bell County Circuit Court," November 9, 1931, Evans Papers, box 1, folder 1.

89. Gaventa, *Power and Powerlessness*, 113; Garland, *Welcome the Traveler Home*, 152; Walker, "'Red' Blood in Kentucky"; Jackson, "Join the CIO."

90. Niebuhr, "Religion and the Class War in Kentucky."

91. Evans Papers, box 4, folder 27; John Dos Passos, "The Free Speech Speakin's."

92. Green, "Poverty Back of Mining Turmoil," notes that employers and miners share patriotism and religion, and are thus united against Communism. Malcolm Ross: "Mr. [W. B.] Smith is of the same race as the mountaineer miners of Bell County. Their vote elected him as the youngest County Attorney ever to take office there. He professes their welfare is his sole aim; he asserts that his suppression of Communist organizers of the National Miners' Union was done for the native miners' benefit" ("A Kentucky Mine Town Speaks Its Mind," *New York Times Magazine*, May 15, 1932). Tillman Cadle cast doubt on Donaldson's motives: "He was a preacher, he was a Klu Kluxer and everything. He is all things to all men, that's what he was. You couldn't trust him" (*Tillman Cadle*). Donaldson had been in the union since the 1917 strike and had composed many labor songs. Tillman Cadle went back with folklorist Elizabeth Barnicle in 1938 to interview him and collect songs and stories from him; see album notes to *It's Just the Same Today: The Barnicle-Cadle Field Recordings*, Tennessee Folklore Society TFS 108. Donaldson's tapes are in Archives of Appalachia, East Tennessee University, Mary Elizabeth Barnicle-Tillman Cadle Collection, Box 10, BC293.

93. Malcolm Ross, "Miners, and Yet Mountaineers at Heart," *New York Times Magazine*, May 15, 1932.

94. Gaventa, *Power and Powerlessness*, 110.

95. Hevener writes that this was an ill-advised gesture and that the black miners felt safer eating separately. On the other hand, had the NMU established segregated soup kitchens, one can imagine that objective and balanced historians would not have missed the opportunity to accuse the Communists of pandering to racism.

96. Levy, "Class War in Kentucky," 34, 36.
97. Aunt Molly Jackson, mimeographed speech, no date, Evans Papers, box 4, folder 27.
98. Draper, "Communists and Miners," 128–30.
99. Ross, "Miners and Yet Mountaineers at Heart"; Green, "Poverty Back of Mining Turmoil."
100. Niebuhr, "Religion and the Class War."
101. "This Week," *New Republic*, October 25, 1933.
102. Ibid.
103. *Knoxville News Sentinel Magazine*, January 7, 1934, C1. The headline also noted: "Only 6 Killers Convicted; Maximum Penalty 15 Years."
104. "Yesterday Joe Lee, a desperate mine guard gunman and the fellow who held up our local union officers of Louellen local and taken their charter and supplies from them, this fellow was shot and killed at Wallins Creek." Lawrence "Peggy" Dwyer to John L. Lewis, August 4, 1934, UMWCF.
105. James L. Lorence, *A Hard Journey: The Life of Don West* (Urbana: University of Illinois Press, 2007), 63–66.
106. James Sherburne, *Stand Like Men* (Boston: Houghton Mifflin, 1973), 264, 267; Bishop, "1931: The Battle of Evarts."

Chapter 10: God, Guns, and Guts

1. Testimony of Lawrence "Peggy" Dwyer, "Violations of Free Speech and Rights of Labor," hearings before a Subcommittee of the Committee on Education and Labor, Harlan, KY, and Washington, DC, U.S. Senate, 75th Congress, April 1936 and April-May 1937 (henceforth "La Follette Committee"), 3459ff.; testimony of B. H. Moses, La Follette Committee, 3640ff.; testimony of the Rev. Carl E. Vogel, La Follette Committee, 3611ff.; John S. Hevener, *Which Side Are You On? The Harlan County Coal Miners, 1931–39* (Urbana: University of Illinois Press, 2002 [1978]), 108–9.
2. Hevener, *Which Side Are You On*, 102; John G. Gorman, Gorman Coal Sales (Lexington: Kentucky, to John L. Lewis, June 26, 1936, United Mine Workers Correspondence Files, District 19 (henceforth UMWCF); John L. Lewis, "Memorandum for the Information of the Labor Relations Board," December 6, 1934, UMWCF.
3. Hevener, *Which Side Are You On*, 99–100; Paul F. Taylor, *Bloody Harlan: The United Mine Workers of America in Harlan County, Kentucky, 1931–1941* (New York: University Press of America, 1990), 47–51.
4. George T. Blakey, *Hard Times and New Deal in Kentucky 1929–1939* (Lexington: University Press of Kentucky, 1986), 157. Organizers explained that by the "president" they meant John L. Lewis.
5. Hevener, *Which Side Are You On*, 95; Melvyn Dubofsky and Warren Van Tine, *John L. Lewis: A Biography* (New York: Quadrangle/New York Times Book Company, 1977), 190–91; Taylor, *Bloody Harlan*, 44–46, 52–55.
6. Hevener, *Which Side Are You On*, 106; Taylor, *Bloody Harlan*, 64–66; testimony of Theodore Middleton, La Follette Committee, 4137.
7. Testimony of Lawrence "Peggy" Dwyer, La Follette Committee, 3468; testimony of William Clontz, La Follette Committee, 3623; Taylor, *Bloody Harlan*, 73–75, 85.
8. George J. Titler, *Hell in Harlan* (Beckley, WV: B. J. Printers, 1972), 138, 140–41; Carletta Bush, "Faith, Power, and Conflict: Miner Preachers and the United Mine Workers of America in the Harlan County Mine Wars, 1931–1939," Ph.D. dissertation, West Virginia University, Morgantown, 2006, 157, 184–231.
9. Bush, *Faith, Power, and Conflict*, 157, 187–202; testimony of B. H. Moses, La Follette Committee, 3495, 3500–1; Titler, *Hell in Harlan*, 73–74.
10. B. H. Moses died in 1939, killed by a slate fall in the mines; Bush, *Faith, Power, and Conflict*, 202.
11. Taylor, *Bloody Harlan*, 78–79.
12. John L. Lewis, "Memorandum for the Information of the Labor Relations Board," December 6, 1934, UMWCF.

13. Report of Governor Laffoon's Investigation. Commission Condemns Outrages in Harlan County Coal Field, Frankfort, Ky., June 7, 1935, Berea College Library, MT Col.—Miners (Harlan and Bell), 1. The report was hotly contested by local politicians and the local paper; Taylor, *Bloody Harlan*, 87–96.

14. Titler, *Hell in Harlan*, 127.

15. Testimony of Rev. Marshall B. Musick, La Follette Committee, 3809; James L. Westmoreland to Governor Ruby Laffoon, November 11, 1934, UMWCF.

16. Lawrence Dwyer to Mrs. Frances Perkins, Secretary of Labor, November 16, 1934, UMWCF.

17. Testimony of Robert Lawson, La Follette Committee, 3833ff.

18. Titler, *Hell in Harlan*, 64–65; testimony of Tom White, La Follette Committee, 3927.

19. Caudill, *The Mountain, the Miner, and the Lord, and Other Tales from a Country Law Office* (Lexington: University Press of Kentucky, 1980), 26–33; Titler, *Hell in Harlan*, 145.

20. Resolution of Lynch UMWA local, November 1934, UMWCF.

21. Hevener, *Which Side Are You On*, 103; Taylor, *Bloody Harlan*, 51.

22. Taylor, *Bloody Harlan*, 42, 47–51; on the activities of the National Guard and its conflict with factions, officials, and the courts in Harlan, 107–12.

23. "Kentucky Feudalism," *Time*, May 3, 1937. While in office, Elmon Middleton had announced that "slot machines would have to go" and "initiated legal actions against moonshiners and bootleggers, operators of bawdy houses, prostitutes, and vagrants": Taylor, *Bloody Harlan*, 66.

24. Hevener, *Which Side Are You On*, 137.

25. Ibid., 15–16; Titler, *Hell in Harlan*, 153–54; William D. Forester, *Harlan County Goes to War* (Harlan: William D. Forester, n.d.), 119.

26. "Chain ballots, whereby voter A would get a ballot, and he would not deposit the ballot in the ballot box: he would take that ballot out to some fellow who was working for whatever interest in the election. That guy would mark the ballot how he would want the vote to be cast. He would pass that ballot on to voter B, who would then take that filled-out ballot into the voting place, get another blank ballot, and take that blank ballot back to that same chap who was out there marking the ballot. He would mark the vote again and give it to voter C; voter C would go in and get another blank ballot, put in the one that had been marked outside, and it went on like that" (*Ewell Balltrip*).

27. Hevener, *Which Side Are You On*, 14–16; Ronald D. Eller, *Miners, Millhands, and Mountaineers: Industrialization of the Appalachian South, 1880–1930* (Knoxville: University of Tennessee Press, 1982), xi; Paul Frederick Cressey, "Social Disorganization and Reorganization in Harlan County, Kentucky," *American Sociological Review* 14, 3 (June 1949): 389–93. On operator control of votes, see William D. Forester, *Before We Forget: Harlan County 1920 Through 1930 with Background Dating Further in Time* (Harlan: William D. Forester, 1983), 112–13; on vote buying in the 1960s and '70s, see Bill Peterson, *Coal Town Revisited: An Appalachian Notebook* (Chicago: Henry Regnery, 1972), 204–6. Melissa Lee, wife of deceased miner Jimmy Lee, testified at a government hearing on mine safety in 2007: "There are too many coal operators who hold office in Harlan County or who benefit from coal mining. There are too many bed partners, is what I like to call them, for the fact being one hand washes the other"; http://bulk.resource.org/gpo.gov/hearings/110h/34100.pdf.

28. "Spinal Meningitis Epidemic Cost Many Lives Here," *Harlan's Heritage*, III, February 28, 1986, 53–55.

29. William Roscoe Thomas, *Life Among the Hills and Mountains of Kentucky* (Louisville: Standard Printing Co., 1930), 152.

30. Forester, *Before We Forget*, 42, 45.

31. Titler, *Hell in Harlan*, 98; testimony of Marshall B. Musick, La Follette Committee, 4229.

32. Hevener, *Which Side Are You On*, 128.

33. Taylor, *Bloody Harlan*, 120–21, 128–30; Hevener, *Which Side Are You On*, 130–31.

34. Blakey, *Hard Times and New Deal in Kentucky*, 161, 177–78. As lieutenant governor, Albert B. Chandler had been in conflict with Governor Ruby Laffoon, especially over the

unpopular sales tax Laffoon had passed in order to support the state budget in the early years of the Depression.

35. Titler, *Hell in Harlan*, 103, 108; testimony of Markham Clouse, La Follette Committee, 4457; testimony of Jasper Clouse, La Follette Committee, 4476; Taylor, *Bloody Harlan*, 152–53.

36. Testimony of Marshall B. Musick, La Follette Committee, 3809.

37. Testimony of Mallie Musick, La Follette Committee, 4237; Taylor, *Bloody Harlan*, 154–56.

38. Testimony of Mallie Musick, La Follette Committee, 4237.

39. Taylor, *Bloody Harlan*, 158; Jerold S. Auerbach, *Labor and Liberty: The La Follette Committee and the New Deal* (Indianapolis: Bobbs-Merrill, 1966), 120.

40. Hevener, *Which Side Are You On*, 146–49.

41. The prosecution did not succeed in proving the allegation that the HCCOA as such was guilty of conspiracy. According to John S. Hevener, while the association's funds had indeed been used to deprive miners of their rights, "knowledge and direction of the plot" was limited to small group of officials; *Which Side Are You On*, 149. Taylor seems convinced that the conspiracy existed and that the hung jury was the result of intimidation of the Clay County jurors; *Bloody Harlan*, 187–204.

42. Taylor, *Bloody Harlan*, 210–11, 217.

43. George S. Titler to John L. Lewis, April 7 and 10, June 13, 1939, UMWCF.

44. G. C. Jones, *Growing Up Hard in Harlan County* (Lexington: University Press of Kentucky, 1985), 166, 132; see also Taylor, *Bloody Harlan*, 219–21.

45. University of Kentucky, Margaret E. King Library, Special Collections, Albert B. Chandler Collection, First Gubernatorial Series, State Correspondence, 1939, box 54, Harlan Miners' Strike (henceforth Chandler Papers); Brig. Gen. Ellerbe W. Carter, Kentucky National Guard, "Report to Governor Chandler on Harlan County Duty," July 22, 1939, Chandler Papers, box 68.

46. "1400 troops are now in the field . . . but they are quartered at the Harlan County country club, which is owned by Bryan Whitfield of Harlan Colleries. The majority of the troops are quartered on the property of mining companies, in their Club Houses and Boarding houses": William Turnblazer to John L. Lewis, May 26, 1939, UMWCF.

47. *London* [KY] *News*, June 1, 1939, Carleton Waldos, "Rule by Bayonets," 1, and editorial, in Chandler Papers, box 54.

48. George Davis, "The Spirit of '39," in George Korson, *Coal Dust on the Fiddle: Songs and Stories of the Bituminous Coal Miners* (Philadelphia: University of Pennsylvania Press, 1943), 434–35.

49. Chandler Papers, box 54, May 14 and 15, 1939.

50. Titler, *Hell in Harlan*, 190; "Picketing and Shooting at Mahan Ellison Coal Corp., Stanfill, Ky., July 12, 1939. Statements Taken at Harlan, July 13, 1939," Chandler Papers, box 68.

51. Titler, *Hell in Harlan*, 192–94; on the killing of Bill Roberts, http://www.rootsweb.ancestry.com/famfile/feehiramsarah.html.

52. Titler, *Hell in Harlan*, 195; Titler to Lewis, July 28, 1939, UMWCF.

53. Harry M. Caudill, *Night Comes to the Cumberlands* (Boston: Little, Brown, 1963), 201–3.

54. "Twenty Tons," text by Samuel Boggs, music by Gene Brooks, *United Mine Workers Journal*, March 15, 1957.

55. Testimony of Marshall B. Musick, La Follette Committee, 3452ff.; Robert B. Lawson, 3833ff.

56. Crandall Shifflett, *Coal Towns: Life, Work, and Culture in Company Towns of Southern Appalachia, 1880–1960* (Knoxville: University of Tennessee Press, 1991), 139.

57. *United Mine Workers Journal*, July 7, 1948.

58. Ibid., January 15, September 15, October 1, 1948.

59. Ibid., January 15, March 1, May 15, 1949; January 15, 1950.

60. Lee Jim Rossie to John L. Lewis, August 13, 1941; Joe Spine to John L. Lewis, December 9, 1940, UMWCF.

61. Cesare Bermani, *Il bambino è servito. Leggende metropolitane in Italia* (Bari: Dedalo, 1991).

62. Tillie Smithers to John L. Lewis, June 4, 1940; John L. Lewis to Tillie Smithers, June 14, 1940, UMWCF.

63. Titler, *Hell in Harlan*, 219; John Gaventa, *Power and Powerlessness: Rebellion and Quiescence in an Appalachian Valley* (Urbana: University of Illinois Press, 1980), 164–201.

64. Bob Hall, interview with Florence Reece, *Southern Exposure* 4, 1–2 (Spring-Summer 1976), 91; Frances "Granny" Hager's quotes about the Battle of Crummies are from the interview with Mike Mullins, March 31, 1973, and March 28, 1978, Appalachian Oral History Project, Alice Lloyd College.

65. William D. Forester, *Harlan County: The Turbulent Thirties* (Harlan: William D. Forester, 1986), 262; Hevener, *Which Side Are You On*, 159–74. An exception is Taylor, *Bloody Harlan*. Yet at the time of this writing, Taylor's book was out of print.

66. Forester, *Harlan County Goes to War*, 52–53.

67. Titler, *Hell in Harlan*, 163.

68. "C.K.W.'s 'Mind Run,'" *Harlan Daily Enterprise*, April 16, 1941.

69. "Roadhouse on Mountain Burns," *Harlan Daily Enterprise*, April 3, 1941; see also Forester, *Harlan County Goes to War*, 55.

70. Titler, *Hell in Harlan*, 160.

71. Ibid., 200–1. The victims were the company president, C. W. Rhodes; the vice president, E. W. Silvers; Bob Robinson, a company guard and former state patrolman; and union miner Sam Evans. The pickets at Fork Ridge included a majority of Harlan County miners: http://www.smithdray1.net/angeltowns/h/mh.htm#Fork%20Ridge%20Coal%20 Mine%20War.

Chapter 11: Harlan on Our Minds

1. Gurney Norman, "Night Ride," in *Kinfolks: The Wilgus Stories* (Frankfort, KY: Gnomon, 1977), 37. The title of this chapter is derived from Henry D. Shapiro's *Appalachia on Our Mind: The Southern Mountains and Mountaineers in the American Consciousness, 1870–1920* (Chapel Hill: University of North Carolina Press, 1979).

2. Walter Tevis, *The Man Who Fell to Earth* (New York: Gold Medal Books, 1963), 65.

3. John Cougar Mellencamp, "You've Got to Stand for Somethin'," *Scarecrow*, Mercury 824-8651; "Leaving Harlan," in the Seldom Scene album *Act Four*, Sugar Hill SH-3709; Kate and Anna McGarrigle, "Goin' Back to Harlan," *Matapedia*, HNCD 1394; Darrell Scott, "You'll Never Leave Harlan Alive" (2004), in *Music of Coal: Mining Songs from the Appalachian Coalfields*, produced by Jack Wright, Lonesome Records, 2007, also recorded by Patty Loveless in *Mountain Soul*, Epic EK 85651, 2005. In the same album, Patty Loveless also includes a version of "Shady Grove" (as "Pretty Little Miss") with the "going back to Harlan" line.

4. On Merle Travis's "Nine Pound Hammer" and the reference to Harlan (derived from the memory of the union battles of the 1930s), see Archie Green, *Only a Miner: Studies in Recorded Coal-Mining Songs* (Urbana: University of Illinois Press, 1972), 357–63. See also Charles Vaught and K. B. Perkins, with assistance from Mary Ann Sheble, "The Devil Went to Georgia: Migration Themes in Southern Music," working paper, Department of Sociology, Virginia Polytechnic Institute and State University, n.d., courtesy of Charles Vaught.

5. Vivian Shipley, "The Snakes in Your Dreams Are Too Green, Their Words Are Unsafe," in *Poems out of Harlan County* (Greenfield Center, NY: Greenfield Review Press, 1989), 15–16; Steve Earle, "Harlan Man," in Steve Earle and the Del McCoury Band, *The Mountain*, Grapevine, GRACO252.

6. The suggestion that the music for "Which Side Are You On" may come from "Jack Munro," via "Lay the Lilies Low," comes from A. L. Lloyd, *United Mine Workers Journal*, November 1, 1964.

7. Leaflets with the text of "Which Side Are You On" were passed around in Harlan during the Brookside strike in 1973–74: Sudie Crusenberry Collection, Southeast Kentucky Community and Technical College, ALC 25 box, 1–4. For an international version from the U.K. miners' strike, see Billy Bragg, *Back to Basics*, Elektra 60726. For a version in the

civil rights movement, see SNCC Freedom Singers, *Voices of the Civil Rights Movement 2*, Smithsonian Collection R 023.

8. Shelly Romalis, *Pistol Packin' Mama: Aunt Molly Jackson and the Politics of Folksong* (Urbana: University of Illinois Press, 1999).

9. John Greenway, *American Folksongs of Protest* (Philadelphia: University of Pennsylvania Press, 1953), 8; *The Songs and Stories of Aunt Molly Jackson*, sung by John Greenway, with stories told by Molly Jackson, Folkways FH 5457.

10. Woody Guthrie, in Alan Lomax, Woody Guthrie, and Pete Seeger, eds., *Hard Hitting Songs for Hard-Hit People* (New York: Oak Publications, 1967), 139.

11. Alan Lomax, "Aunt Molly Jackson: An Appreciation," *Kentucky Folklore Record* 7, 4 (October–December 1961): 131–32; in the same issue (the Molly Jackson memorial issue), see D. K. Wilgus, "Aunt Molly's 'Big Record,'" 171–75.

12. Romalis, *Pistol Packin' Mama*, 58. See also Carolyn Hazlett Adams, "Aunt Molly Jackson: The Benefits of Cussedness," *Appalachian Journal* 26, 3 (Spring 1999): 264–69; John Greenway, "Aunt Molly Jackson as an Informant," *Kentucky Folklore Record* 7, 4 (October–December 1961): 141–46.

13. Molly Jackson, "I Love Coal Miners Blues," *Library of Congress Recordings*, Rounder Records 1002; Romalis, *Pistol Packin' Mama*, 2.

14. Jim Garland, *Welcome the Traveler Home: Jim Garland's Story of the Kentucky Mountains*, ed. Julia Ardery (Lexington: University Press of Kentucky, 1983), 183; Green, *Only a Miner*, 48; Tillman Cadle, in *Dreadful Memories: The Life of Sarah Ogan Gunning*, directed by Mimi Pickering, Appalshop, Whitesburg, KY, 1988. On Garland's "The Murder of Harry Simms," see chapter 9; see also Green, *Only a Miner*, 420–22, and Mary Elizabeth Barnicle, "Harry Simms: The Story Behind this American Ballad," notes to *Songs of Struggle and Protest, 1930–1950*, Folkways FH 5233, 3–4.

15. "I Hate the Capitalist System," *The Silver Dagger*, Rounder Records 0051, 1976. Courtesy of Folk-Legacy Records, Inc., www.folk-legacy.com. See also performances by Barbara Dane, *I Hate the Capitalist System*, Paredon P-1014; and in *L'America della contestazione*, ed. Ferdinando Pellegrini and Alessandro Portelli, Dischi del Sole 179/81/CL. Sarah Ogan was persuaded for a time to change her line to "I hate the company bosses"—which no critic seems to see as a case of manipulation and censorship—but toward the end of her life she was again singing the song as she wrote it. Sarah Ogan sings "I Hate the Company Bosses" in *Girl of Constant Sorrow: Songs from the Kentucky Coal Fields*, Folk Legacy CD-26.

16. Romalis, *Pistol Packin' Mama*, 19.

17. Sarah Ogan Gunning, "Come All You Coal Miners," in *Come All You Coal Miners*, recorded in 1972 at the Highlander Center, Rounder 4005. Courtesy of Folk-Legacy Records, Inc., www.folk-legacy.com.

18. Woody Guthrie, "Leadbelly Is a Hard Name," in Guthrie, *American Folksong* (New York: Oak Publications, 1961), 11.

19. Sarah Ogan Gunning, "A Girl of Constant Sorrow," in *Girl of Constant Sorrow*; "Dreadful Memories," in Pickering, *Dreadful Memories*. Courtesy of Folk-Legacy Records, Inc., www.folk-legacy.com.

20. Jim Garland sings "I Don't Want Your Millions, Mister" and "The Ballad of Harry Simms" on *Newport Broadside*, Vanguard VSD-79144.

21. *Knoxville News Sentinel*, April 20, 1931.

22. Joe Glancy, "Mule Skinnin' Blues" and "Coal Loadin' Blues," recorded at Norton, VA, and Harlan, KY, and George Davis, "Harlan County Blues," recorded at Glomawr, in Perry County, in *Songs and Ballads of the Bituminous Miners*, ed. George Korson, Library of Congress, Archive of American Folk Song LP L60; Richard Lawson, "That Little Lump of Coal," "Coal Buckin' Misery," recorded at Kenvir, and George Davis, "The Spirit of '39," recorded at Glomawr, in George Korson, *Coal Dust on the Fiddle* (Philadelphia: University of Pennsylvania Press, 1943), 123, 185, 434–35. Davis's "The Spirit of '39" is quoted in chapter 10; "Harlan County Blues" is also in *When Kentucky Had No Union Men*, Folkways FW02343. The Mary Barnicle–Tillman Cadle collection is at the Appalachian Studies Center at University of Tennessee, in Johnson City; "Hard Times" is included in the album *It's Just the Same Today: The Barnicle-Cadle Field Recordings from Eastern Tennessee*, Tennessee Folklore Society, TFS 108.

23. In 1914, a miners' strike in Ludlow ended in a massacre in which twenty-five people were killed by the National Guard. Many were children and women (nine were Italians, including six children from four months to six years of age). See Martelle Scott, *Blood Passion: The Ludlow Massacre and Class War in the American West* (New Brunswick, NJ: Rutgers University Press, 2007).

24. George Davis also claimed to be the original author of "Sixteen Tons." A song written in the 1940s and published in 1957 by Closplint miner Samuel Boggs also has echoes of "Sixteen Tons": "I woke up one morning, snow was on the ground, / Picked my shovel right up and went to the mines / Loaded twenty tons of hard-block coal /For only three bucks and that was all," *United Mine Workers Journal*, March 15, 1957. On "Sixteen Tons," see Archie Green, *Only a Miner*, 279–314 and passim; Merle Travis, "I Owe My Soul to the Company Store," *United Mine Workers Journal*, December 1, 1955.

25. Jacob J. Podber, *The Electronic Front Porch: An Oral History of the Arrival of Modern Media in Rural Appalachia and the Melungeon Community* (Macon, GA: Mercer University Press, 2007).

26. Psalms 98:4.

27. Alessandro Portelli and Charles Hardy III, "I Can Almost See the Lights of Home: A Field Trip to Harlan County, Kentucky," *Journal of MultiMedia History* 2 (1999), http://www.albany.edu/jmmh.

28. Becky Ruth Brae's "Coal Mines" can be heard in Portelli and Hardy, "I Can Almost See the Lights of Home." Another of her songs, "I Can Fly," is quoted in chapter 5. Courtesy of Becky Ruth Brae.

29. Mary Lou Layne, "The Battle of Jericol," performed by Reel World String Band, in *They'll Never Keep Us Down: Women's Coal Mining Songs*, Rounder 4012.; Beverly Futtrell, "Cranks Creek," in Reel World String Band, *In Good Time*, Flying Fish FF 335; Si Kahn, "Lawrence Jones," in *New Wood*, June Appal 002. On the Jericol and Brookside strikes, see chapter 14; on the Cranks Creek flood, see chapter 15.

30. Hazel Dickens, "They'll Never Keep Us Down," in *Hard Hitting Songs for Hard Hit People*, Rounder Records 0126. Courtesy of Hazel Dickens.

31. David C. Duke, *Writers and Miners: Activism and Imagery in America* (Lexington: University Press of Kentucky, 2002), 35. Dreiser's concern for Harlan predates his visit: his *Tragic America* (New York: Horace Liveright, 1931) opens on a contrast between Wall Street wealth and the "uncivilized conditions" and "lawless terror" in Harlan, where miners are "denied…privileges guaranteed by Constitution and State laws."

32. Duke, *Writers and Miners*, 26–45; Theodore Dreiser, ed., *Harlan Miners Speak: Report on Terrorism in the Kentucky Coal Fields* (New York: Da Capo Press, 1979 [1932]).

33. Jo Carson, *Preacher with a Horse to Ride: A Play in Two Acts* (1990), in Valetta Anderson and Kathie deNobriga, eds., *Alternate Roots: Plays from the Southern Theater* (Portsmouth, NH: Greenwood Press, 1994), 267–334.

34. John Dos Passos, "The Free Speech Speakin's," in Dreiser, ed., *Harlan Miners Speak*, 277–97.

35. John Dos Passos, *Adventures of a Young Man* (New York: Harcourt, Brace, 1938), 202. See also Daniel Aaron, *Writers on the Left: Episodes in American Literary Communism* (New York: Columbia University Press, 1961), 343–53.

36. Mary Lee Settle, *Choices* (New York: Nan A. Talese/Doubleday, 1995), 90.

37. James Sherburne, *Stand Like Men* (Boston: Houghton Mifflin, 1973), 262, 267, 244.

38. Kurt Vonnegut, *Jailbird* (New York: Dell, 1979), 203; Lee Smith, *Fair and Tender Ladies* (New York: Ballantine, 1988), 183, 244; Elmore Leonard, *Pronto* (New York: Harper Torch, 1993), 200–201. Leonard seems to have a secondhand knowledge of Harlan: for instance, he calls the independent town of Evarts a "coal camp." See also William B. Thesing, *Caverns of Night: Coal Mines in Art, Literature, and Film* (Columbia: University of South Carolina Press, 2000).

39. Robert Schenkkan, "Author's Note," *The Kentucky Cycle* (New York: Plume, 1993), 336, also quoted in Miriam Horn, "The Malignancies of History," *U.S. News and World Report*, September 10, 1993, 72–74; Duke, *Writers and Miners*, 107–9; Bobbie Ann Mason, "Recycling Kentucky," *New Yorker*, November 1, 1993, 50–62; Gurney Norman, "Notes on *The Kentucky Cycle*," in Dwight B. Billings, Gurney Norman, and Katherine Ledford, eds.,

Confronting Appalachian Stereotypes: Back Talk from an American Region (Lexington: University Press of Kentucky, 1999), 327–32, and all the essays in the last section, "Recycling Old Stereotypes: Critical Responses to *The Kentucky Cycle*," 281–332.

40. George Ella Lyon, "Literature in Its Place," *Hemlocks and Balsams* 9 (1989) [Lees-McRae College, Banner Elk, NC], 4–8.

41. Duke, *Writers and Miners*, 169.

42. James B. Goode, "Poets of Darkness," in *Poets of Darkness* (Jackson: University of Mississippi Press, 1981). Also, we ought to at least mention Lee Pennington, who, though not born in Harlan, spent several years teaching there and wrote intense and sensitive poems about it: "Harlan Where I've Been," *Songs of Bloody Harlan* (Fennimore, WI: Westburg Associates, 1975), 38–39.

43. On the origins of the word *hillbilly* (first introduced in a 1900 article in the *New York Journal*), see Anthony Harkins, *Hillbilly: A Cultural History of an American Icon* (New York: Oxford University Press, 2004), 48–50.

44. See W. C. Stump, *The Bloody Harlan Legacy: Harlan County History Like It or Not* (1988), privately printed and available from the Village Gun Shop; the cover features a photograph of the billboard. A souvenir I bought is a small reproduction of a poster that says "Bloody Harlan. Welcome to Kentucky's friendliest town. Everybody is insured by Colt/S&W/Winchester," mounted on a piece of coal. On the "bloody Appalachia" stereotype, see James G. Branscome, "Nonviolence and Violence in Appalachia," in Robert J. Higgs, Ambrose N. Manning, and Jim Wayne Miller, eds., *Appalachia Inside Out*, vol. 1: *Conflict and Change* (Knoxville: University of Tennessee Press, 1995), 308–10.

45. J. W. Williamson, *Hillbillyland: What the Movies Did to the Mountains and What the Mountains Did to the Movies* (Chapel Hill: University of North Carolina Press, 1995), 167.

46. If one Googles "Appalachia incest," the result is 42,400 entries. See Jerome E. Dobson, "Fighting Words About Appalachia," http://www.amergeog.org/newsrelease/dobson-fortwortho8.pdf (Dobson quotes then Vice President Dick Cheney as saying, "We had Cheneys on both sides of the family—and we don't even live in West Virginia"); on Appalachian incest jokes, see Anne Shelby, "The 'R' Word: What's So Funny (and Not So Funny) About Redneck Jokes," in Billings, Norman, and Ledford, eds., *Confronting Appalachian Stereotypes*, 153–60.

47. Henry Kuttner, "Pile of Trouble," in *Head of Time* (New York: Ballantine, 1953); Bob Leman, "The Pilgrimage of Clifford M.," *Magazine of Fantasy and Science-Fiction* 66, 5 (May 1984): 8–30. I have not been able to locate the other story, which I remember reading in a collection of best-of-the-year science fiction stories around 1961 (but the book may have been published earlier). I remember it vividly as my first acquaintance with what passed for Appalachian speech and ways. See also my "Appalachia as Science Fiction," *Appalachian Journal* 16, 1 (Fall 1988): 32–43.

48. Williamson, *Hillbillyland*, 150; Harkins, *Hillbilly*, 205–11. *Strangers and Kin: A History of the Hillbilly Image*, Whitesburg, KY, Appalshop Films, 1984, directed by Herb Smith, identifies four "hillbilly" images, linked to technology (enemies of progress, objects of paternalism) and nature (noble but doomed, preservers of tradition). On the image of "hillbillies" as enemies of progress, see Carol Mason, *Reading Appalachia from Left to Right: Conservatives and the 1974 Kanawha County Textbook Controversy* (Ithaca, NY: Cornell University Press, 2009).

49. Dee Davis, "I veri *hillbillies* e la CBS: storia di una battaglia," *Acoma* [Milan] 27 (2004): 14–24; Harkins, *Hillbilly*, 223–26.

50. Sandra Ballard, "Where Did Hillbillies Come From? Tracing Sources of the Comic Hillbilly Fool in Literature," in Billings, Norman, and Ledford, eds., *Confronting Appalachian Stereotypes*, 138–48 (and *Acoma* 27 [2004]: 25–34); Williamson, *Hillbillyland*, 27, 167 (also see 21–71); Harkins, *Hillbilly*, 86–102 (on *The Beverly Hillbillies*).

51. Edwin T. Arnold, "Al, Abner, and Appalachia," *Appalachian Journal* 17, 3 (Spring 1990): 262–75; Harkins, *Hillbilly*, 133, 135. Al Capp's Dogpatch series first appeared on August 14, 1934, and ended on November 13, 1977. At its peak, it was carried by more than nine thousand newspapers. See Al Capp, *Li'l Abner: Dailies*, 6 vols. (Princeton, WI: Kitchen Sink

Press, 1988–89); Edwin T. Arnold, "Abner Unpinned: Al Capp's Li'l Abner, 1940–1955," *Appalachian Journal* 24, 4 (Summer 1997): 420–35.

Chapter 12: Exodus

1. Elsie Asbury, *Horse Sense Humor in Kentucky* (Lexington: Thorobred Press, 1981), 92. See Jeff Biggers, *United States of Appalachia: How Southern Mountaineers Brought Independence, Culture and Enlightenment to America* (Berkeley, CA: Shoemaker and Hoard, 2005); Harry Caudill, "Hills Historically Have Produced Heroes," Whitesburg *Mountain Eagle*, September 21, 1988, on the famous Appalachian World War I hero Sgt. Alvin York from Fentress County, Tennessee.

2. Ernie Mynatt, teacher and social worker, 1923, Knox County, interviewed by Dan Corathers in Cincinnati, quoted in Malcolm J. Wilson and Dan Corathers, *Perception of Home: The Urban Appalachian Spirit* (Cincinnati: Urban Appalachian Council, 1996).

3. Daniel Bruce, "Howard Played Important Role as Officer During World War II," *Harlan County Heritage*, XVI, March 20, 2003, 6–7, 13; William D. Forester, *Harlan County Goes to War* (Harlan, KY: William D. Forester, n.d.), 41–42.

4. Basil Collins appears in several scenes of Barbara Kopple's 1977 documentary, *Harlan County, U.S.A.* The "Bataan death march" took place in April 1942, when seventy-five thousand prisoners (mostly Filipino, but including more than eleven thousand Americans) were marched for sixty miles to camps in the peninsula of Bataan. They were subjected to abuse and torture, and at least 25 percent died. See Anton Bilek, *No Uncle Sam: The Forgotten of Bataan* (Kent, OH: Kent State University Press, 2003). Forester, *Harlan County Goes to War*, 90–91, lists three Harlan men killed during the Bataan march: Jimmy Shy, Charles Ward, and L. M. Proffitt.

5. All these obituaries, and many more, are from http://www.rootsweb.com/~kyharlan/research.html. Forester, *Harlan County Goes to War*, lists 237 Harlan County dead in World War II.

6. Melvyn Dubofsky and Warren Van Tine, *John L. Lewis: A Biography* (New York: Quadrangle/New York Times Books, 1977), 303.

7. Forester, *Harlan County Goes to War*, 51–64.

8. On rationing and the black market, see Forester, *Harlan County Goes to War*, 158–64.

9. On the wartime and postwar boom-and-bust cycle of locally owned small truck mines, see Ronald Eller, *Uneven Ground: Appalachia Since 1945* (Lexington: University Press of Kentucky, 2008), 14–18.

10. William D. Forester, *From Riches to Rags in Less than a Decade* (Harlan, KY: William D. Forester, 1995), 98–99.

11. Keith Dix, *What's a Coal Miner to Do? The Mechanization of Coal Mining* (Pittsburgh: University of Pittsburgh Press, 1988), 160–64.

12. Dubofsky and Van Tine, *John L. Lewis*, 506; Dix, *What's a Coal Miner to Do;* "A Mechanization Study," *United Mine Workers Journal*, February 1, 1962, 14–17.

13. Tom Bethell, "Conspiracy in Coal," *Washington Monthly*, March 1969, in David S. Walls and John B. Stephenson, comps., *Appalachia in the Sixties: Decade of Reawakening* (Lexington: University Press of Kentucky, 1972), 72–91; Ben A. Franklin, "The Scandal of Death and Injury in the Mines," in Walls and Stephenson, comps., *Appalachia in the Sixties*, 92–108; Joseph E. Finley, *The Corrupt Kingdom: The Rise and Fall of the United Mine Workers* (New York: Simon and Schuster, 1972), 174–75.

14. Dubofsky and Tine, *John L. Lewis*, 506; Brit Hume, *Death and the Mines: Rebellion and Murder in the UMW* (New York: Grossman, 1971), 22. On the acquisition of the National Bank of Washington, see Finley, *The Corrupt Kingdom*, 160–62.

15. "A Mechanization Study." On the background and development of the Joy loader, see Keith Dix, *What's a Coal Miner to Do*, 61–76.

16. Energy Information Administration, "Longwall Mining," 1993, http://tonto.eia.doe.gov/FTPROOT/coal/tr0588.pdf.

17. Franklin, "The Scandal of Death and Injury"; Hume, *Death and the Mines*, 7.

18. Forester, *From Riches to Rags*, 206–8.

19. Richard A. Couto, "The Memory of Miners and the Conscience of Capital. Coal Miners' Strikes as Free Spaces," in Stephen L. Fisher, ed., *Fighting Back in Appalachia: Traditions of Resistance and Change* (Philadelphia: Temple University Press, 1993); Thomas E. Wagner, "Too Few Tomorrows," in Philip J. Obermiller and William W. Philliber, eds., *Too Few Tomorrows: Urban Appalachians in the 1980s* (Boone, NC: Appalachian Consortium Press, 1987), 3-12; Ames S. Brown and George A. Hillery Jr., "The Great Migration, 1940-1960," in Thomas R. Ford, ed., *The Southern Appalachian Region: A Survey* (Lexington: University of Kentucky Press, 1967), 54-78; Willis A. Sutton Jr., and Jerry Russell, *The Social Dimensions of Kentucky Counties*, Kentucky Community Series no. 29 (Lexington: University of Kentucky, Bureau of Community Service, 1964), tables 6 and 10; *United Mine Workers Journal*, April 1, 1954.

20. Forester, *From Riches to Rags*, 180-81; Harry M. Caudill, *Night Comes to the Cumberlands* (Boston: Little, Brown, 1963), 330.

21. Caudill, *Night Comes to the Cumberlands*, 264.

22. On Appalachian migration to Chicago in the 1960s, see Bill Montgomery, "The Uptown Story," *Mountain Life and Work*, September 1968, in Walls and Stephenson, comps., *Appalachia in the Sixties*, 144-53.

23. "Girl Reporter Visits Jungle of Hillbillies," *Chicago Tribune*, March 3, 1957, quoted in Philip J. Obermiller, "Paving the Way: Urban Organizations and the Image of Appalachians," in Dwight Billings, Gurney Norman, and Katherine Ledford, eds., *Confronting Appalachian Stereotypes: Back Talk from an American Region* (Lexington: University Press of Kentucky, 1999), 251-66.

24. Albert N. Votaw, "The Hillbillies Invade Chicago," *Harper's Magazine*, February 1958, 64-67. According to a survey reported by Philip J. Obermiller ("Labeling Urban Appalachians," in Obermiller and Philliber, eds., *Too Few Tomorrows*, 35-42), Appalachian migrants were described on one hand as loyal, religious, familistic, independent, honest, patriotic, and resourceful, and on the other as racist, apathetic, alcoholic, untidy, and violent. See also Clyde B. McCoy and Virginia McCoy Watkins, "Stereotypes of Appalachian Migrants," in William W. Philliber and Clyde B. McCoy, eds., with Harry C. Dillingham, *The Invisible Minority: Urban Appalachians* (Lexington: University Press of Kentucky, 1981), 20-31.

25. Appalachians were also blamed for undermining "the fixity of Northern racial stereotypes" by sharing cultural traits and associating with southern blacks; John Hartigan Jr., "Disgrace to the Race: 'Hillbillies' and the Color Line in Detroit," in Philip Obermiller, Thomas E. Wagner, and Bruce Tucker, eds., *Appalachian Odyssey: Historical Perspectives on the Great Migration* (Westport, CT: Praeger, 2000), 159-80, 143-58.

26. Shirley L. Stewart and Connie L. Rice, "The 'Bird of Passage' Phenomenon in West Virginia's Out-Migration," in Obermiller, Wagner, and Tucker, eds., *Appalachian Odyssey*, 40-47.

27. Quoting Mel Tillis, "Detroit City," the song with the immortal line, "By day I make the cars, by night I make the bars," in Bobby Bare, *Detroit City*, RCA Victor LSP-2776.

28. Kathryn M. Borman, "Lower Price Hill's Children: Family, School, and Neighborhood," in Alan Batteau, ed., *Appalachia and America: Autonomy and Regional Dependence* (Lexington: University Press of Kentucky, 1983), 210-26.

29. In 2001, the African American ghettoes of Cincinnati rebelled after nineteen-year-old Timothy Thomas was killed by a policeman. He was the fifth young black man killed by a police officer in six months, the fifteenth since 1995.

30. Ivana Krajnovic, *From Company Doctors to Managed Care: The United Mine Workers' Noble Experiment* (Ithaca: Cornell University Press, 1997); "Harlan County Medical Setup Still Backward, Medical Advisers Learn; Fund Plans Action," *United Mine Workers Journal*, April 15, 1951, 3-4, denounces "questionable practices" and "grave deficiencies."

31. Curtis Seltzer, with the assistance of Robb Burlage, "Health Care by the Ton," *Health PAC Bulletin* 79 (November-December 1977); on opposition from organized medicine, see Richard P. Mulcahy, *A Social Contract for the Coal Fields: The Rise and Fall of the United Mine Workers of America Welfare and Retirement Fund* (Knoxville: University of Tennessee Press, 2000), 97-127.

32. Seltzer, "Health Care by the Ton."
33. This clause excluded many faithful old-timers: for instance, Jack Collier, a West Virginia miner and UMW stalwart who had lost his legs in the mine in 1939 was denied a pension because he hadn't been working in the last ten years before retirement in 1955. Bill Peterson, *Coal Town Revisited: An Appalachian Notebook* (Chicago: Henry Regnery, 1972), 78–80.
34. Finley, *The Corrupt Kingdom*, 188–93; Kenneth Warren Mirvis, "A Phenomenological Analysis of the Appalachian Coal-Producing Counties," Ph.D. dissertation, Boston University, School of Education and Health, 1981, 122; Krajnovic, *From Company Doctors to Managed Care*, 151–59; Mulcahy, *A Social Contract for the Coal Fields*, 107.
35. Seltzer, "Health Care by the Ton." See also Barbara Ellen Smith, *Digging Our Own Graves: Coal Miners and the Struggle over Black Lung Disease* (Philadelphia: Temple University Press, 1987), 57–66; Joseph E. Finley, *The Corrupt Kingdom*, 178–204. Crandall A. Shifflett argues that undue claims on the health fund by miners and medical personnel contributed to its collapse: *Coal Towns: Life, Work, and Culture in Company Towns of Southern Appalachia, 1880–1960* (Knoxville: University of Tennessee Press, 1991), 209.
36. The fund was broken into separate entities in 1974 and ended direct care after the 1978 strike, continuing only the pension program; Mulcahy, *A Social Contract for the Coal Fields*.
37. *United Mine Workers Journal*, August 15 and September 15, 1951, July 1, 1952, January 1 and May 15, 1953; Finley, *The Corrupt Kingdom*, 144–45.
38. *United Mine Workers Journal*, January 1, 1959.
39. Hume, *Death and the Mines*, 23.
40. *United Mine Workers Journal*, February 15 and March 1, 1954; Finley, *The Corrupt Kingdom*, 154.
41. T. N. Bethell, "Conspiracy in Coal," *Washington Monthly*, March 1969, in Walls and Stephenson, comps., *Appalachia in the Sixties*, 76–91; Paul Nyden, *Coal Miner's Struggle in Eastern Kentucky* (Huntington, WV: Appalachian Movement Press, 1972); Hume, *Death and the Mines*, 18; Peterson, *Coal Town Revisited*, 63–69.
42. Finley, *The Corrupt Kingdom*, 148–52. According to Dubofsky and Van Tine, *John L. Lewis*, 504, the planning and execution of violence was delegated to Lewis's assistant Tony Boyle and District 19 president Albert Pass. Both were later found guilty of conspiracy in the 1969 murder of union insurgent Jock Yablonski.
43. Peg, "A Letter from Perry County, Kentucky," in Jim Axelrod, ed., *Growin' Up Country* (Clintwood, WV: Council of the Southern Mountains, 1973), 40–41.
44. Finley, *The Corrupt Kingdom*, 148–49, mentions the killing of at least one truck driver.
45. *United Mine Workers Journal*, May 1, 1959.
46. For instance, Deaton explained, companies were allowed to hire cleanup crews "under no contract, no obligations with the UMW. They don't have to pay no UMW wages or nothing, until they clean up that section, and when that section [goes] to running coal, get actual coal production" they are promoted to union wages, while the company hires another nonunion crew, and the cycle goes on: "They go in there and work for two dollars an hour, until they get ready to mine the coal, then they go by the office, sign their name over to the Kentucky Jellico Coal Company, their pay goes up, same as the other." See Caudill, *Night Comes to the Cumberlands*, 329; Finley, *The Corrupt Kingdom*, 250.
47. Kate Black, "The Roving Picket Movement and the Appalachian Committee for Full Employment, 1959–1965: A Narrative," *Journal of the Appalachian Studies Association* 2 (1990), 110–27; Finley, *The Corrupt Kingdom*, 196; Paul Good, "Kentucky's Coal Beds of Sedition," *The Nation*, September 4, 1967, in Walls and Stephenson, comps., *Appalachia in the Sixties*, 184–93. In the same year, the miners' pensions were reduced from $100 to $85 per month. In 1965, the union announced that only miners who had worked for the last year in a union mine would be eligible for benefits, thus cutting off faithful old-timers who had been forced by economic circumstances to accept nonunion jobs; Dubofsky and Van Tine, *John L. Lewis*, 519–20.
48. "The Superfluous People of Hazard, Kentucky," *Reporter*, January 3, 1963. See *Harlan Daily Enterprise*, October 31, 1962, November 21 and 28, 1962, January 9 and 21, February 6, 1963, for reports of incidents involving armed confrontations and explosions in Perry, Floyd,

and Letcher counties; for clashes between pickets and working miners, and dynamited bridges, Whitesburg *Mountain Eagle,* November 1 and 29, 1962.

49. *Harlan Daily Enterprise,* November 18, 21, 22, and 28, 1962.

50. Dan Wakefield, "In Hazard," *Commentary,* September 1963, in Walls and Stephenson, comps., *Appalachia in the Sixties,* 11.

51. *Progressive Labor News,* January 1963, in Guy and Candie Caravan, eds., *Voices from the Mountains* (Urbana: University of Illinois Press, 1982), 164.

52. Malvina Reynolds, "Mrs. Clara Sullivan's Letter," in *Little Boxes and Other Handmade Songs* (New York: Oak, 1966); Pete Seeger, *The Complete Carnegie Hall Concert, June 8, 1963,* Columbia CSK-45312, 1989; Carawan and Carawan, eds., *Voices from the Mountains,* 165. Hazel Dickens sings a moving a cappella version of the song in the soundtrack of *Roving Pickets 1962–65,* directed by Anne Lewis, Headwaters-Appalshop, 1991.

53. Phil Ochs, "Hazard, Kentucky," *The Broadside Tapes 1,* Smithsonian Folkways SFW 40008; Eric Andersen, *'Bout Changes and Things,* Vanguard LP VRS- 79206; Tom Paxton, "The High Sheriff of Hazard," *Ramblin' Boy,* Elektra EKL 277. The example of the miners led Tom Paxton and others to organize the short-lived New York Council of Performing Artists; see Josh Dunson, *Freedom in the Air: Song Movements of the 60's* (New York: International Publishers, 1965), 80–81.

54. According to a biographer, Dylan resented the fact that organizers in Harlan, though appreciative of the help, did not pay him much attention. Later, he gave a ride to a miner who was walking down the road; he and his co-travelers "threw questions at him…stereotyping him as The Miner, grooving on him being a real miner, not seeing him as a man with a wife and kids, struggling to get along": Anthony Scaduto, *Bob Dylan* (New York: Grosset and Dunlap, 1971), 164–67.

55. Lewis, dir., *Roving Pickets;* Black, "The Roving Pickets Movement."

Chapter 13: The Other America

1. "They put paper bags on their heads because they said they were the faceless people, they had no voice, they had no face, they were not represented in local politics and they saw no future for themselves there. Also they were somewhat afraid about recriminations from their schools if they presented themselves more openly" (*David Walls*). See T. N. Bethell, Pat Gish, and Tom Gish, "Kennedy Hears of Need," *Mountain Eagle,* February 18, 1968, in David S. Walls and John B. Stephenson, eds., *Appalachia in the Sixties: Decade of Reawakening* (Lexington: University Press of Kentucky, 1972), 64–68.

2. Ronald Eller, *Uneven Ground: Appalachia Since 1945* (Lexington: University Press of Kentucky, 2008), 53ff.

3. Thomas J. Kiffmeyer, "From Self-Help to Sedition: The Appalachian Volunteers in Eastern Kentucky, 1964–1970," *Journal of Southern History,* February 1988; Eller, *Uneven Ground,* 93.

4. Kate Black, "The Roving Picket Movement and the Appalachian Committee for Full Employment, 1959–1965: A Narrative," *Journal of the Appalachian Studies Association* 2 (1990): 110–27.

5. Thomas Kiffmeyer, *Reformers to Radicals: The Appalachian Volunteers and the War on Poverty* (Lexington: University Press of Kentucky, 2008), 18.

6. William H. Crook, *Warriors for the Poor: The Story of VISTA, Volunteers in Service to America* (New York: Morrow, 1969); on refurbishing and renovating schools and curriculum enhancement, see Kiffmeyer, *Reformers to Radicals,* 71–73; on Books for Appalachia, ibid., 83–84.

7. Michael Harrington, *The Other America (Poverty in the United States)* (New York: Macmillan, 1962); Harry M. Caudill, *Night Comes to the Cumberlands: A Biography of a Depressed Area* (Boston: Little, Brown, 1963).

8. Gurney Norman, *Divine Right's Trip* (New York: Dell, 1972). See A. Portelli, "Two 'Peripheries' Look at Each Other: Italy and Appalachian America," *Appalachian Journal* 12, 1 (Fall 1984): 31–33; Annalucia Accardo, "*Divine Right's Trip*: A Folk Tale or Postmodern Novel?" *Appalachian Journal* 12, 1 (Fall 1984): 38–43.

9. David S. Walls, "Internal Colony or Internal Periphery? A Critique of Current Models and an Alternative Formulation," in Helen M. Lewis, Linda Johnson, and Donald Askins, eds.,

Colonialism in Modern America (Boone, NC: Appalachian Consortium Press, 1978, 319-49); Jeff Godell, *Big Coal: The Dirty Secret Behind America's Energy Future* (Boston: Houghton Mifflin, 2007), 31-34.

10. Jack Weller, *Yesterday's People: Life in Contemporary Appalachia* (Lexington: University Press of Kentucky, 1965). See Ronald Eller, *Uneven Ground*, 102; Kiffmeyer, *Reformers to Radicals*, 104; Bruce Jackson, "In the Valley of the Shadows: Kentucky," *Transaction* 8, 8 (June 1971); David E. Whisnant, *Modernizing the Mountaineer* (Knoxville: University of Tennessee Press, 1994), 185-219.

11. Don West, "Romantic Appalachia," in Walls and Stephenson, eds., *Appalachia in the Sixties*, 210-16; Don West, "Appalachian Blues," in *O Mountaineers: A Collection of Poetry* (Huntington, WV: Appalachian Press, 1974), 239-42.

12. On the problems caused by differences in lifestyles and morality standards, see Kiffmeyer, *Reformers to Radicals*, 140-44.

13. Joe Mulloy, quoted in John M. Glen, "The War on Poverty in Appalachia: Oral History from the Top Down and from the Bottom Up," *Oral History Review* 22, 1 (1995): 67-93.

14. "In no place was nepotism more evident than in the Harlan County education system"; Shaunna Scott, *Two Sides to Everything: The Cultural Construction of Class Consciousness in Harlan County, Kentucky* (Albany: State University of New York Press, 1995), 117-18. On education in Appalachia, see James Branscome, *Annihilating the Hillbilly: The Appalachians' Struggle with American Institutions* (Huntington, WV: Appalachian Movement Press, [1971]).

15. Kiffmeyer, *Reformers to Radicals*, 132-35, 151, 173, 187.

16. Paul Good, "Kentucky's Coal Beds of Sedition," *The Nation*, September 4, 1967, in Walls and Stephenson, eds., *Appalachia in the Sixties*, 184-92; Catherine Fosl, *Subversive Southerner: Anne Braden and the Struggle for Racial Justice in the Cold War South* (New York: Palgrave, 2002), 307; Jackson, "In the Valley of the Shadows"; Kiffmeyer, *Reformers to Radicals*, 186-91; Chad Montrie, *To Save the Land and People: A History of Opposition to Surface Coal Mining in Appalachia* (Chapel Hill: University of North Carolina Press, 2003), 93-94: Anne Lewis, director, *Save the Land and People*, Appalshop Film, Whitesburg, KY, 1982. The Office of Economic Opportunity was closed in 1973 by the Nixon administration. Its last head, who prepared and oversaw its demise, was Donald Rumsfeld; Eller, *Uneven Ground*, 155.

17. Kiffmeyer, *Reformers to Radicals*, 187-89, 214; Whisnant, *Modernizing the Mountaineer*, 185-219; Paul Good, "Kentucky's Coal Beds of Sedition," in Walls and Stephenson, eds., *Appalachia in the Sixties*, 184-93; Fosl, *Subversive Southerner*, 306-7.

18. U.S. Department of Agriculture, Economics, Statistics, and Cooperative Services, *Indexes and Ranking of Social Well-Being for U.S. Counties (Statistical Supplement for Rural Development, Research Report No. 10)* (Washington, DC, 1979).

19. Bethell, Gish, and Gish, "Kennedy Hears of Need."

20. Catherine Fosl and Tracy E. K. Meyer, eds., *Freedom on the Border: An Oral History of the Civil Rights Movement in Kentucky* (Lexington: University Press of Kentucky, 2009), 73, 75.

21. [William H. Turner], editorial, *Sojourner Memorial Calendar* (Lynch: Eastern Kentucky Social Club, 1988), n.p.

22. Mildred Shackleford wrote an article in the school paper about the confrontation with the racist teacher and was threatened with expulsion. She had a VISTA legal aide call the principal and stop the sanction, but the teacher gave her an F in the course, which ruined her chances for college.

23. At the 1968 Olympic games in Mexico City, Tommie Smith and Roberto Carlos, winners of the gold and bronze medals in the 200-meter race, raised their fists in the black power salute on the podium.

24. http://quickfacts.census.gov/qfd/states/21/21095.html.

25. In 1974, after a flood caused families to be evacuated from the black community of Georgetown, the city—without consulting the community—announced a plan to redevelop the area, raise it above the flood plain, and build an athletic complex. Georgetown resident Wylda Dean Harbin complained, "The city never seems to think of

us as human beings"; Ewell Balltrip, "The Georgetown Proposal: Met by Residents' Angry Reaction," *Harlan Daily Enterprise*, June 9, 1974.

26. John Middleton, "County's Residents Put Election Behind to Support Obama," *Harlan Daily Enterprise*, November 5, 2008.

27. In one of the musical evenings I attended at the Cranks Creek Survival Center, Anne Napier and guests played Dolly Parton's "Coat of Many Colors" (*Coat of Many Colors*, RCA LSP-4603), a song that tells the same story.

28. Quoted in my *Biografia di una città. Storia e racconto. Terni 1830–1985* (Turin: Einaudi, 1985), 169.

29. G. C. Jones, *Growing Up Hard in Harlan County* (Lexington: University Press of Kentucky, 1985).

30. In 1967, in Jeremiah, Letcher County, Canadian documentary filmmaker Hugh O'Connor was killed by Hobart Isom, a local man on whose property he had been taking pictures. The trial was moved to Harlan, where there was a great deal of sympathy for the defendant. As one local person said, "The old man thought they were laughing and making fun of him, and it was more than he could take"; Calvin Trillin, "A Stranger with a Camera," *New Yorker*, April 29, 1969, in Walls and Stephenson, eds., *Appalachia in the Sixties*, 193–201. See Elizabeth Barret, director, *Stranger with a Camera* (2000), an Appalshop film.

31. Richard J. Callahan suggests that, for instance, the story of John C. C. Mayo might be seen as an example that, as opposed to popular images, not all Appalachians are bound to a fate of poverty and ignorance; *Work and Faith in the Kentucky Coal Fields: Subject to Dust* (Bloomington: Indiana University Press, 2008), 58. Castle Rock Smith, "Harlan Is Slandered Again," *Harlan Daily Enterprise*, January 12, 1972, a response to a report by the *New York Times*' Bill Service, makes the point that there is even worse poverty in New York.

32. See the LP record *Roma. La borgata e la lotta per la casa*, ed. Alessandro Portelli (Milan: Istituto Ernesto De Martino, 1970; AS/SdL 12); A. Portelli et al., *Città di parole. Storia orale di una periferia romana* (Rome: Donzelli, 2006).

33. On "the currency of shame" in the public sphere, see Alan Batteau, "Rituals of Dependence in Appalachian Kentucky," in Batteau, ed., *Appalachia and America: Autonomy and Regional Dependence* (Lexington: University Press of Kentucky, 1983), 142–67.

34. David H. Loof, *Appalachia's Children: The Challenge of Mental Health* (Lexington: University Press of Kentucky, 1971), 33, 36, 42, 28. Child psychiatrist Robert Coles presents an alternative view, based on living with Appalachian families: "The mountain child is allowed a good deal of freedom with his body, his legs and arms, as he learns to explore, climb, run and strike out." Mountain children experience "a greater sense of family, of shared allegiance of parents and grandparents, that somehow makes for relatively more cooperative activity, frolic (and eventually) work than one sees among many other American children": *Migrants, Sharecroppers, Mountaineers* (Boston: Little, Brown, 1971), 500. See also Harry M. Caudill, "The Rise and Fall of Education," in *The Watches of the Night* (Boston: Little, Brown, 1976); Peter Schrag, "The School and Politics," *Appalachian Review*, Fall 1966, in Walls and Stephenson, eds., *Appalachia in the Sixties*, 219–24.

35. Ada F. Haynes, *Poverty in Central Appalachia: Underdevelopment and Exploitation* (New York: Garland, 1997), 65. "Kentucky is now the least literate state in the Union. Forty-six of its counties are at the educational bottom [with] the lowest possible average educational attainment among their citizens": Whitesburg *Mountain Eagle*, October 19, 1988. See also "Huge Illiteracy Problem Remained Well Hidden," *Harlan Daily Enterprise*, October 18, 1986; St. John Hunter and D. Harman, *Adult Illiteracy in the United States* (New York: McGraw-Hill, 1979), quoted in Armando Petrucci, *Scrivere e no. Politiche della scrittura e analfabetismo nel mondo di oggi* (Rome: Editori Riuniti, 1987), 62–63.

36. The Appalachian Land Ownership Task Force, *Who Owns Appalachia: Land Ownership and Its Impact* (Lexington: University Press of Kentucky, 1983), 63. The report explains that the underfinancing of schools depends on the low amount of local taxes, caused in turn by the fact that coal profits are taken, and taxed, out of state. See also Caudill, "The Rise and Fall of Education," 222.

37. "Harlan Boy Chorus Invited to Austria," *Harlan Daily Enterprise*, March 1, 1972; "Harlan High School Musettes Invited to Choral Music Festival in Rome," *Harlan Daily Enterprise*, January 21, 1974; "Boys' Choir Inaugural Performance Captures Nation's Attention," *Harlan Daily Enterprise*, January 21, 1989.

38. Loof, *Appalachia's Children*, 47; William Labov, "The Logic on Nonstandard English," in Louis Kampf and Paul Lauter, eds., *The Politics of Literature* (New York: Pantheon, 1972), 194-244.

39. Robert Pattison, *On Literacy* (New York: Oxford University Press, 1982), ch. 1.

40. In Barbara Kopple's *Harlan County, U.S.A* (1976), Criterion Collection DVD, 2006.

41. See chapter 3. Hiram Day did join the Harlan County Literacy program. The program published a pamphlet of his life memories, transcribed from oral performance: Hiram Day and Mae Hensley, *In Honor of the Old Folks* (Harlan, KY: Harlan County Literacy Materials Project, 1993).

42. Calvin Trillin, "The Logical Thing, Costwise," *New Yorker*, December 27, 1969, in Walls and Stephenson, eds., *Appalachia in the Sixties*, 109-16; T. N. Bethell, "Hot Time Ahead," *Mountain Life and Work*, April 1969, in Walls and Stephenson, eds., *Appalachia in the Sixties*, 116-18.

43. Patrick N. Angel, http://www.osmre.gov/anniversary/employee/patricknangel.htm. The "bench" and the "highwall" are the flat and the vertical cuts created by stripping on a steep hillside.

44. Eller, *Uneven Ground*, 38-39; Lowell L. Harrison and James C. Klotter, *A New History of Kentucky* (Lexington: University Press of Kentucky, 1997), 310; "Strip Mine Output Triples in Past 10 Yrs.," *United Mine Workers Journal*, April 1, 1947; "A Mechanization Study," *United Mine Workers Journal*, February 1, 1962, 14-17; James C. Millstone, "East Kentucky Coal Makes Profits for Owners, Not Region," *St. Louis Post-Dispatch*, November 18 and 20, 1967, in Walls and Stephenson, eds., *Appalachia in the Sixties*, 69-78; James Branscome, "The Federal Government in Appalachia: TVA," in Helen Lewis, Linda Johnson, and Donald Askins, eds., *Colonialism in Modern America: The Appalachian Case* (Boone, NC: Appalachian Consortium Press, 1978), 283-93; Montrie, *To Save the Land and People*, 70-72.

45. Eller, *Uneven Ground*, 145-46; David B. Brooks, "Strip Mining in East Kentucky," *Mountain Life and Work*, Spring 1967, in Walls and Stephenson, eds., *Appalachia in the Sixties*, 119-29.

46. Wendell Berry, quoted in Harrison and Klotter, *A New History of Kentucky*, 428; A. Portelli, "Sacche di povertà," in *Taccuini Americani* (Rome: Manifestolibri, 1991), 18-21; Mary Beth Bingman, "Stopping the Bulldozers. What Difference Did It Make?" in Stephen L. Fisher, ed., *Fighting Back in Appalachia: Traditions of Resistance and Change* (Philadelphia: Temple University Press, 1993), 17-30.

47. See Stephen L. Fisher, "Introduction," in Fisher, ed., *Fighting Back in Appalachia*, 7; Bingman, "Stopping the Bulldozers"; Bethell, "Hot Time Ahead."

48. Montrie, *To Save the Land and People*, 72-73; Rebecca Caudill, *My Appalachia: A Reminiscence*, photographs by Edward Wallowitch (New York: Holt, Rinehart and Winston, 1966), 25-26.

49. Montrie, *To Save the Land and People*, 2, 79, 87-88, 91, 104-5; Bingman, "Stopping the Bulldozers"; Bill Peterson, *Coal Town Revisited: An Appalachian Notebook* (Chicago: Henry Regnery, 1972), 165-70; Gurney Norman, "The Ballad of Dan Gibson," and Jim Wayne Miller, "The Ballad of Jink Ray," in Guy and Candie Carawan, eds., *Voices from the Mountains* (Athens: University of Georgia Press, 1996 [1972]), 46-49.

50. Eller, *Uneven Ground*, 147-8; Montrie, *To Save the Land and People*, 83. The picture of Widow Comb carried away from her field is now in Carawan, *Voices from the Mountains*, 45.

51. Bingman, "Stopping the Bulldozers"; Eller, *Uneven Ground*, 162; Montrie, *To Save the Land and People*, 104-5.

52. Appalachian Land Ownership Task Force, *Who Owns Appalachia*; Eller, *Uneven Ground*, 161-65.

53. Montrie, *To Save the Land and People*, 170-79.

54. Ibid., 179–80: P. N. Angel, http://www.osmre.gov/anniversary/employee/patricknangel. htm. In 1997, Hazel King received the Office of Interior's National Mining Award for her contributions to the community and the environment: www.lrc.ky.gov/RECORD/07S2/ HR11/bill.doc. See also Silas House and Jason Howard, *Something's Rising: Appalachians Fighting Mountaintop Removal* (Lexington: University Press of Kentucky, 2009), 17–18.

55. Bingman, "Stopping the Bulldozers," 20.

Chapter 14: Democracy and the Mines

1. Brit Hume, *Death and the Mines: Rebellion and Murder in the United Mine Workers* (New York: Grossman, 1971), 16.

2. Paul F. Clark, *The Miners' Fight for Democracy: Arnold Miller and the Reform of the United Mine Workers* (Ithaca, NY: Cornell University Press, 1981), 19.

3. John Gaventa, *Power and Powerlessness: Rebellion and Quiescence in an Appalachian Valley* (Urbana: University of Illinois Press, 1980), 198; Hume, *Death and the Mines*, 209, 197–230; Joseph E. Finley, *The Corrupt Kingdom: The Rise and Fall of the United Mine Workers* (New York: Simon and Schuster, 1972), 37–39.

4. Hume, *Death and the Mines*, 245–59; Arthur H. Lewis, *Murder by Contract: The People v. "Tough Tony" Boyle* (New York: Macmillan, 1975); Finley, *The Corrupt Kingdom*, 272–79.

5. Miller had close ties to eastern Kentucky: "My daddy was born in Bell County, in Pineville in East Kentucky, and was forced to migrate out of Kentucky to West Virginia at the age of 14, ostensibly for his organizing activity": Michael Kline, "Growing Up on Cabin Creek: An Interview with Arnold Miller," http://www.wvgenweb.org/wvcoal/miller.html. See also Mary McGory, "Man Who Couldn't Win, Did," *Charleston Gazette*, December 24, 1972. Miller resigned from the presidency for health reasons in 1979 and died in 1985.

6. See Bryan Woolley and Ford Reid, *We Be Here When the Morning Comes* (Lexington: University Press of Kentucky, 1974), 62; Finley, *The Corrupt Kingdom*, 153.

7. Gaventa, *Power and Powerlessness*, 194. On harassment of opposition during the Miners for Democracy campaign, see "Rebel Faction Has Tough Time," *Harlan Daily Enterprise*, September 25, 1972.

8. Hume, *Death and the Mines*, 46–48; Trevor Armbrister, *Act of Vengeance: The Yablonski Murders and Their Solution* (New York: Saturday Review Press, 1975), 45; Finley, *The Corrupt Kingdom*, 34–35, 256; Gaventa, *Power and Powerlessness*, 180.

9. "The UMW pretty well abandoned them. They had gone out on strike but the union only gave them $25 a week for relief, and the district office kept part of that...after that there was a lot of mistrust toward the leadership": "James "Goat" Thomas, UMW organizer, interviewed by Bob Hall, "1974: Contract at Brookside. A Perspective by Tom Bethell with Interviews by Bob Hall," in Marc S. Miller, ed., *Working Lives: The Southern Exposure History of Labor in the South* (New York: Pantheon, 1980), 112–24.

10. Quoted in Guy and Candie Carawan, *Voices from the Mountains* (Athens: University of Georgia Press, 1996 [1972]), 198.

11. Clark, *The Miners' Fight for Democracy*, 117–36. On rank-and-file dissent on the 1974 contract, see *Harlan Daily Enterprise*, January 15, 16, 17, and 19, 1974. Kentucky miners voted against the contract: *Harlan Daily Enterprise*, December 6, 1974.

12. Alessandro Portelli, "15 mesi di lotta nella miniera di Harlan," *il manifesto*, June 6, 1974.

13. Paul H. Sherry, ed., "Harlan County Revisited," special issue, *Journal of Current Social Issues* 11 (Spring 1974): 11; Sally Ward Maggard, "Coalfield Women Making History," in Dwight B. Billings, Gurney Norman, and Katherine Ledford, eds., *Confronting Appalachian Stereotypes: Back Talk from an American Region* (Lexington: University Press of Kentucky, 1999), 228–50.

14. The mine had operated as Harlan Collieries, owned by the Whitfield family, under a union (and later a sweetheart) contract, until it went nonunion after a strike and lockout in 1964: Sally Ward Maggard, *Eastern Kentucky Women on Strike: A Study of Gender, Class, and Political Action in the 1970s* (Ann Arbor, MI: University Microfilms International, 1988), 100–5; Woolley and Reid, *We Be Here When the Morning Comes*, 29; Fred Harris, "Burning Up People to Make Electricity," *The Atlantic*, July 1974, http://www.theatlantic.com/ magazine/archive/1974/07/burning-up-people-to-make-electricity/4563.

15. Linda Ann Ewen, *Which Side Are You On? The Brookside Mine Strike in Harlan County, Kentucky, 1973-1974* (New York: Vanguard, 1979), 32-33. For a detailed chronology of the Brookside strike, its background, and its aftermath, see Maggard, *Eastern Kentucky Women on Strike*, 313-30.

16. In a full-page ad in the *Harlan Daily Enterprise* ("Coal miners of Eastern Kentucky what does the Brookside strike mean to you?") the union stated its demands: portal-to-portal pay ("German prisoners of war who worked in this country's coal mines during World War II were *guaranteed* portal-to-portal pay under the Geneva convention"), "job security, a decent medical program, and the protection of a Umwa safety committee"; *Harlan Daily Enterprise*, September 26, 1973. On POWs in Appalachia, see Richard E. Holl, "Swastikas in the Bluegrass State: Axis Prisoners of War in Kentucky, 1942-46," in Doug Cantrell, Thomas D. Matjasic, Richard E. Holl, Lorie Maltby, and Richard Smoot, eds., *Kentucky Through the Centuries: A Collection of Documents and Essays* (Dubuque, IA: Kendall/Hunt, 2005), 397-416.

17. Ewen, *Which Side Are You On*, 28. Miners from Lynch and Glenbrook who refused to cross picket lines at Brookside were ordered back to work by UMW District 19; *Harlan Daily Enterprise*, October 25, 1973.

18. Woolley and Reid, *We Be Here When the Morning Comes*, 29; "UMW Declares War on Eastover," *Harlan Daily Enterprise*, August 23, 1973.

19. "Picketing Rules Set by Judge," *Harlan Daily Enterprise*, September 14, 1973. On the use of strikebreakers and a security guard with a criminal record, see Harris, "Burning Up People to Make Electricity."

20. Alessandro Portelli, *The Order Has Been Carried Out: History, Memory and Meaning of a Nazi Massacre in Rome* (New York: Palgrave, 2003), 47-48.

21. Bessie Lou Cornett, Lois Scott's daughter, was the treasurer of the Brookside Women's Club during the strike. I quote from "1974: Contract at Brookside," 259-70. On the women's decision to join the strike, see Maggard, *Eastern Kentucky Women on Strike*, 148-50; on their strike actions, 176-79; on the Brookside Women's Club, 158-63.

22. Woolley and Reid, *We Be Here When the Morning Comes*, 30-31; *Harlan Daily Enterprise*, October 17, 1963, May 15, 1974.

23. As seen in Barbara Kopple's *Harlan County, U.S.A.* (1976), Criterion Collection DVD, 2006.

24. "I could remember when I was four years old, the gun thugs was coming in and kicking the door open and shining flashlights in beds to see if my daddy was there. And my daddy had to hide behind a log and have his supper took to him, because the gun thugs were waiting around our house, simply because he wanted the United Mine Workers": Lois Scott, testimony in "Harlan County Revisited," *Journal of Current Social Issues* 11 (Spring 1974): 45.

25. Norman Yarbrough's statement is in Kopple, *Harlan County, U.S.A.*; Lois Scott is quoted in "Harlan County Revisited," 47. "There ain't no way in the world you can act like a lady with a scab": Betty Eldridge, in Maggard, *Eastern Kentucky Women on Strike*, 230. On love as motivation, ibid., 224; on male attitudes, ibid., 238-41.

26. Betty Eldridge and Captain James Cromer, quoted in Harris, "Burning Up People"; see "Eastover Attempt to Go to Work Resisted," *Harlan Daily Enterprise*, March 1, 1974. The women consciously played on male attitudes: thus, they used switches rather than sticks because they were more humiliating and men would not testify in court that they had been whipped: Maggard, *Easter Kentucky Women on Strike*, 229.

27. *Harlan Daily Enterprise*, March 1, 1974.

28. I quote the songs as Sudie Crusenberry read them to me during our interview. The scrapbooks are now in the Appalachian Archive at Southeast Kentucky Community and Technical College, Sudie Crusenberry Collection, ALC 25, box 1-4.

29. The scene is in *Harlan County, U.S.A.*

30. "Commentary," in the Criterion DVD of *Harlan County, U.S.A.* The film was the winner of an Academy Award as the best documentary in 1977; in Italy, it was shown in commercial theaters and during prime time on a national TV network.

31. Peter Biskind, "*Harlan County, U.S.A.*: The Miners' Struggle," *Jump Cut: A Review of Contemporary Media* 14 (1977): 3-4.

32. "Commentary," in the Criterion Collection DVD of *Harlan County, U.S.A.*

33. "Outtakes," in the Criterion Collection DVD of *Harlan County, U.S.A.*

34. *Harlan Daily Enterprise*, July 11, 15, 16, 1974; Ewen, *Which Side Are You On*, 55, 64, 67; Woolley and Reid, *We Be Here When the Morning Comes*, 35.

35. "Commentary," in the Criterion Collection DVD of *Harlan County U.S.A.*

36. Wooley and Reid, *We Be Here When the Morning Comes*, 9.

37. Hazel Dickens, "They'll Never Keep Us Down," on the soundtrack of Barbara Kopple's *Harlan County, U.S.A.*; also in Hazel Dickens, *Hard-Hitting Songs for Hard-Hit People*, Rounder 0126; and in *They'll Never Keep Us Down: Women's Coal Mining Songs*, Rounder 4012. Courtesy of Hazel Dickens.

38. Darrell Deaton, interviewed by Tom Hall, "1974: Contract at Brookside," 112–24.

39. Bernie Aronson, interviewed by Bob Hall, in "1974: Contract at Brookside." The UMW charged (and brought tapes to prove) that Eastover, through SLU officials, had offered $5,000 to two UMW members to break the strike: *Harlan Daily Enterprise*, May 14–15, 1974; on the defeat of the UMW at Highsplint, *Harlan Daily Enterprise*, October 16, 1975.

40. Brookside miner Grover Jennings said he had been accepted for a job at the Mary Helen mine, but that when he went back for his physical an official told him they couldn't hire him: "I've talked to Norman Yarborough, and you ain't bringing no union down here." Fred Harris, "Burning Up People."

41. Ewen, *Which Side Are You On*, 117; *Harlan Daily Enterprise*, September 1 and 15, 1974.

42. James Goode quotes a sign the workers put up at one of the mines: "Dear Jimmy Peanut Carter: we sure as hell would love to see your ass / On a continuous miner." James B. Goode, "100 Days and Counting," in *Poets of Darkness* (Jackson: University of Mississippi Press, 1981), 53.

43. Jeanne Belovitch, "Energy Generator: Harlan County, U.S.A.," http://www.jeanne belovitch.com/articles/coal10.html.

44. *Harlan Daily Enterprise*, March 16, 1979.

45. Ibid., December 4, 2007.

Chapter 15: Staying Alive

1. David Steinman and J. D. Miller, *Clover Fork Clinic: The Case History of a New Rural Health Center* (Washington, DC: Appalachian Regional Commission, 1977).

2. On health in Appalachia, see James Branscome, *Annihilating the Hillbilly: The Appalachians Struggle with America's Institutions* (Huntington, WV: Appalachian Movement Press, [1971]).

3. "But even if you don't have insurance if you go to the emergency room they have to admit you. They cannot say that they refuse you, I don't think so" (*Dr. Albino Nunes*).

4. "Recruiting Doctors a Challenge for Harlan," *Harlan Daily Enterprise*, June 9, 2004; According to *The American Coal Miner: A Report on Community and Living in the Coal Fields: The President's Commission on Coal*, John D. Rockefeller IV, chairman, Washington, DC, 1980, 104, the presence of foreign-trained physicians (ten out of twenty-seven at the Daniel Boone Clinic in Harlan at the time) raised problems of language and cultural communication.

5. Kenneth Warren Mirvis, "A Phenomenological Analysis of the Appalachian Coal-Producing Counties," Ph.D. dissertation, Boston University, School of Education, 1981, ch. 4.

6. Carl Wiesel and Malcolm Arny, "Psychiatric Study of Coal Miners in Eastern Kentucky Area," *American Journal of Psychiatry* 108 (February 1952): 617–24, http://ajp.psychiatryon-line.org/cgi/content/abstract/108/8/617.

7. Richard J. Callahan, *Work and Faith in the Kentucky Coal Fields: Subject to Dust* (Bloomington: Indiana University Press, 2008), 19; Mirvis, "A Phenomenological Analysis," 142. On the acceptance of death in Appalachian culture, see James K. Crissman, *Death and Dying in Central Appalachia: Changing Attitudes and Practices* (Urbana: University of Illinois Press, 1994), ch. 1.

8. See Crissman, *Death and Dying*, 106–9, 120.

9. See Lynwood Montell, *Tales from Kentucky Funeral Homes* (Lexington: University Press of Kentucky, 2009).

10. In Charles Hardy III and Alessandro Portelli, eds., *I Can Almost See the Lights of Home*, an essay in sound, *Journal of MultiMedia History* 2 (1999), www.albany.edu/jmmh/vol2no1/lights.html.

11. On Vietnam and pseudo-Vietnam stories and their meanings, see Bruce Jackson, *The Story Is True: The Art and Meaning of Telling Stories* (Philadelphia: Temple University Press, 2007), 203–30.

12. Nassiriya was the headquarters of the Italian expedition force in Iraq. On November 12, 2003, an insurgent attack resulted in nineteen Italian casualties.

13. Angelo Del Boca, *Italiani brava gente?* (Vicenza: Neri Pozza, 2008).

14. "Capture or kill—that's what we're doing…It's hard to know who the enemy is over there. They talk to you one day and are shooting at you the next"; Michael Foutch, from Cumberland, *Harlan Daily Enterprise*, November 11, 2005. For one Harlan County Iraq casualty, Sgt. Matthew L. Deckard, see *Harlan Daily Enterprise*, September 27, 2005.

15. Edward J. Cabbell, "Black Invisibility and Racism in Appalachia: An Informal Survey," in E. J. Cabbell and William H. Turner, eds., *Blacks in Appalachia* (Lexington: University Press of Kentucky, 1985), 7; *Harlan Daily Enterprise*, December 16, 1972.

16. A. Portelli, "Between Sanctified Hill and Pride Terrace: Urban Ideals and Rural Working-Class Experience in Black Communities in Harlan County, Kentucky," *Storia Americana* 7, 2 (1990): 51–63.

17. Kai T. Erikson, *Everything in Its Path: Destruction and Community in the Buffalo Creek Flood* (New York: Simon and Schuster, 1976); Thomas N. Bethell and David McAteer, "The Pittston Mentality: Manslaughter on Buffalo Creek," in Helen M. Lewis, Linda Johnson, and Donald Askins, eds., *Colonialism in Modern America: The Appalachian Case* (Boone, NC: Appalachian Consortium Press, 1978), 259–75; Mimi Pickering, director, *The Buffalo Creek Flood: An Act of Man*, an Appalshop Film, 1975; Jerry Hard, *Harlan County Flood Report* (Corbin, KY: Science in the Public Interest, 1978), 30.

18. *Harlan Daily Enterprise*, March 11, 12, and 18, 1963.

19. Ronald D. Eller, *Uneven Ground: Appalachia Since 1945* (Lexington: University Press of Kentucky, 2008), 249.

20. Hard, *Harlan County Flood Report*, 47, 35. See *Harlan Daily Enterprise*, March 10, 1977.

21. Dwight B. Billings and Kathleen M. Blee, *The Road to Poverty: The Making of Wealth and Hardship in Appalachia* (New York: Cambridge University Press, 2000), 325.

22. See Melanie Zuercher, *Making History: The Fist Ten Years of KFTC* (Prestonburg, KY: Kentuckians for the Commonwealth, 1991); Appalachian Land Ownership Task Force, *Who Owns Appalachia? Land Ownership and Its Impact* (Lexington: University Press of Kentucky, 1983).

23. The story of the Cranks Creek Survival Center is told in a section of *You Got to Move: Stories of Change in the South* produced by Lucy Massie Phenix, directed and edited by Lucy Massie Phenix and Veronica Selver, Milestone Film, 1985.

24. Zuercher, *Making History*, 40.

25. Eller, *Uneven Ground*, 249–50; Erik Reece, *Lost Mountain: A Year in the Vanishing Wilderness* (New York: Riverhead Books, 2007), 124; Silas House and Jason Howard, *Something's Rising: Appalachians Fighting Mountaintop Removal* (Lexington: University Press of Kentucky, 2009); Larry Wilson, "God Should Have Known Better," *Exquisite Corpse: A Journal of Letters and Life*, 10, http://www.corpse.org/archives/issue_10/broken_news/wilson.html. Other disasters include the 1996 collapse of a Consol Energy coal waste dam near Oakwood, Virginia, which polluted the Levisa Fork of the Big Sandy River for twenty-five miles; the 2001 flood that killed six people in West Virginia; the December 2008 spill near Kingston, Tennessee, which covered more than four hundred acres with over a billion gallons of sludge (House and Howard, *Something's Rising*, 181–4); and many smaller but not insignificant ones.

26. Roy Silver and Concerned Citizens Against Toxic Waste, *Harlan County Almanac*, Harlan County Chapter of Kentuckians for the Commonwealth, 1991, 27–28; "Water Water Everywhere—and Much Too Scared to Drink," *The Public i: Newsletter of the Center for Public Integrity*, Washington, D.C., July-August 1994, http://www.publicintegrity.org/assets/

pdf/pi_1994_07.pdf; "Officials Say the Likelihood of Cancer from Water Is Slim," *Harlan Daily Enterprise*, March 12, 1989. On Joan Robinett, see Robin Epstein, *Citizen Power: Stories of America's New Civic Spirit* (Lexington, KY: Democratic Resource Center, 1999), 32–45; Hardy and Portelli, eds., *I Can Almost See the Lights of Home*.

27. Courtesy of Kenneth Rosenbaum.
28. Sherry Cable, "From Fussin' to Organizing: Individual and Collective Resistance at Yellow Creek," in Stephen L. Fisher, ed., *Fighting Back in Appalachia: Traditions of Resistance and Change* (Philadelphia: Temple University Press, 1993), 69–83; Valerie Miller, "The Struggle at Yellow Creek," *PLA Notes* 43 (2002): 42–44.
29. Phyllis Sargent, "Act Locally. Grassroots Groups in Rural Kentucky Act Up," *Ace Magazine*, January 19, 2000; Joan Robinett, "Who They Were and What They Left Behind," http://www.uky.edu/RGS/AppalCenter/RockefellerWeb/FellowProjects/Robinett.htm. On plant workers' concern, see *Harlan Daily Enterprise*, August 1, 1989.
30. Reece, *Lost Mountain*, 47; Cable, "From Fussin' to Organizing."
31. Reece, *Lost Mountain*, 44.
32. House and Howard, *Something's Rising*, 245.
33. Ibid., 1. See Reece, *Lost Mountain*, 17; Anita Desai, "Montagne scoperchiate," *il manifesto*, Rome, June 25, 2009.
34. *Harlan Daily Enterprise*, December 19, 2005; Joby Warrick, "Appalachia Is Paying Price for White House Rule Change," *Washington Post*, August 16, 2004. See also Lee Mueller, "Bulldozers Slice Open Coalfields Controversy," *Lexington Herald-Leader*, August 9, 1998.
35. Warrick, "Appalachia Is Paying Price"; House and Howard, *Something's Rising*, 2; Michael Downs, "How to Save a Mountain: And a Little Child Shall Lead Them," *Ace Magazine*, December 12–25, 1999, 12–17. According to an EPA study, by 2002 only 3 percent of all mountaintop removal sites had been returned to previous use; Jeff Biggers, "The Coal Field Uprising," September 30, 2009, http://www.thenation.com/doc/20091019/biggers.
36. House and Howard, *Something's Rising*, 2–3; Warrick, "Appalachia Is Paying Price"; Jeff Goodell, *Big Coal: The Dirty Secret About America's Energy Future* (Boston: Houghton Mifflin, 2006), 16, 18–19; *Harlan Daily Enterprise*, August 25, 2008.
37. Jennifer McDaniels, "Mountaintop Mining Focus of Discussion," *Harlan Daily Enterprise*, May 3, 2007.
38. Warrick, "Appalachia Is Paying Price"; *Harlan Daily Enterprise*, August 25, 2008.
39. Jennifer McDaniels, "Plan to Turn Coal to Liquid Could Be in the Region's Future," *Harlan Daily Enterprise*, May 12, 2007 (the industry claims that "it's good for the environment because it's clean"); Tim Huber, "Coals to Liquid Quietly Becomes a Reality in the U.S.," *Harlan Daily Enterprise*, August 14, 2007; Goodell, *Big Coal*, 18–21. For industry's viewpoint, see http://futurecoalfuels.org. For environmentalist criticism, see http://www.saveourenvironment.org/Liquid-Coal.pdfd. Among liquid coal's bipartisan supporters were President Bush and then-senator Barack Obama (from the coal-rich state of Illinois).
40. Dori Hjalmarson, "Mountaintop Mining Debated at Meeting—Friends, Foes of Valley-Fill Permits Heard," *Lexington Herald-Leader*, October 14, 2009.
41. "'Disaster Tourism' Becomes Part of Some Itineraries: Tourists View Mountaintop Mining," *Harlan Daily Enterprise*, December 19, 2005.
42. Downs, "How to Save a Mountain."
43. Ten years later, another symbolic victory was achieved in West Virginia, when Blair Mountain—the site of the historic miners' rebellion in 1921—was saved from mountaintop removal by a citizens' movement that succeeded in having it placed on the National Register of Historic Places: Jeff Biggers, "Big Coal Defeat! Rednecks and Greens Announce Victory at Blair Mountain," http://www.huffingtonpost.com/jeff-biggers/big-coal-defeat-redneck-g_b_180979.html.
44. Paul F. Taylor, *Bloody Harlan: The United Mine Workers of America in Harlan County, Kentucky, 1931–1941* (New York: University Press of America, 1990), 243–44.
45. William Keesler, "Mining Jobs Are Disappearing, and There's Little to Fall On," Louisville *Courier-Journal*, November 12, 1989 (first of the five-part series "Is Coal All there Is?"); on

data from the University of Kentucky Center for Business and Economic Research, see http://www.epodunk.com; on census data, see http://quickfacts.census.gov/qfd/states/21/21095.html.

46. William Kessler, "Diversification Remains an Elusive Goal," Louisville *Courier-Journal*, November 16, 1989; Appalachian Land Ownership Task Force, *Who Owns Appalachia?* (1983).

47. Kentuckians for the Commonwealth, "Understanding Kentucky's Coal Severance Fund," http://kftc.org/our-work/high-road/coal-severance-tax.

48. Ada F. Haynes, *Poverty in Central Appalachia: Underdevelopment and Exploitation* (New York: Garland, 1997), 67; Eller, *Uneven Ground*, 230. Eller notes that United Glove received a $1 million tax credit on the promise to create 100 jobs, and left the state. A biscuit factory opened in 1994 promising to create 106 jobs; until 1999 it never employed more than seven. A sock factory that had received $1.5 million in grants and loans failed in 1998. Sunshine Valley Farms, owned by nonprofit corporations created during the War on Poverty, failed. A furniture factory at Baxter burned down. A ski slope on Big Black Mountain succumbed to several consecutive warm winters. Appalachian Computer Services started in Harlan but moved to London. William Keesler, "Harlan County's Problems: Industry Recruiters Find It Difficult to 'Sell' Region," Louisville *Courier-Journal*, November 13, 1989.

49. John W. Morris, "The Potential of Tourism," in Ford, *The Southern Appalachian Region* (Lexington: University of Kentucky Press, 1967), 136–48; *Harlan Daily Enterprise*, May 11 and December 20, 2004, July 28, 2006.

50. *Harlan Daily Enterprise*, September 16, 2008.

51. "McCain Working to Boost Tourism as Ridge Runners Leader," *Harlan Daily Enterprise*, December 20, 2004; "Evarts Kentucky ATV Trip 2008," http://www.youtube.com/watch?v=C9zcyFL71Wg.

52. Keesler, "Harlan County's Problems."

53. For early warnings: Jim Gibson, "Tranquillizers Said More Danger than Hard Drugs," *Harlan Daily Enterprise*, January 3, 1972; Ewell Balltrip, "Alcohol and Drug Abuse in Harlan Is Hard to Ignore," *Harlan Daily Enterprise*, June 29, 1973.

54. Bill Bishop, "As Poverty Worsens in Appalachia, So Do Drug Abuse and Depression," August 14, 2008, http://www.dailyyonder.com/poverty-worsens-appalachia-so-do-drug-abuse-and-depression; Linda J. Johnson, "Eastern Kentucky: Painkiller Capital," *Lexington Herald-Leader*, January 19, 2003; Linda J. Johnson and C. Ware, "Antidote for Addiction Sits on Shelf," *Lexington Herald-Leader*, February 9, 2003; Debbie Caldwell, "Suit Filed Against Oxy Manufacturers," *Harlan Daily Enterprise*, June 29, 2001. In 2007, Purdue was fined $600 million for misleading the public about the characteristics of the drug; Robert Weissman, "Victories in 2007," December 31, 2007, Multinational Monitor, http://www.multinationalmonitor.org/editorsblog/index.php?/archives/66-Victories-in-2007.html.

55. In 2000, more than 11 percent of the population suffered from some kind of disability; http://quickfacts.census.gov/qfd/states/21/21095.html.

56. Peggy Peck, "'Oxycotton' the New Street Drug of Choice for Many," WebMD Medical News, February 9, 2001, http://www.webmd.com/mental-health/news/20010209/oxycotton-new-street-drug-of-choice-for-many.

57. Debra Rosenberg, "How One Town Got Hooked," *Newsweek*, April 24, 2001; Paul Tough, "The Alchemy of OxyContin," *New York Times*, July 29, 2001.

58. "The OxyContin Epidemic and Crime Panic in Rural Kentucky," *Contemporary Drug Problems*, June 22, 2005, http://goliath.ecnext.com/coms2/gi_0199-5699873/The-OxyContin-epidemic-and-crime.html; Judy Jones and Karen Pratt, "OxyContin: A Prescription Pain 'Killer,'" Kentucky State Office of Rural Health; Adrienne Steinfield, "Overdoses Claimed 11 Deaths in '04," *Harlan Daily Enterprise*, August 3, 2005; Gardiner Harris, "Drug Panel Rejects Pleas to Curb Sales of a Widely Abused Painkiller," *New York Times*, September 9, 2003; Peck, "'Oxycotton' the New Street Drug"; Johnson, "Prescription-Painkiller Capital." For contrary views, "OxyContin the New Drug Plague? Don't Believe the Hype," StopTheDrugWar.org, May 25, 2001, http://stopthedrugwar.org/chronicle-old/187/oxycontinhype.shtml; Trevor

Butterworth, "The Great OxyContin Scare," AlterNet, August 30, 2004, http://www.alternet.org/drugreporter/19707.

59. *Harlan Daily Enterprise*, October 14, 22, and 28, December 26, 2004; for mass arrests, *Harlan Daily Enterprise*, March 25, July 16, August 18, 2004, May 19, 2005, July 15, September 17, December 24, 2006.

60. Charles B. Camp, "Denied in Virginia, Licensed in Kentucky," *Lexington Herald-Leader*, January 31, 2003; *Harlan Daily Enterprise*, May 10 and August 28, 2003, May 30 and September 20, 2007; Debbie Caldwell, "Nashville Doctors Indicted in Kentucky," *Harlan Daily Enterprise*, February 4, 2009. This particular doctor had served jail time in Tennessee for double second-degree murder, after which his license had been reinstated.

61. "The Harlan County Project: Final Report to the Rockefeller Foundation," submitted by Robert Gipe, January 31, 2007. The Listening Project also found misgivings with inequalities in the way the judicial system was treating drug cases, and with certain police investigation tactics based on infiltration and informants.

62. Steinfield, "Overdoses Claimed 11 Deaths in '04." On meth labs and other related news, see *Harlan Daily Enterprise*, Feb 8, 2003, May 10, 2004, November 12 and December 24, 2006.

63. Joan Robinett, quoted in http://www.listeningproject.info/news/projects/HarlanCountyLP_11-05.php.

64. The performance was co-directed by Jerry Metheny. Theresa Osborne and Connie Owens worked as community coordinators, Ann Schertz coordinated the music, Danielle Burke the photography project, Joe Scopa the tile project and the mural. The play was also presented at the 2006 ARC Governors Conference in Pikeville as well as the East Kentucky Leadership Conference and Martin Luther King Jr. Day and African American History Month celebrations in Harlan County. A number of tile and mural projects followed PACT's example in different parts of the county: Gipe, "The Harlan County Project."

65. Brandon Going, "'Higher Ground' to Feature Stories of Harlan Countians," *Harlan Daily Enterprise*, August 19, 2005; Jennifer McDaniels, "Higher Ground Continues to Draw Large Crowds," *Harlan Daily Enterprise*, May 11, 2005.

66. Robert Gipe, "The Appalachian Program at Southeast Kentucky Community and Technical College: Report to the Steele-Reese Foundation," May 15, 2009.

67. *Higher Ground* script, courtesy of Southeast Kentucky Community and Technical College and Robert Gipe, Act One, p. 13; video recording, *Finding Higher Ground*, Kentucky Educational Television, Lexington, 2008.

68. Personal responsibility and community involvement is the theme of PACT's other community play, *Playing with Fire*, presented in April 2009, with an even larger cast and enthusiastic audience response; Gipe, "The Appalachian Program." A third play is due to be presented in 2010.

Index

mine safety, 132
mining death, 144–51, 396 n15
New Deal, 209–10
oil companies competition, 256
and the railroads, 101–3
royalties on, 256
segregation, 174, 288
snake hunting, 23
techniques of, 139–44
tipple, 123, 127, 141, 382n35
ups and downs, 351
wages, 182
during World War II, 252
coal towns, 101–3, 118–21, 123, 128–30, 133–34,
    144–51, 157–61, 168–69, 171
cockfights, 21
Cohen, Lester, 242–43
Cole, Betty, 372
Coles, Robert, 416 n34
Coles, Russell, 145
Collett, Harvey, 205
Colley, Jack, 179, 180, 372
Collins, Basil, 250–51, 315, 321, 331
Columbia University, 6
Combs, Ollie, 303
Committee on Education and Labor, 219
Committee on Manufactures, 198
Commonwealth Labor Training
    Institute, 200
Communists, 3, 11, 90, 193–94, 201–2, 207,
    237, 284–85, 317–18, 403n92. *See also*
    Red-baiting
Community Action Programs (CAPs), 278,
    283–84
company towns. *See* coal towns
Concerned Citizens Against Toxic Waste, 346
Concerned Citizens for Water, 305
Condon, Mabel, 24, 53
Congregationals, 64
Connors, Tom, 193
Consolidation Coal Company (Consol), 123,
    148, 256, 307
Continental Coal Company, 101
Continental Hotel, 198
continuous mining machine, 257
Cook, Iverson Minter, 171, 372
Cook, Leroi, 171
Cooke, John Esten, 64
COPE (Clover Fork Organization to Protect
    the Environment), 343
Corbin, 171
corn shucking, 33
Cornett, Bessie Lou, 298, 313–14, 317
Cornett, Denver, 102
Cornett, Jess, 66

Cornett, Judy, 158
Cornett-Lewis mine, 119, 126, 212, 258, 323
Costigan, Edward P., 198
Costigan Committee, 185
Cotton hollow, 157
Cotton Stocking Row, 130
Council of the Southern Mountains, 279, 282
Cowans, Hugh
    activist, 7
    African American coal miners, 175
    biography, 372
    coal mining, 135, 142
    coal towns, 124
    on Dr. King, 290–91
    Equal Rights Congress, 289
    folk music, 240
    on Lewis, 225, 228
    National Guard, 223
    union organizing, 209
    welfare, 90
    World War II, 251, 253
Cowans, Julia
    African American coal miners, 166–67
    African American strike breakers, 174
    biography, 372
    coal mining, 138
    coal towns, 119
    Equal Rights Congress, 289
    folk music, 240
    integration, 287, 290
    and Lawson, 132
    marriage, 38
    mining death, 150
    miscegenation, 171
    missionaries, 172–73
    moonshining, 114
    on prejudice, 173
    roving pickets, 223
    script, 125
    segregation, 168–70
    slavery, 7–8, 53
Cowley, Malcolm, 187, 199, 242
Coxton hollow, 96, 344
crafts, 67–68, 353
Cranks Creek, Kentucky, 13–15, 19, 30, 31,
    50–51, 53, 68, 71, 93, 105–6, 111, 300,
    304, 342–43
Cranks Creek Survival Center, 5–6, 67, 106,
    240–41, 295, 343–44
Crawford, Bruce, 196
Creech, Robert W., 251
Creech, William (mine owner), 65, 102,
    104–5, 126, 220, 226, 251
Creech Coal Company, 135, 194, 224
Creek, Aunt Sal, 66

THE OXFORD ORAL HISTORY SERIES

J. TODD MOYE (University of North Texas), KATHRYN NASSTROM (University of San Francisco), and ROBERT PERKS (The British Library Sound Archive), *Series Editors*
DONALD A. RITCHIE, *Senior Advisor*

history
literature
music
natural interviews
newss reports — NYT
film — Deliverance
tv — Andy Griffith